# Civil Rights & Liberties in the 21st Century

## SECOND EDITION

## JOHN C. DOMINO
*Sam Houston State University*

New York  San Francisco  Boston
London  Toronto  Sydney  Tokyo  Singapore  Madrid
Mexico City  Munich  Paris  Cape Town  Hong Kong  Montreal

*To my wife, Caroline, and my children, Nicholas and Chloe*
*And, in memory of my brother, Michael S. Domino*

Vice President and Publisher:   Priscilla McGeehon
Executive Editor:   Eric Stano
Senior Marketing Manager:   Megan Galvin-Fak
Senior Production Manager:   Bob Ginsburg
Project Coordination, Text Design, and Electronic Page Makeup:   Sunflower Publishing
    Services
Cover Design Manager:   John Callahan
Cover Designer:   Maria Ilardi
Cover Photo:   © Steve Bronstein/Getty Images/The Image Bank
Publishing Services Manager:   Al Dorsey
Printer and Binder:   The Maple-Vail Book Manufacturing Group
Cover Printer:   Lehigh Press, Inc.

CIP data on file.

Please visit our website at http://www.ablongman.com

ISBN 0-321-08970-7

2345678910—MA—05040302

# Contents

# Preface

In 1992, when the first edition of this book was nearing completion, the U.S. Supreme Court was dominated by justices appointed by three conservative Republican presidents and was on the verge of moving on an even more conservative path, narrowing or overturning many of the Warren and Burger Courts' celebrated rulings on civil rights and liberties. President George H. W. Bush, buoyed by high approval ratings following the Persian Gulf War, was expected to easily win reelection in November 1992 and thus continue to shape the federal judiciary by appointing conservative justices like Clarence Thomas. However, the election of Democrat Bill Clinton in 1992 and his reelection in 1996 slowed this conservative trend. By the late 1990s, Clinton's two High Court appointments—Ruth Bader Ginsberg and Stephen Breyer—were beginning to forge a moderate bloc of justices with the help of Justices Stevens and Souter. During his eight tumultuous years in office, Clinton was also able to influence civil rights and liberties through his selection of lower court judges and executive department officials (such as attorney general, solicitor general, chair of the Equal Employment Opportunity Commission, and secretary of Health and Human Services).

The 1990s was also a decade of extraordinary political events that have had an effect on the judiciary. In the 1994 mid-term congressional elections, Republicans took control of both houses of Congress for the first time in forty years. More conservative than ever before, the new Republican majority promised a social and economic policy revolution and very close scrutiny of any new Clinton judicial appointees who might stand in the way. Leading this revolution was House Speaker Newt Gingrich, who vowed that Congress would now be the agent of change, making President Clinton irrelevant. Clinton fought back and won reelection in 1996, due largely to a booming economy; the lackluster campaign of his challenger, Senator Robert Dole; and a perception that the Republican Party had moved too far to the right. The Democrats were still in position to influence the judiciary, but the Republican-controlled Senate made the appointment of a liberal justice difficult.

Clinton recaptured the agenda from Gingrich and won a few political battles until a series of scandals—most notably the Monica Lewinsky sex scandal—led to an investigation by an independent counsel and his ultimate impeachment in the House for perjury and obstruction of justice. His confidence bolstered by a high approval rating, Clinton refused to resign and was acquitted of all charges in the Senate. The Clinton presidency would forever be tainted by impeachment, but it was the Republicans who suffered in the short run. A majority of Americans were appalled by Clinton's behavior but opposed removing him from office, concluding that many Republicans were driven purely by partisanship and personal animosity. The backlash cost Republicans a few lost seats in Congress in the 1998 off-year elections, narrowing their majority in both houses. The political fallout also led to Gingrich's resignation and contributed to an additional net loss of Republican seats in the House and the loss of control of the Senate in 2001.

On election day 2000, another political first began to unfold. A close race between Texas Governor George W. Bush and Vice President Al Gore was predicted but no one dreamed of the infamous photo finish in Florida, where the presidential race hinged entirely on Florida's twenty-five electoral votes. Early the next morning, it appeared that Bush had won Florida by 1,784 votes, but the results were so close that an automatic machine recount dropped his lead to 537 votes. For weeks after election day, new recounts were initiated, lawsuits were filed, and voter fraud was charged, yet still the president had not been elected. Finally, on December 12, the U.S. Supreme Court ordered an end to all recounts, thus granting Florida's electoral votes to George W. Bush. In one of the most bitterly contested elections in our nation's history, Bush won a narrow electoral college victory even though Gore won the majority of the popular vote nationwide. Thrust into the political fray, the Court—appearing deeply divided along ideological and partisan lines—determined who would become the forty-third president of the United States.

Like his father before him, President George W. Bush will attempt to move the federal judiciary in a more conservative direction.

Less than a year after the political tumult of the 2000 presidential election, America was wracked by the September 11, 2001, terrorist attacks. Americans were shocked and horrified not only by the vicious act of terror and loss of life, but also by the potential threat to freedom and democracy. The looming threat of terrorism as well as new security measures may forever change American society. The challenge of the twenty-first century may well be how to keep Americas safe yet free; that is, how to strike a wise balance between security and liberty.

One theme of the first edition of this book was change—whether the counter-revolution in civil rights and liberties had occurred. If it had not, was the conservative Rehnquist Court poised in the early 1990s to overturn or narrow many of the landmark rulings on abortion, privacy, or due process rights? This remains a valid question for the second edition, as well. Notwithstanding the influence of the most conservative justices—Rehnquist, Scalia, and Thomas—did the principle of *stare decisis*, or respect for precedent, forestall or prevent dramatic change in the voting patterns of the Court? Has the Rehnquist Court taken us in new directions by revisiting issues thought to be well settled? What impact did the Clinton appointees have on the Court?

This edition is an update of cases through the Court's 2000–2001 term, but it also includes a new introductory chapter that focuses on the power and operation of the Court and a short guide to finding the full text of Supreme Court opinions on the World Wide Web. Also added is a discussion of the implications of the campaign finance reform movement on the First Amendment, the regulation of the Internet, and the controversial subject of public funding of the arts. A new section on discrimination on the basis of sexual preference has been added; as well as a section on voting and elections, which culminates with an analysis of the Court's role in determining the outcome of the 2000 presidential race in *Bush v. Gore*.

This book does not pretend to be an exhaustive account of the Court's landmark rulings on civil rights and liberties. As in the first edition, rather than proceeding from a shopping list of cases and topics, I endeavored to organize this book around the issues, controversies, and opinions that in my judgment are highly representative of the most important developments and changes in civil rights and liberties during the Warren, Burger and Rehnquist eras.

I would like to express my indebtedness to my colleagues in the political science department at Sam Houston State University, especially to Professor Robert Biles, for his encouragement and support. I would like to thank the reviewers whose comments on the first edition helped guide the second edition, including Christopher Banks, University of Akron; Justin Halpern, Northeastern State University; and John Kozlowicz, University of Wisconsin–Whitewater. Finally, I would also like to thank Eric Stano, executive editor for political science at Longman Publishers, for his incisive comments and input, as well as others at Longman who have helped bring this second edition into being.

JOHN C. DOMINO

# CHAPTER ONE

# Introduction: Rights and Liberties and the Supreme Court

*A bill of rights is what the people are entitled to against every government on earth, general or particular; and what no just government should refuse, or rest on inference.*

Thomas Jefferson,
Letter to James Madison, December 20, 1787

*It is emphatically the province and duty of the judicial department to say what the law is.*

Chief Justice John Marshall,
*Marbury v. Madison*, 1803

## CIVIL RIGHTS AND LIBERTIES

For more than two centuries civil rights and liberties have been at the center of American political discourse and debate. More than mere words on parchment, rights and liberties are integral elements of our culture and firmly established in the American psyche. Americans possess an atavistic entitlement to liberty—a deeply held belief that rights and liberties are natural and inalienable. Yet, as this book explores, we have struggled to reach a consensus on the definition and scope of these rights and at times have foundered in our commitment to them. Paradoxically, as quickly as we have come to the defense of our freedoms so too have we often been willing to restrict the rights of others, particularly those who are perceived as threats to the prevailing social and political values of the majority.

Although the two terms are often used interchangeably when referring to a broad array of freedoms, *civil rights* and *liberties* actually constitute two distinct areas of constitutional protection. Liberty can be understood simply as the absence of constraints or restrictions upon what a person wants to do. Rights, then, protect liberty by legally defining the boundaries between a person's liberty and the authority of government. In essence, rights limit how far the government can intrude into our lives.[1] *Civil liberties* are the most basic fundamental freedoms protected by the U.S. Constitution: the freedom to speak one's mind or practice a belief system with-

1

out fear of coercion or punishment, the right to move about freely, the freedom to associate with others, and the right to privacy in personal or intimate matters.

Liberty may be fundamental but it is not absolute. Some degree of our personal freedom is restricted in the interest of public safety, national security, or moral decency. We expect our liberty to be protected, but we also expect governmental protection against those who abuse liberty. Living in society we are not at perfect liberty to do as we please, for rights cannot exist without concomitant responsibilities or duties, such as paying taxes, serving in the military if called, and treating fellow citizens with respect and dignity. In a "civil" society we are expected to respect the rights of others and subject our own activities to reasonable governmental restrictions enacted for the good of society.

Whereas civil liberties protect individuals *from* governmental intrusions on fundamental freedoms, the term *civil rights* has come to connote a positive act of government intended to guarantee that each person is treated as an equal member of society. Civil rights, in contrast to individual liberties, guarantee freedom from discrimination, equal access to the polls and the political process, and full citizenship. The U.S. Supreme Court's ruling in *Brown v. Board of Education* (1954), which overturned the doctrine of separate but equal in public schools; the Civil Rights Act (1964); and the Voting Rights Act (1965) are examples of governmental action intended to protect civil rights. Such measures promote equality by prohibiting arbitrary, unreasonable, or discriminatory treatment.

Equal treatment has also come to mean more than the absence of discrimination. Affirmative action programs, for instance, set aside special opportunities for certain classes of people in order to remedy the lingering effects of past discrimination or to promote a more diverse workplace.

## Constitutional Foundations of Civil Rights and Liberties

The first ten amendments to the U.S. Constitution—the Bill of Rights—constitute the primary source of protection for our rights and liberties. However, as originally drafted by the Philadelphia Constitutional Convention of 1787, the Constitution did not have a bill of rights. The constitutional principles of separation of powers, checks and balances, and federalism—intended to act as a bulwark against the concentration and abuse of power—were woven into the Constitution so that one branch of government would not dominate the other branches or that the creation of a strong national (federal) government would not diminish the sovereignty of the states. Yet, one major objection to the proposed Constitution of 1787 was that it did not place sufficient safeguards on certain fundamental rights. The Constitution granted trial by jury in federal cases and prohibited bills of attainder, ex post facto laws, and the suspension of the writ of habeas corpus during times of peace; but as proposed by the Convention of 1787 the new Constitution enumerated no specific guarantees of freedom of speech, press, assembly, and religion. Nor did it address the rights of due process that became the foundation of our current justice system: the prohibition against unreasonable search and seizure and forced confessions, the right to counsel, and protection against cruel and unusual punishment. These rights were intended to place limits on the powers of the state by guarding against the kinds of abuses of power that colonial Americans experienced at the hands of British law enforcement.

Alexander Hamilton and other opponents of a national bill of rights argued that since the Constitution protected fundamental rights and since most state constitutions contained a bill of rights, the inclusion of a national bill of rights would be not only redundant but dangerous. In *The Federalist* (No. 84), Hamilton reasoned that the phrase "Congress shall make no law . . . abridging the freedom of speech, or of the press" might actually imply that the national government had the power to regulate speech or the press as long as it did so without "abridging" those liberties. Nevertheless, on December 15, 1791, a national bill of rights—largely the work of James Madison, who was initially strongly resistant to the idea—was ratified and added to the Constitution. Madison knew that the precise meaning of the rights and liberties in the first ten amendments would always be subject to vigorous debate, but that the adoption and ratification of the Bill of Rights would codify the legal recognition of the existence of those rights.[2]

The framers did not proceed from the assumption that rights are to be granted to the people by the government, but from an understanding that rights exist independently of civil society and government. The First Amendment does not read "The People shall enjoy freedom of speech and press," but rather "Congress shall make no law . . . abridging the freedom of speech, or of the press." Thus, the Bill of Rights codifies these fundamental rights in order to place concrete constitutional limits on governmental authority.

The Bill of Rights was adopted to protect the citizens of the states from the potential abuses of the new federal government; it was not intended to limit the powers of the state governments. Indeed, in 1833 Chief Justice John Marshall argued that had the framers intended the Bill of Rights to limit the powers of the state governments, they would have clearly expressed that intention in plain language.[3] Marshall, who was by no means reluctant to expand the power of the national government, contended that the Supreme Court could not protect the individual's rights from state action.

It was not until the middle of the twentieth century that the Supreme Court "nationalized" the Bill of Rights by selectively applying provisions of the first ten amendments to the states through the Fourteenth Amendment.

After the Civil War, the Thirteenth, Fourteenth, and Fifteenth Amendments were adopted to abolish slavery, to grant citizenship to those who were emancipated, and to protect their right to vote. The amendments were intended by Congress to prohibit the states from imposing hardships on African Americans because of their race, color, or previous condition of servitude. Nearly three quarters of a century would pass, however, before the promise of equal justice for African Americans would even begin to be realized. The revolution in civil rights would finally come in 1954 in *Brown v. Board of Education*, where the Supreme Court ruled that racially segregated public schools violated the equal protection clause of the Fourteenth Amendment. The equal protection clause then became the means by which the Court scrutinized discriminatory state regulations and began to dismantle the legal underpinnings of a segregated society.

## Constitutional Questions

At first glance the rights and liberties set forth in the Constitution seem abundantly clear; but upon closer scrutiny we can appreciate why the language it contains raises more questions than it answers. For example, the First Amendment states: "Congress shall make no law respecting an establishment of religion, or prohibiting the free exercise thereof; or abridging the freedom of speech, or of the press; or the right of the people peaceably to assemble, and to petition the Government for a redress of grievances." Two religion clauses of the First Amendment were intended to safeguard religious liberty and freedom of conscience, but does the phrase "no law respecting an establishment of religion" merely prohibit Congress from establishing or founding an official church or does it also prohibit any state-sanctioned religious practice, such as prayer or Bible reading in public schools? Is the free exercise clause an absolute, prohibiting any restrictions on religious practice or just the restrictions that are unreasonable? What about religious practices that contravene social mores or generally applicable laws? Should members of the Native American Church be allowed to ingest the hallucinogenic cactus peyote, an illegal controlled substance, in order to exercise their long-established religious rituals? The Church of the Lukumi Babalu Aye still sacrifices animals as a part of its religious ceremony. Should freedom of religion supercede animal cruelty laws?

The freedom of speech is a cornerstone of our democratic system because it is essential to the free and open exchange of political ideas and thus to the ability of a people to hold government accountable. More than this, it is essential to the human thirst for self-expression through literature, music, or art. The First Amendment plainly states that the freedom of speech shall not be abridged, but is this right absolute? If not, what kinds of restrictions are permissible? For that matter, how is speech defined? Does it extend beyond spoken words to other forms of expression?

The language in the Fourteenth Amendment raises even more questions than that in the First Amendment: "No State shall make or enforce any law which shall abridge the privileges or immunities of citizens of the United States; nor shall any State deprive any person of life, liberty, or property, without due process of law; nor deny to any person within its jurisdiction the equal protection of the laws." What, precisely, are the privileges and immunities enjoyed by citizens? Are privileges and immunities the same as rights? Does this clause confer additional rights to citizens beyond those in the Bill of Rights? In what ways does the due process clause of the Fourteenth Amendment differ from the identical clause in the Fifth Amendment?

The phrase "no state shall deny persons the equal protection of the laws" appears to need little if any clarification, but it too has proved vexing. Does it require only that all persons have the same legal status as citizens or does it require that all persons be treated equally; that is, free from any kind of discrimination? If the latter is so, does the equal protection clause forbid only state-sponsored discrimination in schools and other state facilities or does it protect against private discrimination by landlords, restaurant owners, and private clubs and organizations? Does it extend to women as well? The equal protection clause of the Fourteenth Amendment was adopted to prohibit states from denying to African Americans the equal protection of the laws. What about other groups of persons who have experienced discrimination on the basis of sex, age, national origin, religion, or sexual preference?

## PURPOSE OF THIS BOOK

*Analysis of Supreme Court Rulings.*   Since the answers to these constitutional questions can be found in the opinions of the U.S. Supreme Court, it is the purpose of this book to undertake a comprehensive analysis of the major Supreme Court rulings that have shaped the nature and scope of our civil rights and liberties. Rather than a collection of abridged opinions found in traditional casebooks, this book offers a detailed examination of the facts, constitutional questions, outcome, reasoning, and significance of those rulings. The intent is to help readers at both the introductory and the advanced levels better understand our civil rights and liberties.

This book's analytical approach includes highlighted major constitutional questions in each chapter to help readers fully understand the reasoning or logic underlying the Court's opinion. The key to understanding constitutional law is not having the right answers but asking the right questions. Simple is the task of associating the right to privacy with *Griswold v. Connecticut* or the abandonment of the separate but equal doctrine with *Brown v. Board of Education.* Far more important and challenging is the task of identifying the constitutional or legal questions raised by each case.

The Supreme Court's written opinions are intended to show that its rulings are rooted in constitutional principles and established legal precedent. It is not enough for the Court to decree that new restrictions on speech are permissible—it must explain how its solution to the dispute is compatible with the Constitution. Examining opinions from the standpoint of constitutional questions fosters a better understanding of the logic behind the expansion and narrowing of rights and liberties; the legal mechanisms employed in this process; and the competing social, economic, and political interests affecting landmark Supreme Court decisions.

This book contains numerous excerpts from influential, eloquent, and controversial opinions. These excerpts illustrate the handiwork of powerful legal minds that have shaped our society; they also remind us that the "Court" is not an abstraction that mechanically produces opinions but is rather a group of nine human beings, each having a distinct judicial philosophy.

For the classroom, this book can serve as a stand-alone discussion of the Court's decisions, but it is also designed to supplement a traditional casebook or collection of opinions (for a constitutional law course, for instance) or to be used in conjunction with the full text of the Court's opinions found at various sites on the World Wide Web. At the end of each chapter readers are provided with web site addresses to these online sources in a sidebar listing the major rulings found in the chapter.

*Competing Judicial Philosophies.*   In addition to its primary purpose, this book also addresses the overarching thesis that *competing judicial philosophies are critical to the development and evolution of civil rights and liberties.* Judicial philosophy refers simply to a justice's substantive policy choices (e.g., a tendency to favor or oppose affirmative action), beliefs about the proper application of the Supreme Court's power (active or restrained), and adopted theory of constitutional interpretation (strict or broad construction).

To say that the definition and extent of our rights depend on a "Court" obscures the fact that individual justices have placed their imprimatur on all of our lives. While it is appropriate to speak of the philosophy of the Warren Court compared with the Burger or Rehnquist Courts (named for the tenure of the particular chief justice), we will see that each justice possesses a distinct judicial philosophy—a set of beliefs that influences an understanding of the judicial role and guides the interpretation of the vaguely worded provisions of the Constitution. Changes in the composition of the Court—due to retirements, deaths, and new presidential appointments—have an impact on the position that the Court will take on a range of issues, such as abortion, race, or homosexuality. There are no shortages of narrowly decided (5–4) rulings where the casting of one vote in the other direction would have a dramatic effect on society.

Competing judicial philosophies[4] have always been critical to the development of civil rights and liberties. Even in the relatively rare instances where the Court hands down a unanimous (9–0) ruling, fundamental divisions among the justices still remain. This theme is woven throughout the chapters in this book and then directly addressed in the concluding chapter. Offered there is an analysis of the judicial philosophies of the current justices and an assessment of whether a dramatic shift in judicial philosophy has led to the modification or abandonment of the major precedents in freedom of expression, due process, privacy, and affirmative action that were produced by the liberal judicial activism of the Warren Court. Has the tenure of conservatives such as Chief Justice William Rehnquist and Justices Antonin Scalia and Clarence Thomas brought about a counterrevolution or has the principle of *stare decisis,* or respect for precedent, and other factors forestalled or prevented any radical change in civil rights and liberties? Has the Rehnquist Court taken us in new directions by revisiting issues thought to be well settled?

Our inquiry begins with many questions. Before proceeding to answer those questions it will be useful to understand how the Supreme Court makes its decisions. Therefore, the remainder of this chapter is a brief primer on the power, operation, and output of the Court, followed by a guide to legal research on the World Wide Web so that readers can locate the full opinions of the cases discussed in this book.

## THE POWER AND OPERATION OF THE SUPREME COURT

### Judicial Review

At the core of the Supreme Court's authority and prestige is the principle of judicial review—the power to review the constitutionality of any federal or state law or regulation, local ordinance, lower judicial ruling, and executive action. The Court exercises this power by weighing the challenged law or governmental action against a superior law or the U.S. Constitution, which is the highest law.

The Court applies the power of judicial review to help define the powers of Congress and the president, shape the relationship between the national government and the states, and expound the scope and nature of our constitutional rights. Judicial review gives the Supreme Court the final word on the meaning of the powers, rights, and privileges set forth in the Constitution. Americans have grown to accept the legitimacy of this power even though the Constitution makes no mention of judicial review. Article III of the Constitution states only that the Supreme Court has "the Judicial Power of the United States" and extends this power "to all cases in Law and Equity arising under this Constitution." Article III, however, is silent on the precise definition of judicial power. Article III also grants the Court irrevocable original jurisdiction in cases affecting ambassadors, public ministers, or consuls, or in cases in which a state is suing another state. More importantly, the Court's power to hear appeals—its appellate jurisdiction—is also granted by Article III, but "with such Exceptions and under such Regulations as Congress shall make."

The Constitution says very little about the Court's powers and responsibilities. The delegates to the 1787 Constitutional Convention devoted relatively little discussion to the powers of the Supreme Court because they considered the proposed judicial branch to be the least powerful and thus potentially the least dangerous branch of the national government.[5]

Nevertheless, a strong consensus existed among the framers that the judiciary be an independent and coequal branch. Though the power of judicial review would not be expressly granted, the Supreme Court would possess the power to strike down legislative acts that were in flagrant violation of the Constitution. This power is based on the fact that the Constitution is superior to ordinary law and that laws that conflict with it are void.[6] *The Federalist* (No. 78) states that because "[t]he interpretation of the laws is the proper and peculiar province of the courts," and courts were designed to keep the legislature from acting outside of their assigned authority, the judicial branch has the power to void unconstitutional laws.[7]

Judicial review is also implied by the national supremacy clause in Article VI, Section 2, which states: The "Constitution, and Laws of the United States which shall be made in Pursuance thereof . . . shall be the supreme Law of the land; and the Judges in every State shall be bound thereby." If "[j]udges in every state" was meant to include justices of the Supreme Court, then the phrase suggests that the framers intended that federal judges could apply the test of constitutionality to national as well as state laws.[8]

The implication of such power in the newly proposed Constitution met with some opposition, but *The Federalist* (No. 81) effectively countered critics of the proposed national judiciary by arguing that nothing in the Constitution directly empowers the Supreme Court to trump the will of the legislature by reviewing the constitutionality of legislation and thus molding the laws into any form that the justices think proper. The legislature is supreme in its authority to make laws. However, if a law is in clear and obvious conflict with the Constitution, it is the duty of the Court to declare the law null and void.[9] This is precisely the point that Chief Justice John Marshall seized upon in *Marbury v. Madison*, 1 Cranch 137 (1803), one of the most significant cases in American history. Marshall found that Congress had enacted a statute that altered the Court's original jurisdiction in Article III and thus conflicted with the Constitution, the highest law of the land. He succinctly reasoned that if it is the role of a court to interpret the law and determine what the law means, and the Constitution is the highest law in the land, then it is the duty of the Supreme Court—the highest court—to say what the Constitution means and, if necessary, to strike down laws or actions that conflict with the highest law. The theory of judicial review may not have originated in *Marbury*, but Marshall's reasoning established a constitutional precedent upon which judicial review exists in fact. Many initially rejected the idea that the Court, rather than Congress, had the final say on the Constitution, but Marshall's logic persisted until, over time, the power of judicial review became a firmly established principle.

Today, the most dramatic exercise of judicial review occurs when the Court overturns an act of Congress because it is negating the actions of another coequal branch of government. Critics of the Court's actions often ask why an undemocratically constituted body of nine elites—not directly accountable to the voters—should be given extraordinary authority to reverse or undo the will of the American people expressed through their elected representatives. Such criticism, however, may miss the point entirely. Arguably, the Supreme Court is in some way accountable to the majority, but the Court's first responsibility is to the Constitution. The justices have no constituency other than the highest law of the land. If the will of the people expressed through law conflicts with the Constitution, then the peoples' will must be undone.[10]

In addition, the Court has used its power sparingly. The Court is a reactive body that hears only a fraction of the tens of thousands of legal disputes tried and resolved by the lower courts. Very few laws are ever challenged. Of the more than 60,000 laws enacted by Congress, the Court has overturned only about 150 federal statutes since 1790.[11] Nevertheless, the cases in which the Court has struck down acts of Congress have had dramatic consequences. Among these laws have been the Missouri Compromise of 1820, intended to forestall a sectional crisis by restricting the westward spread of slavery in the territories;[12] early attempts to regulate industry; laws prohibiting child labor;[13] and many of the popular New Deal programs of the 1930s.[14] More recently, the Court struck down the presidential line-item veto,[15] a law banning guns from schools,[16] and the Religious Freedom Restoration Act as part of a congressional attempt to expand the free exercise clause of the First Amendment.

In many instances, however, the Court strikes down only part of a law, *and* often it applies its power of judicial review to uphold important acts of Congress that have been challenged in the courts.

The Court has also used its power of judicial review to alter the balance of state-federal relations by striking down 1,249 state laws and local ordinances since 1790[17] on the grounds that they conflict with the Constitution, federal law, or contravene the principle of national supremacy.

## An Independent Judiciary

The Supreme Court's authority also rests on the principle of judicial independence—the idea that judges should make impartial decisions free from political pressures exerted by the other branches of government, interest groups, and voters. One of the crown jewels of the America political system, judicial independence did not originate with the adoption of the Constitution. It is deeply rooted in the English common law tradition of the neutral judge or magistrate who has no stake in the issuance of a warrant or in ruling in favor of the farmer over the rancher in a property line dispute.[18] Having witnessed the abuses of judicial power by the king in colonial America, the framers sought to maximize independence by establishing a constitutionally independent and coequal judicial branch.

Just as Article III of the Constitution makes no mention of the power of judicial review, so too is it silent on the principle of an independent judiciary. However, Article III does contain three provisions upon which judicial independence rests. First, the judicial power clause states that "[t]he judicial power of the United Sates, shall be vested in one supreme Court, and in such inferior Courts as the Congress may from time to time ordain and establish." Since "the" judicial power is delegated to the courts and not to Congress or the president, Article III creates a separate and independent judicial authority that is protected from encroachments by the other two branches. Second, the grant of life tenure "during good Behavior" by Article III assures federal judges that they are free to make independent decisions without fear that they might be removed or pressured from office. Third, the compensation clause of Article III that provides a salary "which shall not be diminished during their Continuance in Office" also enables federal judges to act without fear of monetary reprisals.

The terse and rather cryptic account of judicial prerogatives in Article III does diminish the importance the framers attached to the principle of judicial independence. In *The Federalist* (No. 78), Alexander Hamilton argued that an independent judiciary is "an excellent barrier to the encroachments and oppression of the representative body" and "the best expedient which can be devised in any government to secure a steady, upright, and impartial administration of the laws."

Simply put, the principle of judicial independence is a cornerstone of our democratic society because it allows judges to make impartial (and often unpopular) decisions based on the Constitution and the laws of the land. Judicial independence frees judges from the fear of political coercion or threats of punishment so that they can carry out their duty to uphold the laws of the land. As Chief Justice John Marshall so aptly said: "The Greatest scourge an angry Heaven ever inflicted upon an ungrateful and sinning people, was an ignorant, a corrupt, or a dependent Judiciary."[19]

The Court's independence as an institution is not absolute. The Constitution gives Congress the power to impeach and remove "all civil Officers" for "High Crimes and Misdemeanors," to establish and fund lower federal courts, and to subject the Supreme Court's power to hear appeals to "Exceptions" and "Regulations." The Constitution also grants to the president the "power, by and with the Advice and Consent of the Senate," to appoint "Judges of the supreme Court, and all other Officers of the United States."[20] The president can shape the federal judiciary and influence constitutional law. The Senate may use a president's nominee to the Court as a political pawn or refuse to confirm a nominee altogether.[21] The House may refuse to appropriate funds needed for judicial and administrative salaries. Congress will on occasion threaten to "strip" the federal courts of jurisdiction to hear certain kinds of cases or, in rare instances, threaten to impeach judges who make unpopular decisions. "Judge bashing" by candidates from both parties during a heated election campaign is common as well. Candidates have found it tempting to blame "activist" judges for all of society's ills. All of these kinds of threats are taken very seriously by judges and scholars because they undermine the public's understanding and appreciation of the importance of judicial independence.[22]

## The Application of Judicial Review: Judicial Activism and Judicial Restraint

Since the exercise of judicial review has an impact not only on the outcome of a case but also on the final interpretation of the Constitution, the manner in which this awesome power is exercised by the justices is of great importance. Whether the Court confronts or defers to Congress, interprets the First Amendment narrowly or broadly, or follows or overturns established precedent in the name of justice are matters of concern not only to scholars and practitioners, but ultimately, to all Americans.

The terms *judicial activism* and *judicial restraint* are commonly used to characterize the degree to which the power of judicial review is exercised. The two concepts are somewhat limited in what they can explain about judicial philosophy and the many factors that influence decisions, but they are useful tools to introduce readers to the ways that judges apply judicial review.

As the term implies, *judicial activism* (compared with judicial restraint) involves a more active exercise of judicial review. An activist justice is more open to change and innovation, which means a greater willingness to break from precedent or interpret precedent in a manner that allows change. Change suggests a departure from traditional constitutional or legal remedies. When justice or fairness demands, the activist is even willing to rely on unenumerated, or implied, constitutional rights, such as the right to privacy,[23] or the findings of social sciences.[24] Furthermore, when faced with a dispute raising a constitutional challenge to a law, the activist judge is more willing to challenge the legislative branch. The activist proceeds with no automatic presumption that the legislature has acted constitutionally, thus placing the burden squarely on the legislature to prove that there is a compelling basis for the law. Nor does the activist feel constrained to defer to the legislative (or the expressed will of the majority) because the court is a coequal and independent branch of government.

The activist is more likely to broadly, or loosely, interpret the Constitution to resolve a dispute, particularly where rights and liberties are threatened and there are no acceptable remedies found in the existing case law. For instance, a broad interpretation of the term "speech" would protect a wide range of activities or forms of expression protected by the First Amendment. In the real world, this would mean the difference between the flag burner going to jail or walking free. The Constitution is not a rigid document to be interpreted using a history book or a dictionary, but is rather a living document that must be interpreted to meet the needs of each new generation. In contrast, strict construction interprets the Constitution narrowly or by looking at its plain meaning.

Judges are often criticized for addressing moral and political issues rather than just legal ones. However, as in cases involving abortion and homosexuality, legal disputes take on moral and political dimensions. Some judges strive to avoid such moral questions, but activists are more inclined to believe that while a legal solution is preferred, some decisions cannot be made in a moral or political vacuum. In some instances, a ruling based on morality alone might be justifiable, particularly if a "higher law" has been implicated by an ordinary civil law.

The higher law approach to judging is rooted in the natural law tradition embraced by many of the nation's founders.[25] The natural law tradition posits that all laws ought to conform to an immutable natural law, or standard of justice, that is knowable through human reason. A law, then, can be voided not only because it is contrary to the Constitution but also because it is incompatible with the natural law. This school of thought also holds that since these rights exist naturally, they antedate civil society and exist independently of a written constitution. Among these rights, in Thomas Jefferson's words, are life, liberty, and happiness (or property, in John Locke's assessment). A judge who applies a higher law standard (or what might be called natural law judicial review) argues that laws can be declared void not only on the grounds that they violate provisions or rights contained in the Constitution, but also on the grounds of their incompatibility with the natural law.[26]

Turning to the mode of judging known as *judicial restraint*, we find that the judge embraces a more restrained application of judicial review. A dispute should be resolved by strict adherence to the established case law (precedent) and a narrow (strict) reading of the Constitution or laws. In a dispute raising a constitutional challenge to a law, the restraintist proceeds with the presumption that the legislature has acted constitutionally and is more likely to place the burden to prove unconstitutionality on the parties challenging the law.

Restraintists are generally strict constructionists, interpreting the Constitution narrowly (in some case literally). A strict interpretation of the term "speech" would likely result in limits on the kinds of expression protected by the First Amendment. Therefore, governmental restrictions on symbolic forms of expression, such as flag burning or erotic dancing, would more likely be upheld.

Proponents of judicial restraint often attempt to ascertain the intent of the framers—rather than applying modern values or needs—to help them understand the meaning of the Constitution. They might ask, What was the original intent of the framers when drafting the First Amendment? What kinds of activities did they seek to include in the word "speech"?

Restraintists criticize activists for imposing their own subjective assessment or personal values on the Constitution. For, in doing so, the activists exceed the legitimate bounds of judicial review, which in turn leads to a politicization of the law. Judicial activists are also criticized for addressing controversial social and political issues (rather than legal ones), and for "finding" new rights not specifically enumerated in the Constitution. Some argue that they have usurped the power of the legislatures, becoming players in the political process. This politicization of the law also accounts for how confirmation hearings in the Senate have become political debates rather than useful discussions of the nominee's qualifications to be a judge.[27]

Restraintists' behavior suggests the belief that law should not seek to solve moral, political, and social problems, just legal ones, and that decisions ought to be made on the basis of what the law is and not on the basis of what the law ought to be. Courts are instruments of the law—they should not impose their will but only apply the law.

The judicial activism versus restraint discussion is not merely an academic one. Hardly an election cycle passes without at least one candidate accusing federal judges of "legislating from the bench" rather than simply interpreting the Constitution and the laws. Members of Congress have blasted "activist" judges for controversial (and typically liberal) rulings on social issues—such as abortion, affirmative action, and the rights of the accused—or when the courts inject themselves into a political dispute involving campaigns and elections. On the other hand, restraintist judges have been criticized as conservative ideologues who hide behind the cloak of judicial restraint in order to defend the status quo and abdicate the power of judicial review. One challenge of using the activism-restraint dichotomy, therefore, is that in the real world it too has become politicized. A judge who exhibits characteristics of the activist is called a liberal and a restraintist is labeled a conservative. It is true that the rulings of the Warren Court—which established a revolution in civil rights and liberties that continues to shape our society—were supportive of liberal policies, such as the expansion of civil rights and greater restrictions on governmental control over personal freedoms. The Warren Court also paved the way for the judiciary to be more involved and active in solving society's social and political problems.

However, judicial activism and judicial restraint are not inherently liberal or conservative. Early in the twentieth century, an activist Supreme Court broadly interpreted the due process clause of the Fifth Amendment to strike down a range of popular liberal economic reforms, particularly the New Deal programs of President Franklin D. Roosevelt. The Rehnquist Court, dominated by justices appointed by conservative Republican presidents, may be exhibiting the characteristics of judicial activism, striking down acts of Congress and trimming back the many precedents of the Warren and Burger Courts.

While the terms "activist" and "restraintist" help us to classify the approaches that judges take in applying judicial review, they cannot fully explain the judicial philosophies that produce outcomes, or judicial decisions. Nor can political ideology—that is, whether a judge is a liberal or a conservative.[28] Judicial philosophy is shaped by complex factors. Such factors may include (1) the personal beliefs and values that a justice brings to the court; (2) role perceptions (i.e., a justice's understanding of the Court's role in society may affect his or her beliefs and behavior); (3) the influence of institutional values (e.g., the importance of impartiality, respect for precedent, collegiality, and proper application of power); (4) the influence of other justices (i.e., how the internal dynamics of the Court or the leadership of one or more justices can shape the justices' beliefs and behavior); (5) the particular dispute (e.g., hearing an emotional abortion or right to die dispute for the first time may have an impact on a justice's beliefs and values); and (6) pivotal social and political events, such as the unprecedented presidential election in 2000 or the threat to national security posed by the 2001 terrorist attacks on the World Trade Center and the Pentagon.[29]

## OPERATION OF THE SUPREME COURT: HOW THE COURT DECIDES A CASE

### Setting the Court's Agenda

During its term, which runs from October through June, the U.S. Supreme Court is bombarded with thousands of petitions requesting the Court to hear appeals or to review lower court rulings. Petitions for review involve two or more parties (litigants) that disagree with the outcome of a ruling from one of the twelve U.S. courts of appeals,[30] a U.S. district court,[31] or one of the fifty state supreme courts.[32] The majority of litigants are individuals, such as criminal defendants who are challenging convictions on constitutional or procedural grounds, and others who are disputing the outcome of a civil suit involving an award of monetary damages due to harm caused by a defective product or negligent action.

One of the most common kinds of appeals involves litigants seeking a ruling from the Court on the constitutionality of a policy or law. An example of this kind of lawsuit is *Dale v. The Boy Scouts of America*, discussed in chapter 7, where an openly gay scoutmaster challenged the constitutionality of the Boy Scout's policy prohibiting homosexuals from serving as scoutmasters. The Court is more likely to grant appeals in this kind of dispute because cases that involve issues of policy typically have broad ramifications and are of great interest to the justices.[33]

Cases dealing with public policy or constitutional rights are likely to involve interest groups, such as the American Civil Liberties Union (ACLU) and the National Association for the Advancement of Colored People (NAACP) on the liberal side of the spectrum; or more conservative groups, such as Americans for Effective Law Enforcement, and Americans United for Life. These group may submit *amicus curiae* ("friends of the court") briefs, urging the Court to grant an appeal, or they may be more directly involved in the lawsuit.[34]

The federal government is a litigant in about one third of all cases brought to the Supreme Court for review (more than any other party). On appeal, the government may ask the Court to sustain a civil rights policy or regulation against a constitutional challenge or uphold the conviction of a defendant that it prosecuted in a criminal case. In these cases, lawyers from the Solicitor General's Office in the Department of Justice represent the federal government.[35]

#### Requirements for Judicial Review

The Supreme Court possesses awesome power, but like any other court, it is a reactive body that can neither initiate a constitutional dispute nor extend judicial review to any social, legal, or political problem that it feels the need to solve. The Constitution, congressional legislation, and the Court's own self-imposed rules that govern its decision-making process limit the scope of judicial review. Specific guidelines and rules pertaining to jurisdiction and rules of access govern the kinds of disputes that reach the Court.

**Jurisdiction**   Jurisdiction is the power and authority of a court to hear a matter that is in dispute. Courts have jurisdiction over types of cases as well as over geographic areas of a state or nation. While a court may have broad powers to decide a wide range of issues, it cannot hear a case that falls outside of its jurisdiction. Article III of the Constitution grants to the U.S. Supreme Court the authority to hear and decide "all Cases, in Law and Equity, arising under this Constitution, the laws of the United States, and Treaties." It further grants to the Court two kinds of jurisdiction: original, which enables parties to bring a case directly to the Court; and appellate, which empowers it to review and revise the judicial actions and proceedings of lower courts. The Court's original jurisdiction, which is not exercised often, extends to cases affecting ambassadors and other public ministers, disputes to which the U.S. government is a party, disputes between two or more states, disputes between a state and a citizen of another state, and disputes between a state (or citizens of that state) and foreign nations. Since the Court has the power to refuse to hear such disputes, very few cases have come to the Court under its original jurisdiction.[36] Typically, original jurisdiction cases involve lawsuits between two or more states over matters of water rights, mineral deposits, or claimed state boundaries.

More important is the Court's appellate jurisdiction to hear cases challenging the rulings of lower courts. The majority of cases that come to the Supreme Court do so on appeal from U.S. courts of appeal, special three-judge U.S. district courts, and state supreme courts in which rulings involve federal law or the U.S. Constitution.

**Rules of Access**   In addition to jurisdictional rules, a set of legal guidelines or rules of access determine the kinds of cases that the judiciary may hear. These rules fall into three broad categories: case or controversy, standing to sue, and political questions. The rules also determine who has access to the courts, thus determining the kinds of cases that judges believe ought to resolved by the judiciary as opposed to the legislative or the executive branch. The Supreme Court has helped define these rules of access. For example, the Warren Court increased access to the number and kinds of litigants who could bring discrimination or due process suits in the federal courts. The Court's 1954 landmark ruling in *Brown v. Board of Education* is heralded as a powerful denunciation of the separate but equal doctrine, thus ending discrimination in public schools. But *Brown* is equally important for expanding access to the federal courts because it granted standing to victims of discrimination in public schools to sue for relief in the federal courts. Thus *standing*, as one doctrine of access, refers to one's right to bring or join a lawsuit. A party must have a sufficient stake in a controversy in order to get to court. In a constitutional matter, for example, a person must be able to show that he or she was adversely affected by a law before being able to challenge its constitutionality.

Article III of the Constitution states that federal judicial power extends to *"case and controversies."* This rather vague clause has come to mean that before a court can exercise its power a real controversy must exist. The controversy must take the form of a real dispute between adversaries. Therefore, the Court cannot issue advisory opinions to legislatures or executive agencies concerning the constitutionality of a proposed law or regulation; it cannot rule until the law or regulation has been enforced and has injured or affected a person in some concrete way, at which point the case is considered *justiciable*, or ripe for adjudication, and appropriate for judicial consideration. A dispute must have ripened or matured from a theoretical dispute to a real or concrete one. The opposite of ripeness is mootness. *Mootness* means that the Court will refrain from hearing a case that has been filed too late or has been brought after the facts have changed or the problem has been resolved by other means.

The third category of the doctrine of access is called *political questions.* The Court has from time to time imposed limits on its own power by refusing to address certain questions that the justices believe ought to be answered by the political branches of government. Such questions have included issues related to military or foreign policy, ratification of constitutional amendments, naturalization policy, and matters involving voting and elections. The political question doctrine does not mean that the Court refuses to hear cases in which the Constitution and politics intersect, since most matters before the Court affect politics in some way. Rather, the doctrine refers more to the Court's reluctance to cross into the distinct realm of authority of the other two separate branches of government. However, since *Baker v. Carr*,[37] where in 1962 the Court struck down racially motivated schemes that determined boundaries of legislative districts, the political question doctrine has been ignored in disputes involving voting rights and electoral politics. Indeed, the most recent and dramatic illustration of this point was the Court's role in deciding the outcome of the 2000 presidential election in *Bush v. Gore.*

### Granting Certiorari: The Decision to Hear an Appeal

Since the passage of the Judiciary Act of 1925,[38] enacted to relieve the Court's overcrowded docket, most of the cases that come to the Court are through writ of certiorari, or what is known as "cert." Certiorari is an order by an appellate court to hear an appeal.[39] If the writ of certiorari is denied, the lower court judgment remains standing.[40]

The power to grant cert gives the Court nearly absolute discretionary control over its dockets, thereby enhancing its power and prestige. As a result, the Court grants plenary review to less than 5 percent of the more than 7,000 petitions for appeal. Plenary review is full consideration by the Court, which means that the parties are allowed to submit briefs and present oral argument before the Court makes its final decisions. Most cases are decided without oral argument and full consideration. The Court simply affirms, vacates, or reverses the lower court's ruling.[41] As a result, the Court hands down rulings with full opinions in only about seventy-five cases during its nine-month term.[42] Nevertheless the number of petitions has grown dramatically during the past thirty years, doubling since the early

1970s. One reason for this increase, is the number of prisoners filing habeas corpus petitions to appeal their convictions.[43] The Court has responded to its burgeoning caseload by raising its standards for granting certiorari, thus reducing the number of petitions for cert from 105 in 1991 to 81 in 1998. Consequently, the number of signed opinions (cases given plenary review) was also down, from 107 in 1991 to 75 in 1998.[44]

Although the Court issues a lengthy and complex opinion explaining its final decision in a case, the justices are not obligated to make known their reasons to grant or reject an appeal. As a result, we do not know as much as we would like about the dynamics of the decision to grant certiorari. This stage in the process is almost as important as the Court's final ruling, for a refusal to grant certiorari means that the lower court's decision stands.

The justices work closely with their law clerks, typically recent graduates from law school, to assemble a pool of petitions for certiorari that merit further consideration. Each justice's final list of cases is added to the chief justice's "discuss list" for further consideration and debate during the Court's conference. Certiorari is granted only when four of the nine justices agree to do so, a tradition that is called the "Rule of Four." How does the Court "decide to decide"? Although many complex variables influence a justice's decision to grant cert, a few fundamental standards outlined by the Court's Rule 10 must be met before an appeal will be granted. Rule 10 is the only official criterion that the justices follow when evaluating a petition for certiorari.[45] It states that "[a] review on writ of certiorari is not a matter of right, but of judicial discretion[,]" to be granted "only when there are special and important reasons therefor." Rule 10 goes on to say that the Court is to consider granting review when courts around the country have reached conflicting conclusions regarding an important question arising under the Constitution or have ruled in a manner directly opposed to an earlier Supreme Court ruling or precedent. (A precedent is a well-established ruling in a case that offers judges guidance in subsequent cases arising under identical or similar questions of law.) This is particularly true when there is a conflict among federal courts of appeal in any of the twelve circuits.[46] The U.S. courts of appeal hear cases on appeal from federal district courts and administrative agencies, such as the Department of Health and Human Services or the Environmental Protection Agency.

Although there are a limited number of possible answers to a major constitutional question, it is possible for two or more courts to arrive at conflicting interpretations of the Constitution, a law, or prior rulings. If the Supreme Court were to leave standing conflicting interpretations of the Constitution or a federal law, there would be no definitive interpretation of a law or final determination of what the Constitution means. It is also important to note that the Supreme Court will hear only the appeals from state supreme courts that involve cases and controversies involving the U.S. Constitution or federal law.

Rule 10 does not limit the justices' choices; it merely specifies certain types of conflicts that are worthy of review. Beyond those conflicts, Rule 10 was designed by the Court to provide justices with the broadest discretion to determine whether a case should be reviewed. On the downside, lawyers do not have access to hard-and-fast rules to guide their decision to appeal a lower court's ruling. This handicap results in lawyers sending the Court many petitions for certiorari that may be without merit, adding to the Court's job of sorting through petitions.[47]

Justices are also more likely to grant cert when good arguments can be made on both sides of the dispute. A petition for appeal has a better chance of being granted if it contains an argument or a question that offers a unique perspective that is likely to arouse interest in a justice. A justice who has been in the minority on a recurring issue, such as abortion, may vote to grant cert because he or she wishes to use the case to expose other justices to a novel approach to the issue. The unique nature of each dispute always has the potential to lead the justices down a new decisional path.

Since justices are human beings with moral and political preferences, and since the Court is not required to provide written justification of its certiorari decisions, appeals may be granted purely on the basis of personal opinions, policy agendas, or feelings toward the parties or groups involved in the case. For example, a conservative justice who fears further weakening of police powers may vote to deny cert if he or she believes that hearing the case will lead to expansion of the rights of the accused. Justices may also be influenced by the identity of the party petitioning for appeal. Generally, the Court seems more willing to grant an appeal when the government is a party in the dispute or when groups such as the NAACP or the ACLU are petitioners or have filed *amicus curiae* briefs.[48]

While the factors that influence the decision to grant cert are complex, the mechanics of the stages of the cert process are straightforward. The thousands of petitions for certiorari go to the clerk of the Court. Not to be confused with a law clerk who assist the justices, the clerk of the Court sends the petitions and supporting papers to each justice's chamber. The petitions are divided up and randomly assigned to each justice who chooses to be part of the "cert pool." This division of labor is intended to save time by avoiding a duplication of effort on the part of the justices and their law clerks. Each justice's law clerk writes memos summarizing and evaluating the merits of each petition and forwards the memos to the chambers of the chief justice as well as to each justice in the pool. A justice who chooses not to participate in the pool will employ his or her own system for reviewing petitions.

Based on the memos sent to his chambers, the chief justice prepares a "discuss list" of petitions to be reviewed in conference. Other justices may add to the list, but cases left off the list are denied further consideration.[49] The petitions that make the discuss list are "meritorious"; that is, they make strong arguments for further review.

In conference, which is closed to all but the justices, the chief justice initiates a brief discussion of the merits of each case. Then, in order of seniority, the justices vote to grant or deny cert.

The Court has great discretion, and thus broad powers, over nearly all of the petitions for appeals from the lower courts, meaning that it alone determines which appeals it wishes to hear. By selecting the kinds of appeals it wishes to grant, the Court exerts control over its agenda and chooses the legal and constitutional issues that it feels need to be addressed. This prerogative definitely adds to the Court's power but should not be construed to mean that lower courts have little impact on policy. On the contrary, less than 1 percent of all federal and state cases are heard by the Supreme Court. Although the Supreme Court's rulings receive the most attention—because they establish precedent—most cases are ultimately decided by the lower federal courts and the courts of the fifty states. The Supreme Court is a court of last resort, not a reactive body with the power of automatic review.

## Oral Argument

During the certiorari process the justices also determine (by at least four votes) whether to decide the case based solely on legal briefs and other written materials or to convene an oral argument. If a case is accepted for oral argument, the justices convene publicly to hear lawyers from each side of the case present legal or constitutional arguments. The lawyers then submit new written briefs that address the issues to be raised during oral argument. The Court also receives *amicus curiae* briefs from interest groups, the government, and other third parties that have a vested interest in the outcome of the case.[50]

Oral argument is typically scheduled four months after a petition for cert has been granted. Standing before the Court's elevated bench, the attorneys representing each side of the dispute are allotted thirty minutes to present an argument. Although justices have already studied written briefs and materials that the parties have submitted to the Court, oral argument gives the lawyers one last chance to influence the thinking of the justices.[51]

While some court watchers, scholars, and the justices themselves have contended that oral argument is largely a pro forma event staged for the public, others maintain that it has an impact on the outcome of the case.[52] Chief Justice Earl Warren did not believe that oral argument was very persuasive;[53] but Chief Justice William Rehnquist has written:

> [S]peaking for myself, it does make a difference: I think that in a significant minority of cases in which I have heard oral argument, I have left the bench feeling different about the case than I did when I came on the bench. The change is seldom a full one-hundred-and-eighty-degree swing, and I find that it is most likely to occur in case involving areas of the law with which I am least familiar.[54]

During oral argument in *Bush v. Gore*, which decided the 2000 presidential election, Governor George W. Bush's attorney Theodore Olson raised a few points that the justices had not yet considered and, in doing so, influenced the final outcome of the case and the election.[55] Olson was later appointed solicitor general by President Bush. The solicitor general, the third-ranking official in the U.S. Department of Justice, represents the federal government before the Supreme Court. Cases in which the government is a party may exceed one third of the Supreme Court's total caseload during its nine-month term.[56]

During oral argument, a justice may sit passively or may vigorously question counsel with the intent of introducing his or her colleagues to new or different perspectives on a constitutional issue. Indeed, it may be a justice's best opportunity to raise issues about which other members of the Court are unaware or hesitant to address.[57]

## Conference and Vote

On Fridays, the nine justices meet in conference to present their points of view and vote on the cases heard earlier that week. The chief justice presides over the highly structured conference, during which each justice summarizes his or her position, and then casts a vote. The conference is not an open debate or a sharing of ideas whereby the justices make up their minds or attempt to persuade others,[58] but simply a stage in the process where the justices state their positions and vote.[59] This is not to suggest that justices do not try to influence their associates. Justices exert subtle (and not so subtle) influence over their colleagues at every stage in the decisional process. As a "task leader," the chief justice may influence vote outcomes though his power to schedule and manage the workload or to set the agenda during a conference.[60]

The final outcome of the case is determined by a vote of a majority (at least five) of the justices, although a justice may change his or her vote while the final written opinion is being drafted. At this stage, in many ways, the justices' work has really just begun. They must now craft a complex written opinion expressing the Court's final position on the legal or constitutional question(s) in the case.

## The Opinion

The chief justice has the important and influential role of assigning which justice will write the opinion. If the chief justice is in the majority, he may choose to write the opinion, or he may assign another member of the majority to write it. If the chief is in the minority, the senior associate justice in the majority has the discretion to write or assign the opinion. As there is often disagreement among the justices within the majority and minority blocs, distinct coalitions of two, three, or four justices form in nearly every decision that the Court hands down. (These coalitions may differ from issue to issue.)[61]

A justice who joins the majority in the final outcome of the case may write a concurring opinion to express a different position on a point of law or fact. A concurring opinion may also be written to discuss an issue neglected by the majority opinion. Generally, concurring opinions are written by justices who agree with the Court's judgment but disagree with the majority's logic or reasoning. If the justice's disagreement is minor or focuses on a narrow point of law, the concurring opinion may pass into history with little effect. However, if the Court is sharply divided on a ruling, with two or more of the majority taking issue with the reasoning or approach to the problem, then the concurring opinion(s) may have a significant impact on the ultimate fate of the Court's ruling.[62] Compliance with the ruling will be more difficult to secure and, the Court will later be forced to return to the same issue.

The members of the Court in the minority may write a dissenting opinion expressing an alternative point of view. Dissenting opinions have no force of law (i.e., no formal legal or constitutional impact). They are written to express a justice's disagreement and perhaps lay the foundation for a future Court to reverse or modify the present majority's ruling. A dissenting opinion can give us a feel for both sides of the issue. Since they are often written to keep the other side "honest," dissents can help us judge whether the majority's argument is on sound footing.

During a period of several weeks following the conference vote, justices draft and circulate among their colleagues majority, dissenting, and concurring opinions. Memoranda are exchanged until the Court reaches a final decision on the content and wording of the opinion. Justices may change their minds after reading these opinions and memos, thus changing the outcome of the case.[63]

As the Court's term draws to a close, a flurry of opinions are handed down and made public. The author of the majority opinion will announce from the bench the outcome of the case and read a summary of the Court's reasoning. Justices who wrote separate concurring or dissenting opinions will also read portions of their opinions from bench.

## THE IMPORTANCE OF THE COURT'S OPINIONS

As you read the analyses of the Court's opinions throughout this book, bear in mind that the Court chooses it words with great care, demonstrating to the nation that its ruling is rooted in constitutional principles, well-established precedent, and reasoned logic. Opinions are usually written narrowly, focusing on the specific issue or question raised by the dispute. The Court is reluctant to stray beyond the issue at hand to offer its position on anticipated disputes or matters that need clarification. For example, the Court may rule that a law promoting Bible reading in public schools is unconstitutional without ruling directly on whether Bible reading in other public institutions is unconstitutional.

The Court must interpret the vague wording of the Constitution against the backdrop of custom, tradition, and above all, legal precedent in order to maintain the stability of the law and the legitimacy of its own authority. As a precedent-setting civil rights case, *Brown v. Board of Education*, for instance, has provided stability and continuity in civil rights law since 1954. In sum, an opinion must demonstrate that the Court's judgment is respectful of past wisdom while meeting present needs.

Since no two cases present identical facts and circumstances, the Court is not bound to honor every word of prior opinions. It does, however, endeavor to follow the basic holding of the earlier case, including the underlying principles and rules. In addition, by explaining how it reached its decision, the Court is establishing the guidelines by which every judge, lawyer, and legislator ought to interpret the law or the Constitution. The opinion will also shed light on the future of proposed or pending legislation. For instance, it is certain that as soon as the Court hands down a ruling on abortion, anti-abortion rights legislators and advocates begin mapping out strategies for new restrictions on abortion that will pass constitutional muster under the Court's latest guidelines.

The opinions of the Supreme Court educate public officials and society about the nature and scope of our rights and duties. Although the main task of the justices is to resolve the legal questions of the case as narrowly as possible to limit second-guessing of the Court, opinions also offer commentaries on the social, political, and economic conflicts that shape our society and collective morality. The Court often takes a professorial tone in its opinions. But while some observers lampoon the justices as nine demanding law professors or as the philosopher kings of Plato's *Republic*, there is no doubt that through legal reasoning, logic, and a dash of political rhetoric, the Court teaches us not only about the nature and scope of governmental powers and constitutional rights, but also about human dignity, tolerance, and the legitimacy of power.

## COMPLIANCE AND IMPLEMENTATION OF THE COURT'S DECISIONS

The Court's opinions are the final word on constitutional questions. They become the law of the land. However, opinions are subject to much scrutiny, second-guessing, and conflicting interpretation by judges, lawyers, legislators, and scholars.[64] There may even be two or three different interpretations of what the Court said or meant to say by the time the media picks up the story on opinion days. In some instances, it will take years of further litigation to implement a ruling, as in the case of the Court's desegregation decree in *Brown v. Board of Education*[65] or its school prayer ruling in *Engel v. Vitale*(1962).[66] Noncompliance occurs where there is a high degree of resistance in the affected population group—in other words, people are not just going to change their ways overnight.[67] Indeed, nearly thirty years after *Roe v. Wade* (1973), where Justice Harry Blackmun attempted to protect a woman's right to privacy while acknowledging the states' interest in protecting fetal health and the health of the mother, the public remains bitterly divided over the right to an abortion. In fact, almost immediately after the Court's issued its ruling, many legislators, advocacy groups, and others assiduously began working to limit and even circum vent it. This political movement produced new laws and regulations which, in turn, were challenged in the courts by proponents of abortion rights. Indeed, since *Roe* the Court has reviewed dozens of restrictions on abortion enacted by state legislatures and Congress. Such restrictions range from parental consent and spousal notification laws to proscriptions on the use of tax dollars to perform abortions. Other forms of resistance to *Roe*, such as protests at clinics and hospitals, produced a new body of case law dealing with the conflicting rights of anti-abortion activists and women exercising their right to privacy. Ultimately, Congress and the states may choose to pass a constitutional amendment to overturn *Roe v. Wade*.

The Warren Court's 1966 ruling in *Miranda v. Arizona*,[68] which required the police to read criminal suspects their constitutional rights, became standard police practice. Nevertheless, *Miranda* was challenged by members of the law enforcement community for more than thirty years. Although such resistance—in the form of litigation and lobbying—did narrow the practice, the Court ultimately upheld it during its 1999–2000 term.[69]

The Supreme Court's awesome power is tempered by certain factors, such as its nature as a reactive body, the rules of jurisdiction and access, internal norms of judicial behavior, and external political forces. The competing philosophies of judicial power held by the justices themselves also affect the Court's role. Nevertheless, the Court plays an extraordinary role in our society, shaping our rights and liberties as well as helping to define the American experience.

## ORGANIZATION OF THIS BOOK

The main purpose of this book is to help readers develop an understanding of civil rights and liberties by providing a comprehensive examination and analysis of the facts, constitutional questions, outcome, reasoning, and significance of the major Supreme Court rulings that have shaped the nature and scope of our fundamental freedoms.

The substantive discussion of civil rights and liberties begins in chapter 2, where we examine the scope and limits of freedom of expression under the First Amendment. The guiding constitutional question in this chapter is the following: When is it permissible for the government to restrict speech that pushes the limits of our tolerance, threatens order and national security, and is offensive to the majority of citizens? This chapter also discusses the implications of campaign finance reform on the First Amendment.

The discussion of obscenity in chapter 3 raises the following issues: Is the communication of sexually oriented ideas or images protected by the First Amendment? How does the Court determine whether material is obscene and therefore not protected? How has the Court responded to attempts to regulate radio and television broadcasts, erotic dancing, and lewd speech on the Internet?

Chapter 4 focuses on freedom of religion and freedom from religion. The chapter first inquires into the extent of our religious liberty under the free exercise clause by asking: When is it constitutional for the state to ban certain forms of religiously motivated conduct? It then examines issues arising under the establishment clause, such as school prayer, Bible reading, the teaching of creation science, and state aid to religion.

Chapter 5 examines the due process rights of society's most unpopular minority: persons accused of criminal behavior. Topics include the nationalization of the Bill of Rights; searches and seizures (including warrantless searches), electronic eavesdropping, and aerial surveillance; the right to counsel; the privilege against self-incrimination; and the Eighth Amendment's prohibition of cruel and unusual punishment.

Chapter 6 analyzes the growth and development of the right of privacy and how this right affects such issues as abortion, "the right to die" and "assisted suicide," drug testing, and the rights of homosexuals.

Chapter 7 traces the development of the Court's interpretation of the equal protection clause of the Fourteenth Amendment, from finding remedies for race and sex discrimination (including sexual harassment), to issues such as affirmative action and quotas. Also discussed are the Court's rulings that affect discrimination based on sexual preference and the impact of the equal protection clause on how the nation elects its leaders.

The last chapter, chapter 8, addresses a number of questions raised throughout the book: Is it possible to classify the individual and collective judicial philosophy of the Rehnquist Court? Did the Rehnquist Court lead a counterrevolution in civil rights and liberties by bringing about a dramatic shift in judicial philosophy? Were the celebrated rulings of the Warren and Burger eras abandoned? What impact did the Clinton appointees have on the Court?

## FINDING THE FULL TEXT OF U.S. SUPREME COURT OPINIONS ON THE WORLD WIDE WEB

The cases discussed in each chapter are assigned an official citation by the Reporter of the Supreme Court. For example, the famous school prayer case *Engel v. Vitale* is cited as 370 U.S. 421 (1962). This citation tells you that the opinion can be located in volume 370 of the *United States Reporter* on page 421. Before the development of electronic databases and the Internet, researchers had to find the full text of the opinion in the *United States Reporter*—still found in major libraries—and photocopy the document or read the case in the library.

Today, readers can search the Internet and download opinions, which are in the public domain and free of charge. At the end of each chapter in this book, there is a sidebar listing the major opinions discussed in the chapter along with the Internet addresses of the full opinions. Find and bookmark these sites; they have user-friendly search engines that require only that you enter the case name or proper names of one or both parties in the case, such as "*Bush v. Gore*" or "*Roe v. Wade*." Because the content and organization of web sites are always in flux, over time some of these sites may be replaced by more advanced sites or newer electronic means to access opinions.

If you intend to read the full text of the Court's opinions in conjunction with the analysis of the cases found in this book, the following approach is suggested: Read the book or chapter first, then read and study the full opinion. Throughout this book, attention is given to the facts, constitutional or legal questions, ruling or outcome, and the reasoning of the justices in the majority and dissenting opinions. Although there are many ways to "brief" a case, let this framework help guide you through the full opinions.

---

 ## U.S. Supreme Court Opinions on the World Wide Web

1. Findlaw (at www.findlaw.com/casecode/supreme.html) contains a database of Supreme Court opinions since 1863, links to lower federal and state court opinions, and a range of legal research and news.

2. Cornell University's Legal Information Institute (at www.supct.law.cornell.edu/supct) contains a database of Supreme Court opinions since 1890 and a list of cases docketed for the current term (including the constitutional questions at issue).

3. The official web site of the U.S. Supreme Court (at www.supremecourtus.gov) provides general information, the calendar for oral arguments, a list of lawyers and *amicus curiae* involved in the current cases, and full opinions.

4. United States Supreme Court News summarizes decisions for subscribers and has links to the full text of opinions. To subscribe to this free service, send an e-mail message to listproc@willamette.edu. In the first line of the message, write: SUBSCRIBE WLO-USSC [YOUR NAME].

5. Library of Congress (at http://lcWeb.loc.gov/global/judiciary.html#sites) will link you to Supreme Court opinions, as well as to the opinions of other federal and state courts.

6. The Oyez project (at oyez.nwu.edu/), developed by Professor Jerry Goldman of Northwestern University, has a collection of audio recordings of oral arguments and will link you to FindLaw for the full text of opinions.

*Continued*

## U.S. Supreme Court Opinions on the World Wide Web  *Continued*

7. Office of the Solicitor General (at www.usdoj.gov/osg) provides a database of legal briefs filed in the Supreme Court by the solicitor general and also contains information on the solicitor general's office.

8. The Constitution of the United States of America: Analysis and Interpretation (at www.access.gpo.gov/congress/senate/constitution/toc.html) provides summaries of the Court's rulings and interpretation of the Constitution. The site also contains a compilation of all federal, state, and local laws that have been declared unconstitutional by the Court and all of the Court's rulings that have been overruled by later rulings.

9. U.S. Federal Courts Homepage (at www.uscourts.gov) serves as a clearinghouse for information about and from the judicial branch of the federal government.

## NOTES

1. *Black's Law Dictionary*, 7th ed. (St. Paul, MN: West Publishing Co., 1990).
2. *Federalist No. 84*, in Frederick Quinn, ed., *The Federalist Papers Reader* (Seven Locks Press: Washington, D.C., 1997).
3. *Barron v. Baltimore*, 32 U.S. (7 Pet.) 243 (1833).
4. The phrase "competing judicial philosophies" also appears in an important book on the chief justiceship of Warren Burger written by Earl M. Maltz, (*The Chief Justiceship of Warren Burger*, Columbia: University of South Carolina Press, 2000). Professor Maltz uses the phrase mainly to refer to the clash of judicial philosophies during the Burger tenure between newcomers to the Burger Court and holdovers from the Warren era.
5. For an excellent and comprehensive discussion of judicial review, see Christopher Wolfe, *Judicial Activism: Bulwark of Freedom or Precarious Security?* (Pacific Grove, CA: Brooks/Cole Publishing Co., 1990).
6. *Federalist No. 78*, in Quinn, *The Federalist Papers Reader*.
7. *Federalist No. 78*, in Quinn, *The Federalist Papers Reader*.
8. Forrest McDonald, *Novus Ordo Seclorum: The Intellectual Origins of the Constitution* (Lawrence: University of Kansas Press, 1985), 254–256.
9. *Federalist No. 81*, in Quinn, *The Federalist Papers Reader*.
10. See this argument in Elliot Slotnick, "The Place of Judicial Review in the American Tradition," 71 *Judicature* (August-September 1987).
11. Lawrence Baum, *The Supreme Court*, 7th ed. (Washington, D.C.: Congressional Quarterly Press, 2001), 195–198.
12. *Dred Scott v. Sanford*, 60 U.S. 393 (1857).
13. *Hammer v. Dagenhart*, 247 U.S. 251 (1918), and *Bailey v. Drexel Furniture*, 259 U.S. 412 (1922).
14. *United States v. Butler*, 297 U.S. 1 (1936), and *Schechter Poultry Corp. v. United States*, 295 U.S. 495 (1935).
15. *Clinton v. New York City*, http://laws.findlaw.com/us/000/97-1374.html. (1998).
16. *United States v. Lopez*, http://laws.findlaw.com/us/000/v10287.html. (1995).
17. Baum, *The Supreme Court*, 198–200.

18. See classic historical works such as Morton J. Horwitz, *The Transformation of American Law, 1780–1860* (Cambridge, MA: Harvard University Press, 1977); Theodore F. T. Plunkett, *A Concise History of the Common Law*, 5th ed. (Boston: Little, Brown, 1956); and Alexander Bickel, *The Least Dangerous Branch* (Indianapolis: Bobbs-Merrill, 1962).

19. *Proceedings and Debates of the Virginia State Convention of 1829–30*, at 616 (1830).

20. See American Bar Association, *An Independent Judiciary: Report of the Commission on Separation of Powers and Judicial Independence* (Washington, D.C.: American Bar Association, 1997).

21. See *Shaping America: The Politics of Supreme Court Appointments* (New York: HarperCollins, 1995).

22. This issue is taken so seriously that the American Bar Association and other groups have convened commissions and formed committees to educate members of the bar and general public about these threats. See American Bar Association, *An Independent Judiciary*.

23. See discussion of *Griswold v. Connecticut* in chapter 6.

24. See discussion of *Brown v. Board of Education* in chapter 7.

25. For a lively discussion of the impact of natural law on the framers, see the classic work, *The Declaration of Independence: A Study in the History of Political Ideas* (New York: Vintage Books, 1958), 24–79; and McDonald, *Novus Ordo Seclorum*.

26. See Wolfe, *Judicial Activism*.

27. See Robert Bork, *The Tempting of America: The Political Seduction of the Law* (New York: The Free Press, 1990).

28. See Jeffrey A. Segal and Albert D. Cover, "Ideological Values and the Votes of U.S. Supreme Court Justices," 83 *American Political Science Review* (June 1989), 557–565; Jeffrey A. Segal, Lee Epstein, Charles M. Cameron, and Harold Spaeth, "Ideological Values and the Votes of Justices Revisited," 57 *Journal of Politics* 812–823 (August 1995).

29. See Lee Epstein and Jack Knight, *The Choices Justices Make* (Washington, D.C.: Congressional Quarterly Press, 1998).

30. About 75 percent come to the Supreme Court from federal courts of appeals.

31. About 4 percent come directly from U.S. district courts.

32. About 14 percent come directly from state supreme courts.

33. Baum, *The Supreme Court*, 82–91.

34. For a detailed discussion of the role of interest groups, see Lee Epstein, "Interest Group Litigation During the Rehnquist Court Era," 9 *Journal of Law and Politics* (Summer 1993); and Karen O'Connor and Bryant Scott McFall, "Conservative Interest Group Litigation in the Reagan Era and Beyond," in *The Politics of Interests: Interest Groups Transformed*, ed. Mark P. Petracca (Boulder, CO: Westview Press, 1992).

35. H. W. Perry, Jr., *Deciding to Decide: Agenda Setting in the United States Supreme Court* (Cambridge MA: Harvard University Press, 1991), 128–130.

36. In the history of the Court, only about 175 cases have come to the Court under its original jurisdiction. See Vincent L. McKusick, "Discretionary Gatekeeping: The Supreme Court's Management of Its Original Jurisdiction Docket Since 1961," 45 *Maine Law Review* 185–242 (1993).

37. 369 U.S. 186 (1962).

38. 396 U.S., 295–298 (1962).

39. *Black's Law Dictionary*.

40. There are a few other ways to get a case to the Supreme Court, but they are rarely used. See Perry, *Deciding to Decide*, 22–31.

41. See David M. O'Brien, *Storm Center: The Supreme Court in American Politics*, 5th ed. (New York: Norton, 2000), 213–224.

42. "Statistical Recap of the Supreme Court's Workload During Last Three Terms," *United States Law Week*, July 20, 1999.

43. See Lee Epstein, Jeffrey Segal, Harold Spaeth, and Thomas G. Walker, *The Supreme Court Compendium: Data, Decisions, and Developments*, 2d ed. (Washington, D.C.: Congressional Quarterly Press, 1996), 74–76.

44. "Statistical Recap of the Supreme Court's Workload During the Last Three Terms." There has been much scholarly commentary about the drop in the Court's caseload. See Arthur D. Hellman, "The Shrunken Docket of the Rehnquist Court," in *The Supreme Court Review*: 1996, ed. Dennis J. Hutchinson, et al (Chicago: University of Chicago Press, 1997).

45. Perry, *Deciding to Decide*, 28–35.

46. For a diagram of the structure and jurisdiction of the federal courts, see the federal judiciary's official web site; n46 http://www.uscourts.gov/outreach/structure.jps

47. Perry, *Deciding to Decide*, 34–35.

48. Perry, *Deciding to Decide*, at 41–91, for a detailed discussion of these factors based on Perry's interviews with justices and their clerks.

49. Perry, *Deciding to Decide*, at 42 and 216–270.

50. See Lee Epstein, "Interest Group Litigation During the Rehnquist Court Era," 9 *Journal of Law and Politics* 200 (Summer 1993).

51. For a detailed narrative and assessment of oral argument, see O'Brien, *Storm Center*, 253–261.

52. To get a better idea of what transpires in oral argument as well as a chief justice's assessment of the value of this sage of the process, see William H. Rehnquist, *The Supreme Court: How It Was, How It Is* (New York: Morrow, 1987).

53. See Bernard Schwartz, *Super Chief: Earl Warren and His Supreme Court—A Judicial Biography* (New York: New York University Press, 1983).

54. Rehnquist, *The Supreme Court: How It Was, How It Is*, 276.

55. *Bush v. Gore*, oral argument Docket 04-944, December 11, 2000. http://oyez.nwu.edu/dynaram.cgl?case_id=766&res

56. See Rebecca Mae Salokar, *The Solicitor General: The Politics of Law* (Philadelphia: Temple University Press, 1992).

57. Rehnquist, *The Supreme Court: How It Was, How It Is*, 287–289.

58. See Bernard Schwartz, *Decision: How the Supreme Court Decides Cases* (New York: Oxford University Press, 1996).

59. Schwartz, *Decision: How the Supreme Court Decides Cases*; and Rehnquist, *The Supreme Court*, 294–296.

60. For excellent discussions of the dynamics of the conference, as well as a substantial list of scholarly sources, see Henry J. Abraham, *The Judicial Process*, 7th ed. (New York: Oxford University Press, 1998), 213–218, and Baum, *The Supreme Court*, 158–168.

61. Abraham, *The Judicial Process*, 218–246.

62. This was the case in the Court's ruling on quotas in the *Bakke* decision. See chapter 7.

63. Antonin Scalia, "The Dissenting Opinion," *Journal of Supreme Court History*, 4:10, 1994.

64. For the classic discussion on compliance, see Walter Murphy, "Lower Court Checks on Supreme Court Power," 53 *American Political Science Review* 1017–1031, (December 1959).

65. 347 U.S. 483 (1954). See the discussion in chapter 7; and Donald G. Nieman, *Promises to Keep* (New York: Oxford University Press, 1991), 148–227.

66. See, e.g., Robert Birkby, "The Supreme Court and the Bible Belt: Tennessee Reaction to the 'Schempp' Decision," 10 *Midwest Journal of Political Science* 3 (August 1966).

67. Abraham, *The Judicial Process*, 247–254 and 369–371.

68. 384 U.S. 717; and see discussion in chapter 5.

69. See chapter 5's discussion of *Miranda v. Arizona* and *Dickerson v. United States*.

# CHAPTER TWO

# Freedom of Expression

*It is a fundamental principle, long established, that the freedom of speech and of the press which is secured by the Constitution, does not confer an absolute right to speak or publish, without responsibility, whatever one may choose, or an unbridled license that gives immunity for every possible use of language and prevents the punishment of those who abuse this freedom.*

Justice Edward T. Sanford in
*Gitlow v. New York* (1925)[1]

*Accordingly a function of free speech under our system of government is to invite dispute. It may best serve its high purpose when it induces a condition of unrest, creates dissatisfaction with conditions as they are, or even stir people to anger. Speech is often provocative and challenging. It may strike at prejudices and preconceptions and have profound unsettling effects as it presses for acceptance of an idea.*

Justice William O. Douglas in
*Terminello v. Chicago.* (1949)[2]

The First Amendment to the U.S. Constitution provides that "Congress shall make no law . . . abridging the freedom of speech, or of the press." Written more than 200 years ago, these words are deceptively simple and clear. Is the First Amendment absolute? What was its intended role in our democratic society? We know from Madison's unsuccessful attempt to extend the First Amendment to the states that the states fully intended to retain the common law tradition of punishing defamatory and offensive speech. Furthermore, when the First Amendment was ratified in 1791, it was generally understood to be only a safeguard against congressional attempts to use prior restraint censorship on newspapers and political pamphlets, rather than a broad right to speak or publish with impunity.[3]

While a small number of "absolutists," such as Justice Hugo Black,[4] have argued that the First Amendment prohibits any restrictions on speech and press, the U.S. Supreme Court has tirelessly sought to establish a standard or test that would enable it to strike an equitable balance between the individual's freedom of expression and society's interest in regulating harmful speech. Our present corpus of constitutional law on freedom of expression is a product of this effort, for as the Court struggled to establish this balance, it was forced to define the parameters of our First Amendment rights.

Today, the First Amendment's guarantee of free speech extends to a broad array of political, literary, and artistic expression. But the scope of the First Amendment protection is by no means fixed and static. Like the Constitution as a whole, it continues to evolve, affected by the demands of modernity and by the personalities of the justices. But the timeless questions remain. *Is there a limitless variety of expression that can be labeled "speech" solely on the grounds that a person intends to express an idea? What is the precise meaning of the word "speech"? What is the scope of protection afforded to us by the First Amendment? When is it constitutionally permissible for the government to place restrictions on freedom of expression?* This chapter addresses these questions and examines the concept of competing rights, and campaign spending as speech.

## SUBVERSIVE POLITICAL SPEECH: THE EVOLUTION OF THE CLEAR AND PRESENT DANGER DOCTRINE

### The Rise and Fall of the Clear and Present Danger Test

*When is it constitutionally permissible for the government to restrict political speech?*   What is the scope of First Amendment protection afforded to subversive political speech? At the height of World War I, Congress passed the Espionage Act of 1917, which penalized any circulation of false statements made with the intent to cause disloyalty in the armed forces, to obstruct the recruiting of military personnel, or to interfere with military success. Charles T. Schenck, who claimed to be the general secretary of the Socialist party in the United States, was convicted of violating Title 1 of the Espionage Act by attempting to cause insubordination in the armed forces when the United States was at war with Germany. Schenck and his comrades had printed and mailed to draftees nearly 15,000 copies of a pamphlet stating that the draft violated the Thirteenth Amendment's prohibition of slavery and that a conscript is little better than a convict. The pamphlet further stated that the draft was a form of despotism and a crime against humanity, perpetrated by cunning politicians in the interest of "Wall Street's chosen few." The pamphlet advocated peaceful remedies, such as the repeal of the act, but also stated, "Do not submit to intimidation," and "Assert your Rights."

In *Schenck v. United States*, 249 U.S. 47 (1919), the Supreme Court found that the pamphlet was not merely a statement of abstract doctrine, but also an attempt to sow discord in the armed forces, for it would not have been mailed unless it had been intended to influence the actions of persons subject to the draft. Writing for a unanimous Court, Justice Oliver Wendell Holmes affirmed Schenck's conviction, stating that in ordinary times the defendant's actions would have been protected by the First Amendment: "But the character of every act depends upon the circumstances in which it was done." These were not ordinary circumstances—the nation was at war, and Schenck's actions, if not restricted, could have created a clear and present danger to national security, thus hindering the ability of the nation to defend its vital interests. Holmes wrote:

> The question in every case is whether the words used are used in such circumstances and are of such a nature as to create a clear and present danger that they will bring about substantive evils that Congress has a right to prevent. It is a question of proximity and degree. When a nation is at war many things that might be said in time of peace are such a hindrance to its effort that their utterance will not be endured so long as men fight and that no court should regard them as protected by any constitutional right.

Thus, the clear and present danger doctrine that emerged from *Schenck* was used by the Court to determine the conditions under which the government may suppress political expression. *Schenck* is also significant because it provides insights into the Court's early view of the scope of protection afforded by the First Amendment. Holmes quickly disavowed the notion that the First Amendment is absolute, particularly when speech is closely connected to some illegal act, such as "falsely shouting fire in a theater and causing panic" or advocating the obstruction of a legitimate governmental interest. However, before speech can be restricted, the government must look at the circumstances in which the words are spoken and at the nature of the words to be suppressed.

*May the clear and present danger test be invoked even if the government has no proof of dangerous action or conduct?*   The answer is a definite yes. Speech can be restricted if evidence shows that the intent of the speech is to bring about a substantive evil or an illegal action. Holmes noted: "If the act [speaking, or circulating a paper], its tendency and the intent with which it is done are the same, we perceive no ground for saying that success alone warrants making the act a crime."

The clear and present danger test developed in *Schenck* represents one of the Court's first attempts to balance the individual's freedom of political expression and the state's interest in regulating harmful speech. However, regardless of the Court's intent in that case, the vague language used in this deceptively simple test opens the door to a dizzying array of interpretations of what constitutes harmful speech and how one goes about finding the requisite intent. Holmes may have been aware of this problem when he attempted to clarify the clear and present danger test in *Debs v. United States*, 249 U.S. 211 (1919), and in his dissenting opinion in *Abrams v. United States*, 250 U.S. 616 (1919).

Eugene Debs was the Socialist candidate for president in 1912 and in 1920. In 1912, Debs received nearly 6 percent of the popular vote. In June 1918, he made a number of inflammatory antiwar and antidraft speeches with the intention of arousing dissent against U.S. involvement in World War I. In his speeches and pamphlets he called for a program of organized "continuous, active, and public opposition to the war, through demonstrations, mass petitions, and all other means within our power." As a result of his intent to obstruct recruiting and cause insubordination in the armed services, he was indicted and convicted of violating the Espionage Act. Debs's conviction was upheld by the Supreme Court.

Writing for the unanimous court, Holmes argued that while the main theme of the speech was protected by the First Amendment, the intent of the speech could be constitutionally restricted by the Espionage Act. Holmes wrote:

> The main theme of the speech was socialism, its growth, and a prophecy of its ulti-mate success. With that we have nothing to do, but if a part or the manifest intent of the more general utterances was to encourage those present to obstruct the recruiting service and if in passages such encouragement was directly given, the immunity of the general theme may not be enough to protect the speech.

Holmes formulated the following constitutional standard: Debs could not be found guilty for merely advocating his views unless: (1) the words he used had the "natural tendency and reasonable probable effect" to obstruct the draft, and (2) he had the specific intent to obstruct the draft in his mind. Debs had admitted to the jury that he was not merely opposed to war in the abstract, but to the country's involve-ment in the war that was raging at that time.

The Court concluded that his opposition was expressed in such a way that its natural and intended effect would be to obstruct military recruiting. For Holmes, the requisite intent was present, the circumstances (wartime) required by *Schenck* existed, and the probable effect of Debs's words would be obstruction of the draft. As a result, the Court refused to accept the argument that Debs's speech fell under the First Amendment's protection of expressions of conscientious belief. Debs went to prison, but he was released in 1921 by order of President Warren G. Harding.

Holmes attempted a further clarification of the clear and present danger test in *Abrams v. United States*, decided within one week of *Schenck*. In *Abrams*, the Supreme Court sustained the convictions of five Communist sympathizers under the 1918 amendments to the Espionage Act. Russian-born Abrams, who was living in the United States, was convicted of urging the curtailment of military arms produc-tion with the intent to hinder the war effort. Abrams and his codefendants had printed and distributed 5,000 leaflets calling for a general strike of all workers in war-related industries.

Citing *Schenck*, the Court rejected Abrams's First Amendment challenge to the conviction on the grounds that he had distributed the leaflets knowing that a large-scale general strike would likely impede the war effort against Germany. However, Holmes disagreed with the majority, for he could not find the necessary intent in Abrams's words that would sustain the conviction under the clear and present dan-ger test. In the dissent, Holmes and Justice Louis Brandeis attempted to further clar-ify the clear and present danger doctrine.

> [T]o make their conduct criminal the statute requires that it should be "with intent by such curtailment to cripple or hinder the United States in the prosecution of the war." It seems to me that no intent is proved.
>
> . . . It is only the present danger of immediate evil or an intent to bring it about that warrants Congress in setting a limit to the expression of opinion where private rights are not concerned. Congress cannot forbid all effort to change the mind of the country.

Holmes went on to argue that mere advocacy or publication does not present any danger and therefore should be protected. Indeed, a broad reading of the statute could result in punishing a patriot who argued that the country was spending too much money on airplanes or cannons. However, publishing those opinions with the intent of obstructing the war effort would have the "quality of an attempt" to undermine national security. If the intent is to bring about danger and if that intent is of the degree that it can be considered an attempt, then Congress has the right to take the necessary measures to regulate speech. Thus, it is only the present danger of an "immediate evil" or the intent to bring it about that warrants limitations on the expression of an opinion.

For Holmes, the clear and present danger test permitted governmental restrictions on political expression when each of the following conditions was present.

1. **Intent:** The person expressing an opinion has a desire to bring about a substantive evil.
2. **The gravity of evil:** The danger that may result must be of a grave and serious nature.
3. **Proximity of danger:** The danger that may result must be clear and immediate.
4. **Circumstances:** The context of the speech is crucial. The speech must occur in circumstances that will contribute to consequences that would not result in another set of circumstances.

Though it may appear that the Court now had a workable doctrine, no real consensus existed on the nature or role of the clear and present danger test. In fact, as early as 1925 in *Gitlow v. New York*, 268 U.S. 652, the Court found it necessary to temporarily abandon the clear and present danger doctrine and approach the problem from another direction.

*Gitlow* involved First and Fourteenth Amendment challenges to the New York Criminal Anarchy Act, which punished the advocacy of the view that the government should be overthrown by violent means. The act fell into a category of state antisedition laws aimed at both anarchy and criminal syndicalism. The first of these laws was enacted in 1902 after the assassination of President William McKinley.

Benjamin Gitlow was the leader of the "Left Wing Section" of the American Socialist party and was responsible for the publication and dissemination of the "Left Wing Manifesto," a statement of his section's beliefs. The manifesto called for an economic and political movement that would throw off the yoke of capitalism through "mass industrial revolts" and, ultimately, revolutionary action. Since there was no evidence that the manifesto had any effect or led to any criminal action, Gitlow contended that he was being punished merely for advocating an abstract doctrine or philosophy, much as a professor might do in a college classroom.

But the New York State Court of Appeals upheld the constitutionality of the Criminal Anarchy Act and, in doing so, came down hard on any form of anarchist speech. It ruled that criminal anarchy is so dangerous that the state may forbid the mere advocacy of that doctrine without regard to whether there is imminent danger that the advocacy will result in criminal activity.

The U.S. Supreme Court affirmed Gitlow's conviction and upheld the constitutionality of the statute. The Court disagreed with Gitlow's argument that the statute penalized mere political or academic discussion and publication of an abstract doctrine. What it prohibits, wrote Justice Edward T. Sanford, is language advocating, advising, or teaching the overthrow of government by unlawful means. A state has the power to punish those who abuse their freedom of expression by attempting to incite violence, corrupt public morals, or disturb the peace. In a revealing account of the prevailing view of the First Amendment in the early part of the century, Sanford wrote the lines that open this chapter.

*Gitlow* represents a shift away from the clear and present danger test as a judicial tool to draw the line between protected and unprotected speech. In *Gitlow*, the majority based its reasoning on what has come to be called the "bad tendency" test. Certain writings may have a bad tendency to corrupt public morals or disturb the peace. The Court believed that the question in *Gitlow* involved a statute prohibiting certain kinds of language, whereas in *Schenck* the Espionage Act regulated certain acts involving the danger of criminal action, without any reference to the language itself. In *Schenck*, the statute in question was not directly applied to speech but to conduct; in applying the bad tendency test, the Court targeted words. It asked whether the specific language used involved the likelihood of bringing about the substantive evil. Speech may be restricted if the language used has a "natural tendency and probable effect" to bring about a substantive evil, such as the violent overthrow of the government. Recall that in *Schenck* the Court ruled that the question in every case is whether the words used in such circumstances are of such a nature as to create a clear and present danger to national security or public safety.

As a consequence of this doctrinal shift, *Gitlow* empowered the government to restrict the teaching of politically subversive doctrine in the abstract not only when it creates a clear and present danger, but also when the state believes that the language has a tendency to create the mere possibility of a threat—even when the nation is not at war.

In his dissent, Holmes attacked the majority's notion of the role of political expression in a democracy.

> It is said that this manifesto was more than a theory, that it was an incitement. Every idea is an incitement. It offers itself for belief and if believed it is acted on unless some other belief outweighs it or some failure of energy stifles the movement at its birth. The only difference between the expression of an opinion and an incitement in the narrower sense is the speaker's enthusiasm for the result. Eloquence may set fire to reason.

What Holmes elucidated here illustrates what is often called the "marketplace theory" of expression. The parameters or allowable boundaries of discourse in the marketplace are established by the First Amendment. The marketplace presupposes a rational and mature citizenry. Within the marketplace a plenitude of ideas are available for consumption; we are free to advance our political ideas, no matter how unsettling or silly. Offensive speech is then countered by more mainstream ideas. An individual should be able to utter subversive or heretical words and, in turn, others should be able to reject those ideas as offensive or silly. The precise point at which abstract ideas on the violent overthrow of the government (or on the selective breeding of humans, for that matter) go beyond urging people to believe and urging them to act is difficult to ascertain. Also difficult to discern is the precise point at which interests in national security and order are threatened and state action is justified. Yet Holmes could imagine speech going only so far.

*Gitlow* is doubly important because it was the first time that the Court held that freedom of speech and of the press are protected against state action by the due process clause of the Fourteenth Amendment. The First Amendment, like the other nine amendments of the Bill of Rights, were intended by the framers to limit the authority of the federal government, not state governments. Prior to *Gitlow*, the Court maintained that the Fourteenth Amendment did not incorporate any part of the first ten amendments. Justice Sanford wrote this startling passage: "For present purposes we may and do assume that freedom of speech and of the press—which are protected by the First Amendment from abridgement by Congress—are among the fundamental personal rights and 'liberties' protected by the due process clause of the Fourteenth Amendment from impairment by the states."

Under the *Gitlow* standard, if a speaker consistently and passionately implores others to break the law, the state has reason to believe that there is a good probability that the law will be broken. The probability increases when the speaker condones or expresses his or her approval of lawlessness. Finally, when the speech constitutes an incitement to lawlessness, the state is justified in taking action to suppress speech.

Substituting the bad tendency test for the clear and present danger test, the Court placed the burden on the individual to show that the law was not reasonable. It demanded only that the state show that there was a possibility that the speech at issue had a tendency to promote unlawful actions. The burden was not shifted from the individual to the state until the emergence of the "preferred freedoms" doctrine sparked by *Thomas v. Collins*, 323 U.S. 516 (1945), and amplified by the Warren Court's active support of political expression.

## The Red Scare

The widespread fear and paranoia of communism and the Soviet Union, exacerbated by the Korean War, provided the impetus for the application of an array of governmental measures aimed at protecting national security. One of these measures, the 1940 Smith Act, was used by the House Committee on Un-American Activities to investigate Communists, Communist sympathizers, and anyone suspected of advocating any kind of belief even remotely similar to communism. The Smith Act made it unlawful to willfully advocate the overthrow or destruction of any government in the United States by force or violence.[5] In 1948, the Truman administration used the conspiracy provisions of the Smith Act to gain the indictment and conviction of Eugene Dennis and twelve other leaders of the Communist party of the United States. In *Dennis v. United States*, 341 U.S. 494 (1951), Dennis and the twelve convicted Communist party members appealed their convictions, challenging the statute on the grounds that it punished the mere teaching or discussion of the merits of Marxist-Leninist doctrine. The petitioners argued that all they had done was to organize people to teach the Marxist-Leninist ideology derived from four books—*Foundations of Leninism*, by Stalin (1924); *The Communist Manifesto*, by Marx and Engels (1848); *State and Revolution*, by Lenin (1917); and *History of the Communist Party of the Soviet Union* (1939)—all of which could be found in libraries throughout the United States. Dennis further charged that the statute was overly broad, since it was aimed not simply at preventing subversive conduct but also at stifling the mere teaching of unpopular ideas.

But the Court upheld the conviction and sustained the constitutionality of the Smith Act—the requirements of the clear and present danger test had been met. Dennis and his copetitioners had been convicted not for merely advocating abstract doctrine, but also for advocating to overthrow the government as quickly as circumstances would permit. The Court agreed with the Truman administration that even though Dennis's activities between 1945 and 1948 did not result in an attempt to overthrow the government, his group was ready to make an attempt. In short, the group's activities had all of the qualities of an attempt because they were well-planned and organized.

Justice Fred Vinson pointed out that the seriousness of this threat was strengthened because during that time the Communist party of the United States was no ordinary political organization seeking change by peaceful, lawful, and constitutional means. Rather, it openly advocated change by violence, terrorism, and revolution. Vinson wrote:

> [T]he leaders, these petitioners, felt the time had come for action, coupled with the inflammable nature of world conditions, similar uprisings in other countries, and the touch-and-go nature of our relations with countries with whom petitioners were in the very least ideologically attuned, convince us that their convictions were justified.

***Was the purpose and intent of the statute legitimate? Was the statute aimed at preventing any kind of political change or was it aimed at protecting legitimate government from the use of violence to facilitate change? Is there a right to rebellion, as Dennis and his followers imagined?*** The Court held that Congress has a legitimate interest in protecting the existing government, not from change by lawful and constitutional means, but from change through violence and terrorism. The Communists' advocacy of forceful revolution created a clear and present danger that Congress had an interest to prevent. Vinson wrote: "Whatever theoretical merit there may be to the argument that there is a 'right' to rebellion against dictatorial governments is without force where the existing structure of the government provides for peaceful and orderly change. We reject any principle of governmental helplessness in the face of preparation for revolution."

The question for the Court was not whether Congress had the power to protect the existing government, but whether the means that it used conflicted with the First Amendment. Recall that Dennis challenged these means on the grounds that the Smith Act was overly broad and punished the mere advocacy of Marxist-Leninist doctrine. Even though there was no proof of a threat or evidence that Dennis's speech would lead to violence, Vinson argued that it was not necessary to have clear evidence that the conspirator would have been successful. Success or probable success of achieving an end is a factor in determining whether to apply the clear and present danger test, but assurance of success is not needed. Instead, the Court focused on the "gravity of evil." The fact that the organization had not made an attempt did not mean that a danger did not exist. The circumstances had to be weighed before the evil could be discounted. During this time, a number of highly organized Communist uprisings were occurring in other countries.

Suppose there is no clear evidence of intent? Is it necessary to show unlawful intent before making arrests and prosecuting subversives? Vinson said no. "Clear and present danger" does not mean that the government must wait for the revolt to occur before it acts, since it is the existence of the conspiracy that creates the danger.

In a classic exercise of judicial restraint—characterized by a willingness to defer to the majoritarian process—Justice Felix Frankfurter, concurring, argued that the whole issue was a political, not a judicial, question. He admonished his brethren to use restraint and to approach balancing freedom of expression and national security with an open mind and not with an overly rigid judicial doctrine. In fact, according to Frankfurter, Congress, not the courts, should decide how best to balance the needs of free speech and national security. He thought the judiciary should defer to the legislature on most, if not all, questions of national security.

Frankfurter was not arguing that the judiciary should refuse to concern itself with First Amendment rights, but that once the reasonableness of a law is established, the courts should let the legislatures decide how to balance free speech with the needs of national security. He wrote: "Primary responsibility for adjusting the interests which compete in the situation before us of necessity belongs to the Congress. We are to set aside the judgment of those whose responsibility it is to legislate only if there is no reasonable basis for it."

Frankfurter's concurring opinion in *Dennis* provides two excellent examples of his philosophy of judicial restraint: (1) deference on the Court's part to the majoritarian process, and (2) an adherence to the reasonableness standard rather than to the preferred freedoms approach to legislative restrictions on speech. A judge employing the reasonableness standard when a law is challenged proceeds from the presumption that a legislature's actions are constitutional. Suppose a legislature enacts statute X to solve a problem and the constitutionality of that law is challenged in court. The judge asks only whether the legislature acted reasonably in enacting statute X over Y and Z. Provided that the law was duly enacted, the judge does not ask whether the law violates some provision of the Constitution, nor does the judge invoke a greater degree of scrutiny because the challenge to the law is based on a preferred freedom found in the Bill of Rights.

On the other hand, a judge employing the "preferred freedoms" approach does not assume that law X is constitutional simply because the legislature acted reasonably. In doing so, the judge now uses a tougher standard when reviewing laws that may impinge upon civil rights and liberties. These freedoms, or rights, of speech, press, association, and assembly are necessary to a democratic society and are thus preferred over the majority's freedom to enact laws through the legislative process. Thus, reasonableness, or balancing of interests, is a key component of the philosophy of judicial restraint, while the preferred freedoms approach is a central component of the philosophy of judicial activism.[6] Eventually, the preferred freedoms

analysis became known as strict scrutiny, whereby the Court has the duty to scruti-
nize legislation passed by the majority that infringes upon the fundamental rights or
freedoms of political minorities.[7]

Justices Black and William O. Douglas strongly disagreed with Frankfurter's
position. They believed that the Court was jeopardizing freedom of speech by allowing constitutional restrictions based only on fear, opposition, or mere dislike of communism. In their dissenting opinions, neither Black nor Douglas believed that
Dennis's speech created a clear and present danger. While Douglas did not believe
that speech was absolute, he did believe that the majority had made it easier for the
government to show that speech was a threat to the existence of government.
According to Douglas, before speech can be restricted, there must be some "immediate injury to society that is likely if speech is allowed." Black blasted the majority
for retreating to the reasonableness standard to sustain congressional restrictions on
speech and press. He wrote: "Such a doctrine waters down the First Amendment so
that it amounts to little more than an admonition to Congress. The Amendment as so
construed is not likely to protect any but those 'safe' or orthodox views which rarely
need its protection."

According to the majority's application of the clear and present danger test in
*Dennis*, the crime depends not on the words taught but on the intent and identity of
the teacher. For Douglas, "[t]hat is to make freedom of speech turn not on what is
said, but on the intent with which it is said." He admitted that communism was a
force in the international arena, scoffed at the idea that communism threatened
America's internal security, and concluded that as a political movement in the United
States it was a "bogeyman." "Bogeyman" notwithstanding, *Dennis* modified the
clear and present danger test, strengthening Congress's hand in restricting subversive
forms of speech.

Shortly after the Court's decision in *Dennis*, the clear and present danger test
was further modified by *Yates v. United States*, 354 U.S. 298 (1957). Oleta Yates and
thirteen other Communist party members were convicted in a federal district court
for subversive activities. They were fined $10,000 and sentenced to prison for five
years for violating various provisions of the Smith Act. Relying on *Dennis*, the district court judge instructed the jury that it could find the defendants guilty for merely
advocating abstract doctrine regardless of whether or not it was probable that their
advocacy would result in action against the government. They appealed, but their
convictions were affirmed by the U.S. court of appeals.

The petitioners then appealed to the Supreme Court, arguing that the trial
judge's instructions to the jury were flawed. They contended that unless the government could prove the advocacy was a calculated attempt to incite persons to forcibly
overthrow the government, their speech fell under First Amendment protection.

When the Supreme Court heard *Yates* it had four new members appointed by
President Dwight D. Eisenhower: Chief Justice Earl Warren and Associate Justices
Charles Whittaker, John Marshall Harlan, and William Brennan. Popular speculation
held that this new cadre would overturn the Smith Act. Instead, the newly constituted
Court upheld the constitutionality of the Smith Act, arguing that the act did not prohibit the mere advocacy and teaching of an abstract principle as long as such advocacy or teaching was not connected with any attempt to instigate violence.

Advocating the necessity of violent revolution could not be restricted unless it could be proved that an attempt to organize was made with that purpose in mind.

In *Yates*, a complex but important issue emerged. *Should the constitutional dividing line between protected and proscribed speech be drawn between advocacy of an abstract doctrine (protected) and incitement (proscribed) or mere discussion of doctrine (protected) and advocacy of forceful overthrow (proscribed)?*

Under the former, an individual would be free to try to convince an audience of the desirability of Marxist-Leninism, but would be subject to prosecution if the speaker's intent was to urge people to act to bring about revolution. Under the latter, an individual would be free to merely discuss Marxist-Leninism, but not to urge people to believe in the desirability of violent revolution. Which of the two provides a more workable guideline? The first is clearly the more liberal because it permits not only discussion but advocacy. The second protects only discussion and punishes advocacy even without any intent to incite.

Citing Justice Holmes's statement in *Gitlow* that every idea is an incitement, Harlan recognized that it is often difficult for the government to distinguish between inciting people to act and stirring people to believe, the latter of which is protected. It is also difficult to determine the imminence of the threat and whether or not the threat is organized. The Court subsequently ordered new trials for Yates and eight of the codefendants and acquittals for the remaining five.

To the chagrin of Congress, the Court made it more difficult for the government to convict members of the Communist party for expressing belief in the abstract idea of violent political change. After *Yates*, in order for the government to proscribe subversive speech, it would need to demonstrate to a jury that the accused had an intent to overthrow the government or to incite others to do so at present or in the immediate future. Membership in an organization whose purpose was instigating the violent overthrow of the government was still part of the equation. But the Court reaffirmed its view in *Dennis* that the government would have to show that the advocacy was aimed at the indoctrination of a sizable and cohesive group in preparation for some future violent action.

Consider an example that involves a threat to private citizens rather than to the government. A university student organizes a radical political cell on a college campus. The student firmly believes that certain professors are in league with the CIA to assist in covert operations in the Middle East, and delivers a number of inflammatory speeches to comrades who are assembled in the university's auditorium. In the speech on a Monday evening, the student denounces these professors as fascists who should be beaten and hung from the bell tower. A week later, the student delivers the same speech, but this time urges the audience to meet the next night, armed with lead pipes and sturdy rope, and "beat and hang those fascists!" According to Harlan's reasoning in *Yates*, the first speech is protected, whereas the second goes beyond merely advocating a political view to the point of inciting illegal activity.

But suppose that the radical student had not mentioned lead pipes and rope or the time and place in which the assault would take place? Under *Yates*, the government might be able to circumvent the issue of immediate danger to the professors by arguing that the student was an active member of a subversive organization. Indeed, after *Yates* the government used the "membership clause" of the Smith Act to secure a number of convictions of Communists. However, this guilt by association argument was challenged and modified in *Scales v. United States*, 367 U.S. 203 (1961).

## Guilt by Association

*Is it constitutionally permissible to prosecute someone merely because they belong to a subversive organization?*   In *Scales*, the Court affirmed the conviction of Junius Irving Scales, the chairman of the North and South Carolina districts of the Communist party, under the membership clause of the Smith Act. Scales was responsible for recruiting new members into the party and for administering a secret school that trained the party's new members in Communist theory and techniques of infiltration and violence. Among the goals of this vocational school for young Communists were placing young members in key industrial positions and instigating black and poor workers in the South to foment revolution. Under Scales's tutelage, students learned a plethora of practical skills, such as how to kill a person with a pencil—a skill that might be useful against strikebreakers on a picket line. The membership clause of the Smith Act made it a felony to be a willing member of any organization that advocates the overthrow of the federal government by force or violence. Scales challenged the constitutionality of the membership clause on the grounds that it violated the First Amendment rights of expression and association and the Fifth Amendment right against imputing guilt by association.

Writing for the majority, Justice Harlan rejected Scales's constitutional challenge and sustained the membership clause. He argued that it was constitutionally permissible to prosecute someone because of membership in an organization but only if there is clear evidence that a defendant specifically intended to carry out the violent goals of the organization as soon as circumstances would permit.

The Court applied the test formulated in *Dennis* to determine that Scales's speech did not deserve constitutional protection. It also relied on *Yates* to determine whether Scales's language amounted to advocacy of action. As in the earlier cases, Scales was not merely teaching Marxist-Leninism and the inevitability of revolution; he was also explaining the types of illegal techniques needed for revolutionary activity.

The Court also believed that *Dennis* and *Yates* settled the question whether the absence of evidence showing that Scales was calling for immediate action against the government was sufficient to preclude his conviction. Harlan wrote: "Hence this record cannot be considered deficient because it contains no evidence of advocacy of immediate overthrow. The evidence amply showed that Party leaders were continuously preaching during the indictment period the inevitability of eventual forcible overthrow."

The membership rule that emerged from *Scales* holds that a person can be convicted under the Smith Act if there is clear proof that the person is a "knowing, active" member of a subversive organization, having a specific intent to bring about the violent overthrow of the government. Harlan did not believe that this standard implied guilt by association alone. A person joining the subversive group simply because Communist dogma is intriguing or appealing or perhaps because the person is "foolish, deluded, or merely optimistic" will not be affected by the statute if the person lacks the kind of specific intent that Scales exhibited.

It is clear that the Court was approaching the subversive speech issue on a case-by-case basis. On the same day as *Scales* was decided, the Court reviewed another conviction under the membership clause in *Noto v. United States*, 367 U.S. 290 (1961). In *Noto*, the Court reversed the conviction of a Communist worker in New York, ruling that unlike *Scales*, there was insufficient evidence that the petitioner's group did anything more than teach the standard party line of the "inevitable proletarian revolution." For Harlan, who wrote for the unanimous Court, there was insufficient evidence to support the government's charge of "advocacy of action." The evidence of the party's call to action in *Noto* "lacked the compelling quality" that was provided by Scales's speeches and activities as a high party official. Scales, who advocated an illegal action and who was "indisputably active," could be convicted under the membership clause. John Noto, a mere party worker who had advocated a philosophical belief, could not be convicted under the clause.

## Retreat from the Clear and Present Danger Test

Twelve years after *Scales*, the Court backed away from the clear and present danger test and adopted a stricter scrutiny of governmental restrictions on freedom of speech. As American society became somewhat more tolerant of political dissent, the Warren Court became more willing to extend First Amendment protection to political speech regardless of its substance. The Court eventually retreated from the clear and present danger test altogether, and came to rely on the preferred freedoms approach to freedom of expression disputes.

The pivotal case in this retreat was *Brandenburg v. Ohio*, 395 U.S. 444 (1969). Charles Brandenburg, the leader of a local Ku Klux Klan group, was convicted of violating the Ohio Criminal Syndicalism statute, fined $1,000, and given a ten-year prison term. The law proscribed "advocat[ing] the duty, necessity, or propriety of crime, sabotage, violence, or unlawful methods of terrorism as a means of accomplishing industrial or political reform" and for "voluntarily assembl[ing] with any society, group, or assemblage of persons formed to teach or advocate the doctrines of criminal syndicalism." Brandenburg and his group had assembled in a rural field north of Cincinnati. At the rally, a cross was burned and speeches were made. A Cincinnati television reporter covered the rally at the request of Brandenburg.

The state's case rested largely on two films taken by the television reporter showing twelve hooded men standing around a burning cross. Some of the men carried guns, while others carried guns and Bibles. One film showed Brandenburg speaking before those assembled. During his diatribe he announced that if the president, Congress, and the Supreme Court continued "to suppress the white, Caucasian race, it's possible that there might have to be some revenge taken." During a second speech, he added, "Personally, I believe the nigger should be returned to Africa, the Jew returned to Israel." The state also presented as evidence a shotgun, a pistol, a rifle, a Bible, and Brandenburg's red Klan hood.

The U.S. Supreme Court reversed Brandenburg's conviction and struck down the Ohio law. In a *per curiam* ("unsigned") opinion issued during the last year of

Chief Justice Warren's tenure, the Court established that a state may not punish the mere advocacy of force unless it can show that such advocacy is intended to incite imminent illegal action and is likely to produce such action. The Court also cited *Noto*, reiterating the view that "the mere abstract teaching [of] the moral propriety or even moral necessity for a resort to force or violence, is not the same as preparing a group for violence and steeling it to such action."

The Court found the Ohio statute to be overly broad and thus contrary to the First and Fourteenth Amendments because it failed to distinguish between advocacy and incitement to lawless action. It punished the mere advocacy or teaching of doctrine and prohibited assembling with others for the purpose of advocating a doctrine. It even punished those who would publish or circulate a book or paper containing such advocacy.

Brandenburg's threats of violence were directed at two groups of persons, blacks and Jews, and were delivered to a like-minded assemblage consisting of his fellow Klansmen. The rally took place in a remote cornfield in rural Ohio. *What if Brandenburg had delivered his speech in downtown Cincinnati? If the Ohio syndicalism law did not apply, would it have been possible for local authorities to arrest and convict Brandenburg under a disturbing the peace or disorderly conduct ordinance?*

*Brandenburg* is generally regarded as a watershed opinion in the long line of Supreme Court cases involving the balance between speech and order. Scholars often attribute the final fall of the clear and present danger test to *Brandenburg*, just as the inception of the standard is credited to Justice Holmes in *Schenck*. This rise and fall analysis, used for many years, has served well as a kind of intellectual shortcut when we attempt to understand the Court's quest to develop a workable constitutional standard for speech questions. However, the rise and fall approach may be misleading because it implies a purely mechanical view of judicial decision-making. It tempts us to treat the clear and present danger doctrine as a single formula or an equation that was consistently applied to resolve similar legal issues in a disparate set of circumstances. This view also sees a legal doctrine slowly evolve and adapt to each new set of circumstances and problems. The doctrine falls when it is no longer a tenable means of resolving constitutional questions.

The clear and present danger test was modified, reinterpreted, remodified, clarified, and ultimately parts of it were incorporated into the preferred freedoms approach to speech by the Warren Court. The Court never settled on one single formula that would apply to all controversies. Instead, most of the justices serving on the Court between *Schenck* and *Brandenburg* seemed to examine each case on its own merits and in its own particular political circumstances.

The government retained the power to restrict speech but the burden was placed on the government to show why an exercise of a fundamental freedom should be infringed. By adopting the preferred freedoms approach, the Court moved toward a stricter form of judicial scrutiny of governmental restrictions on freedom of speech. And even though the Court has come to rely on the preferred freedoms approach to freedom of expression questions, it has retained the *Brandenburg* modification of the clear and present danger test by relying on the incitement to imminent unlawful action component of the test.

## Inflammatory Words

Consider the situation where inflammatory words are not directed at any one person or group but are spoken in the midst of a crowded public thoroughfare where the likelihood of violence is greater. Would a speech delivered in that context be more likely to produce imminent lawless action? The Court fielded such a question in *Hess v. Indiana*, 414 U.S. 105 (1973), where it applied the *Brandenburg* standard to reverse the disorderly conduct conviction of a Vietnam War protester.

In 1970, Gregory Hess and approximately 100 to 150 other demonstrators on the Indiana University campus in Bloomington marched down a public street, blocking traffic and causing a noisy gathering of bystanders on the sidewalk. After the police moved the demonstrators onto the curbs on both sides of the street, Hess shouted in a loud voice, "We'll take the fucking street later," or "We'll take the fucking street again." A police officer passing by heard Hess's commentary, and the incident resulted in Hess's conviction under Indiana's disorderly conduct statute. The state supreme court affirmed the trial court's finding that Hess's statement was intended to incite further lawless action on the part of the crowd and was likely to produce such action.

Citing *Brandenburg*, the Supreme Court reversed the conviction on the grounds that Hess's language did not fall within any of the "narrowly limited classes of speech" that the state of Indiana could punish without violating the First and Fourteenth Amendments. The Court believed that the words he used were not directed to any person or group and that there was no evidence to suggest that they were intended and likely to produce imminent disorder during the demonstration.

If Hess was advocating unlawful action, then his statement amounted to nothing more than advocacy of an unspecified illegal action at some indefinite future time. Under *Brandenburg*, the advocacy of illegal action is protected under the First Amendment unless it is the intent of the speaker to produce violent acts or other forms of lawless action and the statement is likely to produce such action. The majority believed that Indiana's disorderly conduct statute was applied in this case to punish only Hess's spoken words and not his actions. Particular words cannot be restricted unless they fall into a narrow category of unprotected speech. These limited classes of speech to which the Court was referring included words that can be punished as obscene under *Roth v. United States*, 354 U.S. 476 (1957), or as "fighting words" under *Chaplinsky v. New Hampshire*, 315 U.S. 568 (1942). While Hess's use of the word "fuck" was clearly offensive to the police officer, it was not obscene because it was not intended to have a sexual meaning or connotation appealing only to lustful or prurient interests. Nor did Hess's speech amount to fighting words because they were not directed to any person or group. Hess was probably only blowing off steam. The majority wrote: "At best . . . the statement could be taken as counsel for present moderation; at worst it amounted to nothing more than the advocacy of illegal action at some future time. This is not sufficient to permit the State to punish Hess' speech."

## Loyalty Oaths

***Can a person be compelled to state a belief that he or she does not hold in
order to vote, run for office, or hold a job?***   The imminent lawless action requirement was applied in another post-*Brandenburg* case, this time involving a constitutional challenge to a loyalty oath. In *Communist Party of Indiana v. Whitcomb*, 414
U.S. 441 (1974), the Court heard a challenge to an Indiana statute requiring that

> [no] existing or newly organized political party or organization shall be permitted on
> or to have the names of its candidates printed on the ballot used in any election until
> it has filed an affidavit, by its officers, under oath, that it does not advocate the over-
> throw of local, state or national government by force or violence.

Members of the Communist party of Indiana, including its candidates for president
and vice president in the 1972 election, were denied a place on Indiana's ballot after
refusing to submit to the required oath. When their challenge of the law was rejected,
they filed the required affidavit, but added: "The term *advocate* as used herein has
the meaning given it by the Supreme Court in *Yates v. U.S.*, . . . 'the advocacy and
teaching concrete action for the forcible overthrow of the government, and not of
principles divorced from action.' "

The Indiana Election Board rejected the modified affidavit, and the U.S. district
court sustained the constitutionality of the statute. Upon appeal to the U.S. Supreme
Court, the appellants argued that the loyalty oath provision of the law punished the
mere advocacy of abstract doctrine as well as action. The argument that the law compelled individuals to state a belief they did not possess could also be made. Consider
the matter from the state's perspective: Could the state of Indiana apply the law to
groups that advocate the extermination of a race of people as an abstract doctrine?

The Court unanimously reversed the decision of the district court and overturned
the loyalty oath requirement of the statute. Justice Brennan, writing for the Court,
asserted that the imminent lawless action standard of *Brandenburg* applied not only
to restrictions on political expression or denials of public employment, bar licensing,
and tax exemption, but also to restrictions imposed on an organization's access to the
ballot. He wrote: "At stake are appellants' First and Fourteenth Amendment rights to
associate with others for the common advancement of political beliefs and ideas."

The state of Indiana argued that the loyalty oath did not place any burden on
legitimate political parties, but rather was aimed at denying ballot access to "fraud-
ulent" groups advocating unlawful action. Brennan responded that the state cannot
deny access to the ballot merely because the party urges others to believe in communism or advocates the violent overthrow of the government. The state cannot
automatically assume that any group that advocates violent overthrow as an abstract
doctrine must be regarded as advocating unlawful action.

The Court "perceive[d] no reason to make an exception" to the imminent lawless action standard and simply recognized the standard without making any effort
to modify or clarify it. In fact, Brennan scrutinized the Indiana law from the standpoint of the pre-*Brandenburg* distinction between advocacy of violent overthrow as
an abstract doctrine and advocacy of unlawful conduct.[8]

## Economic Boycotts as Speech

*Is an economic boycott intended to compel political action a protected form of speech and association or is it an illegal conspiracy that illegally imposes financial harm on citizens?*   In 1966, a seven-year boycott by African American citizens of white-owned businesses was initiated in Claiborne County, Mississippi. Its purpose was to persuade white political and economic leaders to comply with a large number of demands for racial justice and equality. During the boycott, numerous speeches were given encouraging citizens to join the boycott or to demonstrate by picketing. Threats of violence and social ostracism were made by a few of the more radical black activists against black citizens who chose not to participate in the boycott.

One boycott leader who made threats against those choosing not to participate was Charles Evers, the NAACP's first secretary and principal organizer in Mississippi. Speaking in support of the boycott, Evers said that blacks who violated the boycott would be "disciplined" by their own people. While a number of personal threats and minor incidents of vandalism were reported, the police made no arrests as a result of Evers's speech or in connection with the picketing and occasional pro-boycott demonstrations.

However, a number of Claiborne County merchants and business owners sued the NAACP and more than 100 individuals to recover more than $1 million dollars in damages that they sustained as the result of the boycott. The Mississippi courts held in favor of the merchants, ruling that as a result of threats of violence and reprisals many blacks had withheld their patronage from white merchants, causing the merchants to suffer substantial financial loss. The state took the position that the entire boycott was an illegal conspiracy because it was based on violence and the threat of violence.

Sixteen years after the NAACP began the boycott, the dispute found its way to the U.S. Supreme Court in *NAACP v. Claiborne Hardware Co.*, 458 U.S. 886 (1982). The Court applied the *Brandenburg* incitement of imminent violence test to reverse the trial court's decision against Evers and other NAACP members, ruling that all boycott activities that were not violent were protected by the freedoms of expression and association. Citing *Brandenburg*, the Court held that although Evers's speech was "strong language" and "emotionally charged," it did not constitute incitement of imminent violence and was therefore constitutionally protected. Justice John Paul Stevens wrote: "An advocate must be free to stimulate his audience with spontaneous and emotional appeals for unity and action in a common cause. When such appeals do not incite lawless action, they must be regarded as protected speech."

The Court also refused to accept the state's characterization of the boycott as a violent conspiracy with the illegitimate purpose of imposing financial harm on the county's merchants and black citizens. It found that Evers's ultimate objectives were "unquestionably legitimate" and that a long-term effort to change the social, political, and economic structure of a local environment cannot be characterized as a violent conspiracy simply because of a few violent acts. In order to legally classify the boycott as a conspiratorial movement, the state would have to prove (1) that Evers and other specific members agreed to use unlawful measures, and (2) that fear rather than constitutionally protected conduct, such as picketing, was the dominant force in the movement. It is worth asking how many beatings would have had to take place before the boycott would have crossed the line from legitimate movement to conspiracy.

The state of Mississippi also sought to impose guilt by association on other NAACP members, reasoning that by not repudiating the actions of Evers, the NAACP had in essence given its tacit approval of the threats of violence. Justice Stevens disagreed. He argued that the First Amendment limits the power of the state to impose sanctions on an individual solely because of his or her association with another. In other words, according to the principles laid down in *Scales* and *Noto*, in order for Mississippi to impose liability on other members of the NAACP by virtue of their association with Evers, it would be necessary to establish that the group itself advocated unlawful goals and that there was clear proof that a member had a specific intent to carry out the goals of the organization by resorting to violence. Stevens maintained that the right to associate does not lose all constitutional protection merely because some members of the group may have participated in conduct or advocated doctrine that is itself not protected.

## Symbolic and Offensive Speech

Judging from *Brandenburg* and subsequent cases, the Court seems willing to extend First Amendment protection to pure political speech regardless of its content. Pure speech involves the oral or written communication of a philosophy, ideology, or body of knowledge that advances society's understanding of the natural, intellectual, or political realm. The best examples of pure speech include delivering a speech or lecture or publishing a pamphlet, news article, or book.

The speech at issue in some cases, however, is not pure political speech; that is, it does not involve the oral or written communication of a political philosophy or set of ideas. Some activities, such as demonstrating, marching, or picketing with signs or banners, are called "speech plus," "symbolic speech," or "expressive conduct" and contain elements of both expression and conduct.

***What forms of action or conduct are protected by the First Amendment, and how much protection do they enjoy?***   Consider a variation of the situation in *Hess v. Indiana*. What if one of Hess's fellow demonstrators had said nothing, but stood conspicuously perched on a curb along the route of the Macy's Thanksgiving Day parade wearing a T-shirt depicting her favorite rock singer in the nude with a gag on his mouth. Under the picture is the slogan "America Sucks" printed in large black letters. Is this display protected by the First Amendment? Is it speech or is it conduct? Is the time, place, or manner in which she attempted to convey her message relevant to the amount of First Amendment protection?

Suppose that the demonstrator is arrested and found guilty of disorderly conduct by a municipal court judge. As a part of the sentence, she is compelled to first place one hand on the Bible and swear that she is not a Communist. Then she is commanded to salute the American flag while reciting the Pledge of Allegiance. She refuses, claiming that the First Amendment gives her the right *not* to speak or to be associated with particular ideas. Is she correct? This section explores some of the cases that address these questions concerning symbolic speech.

## Compulsory Flag Salute

Although the Supreme Court recognized as early as *Stromberg v. California*, 283 U.S. 359 (1931), that protected speech may be nonverbal, it was not until the landmark case of *West Virginia Board of Education v. Barnette*, 319 U.S. 624 (1943), that the Court ruled that the government could not compel a person to participate in a symbolic act. Following *Minersville School District v. Gobitis*, 310 U.S. 586 (1940), in which the Supreme Court sustained the constitutionality of a compulsory flag salute law, the West Virginia legislature passed an act requiring all public schools in the state to conduct classes in civics "for the purpose of teaching, fostering and perpetuating the ideals, principles and spirit of Americanism." In implementing the law, the state board of education directed all teachers and students to recite the Pledge of Allegiance as a part of daily school activities. Students were required to recite the pledge while maintaining the "stiff arm" salute—a symbolic gesture that would soon become unpopular in the United States after the rise of Nazism in Germany. Any student who failed to comply with the rule could be expelled and thereafter treated as a delinquent. Parents of the recalcitrant children were held liable to prosecution and faced a penalty of thirty days in jail and a fine of $50.

Walter Barnette, a Jehovah's Witness, brought suit against the board of education to stop this compulsory flag salute on the grounds that to have his children comply would violate a religious commandment not to worship any graven image. The board dismissed the complaint, but a federal district court ruled in Barnette's favor, putting a stop to the mandatory flag salute policy. The board of education appealed the lower court's decision to the U.S. Supreme Court.

The Court affirmed the district court's decision, ruling that the compulsory flag salute policy violated the First Amendment's guarantees of freedom of belief, conscience, and expression. It is important to point out that while Barnette's religious beliefs compelled him to challenge the law, the Court did not believe that the case turned on the issue of freedom of religion, but rather on freedom of speech and liberty of the individual to be free from such a compulsory rite.

Writing for the majority, Justice Robert Jackson's reasoning focused on the following points. First, there was no question that action, such as a salute or the waving of a flag, should be viewed as speech protected by the First Amendment. The Court had already recognized in *Stromberg* that speech need not be oral to be afforded constitutional protection. In that case, the Court voided state law that punished the display of a red flag as a symbol of opposition to organized government. Pledging allegiance to the American flag is a symbolic act expressing support for the ideal of Americanism. Second, by requiring the Barnette child to salute the American flag, the state had compelled him to declare a belief in the ideals of Americanism. To compel someone to show support for an idea in which he or she does not believe is to compel that person to state a belief that he or she does not have. The state's interest in promoting national unity is "substantial," but the government cannot use this interest to conveniently eliminate dissent or to punish unpatriotic citizens. Jackson wrote:

> To sustain the compulsory flag salute we are required to say that a Bill of Rights which guards an individual's right to speak his own mind, left it open to public authorities to compel him to utter what is not on his mind.
>
> If there is any fixed star in our constitutional constellation, it is that no official, high or petty, can prescribe what shall be orthodox in politics, nationalism, religion, or other matters of opinion or force citizens to confess by word or act their faith therein.

Justice Jackson's words are indeed powerful testimony to the Court's strong disdain for state-compelled beliefs. *But are we to imply from his words that the First Amendment is absolute? Does the Bill of Rights give individuals the right to make all of the final decisions as to what they will learn or what they will say? Is society powerless to affect the choices, opinions, or common language of its members?* While few of us would be comfortable with state-compelled political or religious opinions, most of us recognize that without a sense of obligation, responsibility, and national identity, rights become meaningless. A rights-based society that is not well ordered is much like a shouting match at a baseball game—gratifying to those screaming at the umpire, but mortifying to those who came to enjoy the game. Constitutional rights are possible only when there is some means of promoting and enforcing the obligations of others to respect our rights. We are reminded of this obligation by the libertarian Justices Black and Douglas in their concurring opinion. They wrote:

> No well-ordered society can leave to the individual an absolute right to make final decisions, unassailable by the State, as to everything they will or will not do. The First Amendment does not go so far. Religious faiths, honestly held, do not free individuals from responsibility to conduct themselves obediently to laws.

Nowhere in *Barnette* does it say that the state does not have the authority to promote good citizenship. The state may constitutionally require civics education, but may not compel students to declare a belief that they do not hold to be true. The state may also legitimately proscribe behavior that is disruptive or that conflicts with the rights of others. However, this does not imply that the refusal to participate interferes with these interests or creates a clear and present danger to our national unity that would somehow justify forcing the child to participate. Thus, in *Barnette* the Court made it clear that while national unity and patriotism may be fostered through education, the compulsion of patriotic sentiment was absurd as well as unconstitutional. Justice Black wrote: "To believe that patriotism will not flourish if patriotic ceremonies are voluntary and spontaneous instead of a compulsory routine is to make an unflattering estimate of the appeal of our institutions to free minds."

*Barnette* is also a dramatic reversal of the Court's stand on compulsory flag salutes, which it took just three years earlier in *Minersville School District v. Gobitis*. In *Gobitis*, the Court upheld the school district's policy on the grounds that "[n]ational unity is the basis of national security" and that state authorities have the legitimate power to select the appropriate means for the fostering of national unity. Writing for the majority, Justice Frankfurter argued that religious liberty and freedom of conscience do not exempt citizens from obedience to laws that apply to all Americans. Since the law made no effort to single out Jehovah's Witnesses, he rejected the argument that the Minersville flag salute policy restricted religious beliefs. He warned that unless the Supreme Court wanted to become "the school board of the country," the issue was best left to state authorities.

After reexamining *Gobitis* in *Barnette*, the Court felt that while national unity as an end was justifiable, the means chosen by the state to advance the end was not. Persuasion was permissible, but compulsion was unconstitutional. In his reexamination of *Gobitis*, Jackson wrote of the futility of attempting to compel patriotism:

> Probably no deeper division of our people could proceed from any provocation than from finding it necessary to choose what doctrine and whose program public educational officials shall compel youth to unite in embracing . . . Those who begin coercive elimination of dissent soon find themselves exterminating dissenters. Compulsory unification of opinion achieves only the unanimity of the graveyard.

Why did the Court change its position so quickly? The reversal of *Gobitis* can be explained partly by a change in personnel. Chief Justice Charles Evans Hughes retired in 1941 and was replaced by former Attorney General Robert H. Jackson, who would write the majority opinion in *Barnette*. Justice James F. Byrnes retired in 1942 and was replaced by Wiley Rutledge. It was predicted then that both Jackson and Byrnes would vote along with Justice Harlan Fiske Stone (the lone dissenter in *Gobitis*) to overturn the compulsory flag salute.

Another reason for the change was that, following these appointments, an unusual and dramatic shift in the philosophy of three other justices occurred. In *Jones v. Opelika*, 316 U.S. 584 (1942), a Jehovah's Witness case in which the Court upheld a licensing tax on bookselling, Justices Black, Douglas, and Frank Murphy announced that *Gobitis* had been "wrongly decided." The surprising announcement was made in a terse memorandum following their dissenting opinions. Several months later, the Court reversed itself on the compulsory flag salute question and overturned *Gobitis*.

The dissenting opinion in *Barnette*, ironically handed down on Flag Day 1943, was written by Justice Frankfurter, an outspoken proponent of judicial restraint to the will of the legislature. He chastised the Court for exceeding the boundaries of judicial power and usurping the legislative and political power of the state of West Virginia. If the flag salute law was unwise, he wrote then it was up to the electorate and the legislature to repeal it. He believed that the Court was too quick to strike down a piece of enacted legislation simply because a constitutional rights challenge had been made. For Frankfurter, it was ludicrous for the Court to void a law that promoted the interests of the state's entire citizenry merely because it may have offended the conscience of a handful of people: "[T]o deny the political power of the majority to enact laws concerned with civil matters, simply because they offend the consciences of a minority, really means that the consciences of a minority are more sacred and more enshrined in the Constitution than the consciences of a majority."

In another classic statement of his philosophy of judicial restraint, Frankfurter condemned the Court for writing its "private notions of policy into the Constitution" and for casually striking down laws on the basis of the "spirit of the Constitution." He concluded with a point that is as salient today as it was fifty years ago. He wrote:

> Our constant preoccupation with the constitutionality of legislation rather than with its wisdom tends to be the preoccupation of the American mind with a false value. The tendency of focusing attention on constitutionality is to make constitutionality synonymous with wisdom, to regard a law as all right if it is constitutional.

Americans educated in the public schools after *Barnette* was handed down may not be able to square the Court's decree with their own memories of beginning each school day with the Pledge of Allegiance. Long after *Barnette*, the recitation of the Pledge of Allegiance remained as much a tradition as did Christmas pageants and homecoming parades. Some states adopted voluntary participation clauses so that children who chose not to recite the pledge could not be officially punished. Other states and school boards enacted compulsory flag salute laws in direct violation of the Supreme Court's ruling.

As this shows, compliance to the edicts of the Court is by no means automatic, particularly in cases involving time-honored practices, such as patriotic or religious instruction. The Court is but one institution in a larger political context of federalism, often dependent on state legislatures, lower courts, and administrative units (such as school boards) to implement its decisions. That is why nearly thirty years after the Court ruled categorically that compulsory flag salute policies are unconstitutional, Susan Russo, a high school art teacher in Henrietta, New York, lost her job for standing silently at attention during daily classroom recitation of the Pledge of Allegiance. During the salute, Russo did not disrupt the ceremony, nor did she attempt to sow discord among her students. She stood at attention with her hands at her sides while another homeroom teacher led the class in the salute. Russo's belief was that the phrase "liberty and justice for all" simply did not reflect the quality of life in America at that time.

*Barnette* asserts that schoolchildren may not be compelled to salute the flag. What about high school teachers? Does the responsibility that a teacher voluntarily assumes—to shape and direct the still impressionable minds of students—somehow lessen the First Amendment rights that she would otherwise enjoy? Citing *Barnette*, the U.S. court of appeals ordered Russo reinstated, ruling that her right to remain silent in the face of an illegitimate demand for speech is "as much a part of First Amendment protection as the right to speak out in the face of an illegitimate demand for silence" (*Central School District #1 v. Russo*, 469 F.2d 623 [2nd Circuit (New York) 1972]). The school district appealed the decision to the Supreme Court, but the high court denied certiorari, leaving the final word on the interpretation of *Barnette* to the court of appeals.

Not all flag salute or flag celebration policies are unconstitutional: Those that are drawn narrowly and in the least restrictive way are permissible. Such regulations must be aimed at promoting education, not at stifling dissent or compelling a belief. In practical terms, the best rule of thumb for school boards that desire their students to salute the flag is to provide a process by which students and teachers can seek exemption from the practice without fear of ostracism or punishment.

If the First Amendment protects individuals from being compelled to honor the American flag, does it also protect those who do not wish to be merely associated with a particular ideology, such as individualism or state pride? In *Wooley v. Maynard*, 430 U.S. 705 (1977), the Court ruled that the state of New Hampshire could not constitutionally impose criminal penalties on two Jehovah's Witnesses (a married couple) who used adhesive tape to cover the New Hampshire state motto "Live Free or Die" on the license plate of their car. The Jehovah's Witnesses found the motto repugnant to their religious, moral, and political beliefs. The state argued that the burden placed on the individual's freedom of conscience and religion was minimal and that the issues raised in this case were trivial. But citing *Barnette*, the Supreme Court held that the state's interest in promoting state pride did not outweigh an individual's First Amendment right to avoid being associated with such a message. Nor did the motto have any rational relationship to the state's asserted interest in facilitating identification of passenger vehicles. For Chief Justice Burger, the issue in *Wooley* went far beyond mottoes on license plates. He believed that the New Hampshire law was, in essence, a means to compel the individual to be "an instrument" for an "ideological point of view he finds unacceptable."

## Conduct as Speech: Of Armbands, Draft Cards, and Flag Burning

Symbolism has also been used to protest governmental policies or social values. Many of us have at some time seen individuals engaged in symbolic behavior at political rallies, sporting events, or concerts. Indeed, symbolic conduct that challenges the status quo often has more impact on society than ordinary speeches or pamphlets. During the civil rights movement of the 1950s and 1960s, black civil rights activists brought attention to their cause by quietly sitting at lunch counters in "white only" sections or in the front seats of buses contrary to company or city policy. The Vietnam War spawned a seemingly endless array of symbolic political activities, ranging from "die-ins" to flag burning. One common form of protest was wearing black armbands in public. While probably one of the more subdued and least controversial forms of protest of that period, the practice nevertheless led to an important Supreme Court ruling on symbolic speech in *Tinker v. Des Moines Independent School District*, 393 U.S. 503 (1969).

In 1965, John Tinker, a high school student, and his sister Mary Beth, who was in junior high school, were suspended from school after refusing to remove the black armbands they wore to school to protest U.S. involvement in Vietnam. School officials reasoned that the Tinkers' action was likely to create a disturbance, thus distracting students from their academic work. In addition, authorities simply felt that "the schools are no place for demonstrations." However, outside of a few hostile remarks made to the Tinkers, there were no threats or acts of violence, nor any evidence that academic activities were disrupted.

The Tinkers challenged the school district's armband policy on the grounds it violated their constitutional right to engage in symbolic political expression. Given the particular circumstances and problems endemic to the public school setting, how much First Amendment protection should be extended to the speech and expressive conduct of students? Both a federal district court and a divided U.S. court of appeals agreed with the school district's argument that the right to express a controversial opinion was outweighed by the school district's interest in maintaining a safe and efficient academic environment. But upon appeal, the Supreme Court reversed, ruling that wearing armbands to communicate a political opinion is closely related to pure speech and therefore entitled to First Amendment protection. Writing for the majority, Justice Abe Fortas reminded the school officials: "First Amendment rights, applied in light of the special characteristics of the school environment, are available to students and teachers. It can hardly be argued that either students or teachers shed their constitutional rights to freedom of speech or expression at the schoolhouse gate."

The Court argued that while public schools have a legitimate interest in proscribing aggressive, disruptive action or outrageous modes of dress, they cannot restrict the expression of opinions merely because those opinions are unpleasant or may cause discomfort. The Court found the school authorities' action was not really based on concern that the black armbands would interfere with education, but rather on the grounds that they wished to avoid the potential controversy or embarrassment that might result from the Tinkers' symbolic expression.

In his majority opinion, Justice Fortas established a standard for balancing a school's interest in maintaining order with a student's right of expression. This standard, often referred to as the *Tinker* test, has had a major impact on education law. Fortas wrote: "Certainly where there is no finding and no showing that engaging in the forbidden conduct would 'materially and substantially interfere with the requirements of appropriate discipline in the operation of the school,' the prohibition cannot be sustained."

*Tinker* is a pivotal decision not only because it recognizes a high school student's constitutional right to engage in symbolic speech on school grounds, but also because the ruling was intended to resolve a persistent dilemma faced by school administrators. How can the public schools maintain a safe and efficient education environment for students while at the same time respect and promote freedom of expression and association? Under the *Tinker* test, a student on school grounds is still a person with First Amendment rights. Therefore, a student's expression may not be restricted to the use of officially approved ideas or symbols only. As Fortas wrote, state-operated schools may not be "enclaves of totalitarianism. School officials do not possess absolute authority over their students."

While the Court reminded school officials that students do not "shed their constitutional rights at the schoolhouse gate," this grant of freedom is by no means absolute, since, under the *Tinker* test, students may engage only in those activities that do not (1) "materially and substantively" interfere with the school's requirements of "appropriate discipline" or (2) "collid[e] with the right of others." *Tinker*

does protect student expression from arbitrary restrictions, but since the two conditions are quite vague, the *Tinker* test provides administrators with much discretion.
Forms of expressive conduct that enjoy protection outside of school grounds might
not be permitted because of their disruptive qualities.

For example, under the two conditions of the *Tinker* test, school officials would
be within their rights to prohibit students from wearing "Support the Klan" buttons
at a high school where racial tension is high. However, as illustrated by the federal
district court in *Guzick v. Drebus*, 305 F. Supp. 473 (1969), the school's rule would
have to prohibit the wearing of all buttons and insignia, rather than only racist ones,
in order to survive a constitutional challenge.

Could public school officials punish or discharge teachers for wearing controversial symbols while at school on the grounds that, in view of the teacher's authority, students were compelled to "hear" the message? In *Board of Education v. James*,
409 U.S. 1042 (1972), the Court reaffirmed *Tinker* when it upheld a lower court's
decision allowing an eleventh grade public school teacher to wear a black armband
on Vietnam Moratorium Day.

While *Tinker* provides school officials with a workable standard for determining when it is permissible to restrict expressive conduct, it fails to provide a precise
measure of which forms of symbolic conduct are and are not "closely akin to pure
speech." Expressive conduct falls within the sphere of pure speech when it advances
a comprehensible idea or makes a contribution to a body of knowledge. Hair length,
for example, may be a symbolic expression of individuality, but it is not considered
akin to pure speech.[9]

During the 1960s, many political activists publicly burned their draft cards, hoping that this extreme action would draw national attention to America's military
involvement in Vietnam. *Is the public destruction of a draft card a form of symbolic
expression protected by the First Amendment?* As we have seen, symbolic expression consists of both speech and nonspeech elements. When the government punishes a particular form of symbolic expression because it finds the content or
message of the expression objectionable, the Court will invoke strict scrutiny and
require the government to demonstrate a compelling reason for its interest in prohibiting the expression. When strict scrutiny is applied to a law, the Court is more
likely to rule that the governmental action is contrary to the First Amendment.
However, when the government can demonstrate that its interest in prohibiting the
conduct element of symbolic expression (throwing rocks, for example) has nothing
to do with the content or message of the symbolic expression, the Court will apply
a *balancing of interests* test and be more willing to uphold the law. In the latter
instance, if the governmental interest is "sufficiently important," it may be found to
outweigh the individual's interest in conveying a message through an act of expressive conduct.

The Court's most authoritative explanation of this two-track theory is found in
*United States v. O'Brien*, 391 U.S. 367 (1968), a First Amendment challenge to a
federal selective service law. On March 31, 1966, David Paul O'Brien and three
other demonstrators burned their draft cards on the steps of the South Boston
Courthouse. The event was witnessed by a sizable crowd, including several FBI
agents. O'Brien openly admitted to the agents that he had burned his draft card to

publicly protest the Vietnam War and that he was aware that he was violating the law. He was promptly arrested, whisked off to jail, and convicted under a 1965 amendment to a federal law that made it a felony to knowingly mutilate, alter, or destroy a draft card.

O'Brien challenged the constitutionality of the selective service law on the grounds that his act was a form of symbolic speech. He argued that Congress's purported interest in the administrative necessity of prohibiting the destruction of draft cards was in reality a thinly veiled attempt to suppress public protest against the draft. Why was he being punished? He was not challenging the power of Congress to establish and maintain the draft, but only its power to punish the destruction of a piece of paper that simply serves as a notification of the registrant's status. The law did not even require registrants to keep the card with them at all times, as is the case with a driver's license when operating a motor vehicle. *Was this piece of paper more important than O'Brien's First Amendment rights?*

The U.S. court of appeals overturned his conviction on the grounds that because the law was directed at public, as distinguished from private, destruction of draft cards, it unjustly singled out individuals who were engaged in public protests against the draft. In other words, O'Brien was punished not for destroying the card, but for doing so publicly with the intent to protest the draft.

The Supreme Court flatly rejected the argument that the 1965 amendment to the federal law was unconstitutional because O'Brien's act of burning the card was a form of symbolic speech protected by the First Amendment. Although the Court did not completely reject the contention that such conduct possesses a "communicative element" protected by the First Amendment, it repudiated the theory that a limitless variety of conduct can be labeled speech solely on the grounds that the person engaged in the conduct intends to express an idea. Chief Justice Warren wrote: "However, even on the assumption that the alleged communicative element in O'Brien's conduct is sufficient to bring into play the First Amendment, it does not necessarily follow that the destruction of the registration certificate is constitutionally protected activity."

When speech and nonspeech elements are combined in one's "symbolic" conduct, the Court will allow the regulation of the nonspeech element (burning a draft card) if a "sufficiently important governmental interest" exists. Chief Justice Warren explained a three-part process to determine if a governmental regulation on the First Amendment is permissible:

1. The regulation furthers an important or substantial governmental interest (e.g., keeping order or maintaining accurate selective service records).
2. The governmental interest is unrelated to the suppression of free expression. (For instance, the law must be narrowly drawn to affect only the form of conduct that is deleterious to a legitimate societal interest.)
3. The restriction on the alleged First Amendment freedom is no greater than is necessary to the furtherance of that interest.

Warren believed that the 1965 amendment fulfilled all of these requirements: Congress had a legitimate interest in prohibiting the card's destruction because the card provided evidence of availability for induction in the event of an emergency, and it reminded registrants of their duty to notify their local draft board in the event of a change of address or status. He wrote:

> We think it apparent that the continuing availability to each registrant of his Selective Service certificates substantially furthers the smooth and proper functioning of the system that Congress established to raise armies. . . . When O'Brien deliberately rendered unavailable his registration certificate, he will-fully frustrated this governmental interest.

In sum, Congress may establish a system of registration and record keeping and may require eligible citizens to cooperate. The issuance and regulation of draft cards are a legitimate means to this end.

The Court also rejected O'Brien's argument that the law should be nullified because the real intent of the legislature in enacting the 1965 amendment was to chill freedom of expression. The Court will not strike down an otherwise constitutional law on the basis of an alleged hidden illicit motive on the part of a legislature. While the Court will examine the statements of legislators to aid its interpretation of a law, it will not void a law that is constitutional on its face on the basis of what a few legislators said about the proposed law during floor debate. For example, during congressional debate of the 1965 amendment to the Universal Military Training Act, three members of Congress stated that draft card burning was a brazen display of unpatriotism, and many more members of Congress probably saw the amendment as a means to foster respect for the system. However, reports of the Senate and House Armed Services Committees indicated that most supporters of the law believed that the unrestricted destruction of cards would disrupt the efficient operation of the Selective Service System. If the Court were to examine the legislative purpose, it would focus on this latter, more authoritative source.

*O'Brien* sent the message that if you want to burn a draft card you had better burn a photocopy, and that is what many protesters did. If the Court rejected the view that any form of activity can be labeled speech simply because the person engaged in the conduct intends to express an idea, what activities can be labeled speech? The Court does not answer this question in *O'Brien*. It is clear that O'Brien intended to express an idea—his disdain for the draft. But unlike earlier cases in which individuals were punished for advocating dangerous doctrine or behavior, O'Brien was punished because his actions created administrative problems for the draft board. Since he was not punished for his speech but for the impact of his action, the Court ruled that the regulation was constitutional.

After reinstitution of draft registration in 1980, the Burger Court relied on the *O'Brien* standard to uphold the conviction of an eighteen-year-old who refused to comply with the Military Selective Service Act of 1980 (*Wayte v. United States*, 470 U.S. 598 [1985]). The case began when Wayte, in an attempt to show his disdain for draft registration, wrote several letters to President Ronald Reagan and other government officials admitting that he did not intend to comply with the registration requirement. The letters were put in a file along with similar letters written by other nonregistrants. Following an FBI investigation, Wayte and others who had written letters were prosecuted, but the federal district court refused to convict the defendants. The district court agreed with Wayte's argument that the government's prosecution of only those persons who had openly expressed their opposition to draft registration by writing letters constituted "selective prosecution." Pressing its case in the U.S. court of appeals, the government managed to win a reversal of the district court's ruling.

The major issues in this case can be understood as follows: *Did the government's policy of selectively prosecuting vocal nonregistrants create a "content-based" grounds for enforcing the law? In other words, even though the policy did not explicitly punish protected speech, did it place restrictions on the kinds of communication that Wayte could employ in protesting the law?* Wayte could write letters in protest without fear of prosecution, but could he legally refuse to register as a form of protest? The Supreme Court affirmed the judgment of the court of appeals, ruling that selective enforcement of a law is prohibited only when the government does so using "unjustifiable standards," such as race or religion. Selective enforcement is not prohibited when it is based on known compliance versus noncompliance with a legitimate governmental interest. The government did not investigate or prosecute those who wrote letters criticizing draft registration unless their letters stated that they had refused to comply with the law. Thus, the law punished conduct, not speech.

Earlier in this chapter, we determined that the First Amendment protects an individual against compulsion to honor the American flag and from being forced to be associated with a statement of ideology. *Does the Constitution also protect those who wish to dishonor or desecrate the American flag as a form of political protest?*

In 1966, a Brooklyn bus driver named Sidney Street, an African American, heard on a radio broadcast that civil rights activist James Meredith had been shot by a sniper in Mississippi. Outraged that the government had failed to uphold its promise to protect Meredith, he took an American flag from his apartment and burned it in anger on a nearby street corner. In little time, a small crowd had assembled on the sidewalk to watch Street. As a police officer approached the crowd, he heard Street exclaim, "We don't need no damn flag," and "I burned it!" "If they let this happen to Meredith, we don't need an American flag."

Street was arrested and convicted under a New York statute that made it a misdemeanor to "publicly mutilate, deface, defile, or defy, trample upon, or cast contempt upon [an American flag] either by words or act." His conviction was affirmed by the New York Court of Appeals. On appeal to the U.S. Supreme Court, Street mounted a challenge to the state statute on First and Fourteenth Amendment grounds. The law was unconstitutionally broad, argued Street, because in addition to punishing conduct that may be legitimately proscribed, it also cast a broad net of restriction over conduct protected by the Constitution. In *Street v. New York*, 394 U.S. 576 (1969), a majority of justices agreed with Street's view. Street had been convicted not for burning the flag per se, but for defying and speaking out against the government. He had not been convicted for his conduct but for his words. The Court found that there were no legitimate state interests that justified convicting Street for the content of his speech: (1) he did not incite anyone to commit unlawful acts, (2) his words were not "fighting words," (3) the state cannot protect passersby from offensive words unless the words are legally obscene, and (4) he could not be compelled to show respect for our national emblem.

However, the Court did not determine whether the act of flag burning is protected under the First Amendment, but merely remanded the case to a lower court to decide whether Street could be convicted for the actual desecration of the flag rather than for his speech against the ideas represented by the flag. If New York still desired to criminalize flag burning, it would have to draft a law that punished only the act of physical desecration without affecting the "contemptuous" words that accompanied the act.

Three of the justices in the minority, Chief Justice Warren and Justices Black and Byron White, were clearly agitated by the majority's refusal to attack the flag burning issue head on. Was the deliberate act of burning the American flag as a protest a protected form of speech? Warren believed that Street was convicted for his act and not his words. He also believed that the government had "the power to protect the flag from acts of desecration and disgrace." The fourth dissenter, Justice Fortas, was opposed to even the prospect of elevating flag burning to a form of protected speech. In his dissenting opinion, he adamantly stated that "action, even if clearly for serious protest purposes, is not entitled to the pervasive protection that is given speech alone."

The Court would not give a definitive answer to whether flag burning by itself is a protected form of speech until *Texas v. Johnson*, 491 U.S. 397 (1989). During the 1984 Republican National Convention in Dallas, Gregory Johnson led a political protest against the policies of the Reagan administration and the practices of certain Dallas-based corporations. Following a clamorous march through the city streets, Johnson burned an American flag taken from a flagpole by a fellow protester. While the kerosene-soaked flag burned, the protesters chanted, "Reagan, Mondale, which will it be? Either one means World War III"; "Ronald Reagan, killer of the hour, perfect example of U.S. power"; and "America, the red, white, and blue, we spit on you." At that point, the protesters spit on the burning flag. No one was physically injured or threatened with injury, but several onlookers reported that they were seriously offended by the flag burning. In one poignant scene, a man who had witnessed the act salvaged the burned flag and buried it in his backyard.

Johnson was charged with the desecration of a venerated object in violation of a Texas statute that made "intentionally or knowingly" desecrating a state or national flag "in a way that the actor knows will seriously offend one or more persons likely to observe or discover his actions" a Class A misdemeanor. Johnson was convicted and sentenced to one year in prison and fined $2,000. Citing the sanctity of the flag as a venerated object and the state's interest in guarding against a breach of peace, a state court of appeals affirmed the lower court's decision. However, the Texas Court of Criminal Appeals reversed, ruling that Johnson's actions were protected by the First and Fourteenth Amendments. In turn, the state of Texas petitioned the U.S. Supreme Court for certiorari on the grounds that its interest in preventing imminent lawless action and in preserving the flag as a symbol of national unity outweighed Johnson's interest in burning the flag as a means of communicating his beliefs.

A sharply divided (5–4) Rehnquist Court affirmed the Texas high court's ruling in Johnson's favor. The following questions were raised: *Does flag burning constitute a form of expressive conduct? If Johnson's conduct was expressive, does the state's flag desecration statute suppress the free expression of political ideas?* To answer these questions, the Court employed a test of expressive conduct to determine whether a particular activity possesses a sufficient degree of communication to be considered speech. For example, in a fit of rage after a heated debate on baseball you grab my new American flag and rip it to shreds. You have mutilated the flag but have done so without the intent to convey any coherent message. Beyond knowing that you are upset with me for slandering your favorite team, I have no idea what you are trying to communicate by ripping my flag to pieces. In response to your actions, several neighbors who witnessed your display of rage attack you in my front yard and administer a terrible beating. Is your action expressive conduct? Does the state have a legitimate interest in proscribing such conduct so as to prevent this breach of peace?

In *Texas v. Johnson*, the Court agreed that in the context of the demonstration at the Republican National Convention, the burning of the flag was "sufficiently imbued with elements of communication to implicate the First Amendment." Johnson's intent was to show contempt for authority and the policies of the Reagan administration, and he knew that there was no better way to attract attention to his cause. Was his message understood by the average onlooker? Johnson knew that unless someone in the crowd was from another planet, the spectators and passersby would understand and respond emotionally to the burning of the American flag. Thus, the Court recognized that in some circumstances flag burning is protected speech. Justice Brennan wrote: "The First Amendment literally forbids the abridgment only of 'speech,' but we have long recognized that its protection does not end at the spoken or written word."

Texas argued that under a balancing of interests rationale, Johnson's interest in burning the flag was sufficiently outweighed by the state's interests in preventing its citizens from taking imminent lawless action and using offensive behavior. The Court rejected this claim as contrary to precedents. Brennan wrote:

> Our precedents do not countenance such a presumption. On the contrary, they recognize that a principal "function of free speech under our system of government is to invite dispute. It may indeed best serve its high purpose when it induces a condition of unrest, creates dissatisfaction with conditions as they are, or even stirs people to anger," *Terminello v. Chicago*, 337 U.S. 1 (1949).

Citing *Brandenburg v. Ohio*, the Court also rejected Texas's argument that since every flag burning poses a "potential for breach of peace" because it is so offensive, all flag burning should be suppressed. (Recall that under *Brandenburg* the government can act only if it is shown that the expression is intended to incite imminent lawless action *and* is likely to produce such action.) Texas has other means to keep the peace, wrote Brennan, and need not punish flag desecration to keep the peace when it already has a statute specifically designed for that purpose.

Did *Texas v. Johnson* ring a death knell for all flag desecration statutes, or is it still possible to prosecute flag burners in the name of preserving the flag as a venerated symbol of national unity? The state may preserve the flag as a venerated object as long as the law is not used to compel respect for the flag or restrict unpopular or offensive ideas expressed about the flag. According to the Court, Johnson was convicted not because he had burned the flag, since flag burning is permitted as a means of disposing of a tattered flag, but because he had expressed contempt for the policies of the country. Thus, the restriction placed on Johnson by the law was content-based. If Johnson had burned a tattered flag while saluting and singing the national anthem, he would not have been prosecuted under the law. Therefore, if a state's objective is to prevent breaches of peace, a flag desecration law must be worded narrowly or specifically enough to affect only acts against the flag that are likely to result in serious disturbance of the peace. The difference between *Texas v. Johnson* and *Street v. New York* is that, unlike the law at issue in *Street*, the Texas law does not on its face allow for conviction on the basis of the words uttered. The New York law explicitly punished the act of publicly defying the authority represented by the flag or casting contempt on the flag "either by words or deeds." In *Street* the Court struck down the statute, while in *Johnson* the Court upheld the law, resolving the case on the grounds that the statute as applied to Johnson violated the First Amendment. The Texas statute in itself did not necessarily apply only to expressive conduct. While it is difficult to prosecute an individual for flag desecration, it is not constitutionally impossible. The Court provided a good example: "A tired person might, for example, drag a flag through the mud, knowing that his conduct is likely to offend others, and yet have no thought of expressing any idea."

Brennan concluded his opinion reaffirming the principle that the First Amendment prohibits the government from establishing an orthodoxy of political beliefs or designating the kinds of messages that can be conveyed by our national symbols. If we reject this principle, we admit that the government can prohibit offensive expressive conduct toward a state flag, a copy of the Constitution, the presidential seal, or a picture of George Washington. Which of these symbols merit protection? Who decides: Congress, the Court, the president? Thus, we return to the question addressed in *Barnette*: Does the Constitution permit the use of compulsion to foster national unity and to teach the political beliefs of the majority?

There is also a powerful emotional dimension to the Court's opinion in *Texas v. Johnson*. Brennan seemed quite sympathetic to the pain and anger that Americans feel when they see Old Glory consumed in flames. However, he was steadfast in his belief that the Court's decision in *Texas v. Johnson* honored both the Bill of Rights and the flag. He wrote:

> Our decision is a reaffirmation of the principles of freedom and inclusiveness that the flag best reflects, and of the conviction that our toleration of criticism such as Johnson's is a sign and a source of our strength. We do not consecrate the flag by punishing its desecration, for in doing so we dilute the freedom that this cherished emblem represents.

In his concurring opinion, Justice Anthony Kennedy, a Reagan appointee, seemed to wrestle with the decision he had made. While joining with Brennan without reservation, he admitted that sometimes "we must make decisions we do not like" and that many Americans will be "dismayed" by the decision, especially those "who have had the singular honor of carrying the flag in battle."

Chief Justice Rehnquist, with whom Justices White and Sandra Day O'Connor joined, wrote a dissenting opinion that is more of an appeal to the heart than to the law. In his emotional appeal, Rehnquist cited Ralph Waldo Emerson, John Greenleaf Whittier, and Francis Scott Key. Charging that the Court was ignoring Justice Holmes's aphorism that "a page of history is worth a volume of logic," Rehnquist also cited more than a dozen federal statutes and codes pertaining to the American flag, a seemingly endless list of state laws that protect the flag, and several Supreme Court decisions protecting the flag from commercial exploitation.

Rehnquist's legal argument against flag burning rested on the following premises. The public burning of the American flag is not an essential part of the exposition of ideas, but merely constitutes "fighting words" under *Chaplinsky v. New Hampshire*, (1942). Johnson was free to deliver speeches on such related topics as the evils of blind obedience to what the American flag represents or the rejection of the American ideal. In doing so he was also free to hurl verbal insults at the flag or to burn the flag in privacy if he so desired. As he wrote in his dissenting opinion in *Spence v. Washington*, 418 U.S. 405 (1974), Rehnquist argued in *Johnson* that while the state cannot punish criticism of the flag, the state may remove the flag from the list of symbols and objects that can be used or abused for the purpose of communicating beliefs and opinions. The flag is not just another "thing" or "idea," venerated by some and vilified by others, but a unique national symbol that helps give us our common sense of nationhood. Like Chaplinsky's insults, Johnson's actions were not essential to the exposition of his ideas and were of such minimal social value that they were far outweighed by the state's interest in protecting against a breach of peace. Rehnquist equated flag burning with "grunting." He wrote: "Far from being a case of 'one picture being worth a thousand words,' flag burning is the equivalent of an inarticulate grunt or roar that, it seems fair to say, is most likely to be indulged in not to express any particular idea, but to antagonize others."

The nation's response to *Texas v. Johnson* was immediate and loud. Many Americans who ordinarily would never watch a congressional proceeding tuned in to C-SPAN to watch coverage of emotional congressional debate on the necessity of a new federal law or constitutional amendment prohibiting flag desecration. President George H. W. Bush, who had made respect for the flag a major issue of his 1988 campaign, supported a constitutional amendment because he believed that congressional action, even in the form of a narrowly drafted law, was likely to be overturned by the Court. Shortly after *Johnson* was handed down, Congress passed the Flag Protection Act of 1989.

The law was immediately violated during a protest on the steps of the U.S. Capitol. Citing *Johnson*, the district court held the act unconstitutional and dismissed the charges against the flag burners. The government appealed directly to the Supreme Court, arguing that, unlike the Texas law in *Johnson*, the Flag Protection Act did not punish expressive conduct based on the content of the message. The act, drafted with close attention to *Street* and *Johnson*, prohibited conduct that damages the flag without punishing the actor for his or her motive, message, or effect on those who witness the flag burning.

In *United States v. Eichman*, 496 U.S. 310 (1990), a fragmented Court, reflecting the division in *Johnson*, struck down the act as unconstitutional. Citing *Johnson*,

Brennan again argued that although the law contained no explicit regulation of the content of the message contained in flag burning, the governmental interest underlying the law was concerned with the "communicative impact" of flag burning and not merely with the physical desecration.

The hue and cry that followed *Johnson* was conspicuously absent after *Eichman*, as the national consensus of which members of Congress spoke seemed to shift its attention elsewhere. Soon after these two decisions, Justice Brennan retired after nearly thirty-five years on the Court. Following Brennan's announcement, Judge David Souter of New Hampshire was appointed to the Court by President George H. W. Bush. Bush was given a second opportunity to influence the direction of the Court when Justice Thurgood Marshall, the first African American to serve on the Supreme Court, announced his retirement in 1991. Bush filled Marshall's seat with Clarence Thomas, also an African American, who served as chair of the Equal Employment Opportunity Commission (EEOC) during the Reagan administration and as a U.S. court of appeals judge.

President Bush's attempt to shape the Court has had mixed results. One the one hand, Souter emerged as a moderate, voting more often with the liberal-moderate wing of the Court than with the conservatives. Thomas's voting record, one the other hand, is solidly conservative and has not disappointed those on the right of the spectrum.

President Bill Clinton's two appointments, Justices Ruth Bader Ginsburg and Steven Breyer, have solid liberal-to-moderate records, consistently voting with Justices Stevens and Souter.

While no one can predict with certainty how the current Court would vote on a future flag burning case, if President George W. Bush chooses Justice Steven's successor, the Court could easily reverse the narrowly decided *Texas v. Johnson*.[10]

## OFFENSIVE AND RACIST SPEECH

*Does the First Amendment protect offensive words, such as expletives and racial slurs, that may produce a negative or a violent reaction? Is there a limitless variety of conduct that can be labeled speech, or are there instances where the state has an interest in punishing what it considers offensive or outrageous to the majority of Americans?*

### Vulgar Language

During a period of widespread anti-Vietnam War demonstrations, Paul Robert Cohen was convicted and sentenced to thirty days in jail for wearing a denim jacket bearing the words "Fuck the Draft" while in a corridor of the Los Angeles County Courthouse. The California Penal Code made it a misdemeanor to "maliciously and willfully disturb the peace or quiet of any neighborhood or person . . . by offensive conduct." The California trial court made a point of noting that the presence of women and children in the courthouse made Cohen's message even more offensive. Though there was no evidence that Cohen said anything or created a disturbance, the trial court found his choice of words so outrageous and offensive that it sentenced him to jail. A California appellate court affirmed his conviction.

In *Cohen v. California*, 403 U.S. 15 (1971), the Supreme Court reversed Cohen's conviction in a 5–4 decision. The Court ruled that displaying the words "Fuck the Draft" on a jacket is constitutionally protected symbolic speech. Speaking for the majority, Justice Harlan approached the issue of whether Cohen's words were protected by the First Amendment by attacking five points of the state's case against Cohen. First, the California court's conviction of Cohen was unconstitutional because it rested solely on his speech and not on his conduct, as the state alleged. A law that primarily restricts conduct but also indirectly affects speech cannot be upheld unless its effect on speech is minor in relation to a compelling interest in the control of conduct. Even shocking language, such as that used by Cohen, can have a valuable communicative function. Since his intent was to announce the depth of his opposition to the Vietnam War and the draft, his purpose would not have been served by saying something like "Down with the Draft."

Second, the state could not punish Cohen for his message on the grounds that he intended to incite disobedience or interference with the draft. Nor were Cohen's words fighting words, for he did not endanger himself or any onlookers by causing a violent reaction or noisy disruption.

Third, the state could not employ the "captive audience" theory to restrict Cohen's speech. The Court has recognized that the state may protect captive listeners from offensive language that is thrust into the privacy of the home. However, in a public place, such as a park or a courthouse, the state cannot "silence dissent simply as a matter of personal predilections." Bystanders who witnessed Cohen's display could avoid being offended by averting their eyes, or for that matter, by wearing a shirt bearing the words "I support the draft." In fact, Cohen had removed his jacket when he entered the courthouse. The only person who reported being offended by the expletive was the arresting officer.

Fourth, Cohen's message could not be considered obscene. The "vulgar allusion to the Selective Service System" was not meant to arouse or appeal to interests of a sexual or lustful nature. According to *Roth v. United States*, 354 U.S. 476 (1957), in order for the state to prohibit obscene expression, such expression must be in some way erotic.

Fifth, without a compelling reason, the state of California could not make display of the word "fuck" a criminal offense. The state does not have the right to cleanse public debate by restricting the use of a particular word. While there is little doubt that a large number of Americans find such four-letter words offensive, the majority of the Court felt it is best to leave matters of good taste and style largely up to the individual. Harlan wrote: "For, while the particular four-letter word being litigated here is perhaps more distasteful than most others in its genre, it is nevertheless often true that one man's vulgarity is another's lyric."

*Cohen* established that shocking language that is not legally obscene and is not directed at another person in order to incite a violent reaction is protected by the First Amendment. The Court also acknowledged that even a vulgar message may have valuable "emotive content" because it expresses a heartfelt belief that cannot be adequately expressed intellectually. Many activists and demonstrators know that as a practical matter using shocking language in connection with a political opinion is often the most effective means of communicating with an apathetic public and a news-hungry media.

At a time when antiwar sentiment reached its zenith and many members of the Court felt as if society was pulling itself apart, the case had ramifications far beyond the reversal of Cohen's conviction. Law enforcement officials who felt overwhelmed by massive demonstrations and bizarre means of expression needed to know how far they could go to ensure order and public safety. Antiwar activists saw the case as a symbolically important reaffirmation of the role of free expression in a pluralistic society. Justice Harlan wrote:

> [The] constitutional right of free expression is powerful medicine in a society as diverse and populous as ours. It is designed and intended to remove governmental restraints from the arena of public discussion, putting the decision as to what views shall be voiced largely into the hands of each of us, in the hope that the use of such freedom will ultimately produce a more capable citizenry and more perfect polity.

However powerful, the medicine that Harlan spoke of was for many people (including four members of the Court) hard to swallow. Chief Justice Burger, who refused to allow Cohen's counsel from the American Civil Liberties Union (ACLU) to say "that word" in his courtroom, joined in Blackmun's dissenting opinion calling Cohen's action an "absurd and immature antic . . . mainly conduct and little speech." The dissenters were also angry with the Court's obvious narrowing of the *Chaplinsky* fighting words doctrine, which placed profane speech outside of constitutional protection. If, according to Harlan, one person's vulgarity is another person's lyric, how will it be possible to determine which words fall into the fighting words category?

## HATE SPEECH

If words cannot be banned merely because they are offensive to others, can a symbol be banned if it represents nothing else but genocide, racism, and murder, and is likely to incite violence? Should the swastika, a symbol once used by a dictatorial regime that killed millions, and used today to convey the idea that anti-Semitism is good and that Adolph Hitler was correct, be entitled to constitutional protection under the First Amendment? *Of what value does hate speech have to the search for the truth and the exposition of ideas? Should this variety of speech be suppressed on the grounds that it may lead to, at minimum, psychological harm or to the extremes of violence and bloodshed?*

In 1978, the American Nazi party sought a permit to hold a demonstration and a march through Skokie, Illinois, a suburb of Chicago with a large Jewish population. Indeed, more than 5,000 of the 40,500 Jewish residents were survivors of Nazi death camps. Several Jewish organizations, including the Jewish Defense League and B'nai B'rith, announced that a counterdemonstration would be held. Since city and county officials were almost certain that these demonstrations would lead to violence and bloodshed, a "racial slur" ordinance was passed banning the dissemination of any material promoting or inciting racial or religious hatred. This material was defined to include the "public display of markings and clothing of symbolic significance." A Cook County circuit court upheld the ordinance, ordering the Nazi party not to march. The Nazi party filed two suits challenging the constitutionality of the city's actions.[11]

In *Skokie v. National Socialist Party*, 373 N.E.2d 21 (1978), the Illinois Supreme Court, applying *Cohen v. California*, reversed the lower court's judgment on First Amendment grounds. The court argued that the display of the swastika, "as offensive to the principles of a free nation the memories it recalls may be," is symbolic speech that is intended to convey the political beliefs of the members of the American Nazi party. Displaying the swastika did not amount to fighting words and could not be totally restricted solely on the speculation that it could provoke an emotional or violent reaction on the part of Jewish residents.

In the second suit, *Collin v. Smith*, 578 F.2d 1197 (1978), both the federal district court and U.S. court of appeals dismissed the city's argument that the march was merely conduct and not speech. Both courts found that the racial slur ordinance violated the First and Fourteenth Amendments. The court of appeals rejected the city's argument that it had a duty to ban the use of swastikas and uniforms because their display would inflict psychic trauma on residents who were Holocaust survivors. Because the city did not rely on a fear of imminent violence to justify the ordinance, the court did not believe that the *Brandenburg v. Ohio* standard would apply. Nor did it believe that the ordinance was justified under *Chaplinsky*, since the words did not have "a direct tendency to cause violence by persons to whom, individually, the words were addressed."

Instead, the court of appeals relied on *Street v. New York* and *Terminello v. Chicago* to strike down the ordinance. Recall that in *Street*, the Supreme Court established that the use or abuse of symbols cannot be restricted or criminalized merely because they convey an offensive political opinion. In *Terminello*, the Court argued that the anti-Semitic speech of a radical Catholic priest could not be punished solely on the grounds that his speech could have invited dispute or stirred people to anger.

Finally, the court of appeals addressed the city's contention that the Jewish residents of Skokie were a "captive audience" of the Nazi's offensive ideology and symbols and that the city had an interest in protecting its citizens from being captives of messages against their will. The court rejected this view and ruled: "Absent such intrusion or captivity, there is no justifiable substantive privacy interest to save [the ordinance], when it attempts, by fiat, to declare the entire Village, at all times, a privacy zone that may be sanitized from the offensiveness of Nazi ideology and symbols." The U.S. Supreme Court refused to grant certiorari in either of these cases, allowing the lower court rulings to stand.

**What about speech directed toward a "captive audience?"**    The Court has held that whenever speech is directed toward an audience that cannot easily avoid exposure to the speech, a captive audience exists and certain restrictions on the speech may be permitted. The Court has applied this theory, as well as a private property rationale, to the regulation of pornography and commercial speech. In

*Frisby v. Schultz*, 487 U.S. 474 (1988), for example, the Rehnquist Court ruled that a city may ban all "focused" picketing that occurs in front of a private home so as to protect the residents of that house from hearing, seeing, or smelling unwanted messages. In doing so, the Court upheld an action prohibiting an extended anti-abortion demonstration in front of a physician's home.[12] However, in other situations the Court has told us to avert our eyes from the words that offend us or, in the case of Skokie's Jewish residents, simply to avoid the city hall area for thirty minutes on the Sunday afternoon that the demonstration was to take place.[13]

The debate surrounding hate speech has recently taken on a new dimension. In an attempt to promote tolerance and to guard against discriminatory speech, more than 100 universities have adopted policies prohibiting hate speech on campus. These policies consist of broad codes of behavior that punish comments or jokes that are racist, sexist, or antigay. The rules punish speech that harasses or intimidates persons because of their race, religion, sex, or sexual orientation. While most of these codes of behavior are aimed at punishing serious harassment and intimidation, some may be drafted or interpreted broadly enough to punish any comments or stories that could be construed to place any disadvantaged group in an unfavorable light. On several university campuses, a student or a professor could possibly be disciplined for telling a joke or taking an offensive stand on a racial or gender issue.

Such policies create a dilemma for many individuals and groups that have supported both the ideals of social and political equality *and freedom of speech*. For instance, many members of the ACLU, a group that has tirelessly supported both freedom of speech and equality, were faced with the dilemma of defending speech that promoted bigotry or stereotypes. *Are these codes of behavior constitutional? Should speech that promotes the kinds of hateful attitudes that most citizens find offensive be afforded First Amendment protection? Are there any ways to limit such speech without violating the Constitution?* Many of these questions were answered in *Doe v. University of Michigan*, 721 F. Supp. 852, a 1989 federal district court case involving the University of Michigan at Ann Arbor.

In January 1987, "unknown persons" distributed a flier on campus declaring "open season" on blacks. One month later, a student disk jockey allowed racist jokes to be broadcast on a campus radio program. In an already tense situation, a Ku Klux Klan uniform was prominently displayed from a dormitory window. Matters became worse when the university was neither able to identify the perpetrators nor determine if university students were involved.

Following university inquiries into these incidents, the United Coalition Against Racism (UCAR), a campus antidiscrimination group, announced that it intended to file a class action civil rights suit against the university for not maintaining a "nonracist" atmosphere on campus. After much debate regarding the constitutionality of a proposed antidiscrimination and harassment policy, the University of Michigan's governing Board of Regents unanimously adopted a policy to deal with racial intolerance and discriminatory harassment of students on campus.

The policy prohibited individuals from "stigmatizing or victimizing" persons or groups on the basis of race, ethnicity, religion, sex, sexual orientation, creed, national origin, ancestry, age, marital status, handicap, or Vietnam-era status. Under the plan, stigmatizing could include anything from racist or sexist comments or displaying the Confederate flag to jokes about gay men or women. The policy also included a provision punishing anyone creating an "intimidating, hostile, or demeaning environment for educational pursuits." Sanctions ranged from a formal reprimand to suspension or expulsion from the university. The policy was published in a simplified form and issued as a guide for students.

"John Doe," a psychology graduate student and teaching assistant who specialized in biopsychology, brought suit challenging the constitutionality of the policy. Although he had not been disciplined, he believed that one section of the policy infringed upon his academic freedom to conduct a classroom discussion of certain controversial theories on the biological differences between sexes and races. One theory he discussed in the classroom focused on sex differences in mental abilities to explain why more men than women chose to enter the engineering profession.

Since these theories had already been pronounced sexist or racist by some professors and students, Doe feared that his discussion of these theories might result in some form of punishment under the policy. He felt that his right to discuss these theories was "impermissibly chilled," or restricted prior to his entering the classroom. As a consequence, Doe asked the court to declare the policy unconstitutional on the grounds that it cast a vague and overly broad restriction on his First Amendment right.

Since Doe was not punished by the university, did he have standing to sue under the "cases and controversies" provision in Article III of the Constitution?[14] The court answered affirmatively because Doe demonstrated a "realistic and credible threat of enforcement" of the policy by the university. The mere possibility that Doe would be subject to punishment is insufficient to challenge the constitutionality of a policy, but the record had shown that students like Doe had been disciplined in the past year for discussing in the classroom ideas that offended others.

The district court blasted the policy as unconstitutionally broad and vague, constituting a violation of Doe's freedom of speech and academic freedom. Any law regulating speech will be ruled overbroad if it affects protected speech along with the words that it may legitimately regulate. The judge wrote: "A law regulating speech will be deemed overbroad if it sweeps within its ambit a substantial amount of protected speech along with that which it may legitimately regulate."

The rule established in *Doe* is as follows: If the university wishes to enact and enforce policies aimed at combating racial or sexual harassment, it must place restrictions only on those statements that constitute epithets under the fighting words doctrine; that is, words that are intended and likely to cause physical or psychological harm. To pass constitutional muster, only discriminatory statements that are directed at individuals can be punished. In the past, laws making it a criminal offense to commit an act of "ethnic intimidation" have passed constitutional scrutiny because they were narrowly drawn to punish the act of intimidation and not the conveyance of ideas of value.

The irony of the Michigan case was that many of the proponents of the university's policy were staunch supporters of the reasoning used by the Supreme Court in flag-burning cases and other offensive speech cases. As we have seen in *Street* and

*Texas v. Johnson*, speech cannot be banned merely because it is offensive to some group or ideology. The district court judge wrote: "The apparent willingness to dilute the values of free speech is ironic in light of the University's previous statements of policy [antiwar protester's rights] on this matter."

While the university owes its students, faculty, and staff an environment in which differences are tolerated and not vilified, the policy placed a frightening burden on the free exchange of ideas much like that imposed on professors and students during the days when *in loco parentis* (acting as students' parents) was official university policy. Indeed, criticism of the policy itself could be regarded by some to be racist, sexist, or antigay.

Three years after the Michigan decision, the Supreme Court dealt a death blow for many similar hate speech codes and ordinances in *R.A.V. v. City of St. Paul*, 505 U.S. 377 (1992). The city of St. Paul, Minnesota, made it a misdemeanor to place on public or private property any symbol, object, or graffiti, including a burning cross or Nazi swastika, that one knows will arouse anger, alarm, or resentment on the basis of race, color, creed, religion, or gender. In 1990, Robert A. Viktora and others were convicted under the ordinance for burning a crudely assembled cross inside the fenced yard of a black family. He successfully challenged his conviction in a state trial court on the grounds that the St. Paul ordinance constituted an overbroad and content-based restriction of speech. But the Minnesota Supreme Court reversed, rejecting Viktora's overbreadth claim because the phrase "arouses anger, alarm or resentment in others" narrowly tailored the reach of the ordinance to fighting words.

However, in a sharply divided opinion, the U.S. Supreme Court reversed the Minnesota high court's ruling on the grounds that the St. Paul ordinance was intended to apply only to those fighting words that insult or provoke violence on the basis of race, color, creed, religion, or gender. According to the logic of the St. Paul ordinance, all displays of expression, no matter how hateful, were permissible unless they were directed at one of the city's protected groups or taboo topics. For example, hostile speech directed toward Republicans, members of unions, homosexuals, or any other group not included in the ordinance was permissible, while hateful speech directed at traditionally disadvantaged groups, such as blacks, Jews, or women, was impermissible. Writing for the Court, Justice Scalia emphasized:

> What we have here . . . is not a prohibition of fighting words that are directed at certain persons or groups (which would be facially valid if it met the requirements of the Equal Protection Clause); but rather, a prohibition of fighting words that contain . . . messages of "bias motivated" hatred . . . "based on virulent notions of racial supremacy."

St. Paul argued that even if the ordinance was content-based, it was constitutional because it served the compelling interest of ensuring the basic human rights of persons who have been historically subjected to discrimination. But Scalia disagreed and reasoned that if the city of St. Paul wishes to ban the reprehensible act of burning a cross in someone's yard it may do so through statutes penalizing terroristic threats, arson, and property damage and not through regulations based on the content or idea contained in a message. He compared fighting words to a noisy sound-truck driving through the streets of a city broadcasting messages. The city may restrict the right of the sound-truck to make loud noises in the streets, but it may not pass ordinances based on the content of the sound-truck's message. In sum, the majority was not willing to adopt St. Paul's more flexible approach to restrictions on hate speech merely because of a purported compelling interest in protecting persons who have had long and painful experience with discrimination.

As a result of this opinion, many hate speech codes enacted to protect certain groups had to be reexamined and modified, forcing a return to more traditional rules of conduct that punish either the intentional infliction of emotional distress or the disruption of the educational mission of the university or college.

Since modern First Amendment law offers broad protection to an almost unlimited array of speech, it is very difficult—though not impossible—for educational institutions or local governments to place restrictions on racist, sexist, or anti-Semitic speech. This is one of the dilemmas of our liberal-democratic society: a powerful simultaneous, but often contradictory, devotion to both freedom of expression *and* equality, the latter being understood as protection of disadvantaged minorities.[15]

"Hate crime" laws have garnered much attention from lawmakers and the media. Therefore, it is worth noting the Court recognizes the distinction between hate speech and hate crimes. In *Wisconsin v. Mitchell*, 508 U.S. 476 (1993), the Court upheld a law that increased the punishment of a crime if a defendant chose the victim on the basis of race, religion, or some other status. The city ordinance struck down in *R.A.V.* was intended to restrict speech but the law upheld in *Mitchell* was aimed at "bias-inspired" criminal conduct.

***How far does First Amendment protection of subversive political speech extend?***   Communism is no longer a perceived threat, but other groups—such as militias, white supremacists, and radical anti-abortion activists—continue to push the limits of the First Amendment. Domestic communism was but a phantom compared to the threats of terrorism that we face today. *Does the First Amendment protect the advocacy of terrorism as a legitimate means of political change?* Under current precedent, the answer is yes, unless the speaker intends to produce violent acts or other forms of lawless action and it is likely that such action will occur. In order for the government to constitutionally restrict your invective, it must be shown that your advocacy of violence was directed at producing unlawful action and is likely to produce such action. However, in light of the government's response to the September 11, 2001, terrorist attacks on the World Trade Center and the Pentagon, such speech would most assuredly necessitate an investigation by the FBI and other law enforcement agencies. Suppose that the author of an online newsletter supporting the philosophy of Osama bin Laden was apprehended, indicted, and tried. Would his or her speech receive the same First Amendment protection as Communists, Nazis, or Klansmen? Could prosecutors rely on *Schenck*? As Justice Holmes said, "When a nation is at war many things that might be said in times of peace are such a hindrance to its effort that their utterance will not be endured." Would this axiom apply to peace activists who are critical of the war on terrorism?

## COMPETING RIGHTS: ABORTION CLINIC PROTESTS

One of the more challenging problems associated with the First Amendment arises when freedom of expression competes not only with society's interest in safety or public order—as we have seen in earlier cases—but with another constitutional right, such as a woman's right to have an abortion. Media reports regularly document this competition of rights taking place at abortion clinic protests around the nation.

According to the U. S. Supreme Court, a woman's constitutional right to an abortion implies that no "undue burden" is placed on that right and that she has access to a physician and facility so that the abortion can be performed.[16] On the other hand, people have the First Amendment right to express their opposition to abortion and to dissuade women and physicians from taking part in an act that they believe to be morally wrong. Public officials find themselves in the middle of two competing constitutional rights. The right to express opposition to abortion is never called into question but the manner in which it is done has generated much controversy. Many anti-abortion protestors have been known to employ a range of tactics—far exceeding mere speech and pamphleteering—that interfere with a legal medical procedure and threaten safety and order. Such tactics have included marching, kneeling, sitting, and laying in clinic parking lots, driveways, and doorways. Activists have hindered women and clinic employees from entering clinics. Many have disrupted clinic operation by crowding around cars. Others have surrounded, jostled, grabbed, pushed, shoved, cursed, thrown blood on, and spat at women entering the clinics. Protesters have used bullhorns and loudspeakers to ensure that patients and employees in the clinics could hear their words. And, most tragically, there have also been fatal shootings and fire bombings at clinics. It is estimated that one third of the nearly 1,000 abortion clinics in the country are protected by court-ordered buffer zones.[17]

The problem had become so serious that in 1993 Congress passed the Freedom of Access to Clinics Entrances Act,[18] making it a crime to use force or the threat of force to intimidate women seeking abortion services or the clinic physicians and staff who provide those services. Prior to the law, women and clinic staff were totally dependent on local law enforcement authorities, many of whom were sympathetic to the anti-abortion activists. Violations of the act can incur a range of penalties, from a $10,000 fine or six months' imprisonment, or both, for first-time nonviolent intimidation to a fine of $25,000 fine or three years' imprisonment, or both, for a repeat conviction for violent intimidation. Injured parties are also authorized to bring civil suits for compensatory and punitive damages. So as not to be used to restrict freedom of expression, it is stated very clearly that nothing in the law should be construed to prohibit any expressive conduct, including peaceful picketing or demonstration. The federal courts have upheld the act[19] and the Supreme Court has chosen not to review the lower courts' rulings.

The law may provide a uniform nationwide punishment for intimidation and violence but by no means does it resolve the First Amendment issues that concern us here. *For instance, what permissible restrictions can authorities place on the expressive conduct of the protesters? Should there be restrictions on what they can*

*say, how they say it, and where they can say it? Just how far can the protesters go*
*before they cross the line between expressive conduct and fighting words?*

The U. S. Supreme Court addressed these questions in a case that originated in upstate New York, where clinics were besieged by protesters calling themselves "sidewalk counselors," who approached women on their way into the clinic and employed various tactics to dissuade women from having abortions. On some occasions, anti-abortion protesters demonstrated outside a physician's home or in front of schools attended by the children of physicians who performed abortions. Even the police who protected the patients and clinic employees were harassed by protesters verbally and by mail.

To deal with these problems occurring at clinics in and around Buffalo and Rochester, New York, a federal district court issued an injunction that prohibited protesters from engaging in such activities at the clinics. The district court based its decision on the 1994 case *Madsen v. Women's Health Center*, 512 U.S. 753, where the Supreme Court allowed the establishment of a thirty-six-foot buffer zone around an abortion clinic but struck down as unconstitutional a 300-foot "no-approach zone" around the clinic.

Contrary to the First Amendment claims of the protesters, the district court's injunction ordered the creation of "fixed buffer zones" to ban demonstrations within fifteen feet (the distance of about five long strides) of all doorways and entrances (including parking lots) and "floating buffer zones" within fifteen feet of any person or vehicle entering or leaving the clinics. The two sidewalk counselors were allowed inside the buffer zones, but the injunction required them to "cease and desist" their counseling if the women so requested. At that point, the counselors would have to abide by the fixed buffer zone. The court of appeals upheld the district court's injunction, and the protesters appealed to the U.S. Supreme Court.

In *Schenck v. Pro-Choice Network of Western New York*, 519 U. S. 357 (1997), the Court reaffirmed its earlier ruling in *Madsen* to uphold[20] the fixed buffer zone (including the cease and desist rule) limitation as constitutional but struck down the floating buffer zone as a restriction on speech that went far beyond what was necessary to serve the significant government interest of order and safety.[21] Writing for the majority, Chief Justice Rehnquist argued that ensuring public safety and order, promoting the free flow of traffic on streets and sidewalks, protecting property rights, and protecting a woman's freedom to seek pregnancy-related services are significant enough to justify an "appropriately tailored" injunction that enables unimpeded access to the clinics. However, the floating buffer zones burdened more speech than is necessary to serve the relevant governmental interests. Such zones around people prevent the protesters (except for the two sidewalk counselors) from communicating a message from a normal conversational distance or handing out leaflets on the public sidewalks. Protesters who wished to communicate their message to a particular individual would have to move along with that person while maintaining a distance of fifteen feet.

Rehnquist felt that this would be difficult to accomplish. He argued that floating buffer zones around vehicles are unconstitutional as well, since they would restrict the speech of those who simply lined the sidewalk in order to hold signs or chant as the vehicles drove past. The uncertainty of whether one is maintaining the proper legal distance places a "chill" on freedom of expression. A protester who did not wish to be fined or jailed for violating an injunction might be reluctant to speak because of this uncertainty. Rehnquist wrote:

> We strike down the floating buffer zones around people entering and leaving clinics because they burden more speech than is necessary to serve the relevant governmental interests.
>
> The floating buffer zones prevent defendants—except for the two sidewalk counselors, while they are tolerated by the targeted individual—from communicating a message from a normal conversational distance or handing leaflets to people entering or leaving the clinics who are walking on the public sidewalks. . . . Leafleting and commenting on matters of public concern are classic forms of speech that lie at the heart of the First Amendment, and speech in public areas is at its most protected on public sidewalks, a prototypical example of a traditional public forum.

For this reason the Court believed that it was necessary to run the risk of the sidewalk counselors harassing the patients and clinic workers entering the clinic. The issue of the sidewalk counselors created a dilemma for some of the justices. On the one hand, something had to be done to stop counselors who were known to employ "in your face" tactics, like screaming at women (even after they entered the clinics). One the other hand, the Court believed that it was inappropriate to prohibit all opportunities for protesters to approach women in order to hand out leaflets or communicate a message. The anti-abortion protesters argued that the cease and desist provision was unconstitutional because it was content-based restriction of speech, that is, it allowed the woman entering the clinic the right to terminate the protester's speech if she disagreed with the content of the speech. But the Court disagreed, since the counselors were free to espouse their message outside of the fifteen-foot zone. Furthermore, the cease and desist provision applied because many of the counselors had previously been arrested for harassing patients.

The Court has ruled in the past that speech taking place on public streets and sidewalks receives the most protection because streets and sidewalks are traditional public forums.[22] Any laws or regulations that impose restrictions on expression in a "traditional public forum" or in a "designated public forum" are subject to the Court's most strict scrutiny.[23] Places such as jails, post offices, and military bases, however, are not considered public forums.[24]

## THE FIRST AMENDMENT AND CAMPAIGN FINANCE REFORM

Every four years Americans go to the polls to elect a new president. They also vote for members of Congress, state legislators, judges, and other officials, and on ballot initiatives. Citizens also contribute their time and money to candidates, causes, and political organizations. We all know that speaking out on political issues is protected by the First Amendment, but few people realize that spending money to get a message across is also a form of protected speech. A person is free to spend an unlimited amount of personal wealth on whatever political message he or she wishes to communicate. You could spend millions of dollars on prime-time infomercials, rent Yankee Stadium so that you could speak to thousands, or purchase a radio station devoted to communicating your message across the airwaves.

In most instances, however, people attempt to influence the political process by donating money to candidates, political parties, interest groups, and political action committees (PACs). Donations are made with the intent of shaping or changing public policy. Individuals and corporations give money to like-minded candidates and organizations that promise something in return, whether it is merely adherence to compatible ideology or a favorable stance on a specific policy issue. Public confidence in the political process is shaken, however, when it becomes apparent that the wealthiest donors have the greatest say over public policy or when politicians become fixated on raising money for their campaigns. In the 2000 election campaign, spending by all presidential and congressional candidates may have topped $3 billion. In the primary and general election of 2000, more than $600 million was spent. George W. Bush spent more than $200 million to win the presidency.[25]

Public opinion polls show that Americans are outraged by the amount of money that flows into political campaigns and that they support proposed measures to limit campaign spending. A 2001 poll found widespread public support for some type of limit on campaign contributions. Seventy-six percent of Americans favor new federal laws limiting the amount of money that an individual or group can contribute.[26]

Senator John McCain (R-Ariz.) made campaign finance reform a cornerstone of his bid for the Republican nomination for president in 2000. He passionately argued that the influence of money is corrupting our ability to address many of the nation's social and economic problems. Although he lost the Republican nomination to Texas Governor George W. Bush, McCain quickly became one of the most popular political figures in the nation. He leveraged his popularity into a renewed debate on the excesses of campaign finance and won passage of the first campaign finance law in twenty-one years. The new reform forces secretive tax-exempt PACs, which raise unlimited funds from undisclosed contributors, to disclose the names of those who are funding television and radio ads for candidates. The law is modest in scope signalled a willingness among some members of Congress to address McCain's primary target: "soft money"; that is, unrestricted contributions from interest groups, PACs, and individuals used to fund campaign activities independently of the candidate's official campaigns. All of those fundraisers that we hear so much about are geared not so much as collecting direct (regulated) contributions to the candidates but toward gathering unlimited sums of money to be used for "independent" activities.

While most Americans support campaign finance reform, they may not realize that such regulations may potentially violate the First Amendment. So, while McCain and his followers gain support for new restrictions on campaign finance, his opponents from both parties are gearing up for new constitutional challenges that will ultimately be heard by the Supreme Court. We can attempt to predict whether new laws will withstand judicial scrutiny by examining some of the Court's previous rulings on this issue, beginning with its landmark ruling in *Buckley v. Valeo*, 424 U.S. 1 (1976).

By the early 1970s, campaign costs skyrocketed as candidates for national office began to rely on expensive television and radio ads, scientific polling, and mass mailing of campaign materials. As the cost of campaigns climbed, it became necessary for candidates to raise large sums of money. Most of this money came from wealthy individuals and corporations that sought to influence the candidates or incumbent politicians. At least a million dollars was given to President Richard Nixon's 1972 reelection campaign by wealthy industrialist Howard Hughes.

Concerned with actual *quid pro quo* arrangements between contributors and candidates as well as with the mere appearance of corruption, Congress passed the nation's most comprehensive campaign reform legislation. The Federal Election Campaign Act (FECA) of 1974 created the present system of limits on federal campaign contributions and expenditures. The legislation was Congress's response to disclosures (during the Watergate hearings) of illegal contributions to President Richard Nixon's campaign for reelection in 1972. Its primary purpose was to equalize the relative ability of all voters to affect the outcome of elections by placing a ceiling on expenditures for political expression by citizens and groups

The Federal Election Campaign Act of 1974 consists of a number of provisions that

1. limited political contributions to candidates for federal office by an individual or group to $1,000 and by a political committee to $5,000 to any single candidate per election, with an overall annual limitation of $25,000 by an individual contributor;

2. limited expenditures from a candidate's personal or family funds for his or her campaign (the amounts depending on the federal office sought);

3. limited expenditures from an individual or group "relative to a clearly identified candidate" to $1,000 per election (e.g., paying for an ad in a newspaper or hiring a bus or an airplane);

4. required political committees to keep detailed records of contributions and expenditures (including the name, address, and occupation of the contributor) and to file quarterly reports with the Federal Election Commission (FEC) disclosing the source of every contribution more than $100, as well as requireing contributors of more than $1,000 to file a statement with the commission;

5. created an eight-member FEC with record-keeping, investigatory, rulemaking, and enforcement powers; and

6. amended the Internal Revenue Code to provide for public financing of presidential primary and general elections, which included matching funds for candidates who raise $5,000 from private sources in each of twenty states. Major party candidates were to receive "full" funding and "minor" and "new" party candidates were to receive a reduced proportion of funding.

Shortly after the act's passage, Senator James Buckley (R-N.Y.); former Senator Eugene McCarthy (D-Minn.), a third-party candidate in the 1976 presidential election; and others brought suit challenging the constitutionality of the act. They argued that it was unconstitutional on the grounds that (1) limiting the use of money for political purposes constitutes a restriction on communication violative of the First Amendment, since all meaningful political communication costs money, (2) the reporting and disclosure provisions of the act impinge upon the right of freedom of association protected by the First Amendment; and (3) public financing of campaigns violates the First and Fifth Amendments.

In *Buckley v. Valeo*—a complex and wordy *per curiam*—the Court recognized that any law restricting campaign contributions implicates the contributors' freedom of political association. The right of association has long been recognized as a basic constitutional freedom closely connected to freedom of speech. However, the right to associate or the right to participate in political activities can be restricted if that restriction advances a "sufficiently important interest." In this instance, the act's restrictions on political association were "appropriate legislative weapons" against the reality or appearance of improper influence of large contributions on candidates.

According to the Court, the specific limits imposed by the act advanced a "basic governmental interest" in protecting the integrity of the electoral process without infringing upon the rights of citizens and candidates to engage in debate and discussion. The caps on contributions to candidates by individuals and groups are constitutional because they limit the undue influence of wealthy persons and work to equalize the relative influence of all voters to affect the outcomes of elections. The caps also serve as a "brake" on the increasing costs of political campaigns without restricting one's right to engage in political expression or volunteer services, or to join a candidate's election committee or political party.

The law's disclosure provisions, as well as the disclosure and record-keeping guidelines, and the system of public financing were also found to be constitutional.

The act, however, did not survive judicial review unscathed: two of its provisions were struck down. Although the Court upheld the act's $1,000 cap on campaign *contributions*, it struck down a $1,000 cap on campaign *expenditures*, because the latter failed to serve any governmental interest in curtailing the existence or appearance of corruption in political campaigns while placing a burden on freedom of expression. In other words, while the government can limit the amount of money a candidate can receive from a contributor (for fear of undue influence), the government cannot limit the amount of money a group or individual spends to get a message across. Individuals and groups are free to spend as much as they like to promote the candidate and his or her views as long as they refrain from expressly advocating the election or defeat of a "clearly identified candidate." The Court also struck down the act's cap on the use of personal funds by candidates on their own behalf because it imposed a restraint on the ability of persons to engage in public discussion. The Court explained:

> The candidate, no less than any other person, has a First Amendment right to engage in the discussion of public issues and vigorously and tirelessly to advocate his own election and the election of other candidates.
>
> A restriction on the amount of money a person or group can spend on political communication during a campaign necessarily reduces the quantity of expression by

restricting the number of issues discussed, the depth of their exploration, and the size of the audience reached. This is because virtually every means of communicating ideas in today's mass society requires the expenditure of money.

In sum, while you may not contribute more than $1,000 to a candidate, you may spend an unlimited amount of money promoting his or her positions. In addition, the First Amendment allows the candidate to spend an unlimited amount of personal or family wealth to campaign for elected office. In fact, as the Court points out, the use of personal funds reduces the likelihood of the candidate's dependence on wealthy contributors. Congress's interest in leveling the playing field by equalizing the relative financial resources of candidates is not sufficient to justify the restriction of First Amendment rights.

Chief Justice Burger, who believed that Congress was rationing political expression, was opposed to all limits on small contributions, disclosures of contributions, and public financing of presidential campaigns because in his mind they were an "impermissible intrusion of by the Government into the traditionally private political process."

Also dissenting, Justice White thought it made little sense for the Court to permit a limit on the amount an individual may contribute or spend with the candidate's approval but strike down a limit on the amount that could be spent on the candidate's behalf.

The Presidential Election Campaign Fund Act,[27] allows presidential candidates of the major political parties the option of receiving public financing for their general election campaigns. Under one provision of the act—section 9012(f)—an independent political action committee may not spend more than $1,000 to promote the candidate's election if the candidate chooses public financing. In 1984, the Democratic Party, the Democratic National Committee, and the FEC brought suit in a federal district court seeking to prevent the National Conservative Political Action Committee (NCPAC) from making a substantial expenditure in support of President Reagan's bid for reelection. NCPAC was an ideological organization that supported conservative candidates and causes. Members raised money to purchase radio and television ads that encouraged voters to reelect Reagan. Their expenditures were "independent," that is, not made at the request of the official Reagan election campaign committee.

Arguing before the district court, the FEC offered evidence of possible corruption or the appearance of corruption by showing a connection between high-level appointments in the Reagan administration of persons connected to PACs that supported Reagan's reelection. However, the district court cited most of the evidence as irrelevant and held that section 9012(f) was an unconstitutional violation of First Amendment freedoms of speech and association. On appeal the U.S. Supreme Court agreed.

In *Federal Election Commission v. National Conservative Political Action Committee (NCPAC)*, 470 U.S. 480 (1985), the Court argued that absent any evidence that independent contributions by PACs corrupt or give the appearance of corrupting the political process, the First Amendment prohibits Congress from limiting such expenditures. Even if huge and wealthy PACs have a tendency to corrupt the process, section 9012(f) is an unconstitutionally overboard response to the problem because it makes no distinction between multimillion-dollar expenditures from wealthy PACs and contributions from informal neighborhood groups that solicit contributions to promote a presidential candidate. Since PACs are organizations designed to participate in the political debate and not to bring about economic gain as a result of their support, Congress may not prohibit them from making contributions to candidates.

Citing *Buckley v. Valeo*, Chief Justice Rehnquist (writing for the majority) concluded that allowing PACs to present their views while forbidding them to spend more than $1,000 is akin to "allowing a speaker in a public hall to express his views while denying him the use of an amplifying system." In further praise of PACs, Rehnquist stated that ordinary citizens who individually can have little impact use PACs to amplify their voices, thus competing with those who can afford expensive media ads. *What then is the government's interest in placing restrictions on PACs?* In *Buckley, NCPAC*, and other cases,[28] the Court has held that preventing corruption or the appearance of corruption are the only permissible governmental interests for restricting campaign finance. Corruption occurs when elected officials are influenced to act contrary to the public trust by the enticement of personal financial gain or large sums of money donated to their election campaigns.

But the real issue is not contributions to the candidate but independent expenditures in support of the candidate. Most contributions to PACs are very small amounts, well under the $1,000 limits upheld in *Buckley*. PACs are designed expressly to participate in political debate and are quite different from unions and corporations that seek economic gain and have large resources.

The dissenting justices believed that the majority overzealously applied the First Amendment to "dismember" congressional efforts to curtail the influence of money on politics. The First Amendment protects the right to speak, "not the right to spend," wrote Justice White,[29] and "limitations on the amount of money that can be spent are not the same as restrictions on speaking." Campaign contributions may produce speech, but they are not speech itself. Furthermore, wrote White, the burden on actual speech imposed by spending limitations is minimal, since the fundamental rights of political expression, advocacy, and association are not restrained in any way.

White also argued that the majority was naïve in its belief that PACs are politically pure organizations devoted to political speech and not coordinated with a candidate's campaign. "PACs do not operate in an anonymous vacuum," he commented, candidates know of the efforts undertaken "independently" on their behalf. For this reason, these so-called independent expenditures must be closely regulated. White lamented that as a result of the Court's action in *Buckley* and *NCPAC* "the same old system remains essentially intact, but that much more money is being spent."

Even in light of public renewed interest and state action regulating campaign finance, the Supreme Court furthered eviscerated FECA in 1996. Responding to a First Amendment challenge in *Colorado Republican Federal Campaign*

*Committee v. Federal Election Commission*, 518 U.S.604 (1996), the Court concluded that campaign expenditures occurring before the Republican party nominated its candidate could not be limited because the expenditures could not have been coordinated with any candidate's knowledge or approval. As an "independent" expenditure, the money spent to buy radio time to attack whoever the Republican's opponent might be was protected by the First Amendment. Again, the Court reasoned that the regulation did not advance any "compelling governmental interest" in "avoiding the appearance of reality of corruption" of the election system.

However, the Court returned to the *Colorado Republican* ruling in its 2001 term, where it upheld FEC limits on the Republican party's unlimited coordinated spending to aid specific candidates. The Court also made an important distinction between Congress' power to regulate political expenditures as compared to political contributions. The Court gives closer constitutional scrutiny to expenditure limits because such restrictions place more of a burden on "expressive and associational activity" than do limits on campaign contributions.[30]

The Court also struck down a ban on federal employees accepting any compensation for writing articles and making speeches[31] and the prohibition on the distribution of anonymously published campaign literature.[32]

Senator McCain's long struggle for major campaign finance reform succeeded in 2002 when Congress enacted the Bipartisan Campaign Reform Act of 2002, which amends the Federal Election Campaign Act.[33] The law goes into effect on November 6, 2002, one day after election day. The major provisions of the law include

1. A prohibition on national parties from raising or spending soft money. Soft money refers to the unlimited and unregulated contributions to political parties from corporations, unions, and individuals that are used to provide indirect support to federal candidates.

2. A ban on corporations and unions from spending unlimited money on pre-election television or radio "issue ads" that indirectly supports candidates without explicitly naming them. Also prohibited within 60 days of a general election or 30 days of a primary are television and radio ads that support a clearly identifiable candidate. No restriction exists on print, mass mail, or internet communications.

3. Increases on the limits on "hard" money contributions to federal candidates from $1,000 per election to $2,000 for Senate and presidential candidates ($4,000 for both primary and general election), but not for House candidates.

Just moments after its passage, critics threatened to challenge the constitutionality of the law. Indeed, the law even contains provisions that expedite review by the federal courts. It is uncertain which provisions of the law will withstand First Amendment scrutiny. *Buckley, NCPAC, and Colorado Republican* support restrictions on campaign finance when such restrictions are necessary to prevent corruption or the appearance of corruption. Yet, these rulings also demonstrate that while the Court is willing to uphold limits on direct campaign contributions, it is hesitant to allow restrictions on expenditures, which receive greater First Amendment protection. Less certain is the fate of bans on indirect expenditures ("soft" money) by corporations, unions, PACs, and individuals that are used to build party "war chests" and run costly "issue ads" prior to elections. Supporters of it will have to show direct evidence that the contributions corrupt or give the appearance of corrupting the political process. And, unlike McCain's broad definition of corruption, the Court has defined corruption very narrowly; that is, when money influences elected officials to act contrary to the public trust.

## CONCLUDING COMMENTS

This chapter began with an inquiry into the definition, nature, and scope of protected expression under the First Amendment. Justice Black, the most influential member of the absolutist school of thought, believed that the First Amendment should be taken literally, serving as a barrier against all governmental intrusions on speech. But not even Black would argue that the First Amendment gives us the right to say anything we please or to incite violence or advocate murder. Surely he did not believe that the First Amendment protects libel and slander, misrepresentation, and conspiracy.

Justice Harlan wrote of the absurdity of interpreting the First Amendment with a dictionary only and without regard for the history of freedom of speech in America. Justice Holmes, the great proponent of judicial restraint, could not bring himself to admit that the absolutist position was even worthy of serious consideration. So, through the years, the Court has made it clear that there are numerous kinds of communications that do not deserve protection because they are unrelated to the activity of democratic politics and government.

The First Amendment protects the right to engage in forms of expression that are intended to push the limits of tolerance, to invite dispute, and to challenge the beliefs of the majority. It even protects the right to spend money on a candidate or cause. Venerated as well as vilified for the protection of that right, the Supreme Court has granted constitutional protection to hate speech, flag burning, and cross burning. It has done so not because society has collectively recognized some inherent value in those activities or because of some talismanic devotion to the First Amendment, but because without constitutional protection of diverse points of view, no matter how half-baked they appear, the cornerstone of a free society—the free exchange of ideas—cannot be maintained.

In the long term, restrictions on the exchange of ideas based on the present direction of the political winds may prevent a nation from prospering, a self-defeating foreign policy from being challenged, or a cure for AIDS from being developed. The same impulse to censor racists may ultimately suppress civil rights and environmental activists. The same law that compels patriotism and obedience by punishing iconoclasts can be applied equally, at a later time, to round up those who express opposition to a gun-control measure.

# Finding the Full Text of the U.S. Supreme Court Opinions Cited in Chapter 2

The full opinion of the U.S. Supreme Court's rulings discussed in this chapter can be found at the Findlaw URL address following each case listed below, or by using the case name (e.g., *Schenck*) or citation (e.g., 249 U.S. 47). Other web sites where opinions can be found are listed at the end of chapter 1.

## Subversive Political Speech

### *The Rise and Fall of the Clear and Present Danger Test*

*Schenck v. United States* (1919), http://laws.findlaw.com/us/249/47.html

*Debs v. United States* (1919), http://laws.findlaw.com/us/249/211.html

*Abrams v. United States* (1919), http://laws.findlaw.com/us/250/616.html

*Gitlow v. New York* (1925), http://laws.findlaw.com/us/268/652.html

### *The Red Scare*

*Dennis v. United States* (1951), http://laws.findlaw.com/us/341/494.html

*Yates v. United States* (1957), http://laws.findlaw.com/us/354/298.html

*Scales v. United States* (1961), http://laws.findlaw.com/us/367/203.html

### *Guilt by Association*

*Noto v. United States* (1961), http://laws.findlaw.com/us/367/290.html

### *Retreat From the Clear and Present Danger Test*

*Brandenburg v. Ohio* (1969), http://laws.findlaw.com/us/395/444.html

### *Inflammatory Words*

*Hess v. Indiana* (1973), http://laws.findlaw.com/us/414/105.html

*Roth v. United States* (1957), http://laws.findlaw.com/us/354/476.html

*Chaplinsky v. New Hampshire* (1942), http://laws.findlaw.com/us/315/568.html

### *Loyalty Oaths*

*Communist Party of Indiana v. Whitcomb* (1974), http://laws.findlaw.com/us/414/441.html

### *Economic Boycotts as Speech*

*NAACP v. Claiborne Hardware Co.* (1982), http://laws.findlaw.com/us/458/886.html

*Continued*

## Finding the Full Text of the U.S. Supreme Court Opinions Cited in Chapter 2    *Continued*

### Symbolic and Offensive Speech

#### *Compulsory Flag Salute*

*Stromberg v. California* (1931), http://laws.findlaw.com/us/283/359.html

*West Virginia Board of Education v. Barnette* (1943), http://laws.findlaw.com/us/319/586.html

*Minersville School District v. Gobitis* (1940), http://laws.findlaw.com/us/310/586.html

*Jones v. Opelika* (1942), http://laws.findlaw.com/us/316/584.html

*Wooley v. Maynard* (1977), http://laws.findlaw.com/us/430/705.html

#### *Conduct as Speech*

*Tinker v. Des Moines Independent School District* (1969), http://laws.findlaw.com/us/393/ 503.html

*Board of Education v. James* (1972), http://laws.findlaw.com/us/409/ 1042.html

*United States v. O'Brien* (1968), http://laws.findlaw.com/us/391/367.html

*Wayte v. United States* (1985), http://laws.findlaw.com/us/470/598.html

*Street v. New York* (1969), http://laws.findlaw.com/us/394/596.html

*Texas v. Johnson* (1989), http://laws.findlaw.com/us/491/397.html

*Terminello v. Chicago* (1949), http://laws.findlaw.com/us/337/1.html

*Spence v. Washington* (1974), http://laws.findlaw.com/us/418/405.html

*United States v. Eichman* (1990), http://laws.findlaw.com/us/496/310.html

### Offensive and Racist Speech

#### *Vulgar Language*

*Cohen v. California* (1971), http://laws.findlaw.com/us/403/15.html

#### *Hate Speech*

*Frisby v. Schultz* (1988), http://laws.findlaw.com/us/487/474.html

*R.A.V. v. City of St. Paul* (1992), http://laws.findlaw.com/us/505/377.html

*Wisconsin v. Mitchell* (1993), http://laws.findlaw.com/us/508/476.html

### Competing Rights

*Madsen v. Women's Health Center* (1994), http://laws.findlaw.com/us/512/753.html

*Schenck v. Pro-Choice Network of Western New York* (1997), http://laws.findlaw.com/us/519/357.html

## The First Amendment and Campaign Finance Reform

*Buckley v. Valeo* (1976), http://laws.findlaw.com/us/424/1.html

*Federal Election Commission v. National Conservative Political Action Committee* (1985), http://laws.findlaw.com/us/470/480.html

*Colorado Republican Federal Campaign Committee v. Federal Election Commission* (1996), http://laws.findlaw.com/us/518/604.html

*Colorado Republican Federal Campaign Committee v. FEC* (2001), http://laws.findlaw.com/us/p00/00-191.html.

## NOTES

1. 268 U.S. 652 (1925).
2. 337 U.S. 1 (1949).
3. James Madison, *The Writings of James Madison*, ed. Hilliard Hunt, vol. 6 (New York: Putnam, 1906–1910), 336.
4. For a detailed discussion of Black's absolutism, see Black's autobiography, *A Constitutional Faith* (New York: Alfred Knopf, 1969); and Craig R. Ducat, *Modes of Constitutional Interoperation* (St. Paul, MN: West Publishing, 1978), 67–76.
5. See Lee Bollinger's classic work, *The Tolerant Society: Freedom of Speech and Extremist Speech in America* (Knoxville: University of Tennessee Press, 1973).
6. In a celebrated footnote in *United States v. Carolene Products*, 304 U.S. 144 (1938), Justice Harlan Stone identified a constitutionally shielded area of "preferred freedom." This theory also emerged in *Thomas v Collins*, 323 U.S. 516 (1945).
7. See Craig R. Ducat's brief yet excellent essay in *Constitutional Interpretation*, 7th ed. (Belmont, CA: Wadsworth, 2000), E1–E16.
8. For a discussion of loyalty oaths, see Stanford Levinson, *Constitutional Faith* (Princeton, NJ: Princeton University Press, 1988).
9. See *New Rider v. Board of Education*, 414 U.S.1097 (1974).
10. For two discussions of flag burning written shortly after the two landmark cases, see John Ely, "Flag Desecration," 88 *Harvard Law Review* 1482 (1975); and J. Greenawalt, "O'er the Land of the Free: Flag Burning as Speech," 37 *UCLA Law Review* 925 (1990).
11. See Philippa Strum, *When the Nazis Came to Skokie* (Lawrence: University of Kansas Press, 1999).
12. See *Organization for a Better Austin v. Keefe*, 402 U.S. 415 (1971).
13. See D. A. Downs, *Nazis in Skokie: Freedom, Communication and the First Amendment* (South Bend, IN: Notre Dame University Press, 1985).
14. See discussion in chapter 1.
15. See James Weinstein, *Hate Speech, Pornography, and the Radical Attack on Free Speech Doctrine* (Boulder, CO: Westview Press, 1999).
16. See discussion of *Planned Parenthood v. Casey*, 505 U.S. 833 (1992), in chapter 6.
17. See Leslie Jacobs, "Nonviolent Abortion Clinic Protests: Reevaluation of Some Current Assumptions About the Proper Scope of Governmental Regulations," 70 *Tulane Law Review* 1359 (1996).
18. The act was passed by a Democratic-controlled Congress and signed by President Clinton the year before the Republican Party won control of both houses of Congress.

19. See, e.g., *American Life League v. Reno*, 47 F.3d 642 (4th Cir. 1995); and *Cheffer v. Reno*, 55 F.3d 1517 (11th Cir. 1995).

20. The vote was 6–3 to uphold the fixed buffer zones (with Justices Thomas, Scalia, and Kennedy dissenting) and 8–1 to strike down the floating buffer zones (with Justice Breyer dissenting).

21. The Court relied on the earlier case *Madsen v. Women's Health Center, Inc.*, 512 U.S. 753 (1994), where the Court ruled that the standard "time, place, and manner" test was not adequate for evaluating "content neutral" injunctions that restrict speech. Instead, it held that the test is whether the challenged provisions burden no more speech than is necessary to serve a significant governmental interest.

22. The Court's assertion is based on *Boos v. Barry*, 485 U.S. 312 (1988).

23. See *Lee v. International Society for Krishna Consciousness, Inc.*, 112 S. Ct. 2709 (1992).

24. See *Adderly v. Florida*, 385 U.S. 39 (1966).

25. See Robert DiClerico, ed., *Campaigns and Elections in America* (Upper Saddle River, NJ: Prentice Hall, 2000); and Federal Election Commission data reported by *Congressional Quarterly Weekly* (Washington, D.C.: Congressional Quarterly Press, 2000).

26. See The Gallup Organization, "Widespread Public Support for Campaign Finance Reform," (March 2001), http://www.gallup.com/Poll/releases/pr010320.asp.

27. 26 U.S.C.A. sec. 9012.

28. See *Citizens Against Rent Control v. Berkeley*, 454 U.S. 290 (1981).

29. Joined in part by Justices Brennan and Marshall.

30. The 1996 *Colorado Republican* ruling remanded the Party's broader claim that all limits on expenditures are unconstitutional. On remand the district court held for the party and the court of appeals affirmed. The Supreme Court agreed in *Federal Election Commission v. Colorado Republican Federal Campaign Committee* in 2001, http://laws.findlaw.com/us/000/00-191.html.

31. *United States v. National Treasury Employees Union*, 513 U.S. 454 (1995).

32. *McIntyre v. Ohio Elections Commission*, 514 U.S. 334 (1995).

33. The law is also known as McCain-Feingold in the Senate and Shays-Meehan in the House. Its final form can be seen in H.R. 2357, 107th Congress; see also Public citizen for a good overview and discussion of the law, http://www.citizen.org.

# CHAPTER THREE

# Obscenity and Offensive Speech: The Limits of Sexually Oriented Expression

*Apart from the initial formulation in the* Roth *case, no majority of the Court has at any given time been able to agree on a standard to determine what constitutes obscene, pornographic material subject to regulation under the State's police power.*

Chief Justice Warren Burger in
*Miller v. California* (1973)

*What shocks me may be sustenance for my neighbor. What causes one person to boil up in rage over one pamphlet or movie may reflect only his neurosis, not shared by others.*

Justice William O. Douglas, dissenting in
*Miller v. California* (1973)

In addition to protecting political expression, the First Amendment's guarantee of free speech and press extends to a broad array of artistic and literary expression, including literature, painting, sculpture, dance, music, photography, and film. In most instances, the flow of artistic expression is regulated only by the "marketplace of ideas" or by the personal tastes and preferences of individuals. These days the marketplace is saturated with sexual images. But when the content of the communication is sexual in nature and runs contrary to contemporary standards of decency, governmental officials and community leaders are empowered by the majority to impose restrictions on particular sexual images and ideas. ***When can sexually explicit materials claim First Amendment protection? What is the permissible scope of governmental regulation of sexually oriented material?*** The key to answering these questions is found in the Supreme Court's struggle to define obscenity and to determine which erotic and pornographic materials are obscene and therefore subject to restrictions.[1]

## EARLY ATTEMPTS TO DEFINE OBSCENITY

In the mid–1950s, Samuel Roth made his living publishing and purveying sexually explicit books, magazines, and photographs. Among the materials he advertised and peddled was a quarterly magazine of "literary erotica" entitled *American Aphrodite*.

Roth was convicted in U.S. district court under the federal Comstock Act of 1873 for sending "obscene, lewd, lascivious, or filthy" circulars and advertisements in the mail. A U.S. court of appeals affirmed his conviction.

Roth challenged his conviction on the grounds that the federal obscenity statute violated the First Amendment provision that Congress shall make no law abridging the freedom of speech and press. In *Roth v. United States*, 354 U.S. 476 (1957), the Supreme Court disagreed, voting 6–3 to sustain Roth's conviction and to uphold the Comstock Act. Writing the first of many obscenity opinions, Justice Brennan flatly rejected Roth's argument on the grounds that there was no evidence suggesting that the framers of the Bill of Rights had ever intended to extend First Amendment protection to obscenity. The purpose of the First Amendment, according to Brennan, is to protect ideas of even the slightest socially redeeming importance, and obscenity contains no ideas worth protecting and is not essential to the exposition of ideas. Brennan wrote:

> There are certain well-defined and narrowly limited classes of speech, the prevention and punishment of which have never been thought to raise any Constitutional problem. These include the lewd and obscene. . . . It has been well observed that such utterances are no essential part of any exposition of ideas, and are of such slight social value as a step to the truth that any benefit that may be derived from them is clearly outweighed by the social interest in order and morality.

Brennan went on to define obscenity as material that deals with sex in a manner appealing to "prurient interests"; that is, intended only to arouse lustful desires. Thus, obscenity is immoral, sexually impure, and intended to arouse lustful desires in readers and viewers.

However, after justifying the government's power to ban obscenity, Brennan extended a broad grant of First Amendment protection to the communication of sexual ideas in a variety of mediums. He argued that sex and obscenity are not synonymous and that the portrayal of sex in works of art and literature is protected by the freedoms of speech and press. Sex, a "subject of absorbing interest to mankind throughout the ages," is protected speech as long as it is not treated in a manner appealing only to prurient interests. Thus, after arguing that obscene ideas are by definition utterly without redeeming social importance and therefore subject to federal and state restriction, Brennan argued that sexual ideas having even the slightest redeeming social importance are protected from governmental censorship.

The test of obscenity adopted in *Roth* asks whether, to the average person and applying contemporary community standards, the dominant theme of the material taken as a whole appeals to prurient interests. In obscenity trials, jurors were asked to consider the evidence and make their judgments based on this standard. One example of prurient interests, according to Brennan, is "impure sexual thoughts" or materials that have a tendency to excite lustful thoughts. Furthermore, if material is to be given constitutional protection, it must be shown that it has the "slightest redeeming social importance."

This more permissive test replaced the nineteenth-century *Hicklin* test, which judged obscenity on the grounds of whether isolated passages have the tendency to deprave and corrupt the minds of "particularly susceptible persons."[2] Brennan rejected the *Hicklin* test as unconstitutional because it was broad enough to allow for the restriction of literature and art that treats sex in a legitimate way. Brennan's intent was to strike a fair balance between the government's interest in regulating obscenity and the First Amendment's guarantee that all ideas having the slightest social importance are protected. The *Roth* test, in Brennan's mind, would make it much more difficult for the government to prove that material was obscene. Prosecutors were then forced to show the jury that the material was completely worthless (void of ideas) and that the material appealed only to prurient interests. Thus, in rejecting the *Hicklin* test and adopting the *Roth* standard, the Court extended protection to a vast array of previously banned erotic literature, film, and photographs.

Although he concurred that the federal obscenity law was valid, Chief Justice Warren was very uneasy about extending First Amendment protection to such materials, no matter how they were defined. In fact, the Court never dealt with the question whether the particular materials involved in the case were obscene. Warren was aware of the folly of attempting to define obscenity, and he would have preferred that the Court address which state and federal interests justify restricting obscenity.

Normally a strong coalition-builder, Warren's strong personal distaste for pornography limited his role in bringing the justices together. As a result, the opinion was sharply divided, and Brennan's quest for a workable definition of obscenity was off to a shaky start. Warren's concurring statement illustrates his opposition to what he called "smut." He wrote that the defendants were "engaged in the commercial exploitation of the morbid and shameful craving for materials with prurient effect I believe that the [government] can constitutionally punish such conduct. That is all we need to decide."

Indeed, Warren's squeamishness toward pornography prevented him from watching films and examining materials in obscenity cases. Rather than be subjected to such "garbage," the Chief Justice sent his law clerks to view the films or relied on his associate's comments.[3]

Justice Harlan, dissenting in *Roth*, took issue with two elements of Brennan's argument. First, he flatly rejected the view that obscenity falls within a distinct and recognizable "peculiar genus" of speech and press to which judicial scrutiny should be applied for the purpose of determining its worth and value. Instead of casting a wide net through the use of some broad standard of constitutionally permissible restrictions, Harlan argued that each communication must be regarded independently and judged for its own value. The censoring of a book or other tangible form of communication creates a distinct constitutional question in which each court must determine for itself whether the restriction is constitutional.

Second, Harlan did not believe that Congress had the power to set national obscenity standards. Under the federal system, the national government has the power to regulate forms of human activity, such as seditious speech, that might undermine its power to protect itself against insurrection. It also has the power to regulate what is sent through the mail, as it did through the statute at issue in *Roth*. But Congress, according to Harlan, has no power over questions concerning sexual morality. Questions of this nature, such as the interests addressed by obscenity laws, are largely the domain of the states and their communities. Each state has its own distinct culture and attitudes toward the communication of sexual ideas. A book that might be classified obscene in one state might be read freely in another. While the citizens of a few states might not have immediate access to a work of literature, such a situation is preferable to one in which a uniform standard is used to permit or suppress the work nationwide.

Justice Douglas, joined by Justice Black, dissented from the Court's view that "obscenity is not expression protected by the First Amendment." Douglas did not believe that the solution to the problem of obscenity regulation could be found in an attempt to base the legality of a publication on whether or not it excites lustful thoughts in some readers or has "no redeeming social importance." Douglas found it absurd to obtain a conviction on the grounds that a publication aroused sexual thoughts. He wrote:

> If we were certain that impurity of sexual thoughts impelled to action, we would be on less dangerous ground in punishing the distributors of this sex literature. But it is by no means clear that obscene literature, as so defined, is a significant factor in influencing substantial deviations from the community standards.

Douglas was saying that since there was no reliable evidence concerning the effect of obscene literature on social deviance, the Court should concern itself with protecting "society's interest in literature." No restrictions should be placed on such literature unless it could be demonstrated that its publication results in some measurable harmful action against which government should guard.

Douglas also brought up one problem that was to plague Brennan's many attempts to formulate a workable definition of obscenity: Basing any test of permissible speech on what is offensive to the community's standards leads to censorship in its worst form. It allows officials to proscribe materials and juries to convict individuals on the basis of personal views of the acceptable way of communicating sexual ideas or on the grounds that such material will lead to sexual arousal. In his own acerbic way, Douglas wrote that such censorship "creates a regime where in the battle between the literati and the Philistines, the Philistines are certain to win."

Douglas's opinion was that the whole issue should be left up to the marketplace of ideas. Comments about Philistines notwithstanding, he seemed to have great faith in the ability of the American people to reject "noxious literature" just as they could "sort out the true from the false in theology, economics, politics, or any other field."

While the *Roth* test made it difficult for the government to place arbitrary restrictions on erotic literature and other tangible forms of communication found to be offensive, the vagueness of its language and the lack of direct reference to the particular kinds of materials at issue in the case resulted in a wide variety of interpretations by state and federal officials. Brennan's use of such vague concepts as "average person," "contemporary community standards," and "prurient interests" led to great inconsistency in the prosecution of individuals accused of violating obscenity statutes. Indeed, it was also unclear where the "redeeming social importance" requirement would fit in the test.

The *Roth* decision led to much criticism of both Brennan's ambivalence toward the degree of protection granted to the communication of sexual ideas and Warren's reluctance to offer any leadership on the question of obscenity. The Court's somewhat academic preoccupation with the formulation of a modern definition left it up to the legislatures to define new justifications for obscenity regulations. Brennan would spend the next sixteen years trying to clarify and give greater precision to the *Roth* standard.[4]

The process began five years after *Roth*, in *Manual Enterprises v. Day*, 370 U.S. 478 (1962), where the Court ruled that in order for photographs of nude males to be ruled obscene, it would have to be shown that the photos were "patently offensive" in addition to appealing to "prurient interests." More importantly, two years later, in *Jacobellis v. Ohio*, 378 U.S. 184 (1964), a ruling that extended protection to an erotic French film entitled *The Lovers*, Brennan clarified his community standards requirement by pointing out that by "contemporary community standards" he had not meant a particular state or local community standard, but a national standard. This clarification made it tougher for cities in the Bible Belt region of the country, for instance, to ban a book or a film that was already available in other parts of the country.

*Jacobellis* was significant also because it used *Roth*'s "utterly without social importance" requirement for the first time to provide constitutional protection for an erotic film. The case also made a lasting contribution to Court humor, as it was on this occasion when Justice Stewart made his famous admission that although it was unlikely that he would ever succeed in defining hard-core pornography, he knew it when he saw it.[5]

In 1966, the Court handed down two decisions that had a major impact on the application and further refinement of the *Roth* criteria: *Memoirs v. Massachusetts*, 383 U.S. 413, and *Ginzburg v. United States*, 383 U.S. 463. In the first case, John Clelland's novel *Memoirs of a Woman of Pleasure (Fanny Hill)* was ruled obscene by the Massachusetts Supreme Judicial Court. Recognized as marginally significant to the development of the English novel, the book is a story of the adventures of an English prostitute that ends with the moral that sex with love is superior to sex in a house of ill-repute.

The Supreme Court reversed the ruling of the Massachusetts court on the grounds it had misinterpreted the *Roth* social value standard. Brennan rejected the lower court's view that if a book appeals to prurient interest and is patently offensive, it does not have to be completely "worthless" before it can be deemed obscene. Writing for the majority, he set forth the following modified *Roth* test, in which three elements must be met before a book is deemed obscene:

1. The dominant theme of the material taken as a whole appeals to a prurient interest in sex.
2. The material is patently offensive because it affronts contemporary community standards.
3. The material is *utterly* without redeeming social value.

The third element meant that the social value of a work could not be canceled by its prurient appeal or patent offensiveness. Each of the three elements of the test must be applied independently.

Suppose that a work has some social value or that it is on the borderline between valuable and worthless speech. Can the material be subject to restrictions on the basis of the manner in which it is sold or distributed? The answer is found in the "variable" approach to obscenity: Constitutional protection depends on the circumstances of its production, sale, and publicity. Brennan wrote in *Memoirs*: "Evidence that the book was commercially exploited for the sake of prurient appeal, to the exclusion of all other values, might justify the conclusion that the book was utterly without redeeming social importance." Thus, material that is not in itself obscene can be subject to restriction if it is displayed in a porn shop, rather than in a legitimate bookstore, or if it is mailed unsolicited to a "captive audience" or sold to a minor.

This variable approach was adopted by the Court in *Ginzburg*, decided during the same term as *Memoirs*. Ralph Ginzburg, the publisher of *Eros, Liaison, The Housewife's Guide to Selective Promiscuity*, and other magazines devoted to erotica, was convicted in federal district court under the Comstock Act, which prohibited mailing erotic publications and related advertisements, and was sentenced to five years in prison. The magazines contained articles and photo essays on love and sex, including an interview with a psychotherapist and two articles that had appeared in professional journals. A key piece of evidence used by the prosecution was Ginzburg's promotional scheme. To boost sales, Ginzburg sought mailing privileges from the postmasters of Intercourse and Blue Ball, Pennsylvania, and Middlesex, New Jersey.

The Supreme Court upheld Ginzburg's conviction not because the material itself was obscene, but because of the titillating manner in which it was advertised and distributed. Justice Brennan argued that some of the publications might have been protected had Ginzburg not deliberately represented his publications as "erotically arousing," made evident by the provocative advertisements Ginzburg sent and by his attempts to mail the materials from towns with those particular names. If the books had intellectual, educational, or therapeutic value, they were not advertised as such. Brennan wrote: "Where the purveyor's sole emphasis is on the sexually provocative aspects of his publication, that fact may be decisive in the determination of obscenity." Brennan concluded that in cases involving borderline obscenity, the decisive factor in satisfying the *Roth* test is the manner in which the material is represented. Where there is "titillation by pornography," material that might escape condemnation in another context may be declared obscene.

In a dissenting opinion, Justice Black shot back that Brennan's criteria was so "vague and meaningless" that it left the fate of the defendant to "the unbridled discretion, whim and caprice of the judge or jury which tries him." Ginzburg was not being sent to prison because his publications were obscene, added Justice Harlan, but merely because they "offend[ed] a judge's esthetic sensibilities." Justice Stewart, also dissenting, was frustrated by the Court's continuing predilection to offer broad standards without naming the particular kinds of materials to be deemed obscene. Arguing that only hard-core pornography should be suppressed, Stewart named examples of the kinds of materials that "[cannot] conceivably be characterized as embodying communication of idea or artistic values." Such materials include

1. Photographs and film, without any pretense of artistic value, graphically depicting acts of sexual intercourse (this would include acts of sodomy and sadism, and scenes of orgy-like character); and

2. Pamphlets and books, sometimes with photographic illustrations, verbally describing such activities in a bizarre manner with no attempt to develop characters or a plot and with no pretense to literary value.

## PRIVATE POSSESSION OF OBSCENE MATERIAL

*Can the mere possession of obscene materials can be made a crime?*    This question was addressed by the Court in *Stanley v. Georgia*, 394 U.S. 557 in 1969. In 1967, federal and state agents searched the home of Robert Stanley for evidence of bookmaking activity. During the search, they stumbled upon three rolls of movie film depicting orgies, sodomy, and sexual intercourse. As a result, Stanley was convicted and sentenced to a year in prison for violating a paternalistic Georgia statute forbidding private possession of obscene material. The Georgia Supreme Court upheld his conviction on the grounds that Stanley did not have an absolute right to read or observe what he pleased, even in the privacy of his home. There were certain kinds of images or words that the state has an interest in restricting: in this instance, the right to protect Stanley's mind from the effects of obscenity.

The Supreme Court reversed the judgment, ruling that the mere private possession of obscene matter cannot constitutionally be made a crime. Justice Marshall, writing for the majority, based his reasoning on an unusual combination of the First Amendment as applied to the states through the Fourteenth Amendment, and the right of privacy as defined in *Griswold v. Connecticut*, 381 U.S. 479 (1965).[6] The right to receive information and ideas is fundamental, wrote Marshall, as is the right to be free from unwanted intrusions into the privacy of one's home. The state does not have the right to control the moral contents of a person's thoughts:

> Whatever may be the justification for other statutes regulating obscenity, we do not think they reach into the privacy of one's home. If the First Amendment means anything, it means that a State has no business telling a man, sitting alone in his own house, what books he may read or what films he may watch.

Citing *Roth*, Georgia also asserted the right to restrict access to obscenity on the grounds that such materials are for mere entertainment purposes and are devoid of any ideas or "ideological content." However, there was no guiding precedent or standard distinguishing between ideas and entertainment, and the Court had no desire to draw such a line in *Stanley*. Thus, the Court refused to apply *Roth* to uphold the Georgia obscenity law because in *Roth* the issue was public distribution of obscene materials, whereas in *Stanley* the issue was private consumption. Thus, while the Court left *Roth* in place and maintained the states' "broad power" to regulate public distribution of obscenity, Marshall refused to recognize any state interest in criminalizing private possession of obscene material.

The constitutional issue that immediately arose from *Stanley* was the tension between the right to use obscene materials in the privacy of one's home and the state's recognized interest in restricting the mailing or commercial exchange of obscene materials. Can we infer from *Stanley* that if one has the right to use obscene materials in private, then one also has the right to purchase or receive obscene materials for personal use? What if you receive an obscene video from a friend who bought it from a commercial supplier? Another constitutional issue that surfaced in this case was whether the right against intrusion into the home is broad enough to protect sexual conduct in addition to sexual communication and entertainment. This issue is examined in the right of privacy discussion in chapter 6.

## THE *MILLER* TEST

When Warren Burger became Chief Justice in 1969, he actively led a reexamination of the various obscenity standards and tests established by the Warren Court. The most successful and enduring product of the Burger Court's efforts emerged in *Miller v. California*, 413 U.S. 15 (1973). Sixteen years after *Roth v. United States*, Miller, a porn dealer, was arrested and convicted for conducting a mass mailing of advertisements for illustrated pornographic books to a "captive audience"; that is, to unwilling recipients. The brochures advertised four books: *Intercourse, Man-Woman, Sex Orgies Illustrated*, and *Illustrated History of Pornography*. Though the brochures contained some printed material, they consisted primarily of explicit photographs and drawings of people engaged in sexual activities. Miller appealed to the Supreme Court after his conviction was affirmed by a state appellate court.

Chief Justice Burger, delivering the opinion of the Court, recognized that the time had come for a new obscenity standard. He wrote: "Apart from the initial formulation in the *Roth* case, no majority of the Court has at any given time been able to agree on a standard to determine what constitutes obscene, pornographic material subject to regulation under the State's police power."

In *Miller*, Burger attributed this lack of consensus to the fact that freedom of expression does not lend itself to many "eternal verities," or fixed standards by which the Court can easily determine which kinds of expressions deserve protection. Nonetheless, Burger believed that the Court had to formulate such a test. Since Miller's case was tried on the basis of *Memoirs*, Burger ordered the state court's decision vacated and remanded for further deliberation under a new definition of obscenity. This new definition, which has survived into the 21st century and is called the *Miller* test, is based on a modification of *Roth* and rejects the "utterly without redeeming social value" test of *Memoirs*.

Under *Miller*, a state may regulate expression if all of the following conditions are satisfied:

1.  Whether the average person, applying contemporary community standards, would find that the work, taken as a whole, appeals to the prurient interest;
2.  Whether the work depicts or describes, in a patently offensive way, sexual conduct specifically defined by the applicable state law; and
3.  Whether the work, taken as a whole, lacks serious literary, artistic, political, or scientific value.

Burger was sensitive to the fact that in addition to its failure to reach a consensus on the definition of obscenity, the Warren Court had never provided specific examples of what kinds of sexual conduct could be subject to restriction as obscene.[7] Burger categorized obscene hard-core sexual conduct to include patently or clearly offensive representations or descriptions of real or simulated sexual acts, either normal or perverted. Also included were patently offensive representations or descriptions of masturbation, excretory functions, and lewd exhibition of the genitals.

Chief Justice Burger also addressed the question whether the concept of community standards should be defined as a fixed national standard of decency, as Brennan had set forth in *Memoirs*, or as a standard that could vary from community to community. In *Miller*, the state of California never applied a national standard, and the jury was instructed to apply statewide standards; this was one reason the case came before the Supreme Court. Burger argued that while First Amendment limitations on the states do not vary from place to place, it would be an exercise in futility to expect lay jurors from the diverse communities to apply a single definition of "appealing to prurient interests" or "patently offensive." Furthermore, Burger believed that the First Amendment was intended to protect only works that contribute to the free exchange of ideas and have serious literary, artistic, political, or scientific value. Freedom of expression does not extend to "the public portrayal of hard core sexual conduct for its own sake, and for the ensuing commercial gain."

Justice Douglas, dissenting in *Miller*, held fast to his view that there are no constitutional guidelines for ascertaining what is obscene, and any excursion into this area of constitutional law brings one face to face with personal tastes and preferences in art and literature. As Douglas put it: "What shocks me may be sustenance for my neighbor. What causes one person to boil up in rage over one pamphlet or movie may reflect only his neurosis, not shared by others." Therefore, since obscenity could not be defined, no restrictions should be enacted that would deny consenting adults access to pornographic materials.

After sixteen years of trying to formulate a workable standard of what constitutes obscene material, Brennan abandoned the task and adopted a philosophy much like that of Douglas. In his dissenting opinion in *Paris Adult Theatre I v. Slaton*, 413 U.S. 49 (1973), handed down during the same term as *Miller*, Brennan confessed that neither *Roth* nor any of the other tests of obscenity were adequate for drawing a constitutionally acceptable line between obscenity and protected speech. He believed that concepts such as prurient interests, patent offensiveness, and serious literary value were too indefinite and vague to serve as standards on which to base permissible First Amendment restrictions.

Is *Miller* any less vague than *Roth* and *Memoirs*? Brennan charged that the *Miller* SLAPS test (which permits suppression if the work lacks any "serious literary, artistic, political, or scientific value") is flawed as well because it allows the state to use some "unspecified standard" to show that the work was not sufficiently serious to deserve First Amendment protection. He concluded that virtually no interests can justify suppression of sexually oriented materials simply because they may have been deemed obscene. Dissenting in *Paris*, he wrote: "I would hold, therefore, that at least in the absence of distribution to juveniles or obtrusive exposure to nonconsenting adults, the [First Amendment prohibits governments] from attempting wholly to suppress sexually oriented materials on the basis of their allegedly 'obscene' contents."

*Miller v. California* has served as *the* obscenity standard for almost thirty years. *The question, however, that begs our attention is whether* Miller *has made it more difficult for the state to suppress obscenity, thus affording greater First Amendment protection to sexually oriented expression?* On the one hand, *Miller* made it much more difficult for a state to successfully prosecute pornographers because the Court rejected the "utterly without redeeming social value" test of *Memoirs* and adopted the SLAPS test, permitting restrictions only if the state can prove that the work taken as a whole lacks any serious literary, artistic, political, or scientific value. Even in some of the least tolerant communities, it is often very difficult to convince twelve jurors that a work lacks some value. The Burger Court also adopted a "physical conduct" test, thus limiting the definition of obscenity to depictions of physical conduct and explicit sexual acts.

On the other hand, by allowing prosecutors to instruct juries to apply community standards (rather than a national standard) of morality in determining what appeals to prurient interests and what is patently offensive, *Miller* can be understood as having a more conservative outcome than *Roth*. Under *Miller*, much discretionary power is given to state and local officials to draft ordinances and prosecute offenders in a manner consistent with the assumptions about sex and morality that prevail in a particular state or community. What resulted was a high degree of variation in First Amendment protection for sexually oriented material from one community to another.[8] But four years later, in *Smith v. United States*, 431 U.S. 271 (1977), the Court unanimously ruled that the literary, artistic, political, or scientific elements of the *Miller* test in determining whether the work has value could not be determined by community standards. Only two factors of the test—appeal to prurient interests and patent offensiveness—are to be determined by a jury applying contemporary community standards.

The Rehnquist Court affirmed this view in *Pope v. Illinois*, 481 U.S. 497 (1987), where the Court was asked to review the convictions of several employees of two adult bookstores in Rockford, Illinois. Overturning the state appellate court's decision, the Supreme Court held that the question whether sexually oriented material passed or failed the SLAPS test was to be judged not by community standards but by what a "reasonable person" would find, the reasonable person being "an ordinary member of *any* community." Justice White believed that the advantage of this approach lies in its creation of a standard of value that does not depend on the degree of community acceptance that a work possesses. White wrote: "Just as the ideas a work represents need not obtain community approval to merit protection, neither, insofar as the First Amendment is concerned, does the value of the work vary from community to community."

Justice Scalia, serving his first term on the Court, joined in White's assessment of *Miller*, but argued that it is futile to attempt to objectively assess the literary or artistic value of a work using the hypothetical "reasonable man" standard. Since modern tastes in art and literature vary so greatly, the "fabled reasonable man," Scalia quipped, might be replaced with the man of "tolerably good taste." He wrote: "I think we would be better advised to adopt as a legal maxim what has long been the wisdom of mankind: *De gustibus non est disputandum*. Just as there is no arguing about taste, there is no use in litigating about it." For Scalia, it is absurd for the courts to attempt to decide what constitutes beauty.

Dissenting in *Pope*, Justice Stevens (joined by Marshall) also found the reasonable person standard deficient because it was based on the subjective literary tastes of jurors. Does a juror "create" a reasonable person on the basis of the majority of the population who find no value in a book or the minority who do find value? Some books, such as *Ulysses* by James Joyce or Henry Miller's *Tropic of Cancer*, may have no literary appeal to the majority of Americans. Thus, it is dangerous to extend First Amendment protection to a work on the basis of a juror's understanding of what a reasonable person might do.

As he had in *Miller*, Justice Brennan, dissenting in *Pope*, refused to get tangled in any attempt to define permissible restrictions on sexually oriented material. He again categorically rejected any attempt by the state to interfere with the distribution of obscene materials to consenting adults.

*May a community ban certain materials or communications under local obscenity standards even though they have been judged not obscene in other communities?*  The answer is yes. Even though *Pope* ruled that the literary, artistic, political, or scientific elements of the *Miller* test could not be determined by local community values, the other two factors of the test—appeal to prurient interests and patent offensiveness—may be determined by a jury applying contemporary community standards. This places the burden on the publisher or distributor of the materials to either create the work in accordance with the most restrictive of communities or tailor distribution so as to send different kinds of erotic materials to different kinds of communities—each of which has its own obscenity laws.[9]

## CHILD PORNOGRAPHY

Whereas there is little disagreement over whether the state has the power to regulate pornographic material harmful to children, there is considerable debate on the proper scope of the legislation or regulation enacted to achieve that interest. Before further examination of this debate can take place, it is important to distinguish between "juvenile obscenity" (at issue in *Ginsburg* and *Sable*, discussed later in this chapter), defined as erotic or indecent materials that may have a deleterious effect on minors, and child pornography, the distribution and possession of indecent or obscene depictions of minors.

The federal and state governments have enacted tough measures to deal with child pornography. Many of these laws criminalize the distribution of materials depicting minors in the nude or engaged in sexual conduct without requiring that the materials be legally obscene under the standards of traditional obscenity law.[10] In *Ferber v. New York*, 458 U.S. 747 (1982), the Burger Court unanimously ruled that in order to protect children from psychological or physical harm, the state could constitutionally prohibit the distribution of films depicting children engaged in sexual activity, even though the films might not be obscene under traditional obscenity law.

In short, child pornography is afforded absolutely no protection by the First Amendment. Does the 1973 *Miller* obscenity test provide an adequate standard in the area of child pornography? The answer is no, according to Justice White, since *Miller* does not take into consideration the more compelling interest in punishing those who sexually exploit children. The *Miller* test's question whether a work, taken as a whole, has value or whether it appeals merely to the prurient interests of the average person is irrelevant when the real issue is whether the child has been psychologically or physically harmed.

***What about the argument that an overbroad child pornography law might restrict certain forms of protected expression that happens to depict children in the nude or in a way that could be construed to be sexual conduct?*** Legitimate photographic art, medical textbooks, illustrations, photographs in *National Geographic*, or other works of value could be affected by the law. But in *Ferber*, the Court rejected the argument that the New York statute went beyond its intent of protecting children from indecency and exploitation to the point of unconstitutionally censoring a literary or artistic theme or idea of value. White, delivering the opinion of the Court, did not believe that the minimal value of permitting live performances and photographic reproductions of children engaged in lewd sexual conduct was substantial enough to warrant First Amendment protection. White wrote: "We consider it unlikely that visual depictions of children performing sexual acts or lewdly exhibiting their genitals would often constitute an important and necessary part of a literary performance or scientific or educational work."

In addition, the Court ruled that the law was not overbroad or vague because the prohibited conduct was specifically defined, restricting only works that visually depict sexual conduct involving children. Descriptions of sexual conduct, such as literature, or other depictions not involving live performances or visual reproduction of live performances, are protected by the First Amendment.

Justice O'Connor, while concurring with the judgment of the Court in *Ferber*, issued a caveat by pointing out several failings of White's analysis. The Court placed freedom of expression in jeopardy by not explicitly requiring New York to exempt material with serious literary, scientific, or educational value from the kinds of depictions proscribed under the statute. Theoretically, New York might ban the distribution of works depicting minors engaged in sexual conduct "regardless of the social value of the depictions." O'Connor, as well as Brennan, recognized that the Court was too quick to gloss over the fact that some depictions of minors involved in sexual conduct do have serious literary, artistic, scientific, or medical value. This is an important admission. Unfortunately, neither of the two justices provided an example of the kinds of depictions that warrant protection.

The Rehnquist Court refused to strike down a highly restrictive child pornography statute in *Massachusetts v. Oakes*, 491 U.S. 576 (1989). The statute not only prohibited the depiction of minors engaged in sexual conduct, but also criminalized posing and photographing a nude minor. Douglas Oakes was convicted under the Massachusetts law and sentenced to ten years in prison for posing and taking photographs of his partially nude fourteen-year-old stepdaughter. It was reported that at the time of the photo session, his stepdaughter, T.S., was "physically mature" and enrolled in modeling school. Oakes claimed that T.S. had agreed to be photographed and that his interest was purely artistic and professional. In an *amicus curiae* brief, the Law and Humanities Institute referred to the photographs not as pornography but as pin-up art.

During Oakes's appeal, the Massachusetts legislature amended the broad statute to add a lascivious intent requirement to the nudity component of the law. The state hoped that by adding this provision it could successfully rebuff any constitutional challenges based on the overbreadth doctrine. The Supreme Court heard the challenge to the original law after the legislature had amended it to be more specific in the kinds of proscribed conduct.

The Massachusetts Supreme Judicial Court reversed Oakes's conviction on the grounds that the expressive process of taking a photograph is protected by the First Amendment. In doing so, the state high court also struck down the law as overbroad, concluding that the law makes "a criminal of a parent who takes a frontal view picture of his or her naked one-year-old running on a beach or romping in a wading pool." Under the First Amendment doctrine of substantial overbreadth, a law is unconstitutionally overbroad when it causes a person to refrain from communicating constitutionally protected ideas out of fear of punishment. It can be argued that with or without the lascivious intent provision, knowledge of the law could cause parents, artists, or scientists to refrain from photographing nude children.

In a sharply divided opinion, the Supreme Court left the law standing but vacated the Massachusetts high court's decision on two grounds. First, the Court rejected Oakes's freedom of expression challenge because his conduct was not protected under any traditional First Amendment interpretations. Second, the overbreadth challenge was moot because the Massachusetts law was amended by the legislature during Oakes's appeal. The majority of the Court was convinced that under this amendment, conduct such as taking family photographs of nude infants could not be criminalized.

The Court then remanded the case to the lower court to determine whether the former (unamended) version of the law could be constitutionally applied to Oakes's actions. The amended version could not be applied because the state could not show lascivious intent on Oakes's part.

Thus, out of the fractious and complex *Oakes* opinion emerged a justification for one of the toughest child pornography laws to date. By refusing to strike down this highly restrictive statute, the Court left to the states the prohibition and criminalization not only of the depiction of minors engaged in sexual conduct, but also of the posing and photographing of nude minors.

In his dissenting opinion in *Oakes*, Brennan, joined by Marshall and Stevens, argued that the unamended Massachusetts law was so broad that it criminalized expression protected by the First Amendment. Citing *Ferber*, he agreed with Scalia that lewd depictions of children may be restricted even though they are not obscene. But he concluded that some nonobscene nude depictions of minors are protected by the Constitution. Brennan objected to the law because "[its] prohibition extends to posing or exhibiting children 'in a state of nudity,' rather than merely to their participation in live or simulated sexual conduct."

Thus, in Brennan's view, parents who photograph their small children naked on the beach or who join nudist clubs and take photographs of children on family outings *may* be threatened with prosecution under the law. The law also may be applied to punish legitimate professional acting or modeling by teenagers who are partially clad. It could also prohibit an anthropologist or a journalist from taking and distributing photographs of children in a culture in which nudity is acceptable. While the state can prohibit depictions of children engaged in sexual conduct, the First Amendment prohibits the state from banning all nudity. As the Court ruled in *Erznoznik v. City of Jacksonville*, 422 U.S. 205 (1975), "[n]udity, without more" is protected expression.

In *Osborne v. Ohio*, 495 U.S. 103, a child pornography case argued later in the 1989 term, the Rehnquist Court refused to extend *Stanley v. Georgia* to invalidate an Ohio law that criminalized the private possession of child pornography. Writing for the 6–3 majority, Justice White argued that the state's interests in protecting the well-being of minors by regulating child pornography outweighed Osborne's right to possess and view such material. In *Stanley*, the Court struck down a Georgia law that criminalized private possession of obscene material. However, White argued that if *Stanley* is read narrowly, the ruling applies only to paternalistic laws that seek to protect the minds of viewers. *Osborne* is different because the Ohio law was enacted to protect children by attempting to eliminate the demand or market for child pornography. The Ohio law was not aimed at regulating Osborne's morals, but rather at decreasing the production and distribution of child pornography by penalizing those who view the product.

Couldn't the state use less draconian measures in protecting victims of child pornography? Was it necessary to penalize possession to stem the tide of child pornography? White responded that, given the importance of the state's interest:

> [W]e cannot fault Ohio for attempting to stamp out this vice at all levels in the distribution chain. . . . since the time of our decision in *Ferber*, much of the child pornography market has been driven underground; as a result, it is now difficult, if not impossible, to solve the child pornography problem by only attacking production and distribution.

In *Osborne*, the Court cited the controversial *Report of the Attorney General's Commission on Pornography* (1986) in further justifying the Ohio ban on private possession. According to the commission's report, child pornography is used to entreat other children into sexual activity. Thus, by criminalizing the private possession of child pornography, the state encourages the possessor to destroy one of the tools used by pedophiles to lure other children into posing nude or engaging in sexual activity.[11]

Justice Brennan attacked the majority for its refusal to respect *Stanley* and for its reliance on the mere supposition that a ban on possession will lead to decreased production of child pornography. While the exploitation of children is disquieting, wrote Brennan, there are better ways of dealing with child pornography than banning mere possession. "I do not believe that [the Court] has struck the proper balance between the First Amendment and the state's interest, especially in light of the other means available to Ohio."

Brennan also charged that the "lewdness" and "graphic focus" language of the statute was vague enough to allow the state to proscribe possession of something akin to the well-known advertisement for suntan lotion showing a small girl's bare untanned bottom.

## Mainstream Forms of Sexual Communication

Most people would not be shocked by the realization that some movie theaters in small communities regularly decide not to show the more sexually explicit or offensive of Hollywood's mainstream film productions. It would be surprising, however, if a state's highest court were to uphold the obscenity conviction of a theater owner for showing a "fully legitimate" film starring Tom Cruise or Nicole Kidman. *May communities apply state or local obscenity laws to sexually oriented materials that are considered mainstream by national tastes, but indecent or obscene by local community standards? Does the fact that they are mainstream have any impact on judicial decision-making?*

In a highly publicized case, the Georgia Supreme Court affirmed the 1972 obscenity conviction of a theater manager in Albany, Georgia, for showing the highly acclaimed film *Carnal Knowledge*, starring Jack Nicholson, Art Garfunkel, Candice Bergen, and Academy Award nominee Ann-Margaret. As its title suggests, the film deals with sexual relationships and contains depictions of sexual acts. But despite its racy title, the film does not show the actors' genitals or any actual "ultimate" sexual acts.

After viewing the film during conference and reading several film reviews, the Supreme Court unanimously overturned the Georgia court's ruling in *Jenkins v. Georgia*, 418 U.S. 153 (1974), holding that the film was not obscene because it did not depict or describe hard-core sexual conduct as demanded by the *Miller* test. The main flaw in the state's case was the jury's misapplication of the *Miller* test. The Court argued that even though a jury may be instructed to consider whether the film appealed to prurient interests or was patently offensive, the community standards component of the *Miller* test does not give juries absolute discretion in determining what is patently offensive. This determination must be made within the parameters set forth in *Miller*. The state prosecutor's instructions to the jury gave the panel enough leeway to convict for obscenity "based upon a defendant's depiction of a woman with a bare midriff."

The Court acknowledged that the film had serious artistic value, but it did not overturn Jenkins's conviction on this basis. Rather, it did so mainly on the state court's erroneous application of *Miller*. Furthermore, much to the chagrin of civil libertarians, the Court did not address whether a film should receive heightened protection because it is a "legitimate" Hollywood production rather than a low-budget, amateurish creation that may contain similar ideas and representations. However, it settled an issue on the minds of many Americans: whether nudity or depictions of sexual activity alone are enough to make a film lose its First Amendment protection. Based on *Jenkins*, regardless of local standards, it is less likely that the Court will permit mainstream sexually oriented materials to be subjected to censorship under obscenity laws.

## TECHNOLOGY AND OBSCENITY

### Telephone Pornography

Modern technology makes it possible to instantaneously communicate sexual messages (for commercial gain) to a huge audience comprised of individuals living in communities having different obscenity standards. "Dial-a-porn" entrepreneurs have used local and long-distance telephone services to tap into a multimillion-dollar market for "phone sex."

In 1988, Congress responded to the need for regulation in this area by amending the Communications Act of 1934, imposing a ban on indecent as well as obscene interstate commercial telephone messages. Sable Communications brought suit challenging the 1988 amendments on two grounds. First, Sable argued that the amendments broadly imposed an unconstitutional ban on protected erotic expression—going beyond the ban on commercial telephone messages that are legally obscene. Second, Congress created a national standard of obscenity contrary to the Supreme Court's decree in *Miller*, thus forcing the message sender to tailor all messages to the least tolerant community.

The U.S. district court rejected the argument that the statute created an unconstitutional national standard, but struck down as overbroad the "indecent speech" provision of the law. In *Sable Communications v. FCC*, 492 U.S.115 (1989), the Rehnquist Court affirmed the lower court's decision, rejecting Sable's contention that the federal law contravened *Miller*. The Court also posited that when distributors of obscene materials are prosecuted under federal law, the defendants may be subjected to the varying community standards within the various federal judicial districts in which they are tried. In other words, if Sable's audience consists of different towns and cities having different moral standards, Sable bears the burden of tailoring the contents of its messages to suit the standards of the respective communities. Justice White wrote: "There is no constitutional barrier under *Miller* to prohibiting communications that are obscene in some communities under local standards even though they are not obscene in others."

***Are there any situations in which indecent but not obscene sexual communication may be constitutionally restricted?***   White ruled that the government may not criminalize sexually oriented material simply because it is indecent, but constitutionally protected sexual expression may be regulated in order to "promote a compelling interest," such as the physical and psychological well-being of children. As the Court established in *Ginsberg v. United States* 390 U.S. 629 (1968), this compelling interest justifies shielding minors from the influence of sexually oriented communication that is not legally obscene by "adult standards." The variable approach of *Ginsburg* states that material that would not be obscene when read or viewed by an adult is obscene when read or viewed by a minor.

***Did the Miller test still apply?***   The answer is yes, although it could now be called the *Miller* "junior" test: A film or publication is obscene only if taken as a whole it lacks serious literary, artistic, scientific, or political value to *minors*, and if it has prurient interest to *minors*, and is patently offensive to *minors*.

In *Sable*, while the Court acknowledged the compelling interest of protecting minors, it ruled that any regulations on the content of constitutionally protected speech must be drawn narrowly. A law aiming to protect children from a particular form of communication must be constructed so that it protects children without denying access to adults. For example, the Federal Communications Commission (FCC) now mandates the use of credit cards, special access codes, scrambling, and other procedures that are the "least restrictive" means of denying minors access to dial-a-porn messages. This approach contrasts with the FCC's position before *Sable*, which held that since these procedures would probably not succeed in preventing more enterprising children from gaining access to the messages, a blanket prohibition on all indecent communications is justified. This blanket approach is considered constitutionally overbroad because in seeking to protect children it denies adults access to constitutionally protected material that is not suited for children. As Justice Scalia wrote in his concurring opinion in *Sable*: "I join the Court's opinion because I think it is correct that a wholesale prohibition upon adult access to indecent speech cannot be adopted merely because the FCC's alternate proposal could be circumvented by as few children as the evidence suggests."

## Radio Broadcasts

*What degree of First Amendment protection is extended to radio broadcasts that include sexually explicit music lyrics or commentary?* This question was addressed in *FCC v. Pacifica Foundation*, 438 U.S. 726 (1978), a case involving the radio broadcast of social satire by a comedian generally regarded as mainstream by many critics. The case originated in 1973, when a New York City radio station aired a selection from an album by George Carlin. The selection, entitled "Filthy Words," began with a monologue about the seven words you cannot say on the public airwaves. In the monologue, recorded in front of a live audience, Carlin listed the words "shit," "piss," "fuck," "motherfucker," "cocksucker," "cunt," and "tits." Carlin repeated these words over and over for shock effect, intending to provide a commentary on contemporary society's attitudes toward the public use of "offensive" words and to present the point of view that the seven words are harmless and that society's attitudes toward them are "essentially silly."

The FCC received a single complaint from a man who had heard the early afternoon broadcast of the monologue while driving in his car with his young son. Although the station warned its listeners that the program would contain offensive language, the listener argued that he and his son had become a captive audience to indecent language because they had tuned in to the monologue after the station's warning was given. The FCC then issued an order that was, in essence, a warning to the station that if subsequent complaints were received, the station's license might be revoked. The FCC found that the language in the monologue was "indecent" and "patently offensive" (though not necessarily obscene) and therefore in violation of a federal law[12] prohibiting the radio broadcast of "any obscene, indecent, or profane language." The FCC was quick to point out that it "never intended to place an absolute prohibition" on such language, but sought to restrict it to the times of day when "children most likely would not be exposed to it."

Pacifica argued that the FCC's actions were unconstitutional and needless since the station, WBAI, was not a commercial top-40 station, but a member-supported station that directed its programming at politically liberal-to-left leaning adults. It was very unlikely that many children were listening, since at the time of the broadcast five- to seventeen-year-old children were in school. Since the recording was not obscene under *Miller*, the First Amendment protected the station's right to broadcast it on the radio. Even if the Carlin monologue was not protected, argued Pacifica, the FCC's interpretation of the statute was unconstitutionally overbroad because it cast a broad net of censorship over various forms of sexually explicit and profane language that are protected. As interpreted, the statute could be applied to a radio reading of a host of literary classics containing one or more of the seven words.

Three major constitutional questions surfaced. *Were the words of Carlin's monologue "speech" within the definition of the First Amendment? Did the FCC restrict the broadcast solely on the basis of the offensiveness of the monologue's content rather than on the claimed basis of indecent language? Did the privacy rights of the captive audience outweigh the First Amendment rights of the speaker?*

Despite its recognition that Carlin's words were indeed speech and that the Commission's decision could not be based on the content of the monologue alone, the Supreme Court sustained the FCC's action against Pacifica on the grounds that the medium and circumstances of communication made it constitutionally permissible to restrict the broadcast. In other words, the government could permissibly prohibit Carlin's monologue because it was communicated through the medium of radio and broadcast at a time when children might become a captive audience. On radio broadcasting in general, Justice Stevens wrote: "We have long recognized that each medium of expression presents special First Amendment problems. And of all forms of communication, it is broadcasting that has received the most limited First Amendment [protection]." This traditional view of radio as well as television broadcasts can be explained by the "scarcity" doctrine. Since there is a finite broadcasting spectrum and most individuals have limited ability to gain access to the airwaves, the government has the legitimate power to place stricter regulations on the electronic broadcasting of ideas and images. Today, with the availability of cable and satellite broadcasting, as well as the Internet, the scarcity doctrine may be outdated.

Another justification can be found in a privacy approach to the problem. In this instance, the listeners had not ventured out to theaters or record stores seeking Carlin's words, but had become an unwilling audience to patently offensive words broadcast over the airwaves into the privacy of their car. In one's car or home, Stevens argued in an earlier case, "the individual's right to be let alone plainly outweighs the First Amendment rights of an intruder."[13] A person who had tuned in after Pacifica's warning about the nature of the monologue would not have been able to "turn away" before being confronted with indecent speech. For this reason, the person becomes a captive audience.

The captive audience doctrine, however, is not without limits. As the Court argued in *Erznoznik*, when a person gives up the expectation of privacy by leaving the home or, to a lesser degree, the car, the First Amendment may demand that the offended listener turn his or her ear away from the speaker's words.

The Court believed that its ruling was compatible with the First Amendment because it did not intend to prevent Carlin from performing or to prevent willing adults from attending his performances. The ruling merely restricted his monologue from being broadcast at times of the day when children might be listening.

Justice Brennan, dissenting, believed that the majority's solution to the problem was contradictory because it allowed the FCC ruling to stand even while recognizing both the social value of the monologue and the fact that Carlin's words were neither fighting words nor obscene. Brennan also blasted the majority's opinion that the right of privacy protected the listener from uninvited radio communications in the home and car. Brennan took a completely different approach to the privacy argument. He argued that unlike a telephone call or an unsolicited advertisement for pornography, as in *Rowan*, radio broadcasts are transmitted over public airwaves and are directed at the public at-large. The radio is a public medium, like a street or a park. Just as people take a chance at hearing something offensive to them when they walk through a park or see someone's jacket, for instance, they take a chance when they turn on the radio. They still retain privacy interests, but privacy is outweighed by the broadcaster's protected First Amendment rights. In other words, we should not ban otherwise protected speech merely because it may be offensive to people who are scanning the airwaves. Instead, we should expect the listener to change the channel or switch off the set. Brennan wrote: "The Court's balance . . . permits majoritarian tastes completely to preclude a protected message from entering the homes of a receptive, unoffended minority. No [past] decision of this Court supports such a result."

After *Pacifica*, the government proceeded from the assumption that since the electronic media are a uniquely powerful means of communication and that because we are often captives to their transmissions, radio and television broadcasts deserve the least amount of First Amendment protection. This means that material considered protected speech when communicated in a concert hall or contained on a compact disc may be subject to strict regulation or an outright ban when communicated over the airwaves. Material need not be legally obscene, but merely indecent or patently offensive to be subject to regulation.

In 1987, the FCC announced that future restrictions on radio indecency would not be limited to specific words, like those in Carlin's monologue, but would be imposed on any broadcast that contained language or material depicting or describing sexual or excretory functions of organs in a patently offensive manner. Even a broadcast that used innuendo or *double entendre* could be subject to such regulation.[14] The following year, the FCC was authorized by Congress to restrict obscene or indecent radio or television broadcasts not only when there was a reasonable risk that children were listening, but twenty-four hours a day.[15] While even works of merit may theoretically be subject to such regulation, the FCC refused to restrict Pacifica's 1987 broadcast of excerpts from James Joyce's *Ulysses*, which contains numerous explicit references to sexual organs in ways that could be patently offensive to listeners.[16]

*Will the community standards rationale serve as a workable doctrine for the FCC given the fact that cable programming has a national rather than localized audience? Will the FCC have to tailor its national regulations to reflect the values of the least tolerant community? Should all FCC restrictions take into account a captive audience of children, since it is likely that the eyes of millions of unattended children are glued to cable television at any given time?* The Court addressed these issues in *United States v. Playboy, Inc.*, 529 U.S. 803 (1998). There, it struck down (5–4) section 505 of the Telecommunications Act of 1996, which required cable television operators to either fully scramble or block adult channels when children are likely to be viewing television (between 6:00 a.m. and 9:00 p.m.). Prior to the law, cable operators used signal scrambling to limit access to certain programs, but often visual or audio portions of the broadcast might "bleed" through for a few seconds allowing children to see or hear portions of the Playboy Channel's broadcasts. Although this was not a widespread problem, section 505's time restrictions were adopted.

Citing *Sable Communications*, the Court recognized the legitimate reasons for regulating the broadcasts but ruled that section 505 constituted a content-based restriction on speech that was not the "least restrictive" means to regulate Playboy's programs. The restrictions placed on the broadcasts were content-based not only because section 505 of the act singled out certain kinds of programming, it also singled out certain programmers, such as Playboy. Laws that are intended to suppress the expression of certain speakers violate First Amendment principles. Writing for the narrow majority, Justice Kennedy reasoned: "Cable television, like broadcast media, presents unique problems, but even where speech is indecent and enters the home, the objective of shielding children does not suffice to support a blanket ban if the protection can be obtained by a less restrictive alternative."

Target blocking, whereby cable operators are required by the subscriber to block the channel completely[17] rather than banning broadcasts during certain hours, is the best way of guarding children from objectionable broadcasts while maintaining Playboy's constitutional protections.

## The Internet and Obscenity

The development and growth of the Internet and the World Wide Web are arguably among the most important cultural and economic events of the twentieth century. This revolution has forever changed—and continues to change—communication, commerce, and culture. Tens of millions of people around the globe now communicate instantaneously with one another in cyberspace. The Internet makes it possible for a person to complete a college degree, find a job, and generate income without leaving home.

Political activists, artists, and entertainers who once aspired to reach an audience of hundreds can now communicate their ideas or works to potentially hundreds of millions of people around the world. Cyberspace has become a limitless marketplace of ideas, regulated only by our tastes, opinions, and interests. This means that ideas that are subversive, unpopular, offensive, or obscene—the subjects of the first two chapters of this book—can now be communicated to a much wider audience with little or no fear of governmental restriction. Imagine for a moment if the Internet had been available to Charles Schenck and his antiwar rhetoric during World War I or to Yates and her fellow travelers. *Will the government try to prose-*

*cute such people today? What about sexual communication? As the online adult entertainment industry grows exponentially, what role should the government play in punishing obscene speech?* Until the early 1990s, those who wished to either publish or peruse sexual images did so through the use of the mail or at adult video-stores or bookstores. Today, one needs only a personal computer and an Internet connection to gain immediate access to the most hard-core images. This makes it much more difficult, if not impossible, for government to promote society's interests in regulating this form of speech.

By the mid-1990s, scholars, lawyers, judges, and public officials began to wonder if it was even possible for Congress to regulate speech on the Internet. *Do rulings such as* Miller *and* Ferber *even apply? Should Internet-based speech be analyzed from the standpoint of telephone pornography, as in* Sable Communications, *or radio broadcasts as in* Pacifica? Can cyberspace be compared to a public place, such as a street corner or a public park. *Or, is communication via the Internet more like a telephone conversation? Should we have the same expectations of privacy when entering a electronic chat room or sending an e-mail as we do when we make a telephone call?*

Outraged parents have argued that the unregulated Internet has the potential to give children a ticket to the equivalent of every adult bookstore and movie theater in the world.[18] In response to this outrage, Congress moved to enact legislation designed to protect children from being exploited by Internet-based activities. The Communications Decency Act (CDA) was enacted by Congress in 1996 to protect minors from harmful material on the Internet by criminalizing the "knowing" transmission of "obscene or indecent" messages to any recipient under eighteen years of age. The act also allows the prosecution of those who "knowing[ly]" send or display to a person under age eighteen any message that "depicts or describes, in terms patently offensive as measured by contemporary community standards, sexual or excretory activities or organs." To be prosecuted under the law, the government must show that the sender intentionally sent the information and failed to take "good faith . . . effective actions" to restrict access by minors. Such good-faith efforts included measures aimed at screening minors by showing proof of age through credit cards or adult identification numbers.

The American Civil Liberties Union (ACLU), the American Library Association, and other free speech advocates challenged the constitutionality of the law on the grounds that in its attempt to protect children the CDA was censoring adult speech. They also argued that the CDA's "indecent transmission" and "patently offensive display" provisions were overly broad and therefore violated freedom of speech. The district court agreed, but the government countered, basing its argument on *Ginsberg v. New York, FCC v. Pacifica*, and *Renton v. Playtime Theatres.*

In its first ruling dealing with the Internet, *Reno v. American Civil Liberties Union*, 519 U.S. 1025 (1997), the U.S. Supreme Court affirmed (7–2) the lower court's ruling and rejected the government's argument that these earlier rulings applied to the Internet. The Court pronounced that online speech and publications receive the same First Amendment protections as do newspapers and books. Writing for the majority, Justice Stevens explained that the CDA differed from the laws and regulations upheld in the earlier rulings because unlike radio, television, movie theaters, or dance clubs (that are all subject to restrictions), the Internet is a unique medium that receives full First Amendment protection. Furthermore, the CDA was unconstitutionally vague, since it contained no definition of the term "indecent" nor any requirement that in order for material to be considered "patently offensive," it must clearly lack socially redeeming value. (Note that the ruling does not bar prohibitions on obscene materials. Obscenity in any form is illegal and receives no First Amendment protection.)

The Court argued that the First Amendment requires Congress to carefully and precisely tailor any restrictions on speech. As we have discovered in earlier cases, the Court does not look kindly on the "chilling effect" of vague terms that may cause uncertainty in speakers, especially when the speaker runs the risk of criminal prosecution. Stevens writes: "We are persuaded that the CDA lacks the precision that the First Amendment requires when a statute regulates the content of speech. In order to deny minors access to potentially harmful speech, the CDA effectively suppresses a large amount of speech that adults have a constitutional right to receive and to address to one another."

In other words, the act's restrictions were overkill. In its attempt to prevent obscene material from reaching twelve-year-olds, it treated everyone like twelve-year-olds. While the Court has allowed such an approach for radio broadcasts, it would not do so for the Internet. Instead of governmental regulation, argued Stevens, children can be protected from inappropriate material through the use of currently available user-based software. Furthermore, unlike radio or television where a child can easily switch channels, it is unlikely that an Internet user can accidentally become a "captive audience" to an indecent web site. Internet communications do not invade one's home unbidden. It takes a number of deliberate steps to conduct a search and open a site. Even if one stumbles across such a site, almost all sexual images are preceded by warnings as to the nature and content of the site. (To obviate the possibility of accidentally opening such a site, parents, librarians, and others employ software that block access to inappropriate sites or open only designated sites.)

*Does the provision of the CDA that limits prosecution to only those who "knowingly" send obscene or indecent messages to a specific person under eighteen years of age protect the First Amendment rights of adults?*   The Court says no, since most Internet forums, chat rooms, and even college computer labs are open to a very wide audience. The sender would always be reluctant to send a message for fear that someone under age eighteen might receive the communication. Indeed, under the CDA, parents who sent their seventeen-year-old college freshman birth control information or an article on rape in prison could be prosecuted if the college town's community found the material to be indecent or patently offensive.

For Stevens, the CDA deviated from the *Miller* standard in three ways. First, the law's definition of obscenity was different from that set forth in the *Miller* test, banning not only descriptions of sexual conduct that were patently offensive but also descriptions of sexual organs. Second, the law did not provide protection for material passing the SLAPS test; that is, material that has serious literary, artistic, political, and scientific value. Third, the law made it possible to judge material available to a national audience by the standards of the community "most likely to be offended by the message."

Stevens also wrote that the law bestowed a "heckler's veto" upon any opponent of indecent speech. A heckler's veto occurs when someone in the audience (or community) who does not like the speech or speaker can disrupt or censor the communication of ideas. Similarly, if speech directed at a chat room or library computer with an Internet connection is tailored for fear that it might offend one person, then that one person has, in essence, shut down a whole range of ideas for the rest of us.

There is little doubt that the Court has grasped the importance of the Internet as "this new marketplace of ideas." Stevens concluded:

> [T]he growth of the Internet has been and continues to be phenomenal. As a matter of constitutional tradition, in the absence of evidence to the contrary, we presume that governmental regulation of the content of speech is more likely to interfere with the free exchange of ideas than to encourage it. The interest in encouraging freedom of expression in a democratic society outweighs any theoretical but unproven benefit of censorship.

The ruling was a clear victory for freedom of expression in cyberspace. *But what about the millions of parents, educators, and others who remain concerned about the Internet's influence on children? Does* Reno v. ACLU *close the door on the possibility of commonsense restrictions?* Not at all. The Communications Decency Act was doomed from the start not because the federal courts have taken an absolutist position on cyber speech, but because the law was poorly written. There is no language in the Court's opinion that prevents Congress from enacting a more specific, narrowly written law that creates "adult zones" on the Internet, much like bookstores and newsstands have adult sections off limits to minors. In their dissenting opinion, Justice O'Connor and Chief Justice Rehnquist advocate this "zoning" approach along with a mandated use of "filtering" or "screening" software to limit access to sexually explicit and inappropriate web sites.

Following *Reno v. ACLU,* lawmakers have turned their attention not to banning certain web sites or kinds of communications, but rather to whether states or school boards can allow restrictions on Internet access in public or school libraries.

## EROTIC DANCE AND OFFENSIVE MUSIC

### Erotic Dance as Speech

Topless and nude dance clubs constitute a substantial portion of the adult entertainment industry. Many communities have enacted and enforced stringent regulations on live music and dance performances considered offensive or indecent. For instance, South Bend, Indiana, banned totally nude exotic dancing by enacting a public indecency law that requires dancers to wear pasties and a G-string. An erotic dancer at the Kitty Kat Lounge challenged the law in *Barnes v. Glen Theatre,* 501 U.S. 560 (1991). *Is nude dancing a form of expressive conduct protected by the First Amendment? Does the First Amendment prohibit the government from enforcing its public indecency law to prevent this form of dancing?*

After the Court decided to grant certiorari in *Barnes,* there was much speculation by dancers, artists, and Court watchers that an unfavorable ruling could have a chilling effect on all forms of artistic dance that is erotic and not merely on the genre of dance found in "strip joints."

In a 5–4 decision, the Rehnquist Court rejected the argument that the intent of the statute was to stifle the messages of eroticism and sexuality conveyed by erotic dancers. Chief Justice Rehnquist, writing for the majority, applied the "time, place, or manner" test of *O'Brien*, arguing that when speech and nonspeech elements are combined in some conduct, such as dancing, a "sufficiently important" governmental interest in restricting the nonspeech element—public nudity—can justify limitations on the First Amendment. As in *O'Brien*, Indiana's interest in protecting order and morality was unrelated to the suppression of free expression. According to Rehnquist, Indiana was not seeking to restrict erotic dancing per se, but rather public nudity. Rehnquist refused to accept the view that an "apparently limitless variety of conduct can be labeled speech" whenever a person intends to express an idea or opinion. He wrote: "Some may view restricting nudity on moral grounds as necessarily related to expression. We disagree. . . . People who go about in the nude in public may be expressing something about themselves by doing so. But the court rejected this expansive notion of 'expressive conduct' in *O'Brien*."

Nude dancing as a form of expressive conduct is protected, just as O'Brien's act of burning his draft card brought the First Amendment into play. But also like O'Brien, the dancer at the Kitty Kat Lounge was not prosecuted for the communicative element of her conduct (erotic message), but rather for the noncommunicative element (public nudity). Thus, Rehnquist concluded that the requirement that the dancers wear pasties and G-strings was only a modest limitation and did not deprive the dance of its erotic message. In other words, the dancers did not have to be totally nude to convey their messages.

Justice Scalia, concurring, refused to admit that erotic dance received even a modicum of protection from the First Amendment. Glossing over the First Amendment issue, he devoted the bulk of his opinion to the issue of state authority to enact laws prohibiting immoral conduct. He argued that Indiana's authority in these matters was securely rooted in a long tradition of laws against public nudity dating back to 1831. His reasoning was much like that employed by Justice White in *Bowers v. Hardwick*, 478 U.S. 186 (1986), which upheld Georgia's prohibition of homosexual sodomy.[19] Furthermore, since public nudity, like homosexual conduct, is not a fundamental right, the state needs only a rational basis—"moral opposition to public nudity"—to comply with the due process clause.

Justice Souter concurred with the ruling of the Court, but not on the grounds that the state's moral views justified the restrictions on nude dancing. Instead, he took a more sociological approach. Citing *Renton v. Playtime Theatres*, 475 U.S. 41 (1986), Souter argued that it is the "secondary effects of adult entertainment," such as prostitution, degradation of women, and sexual assault, that provide the rational basis for the law.[20] In *Renton*, the Court ruled that a city was not compelled to justify its actions by conducting studies aimed at discovering the correlation between porn and crime, but could rely on the experience of other cities showing the negative secondary effects associated with adult theaters.

However, much to the relief of many civil libertarians, Souter, who was expected to hold a more conservative judicial philosophy, adopted a more expansive interpretation of expressive conduct than was predicted. He agreed with the proposition that erotic dancing possesses a degree of First Amendment protection, and wrote that even if the message expressed is merely eroticism or the endorsement of an erotic experience, nude dancing is protected as expressive conduct. Even in light of these revelations on expressive conduct, Souter did not believe that nudity per se was expressive and voted to uphold the Indiana law. He wrote: "Pasties and a G-string moderate the expression to some degree, to be sure, but only to a degree. Dropping the final stitch is prohibited, but the limitation is minor when measured against the dancer's remaining capacity and opportunity to express the erotic message."

In a strong dissent, Justice White argued that the Court's ruling was based on its own subjective judgment of what is art, and not on the basis of established constitutional law: "That the performances in the Kitty Kat Lounge may not be high art, to say the least, and may not appeal to the Court, is hardly an excuse for distorting and ignoring settled doctrine." He also attacked the various rationales for the law that were set forth by the state and embraced by the majority. The state did not base its restrictions on nude dancing on its fear of the effects it would have on public safety, he argued, but only because the state sought to prevent the dancers from generating ideas or feelings of eroticism among audience members. Thus, the state was placing restrictions on the content of the expression and not merely on the effects, as the majority argued. In upholding the law, White argued, the majority had broken with the established principles of *O'Brien* and *Texas v. Johnson*.

Although the Court did not rule on whether the Indiana law would be valid in other contexts, many people in the art community worry that this new precedent could easily be applied to mainstream productions, such as *Hair* or *Equus*, both of which contain a great deal of nudity. Theoretically, under Rehnquist's rationale a state could demand that the actors in *Hair* or *Equus* wear pasties and G-strings simply because of the state's moral opposition to nudity. Under Souter's secondary effects approach, it would be very difficult for a city or state to prove that the performance of such mainstream plays in places other than seedy adult clubs and theaters posed a threat to public safety. Prosecutors would have to show that such performances attracted disruptive motorcycle gangs, roughnecks, and prostitutes to the local dramatic theater before shutting down the production. In any event, the Court took a narrow approach to the issue, leaving intact the view that nude dancing in nightclubs is expressive conduct, if only "within the outer perimeters of the First Amendment."

This case is a classic example of how the retirement of one justice can change constitutional law. Had Justice Brennan not retired after the Court's 1989–1990 term, the Court would most assuredly have ruled against the Indiana statute.

The Court returned to the issue of nude dance in *City of Erie v. Pap's A.M.*, 120 S. Ct. 1382 in 2000.[21] The City of Erie, Pennsylvania, enacted an ordinance prohibiting totally nude dancing. As in the earlier case of *Barnes*, the ordinance required dancers at Kandyland to wear pasties and a G-string. However, the Pennsylvania Supreme Court struck down the ordinance as a content-based violation of freedom of expression because it believed that the city was not merely combating the negative secondary effects of nude dancing, but also, the court suspected, of indirectly attempting to restrict the erotic message of the dance.

On appeal, the U.S. Supreme Court reversed the state supreme court. Writing for the majority (7–2), Justice O'Connor argued that Erie's ordinance does not unconstitutionally target the erotic message, but rather bans all public nudity, regardless of whether that nudity is accompanied by expressive conduct. As established in *Barnes*, the requirement that dancers not drop the "last stitch" of clothing has a minimal effect on the overall expression.

*Why, then, did the Court reverse the Pennsylvania high court? Was the Court prepared to modify or overturn* Barnes *or was it dissatisfied with the state court's interpretation of precedent?*    The Pennsylvania high court concluded that *Barnes*, which admittedly is a fragmented opinion, did not offer a definitive rule or standard by which to judge the Erie ordinance. Therefore, it conducted an independent inquiry and concluded that the ordinance constituted content-based suppression of speech. The Supreme Court took the appeal with the intent of clarifying *Barnes* and then remanding the case back to Pennsylvania for further consideration.

O'Connor wrote that governmental restrictions on public nudity should be evaluated not under *Barnes* but under *United States v. O'Brien*. Recall that O'Brien was convicted under a federal law for burning his draft card as a public statement of his antiwar views. The Supreme Court rejected his claim that the law violated his freedom of expression because the law punished him for the "noncommunicative impact of his conduct" (destroying his draft card). Similarly, the Erie ordinance prohibiting public nudity is aimed at combating crime and the other secondary negative effects caused by the presence of nude dance clubs and not at suppressing the erotic message of the dancer.

The standard that emerges from *Pap's A.M.* is a reiteration of *O'Brien*. For our purposes it can be labeled the *Barnes-O'Brien* test, which can be understood as follows: Since erotic dance *is* protected speech *(Barnes),* regulations on erotic dance establishments are justified only when they are content neutral, aimed only at combating negative secondary effects of the nude dancing such as prostitution, public intoxication, gang violence, or threats to public health *(O'Brien)*. Furthermore, the government should have "sufficient leeway" to justify a restriction based on secondary effects without expecting it to develop a specific evidentiary record showing the negative secondary effects.

## Offensive Music

*Is music a form of speech protected under the First Amendment? Can a musical work be found obscene if it meets the* **Miller** *test?*    Throughout human experience, music has served as a means of social or political communication as well as entertainment. Plato, in the *Republic*, speaks of the need to censor the music of the youth in the name of virtue and patriotism. The black spirituals sung by both slaves and civil rights activists contain political messages concealed in allusions to Christian doctrine. The rock music of the 1960s and early 1970s made no attempt to veil its antiwar and counterculture message to its young listeners. Today, the political and social commentary of many rap musicians is made doubly controversial by its graphic portrayal of violent sex and criminal conduct.

Modern attempts to place legal restrictions on popular music have generally tried to separate the lyrics from the total musical work in order to ban lyrics having an indecent message or containing obscene language. While there are few people who argue that the use of obscenity for obscenity's sake is essential to the exposition of ideas, some modern musicians use obscene lyrics to draw attention to their social and political messages much like Cohen used his "Fuck the Draft" jacket to draw attention to his political views. Many rap groups have used such First Amendment arguments to challenge attempts by local authorities to shut down their live performances and prohibit the sale of their music. While the Supreme Court has not yet heard a case involving obscene music lyrics, the U.S. court of appeals had an opportunity to do so in *Luke Records, Inc. v. Navarro*, 960 F.2d 134 (1992). This decision is important because it addresses whether a musical work can be found obscene under *Miller* and gives some indication of how the Supreme Court might rule in such a case.

In 1989, the rap group 2 Live Crew released the recording *As Nasty as They Wanna Be*. The album's lyrics and song titles contain references to "male and female genitalia, human sexual excretion, oral-anal contact, fellatio, group sex, specific sexual positions, sado-masochism, the turgid state of the male sexual organ, masturbation, cunnilingus, sexual intercourse, and the sounds of moaning." The recording was intended to be sold to the general public, and 2 Live Crew included a small statement on the recording that read, "Warning: Explicit Language Contained."

In February 1990, the Broward County Sheriff's Office responded to complaints by South Florida residents that the recording was being sold to all customers, regardless of age, from an open rack at a number of retail music stores throughout the county. After a Broward County judge found probable cause to believe that the recording was obscene under Florida law, the Sheriff's Office began to warn all store managers that their arrest was imminent if they continued to sell the recording to minors or adults. The police proceeded under a Florida law that criminalized the distribution, sale, or production of any obscene recording, musical or otherwise.

The warnings were apparently quite effective, as within a week all retail stores in the county took the recording off their shelves. No further action was taken by the Sheriff's Office against either local merchants or 2 Live Crew.

However, within days, Skywalker Records and members of 2 Live Crew brought suit in U.S. district court challenging the law on First Amendment grounds. The group argued that regardless of whether the recording is obscene, it is protected speech under the First Amendment. The obscenity or nonobscenity of any material should not be a concern for the state, but left to the marketplace of ideas. The group contended that to promote its message as rap artists, it needed the vulgar lyrics. However, this absolutist freedom of artistic expression argument did not fall upon receptive judicial ears.

The district court rejected the group's First Amendment challenge to Florida's obscenity statutes, relying on Supreme Court rulings in *Paris Adult Theatre I* and *Miller*. It rejected the notion that the government cannot legitimately impede an individual's desire to see or acquire obscene plays, movies, or books: With or without 2

Live Crew's warnings, obscenity is not protected speech and the people of Florida have the right to make obscenity a crime.

The district court found that the recording was obscene under *Miller* because the references in its lyrics were aimed at inciting lustful thoughts and luring listeners into sexual acts. The style of commercial advertising used to market the recording contributed to this conclusion, since it was done in a manner designed to titillate and not merely to inform. And the fact that the work was music also contributed to the court's conclusion that it should be restricted. Music, since it is played aloud, is more intrusive to the unwilling audience than a videotape or a book. Thus, it is more difficult for the unwilling listener to escape the message of the speaker. The court also rejected 2 Live Crew's argument that obscenity is a necessary element of rap music.

The U.S. court of appeals reversed the district court's ruling and held that the musical recording was not obscene under *Miller*. The district court judge improperly applied *Miller* by using his own expertise, without a jury, to determine that the recording had no serious artistic value. He also applied his understanding of the tastes and values of the South Florida community to determine that the recording appealed to prurient interests (applying community standards) and patent offensiveness as defined by Florida law.

The court of appeals relied on the testimony of a psychologist, several music critics, and Professor Carlton Long, a Rhodes scholar and expert on African American culture. Long testified that the recording should receive protection because it contained several political statements and literary devices relevant to the African American experience.

The court of appeals found no evidence to contradict the testimony that the recording *As Nasty as They Wanna Be* is protected by the First Amendment and rejected the argument that simply by listening to the recording the district court judge could determine that the work had no serious artistic value.

The court of appeals upheld the district court's injunction prohibiting the Sheriff's Office from employing prior restraint censorship; that is, using the threat of arrest to prevent local retailers from making the recording available prior to an obscenity ruling and prior to the actual sale of the recording to the public. Prior restraint censorship can take the form of licensing requirements or prepublication submission of materials for approval. As the Supreme Court ruled in *Near v. Minnesota*, 283 U.S. 697 (1931), the First Amendment prohibits restrictions on speech prior to publication except where a threat to national security is present or when a work is legally obscene.

Although *Near* is an important and fascinating decision, this book does not treat the massive body of case law and commentary on prior restraint censorship and censorship of the press. Any investigation of these issues must begin with *Near, New York Times v. Sullivan*, 376 U.S. 254 (1964), and *New York Times v. United States*, 403 U.S. 713 (1971).[22]

## PUBLIC FUNDING OF OFFENSIVE ART

Angered by artists who have used government grants to produce photographs that are offensive or indecent, many Americans have urged Congress to place greater restrictions on artists who receive such grants. Indeed, many members of

Congress have sought to eliminate federal funding for the arts completely. Others, however, have argued that the government has an obligation to support the arts.

***Should there a distinction between the degree of artistic expression enjoyed by an artist who uses private funds and an artist who utilizes public funding?*** Imagine an artist's photograph or sculpture that conveys an offensive or sexual message. Unless her work is obscene under *Miller* or depicts children in an indecent manner, she is free to produce and exhibit her work. *But what if she applies for a government grant to produce her work? Can the grantor place limits on the content of her message; that is, insist that her final product must neither be offensive nor indecent?* After all, one might argue that by funding the art, the government (or the people it represents) becomes the advocate of the subsidized expression. This issue received much attention in the early to mid-1990s, particularly after the Institute of Contemporary Art at the University of Pennsylvania used a $30,000 federal grant to exhibit a retrospective of photographer Robert Mapplethorpe's work, including homoerotic photographs that many condemned as pornographic. Also criticized was the Southwest Center for Contemporary Art for displaying Andres Serrano's work *Piss Christ*, a photograph of a crucifix immersed in a substance resembling urine. This work was considered blasphemous to a range of Christian groups, although Serrano's supporters argued that his intent was to depict what modern organized religion has done to Christianity. In both instances the works were supported by the publicly supported National Endowment for the Arts (NEA).[23]

The National Foundation on Arts and Humanities Act was passed by Congress in 1965 to provide financial support for the arts in the United States. The act pledges federal funds to "help create and sustain not only a climate encouraging freedom of thought, imagination, and inquiry but also the material conditions facilitating the release of . . . creative talent." The act vests the NEA with broad discretion to award grants to artists engaged in a wide variety of creative activity, including the encouragement of public education and appreciation of the arts.

All applications for NEA grants are initially reviewed by an advisory panel of experts who narrow the list and make recommendations to the National Council on the Arts. In turn, the Council advises the NEA chairperson, who makes the final determination for funding.[24]

Since 1965, only a fraction of the more than 100,000 grants have generated formal complaints. However, in the late 1980s the controversial photographs of Mapplethorpe and Serrano that were exhibited in two NEA-funded exhibits caused public outcries.

While no serious attempt was made to ban the artists' photographs, Congress responded to the controversy by amending the NEA's reauthorization bill, giving more discretion to the chairperson to screen out works that might be considered indecent or offensive by the American public. Specifically, the amendment directed the chairperson to ensure that "artistic excellence and artistic merit are the criteria by which applications are judged, taking into consideration general standards of decency and respect for the diverse beliefs of the American public." The amendment also stipulated that no NEA funds may be used to promote, disseminate, or produce materials which in the judgement of [the NEA] may be considered obscene, including but not limited to, depictions of sadomasochism, homoeroticism, the sexual exploitation of children, or individuals engaged in sex acts and which, when taken as a whole, do not have serious literary, artistic, political, or scientific value.[25]

The 1990 amendment in its final form was a bipartisan compromise introduced to "save" the NEA's funding from attempts by many conservatives to eliminate the NEA completely.

Karen Findley, and three other performance artists, applied for NEA grants before the amendment was enacted. An advisory panel recommended approval, but the Council rejected the proposals. The artists filed suit, claiming that the NEA had violated their First Amendment rights, asking for reconsideration of their grant applications, and challenging the new guidelines. The district court and the court of appeals ruled in favor of the artists, arguing that the amendment impermissibly discriminates on the basis of viewpoint and is void for vagueness under the First Amendment. Recall from our earlier discussions that viewpoint-based suppression of speech occurs when the expression is curtailed because it conveys a particular message that the government does not wish society to hear (e.g., speech or expression that disparages minorities or religion). Under the vagueness doctrine, a law is unconstitutional if it does not fairly inform a person of what is commanded or prohibited.

In *NEA v. Findley*, 569 U.S. 524 (1998), the Supreme Court disagreed with the lower courts and upheld the amendment. Writing for the (8–1) majority, Justice O'Connor disagreed with the artist's contention that the amendment constrained the NEA's ability to fund certain categories of artistic expression. She argued that the amendment does not preclude grant awards to projects that might be considered "indecent" or "disrespectful," but simply asks the NEA to consider the general standards of decency and diverse beliefs of the public.

The Court did not believe that there was a realistic danger that the amendment would be used to prevent or punish the expression of particular views contained in artistic activity. The Court is more likely to strike down legislation as unconstitutionally vague when the "dangers are both more evident and more substantial," as in *R.A.V. v. City of St. Paul*, where a municipal ordinance punished all speech that might cause resentment in others on the basis of race, color, creed, religion, or gender.

Furthermore, unlike other instances where laws or policies suppress speech on the basis of content, such as where the Court overturned a university's denial of funding to all student publications having religious viewpoints,[26] the subjective nature of arts funding must always be taken into account because the NEA has limited resources to allocate among many "artistically excellent" projects. And, as Chief Justice Rehnquist has reminded us in the past, there is no right to receive public money. For example, there may be a right to have an abortion but there is no concomitant right to have the government pay for it.[27] Since *Finley* involves freedom of expression, the First Amendment *does* apply. However, where subsidies are involved, Congress has broad discretion to require specific guidelines to determine which programs or projects receive tax dollars. The Court has determined that since the NEA has limited resources, it must deny the majority of grant applications it receives, including those that propose "artistically excellent" projects. In a highly competitive and selective grant application process, a large amount of constitutionally protected expression will go unfunded. The NEA may consider the proposed project's relevance, suitability to special audiences, and educational value, but it may not use its discretion to deny funding to projects that advance particular disfavored viewpoints or raise offensive or subversive ideas.

*Findley* did not address whether the government can directly regulate or punish speech, but merely whether the government may establish a criteria by which to allocate competitive public funding of artistic expression. According to the Court, the government has not discriminated on the basis of viewpoint but has merely chosen to fund one activity to the exclusion of the other.

In his lone dissent, Justice Souter disagreed with the majority's findings that the statute is flexible enough not to require viewpoint-based suppression of speech. Souter argued that the decency and respect provision of the amendment *requires* the NEA to make viewpoint-based decisions in the allocation of governmental funding for the arts. The new amendment was passed because members of Congress had listened to their constituents' desire to make sure that exhibits like Serrano's and Mapplethorpe's were not funded again. Souter continued:

> [A] statute disfavoring speech that fails to respect America's "diverse beliefs and values" is the very model of viewpoint discrimination; it penalizes any view disrespectful to any belief or value espoused by someone in the American populace. Boiled down to its practical essence, the limitation obviously means that art that disrespects the ideology, opinions, or convictions of a significant segment of the American public is to be disfavored, whereas art that reinforces those values is not.

Souter also disagreed with the majority's view that where subsidies are involved Congress has discretion to place restrictions on the First Amendment. When the government acts as a patron of the arts, subsidizing the expression of others, it may not prefer one view over another. So long as Congress chooses to subsidize artistic expression, it has no business requiring the NEA to reject grant applications of artists who wish to defy the tastes, beliefs, and values of the majority of Americans. In sum, Congress may not use the power of the purse to suppress offensive ideas.

## CONCLUDING COMMENTS

Restrictions on sexually oriented materials are often so vague and subjective that they may "chill artistic expression"; that is, affect a legitimate photographic artist's decision to publish a photograph that communicates a sexual message. Artists, as well as gallery and theater owners, have made decisions not to create and show certain sexually explicit works because of the possibility that vaguely worded obscenity codes might be applied to crack down on explicit photography and film. In doing so, some communities have banned not only obscene material, but also public and private exhibits of erotic or avant-garde photography as well. A resurgence of these crackdowns seemed to coincide with the prosecution of a Cincinnati art gallery for exhibiting the controversial homoerotic photographs of the late Robert

Mapplethorpe.[28] Despite the prosecution's argument that several of the photographs were obscene under local and state statutes, the jury acquitted, ruling that taken as a whole the collection of photographs had serious artistic value under the *Miller* test. Cognizant of the monetary loss and negative publicity that obscenity charges could precipitate, many galleries around the country have hesitated to show the kind of work falling into the Mapplethorpe genre—at least until the controversy dies down.

Justice Brennan, who abandoned his quest for a viable definition of obscenity years before he retired from the Court, had long argued that vague standards fail to provide individuals with adequate guidelines of what is permissible or proscribable activity. In the area of speech or press, specificity is crucial because statutory vagueness creates a chilling effect—an uncertainty, prior to speaking, of whether one's expression is protected by the First Amendment. As a consequence of this uncertainty, the individual imposes self-censorship rather than risking punishment. Statutory vagueness also leads to what Justice Brennan calls institutional stress on the judicial system: confusion in the state courts, resulting in endless appeals and a constant review of state court decisions by federal courts.

For some, the 1960s and 1970s represent an exciting departure from the stodgy tastes and values of the status quo. To others, those years represent a period of silly self-indulgence or chaos, best characterized by a kind of reluctant acceptance of the inevitability of an "anything goes" vulgar popular culture. One thing is certain: The decisions of both the Warren and Burger Courts helped to shift power away from the majority, thus enabling individuals, as well as political and racial minorities, to influence American tastes in art, literature, theater, and music. The conservative movement of the last two decades witnessed a sustained effort by lawmakers to return power to the majoritarian process so that a more traditional balance between individual tastes and community values could be reestablished. This ongoing movement has been frustrated by the influence of popular culture and the Internet, as well as by the Court's reluctance to sustain regulations on sexual expression.

# Finding the Full Text of the U.S. Supreme Court Opinions Cited in Chapter 3

The full opinion of the U.S. Supreme Court's rulings discussed in this chapter can be found at the Findlaw URL address following each case listed below, or by using the case name (e.g., *Schenck*) or citation (e.g., 249 U.S. 47). Other web sites where opinions can be found are listed at the end of chapter 1.

## Early Attempts to Define Obscenity

*Roth v. United States* (1957), http://laws.findlaw.com/us/354/476.html

*Manual Enterprises v. Day* (1962), http://laws.findlaw.com/us/370/478.html

*Jacobellis v. Ohio* (1964), http://laws.findlaw.com/us/378/184.html

*Memoirs v. Massachusetts* (1966), http://laws.findlaw.com/us/383/413.html

*Ginzburg v. United States* (1966), http://laws.findlaw.com/us/383/463.html

## Private Possession of Obscene Material

*Stanley v. Georgia* (1969), http://laws.findlaw.com/us/394/557.html

## The *Miller* Test

*Miller v. California* (1973), http://laws.findlaw.com/us/413/15.html

*Paris Adult Theatre I v. Slaton* (1973), http://laws.findlaw.com/us/413/49.html

*Smith v. United States* (1977), http://laws.findlaw.com/us/431/271.html

*Pope v. Illinois* (1987), http://laws.findlaw.com/us/481/497.html

## Child Pornography

*Ferber v. New York* (1982), http://laws.findlaw.com/us/485/747.html

*Massachusetts v. Oakes* (1989), http://laws.findlaw.com/us/491/576.html

*Osborne v. Ohio* (1989), http://laws.findlaw.com/us/495/103.html

## Mainstream Forms of Sexual Communication

*Jenkins v. Georgia* (1974), http://laws.findlaw.com/us/418/153.html

## Technology and Obscenity

### Telephone Pornography

*Sable Communications v. FCC* (1989), http://laws.findlaw.com/us/492/115.html

*Ginsberg v. United States* (1968), http://laws.findlaw.com/us/390/629.html

### Radio Broadcasts

*FCC v. Pacifica Foundation* (1978), http://laws.findlaw.com/us/438/726.html

*United States v. Playboy, Inc.* (2000), http://laws.findlaw.com/us/000/98-1682.html

### The Internet and Obscenity

*Reno v. American Civil Liberties Union* (1996), http://laws.findlaw.com/us/000/96-511.html

## Erotic Dance and Offensive Music

### Erotic Dance as Speech

*Barnes, v. Glen Theatre* (1991), http://laws.findlaw.com/us/501/560.html

*Continued*

---

### Finding the Full Text of the U.S. Supreme Court Opinions Cited in this Chapter 3   *Continued*

*Renton v. Playtime Theatres* (1986), http://laws.findlaw.com/us/475/41.html

*City of Erie v. Pap's A.M.* (1998), http://laws.findlaw.com/us/000/98-1161.html

#### Offensive Music

*Near v. Minnesota* (1931), http://laws.findlaw.com/us/283/697.html

*New York Times v. Sullivan* (1964), http://laws.findlaw.com/us/376/254.html

*New York Times v. United States* (1971),
    http://laws.findlaw.com/us/403/713.html

#### Public Funding of Offensive Art

*National Endowment for the Arts v. Findley* (1998),
    http://laws.findlaw.com/us/569/524.html

---

## NOTES

1. For background on the subject, see Harry Clor, *Obscenity and Public Morality* (Chicago: University of Chicago Press, 1969); Donald Downs, *The New Politics of Pornography* (Chicago: University of Chicago Press, 1989); and Nadine Stossen, *Defending Pornography* (New York: Scribner Press, 1995).
2. This English common law test for obscenity was established in *Regina v. Hicklin*, L.R. 2 Q.B. 360 (1868).
3. See Bernard Schwartz, *Super Chief: Earl Warren and His Supreme Court—A Judicial Biography* (New York: New York University Press, 1983), 221–222.
4. See David O'Brien, *Storm Center: The Supreme Court in American Politics*, 5th ed. (New York: Norton, 2000), 221.
5. See Earl Maltz, *The Chief Justiceship of Warren Burger* (Columbia: University of South Carolina Press, 2000), 97–100.
6. See discussion of right to privacy in chapter 6.
7. Maltz, *The Chief Justiceship of Warren Burger*, 97–100.
8. For more discussion on the impact of *Miller* and other obscenity standards, see Richard F. Hixon, *Pornography and the Justices: The Supreme Court and the Intractable Obscenity Problem* (Carbondale: Southern Illinois University Press, 1996).
9. See Downs, *The New Politics of Pornography*.
10. See Anthony Miranda, "Current Developments in the Law: A Survey of Federal Cases Involving the Child Pornography Prevention Act of 1996," *Boston University Public Interest Law Journal* 483 (Spring 2000).
11. See James Weinstein, *Hate Speech, Pornography and the Radical Attack on Free Speech Doctrine* (Boulder, Co: Westview Press, 1999), 192.
12. 18 U.S.C. sec. 1464.

13. *Rowan v. Post Office*, 397 U.S. 728 (1970).
14. 52 *Federal Register*. 1635.
15. Pub. L. No. 100–459.
16. FCC Record 930 (1987).
17. Mandated by section 504 of the act.
18. See Kelly M. Doherty, "An Analysis of Obscenity and Indecency Regulation on the Internet," 332 *Akron Law Review* 259 (1999).
19. See chapter 6.
20. For more discussion on the secondary effects of adult entertainment see S. A. Rubin and L. B. Alexander, "Regulating Pornography: The Feminist Influence," 18 *Communications and the Law* 73–94 (December 1996).
21. *United States Reporter:* http://laws.findlaws.com/us/000/98-1181-html
22. A good place to begin such an inquiry is Craig R. Ducat's excellent casebook, *Constitutional Interpretation*, 7th ed., (Belmont, CA: West Wadsworth, 2000), 984–1109.
23. See Elizabeth Megan Ray, "Comment: 'I May Not Know Art, But I Know What I'll Pay For,' The Government's Role in Arts Funding Following *National Endowment of the Arts v. Findley*," 2 *University of Pennsylvania Journal of Constitutional Law* 497 (March 2000).
24. See facts as stated in *NEA v. Findley*, 569 U.S. 524 (1998).
25. *NEA v. Findley*, 569 U.S. 524.
26. *Rosenberger v. Rector and Visitors of University of Virginia*, 515 U.S. 819 (1995).
27. See discussion of abortion in chapter 6.
28. Two companion suits were brought in the Hamilton County, Ohio Municipal Court : *Ohio v. Contemporary Arts Center and Ohio v. Dennis Barrie*. The ACLU of Ohio and the Cincinnati Chapter of the ACLU filed an *amicus curiae brief*.

# CHAPTER FOUR

# Freedom of Religion and Freedom from Religion

*A critical function of the Religion Clauses of the First Amendment is to pro-
tect the rights of members of minority religions against quiet erosion by
majoritarian social institutions that dismiss minority beliefs and practices
as unimportant, because unfamiliar.* It is the constitutional role of this
Court to ensure that this purpose of the First Amendment be realized
*[emphasis added].*

Justice William Brennan, dissenting in
*Goldman v. Weinberger* (1986)

## FREE EXERCISE OF RELIGION

The free exercise clause of the First Amendment declares that Congress shall make
no law prohibiting the free exercise of religion. This brief clause reflects the philosophy that religion is a highly personal matter that should be placed beyond the reach
of government. The framers of the Bill of Rights intended the clause to prevent only
the national government from restricting religion. However, since *Cantwell v.
Connecticut*, 310 U.S. 296 (1940), the U.S. Supreme Court has extended the clause
to state action by selectively incorporating its protection into the Fourteenth
Amendment. In a wide variety of rulings, rich with colorful claims and complex constitutional arguments, the Supreme Court has ruled that the free exercise clause protects our right to believe or to not believe in any religious doctrine, prohibits all
governmental regulation of religious beliefs, forbids the government from compelling us to worship, prohibits the punishment of religious beliefs that the government believes to be false, and denies to the state the power to grant benefits or place
burdens on the basis of religious beliefs or status.

## Balancing Religious Liberty With the Needs of Society

*Is the First Amendment's protection of religion absolute?*    To answer this question we must understand that there is more to religion than one's beliefs and the
expression of those beliefs. Although the First Amendment explicitly recognizes

116

"religion," religious *conduct* is an integral facet of the "exercise of religion." Thus, no less difficult than defining religion is the task of determining what forms of religiously motivated conduct are necessary elements of an individual's religious beliefs. In our pluralistic society, religion may involve activities that run counter to the beliefs of the majority or practices that contradict laws aimed at serving the public interest. Such religious activities go beyond taking the sacraments to taking multiple wives; from proselytizing in front of public schools to refusing to attend school.

## Religious Exemptions to the Law

Whereas many minority religious beliefs and practices have at some time suffered ridicule or condemnation from intolerant individuals or groups, most legal or governmental restrictions on such beliefs and practices have not taken the form of direct bans. Instead, they have resulted from the indirect effects of seemingly legitimate exercises of governmental power. Indeed, it would be difficult to find laws that have imposed outright bans on activities or abstentions from activities solely on the basis of religious beliefs. Selective service laws, for example, are not aimed at Jehovah's Witnesses, but they may infringe upon their religious liberty if adherents are compelled to act contrary to their faith. And while there are no laws specifically prohibiting public nudity as a form of religious worship, many laws proscribe public nudity of any kind. Thus, an adherent to a "Church of Nature," for example, may be prohibited from proselytizing in the nude not because of a ban on nude religious worship or on "Fifth Day Naturalists," if you will, but because of a state's interest in decency and safety. A religious exemption to the public nudity law could be sought, but it would be highly unlikely that a successful challenge to the ban could be made on First Amendment grounds. Among the questions that the Court might ask in this hypothetical case would be how important or compelling is the governmental interest of public decency. The Court might also ask if the ban on all public nudity is the least restrictive means of achieving the state's interest.

Although the Supreme Court has granted exemptions to conduct mandated or proscribed by government to "well-organized" sects, such as the Jehovah's Witnesses and the Amish, it has on balance been much more circumspect with free exercise claims made by individuals whose beliefs balance on the fine line between religion and personal philosophy.[1] For example, you would be more likely to succeed in challenging a selective service law if you are a Jehovah's Witness than if you are an adherent to the philosophy of nonviolence espoused by Gandhi. In assuming the role of balancing the constitutional claims of religious minorities and the will of the majority, the Court has also shouldered the burden of actually defining religion. In one of its earliest major decisions on the free exercise clause, *Davis v. Beason*, 133 U.S. 333 (1890), the Court defined religion broadly as "one's view of his relations to his Creator, and the obligations they impose." *Davis* sustained an Idaho territorial law disqualifying polygamists from voting. However, Justice Steven Field reasoned in no uncertain terms that definite limits could be placed on religious obligations and practices when those practices interfered with "the laws of society, designed to secure peace and prosperity, and the morals of its people."[2]

In granting religious exemptions from military service to conscientious objectors (COs), the Court has expanded Congress's definition of religion to include views that recognize a "supreme being," rather than "God," as the source or inspiration of beliefs against killing or war.[3] Yet this broad definition has rarely included the use of essentially philosophical, political, or sociological arguments for CO status. However, the Court has made exceptions for those whose views do not necessarily recognize a supreme being but who are religious in the ethical sense of the word. As Justice Black wrote:

> [E]xclusion of those persons [seeking exemption from military service] with "essentially political, sociological, or philosophical views or a merely personal moral code" should [not] be read to exclude those who hold strong beliefs about our domestic and foreign affairs or even those whose conscientious objection to participation in all wars is founded to a substantial extent upon considerations of public policy.[4]

The kinds of personal beliefs that do not fall within these definitions produce aversion to military service or war solely on, in Black's words, "policy, pragmatism, or expediency" rather than on religious, moral, or ethical principles.

*When are a state's actions to advance a legitimate governmental interest, such as safety, contrary to the protections afforded to citizens under the free exercise clause of the First Amendment? Must these actions be directly intended to curtail the effects of religiously motivated conduct in order to run afoul of our right to freely exercise religious beliefs?*  In 1959, a textile mill in Spartanburg, South Carolina, announced that for all three shifts working at the mill, the workweek would be increased to six days, including Saturdays. While most workers were pleased by the prospect of overtime pay, Mrs. Sherbert, a member of the Seventh-Day Adventist Church for more than two years, was upset with her employer for compelling her to work on her Sabbath. Upon hearing of her refusal to work on Saturdays, her employer discharged her. Since all of the other mills in the area required their employees to work a six-day workweek, Sherbert filed for unemployment benefits with the South Carolina Employment Security Commission. She made it clear to the commission that she would accept a job in another industry so long as she was not required to work on Saturdays. However, her claim for unemployment compensation was denied, since under an eligibility provision of the Unemployment Compensation Act she had failed to show good cause for not accepting "suitable work when offered." Ironically, had she been a Sunday worshiper, she would have been granted a statutory exemption from Sunday employment in the textile mills.

*Did the state's denial of benefits to Sherbert impose an unconstitutional burden on her freedom of religion?*  As counsel for the state of South Carolina argued, the state neither forbade her from practicing her beliefs nor directly compelled her to work on Saturdays. The statute did not single out any religious group, but was concerned merely with preventing abuses of the state's unemployment compensation system by individuals who were offered employment but were not willing to work. The question state officials posed was whether the state was obligated to tailor each of its statutes to the religious beliefs of individuals or groups, or whether the burden fell on the individual to bend in light of legitimate state interests.

The South Carolina Supreme Court sustained the commission's denial of unemployment benefits, rejecting Sherbert's argument that the unemployment act abridged her religious liberty. The court maintained that the statute was constitutional because it imposed no restrictions on either Sherbert's religious beliefs or her freedom to exercise those beliefs. On appeal in *Sherbert v. Verner*, 374 U.S. 398 (1963), the U.S. Supreme Court reversed the judgment of the lower court by a vote of 7–2 on the grounds that the statute violated the free exercise clause of the First Amendment as applied to the state through the Fourteenth Amendment. Writing for the majority, Justice Brennan recognized that while the state did not impose criminal sanctions on Sherbert to force her to work on Saturdays, her ineligibility for unemployment compensation was based solely on her religious practice. By its denial of benefits, the state pressured her to either abandon her religious beliefs or go hungry, which is no different than directly imposing a fine for worshiping on Saturday. Brennan wrote:

> [C]onditions upon public benefits cannot be sustained if they so operate, whatever their purpose, as to inhibit or deter the exercise of First Amendment freedoms. . . . [T]o condition the availability of benefits upon this appellant's willingness to violate a cardinal principle of her religious faith effectively penalizes the free exercise of her constitutional liberties.

***Doesn't the state have a legitimate interest in denying unemployment compensation to individuals who are given the opportunity to work but refuse to do so for religious reasons?*** The state asserted that by granting religious exemptions to the good cause eligibility provision of the law, the unemployment compensation fund could be depleted by "unscrupulous" individuals alleging religious objections to Saturday work or other kinds of employment conditions. But the Supreme Court found that the state's asserted interest was weak and not compelling enough to justify an infringement of Sherbert's religious liberty. Even if the unemployment insurance fund had been threatened by unscrupulous claims, the burden would still fall on the state to demonstrate that the eligibility provisions of the law were the least restrictive means of regulating the program. The state would have had to show that the fairness and financial integrity of the system could have been achieved only by these strict eligibility provisions. For example, two years earlier in *Braunfeld v. Brown*, 366 U.S. 599 (1961), the Court rejected a free exercise challenge to a Sunday closing law, or "blue law," brought by Orthodox Jewish merchants. Sunday is one of the busiest days for Orthodox Jewish merchants, and because their religious beliefs prohibit work on Saturday, the Sunday closing law seriously impaired their ability to earn a living. In essence, they were being punished for their religious beliefs. However, the Court rejected that argument and held that the state's interest in having one uniform day of rest for all workers justified the indirect burden on the Orthodox Jews. Unlike the unemployment law in *Sherbert*, the state's asserted interest in *Braunfeld* could be achieved only by declaring Sunday to be the day of rest. There was no least restrictive means available to the state in advancing its interest in a uniform day of rest.[5]

The tension between the two religious clauses of the First Amendment is evident in *Sherbert*. One might argue that by ordering the state to provide benefits to Sherbert, the Court ran afoul of the establishment clause by fostering the establishment of the Seventh-Day Adventist religion. Did the Sabbatarians receive benefits solely on the basis of their religious beliefs? If so, did the Court advance the interests of one religion over another? In defense of what he believed to be a neutral position, Brennan wrote:

> [F]or the extension of unemployment benefits to Sabbatarians in common with Sunday worshipers reflects nothing more than the government's obligation of neutrality in the face of religious differences, and does not represent that involvement of religious with secular institutions which it is the object of the establishment clause to forestall.

Justice Harlan, dissenting, was disturbed by what he believed to be the outright rejection of the two-year-old *Braunfeld* decision. Just like the Sunday closing law, the South Carolina unemployment insurance statute served a perfectly legitimate secular interest: to provide unemployment benefits to those who were involuntarily unemployed during periods when work was unavailable. There was no constitutional reason why the state had to provide benefits for those who became unavailable for work because of personal reasons. The fact that these personal reasons were based on religious beliefs was irrelevant to the state's application of the law, since the law was applied evenly and without regard to religious beliefs or practices. Adopting a very narrow interpretation of the free exercise clause, Harlan argued that the purpose of the clause is not to require the state to make exemptions to its laws on the basis of religious beliefs, but to guard against direct legal prohibitions imposed on religious beliefs or practices. By broadly interpreting the free exercise clause, the majority compels the state to breach the establishment clause by "singl[ing] out for financial assistance those whose behavior is religiously motivated, even though it denies such assistance to those whose identical behavior (in this case, inability to work on Saturdays) is not religiously motivated."

***Can a state compel all school-age children to attend school against the religious objections of their parents? How far must the state go in accommodating the religious beliefs of people who constitute a small percentage of the population?*** In a dispute involving a compulsory school attendance law, Jonas Yoder, a member of the Old Order Amish religion, refused to send his daughter to school beyond the eighth grade, believing that high school attendance was contrary to the Amish religion and way of life. The Amish objection to formal education is based on the view that high school tends to emphasize intellectual and scientific achievement, competitiveness, and worldly success, whereas the Amish way of life values goodness, simplicity, and learning through doing. The Amish have traditionally provided their children with a continuing religious-vocational education after eighth grade.

Wisconsin's compulsory school attendance law requires attendance until age sixteen regardless of the wishes of the child's parents. After school administrators learned of Yoder's actions, a complaint was filed, and the Green County Court found Yoder to be in violation of the state law. The Wisconsin Supreme Court reversed the conviction on the grounds that the state law violated Yoder's rights under the free exercise clause of the First Amendment, as applied to the states by the Fourteenth Amendment. Wisconsin sought review of that decision by the U.S. Supreme Court, arguing that compulsory attendance until age sixteen is a "reasonable and constitutional" means to advance the state's interest in universal education and that this interest overrode Yoder's right to freely practice his religious beliefs. The state cited, *Garber v. Kansas*, 389 U.S. 51, (1967), in which the Supreme Court rejected an Amish free exercise claim of a right to have their children totally exempted from compulsory education.

On appeal in *Wisconsin v. Yoder*, 406 U.S. 205 (1972), the Supreme Court sustained the state supreme court's ruling, arguing that the compulsory attendance law imposed an unconstitutional burden on Yoder, compelling the Amish to act in a manner inconsistent with the fundamental tenets of their religious beliefs. Because they do not draw a neat distinction between religious belief and practice, the Amish must honor a prescribed way of life in order to remain faithful to their religion. The Court found that the state seriously threatened to undermine the Amish religion because the law forced them to either abandon their beliefs and assimilate into society or move to a more tolerant state or region having no such laws.

The state also argued that the compulsory attendance law did not violate the free exercise clause because it did not regulate religious beliefs but merely conduct. In other words, belief in the tenets of the Amish religion was in no way restricted. The state maintained that religiously motivated actions, such as refusing to send a child to school, were placed outside the protection of the First Amendment. However, as it had in *Braunfeld* and *Sherbert*, the Court rejected this narrow interpretation of the free exercise clause. Although the behavior of individuals may be regulated in order to promote the health, safety, and general welfare of citizens, there are forms of conduct that *are* protected under the free exercise clause. As Justice Burger wrote: "This case, therefore, does not become easier because respondents were convicted for their 'actions' in refusing to send their children to the public high school; in this context belief and action cannot be neatly confined in logic-tight compartments."

Thus, conduct grounded in religious beliefs is exempt from regulation unless the state can demonstrate that such regulation advances state interests of the "highest order." What if the Amish were not educating their children at all or if the Amish community was losing members by attrition? Would the Court have ruled as it had? Burger's reasoning relied heavily on the facts that the Amish community provided an informal vocational education for its young people, that the Amish had existed as a law-abiding and "highly successful social unit" for 300 years, and that there was no evidence that upon leaving the fold the Amish children would become burdens on society. In light of these facts, it mattered little whether the child received an additional year or two of formal education.[6]

Suppose that an adherent of Henry David Thoreau's philosophy of self-reliance and rejection of contemporary social values sought an exemption to the Wisconsin compulsory attendance law. Would this person's claim be successful under *Yoder*? This scenario is highly unlikely since, according to Burger, the concept of religious liberty contained in the First Amendment does not protect philosophical or personal beliefs. Such beliefs, or conduct following from such beliefs, must be based on long-held religious convictions and shared by an organized group.

What if the child wishes to leave her simple life with the Amish and practice another religion or no religion whatsoever? Does the child have the same degree of religious liberty as her parents? Justice Douglas, who dissented in part, believed that by allowing Yoder a religious exemption to the law, the Court had allowed the parent to impose his beliefs on the child without regard to the child's religious liberty. While Yoder's daughter had testified that she did not want to attend high school, Douglas felt that the other Amish children affected by the Court's decision might want to attend high school against their parents' wishes. The Court had already recognized in *In re Gault*, 387 U.S. 1 (1967), that "neither the Fourteenth Amendment nor the Bill of Rights is for adults alone"; and in *In re Winship*, 397 U.S. 358 (1970), that a twelve-year-old boy was protected by the Sixth Amendment. In *Yoder*, Douglas wrote: "While the parents, absent dissent, normally speak for the entire family, the education of the child is a matter on which the child will often have decided views. He may want to be a pianist or an astronaut or an oceanographer. To do so he will have to break from the Amish tradition."

Eighteen years after *Sherbert*, the Burger Court granted certiorari to hear *Thomas v. Indiana Employment Security Review Board*, 450 U.S. 707 (1981), an appeal from a lower court action involving a free exercise challenge to another state unemployment compensation policy. However, in this instance, the free exercise claimant was not fired from his position, but voluntarily terminated his employment when his work became objectionable to his religious convictions.

Thomas, a Jehovah's Witness, was hired by the Blaw-Knox Foundry and Machinery Company. He was informed that the foundry, which rolled sheet steel for a variety of uses, would be closed and that he would be transferred to a division of the company responsible for manufacturing military tank turrets. Since Thomas found it religiously objectionable to build weapons, he pleaded for a transfer to a division that did not produce armaments. Informed that all other departments were engaged in weapons manufacture, Thomas asked for a layoff so that he could collect unemployment compensation while looking for a new job. When his request was denied, he left the company on the grounds that his religious beliefs would not permit him to build weapons of war.

The Indiana Employment Security Review Board rejected Thomas's application for unemployment compensation, stating that his reasons for quitting were not based on a "good cause [arising] in connection with [his] work" as required by state law. A state appellate court, however, reversed and ordered the board to grant Thomas his benefits on the grounds that by failing to do so the state placed an unconstitutional burden on his free exercise of religious beliefs. Thomas's hopes were dashed, however, when the Indiana Supreme Court overturned the lower court's ruling. Counsel for Indiana hoped that the Burger Court would reexamine the Warren Court's reasoning in *Sherbert* and evaluate the policy from the standpoint of a much narrower interpretation of the free exercise clause.

The U.S. Supreme Court ruled 8–1 to overturn the Indiana Supreme Court's denial of benefits, raising four questions in examining the case: (1) Was Thomas's decision to quit based on religious beliefs or on a personal philosophical choice? (2) Was the board's policy an unconstitutional infringement of Thomas's freedom of religion? (3) Did the state's interest in maintaining the financial integrity of the insurance fund outweigh the burden placed on Thomas's religious freedoms? (4) More broadly, does the policy of compensating an individual who quit his job for religious reasons violate the establishment clause?

Citing *Sherbert* and *Yoder*, Chief Justice Burger disputed the Indiana Supreme Court's contention that Thomas's aversion to war was based solely on philosophical rather than religious beliefs. Counsel for Indiana had raised doubts about Thomas's understanding of the tenets of his faith. Evidently, Thomas had great difficulty articulating his beliefs and his testimony was riddled with contradiction. He had testified that he would not object to producing the raw materials necessary for weapons but that his religious convictions clearly forbade him from building the actual weapons. The Indiana high court found this testimony to be contradictory. Furthermore, on his application for employment, Thomas indicated that he was a member of the Jehovah's Witnesses but denied that he had an aversion to any particular kind of work. Counsel for the state also pointed out that since another member of the Jehovah's Witnesses at the factory had no objections to working on tank turrets, it was really not "scripturally" unacceptable for Thomas to work on military equipment at the factory. The Indiana court had therefore concluded that Thomas's aversion to his work was based not on established religious tenets but on personal philosophical beliefs.

Chief Justice Burger reasoned that while it was within the power of the state court to determine whether Thomas's beliefs were rooted in a coherent religious doctrine and whether he had lived by those beliefs prior to the incident at the foundry, the state supreme court had erred by employing a "microscopic examination" of Thomas's beliefs. Burger also discounted the state's "[i]ntrafaith differences" argument that was employed to attack the credibility of Thomas's convictions. Thomas had adequately demonstrated "an honest conviction that such work was forbidden by his religion." Burger wrote: "Courts should not undertake to dissect religious beliefs because the believer admits that he is 'struggling' with his position or because his beliefs are not articulated with the clarity and precision that a more sophisticated person might employ."

*Is there, then, an established formula by which to determine what constitutes a religious belief?*    According to Burger, since religious beliefs need not be "acceptable, logical, consistent, or comprehensible," religious liberty claims must be examined on a case-by-case basis guided by precedent. The Court gives us only the following rule: In order to be entitled to protection under the free exercise clause, an individual must show an "honest conviction" that an activity is forbidden by the religion. In short, claimants whose beliefs are "bizarre" or "clearly nonreligious in motivation" need not apply.

A direct restriction on Thomas's religious beliefs was not imposed nor was he compelled to act in a manner contrary to his conscience. The government did not conscript Thomas into military service, nor did it directly prohibit Jehovah's Witnesses from collecting unemployment compensation. However, Burger reasoned that because Thomas knew that he would not receive unemployment insurance if he quit for religious reasons, it put pressure on him to hedge or sidestep the teachings of his faith in order to keep his job at the factory. The state's action forced him to choose between fidelity to his beliefs and being unemployed and without income. Burger wrote: "Where the state conditions receipt of an important benefit upon conduct proscribed by a religious faith, or where it denies such a benefit because of conduct mandated by religious belief, thereby putting substantial pressure on an adherent to modify his behavior and to violate his beliefs, a burden upon religion exists."

To help us understand the problem, suppose that Ezekiel, who is also a Jehovah's Witness, decides to attend college after leaving the armaments factory and applies for a federally insured student loan to cover the cost of his tuition. Further suppose that the student loan is contingent on his signing an affidavit swearing allegiance to the United States. If Ezekiel refuses, he forfeits his chance of attending college. If he complies, he acts against his faith's prohibition against swearing oaths or worshiping graven images. Does this policy violate the free exercise of religious beliefs? Are the ethical and legal issues in Ezekiel's case comparable to those in *Thomas*?

Indiana also argued that *Sherbert* did not apply to Thomas's case because unlike Sherbert, who was fired after refusing to work on Saturdays, Thomas voluntarily resigned after finding his new responsibilities objectionable. The Supreme Court, however, found little difference between the cases, for in both instances the termination of employment occurred after the position became "religiously objectionable." In other words, when Sherbert and Thomas took their respective jobs, the terms or conditions of employment were not hostile to their religious beliefs. It was only later, once employed, that their jobs became religiously objectionable.

What if large numbers of workers quit their jobs for religious reasons at a time when a record number of steelworkers were already unemployed? Didn't Indiana's interest in preventing the depletion of the insurance fund outweigh the indirect burden placed on religious freedom? While the state does have a legitimate interest in maintaining the fairness and financial integrity of any of its programs, it must use the least restrictive means of carrying out a compelling state interest when a fundamental freedom such as religious liberty is affected. In other words, the state could have maintained the financial integrity of its unemployment insurance program without refusing to grant exemptions to the handful of workers who voluntarily left their jobs for legitimate religious reasons. Since there was no real threat of hundreds of petitions for religious exemptions, the state could not justify its actions on grounds that one exemption would threaten the solvency of the system. As the Court said in *Yoder*, only state interests of the highest order can balance out legitimate claims of religious freedom. Burger wrote: "Neither of the interests advanced is sufficiently compelling to justify the burden upon Thomas's religious liberty. Accordingly, Thomas is entitled to receive benefits unless, as . . . the Indiana court held, such payment would violate the establishment clause."

While many heralded *Thomas* as a just decision, Justice Rehnquist immediately pointed out that by ruling for the Jehovah's Witness, the Court had run afoul of the establishment clause. Is the Court fostering a religion by ordering the state to provide unemployment benefits to Thomas, or is it remaining neutral, as Burger contended, and neither fostering nor inhibiting? If it does nothing, the state violates religious liberty. If it protects religious liberty, it grants a material benefit to an individual on the basis of religious beliefs, thus entangling government and religion. Burger recognized this dilemma as an inevitable result of the tension between the free exercise and establishment clauses, but made no attempt to resolve it.

Justice Rehnquist, on the other hand, reasoned that the tension was not natural or inevitable, but largely a product of the Court's misinterpretation of the two religious clauses. The Court had interpreted free exercise more broadly than the framers had intended. In doing so, contrary to the its purported "neutrality" in *Thomas*, the Court had constitutionally required Indiana to provide financial assistance to an individual "solely on the basis of his religious beliefs," thus violating the establishment clause. Rehnquist adopted a narrower, more literal interpretation of the free exercise clause, much like that employed by the Warren Court prior to *Sherbert* in *Braunfeld*. For Rehnquist, the free exercise clause applies only to laws that make religious practices unlawful. Indiana did not deny benefits to Thomas because he was a Jehovah's Witness, but merely enacted a generally applicable law aimed at achieving a compelling governmental interest. The law did not proscribe religion, but simply made it a bit more expensive to practice one's religious beliefs in a manner unfettered from all legitimate social interests. According to Rehnquist, the free exercise clause does not prohibit legislatures from imposing an indirect burden on the exercise of religion as long as the law does not prohibit the religious practice itself. The free exercise clause does not require the government to conform each law to the religious views of any group or individual. Rehnquist wrote: "I believe that although a State could choose to grant religious exemptions to religious persons from state unemployment regulations, a State is not constitutionally compelled to do so."

In order to live in society one must often subordinate the need to engage in religiously motivated conduct to the needs of the majority. Society cannot be expected to conform itself to the religious beliefs of each of its members.

## A Narrowing Interpretation of the Free Exercise Clause

By the time President Reagan elevated William Rehnquist to chief justice in 1986, a new conservative voting bloc composed of Justices Rehnquist, O'Connor, and Scalia was already coalescing. Consequently, Rehnquist's narrow interpretivist and original intent theories were no longer merely those of a lone dissenter, but of a leader who could potentially mold a new conservative bloc of justices. Under this leadership, the Court could reassess whether there are circumstances or governmental interests that outweigh an individual's religious freedom. This reassessment of constitutional theory surfaced in *Goldman v. Weinberger*, 475 U.S. 503 (1986), where the Rehnquist Court ruled 5–4 that the First Amendment does not prohibit the U.S. Air Force from restricting the wearing of religious apparel as a form of worship or devotion. The case originated when S. Simcha Goldman, an officer and clinical psychologist at March Air Force Base in Riverside, California, refused to remove his yarmulke while on duty. For Goldman, who is an Orthodox Jew and ordained rabbi, it is a sin not to cover his head in the presence of God. For years, Goldman avoided controversy by wearing his service cap over the yarmulke when he left the mental health clinic to walk across the base. However, after he was observed wearing his yarmulke in a courtroom while testifying as a witness for the defense in a court-martial, a complaint was filed by another officer, and Goldman was found to be in violation of an Air Force regulation (AFR 35–10) prohibiting the wearing of head-gear indoors except by armed security police.[7] After being informed of an imminent court-martial, Goldman sued Secretary of Defense Caspar Weinberger and others, charging that by prohibiting the wearing of a yarmulke, the Air Force had violated his freedom to exercise his religious beliefs. The District Court for the District of Columbia ruled for Goldman, but the District of Columbia Circuit Court reversed on the grounds that the regulation served a legitimate military interest in discipline out-weighing Goldman's right to wear the yarmulke while in uniform. Goldman argued that the regulation should be examined under *Sherbert, Yoder*, and *Thomas* because it prohibited religiously motivated conduct, but the Supreme Court rejected this argument outright, citing numerous rulings in which the Court recognized that the "military is, by necessity, a specialized society separate from civilian society."[8]

Indeed, the Court has traditionally used a more deferential standard of judicial review when examining constitutional challenges to military regulations as opposed to similar regulations or statutes in civilian society. In other words, when constitu-tional challenges are brought against military regulations or congressional action concerning national security, such as the draft, the Court is more likely to apply a balancing of interests approach than a strict scrutiny approach to the regulation or law. As Chief Justice Rehnquist pronounced: "Our review of military regulations challenged on First Amendment grounds is far more deferential than constitutional review of similar laws or regulations designed for civilian society. The military need not encourage debate or tolerate protest to the extent that such tolerance is required of the civilian state by the first Amendment."

It is not that the individual in the military has no First Amendment rights, but that those rights must be balanced with and occasionally subordinated to the military values of obedience, discipline, and commitment. Five years earlier the Court had used such judicial deference in upholding the present system of draft registration in *Rostker v. Goldberg*, 453 U.S. 57 (1981).[9]

As an officer, Goldman recognized the need for a uniform dress code, but he took exception to the Air Force's reasoning that his religious headgear posed a threat to discipline and esprit de corps. He testified that his yarmulke was a familiar sight that had never caused a disruption or breach of decorum. In fact, the Air Force already had several exceptions to accommodate certain pieces of religious jewelry and hairstyles. Yarmulkes were permitted to be worn indoors for on-base religious services. Goldman was even willing to wear whatever color yarmulke the Air Force desired. Since the yarmulke posed no clear danger of undermining military values, he believed the free exercise clause required the Air Force to make an exception to its regulation against wearing headgear indoors. By refusing to do so, the Air Force was making Goldman choose between his duty as an officer and his obligations to his religion. Nevertheless, the majority was intractable in its support of the Air Force's prohibition of visible religious apparel. The Court ruled that while the Air

Force could not directly place restrictions on Goldman's beliefs, it could prohibit certain forms of religious conduct associated with his religion if that conduct interfered with legitimate military interests.

When constitutional challenges are brought against military regulations or congressional action concerning national security, the Court is more willing to defer to the professional judgment of the military and intelligence establishment. Nevertheless, we can still ask whether the Court was too deferent to the Air Force in this instance. Justice Brennan, joined by Justice Marshall, strongly dissented against the Court's "abdicat[ion]" of its role as guardian of the Bill of Rights. Brennan believed that the majority had gone far beyond the Court's tradition of upholding the military's need to limit certain liberties, completely abdicating its obligation to review the constitutionality of governmental actions. In doing so, the Court adopted what Brennan called a "subrational-basis standard" of judicial review: an absolute uncritical deference to the military's discretion to rule on the constitutionality of its own regulations. He reasoned:

> A deferential standard of review, however, need not, and should not, mean that the Court must credit arguments that defy common sense. When a military service burdens the free exercise rights of its members in the name of necessity, it must provide, as an initial matter and at minimum, a *credible* explanation of how the contested practice is likely to interfere with the protected military interest. Unabashed *ipse dixit* cannot outweigh a constitutional right. [emphasis added.]

According to Brennan, the Court simply accepted the word of military authorities without providing any explanation of how Goldman's conduct threatened Air Force interests. There was no evidence that there would have been a complete breakdown of discipline and military preparedness if Goldman and other Orthodox Jews were permitted to wear their yarmulkes. The Air Force offered no legitimate reason an exception to Goldman could not be granted. Curiously, the Air Force's interest in conformity did not go so far as to bar religious and cultural differences from being expressed on base. Personnel were allowed to express their religious beliefs by attending on-base services and by wearing nonuniform religious jewelry while on duty, so there was no attempt to conceal the religious or cultural differences among Air Force personnel. In addition, the yarmulke did not fall into that category of dress or appearance that could cause problems on the battlefield. Thus, the dissenters found it unusual that the Air Force could give no rational reason for its prohibition of yarmulkes, and stranger still that the Court asked for no explanation.

Brennan's closing comments cut to the heart of the concerns expressed by those who are apprehensive of the Rehnquist Court's predilection for judicial restraint in such cases. Brennan wrote that while guardianship of religious liberty is not the exclusive domain of the federal courts,

> [o]ur Nation has preserved freedom of religion, not through trusting to the good faith of individual agencies of government alone, but through the constitutionally mandated vigilant oversight and checking authority of the judiciary.
>
> A critical function of the religion clauses of the First Amendment is to protect the rights of members of minority religions against quiet erosion by majoritarian

social institutions that dismiss minority beliefs and practices as unimportant, because unfamiliar. *It is the constitutional role of this Court to ensure that this purpose of the First Amendment be realized* [emphasis added].

Justice O'Connor, who has been a moderate voice in many opinions, also attacked the majority's complete deference to the prerogatives of military doctrine. In her dissenting opinion, she was very disturbed by the majority's outright rejection of Goldman's appeal without even the slightest attempt to apply or develop a standard or rule for determining when military interests outweigh religious liberty. For example, in *Yoder*, the Court ruled that only interests of the highest order can outweigh legitimate claims to free exercise of religion. In *United States v. Lee*, 455 U.S. 252 (1982), the Court stated that a restriction on religious liberty is justified if it is "essential to accomplish an overriding governmental interest." But in *Goldman*, the Court did not apply these standards, or any others, to review the Air Force's actions.

While it is true that the Court has long recognized that upon joining the military an individual must willingly subordinate many personal interests to esprit de corps and discipline, it has also ruled that military personnel are still citizens and thus do not give up their fundamental rights merely because they are in uniform (*Chappell v. Wallace*, 462 U.S. 296 [1983]). Brennan believed that Goldman was not merely inconvenienced by the regulation, he was barred from fulfilling part of his religious obligation. While mere personal preferences in dress are not constitutionally protected, the free exercise clause prohibits the government from punishing an adherent to a faith for wearing an item of dress that is central to the practice of that religion.

## The Use of Illegal Drugs as a Religious Practice

When President George H. W. Bush declared a war on drugs shortly after assuming office in 1989, many states adopted a "zero tolerance" approach in drafting new laws or enforcing existing controlled substance statutes. In light of society's heightened awareness of the drug problem, it was no surprise when a number of religious practices involving the use of marijuana and peyote came under attack in state legislatures. With the exception of the religious use of peyote by Native Americans in some states, no religious sects or organizations have been exempted from controlled substance laws on religious grounds.[10]

***Can members of particular religions be granted immunity from prosecution under drug laws on the grounds that such laws violate their religious liberty?***
The U.S. Supreme Court addressed this issue in *Employment Division, Department of Human Resources v. Smith*, 494 U.S. 872 (1990). Alfred Smith and Galen Black were fired from their jobs at a private drug rehabilitation center in Oregon after it was discovered that they had used peyote at a ceremony at the Native American Church. Peyote, a hallucinogenic plant, is a traditional sacrament of the Native American Church. Using the hallucinogenic cactus is considered an act of worship and communion because it is believed that the Great Spirit is embodied in the plant. Smith and Black were denied unemployment benefits by the Employment Division of Oregon's Department of Human Resources because they were terminated for

work-related "misconduct" and for violating state drug laws. They then challenged the state's action on the grounds that the free exercise clause prohibited applying Oregon's drug laws to the ceremonial use of peyote.

Citing *Sherbert* and *Thomas*, the Oregon Supreme Court reasoned that since the ceremonial ingestion of peyote is protected by the free exercise clause, unemployment compensation should not be denied to Smith and Black. However, the U.S. Supreme Court reversed the Oregon court's decision, ruling that the free exercise clause neither prohibited the state from applying its drug laws to the sacramental use of peyote nor from denying unemployment benefits to those fired for using the drug. Writing for the 6–3 majority, Justice Scalia reasoned that although Oregon is constitutionally prohibited from banning conduct solely because it is religiously motivated, the state may forbid conduct that is an expression of a religious belief if the law does not directly target the religious practice and is applied evenly to those who commit the same activity for nonreligious reasons. In other words, there was nothing in the controlled substance statute that was directed specifically at members of the Native American Church; it just so happened that the activities of the Native Americans fell within the scope of the controlled substance law.

Scalia rejected the argument that the state was "prohibiting the free exercise of religion" by requiring Smith and Black to obey a law that forbade conduct that their religion requires. In doing so, he adopted a narrow view of the free exercise clause much like that espoused by Chief Justice Rehnquist. Scalia wrote:

> As a textual matter, we do not think the words must be given that meaning. It is no more necessary to regard the collection of a general tax, for example, as "prohibiting the free exercise [of religion]" by those citizens who believe support of organized government to be sinful, than it is to regard the same tax as "abridging the freedom . . . of the press" of those publishing companies that must pay tax as a condition of staying in business.

Thus, for Scalia the objective of the criminal statute is not to restrict religion but to carry out a legitimate state interest, and the restriction on Smith and Black's religion was only incidental, not direct. Scalia went all the way back to Justice Frankfurter's argument in *Minersville v. Gobitis* to support his reasoning. (In *Gobitis*, Frankfurter vigorously denied that the "mere possession of religious convictions" exempts an individual from civic responsibilities.) Scalia also relied on *United States v. Lee*, where the Court rejected an Amish businessman's request for a religious exemption from the collection and payment of Social Security taxes. In that case, Chief Justice Burger argued that religious liberty may be limited when the state can show that such limitation is essential to an overriding governmental interest. If religious groups were permitted to exempt themselves from paying taxes because they objected to the way their tax dollars were spent, the entire tax system would eventually crumble.

Scalia indicated that he would have been more willing to apply a stricter level of scrutiny to the neutral and generally applicable law in *Smith* only if the asserted free exercise claim had been connected with a freedom of expression claim. For example, in *Cantwell v. Connecticut*, 310 U.S. 296 (1940), the Court employed a combination free exercise and freedom of speech argument to overturn a licensing policy for religious and charitable organizations that allowed officials to use their discretionary authority to deny a license to a group they deemed nonreligious. Similarly, in *Wooley v. Maynard*, 430 U.S. 705 (1977), the Court invalidated the state-compelled display of a motto that offended religious beliefs.[11] But unlike hybrid cases that combine free exercise claims with freedom of expression issues, Oregon's controlled substance law was held to be constitutional because it made no attempt to regulate religious expression or compel either ideas or behavior offensive to religion.

Surprisingly, Scalia refused to apply *Sherbert* and *Thomas* in evaluating the Oregon law even though the Court had applied the two precedents just four years earlier in *Bowen v. Roy*, 476 U.S. 693 (1986). In *Bowen*, the Court ruled 5–4 to exempt the parents of a Native American girl from a federal unemployment compensation requirement that she provide her Social Security number on her application for benefits. Justice O'Connor reasoned that granting a religious exemption to the girl and to the "handful of others" who might apply would not undermine the government's ability to combat welfare fraud. The Court also applied *Sherbert* in *Hobbie v. Unemployment Appeals Commission*, 480 U.S. 136 (1987), where it found that even though Hobbie became a Sabbatarian during the course of her employment, the state's refusal to grant unemployment insurance benefits constituted an undue burden on her religious freedom.

Scalia's reluctance to apply *Sherbert* and *Thomas* in *Smith* may be explained by the fact that the Court was asked to make an exception to a criminal law. He did not believe he was departing from established precedent because the Court had never applied *Sherbert* to grant a religious exemption outside the area of unemployment compensation, much less to grant an exemption to a criminal law. He noted that the Court had declined to apply *Sherbert* in *Lyng v. Northwest Indian Cemetery Protective Association*, 485 U.S. 439 (1988), to block the government's logging of timber in a portion of a national forest that traditionally had been used for religious worship by several Native American tribes. Thus, in *Smith* he reasoned that because the ingestion of peyote was prohibited under Oregon law, and because an exemption would undermine Oregon's compelling interest in prohibiting possession and trafficking of peyote, the free exercise clause did not prohibit Oregon from denying unemployment compensation when a dismissal resulted from the illegal use of a controlled substance.

Justice O'Connor, who agreed with the judgment of the Court but not with Scalia's reasoning, argued that the Court's decision is indeed a dramatic break from established precedent because it allowed Oregon to prohibit religiously motivated conduct by simply showing that the law was applicable to all citizens.[12] The rule from which Scalia deviated was the compelling interest test. That test, set forth in a long string of cases—including *Thomas, Yoder*, and *Sherbert*—requires the government to justify any substantial incursion on religiously motivated conduct by showing that it has a clear and compelling interest and that this interest is achieved by means that are narrowly drawn to achieve only those interests.

O'Connor attacked what she saw as a fallacy in the Court's argument. Scalia reasoned that the Oregon law was constitutional because it was a generally applicable law that only incidentally or indirectly placed a burden on religious liberty, and implied that the free exercise clause was intended to prohibit only direct restrictions on religious practice. O'Connor strongly disagreed and wrote:

> The Court responds that generally applicable laws are "one large step" removed from laws aimed at specific religious practices. The First Amendment, however, does not distinguish between laws that are generally applicable and laws that target particular religious practices. *Indeed, few States would be so naive as to enact a law directly prohibiting or burdening a religious practice as such* [emphasis added].

According to Justice Blackmun, who was joined by Justices Brennan and Marshall in his dissent, Scalia's interpretation of free exercise doctrine was "distorted." The three dissenters concurred with O'Connor, but added that the majority demonstrated a "distorted view of our precedents" by refusing to apply the free exercise clause to criminal prohibitions that infringe upon religious conduct. The majority limited the application of *Sherbert* to only those cases involving governmental "conditions on the receipt of benefits." In doing so, Blackmun believed that the Court wrought a complete reversal of precedent by "effectuat[ing] a wholesale overturning of settled law concerning the religion clauses of our Constitution. One hopes that the Court is aware of the consequences, and that its result is not a product of overreaction to the serious problems the country's drug crisis has generated."

Was the state's interest in enforcing the ban on peyote legitimate, or was it merely a symbolic overreaction and not based on any real threat to undermine the state's war on drugs? In order for a state's interest to outweigh a free exercise claim, it must be shown that the religious exemption would in some way threaten the state's antidrug program. In other words, the state cannot balance a preferred freedom, such as religious liberty, with an abstract policy goal—the countervailing interest must be a real threat of widespread drug use. Testimony in *Smith* showed that there was no such threat; in fact, the state had made no attempt to enforce the law against the Native Americans, peyote was not even classified as a dangerous drug by the federal government, and twenty-three states and the federal government have religious exemptions in their drug laws for peyote.[13] If Oregon's interest in enforcing its drug laws was not sufficient to outweigh free exercise claims, then it was unconstitutional to deny unemployment benefits because of religiously motivated "misconduct."

## Animal Sacrifice as Religious Conduct

In its first major free exercise case after *Smith*, the city of Hialeah, Florida, asked the Court to uphold a ban on animal sacrifices by the Church of the Lukumi Babalu Aye. The church, which practices the Santeria faith, sacrificed chickens, pigeons, doves, ducks, guinea pigs, goats, sheep, and turtles to mark special occasions, such as births, marriages, and deaths. After the animals throats are cut, they are cooked and eaten. The Santeria faith, which combines African beliefs with Catholicism, originated in the people of eastern African who were brought as slaves to the islands of Caribbean region.

The city of Hialeah passed several ordinances prohibiting animal sacrifices, "expressing concern over religious practices inconsistent with public morals, peace, or safety." The ordinances defined a sacrifice as the unnecessary and ritualistic killing of animals not for the primary purpose for food consumption.

The church argued that the city ordinances violated the First Amendment's guarantee of freedom of religion. A federal district court and a court of appeals upheld the ordinances, and the church attorneys appealed to the U.S. Supreme Court. In *Church of the Lukumi Babalu Aye v. City of Hialeah*, 508 U.S. 520 (1993), a unanimous Court struck down the ordinances on the grounds that the city council had acted expressly to restrict the practices of one religious group. Under *Smith*, a law that is neutral and of general applicability need not be justified by a compelling governmental interest even if the law has the incidental effect of burdening a particular religious practice. However, the Hialeah ordinances were neither neutral nor generally applicable. Because the ordinances used the words "sacrifice" and "ritual," it was obvious that they targeted those of the Santeria faith. The interest in protecting the public health and preventing cruelty to animals must be advanced in a neutral manner using means that are the least restrictive on religious expression.

This does not mean that the city is prohibited from passing animal cruelty laws. It means only that the city must find a way of protecting animals without classifying or burdening particular religious practices. Justice Kennedy concluded: "A law burdening religious practice that is not neutral or not of general application must undergo the most rigorous of scrutiny. To satisfy the commands of the First Amendment, a law restrictive of religious practice must advance 'interests of the highest order' and must be narrowly tailored."

The *Lukumi Babalu* ruling was clearly supportive of religious liberty, but many members of Congress did not approve of the Court's cramped interpretation of the free exercise clause in *Smith*. In a direct attempt to overturn *Smith* and return to the *Sherbert* test in free exercise doctrine, Congress enacted the Religious Freedom Restoration Act (RFRA) of 1993,[14] which prohibits the government from substantially burdening a person's exercise of religion even if the burden results from a generally applicable law. Restrictions on religious liberty are allowed only if the government can demonstrate that the burden advances a compelling interest and is the least restrictive means of furthering that interest. Congress passed RFRA using its Fourteenth Amendment power to enforce provisions of the Constitution—in this case the free exercise clause of the First Amendment.

However, the constitutionality of RFRA was challenged after the city of Boerne, Texas, denied the Catholic archbishop of San Antonio a building permit to enlarge a historic church. The archbishop challenged the permit denial under RFRA, arguing that his religious freedom outweighed a city ordinance governing the preservation of historic structures. A federal district court concluded that RFRA was unconstitutional, but the circuit court of appeals reversed.

On appeal in *City of Boerne v. Flores*, 521 U.S. 507 (1997), the Supreme Court ruled that Congress had impermissibly rewritten free exercise jurisprudence and had exceeded its power to enforce the First Amendment. Writing for the majority, Justice Kennedy argued that congressional enforcement legislation must be remedial in nature. Legislation that deters or remedies specific constitutional violations by the states falls within Congress's Fourteenth Amendment enforcement power even "if in the process it prohibits conduct which is not itself unconstitutional and intrudes into legislative spheres of autonomy previously reserved to the States." However, in enacting RFRA, Congress used its enforcement power to make substantive changes in the Constitution, thus altering the Court's ability to say what the free exercise clause means. In other words, Congress was not successful in returning to the compelling interest test in *Sherbert*. *Smith*, and its rules of general applicability and neutrality, would stand, making it easier for the government to place indirect restrictions on religious conduct if such conduct runs afoul of the law.

## THE ESTABLISHMENT CLAUSE AND STATE-SPONSORED RELIGION

### The Wall of Separation

The establishment clause of the First Amendment was forged in the fires of religious persecution and government-controlled religion in England and colonial America. In the sixteenth century, the English Parliament promulgated the Book of Common Prayer, which outlined the required form and content of prayer to be used by the Church of England. Though the nature of the prayers varied from time to time, they largely depended on whatever factions wielded the most control over lawmakers. Many adherents to minority religions, persecuted and denied access to power, fled to the American colonies to escape state-established religion or religion in general.[15]

In 1776, eight of the thirteen newly independent American states had established state churches, while four had governmentally sanctioned religions. However, this practice did not persist for long after the Revolution, as minority religious groups—including Presbyterians, Lutherans, Quakers, and Baptists—gained sufficient political clout to successfully challenge these traditions. With the wisdom and stewardship of James Madison and Thomas Jefferson, this movement for greater tolerance and against religious establishment culminated in the Virginia Bill for Religious Liberty and similar laws enacted throughout the states. The First Amendment, ratified in 1791, was framed with the purpose of prohibiting the federal government from using its power to support, influence, or regulate prayer. Expanding on this principle, Jefferson and Madison advocated the construction of a constitutional wall of separation between church and state to preserve the integrity of both religious liberty and democratic government. The ultimate result of this movement was the establishment clause of the First Amendment.[16]

By no stretch of the imagination did controversy end when the First Amendment was ratified. Notwithstanding the intent of the framers—and not yet affected by the eventual application of the First Amendment to state action—the states routinely accommodated Christianity by adorning public symbols with religious allusions, employing public chaplains, and infusing religious imagery in public pronouncements and laws. As the public school system emerged, religious leaders regularly affected curriculum decisions and the hiring and firing of teachers on the basis of religious orthodoxy.

While the establishment clause barred the federal government from establishing religion, the states were constitutionally free to do so until *Everson v. Board of Education*, 330 U.S. 1 (1947).[17] Although *Everson* did not strike down the practice of reimbursing private religious schools for transporting students to and from school, the Supreme Court recognized for the first time that the establishment clause applied to the states through the Fourteenth Amendment and was intended to erect a wall of separation between church and state that "must be kept high and impregnable." In *Everson*, Justice Black reasoned that the New Jersey law did not breach that wall because it served a neutral purpose: It paid the bus fares of parochial school students as part of a general program covering the transportation costs of all children attending school in New Jersey. However, Black asserted that no tax can be levied to support any religious activity or instruction, nor can a religious organization participate in the public policy-making process. Invoking the spirit of Jefferson and Madison, Black adopted a broad interpretation of establishment. He wrote:

> Neither a state nor the Federal Government can set up a church. Neither can pass laws which aid one religion, aid all religions, or prefer one religion over another. Neither can force nor influence nor influence a person to go or to remain away from church against his will or force him to profess a belief or disbelief in any religion. . . . No tax in any amount, large or small, can be levied to support any religious activities or institutions, whatever they be called, or whatever form they may adopt to teach or practice religion.

## School Prayer

Justice Black's pronouncement in *Everson* casts doubt on the constitutionality of the long tradition of compulsory prayer and Bible reading in public schools. With the growing diversity of American society and expanding public school enrollments following World War II, government officials were under increasing pressure to limit the amount of religious activity in the classroom. A number of lawsuits in the lower courts were forcing school boards to provide students with exemptions to morning prayers and to adopt only nondenominational prayers and hymns.

In 1962, the Supreme Court handed down a ruling on school prayer that was destined to generate much more controversy than its rulings on state aid and tax credits to parochial schools. It is safe to say that more Americans have felt the effect of *Engel v. Vitale*, 370 U.S. 421, than any other church/state case. As in the Court's desegregation ruling in *Brown v. Board of Education*, its ruling in *Engel* had a direct impact on a social practice: It affected how communities could educate and socialize their children. Also like *Brown*, the ruling in *Engel* placed the Court itself on trial and drew angry promises of noncompliance from citizens and government officials. The ruling was effectively implemented only after a long string of school prayer and moment-of-silence cases. As many studies and anecdotes testify, large-scale resistance to *Engel* continued well into the 1970s and pockets of noncompliance continue in the twenty-first century.[18]

*Engel* originated when the New Hyde Park, New York Union Free School District ordered principals to direct all students to recite a nondenominational prayer at the beginning of each school day. The prayer was to be said aloud in the presence of a teacher: "Almighty God, we acknowledge our dependence upon Thee, and we beg Thy blessings upon us, our parents, our teachers, and our Country."

The policy was ordered by the New York State Board of Regents, a governmental agency possessing broad administrative powers over New York's public schools. The prayer, which was composed by the regents, was part of a policy intended to promote moral and spiritual training in the public schools. While the rule mandated the reading of the prayer, it stipulated: "Neither teachers nor any school authority shall comment on participation or nonparticipation." There was also a provision for excusing children from the room while the prayer was being recited. Furthermore, there was no record of any coercion or social ostracism of children.

Soon after the first prayer was uttered by the students of Hyde Park, Steven Engel and ten other parents of pupils enrolled in the school challenged the constitutionality of the state law that authorized the prayer and the action taken by William Vitale and other members of the board of regents to implement the policy. Engel and the other parents argued that the use of prayer in public schools violated the First Amendment prohibition on Congress from establishing religion and that this prohibition of government-sponsored religion was applicable to state action through the Fourteenth Amendment.

*Did the prayer constitute an establishment of religion in the historical and narrow meaning of those words?* If it did not, could a successful free exercise claim be brought against the state if it was shown that students were compelled to recite the prayer under threat of punishment?

The New York high court ruled that the practice was constitutional as long as the schools did not coerce or compel students to pray against their will or over their parents' objection. The state court insisted that the board of education devise a procedure to exempt those who did not care to pray and to protect them against "embarrassments and pressures." However, the U.S. Supreme Court voted 6–1 to overturn the state court's ruling, finding the regents' prayer to be a state-sponsored religious activity "wholly inconsistent" with the establishment clause. Writing for the majority, Justice Black argued that the state law authorizing the use of the board of regents' prayer violated the establishment clause because it was composed by governmental officials for the sole purpose of fostering religious beliefs. This practice, wrote Black, breached the constitutional wall between church and state: "[W]e think that the constitutional prohibition against laws respecting an establishment of religion must at least mean that in this country it is no business of government to compose official prayers for any group of the American people to recite as a part of a religious program carried on by government."

Thus, even if a prayer is nondenominational and students have the option to remain silent or be excused from the room while the prayer is recited, the establishment clause prohibits public officials from composing an official state prayer and requiring that it be recited in the state's public schools. It matters not whether it can be shown that the student was under coercion to participate, since unlike the free exercise clause, the establishment clause does not require proof of any direct governmental compulsion of a particular belief or religious activity. Rather, the establishment clause is violated when laws are enacted that endorse or officially recognize religion whether or not it can be proved that such laws coerce those who choose not to participate. Yet, even laws that provide for de jure exemptions to state-required religious activity may involve some degree of de facto coercion. In every situation where the government endorses religion, the pressure on the minority of nonpartici-pants to conform to majority practice hangs heavy in the air regardless of any stated procedural safeguards. Even in those situations where children are technically excused from the practice, there exists the possibility of social ostracism by their peers or outright persecution from zealous teachers.

*Engel* was a dramatic break from the long-held position that prayer does not constitute an establishment of religion as such. However, Black relied heavily on what he believed to be the intent of the framers in justifying his argument. Indeed, Black's opinion in *Engel* is mostly an historical excursion from the sixteenth century forward, recalling the evils of government involvement in religion. In the spirit of James Madison's strong remonstrances against government entanglement in reli-gion, Black wrote:

> When the power, prestige, and financial support of government is placed behind a particular religious belief, the indirect coercive pressure upon religious minorities to conform to the prevailing officially approved religion is plain. But the purposes underlying the Establishment Clause go much further than that. Its first and most immediate purpose rested on the belief that a union of government and religion tends to destroy government and to degrade religion.

Black was sensitive to the fact that his opinion would bring charges that the Court was hostile toward prayer and religion. Indeed, many major newspapers ran headlines such as "Court Outlaws God" after *Engel* was handed down, and the vol-ume of mail attacking the decision was the largest in the history of the Court. Sensing the ill will engendered by the opinion, President John F. Kennedy took to the presidential pulpit to defend *Engel* and urged all Americans to comply with the Supreme Court's ruling. Kennedy commented that there was "a very easy remedy" for those who worried about the impact of the Court's ruling:

> and that is to pray ourselves, and I would think it would be a welcome reminder to every American family that we can pray a great deal more at home and attend our churches with a good deal more fidelity, and we can make the true meaning of prayer much more important in the lives of all our children.[19]

Evangelist Billy Graham declared at his revivals that he was "shocked and dis-appointed," and when Chief Justice Warren announced his resignation seven years later in 1968, the still-embittered Graham called on President Lyndon B. Johnson to balance the Court with conservatives.[20]

Nothing in Black's opinion prohibits children and teachers from praying silently to themselves. In fact, the opinion urged people to look beyond their selfish and shortsighted desire to use the public schools as a convenient forum for promoting religion as a solution to some perceived decay in values. Respect for religion and the role it plays in American society is best served by a separation of church and state.

One need look only at the destruction wrought in the name of religion throughout history to understand the framers' intent to safeguard government from religion and religion from government. Black concluded: "It is neither sacrilegious nor antireligious to say that each separate government in this country should stay out of the business of writing or sanctioning official prayers and leave that purely religious function to the people themselves and to those the people choose to look to for religious guidance."

Although Justice Douglas examined the issues in *Engel* from a somewhat narrower perspective, his concurring opinion gives added insight into why school prayer is unconstitutional. For him, the New York policy did not involve government compulsion or coercion to foster an official prayer, for the board of regents' policy provided ample opportunity for students to exempt themselves from participation and there was no evidence that students were forced to say the prayer. Douglas pointed out that the only person required to utter the prayer was the teacher, and since no teacher complained, the question of compulsion was not an issue. Nor did Douglas agree with Black's argument that to authorize the regents' prayer was to establish a religion in the strict historic meaning of those words. However, for Douglas, the state did run afoul of the establishment clause by using public dollars to finance a religious exercise. In doing so, the government entangled itself in religious affairs in a way antithetical to the spirit of the establishment clause. Prayers composed by governments will invariably tend to favor one religious sect over another, or religious over nonreligious beliefs. Even though it upheld the law, the New York State Supreme Court admitted that the prayer did not conform to all of the teachings of all of the members of the community, such as Jews and Unitarians. If we know anything about the intent of the framers, wrote Douglas, it is that they sought to prohibit the government from using its power and resources to favor one sect over another and set the standards of religious worship.

Justice Stewart, dissenting, argued that the Court had misapplied the establishment clause. Taking a strictly literal view of the establishment clause, he could not understand how the inclusion of a twenty-word prayer in the school's activities could possibly establish an official religion. For Stewart, the establishment clause serves only to prohibit the establishment of a state church or official religion and nothing more. In fact, the Court's action had actually violated the rights of children who wished to join in reciting prayer, argued Stewart, and in doing so ran contrary to the nation's "spiritual heritage." He noted that this heritage has included prayer at the opening of each day's session of the Supreme Court and both houses of Congress, led by official chaplains who are paid with public money. Each president has asked for the protection and help of God in his inaugural address and, a decade earlier, the Court itself recognized that "[w]e are a religious people whose institutions presuppose a Supreme Being," *Zorach v. Clauson*, 343 U.S. 306 (1951). Stewart was not prepared to break with this heritage in the name of a judicially created wall of separation.

## Bible Reading

*Is there any way around* Engel? *Was the Regents' prayer unconstitutional only because it was written and sanctioned by public officials? Suppose teachers read aloud from the King James Bible at the beginning of each school day? Would this practice pass constitutional muster under* **Engel?**    These questions were raised in a challenge to a Pennsylvania law that required Bible readings at the outset of each school day. As in the case of the New York prayer, student participation was voluntary. However, unlike the prayer, the verses were not composed by any public official or state employee, but were taken directly from the Bible. The Pennsylvania law provided that "[a]t least ten verses from the Holy Bible be read, without comment, at the opening of each public school on each school day. Any child shall be excused from such Bible reading, or attending such Bible reading, upon the written request of his parent or guardian."

The Schempp family, members of the Unitarian Church, challenged the constitutionality of a high school policy requiring Bible reading and reciting the Lord's Prayer. A three-judge federal district court found the law to be an abridgment of the establishment clause as applied to the states through the Fourteenth Amendment. On appeal to the Supreme Court in *Abington v. Schempp*, 374 U.S. 203 (1963), a majority of eight justices affirmed the district court's decision and struck down the Pennsylvania law. Writing for the majority, Justice Tom Clark proposed three reasons the government must remain neutral with regard to religion: (1) influential religious sects might bring about a fusion of governmental and religious functions, serving their own social or political interests; (2) a lack of neutrality on the part of government toward religion may create a dependency of one upon the other, degrading both in the process; and (3) the use of government to advance religious activity violates the concept of personal choice and freedom from compulsion in matters of religion as protected by the free exercise clause.

More importantly, Clark established a test for determining when governmental action implicates the establishment clause. First, what is the purpose and primary effect of the policy? If its purpose is either advancement or inhibition of religion, then the policy exceeds constitutional limits on governmental powers. Second, to be considered constitutional under the establishment clause there must be a secular legislative purpose and a primary effect that neither advances nor inhibits religion. On the other hand, the purpose of the free exercise clause is to secure religious liberty for the individual by prohibiting governmental invasions. In a free exercise case, it is necessary to prove that the policy has a coercive effect on religious practice; in an establishment case, merely a breach of the secular purpose test must be shown, rather than governmental coercion. Thus, allowing students to be excused from religious exercises is no defense to a constitutional challenge. Clark also used a slippery slope analogy to deflect the assertion that these kinds of religious activities are minor encroachments on the First Amendment. He wrote: "The breach of neutrality that is today a trickling stream may all too soon become a raging torrent."

One criticism of this neutrality standard was that by prohibiting all religious exercises, the Court was demonstrating hostility toward religion and establishing what would later be called a religion of secularism or secular humanism. Clark countered that the concept of neutrality does not collide with the majority's right to exercise religious liberty, but only with the majority's desire to "use the machinery of the state to practice its beliefs." *Schempp* did not prohibit studying the Bible or religion as part of the secular curriculum. If schools wanted to offer courses on the religions of the world or to use the Bible in a literature or history class, they were free to do so.[21]

Both the regents' prayer and Bible-reading policies in *Engel* and *Schempp*, respectively, contained specific provisions to excuse students from participating in the daily religious exercises. These provisions were unsuccessful attempts by officials to slide the practice of religious instruction past any allegations of coercion or compulsion. Since the Court ruled that it was not necessary to show coercion before invoking the establishment clause, these provisions were rendered moot. Even today some contend that such provisions are a practical way of putting prayer or moments of silence back into the classroom. However, if many administrators and teachers were willing to openly flout prohibitions on religious instruction, it seems likely that so too might they ignore these exemptions. Even if students avail themselves of the opportunity not to participate, they still leave themselves open to subtle harassment by teachers and ostracism by fellow students. In small, homogeneous communities, where it is unlikely that the majority will offer any opposition to school prayer, those who would prefer to have their children spared state-sponsored religion have much to lose by complaining about the school's unconstitutional activities. Imagine being a successful Jewish or Moslem physician in a small town dominated by Christian fundamentalists.

Recall that in *Engel*, Black argued that the state law authorizing the use of the board of regents' prayer was a violation of the establishment clause because it was composed by governmental officials for the sole purpose of fostering religious beliefs. This practice, wrote Black, breaches the constitutional wall of separation between church and state. In *Schempp*, Clark's reasoning was more analytical and detailed. He carefully outlined the purpose of the establishment clause and offered a straightforward standard for adjudicating future cases.

## Financial Support of Religion

*When is the transfer of public dollars to private religious schools constitutional?*     The wall of separation between church and state is often blurred by policies providing financial aid to parochial schools in the form of tax breaks,[22] bus transportation,[23] and money to offset the costs of administering state-mandated aptitude tests.[24] In 1968, during a period of fiscal austerity, the Pennsylvania legislature authorized the state superintendent of public instruction to "purchase" a number of "secular educational services" from private schools. In doing so, the state directly reimbursed those schools for textbooks, instructional materials, and teachers' salaries. The materials and services purchased were to be restricted to those of a secular nature, and no payment was to be made for any course containing religious teaching. Thus, students who would normally attend public schools would attend private schools for some or all of their instruction.

Similarly, one year later in Rhode Island, in an attempt to improve the quality of nonpublic education, the legislature authorized a 15 percent salary supplement to be paid to teachers in private schools where the average per-pupil state expenditure was below the average found in the public schools. The act required that the teachers be state certified and that they teach only those secular subjects offered in the public schools.

In both instances, the respective legislatures were careful to provide specific mechanisms for supervising and auditing the private schools so that no tax dollars could be used for religious instruction. However, in separate actions in federal district courts, concerned citizens, taxpayers, and parents brought suit to have the laws declared unconstitutional on the ground that these policies violated the establishment and free exercise clauses. If the legislatures' purpose was secular—not to endorse or finance religion—wouldn't it be difficult to successfully challenge the constitutionality of the two laws?

The two cases were heard together by the Supreme Court in the landmark case *Lemon v. Kurtzman*, 403 U.S. 602 (1971), where both state laws were declared unconstitutional.

Writing for the majority, Chief Justice Burger began by attacking the narrow, literalist approach to the establishment clause that contends the sole purpose of the clause is to prevent government from establishing a state church or a state religion. The framers intended for the clause to go beyond that interpretation, intending that there should be no law *respecting* establishment of religion. A law does not have to establish or attempt to establish a religion to be unconstitutional, for the establishment clause may be violated if a law is in some way related to or concerned with the establishment of religion. Burger wrote:

> The language of the religion clauses of the First Amendment is at best opaque. . . . In the absence of precisely stated constitutional prohibitions, we must draw lines with reference to the three main evils against which the establishment clause was intended to afford protection: "sponsorship, financial support, and active involvement of the sovereign in religious activity.[25]

The chief justice then posited a three-pronged standard for analyzing establishment clause cases. This standard, which has come to be known as the *Lemon* test, consists of several rules developed by the Court over time.[26] Under this test, a statute is constitutional under the establishment clause if: (1) it has a secular legislative purpose, (2) its principal or primary effect neither advances nor inhibits religion, and (3) it does not foster excessive governmental entanglement with religion.

Applying this three-pronged standard, the Court found that both the Pennsylvania and Rhode Island statutes met the first requirement: There was no reason to believe that either legislature intended to advance religion. As for the second prong, both statutes were intended to improve the quality of secular education. However, the cumulative effect of the programs violated the third prong of the test: They both involved "an excessive entanglement between government and religion." In particular, the Rhode Island program allowed public school students to receive secular instruction from nuns in Catholic school buildings containing religious symbols such as crucifixes and paintings. Even though the instruction was in secular subjects, such as mathematics, the atmosphere in which the young impressionable pupils spent their day was extremely religious in nature. Burger wrote:

> The substantial religious character of these church-related schools gives rise to entangling church-state relationships of the kind the religious clauses sought to avoid. Although the District Court found that concern for religious values did not inevitably or necessarily intrude into the content of secular subjects, the considerable religious

activities of these schools led the legislature to provide for careful governmental controls and surveillance by state authorities in order to ensure that state aid supports only secular education.

Although the two state legislatures had set up extensive provisions for monitoring possible religious inculcation, these safeguards were not adequate to offset the cumulative religious impact that the programs had on children. An enormous difference exists between a program that allows states to provide parochial schools with money for textbooks, as the Court had allowed in *Board of Education v. Allen*, 392 U.S. 236 (1968), and a program that pays parochial school teachers to teach public school students. It is relatively easy to prevent the church schools from spending tax dollars on books with a religious content, but difficult to monitor the way a teacher handles a subject in the confines of a classroom. Unlike textbooks, teachers cannot be read to determine whether they will impose personal beliefs on students. In providing public money to teachers under religious control, we run the risk of subsidizing and thus promoting religious instruction.

The chief justice concluded his opinion by raising a subtle point regarding another danger of infusing religion into public policy-making. The two programs of state aid to parochial schools ran afoul of the Constitution because they forced the citizens of those states to align themselves with candidates and parties on the basis of their religious beliefs, which is exactly what the framers hoped to avoid. Supporters of such policies will vote for candidates who promise to enact or perpetuate state support of religion, while opponents of any form of state aid to religion will line up on the other side of the political fence. What results is two (or more) religious factions that are vying for state aid, or religious and secular factions seeking control of the legislature or courthouse. Burger reasoned:

> Ordinary political debate and division, however vigorous or even partisan, are normal and healthy manifestations of our democratic system of government, but political division along religious lines was one of the principal evils against which the First Amendment was intended to protect. The potential for political divisiveness related to religious belief and practice is aggravated in these two statutory programs by the need for continuing annual appropriations and the likelihood of larger and larger demands as costs and populations grow.

Does *Lemon* absolutely proscribe entanglement or does it permit some accommodation? At first reading, it appears to be a strong statement of the Court's commitment to the principle of government neutrality toward religious instruction and that churches ought to be excluded from the policy-making process. Yet Burger stopped short of advocating total separation of church and state, and actually backed away from the wall of separation metaphor recognized in earlier cases such as *Everson*. He argued that in some situations the separation is a "blurred, indistinct, and variable barrier" rather than a wall. Because of our nation's long tradition of publicly celebrating religious events and employing religious symbols and metaphors in political or economic activity, Burger was not willing to impose a strict and clear boundary separating the secular from the sectarian. Depending on the circumstances, the Court could continue to accommodate some state aid to religious institutions, such as bus transportation, meals, and secular textbooks for underfunded schools, as long as governmental entanglement was not excessive.

Superficially, the three-pronged *Lemon* test appears to be straightforward. However, the vague "excessive entanglement" provision of the third prong puts us back almost to square one. What is "excessive"? Burger tells us only to look at the "character and purposes" of the institutions benefited by the aid, the "nature of aid," and the "resulting relationships" between government and the religious institution.

The murky nature of this standard has led to a long line of inconsistent rulings. Although it struck down the Pennsylvania and Rhode Island laws in *Lemon*, a divided Court voted 5–4 in a companion case to uphold a federal statute authorizing $240 million to help build new academic facilities on the campuses of private colleges, many of which were church-affiliated.[27] In this case, *Tilton v. Richardson*, 403 U.S. 672 (1971), Burger justified the apparent departure from *Lemon* by drawing a distinction between higher education and elementary and secondary education: One of the main purposes of precollege religious instruction is to ensure the continuance of the religion by adding prospective followers or adherents to the faith—adding to the flock, so to speak. Recognizing that young children are more impressionable than college students, parochial education at the elementary and secondary levels tends to be more infused with religious indoctrination than at church-affiliated colleges and universities. Since college students are less impressionable and higher education focuses more on academic skills and professional training, church-affiliated colleges spend far less time teaching religion. This lessens the chance that an academic building intended to be used for secular purposes, such as a library or science lab, will be used for religious instruction or activity. Combined with the fact that the federal dollars were not to be spent for professors' salaries or for textbooks, the difference between the educational processes occurring in higher education compared with precollege schooling lessened the risk of governmental aid to religion.

The likelihood that excessive entanglement between government and religion would occur in this case was further minimized by the one-time, single-purpose nature of the appropriation. The program did not create an ongoing financial relationship as did the two programs at issue in *Lemon*. Unlike the circumstances of *Lemon*, all of these factors—the nature of higher education, the nonideological nature of the aid, the noncontinuing relationship—enabled the program to pass the excessive entanglement test.

The dissenting justices, however, saw little difference between the two state programs in *Lemon* and the federal grant in *Tilton*. They were skeptical of the claim that the risk of sectarian instruction in a college-level course was lessened by the fact that somehow college students were less impressionable and that college courses were "less susceptible to religious permeation." The strict policing guidelines on building usage attested to the fact that the federal government recognized the possibility of religious teaching in the federally funded buildings. Indeed, the same kind of policing program was struck down in *Lemon*. Mindful of the historical precedents against state aid to sectarian schools, Justice Brennan wrote:

In sharp contrast to the "undeviating acceptance given religious tax exemptions from our earliest days as a Nation," subsidy of sectarian educational institutions became embroiled in bitter controversies very soon after the nation was formed. [After the 1840s] States added provisions to their constitutions prohibiting the use of public school funds to aid sectarian schools, and [t]oday fewer than a half-dozen states omit such provisions from their constitutions. [If] this history is not itself compelling, [other] forms of governmental involvement which each of the three statutes requires tips the scales in my view against the validity of each of them.

Using the precollege/college dichotomy, the Court also upheld (6–3) a South Carolina bond issue for the construction of academic buildings (for nonreligious use) by private religious schools.[28] The Court upheld the loan of secular textbooks from public schools to private religious schools,[29] and voted 5–4 to uphold an annual tax deduction of $700 for parents of children in elementary and secondary schools run by religious organizations.[30] On the other hand, the Court struck down (8–1) an Ohio law authorizing an annual $90-per-child tuition voucher for parents who send their children to precollege parochial schools,[31] direct reimbursement to parochial schools for record-keeping and testing services (6–3),[32] and state-funded instructional services on parochial school grounds (5–4).[33] In *Aguilar v. Felton*, 473 U.S. 402 (1985), the Court held that the New York City program that used "Title I" federal money to send public school teachers into parochial schools in order to provide remedial education to disadvantaged children constituted an excessive entanglement of church and state. It made no difference to the Court at the time that the aid came with complex guidelines to ensure that only secular instruction would occur and that the funds were not to be used to provide services on a school-wide basis but only to those students eligible for aid.

To comply with *Aguilar*, the school board provided Title I instruction only at public school sites, at leased sites, or in converted vans parked near the religious schools. In doing so the school district incurred huge costs that were deducted from the federal grants even before any money was spent helping disadvantaged students. As a result, fewer disadvantaged students benefited from the program.

Ten years later the original parties bound by the court order in *Aguilar* filed suit again, asking the Court to reconsider its ruling. They argued that the cost of complying with the ruling was excessive and that *Aguilar* was no longer good law since during the past decade the Court had softened its position on excessive entanglement and five justices had argued that the original premise of *Aguilar* ought to be reconsidered.[34]

In *Agostini v. Felton*, 521 U.S. 203 (1997), the Court agreed and overturned *Aguilar*. Writing for the 5–4 majority, Justice O'Connor argued that placing full-time public school teachers in parochial schools does not necessarily amount to unconstitutional religious indoctrination. Since there was no evidence that any New York City teacher ever attempted to inculcate religion in students while teaching on parochial school premises, the federal program[35] under which the public school teachers were sent into parochial schools should be upheld. O'Connor stated that the program served a secular purpose and did not create an excessive entanglement of government and religion. Under the old standard used in *Aguilar*, excessive entanglement occurred if: (1) the education program would require "pervasive monitoring by public authorities" to ensure that public employees did not teach religion, (2) the program required "administrative cooperation" between the government and parochial schools, and (3) the program might increase the dangers of "political divisiveness." However, under the Court's current establishment clause doctrine, the second and third factors are insufficient to create an excessive entanglement. Thus, programs using public dollars for programs in parochial schools advance religion only if they: (1) result in governmental indoctrination, (2) define recipients by reference to religion, (3) create an excessive entanglement of church and state, or (4) endorse religion.

Furthermore, the Court also abandoned its position that the placement of public employees on parochial school grounds inevitably results in a union between government and religion. For example, it was permissible for a deaf student to bring his state-employed sign language interpreter with him to Catholic high school[36] and for a state to issue a vocational tuition grant to a blind person who wished to attend a Christian college and become a pastor.[37] These services, like those provided in New York City under Title I, were allocated using criteria that neither favored nor disfavored religion, but were made available to all children who met the eligibility requirements, regardless of their religious beliefs or the kind of school they attend. Returning to the question of "entanglements" and whether they are "excessive," O'Connor wrote in *Agostini*: "Not all entanglements, of course, have the effect of advancing or inhibiting religion. Interaction between church and state is inevitable . . . and we have always tolerated some level of involvement between the two. Entanglement must be 'excessive' before it runs afoul of the Establishment Clause."

Dissenting, Justice Souter (joined by Justices Stevens, Ginsburg, and Breyer), believed that the majority unwisely violated the principle of *stare decisis* by overturning *Aguilar*. Souter held fast to the position that just as the state is forbidden to subsidize religion directly so too is it forbidden to act in any way that could be reasonably viewed as religious endorsement. One might ask, how is the government endorsing religion by sending a state-paid remedial math teacher into a parochial school? Souter's objections can be illustrated as follows. Suppose that Ms. Smith, a state-paid teacher who is Catholic, is sent to Catholic school in the Bronx to teach English as a second language. She finds herself in a religious setting surrounded by students, faculty, staff, and parents who share similar views. Soon, Ms. Smith's lessons begin to reflect the school's religious mission. Mindful of this, the school district sends over a state-paid monitor to make certain that Ms. Smith is not teaching religion. Not only do we have a direct transfer of money to bail out or support a financially strapped school with a religious mission but we have fostered an entanglement between the church and state by having to send in a monitor to make certain that no religion is interjected into the curriculum. Souter admits, however, that the entanglement argument is the weaker of the two. Furthermore, the state's subsidy of the Catholic school would generate resentment in other members of the religious community whose schools did not qualify for public subsidies. Souter writes:

> [T]he flat ban on subsidization antedates the Bill of Rights and has been an unwavering rule in Establishment Clause cases. . . . The rule expresses the hard lesson learned over and over again in the American past and in the experiences of the coun-

tries from which we have come, that religions supported by governments are compromised just as surely as the religious freedom of dissenters is burdened when the government supports religion.

The inconsistency of rulings on aid to education since *Lemon* underscore the philosophical cleavage between the justices who argue for a strict wall of separation and those who contend that the Court should take a more accommodating stand on government aid to religion. Indeed, these competing philosophies continue to present a real problem for courts as well as legislatures in determining where to draw the line.

## Moment of Silence

The Court returned to the issue of school prayer in *Wallace v. Jaffree*, 472 U.S. 38 (1985), where it struck down by a 6–3 vote an Alabama law requiring a moment of silence in all public schools for meditation or silent prayer.[38] The case originated when Ishmael Jaffree, a resident of Mobile County, Alabama, filed a complaint against Governor George Wallace, various other officials, and public school teachers on behalf of his three school-age children. Jaffree charged that contrary to *Engel*, teachers led their classes in prayer on a daily basis, and two of his children had been subjected to religious indoctrination and had been ostracized by their peers because they did not participate. In a rather unusual ruling, a federal district court in Alabama held the statute to be constitutional because, in its view, the Supreme Court had erred in *Engel* and that Alabama had the power to establish a state religion if it so chose. However, the court of appeals rejected this argument and reversed the district court's ruling on the grounds that according to precedent the teacher's religious activities violated the establishment clause.

The U.S. Supreme Court affirmed the ruling of the court of appeals, holding that contrary to the first prong of the *Lemon* test, the enactment of the Alabama statute was not motivated by any secular purpose. An earlier version of the law, calling only for a minute of silence for meditation, met the secular purpose requirement and was left unchallenged. However, Alabama state legislators were not satisfied with this law and pushed for the inclusion of the words "or voluntary prayer" (ostensibly to protect students' right to pray) after many had come under pressure by politically active Christian fundamentalists. However, Justice Stevens, writing for the majority, argued that the sole purpose of the law was to reintroduce state-sponsored prayer into public schools by encouraging praying out loud during the period of time set aside. A student's right to pray silently was never in question, since it was protected by the free exercise clause and by the earlier Alabama meditation statute.

The Court found it "remarkable" that, contrary to a long line of cases in which the establishment clause was applied to the states via the Fourteenth Amendment, a federal district court judge actually concluded that Alabama was free to establish a state religion. Apparently, the district court had its own political or religious agenda when it ruled that the Supreme Court had erred in its decisions over the preceding fifty years and that *stare decisis* notwithstanding it was free to accommodate the will of the Alabama legislature.

Justice Stevens argued that the religious clauses of the First Amendment prevent the state from fostering adherence to a religious or ideological point of view and from using an individual as an instrument to that end. The establishment clause does much more than prohibit the state from establishing a religion: It protects our right to refrain from accepting the majority's creed or prescribed practices. Stevens wrote:

> At one time it was thought that this right [freedom from religion] merely proscribed the preference of one Christian sect over another, but would not require equal respect for the conscience of the infidel, the atheist, or the adherent of a non-Christian faith such as Islam or Judaism. But when the underlying principle has been examined in the crucible of litigation, the Court has unambiguously concluded that the individual freedom of conscience protected by the First Amendment embraces the right to select any religious faith or none at all.

Although she concurred with the majority opinion, Justice O'Connor raised the concern that the *Lemon* test may have outlived its usefulness and should be reexamined and redefined. Since the test had been modified, questioned, and occasionally ignored in cases subsequent to its origins in 1971, it did not easily lend itself to "consistent application to the relevant problems." O'Connor recommended that a *Lemon* "endorsement test" had the most value. Using this approach, the Court inquires as to the purpose and effect of legislation in order to determine if the government's purpose is to endorse religion and whether the law conveys a message of endorsement. For O'Connor, public policy that serves to endorse religion is unconstitutional under the endorsement test because it creates two camps within the political community— favored insiders and disfavored outsiders. Other laws that merely have an "incidental effect" on religion do not necessarily run afoul of the endorsement test. Laws that criminalize murder, for example, are secular in purpose but promote the biblical command against killing. In sum, O'Connor's proposed endorsement test does not prohibit government from acknowledging religion or from "taking religion into account" in making law and policy. But it does prohibit government from "conveying or attempting to convey a message that religion or a particular religious belief is favored or preferred."

O'Connor decided to take a straight-on look at whether the moment-of-silence policy is permissible under established law. She reasoned that a state-sponsored moment of silence in the classroom is constitutional as long as: (1) it is not associated with any religious activity, such as prayer or Bible reading; (2) it is not used by the state to endorse religious activity; and (3) students need not compromise their beliefs. The problem with this rule is that within the confines of a classroom and in the setting of a small community far from Washington, D.C., a teacher may employ a secular moment-of-silence law to reintroduce coerced prayer to the classroom.

In his dissenting opinion, Justice Rehnquist called for a complete abandonment of *Lemon* and a reassessment of establishment clause doctrine. He thought *Lemon* should be abandoned not only because it produced inconsistent results but also because it was based on an erroneous interpretation of the history of the establishment clause—an interpretation supporting the wall of separation metaphor. Rehnquist's original intent construction of the clause called for a literal-historical reading of "establishment" and a maximum accommodation of religious practices, including vocal prayer in public schools.[39] Thus, according to Rehnquist, the establishment clause "does not prohibit Congress or the states from pursuing legitimate secular ends through nondiscriminatory sectarian means."

## Teaching Creation Science

From the days of the famous *Scopes* trial in 1927, many Americans have taken the position that the teaching of evolution[40] in science classes will somehow undermine children's religious beliefs.[41] Consequently, many school districts and states have either omitted from their curriculum any reference to evolution or have called for the teaching of creationism. Even in the late 1990s, in an attempt to offset the influence of scientific theories perceived to be hostile to religion, a few states and school boards took legislative action to promote "balanced treatment" of creationism and evolution.[42]

Forty-one years after the *Scopes* trial, the Supreme Court heard a challenge to Arkansas's "monkey law" in *Epperson v. Arkansas*, 393 U.S. 97 (1968). The dispute arose when Susan Epperson, who had obtained her master's degree in zoology at the University of Illinois in 1964, returned home to teach tenth-grade biology at Central High School in Little Rock, Arkansas. At the beginning of the 1965–1966 academic year, however, she was faced with a problem: If she taught from a biology textbook that contained a chapter on how humans evolved from a lower form of animal, she would be dismissed and convicted of a misdemeanor under a 1929 law prohibiting the teaching of Darwinian theory. The Arkansas law made it unlawful for a teacher or instructor in any state-supported school or university "to teach the theory or doctrine that mankind ascended or descended from a lower form of animals" or "to adopt or use in any such institution a textbook that teaches" Darwinian theory. The Arkansas statute, a product of 1920s Christian fundamentalism, was based on the Tennessee "monkey law" that was upheld by the Tennessee Supreme Court in 1927 after the famous *Scopes* trial. Unlike Tennessee's law, however, it did not require the teaching of Divine Creation, but merely the omission of evolutionary theory in all discussions of biology. During the 1960s, only Arkansas and Mississippi had such laws, and there was no evidence that anyone in Arkansas had been prosecuted. The majority of such schools in the South avoided the controversy by simply not teaching Darwinian theory—a practice that still persists in many small school districts today. Students graduate high school without ever hearing about evolutionary biology or natural selection.

*Is it constitutional to omit a body of knowledge from a school curriculum merely because it is offensive to certain religious sects?*     Fearful that the state might punish her, Epperson, joined by a parent of two school-age sons, asked the chancery court to declare the law void and enjoin the state from dismissing her. In a decision that no doubt brought the condemnation of his community upon him, the chancery court judge held that the statute violated the First and Fourteenth Amendments of the U.S. Constitution. On appeal, the Arkansas Supreme Court reversed and, in a two-sentence opinion, sustained the law as an appropriate exercise of the state's power to determine the curriculum in the public schools. However, in *Epperson* the U.S. Supreme Court reversed the state high court's ruling on the grounds that the Arkansas law was in conflict with the constitutional prohibition on the establishment of religion. The Arkansas legislature selectively prohibited the teaching of a body of knowledge solely because it was deemed to conflict with one particular sect's interpretation of the Book of Genesis. Under fundamentalist pressures, the state legislature had passed a law governing the orthodoxy of ideas in the classroom. Calling for governmental neutrality toward religion, Justice Fortas wrote for the majority:

> Government in our democracy, state and national, must be neutral in matters of religious theory, doctrine, and practice. It may not be hostile to any religion or to the advocacy of nonreligion; and it may not aid, foster, or promote one religion or religious theory against another or even against the militant opposite. The First Amendment mandates governmental neutrality between religion and religion, and between religion and nonreligion.

Contrary to the state's contention, the Arkansas law was not neutral toward religion: Its opposition to teaching a legitimate scientific theory was based solely on a religious hostility to any theory contradicting Divine Creation. It was clear that, in addition, the law embodied the religious preferences and influences of sects falling under the rubric of fundamentalism.

The Court was sensitive to the fact that it might be intruding upon educational policy—a realm of policy traditionally left to the states and local communities. Fortas recognized the fact that public education should be controlled by state and local entities unless the fundamental values of freedom of speech, intellectual inquiry, and religious belief are threatened. Fortas found this position firmly anchored in precedent:

> Judicial interposition in the operation of the public school system of the Nation raises problems requiring care and restraint . . . On the other hand, "[t]he vigilant protection of constitutional freedoms is nowhere more vital than in the community of American schools," *Shelton v. Tucker*, 364 U.S. 479, 487 (1960). As this Court said in *Keyishian v. Board of Regents*, the First Amendment "does not tolerate laws that cast a pall of orthodoxy over the classroom."

Thus, the time-honored tradition of local control over public education may be restricted when state or school authorities place criminal penalties on the teaching of one scientific theory solely because it is considered blasphemy by a handful of influential citizens.

During the 1980s, a new wave of Christian fundamentalism forced the Court to return to the issue of creationism in the public schools. In *Edwards v. Aguillard*, 482 U.S. 578 (1987), the Court struck down a 1982 Louisiana "Creationism Act" that proscribed teaching the theory of evolution in public schools unless creation science was taught as well. While no school was required to teach evolution or creation, if either was taught then the other must also be taught. The express purpose of the legislature was to ensure a balanced treatment for both theories in public school instruction. Proponents of the bill argued that by not including creation science in the curriculum, the state had censored a body of "educationally valuable scientific data" on the origins of humans. They insisted that this body of knowledge had been censored from the classrooms by a "biased" and "embarrassed" scientific community that clung to evolution as a religion in itself.

Opponents of the bill, including many parents, teachers, and religious leaders, argued that creation science is not science at all, but merely a thinly veiled religious doctrine lifted from the Book of Genesis, and bad theology as well.[43] Challengers also contended that the act did not further its stated secular purpose of "protecting academic freedom," nor did it enhance the pedagogical goal of "teaching all of the evidence." The law did not foster comprehensive scientific education because it forbade teaching evolution where creation science was not taught, and it was biased in favor of creation science insofar as it required development of teaching guides and resources for creationism but not for evolution.

*Who was right? Was the law truly intended to advance the purported secular purpose of fostering a balanced treatment of the two theories, or was the teaching of Divine Creation aimed at discrediting a body of scientific knowledge that was deemed offensive by fundamentalists?*    Both the district court and court of appeals agreed that the primary purpose of the act was to advance religion and not merely to offer a balanced treatment of both theories. Neither court was able to determine a secular purpose for the law and, therefore, under the first prong of the *Lemon* test, struck down the act as unconstitutional. The court of appeals observed that the Louisiana legislature's real intent was "to discredit evolution by counterbalancing its teaching at every turn with the teaching of creationism, a religious belief."

On appeal, the U.S. Supreme Court agreed with the two lower courts and voted 7–2 to strike down the act as unconstitutional. Writing for the majority, Justice Brennan held that the act violated the establishment clause because it fell short of satisfying the first prong of the *Lemon* test: The legislature did not have a secular purpose in adopting the law. According to Brennan's reasoning, the act's stated purpose of promoting academic freedom or "fairness" and a more comprehensive science curriculum was really a sham, for these two goals cannot be advanced by outlawing the teaching of evolution or by requiring the teaching of creationism. Based on the statements of the bill's sponsor, state Senator Bill Keith, the purpose of the act was to narrow the science curriculum. In fact, as Brennan pointed out, Keith stated: "My preference would be that neither [creationism or evolution] be taught." In essence, the purpose of the act was to undermine academic freedom and curtail science education in the Louisiana public schools.

That the purpose of the act was not "fairness" was also evident, since it forbade the school board from discriminating against creation scientists, but failed to protect those who taught evolution. As Arkansas had done in *Epperson* in 1968, Louisiana attempted to protect particular religious sects from scientific views that are threatening or distasteful. Examining the legislative history of the act attests to the fact that the legislature's principal purpose was to change the science curriculum to indoctrinate students to the religious belief that a supernatural being was responsible for the creation of humankind. Keith expressed his dislike for evolutionary theory and admitted that evolution was contrary to his own religious beliefs. Brennan wrote:

> The legislation therefore sought to alter the science curriculum to reflect endorsement of a religious view that is antagonistic to the theory of evolution. . . . In this case, the purpose of the Creationism Act was to structure the science curriculum to conform with a particular religious viewpoint. . . . As in *Epperson*, the legislature passed the Act to give preference to *those* religious groups which have as one of their tenets the creation of humankind by a divine creator [emphasis added].

Theoretically, could creationism be offered in the public schools without implicating the First Amendment? Brennan said yes, if such theories are presented with the "clear secular intent" of improving science instruction. This was not the case with the creationism act.

In sum, the creationism act was intended to promote a religion-based theory and censor the teaching of a scientific theory merely because it was disagreeable to a number of Christian sects. As it turned out, many school board officials concluded that the best way to avoid political pressures from fundamentalists was to discourage all science instruction in the public schools. Some believed that if children were to receive their religious instruction only at home, then it was only fair that they should get their science instruction from the same place.[44]

While the decision was heralded as a resounding victory for science education, two members of the Court, Justices Scalia and Rehnquist, believed that the creationism act had a sincere secular purpose and should have remained in force in Louisiana. Scalia attacked the Court for second-guessing the legislature's purpose in enacting what he called the "balanced treatment act." For Scalia, the establishment clause does not forbid legislators from acting upon their religious convictions; if it did, then a law enacted to feed the hungry or shelter the homeless would have to be stricken from the books if it were shown that the legislators were motivated by their religious beliefs. Scalia held that the Court should not assume that the act's sole purpose was to advance religion simply because it happens to be compatible with the beliefs of one or more religions or because its secular purpose indirectly benefits religion. He looked at the issue differently: If the state feels that science teachers are opposed to creationism because of their hostility toward religion, then there is nothing to stop the legislature from enacting a balanced treatment act. In short, there is nothing in any of the Court's establishment clause rulings that precluded Louisiana from acting to eliminate teaching that is hostile to religion.

A substantial amount of the testimony to the legislature in support of the bill was from scientists and educators who believed in creation science. Although Scalia made clear that he did not endorse the accuracy of the testimony of the bill's supporters, he included four pages of their testimony in his opinion to demonstrate his belief that the legislature sincerely believed creation science was a legitimate body of scientific knowledge that should be included in the state's public school curriculum. It is clear that Scalia believes that regardless of its veracity, creationism is a "collection of scientific data supporting the theory that life abruptly appeared on earth." It matters little that the "scientific data" of which he speaks are derived from the Book of Genesis and posit a creator who is the object of religious worship. According to this logic, the legislature has the right to require the teaching of flat earth theory or the of existence of UFOs if powerful groups in the majority have the political clout to convince the legislature of the merits of their theories.

Scalia also attacked *Lemon*'s secular-purpose prong in his dissenting opinion. Much like Rehnquist's critique in *Wallace v. Jaffree*, Scalia reasoned that while it is possible to find the express purpose of a statute or even the legislature's motivation as recorded in the legislative proceedings, discovering the subjective motivation (either good or bad) of those sponsoring the statute is almost always an "impossible task." There may be a hundred reasons why a bill receives a majority of support. He asked:

> If a state senate approves a bill by a vote of 26 to 25, and only one of the 26 intended solely to advance religion, is the law unconstitutional? What if 13 of the 26 had the intent, but 3 of the 25 voting against the bill were motivated by religious hostility. . .? Or is it possible that the intent of the bill's sponsor is alone enough to invalidate it . . .?

Because of the impossibility of discerning the subjective intent of legislators, and because the *Lemon* purpose test worsens the tension between the two religious clauses, Scalia concluded that the *Lemon* purpose test should be abandoned. It is apparent that Scalia is not alone in his desire to scrap all or part of *Lemon*. If this should occur, what would the Court use in its place? How might *Lemon* be modified?

## State-Supported Displays of Religious Symbols

Outside of the schoolhouse gate, public dollars are routinely employed to recognize and celebrate the nation's religious heritage. Chaplains are hired by legislatures, religious symbols are minted on legal tender, and an impressive frieze depicting Moses receiving God's commandments watches over the Supreme Court building in Washington, D.C. *Does the mere display of a religious message on public or government property constitute excessive entanglement of government and religion?*

Almost without exception, during the Christmas season communities across the country deck the halls not only with boughs of holly, but with a myriad of symbols, both secular and religious. The city of Pawtucket, Rhode Island, annually erected a Christmas display that included Santa Claus, his house, reindeer pulling Santa's sleigh, a Christmas tree, a teddy bear, hundreds of colored lights, and a crèche consisting of the infant Jesus, Mary, Joseph, angels, kings, shepherds, sheep, and rabbits. The figures in and around the manger ranged from five inches to five feet tall, so they could be seen by passersby on the sidewalk and street. The city originally paid $1,365 for the scene in 1973, and it spent about $20 a year to assemble, dismantle, and light the display. The city claimed that its purpose in erecting the display was not religious, but secular. In keeping with the tradition, the city wished to participate in the celebration of a national holiday, to foster goodwill and neighborliness, and to promote holiday retail sales in the downtown area.

A suit was brought in federal district court against the city, charging that by including the crèche in the seasonal display the city violated the establishment clause by conferring a substantial and unconstitutional benefit on religion in general and on the Christian faith in particular. The district court agreed and ruled that displaying the crèche was a governmental endorsement of Christianity having no secular purpose whatsoever.

In *Lynch v. Donnelly*, 465 U.S. 668 (1984), the justices voted 5–4 to reverse the ruling of the district court, arguing that when viewed in the appropriate context of the holiday season, there was insufficient evidence to establish that the display of the crèche was an intentional effort on the part of the city to endorse or advocate a particular religious message. Even though the crèche had obvious religious connotations, the display passed the *Lemon* test because the city had a "legitimate secular purpose": to recognize and celebrate a holiday that in some way touches the lives of the large majority of the city's residents. The Court recognized that Pawtucket's purposes were not "exclusively secular," or else it would not have included the crèche among the other holiday symbols. However, in order to pass the *Lemon* test, legislation or governmental conduct need not be exclusively secular (have no impact on religion), but must simply be intended to serve a legitimate secular purpose. Thus, as confusing as it may sound, a religious object can serve a secular legislative purpose.

Writing for the majority, Chief Justice Burger employed a historical justification of the Court's accommodation of Pawtucket's Christmas display. He reasoned that throughout our nation's history, presidents and Congress have proclaimed Christmas and Thanksgiving—celebrations having religious overtones—to be national holidays. On those days, federal and state employees, who are paid through public revenues, are released from their duties with pay. Other examples of how the nation's religious heritage is recognized or supported by public revenues include such things as our national motto—"In God We Trust"—which appears on coin and currency, and governmental support of The National Gallery in Washington, D.C., which exhibits masterpieces depicting religious figures and events such as the Last Supper and the Crucifixion and Resurrection of Christ. Burger wrote:

> This history may help explain why the Court consistently has declined to take a rigid, absolutist view of the establishment clause. [In] the line-drawing process we have often found it useful to inquire whether the challenged law or conduct has a secular purpose, whether its principal or primary effect is to advance or inhibit religion, and whether it creates an excessive entanglement of government and religion.

In sum, the display of the crèche is no more an endorsement or advancement of religion than the designation of Thanksgiving and Christmas as national holidays or Congress's support of art having a religious connotation. Is Christmas more of a secular seasonal celebration than a religious one? While the Court did not address this question directly, the majority did say that despite the crèche's religious connotations it is merely a representation of a historic religious event that is one part of a larger secular seasonal celebration that we have come to know as the holiday season.

Justice Brennan, writing for a bloc of four dissenters, rejected the view that Christmas is merely a seasonal celebration and was skeptical of Pawtucket's claim that its purposes were exclusively secular. If Pawtucket's purposes were merely to recognize the holiday season, to attract shoppers downtown, and to foster goodwill and neighborliness, it could have done so without depicting the birth of Christ in its display. Brennan was convinced that, contrary to their rhetoric, the city's leaders plainly understood that the inclusion of the crèche would serve the purpose of "keeping Christ in Christmas." By doing so, a message is conveyed to non-Christian religious groups or to individuals who do not wish to be exposed to religion that Christianity is the recognized religion of the city of Pawtucket, which surely must be an excessive entanglement of government and religion. After the Court's decision in *Lynch*, wrote Brennan: "Jews and other non-Christian groups, prompted perhaps by the Mayor's remark that he will include a Menorah in future displays, can be expected to press government for inclusion of their symbols, and faced with such requests, government will have to become involved in accommodating the various demands."

It would appear that according to *Lynch*, government-supported Christmas scenes and crèches were permissible. However, four years later in *County of Allegeny v. ACLU*, 492 U.S. 573 (1988), the Court found (5–4) that a crèche on county property did violate the establishment clause because it was displayed by itself next to a banner endorsing a patently religious message: *Gloria in Excelsis Deo*. The crèche was not part of a larger seasonal display and was prominently displayed in the main lobby of a government building. The Court felt that Allegheny County was sending an unmistakable message that it endorses Christianity.[45] Justice Blackmun, delivering the opinion of the Court, explained the difference between this case and *Lynch* in the following terms:

> In sum, *Lynch* teaches that government may celebrate Christmas in some manner and form, but not in a way that endorses Christian doctrine. Here, Allegheny County has transgressed this line. It has chosen to celebrate Christmas in a way that has the effect of endorsing a patently Christian message: Glory to God for the birth of Jesus Christ. Under *Lynch*, and the rest of our cases, nothing more is required to demonstrate a violation of the establishment clause.

While the Court has recognized the need to accommodate some state-sponsored religion, to what extent may government incorporate religious symbols into public ceremonies and politics? Based on the Court's prior decisions, Brennan derived three principles that may help us determine when government may accommodate religion without running afoul of the establishment clause:

1. The government may accommodate the opportunities of individuals to practice their religion by declaring such days as Christmas or Chanukah as national holidays if it so chooses. It may also provide exemptions to a required seven-day workweek or provide unemployment compensation to those who leave their jobs for religious reasons.

2. Governmental practices that are derived from religious practices and convey a religious message are constitutional when they are continued for secular reasons. The public recognition of Thanksgiving Day as a national holiday is an example of such a practice, since today, most people understand Thanksgiving as a time to celebrate personal and national good fortune.

3. Practices such as the issuance of coins with "In God We Trust" minted on them or references to God in the Pledge of Allegiance do not violate the establishment clause because they are a form of ceremonial deism, activities that "have lost through rote repetition any significant religious content." While the recognition of these practices may offend the sensibilities of some individuals, such allusions to religion are unlikely to foster an excessive entanglement or cause political divisiveness along religious lines.

## Use of Public School Facilities for Religious Activities

In an important though less-controversial area of the establishment clause debate, the Court was asked to rule on whether religious organizations may use public school facilities for school-sponsored events and activities. In the midst of charges that Bible-reading clubs were denied access to public facilities while organizations such as witchcraft clubs were allowed, Congress passed the Equal Access Act in 1984. The statute prohibited public schools that receive federal dollars from denying equal access to or discriminating against student groups "on the basis of their religious, political, philosophical, or other content of the speech at [their] meetings." The federal law was challenged on the grounds that because student religious meetings are held on campus and because school attendance is compulsory, the state is in reality providing a ready-made audience for student evangelists. Consequently, a neutral or nonreligious student will be under the impression that the school has officially sponsored the religious activity in a manner that is not much different than posting the Ten Commandments or requiring a moment of silent meditation for prayer.

But the Rehnquist Court disagreed and upheld (8–1) the Equal Access Act in *Board of Education v. Mergens*, 496 U.S. 226 (1990). Writing for the majority, Justice O'Connor reasoned that notwithstanding the prohibition placed on religious activities in the classroom, the establishment clause does not prohibit a public high school from including a Christian club or a Bible-reading club among a school's thirty or so recognized student organizations. Indeed, a prohibition on the basis of the establishment clause would conflict with the free exercise clause. O'Connor pointed out that this was a case of private speech endorsing religion, which the free exercise clause protects, and not government speech endorsing religion, which is prohibited by the establishment clause. Secondary school students are mature enough not to mistake an extracurricular religious club for a school-endorsed religious activity. The risk of official endorsement was further minimized by the fact that the act categorically limits school officials in the role they can play at the meetings of the student religious groups and demands that any such meetings be held during "noninstructional time." In doing so, the act avoids two problems addressed in *Aquillard* and *McCollum*, respectively: students' emulation of teachers as role models and mandatory attendance requirements. Any possible message of official endorsement of a particular religion is further minimized by the fact that students are free to organize other kinds of clubs to counteract any possible religious message.

The Court based its reasoning in *Mergens* on *Widmar v. Vincent*, 454 U.S. 263 (1981), where it held that a similar equal access policy at the university level does not violate the establishment clause. Under the *Lemon* test, an open forum policy has a secular purpose, according to O'Connor, and would actually avoid governmental entanglement in religion by allowing prayer and Bible reading after school free from the kind of coercion that exists when such activities are promoted in the classroom. The school or university would be more likely to risk entanglement by enforcing a policy prohibiting religious worship or religious speech on campus.

Are the justices aware of the possibility that in the real world teachers or administrators may use the equal access law to endorse religion? The concurring opinions all seem to advise school officials to use caution in sanctioning religious clubs and organizations. Justice Kennedy, joined by Justice Scalia, saw little value in the plurality's use of an endorsement test because any school-recognized club or organization is implicitly endorsed as a permissible extracurricular activity. Similarly, in a secondary school environment it is difficult to determine whether or not the school uses coercion to influence students to join a particular organization.

Justices Marshall and Brennan concurred with the judgment of the Court, but cautioned that schools must take all precautions to avoid appearing to endorse the goals of a religious club. Religious clubs are not the same as other student organizations. Marshall wrote: "[A]lthough a school may permissibly encourage its students to become well-rounded as student-athletes, student-musicians, and student-tutors, the Constitution forbids schools to encourage students to become well-rounded student-worshipers."

In an environment where there is a wide variety of "ideological" groups, it is unlikely that students will perceive official endorsement of any particular group. However, if the religious organization is the only "advocacy" group among the school-sponsored groups, and school officials encourage membership as a means to help the community, for instance, then the school runs the risk of officially endorsing religious activity. In sum, a school board minimizes the risk of an establishment clause challenge if it discourages its faculty and administrators from encouraging membership as well as participation in the club's activities.

Justice Stevens, the lone dissenter, was obviously not convinced that the act was neutral or that it provided adequate safeguards against state-sponsored religion. He wrote:

> Under the Court's interpretation of the Act, Congress has imposed a difficult choice on public high schools receiving federal assistance. If such a school continues to allow students to participate in such familiar and innocuous activities as a school chess or scuba diving club, it must also allow religious groups to make use of school facilities . . . [T]he Act, as construed by the majority, comes perilously close to an outright command to allow organized prayer, and perhaps the kind of religious ceremonies involved in *Widmar*, on school premises.

Stevens believed that in deciding as it had, the Court, unlike the proverbial Dutch boy, pulled its finger from the dike. Portending at first only a trickle of religion in the schools, the decision would eventually lead to a flood of various ceremonies and, ultimately, a return to school prayer itself.

The logic of this decision seemingly allows any group to meet on school grounds. But what about the practical application of the policy? Suppose the Student Atheists of America sought to counteract the influence of numerous religious organizations at a high school located in a very religious community. Since atheists are a relatively unpopular group in most communities, school officials would probably be pressured by parents to disband the offensive group. Would officials have to ban all groups in order to rid the school of the least favored ones? Or would it again come down to majority preferences?

## Prayer at Football Games

Santa Fe Independent School District, located in a small community in southeastern Texas, allowed the practice of student-led prayer at high school football games. The games were well attended since in Santa Fe, as in Texas generally, high school football enjoys a great deal of community support. Indeed, for many Texans, high school football games overshadow collegiate and professional games. The prayer was delivered by a student (elected to the office of student council chaplain) over a public address system at the beginning of every football game. However, in April 1995, Catholic and Mormon families brought suit challenging the constitutionality of the practice. In their lawsuit, the Does, as they were called to protect them from harassment and intimidation, sought a court order preventing the school district from violating the establishment clause at the forthcoming graduation convocation. The Does stated that the school district had allowed overtly Christian prayers at graduation ceremonies and football games and had engaged in several proselytizing practices, such as promoting attendance at a Baptist revival meeting, encouraging membership in religious clubs, and harassing students who held minority religious beliefs.[46] While the suit was pending in a federal district court, the school district adopted a new policy that allowed voluntary, student-initiated, and student-led prayers at home games.

In May 1995, just prior to graduation, the district court ordered that a "nondenominational, non-proselytizing prayer" consisting of "an invocation and/or benediction" could be presented by a graduating senior selected by members of the graduating class if the content of the prayer was determined by the students without any involvement of school officials.

Following the court order, the school district adopted several policies dealing with prayer at graduation ceremonies and football games. The graduation policy permitted the graduating senior class to vote on whether or not a prayer should be part of the graduation ceremonies and to elect a student to deliver the prayer. The second policy, entitled "Prayer at Football Games," was similar to the graduation policy. On August 31, 1995, the senior class at Santa Fe High voted to allow a student to say a prayer over the public address system at varsity football games.

The district court then reviewed the new school district policy to determine whether it was compatible with the Supreme Court's ruling in *Lee v. Weisman*. The court found it was not and ordered the school district not to implement the two policies because the prayers not only appealed to distinctly evangelical Christian beliefs but also because the prayers coerced students to participate in religious events. Spectators did not sit in the stands in anonymity. Community members are keenly aware of what their neighbors do or refrain from doing.

The school district then changed its "Prayer at Football Games" policy, omitting the word "prayer" and using the terms "messages," "statements," and "invocations." Both parties then appealed the district court's ruling.

The U.S. court of appeals for the Fifth Circuit held that student-led nonsectarian and nonprosleytizing prayer was permissible at graduating ceremonies but not at school-related sporting events. Based on two earlier Fifth Circuit rulings,[47] the court of appeals reasoned that high school graduation was a solemn one-time event that contrasted with athletic events that took place in settings that were "far less solemn and extraordinary."

The U.S. Supreme Court granted certiorari to address only whether Santa Fe's policy of permitting prayer at football games violates the establishment clause. Since the Court had never ruled directly on this issue, it would have to revisit its 1992 ruling in *Lee v. Weisman* to determine whether its ruling striking down a prayer delivered by a rabbi at a middle school graduation ceremony applied to prayer at sporting events. The justices would also have to determine whether the two Fifth Circuit prayer rulings conflicted or were compatible with Supreme Court precedent.

The school district argued that student-led prayers at football games are constitutional because they constitute private religious speech protected by the free exercise clause. The school district, a governmental entity, was not endorsing religious speech, but merely allowing students to exercise their free speech[48] in a kind of public forum.

But in *Santa Fe Independent School District v. Doe*[49] in 2000 the Court rejected (6–3) Santa Fe's argument and struck down the policy. As in *Lee v. Weisman*, the Court stated that the student's free exercise of religion, while important, does not supercede the limitations imposed on the government by the establishment clause. The invocations or prayers at football games were not private speech; they were authorized by a governmental policy and took place on governmental property during a government-sponsored school-related event. This does not mean that all religious speech at Santa Fe's football games is government-sponsored speech, but it is clear that the school officials did not intend to open up the pregame ceremony to all spectators for religious or political debate. In other words, the pregame ceremonies were not a government-created public forum, examples of which would be student organizations that meet on school property or a school-sponsored mock presidential election. If different students with differing points of view were allowed to take the stage at each of the season's football games, then it could be argued that a public forum exists and that the speakers were engaged in private speech. But Santa Fe allows only one student to deliver a prayer during the entire football season. There is no rebuttal or discussion; nor is there an opportunity for students with different faiths or philosophies to utter words during the pregame ceremonies. In Justice Stevens' words: "Santa Fe's student election system ensures that only those messages deemed 'appropriate' under the District's policy may be delivered. That is, the majoritarian process implemented by the District guarantees, by definition, that minority candidates will never prevail and that their views will be effectively silenced."

The Court cited a related case where it ruled that student elections that determine, by majority vote, which "expressive activities" should receive or not receive school funding and benefits were usually unconstitutional. Government entities, such as schools or colleges, that support art, music, or speech must remain viewpoint neutral. A majority vote to determine who gets the microphone (e.g., access to a public forum) violates the principle of view point neutrality. In sum, minority views must be treated with the same respect as majority views.[50]

So badly did Santa Fe High School authorities want to continue prayer at football games that they concocted a complex process of student elections in order to disentangle themselves from any responsibility for continuing the tradition. Then they embraced a public forum argument in which private persons (students) took the initiative to deliver religious messages and then argued that preventing them from doing so constituted a violation of the First Amendment.

Santa Fe further argued that the policy was neutral because it merely permitted a student to deliver a brief invocation and/or message so as to promote fair competition and "good citizenship." But the Court found that since the policy's purpose is to "solemnize the event," a religious message is the most obvious method of doing so. The term "invocation" does not suggest a discussion of political or civic issues, but an appeal to God. The school district knew full well that the purpose of the policy was to promote the Santa Fe community's brand of Christianity; it knew that the student election would produce a decision to include prayer and that the elected student would say a Christian prayer.

Nor did the majority of the Court believe that this was a private expression of religious sentiments. To an objective spectator this would appear to be a state endorsement of prayer in the schools. Neither was this a moment of silence. The prayer would take place at every home game delivered to a large captive audience booming out to the audience over the school's public address system, which is controlled by school officials. At every home game during the football season all spectators, regardless of creed or belief, would hear a state-endorsed evangelical Christian prayer. This activity cannot be viewed as private speech, as the school district maintained. School sponsorship of a religious message is impermissible because it sends the message to students who are not adherants or believers "that they are outsiders, not fully members of the political community, and an accompanying message to adherants that they are insiders, favored members of the political community."[51]

Santa Fe also argued that those who did not wish to hear the prayer were free to stay away. After all, unlike daily classes where attendance is mandatory, students were not being coerced into attending football games. This scenario might pose a problem for those on the football team, on the cheerleading squad, and in the band. Furthermore, high school students feel immense pressure from their peers to conform—not to stand out. With all eyes upon them, some students would have to wrestle with the choice between uttering a prayer that is contrary to their convictions *and* losing their peer approval. As we have seen in *Barnette*, the Constitution requires that we do not force this choice upon young people. As the Court wrote in *Lee v. Weisman*: "What to most believers may seem nothing more than a reasonable request that the nonbeliever respects their religious practices, in a school context may appear to the nonbeliever or dissenter to be an attempt to employ the machinery of the State to enforce a religious orthodoxy." Stevens concluded the *Santa Fe* opinion by reiterating what the Court has established in previous rulings, *nothing in any of the Court's rul-*

*ings prohibits any student from voluntarily praying at any time before, during, or after school.*

In his dissenting opinion, Chief Justice Rehnquist (joined by Scalia and Thomas) felt that the Court was once again taking an overly rigid view of the establishment clause. He accused the majority not only of distorting precedent in order to find fault with the football prayer, but also of being hostile "to all things religious in public life." Not surprisingly, the three conservatives relied on a common theme: what might be called the George Washington theory of religious accommodation. Beginning with the first president's proclamation of a day of public thanksgiving and prayer, American have traditionally turned to expressions of religion to solemnize public ceremonies. So it is that we should be more accommodating of such expressions of religion in public life.

More specifically, Rehnquist believed that the majority erred by, first, striking down Santa Fe's policy even before the outcome of the student vote was known. In other words, the Court struck down the policy even before it was put into practice. Second, it was plausible that the policy had a plausible secular purpose; that is, "to solemnize the event and promote good sportsmanship and student safety." Third, Rehnquist believed that *Santa Fe* was different from the graduation prayer at issue in *Lee v. Weisman* because the prayer in *Lee* was directed and controlled by a school official. The speech at issue in *Lee* was government speech, but the speech in *Santa Fe* was private student speech protected by the First Amendment.

## CONCLUDING COMMENTS

On balance, the Supreme Court has ruled that the free exercise clause not only protects against direct governmental restrictions on religious beliefs, but also protects certain forms of religiously motivated conduct that may conflict with legitimate governmental interests, such as selective service policy or compulsory attendance rules for the nation's public schools. The Court has also broadly interpreted religious liberty so as to prohibit the state from conditioning receipt of financial benefits upon a person's willingness to bend or violate religious convictions. Unless a person's exemption from a social duty or generally applicable law presents a significant threat to the state's ability to promote a social good or prevent criminality, the free exercise clause demands that the person should be granted an exemption from that duty or law rather than be compelled to compromise religious beliefs. The state does have a legitimate interest in promoting the public welfare and protecting its citizenry. However, when legitimate religious interests are threatened, the government must use the least restrictive methods of carrying out the public's interests.

However, this broad interpretation of religious liberty is not universally accepted. Proponents of a narrow interpretation of free exercise, like Chief Justice Rehnquist and Justice Scalia, have vigorously argued that the purpose of the free exercise clause is only to guard against direct legal prohibitions imposed on religious beliefs and practices: The state is not constitutionally required to grant religious exemptions to laws that apply equally to all citizens. When the courts grant such exceptions, they interpret the free exercise clause more broadly than the framers intended, and in doing so provide some benefit to an individual solely on the basis of religious beliefs, thus violating the establishment clause. Furthermore, the free exercise clause does not require the government to conform each law to the religious views of any group or individual. The religious freedom of the individual must be balanced with the tastes and legitimate goals of the majority.

In the area of establishment clause jurisprudence, the Court has traditionally been divided between the justices who rely more on the wall of separation approach, legitimized by the writings of Madison and Jefferson, and the justices who eschew the original intent argument for a more accommodationist view, rooted in the recognition of the nation's religious heritage. The debate has been cast not only in terms of a broad or narrow interpretation of the two religion clauses of the First Amendment but, ironically, also in terms of conflicting historical images of the intent of the framers. Those seeking to protect the individual from the majority conjure up images of hundreds of years of religious persecution in England and postcolonial America. Supporters of the latter position remind us of the Judeo-Christian foundations of the American experience and cite images of George Washington invoking God's name in the first inaugural address or of the role of religion in the civil rights movement. This disagreement, coupled with a string of problematic and inconsistent rulings since *Lemon*, presents a real problem for those policymakers, such as school officials, who are responsible for drawing the line between government neutrality and accommodation of state-supported religion.

No decision of the Supreme Court is made in a political or cultural vacuum. The landmark church-state decisions have been argued, crafted, and penned amidst great social and political debate. Opinions tell a complex and colorful American story, characterized by uneasy coexistence between individuals who wish to adhere to a set of beliefs free from governmental or societal disapprobation and those who draw their comfort from a shared orthodoxy of values and beliefs and would like to see public policy reflect those values and beliefs. The debate continues long after the final written opinion is posted online and sent to the Government Printing Office. Policymakers at the national, state, and local levels share the responsibility of applying the Court's rulings on religion to new cases and controversies. Legislators and lower court judges, as well as welfare administrators and university presidents, must wrestle with constitutional standards and tests that are often ill-defined, vague, and, at times, perplexing.

Notwithstanding Justice Rehnquist's call for an abandonment of *Lemon* and his preference of a more accommodating approach toward majoritarian positions on religion, it is still not clear whether nearly forty years after *Engel* the Court will allow a trickle of accommodation or a torrent of state-sponsored sectarianism. At present, the majority of justices appear to be standing fast against the strategies of many legislators, school officials, and interest groups that wish to put religious instruction of some kind directly into the classroom.

# Finding the Full Text of the U.S. Supreme Court Opinions Cited in Chapter 4

The full opinion of the U.S. Supreme Court's rulings discussed in this chapter can be found at the Findlaw URL address following each case listed below, or, by using the case name (e.g., *Schenck*) or citation (e.g., 249 U.S. 47). Other web sites where opinions can be found are listed at the end of chapter 1.

## Free Exercise of Religion

*Cantwell v. Connecticut* (1940), http://laws.findlaw.com/us/310/296.html

### Balancing Religious Liberty With the Needs of Society

*Davis v. Beason* (1890), http://laws.findlaw.com/us/133/333.html

*Sherbert v. Verner* (1963), http://laws.findlaw.com/us/374/398.html

*Braunfeld v. Brown* (1961), http://laws.findlaw.com/us/366/599.html

*Garber v. Kansas* (1967), http://laws.findlaw.com/us/389/51.html

*Wisconsin v. Yoder* (1972), http://laws.findlaw.com/us/406/205.html

*Thomas v. Indiana Employment Security Review Board* (1981), http://laws.findlaw .com/us/.html

### A Narrowing Interpretation of the Free Exercise Clause

*Goldman v. Weinberger* (1986), http://laws.findlaw.com/us/475/503.html

*Rostker v. Goldberg* (1981), http://laws.findlaw.com/us/453/57.html

*United States v. Lee* (1982), http://laws.findlaw.com/us/455/252.html

*Chappell v. Wallace* (1983), http://laws.findlaw.com/us/462/296.html

### The Use of Illegal Drugs as a Religious Practice

*Employment Division v. Smith* (1990), http://laws.findlaw.com/us/494/872.html

*Cantwell v. Connecticut* (1940), http://laws.findlaw.com/us/310/296.html

*Wooley v. Maynard* (1977), http://laws.findlaw.com/us/430/705.html

*Bowen v. Roy* (1986), http://laws.findlaw.com/us/476/693.html

*Hobbie v. Unemployment Appeals Commission* (1987), http://laws.findlaw.com/us/480/136.html

*Lyng v. Northwest Indian Cemetery Protective Association* (1988), http://laws .findlaw.com/us485/439/.html

### Animal Sacrifice as Religious Conduct

*Church of the Lukami Babalu Aye v. City of Hialeah* (1993), http://laws.findlaw .com/us/508/520.html

*Continued*

# Finding the Full Text of the U.S. Supreme Court Opinions Cited in Chapter 4   *Continued*

*City of Boerne v. Flores* (1997), http://laws.findlaw.com/us/521/507.html

## The Establishment Clause and State-Sponsored Religion

### *The Wall of Separation*
*Everson v. Board of Education* (1947), http://laws.findlaw.com/us/330/1.html

### *School Prayer*
*Engel v. Vitale* (1962), http://laws.findlaw.com/us/370/421.html
*Zorach v. Clauson* (1951), http://laws.findlaw.com/us/343/306.html

### *Bible Reading*
*Abington v. Schempp* (1963), http://laws.findlaw.com/us/374/203.html

### *Financial Support of Religion*
*Lemon v. Kurtzman* (1971), http://laws.findlaw.com/us/403/602.html
*Board of Education v. Allen* (1968), http://laws.findlaw.com/us/392/236.html
*Tilton v. Richardson* (1971), http://laws.findlaw.com/us/403/672.html
*Aguilar v. Felton* (1985), http://laws.findlaw.com/us/473/402.html
*Agostini v. Felton* (1997), http://laws.findlaw.com/us/521/203.html

### *Moment of Silence*
*Wallace v. Jaffree* (1985), http://laws.findlaw.com/us/472/38.html

### *Teaching Creation Science*
*Epperson v. Arkansas* (1968), http://laws.findlaw.com/us/393/97.html
*Edwards v. Aguillard* (1987), http://laws.findlaw.com/us/482/578.html

### *State-Supported Displays of Religious Symbols*
*Lynch v. Donnelly* (1984), http://laws.findlaw.com/us465/668/.html
*County of Allegeny v. ACLU* (1988), http://laws.findlaw.com/us/492/573.html

### *Use of Public School Facilities for Religious Activities*
*Board of Education v. Mergens* (1990), http://laws.findlaw.com/us/496/226.html
*Widmar v. Vincent (1981)*, http://laws.findlaw.com/us/454/263.html

### *Prayer at Football Games*
*Santa Fe Independent School District v. Doe* (2000), http://laws.findlaw.com/us/
    000/99-62.html

## NOTES

1. For further analysis, see some of the conscientious objector cases, such as *Mitchell v. United States*, 386 U.S. 972 (1967); and *Massachusetts v. Laird*, 400 U.S. 886 (1970). In *United States v. Ballard*, 332 U.S. 78 (1944), the Court ruled that the veracity of religious beliefs may not be determined by a jury. See also Jesse Choper, "Defining Religion in the First Amendment," 15 *University of Illinois Law Review* 3 (1982).
2. *Davis v. Beason*, 133 U.S. 333 (1890). The Court had unanimously upheld a federal statute banning polygamy over the free exercise claims of Mormons in 1879 in *Reynolds v. United States*, 90 U.S. 145, its earliest major free exercise decision.
3. *United States v. Seeger*, 380 U.S. 163 (1965).
4. *Welsh v. United States*, 398 U.S. 333 (1970).
5. Other oft-cited blue law cases include *McGowan v. Maryland*, 366 U.S. 420 (1961); *Two Guys From Harrison-Allentown, Inc. v. McGinley*, 366 U.S. 582 (1961); and *Gallagher v. Crown Kosher Super Market of Massachusetts*, 366 U.S. 617 (1961). See also Paul G. Kauper, *Religion and the Constitution* (Baton Rouge: Louisiana State University Press, 1964).
6. In 1990, the Rehnquist Court ruled that the Amish are not exempted from complying with Minnesota highway safety laws; *Minnesota v. Hershberger*, 110 S. Ct. 1918.
7. Prior to that trial, Goldman was never questioned about his religious practice and was given extremely high ratings.
8. Rehnquist cited *Parker v. Levy*, 417 U.S. 733 (1974); *Chappell v. Wallace*, 462 U.S. 296 (1983); *Schlesinger v. Councilman*, 420 U.S. 738 (1975); and *Orloff v. Willoughby*, 345 U.S. 83 (1953).
9. See chapter 2 for more discussion of judicial deference in military matters.
10. See *Olsen v. Iowa*, 808 F.2d 652 (1986), involving the much-publicized use of marijuana by the Zion Coptic Church.
11. See discussion of symbolic speech in chapter 2.
12. Justices Brennan, Marshall, and Blackmun, dissenting, agreed with O'Connor's reasoning.
13. See also *Olsen v. Drug Enforcement Administration*, 279 U.S. App. D.C. 1 (1989).
14. 107 Stat. 1488.
15. See Sidney Ehler, *Twenty Centuries of Church and State* (Westminster, MD: Newman Press, 1957); and Thomas Buckley, *Church and State in Revolutionary Virginia: 1776–1787* (Charlottesville: University Press of Virginia, 1977).
16. Buckley, *Church and State in Revolutionary Virginia: 1776–1787*. For two of the best collections of the writings of Jefferson and Madison on religion, see Albert Bergh, ed., *Thomas Jefferson Autobiography; Writings* (Washington, D.C.: Jefferson Memorial Association, 1907); and William Hutchison and William Rachal, eds., *James Madison, Papers* (Chicago: University of Chicago Press, 1962).
17. In the Court's first decision dealing with financial assistance to parochial schools, *Bradfield v. Roberts*, 175 U.S. 291 (1899), it upheld a federal allocation of funds to build a public hospital ward to be administered by the Catholic Church. In *Quick Bear v. Leupp*, 210 U.S. 50 (1908), the Court sustained federal payments to private religious schools for the benefit of members of the Sioux Indian tribe. In neither of these cases did the Court address whether such aid was constitutional.
18. See Robert H. Birkby, "The Supreme Court and the Bible Belt: Tennessee Reaction to the 'Schempp' Decision," 10 *Midwest Journal of Political Science* 304–319 (August 1966); Roald Y. Mykkeltvedt, "The Response of Georgia's Public School Systems to the School Prayer Decisions: 'Whipping a Dead Horse,'" *Georgia State Bar Journal*

425–441 (May 1973); and Micael W. La Morte and Fred N. Dorminy, "Compliance with the *Schempp* Decision: A Decade Later," *Journal of Law and Education* 399–407 (July 1974).

19. See Bernard Schwartz's excellent biography of Earl Warren, *Super Chief: Earl Warren and this Supreme Court—A Judicial Biography* (New York: New York University Press, 1983), 440–443.

20. Schwartz, *Super Chief.*

21. The case *Murray v. CURLett*, a Maryland case, was decided together with *Schempp*. Madeline Murray and her son, both "professed atheists," successfully challenged a Baltimore school's policy of voluntary Bible reading and recitation of the Lord's Prayer.

22. See *Walz v. Tax Commission of the City of New York*, 397 U.S. 664 (1970).

23. See *Everson v. Board of Education*, 330 U.S. 1 (1947).

24. See *Wolman v. Walter*, 433 U.S. 229 (1977); and *Committee for Public Education and Religious Liberty v. Regan*, 444 U.S. 646 (1980).

25. See *Walz v. Tax Commission*, 397 U.S. 664, in which the Court upheld tax exemptions for real property owned by religious organizations used for religious worship.

26. In his formulation of the *Lemon* test, Burger cited *Board of Education v. Allen*, 392 U.S. 236 (1968); and *Walz v. Tax Commission*, 397 U.S. 664 (1970).

27. Title I of the Higher Education Facilities Act of 1963 authorizes grants for buildings and facilities used only for secular educational purposes. The United States retains a twenty-year interest in any facility constructed with Title I funds so that if the recipient violates the conditions of use, the United States is entitled to recover its initial investment.

28. *Hunt v. McNair*, 413 U.S. 734 (1973).

29. *Meek v. Pittenger*, 413 U.S. 349 (1973).

30. *Mueller v. Allen*, 463 U.S. 388 (1983).

31. *Essex v. Wolman*, 409 U.S. 808 (1972).

32. *New York v. Cathedral Academy*, 434 U.S. 808 (1972).

33. *Aguilar v. Felton*, 473 U.S. 402 (1985).

34. *Board of Education of Kiryas Joel Village School District v. Grumet*, 512 U.S. 687 (1994).

35. In 1965, Congress enacted Title I of the Elementary and Secondary Education Act of 1965 "to provid[e] full educational opportunity to every child regardless of economic background," 79 Stat. 27, as modified by 20 U.S.C. sec. 6301.

36. *Zobrest v. Catalina Foothills School District*, 509 U.S. 1 (1993).

37. See *Committee for Public Education & Religious Liberty v. Nyquist*, 413 U.S. 756 (1973).

38. The statute in question (Alabama Code secs. 16.1–20.1) provided that "[a]t the commencement of the first class of each day in all grades in all public schools the teacher in charge of the room . . . may announce that a period of silence not to exceed one minute in duration shall be observed for meditation or voluntary prayer."

39. For an analysis of Chief Justice Rehnquist's theory of original intent, see Derek Davis, *Original Intent: Chief Justice Rehnquist and the Course of American Church/State Relations* (Buffalo, NY: Prometheus Books, 1991).

40. The main tenet of evolutionary biology is that all living organisms change over time in response to changes in the environment. For a good overview of the subject, see Carl Zimmer, *Evolution: The Triumph of an Idea* (New York: HarperCollins Publishers, 2001).

41. See E. J. Larson, *Summer for the Gods: The Scopes Trial and America's Continuing Debate Over Science and Religion* (Cambridge, MA: Harvard University Press, 1998).

42. Larson, *Summer for the Gods*; and National Academy of the Sciences. *Science and Creationism: A View From the National Academy of Science* (Washington, D.C.: National Academy Press, 1999).

43. Larson, *Summer for the Gods*; National Academy of the Sciences, *Science and Creationism*; and R. L. Number, *The Creationists* (New York: Knopf, 1992).
44. See facts as stated in *Edwards v. Aguillard*, 482 U.S. 578.
45. The fact that the display bore a little sign disclosing its ownership by the Roman Catholic Church did not alter the Court's conclusion.
46. The district court noted that many school officials, teachers, parents, and students were trying to find out the identity of the plaintiffs by using bogus petitions, questionnaires, and "snooping." The district court judge promised contempt charges for anyone attempting to intimidate or harm the opponents of this policy.
47. Prayer at high school graduation ceremonies was upheld in *Jones v. Clear Creek Independent School District*, 977 F.2d 963 (5th Cir. 1992); but prayer at football games was struck down in *Duncanville Independent School District*, 70 F.3d 402 (5th Cir. 1995).
48. The school district relied on *Rosenberger v. Rector and Visitors of University of Virginia*, 515 U.S. 819 (1995).
49. www.http://laws.com/us/000/99-62.html
50. See *Board of Regents of University of Wisconsin System v. Southworth*, http://laws .findlaw.com/us/000/98-1189.htm.
51. Quoting Justice O'Connor in *Lynch v. Donnelly*.

# CHAPTER FIVE

# Due Process Rights and Criminal Justice

*He that excuses the guilty, condemns the innocent.*

Francis Quarles (1592–1644)

*It is better that ten guilty persons escape, than that one innocent suffer.*

Sir William Blackstone (1723–1780)

No area of constitutional law has evolved more than the due process rights of persons suspected or accused of criminal wrongdoing. The prohibition of unreasonable searches and seizure, the right against self-incrimination, the assistance of counsel, and the protection against cruel and unusual punishment are among the safeguards guaranteed by "procedural due process" in the Fourth through Eighth and the Fourteenth Amendments.

This chapter first focuses on a small though significant slice of procedural due process, particularly the landmark rulings of the Warren Court during the 1960s. It then examines how these rulings have weathered a "counterrevolution" in due process jurisprudence brought about by competing judicial philosophies on the Supreme Court.

## DUE PROCESS AND INCORPORATION

***Was the Bill of Rights intended to restrict the powers of state governments or just the power of the national government?*** We take for granted that the procedural safeguards embodied in the Bill of Rights protect us not only against unreasonable or arbitrary actions by the federal government but also against our local and state police officers, prosecutors, and judges. While the corpus of federal criminal law is growing, most criminal law is state law and most investigations and trials are handled by officials at the state level. For a long time, prevailing wisdom held that the framers intended the first ten amendments to limit the powers of the federal government only, and not those of the states. As earlier chapters have shown, the Court gradually applied the freedom of speech, press, and religion to the actions of the states via the Fourteenth Amendment. We now turn to a discussion of how the Court ultimately came to employ the due process clause of the Fourteenth Amendment as a means by which the procedural safeguards that govern federal law enforcement are applied to the criminal justice process in the states.[1]

In 1833, Chief Justice Marshall ruled in *Barron v. Baltimore*[2] that had the framers intended the Bill of Rights to limit the powers of the state governments, they would have clearly expressed that intention in plain language. Marshall, who was by no means reluctant to expand the power of the national government, held in *Barron* that the Supreme Court could not protect the individual's rights from state action.[3] On the Bill of Rights, he wrote: "Each state established a constitution for itself, and, in that constitution, provided such limitations and restrictions on the powers of its particular government as its judgment dictated. . . . These amendments contain no expression indicating an intention to apply them to the state governments. This court cannot so apply them."

But the Fourteenth Amendment, adopted after the Civil War, would change this time-honored principle by providing the constitutional mechanism by which the Court would "nationalize" the Bill of Rights. The Fourteenth Amendment, ratified roughly three years after the Thirteenth Amendment banned slavery, guaranteed the following to "[a]ll persons born or naturalized in the United States": citizenship, the "privileges or immunities" of citizenship, "due process of law," and "equal protection of the laws." This amendment overturned the *Dred Scott*[4] decision by making all persons born within the United States citizens of the United States. Following the Civil War, a precondition for full restoration of southern state governments set by Congress was ratification of the Fourteenth Amendment. While its express purpose was to grant citizenship to freed slaves and to protect them from their former masters,[5] many in Congress believed that the privileges and immunities clause would protect all individuals from injuries to their rights that result from state actions. But this hope went unrealized for many years. In its earliest interpretation of the Fourteenth Amendment, the famous *Slaughterhouse* cases of 1873,[6] the Supreme Court reaffirmed Marshall's opinion in *Barron* that the guarantees in the Bill of Rights and Fourteenth Amendment were not to be construed to apply to the states.

In the *Slaughterhouse* cases, the Court was asked to recognize certain national substantive economic rights embodied by the Fourteenth Amendment, in particular the right to practice one's profession or occupation. The famous cases originated when, during a cholera epidemic in 1869, Louisiana enacted a statute to clean up the polluted Mississippi River. Slaughterhouses in the New Orleans area regularly dumped animal renderings and other wastes into the river. To stop independent butchering facilities from flouting similar city ordinances, the state prohibited all landing and slaughtering of livestock within the city and surrounding parishes except at one huge facility that was granted an exclusive twenty-five-year franchise by Louisiana. The Butcher's Benevolent Association, a group of independent slaughterers who, as a result of the statute, were suddenly unemployed or displaced, challenged the act on the grounds that it deprived them of the right to make full use of their profession. This claimed right was based on a rather unspecific constellation of economic and property rights protected by the privileges and immunities, due process, and equal protection clauses of the Fourteenth Amendment. But the Court rejected their claim and ruled 5–4 that the Fourteenth Amendment protects only citizens of the United States and not citizens of the several states.

The purpose of the Civil War amendments, wrote Justice Samuel Miller, was to guarantee freedom and citizenship to blacks, no more and no less. Justice Miller believed that the Fourteenth Amendment was not intended as a protection against the legislative power of a citizen's own state, but was protection against the actions of the national government that affect the individual in the capacity of citizen of the United States. To interpret the Fourteenth Amendment in a way that would extend the constitutional rights of citizens of the United States to citizens of the several states would radically alter the constitutional balance between the federal government and the states. The decision gave credence to the position that by protecting only the privileges and immunities of citizens of the United States and not citizens of the several states, the Fourteenth Amendment maintains a system of dual citizenship.

Article IV, Section 2 of the Constitution states: "The citizens of each State shall be entitled to all privileges and immunities of citizens in the several States." Doesn't this clause imply the existence of "national rights" that limit the power of state as well as national governments? Justice Miller did recognize fundamental privileges and immunities enjoyed by citizens of all free governments: the right to governmental protection, the right to acquire and possess property, and the right to pursue and obtain happiness and safety. However, Article IV, Section 2 did not create those rights, nor was it intended to control the power of state governments over the rights of its own citizens. Its "sole purpose," wrote Miller, was to declare to the states that whatever rights they chose to grant, limit, or qualify, they had to do the same for citizens of other states living within their borders. Thus, citizens may seek redress of grievances against the national government through the U.S. Constitution, but they must depend on their own state's statutes and constitution for whatever procedural safeguards and substantive rights they enjoy as citizens of their respective state. The majority refused to rule that the state could not deny to the citizens residing within a state any of the rights that are guaranteed to citizens of the United States.

The four dissenters, led by Justice Stephen Field, embraced a different approach to the problem. Field argued categorically that the Fourteenth Amendment did protect citizens of the United States against the deprivation of their rights by state governments. Although the dissenters were concerned primarily with the vindication of certain substantive economic rights, they took a stand that would greatly influence future discussions on the applicability of the Constitution to the states. Justice Field argued: "[T]he amendment does not attempt to confer any new privileges or immunities upon citizens, or to enumerate or define those already existing. It assumes that there are such privileges and immunities which belong of right to citizens as such, and ordains that they shall not be abridged by State legislation."

Field contended that the Fourteenth Amendment does for the U.S. citizen what Article IV, Section 2 does for the citizens of the several states: It protects the privileges and immunities of all citizens at all times against the hostile or discriminatory actions of the states. But Field's argument would not be vindicated until many years later. Meanwhile, Justice Miller's view would prevail: The Fourteenth

Amendment—as well as the other Civil War amendments—was to be read narrowly and not in such a way that "radically changes the whole theory of the relations of the state and federal governments to each other and both of these governments to the people." Nor should the Court employ the amendments to be "a perpetual censor upon all legislation of the States."

The *Slaughterhouse* cases effectively rendered the privileges and immunities clause useless for nationalizing the Bill of Rights. Later efforts to apply the procedural safeguards of the Bill of Rights to state criminal proceedings focused on the due process clause of the Fourteenth Amendment as a generally applicable standard of fundamental fairness and as a mechanism through which the guarantees of the Bill of Rights could be selectively incorporated.

One way of approaching this issue is to argue that there are certain due process rights protected by the Fifth and Fourteenth Amendments that can be traced in common law back to the Magna Carta. Because these rights are so fundamental to due process of law, a state may not make exception to them in its criminal proceedings. Is this a valid argument? If so, how far can it be taken? *Do the states have the authority to make exceptions to the fundamental principles of justice contained in the Fifth and Fourteenth Amendments?* May a state use its reserved powers (Tenth Amendment), for instance, exerted within the general bounds of due process, to employ procedural means other than those contained in the Fifth and Fourteenth Amendments to prosecute and convict defendants?

In *Hurtado v. California*, 110 U.S. 516 (1884), the Court attempted to answer these questions and give meaning to the due process clause. A provision of the 1879 California Constitution stated that an individual could be prosecuted for a crime on the basis of "an information"; that is, a formal accusation drawn up by a prosecutor after review by a neutral magistrate. The provision circumvented the federal constitutional requirement that an indictment of a grand jury was necessary before a defendant could be prosecuted, particularly in capital cases. A California district attorney filed an information against Hurtado, charging him with murder. He was convicted of the crime and sentenced to death. Hurtado appealed on the grounds that in felony cases, a state may not dispense with an indictment by a grand jury in its criminal proceedings without violating the due process clauses of the Fifth and Fourteenth Amendments. The Fifth Amendment declares: "No person shall be held to answer for a capital, or otherwise infamous crime, unless on a presentment or indictment of a Grand Jury." Hurtado further argued that indictment by grand jury is an essential part of due process, for without it an individual may be harassed and destroyed by prosecutions based only on popular prejudice or hatred.

The U.S. Supreme Court answered that due process of law does not demand an indictment by a grand jury. A state may use the discretion of its legislative power to employ any legal proceeding it chooses as long as that process preserves the "principles of liberty and justice which lie at the base of all our civil and political institutions." California's substitution of a proceeding by information for an indictment by grand jury is constitutional because a magistrate certified the probable guilt of the defendant, counsel was provided, and a cross-examination of the witnesses took place.

In one of his many dissents against the Court's refusal to extend the full protection of the Bill of Rights to the states, Justice John Marshall Harlan, Sr. insisted that due process of the law has only a single definition. It does not mean one thing with regard to the powers of the states and another with regard to the powers of the federal government. The Fourteenth Amendment required that Hurtado receive the same kind of due process in a state proceeding as he would receive in a federal trial. Harlan wrote: "The words 'due process of law,' in the latter amendment, must receive the same interpretation they had at the common law from which they were derived, and which was given to them at the formation of the [federal] government."

A result of *Hurtado* was the adoption of a flexible definition of the due process clause. The majority held the state only to a loosely defined standard of procedural due process—fundamental fairness in light of the totality of all procedures used in a state criminal proceeding; it did not require the Bill of Rights to be applied to the states. Following *Hurtado*, the Court used this vague standard on a case-by-case basis in determining whether states acted constitutionally. For example, in *Maxwell v. Dow*, 176 U.S. 581 (1900), the Court upheld a Utah statute providing for a trial before a jury of eight rather than twelve persons because the policy was compatible with the notion of fundamental fairness. In *Twining v. New Jersey*, 211 U.S. 78 (1908), the Court upheld the action in a state trial court of a judge who, in front of a jury, verbally attacked two defendants who refused to take the stand. After being convicted, the two defendants appealed on the grounds that the judge violated their Fifth Amendment right against self-incrimination, which, under the Fourteenth Amendment, the states were forbidden to abridge. The Court, however, ruled that the exemption from self-incrimination did not apply in state criminal proceedings because, under the standard of fundamental fairness, the exemption was "not fundamental in due process of law, nor an essential part of it." Dissenting as he had in *Hurtado*, Justice Harlan forcefully reiterated his position that the Bill of Rights must be applicable to the states.

By the early 1900s, the Court had three major options: (1) continue applying the fundamental fairness standard whenever appropriate, (2) adopt the doctrine of total incorporation by ruling that the Fourteenth Amendment nationalizes the Bill of Rights in its totality, or (3) embrace the doctrine of selective incorporation, whereby selected provisions of the first ten amendments are made applicable to the states through the Fourteenth. Pivotal in this debate was the 1937 case *Palko v. Connecticut*, 320 U.S. 319.

**Why was Palko so important?**    By the time it appeared on the Court's docket, freedom of speech[7] and press,[8] freedom of religion,[9] and fair trial and right to counsel in capital cases[10] had already been selectively incorporated. However, the Court had nationalized these rights through a piecemeal approach without any clearly developed theory of incorporation. *Palko* moved beyond this approach and established a clear dividing line between the rights contained in the Bill of Rights that are so fundamental that they must be applied uniformly to the states and the rights that are not so fundamental. In the latter category, the Court is more willing to countenance certain kinds of discretionary restrictions or modifications of defendants' procedural rights in state criminal trials.

This landmark case deserves close scrutiny. Frank Palko was convicted of murder in the second degree and sentenced to life in prison. Under a state statute that granted to the state the same right to appeal as the accused if permission was given by the trial court, the state of Connecticut proceeded to retry Palko using evidence that was erroneously withheld from the jury in his original trial. The jury at the second trial returned a judgment of first degree murder, and Palko was sentenced to death. Palko appealed the second verdict on the grounds that it violated the Fifth Amendment's prohibition against being put in jeopardy twice for the same offense, applicable to the actions of the states by the due process clause of the Fourteenth Amendment. He further contended that not only did the Fourteenth Amendment embody the prohibitions of the Fifth, but that the First through Eighth Amendments restrict the states in the same way that they restrict the federal government.

Palko's contentions were not to be upheld. The Court, through Justice Benjamin Cardozo, countered that the double jeopardy clause is meant to apply only to the federal government. Since there was no general rule of total incorporation, the states could make exceptions to the Fifth Amendment just as they had made exceptions to the requirement of a jury trial in all criminal and in civil cases as set forth by the Sixth and Seventh Amendments. However, there were certain rights that the states could not abridge, including speech, press, free exercise of religion, peaceable assembly, and counsel. Because these rights were considered fundamental, they were as valid against the states as they were against the federal government. But why were some of the protections contained in the Bill of Rights applicable to the states while others were not? Justice Cardozo reasoned that even though the right to trial by jury, immunity from prosecution except as the result of indictment, and protection against self-incrimination and double jeopardy are important, they are not "of the very essence of a scheme of ordered liberty" that is considered "fundamental." Liberty and justice would certainly exist without these protections, but would perish without such rights as freedom of thought and speech. Cardozo wrote: "Of that freedom [thought and speech] one may say that it is the matrix, the indispensable condition, of nearly every other form of freedom. With rare aberrations a pervasive recognition of that truth can be traced in our history, political and legal."

Thus, the kind of double jeopardy to which Palko was subjected did not violate the fundamental principles of liberty and justice "which lie at the base of all our civil and political institutions." However, Cardozo did intimate that if the state tried Palko repeatedly for punitive reasons alone or for the purpose of wearing him down, then the Court might limit the state's actions by applying the double jeopardy clause. He continued:

> We reach a different plane of social and moral values when we pass to [those guarantees of the Bill of Rights] brought within the [Fourteenth Amendment] by a process of absorption. These in their origin were effective against the federal government alone. . . . [T]he process of absorption has had its source in the belief that neither liberty nor justice would exist if they were sacrificed. This is true, for illustration, of freedom of thought and speech.

Cardozo's carefully crafted opinion has long been regarded as a catalyst in the nationalization of the rights of the accused, as it established categorically that the states are obligated to the fundamental imperatives of the Bill of Rights through the

Fourteenth Amendment. Cardozo distinguished rights that are fundamental—"the very essence of a scheme of ordered liberty"—from rights that are not quite so fundamental. Like freedom of thought and expression, these rights are central to all of our civil and political institutions. Other rights not quite as fundamental but nonetheless important are "formal" rights, such as trial by jury, and rights that are chiefly procedural. Fundamental rights must always be applied to the states, whereas others may be applied to the states only when state action violates the due process clause of the Fourteenth Amendment. In other words, states may use their discretion to ensure effective law enforcement and efficient criminal justice unless they fail to guarantee due process of law in trying and convicting a defendant.

Cardozo's theory of selective incorporation in *Palko* remained untouched for twenty-four years. During that time the Court added the establishment clause's protection against state-sponsored religion[11] and the right to a public trial[12] to the list of rights that merit incorporation by the Fourteenth Amendment. But the true revolution in criminal due process would not come until the judicial activism of the Warren Court.

## SEARCHES AND SEIZURES

The Fourth Amendment states: "The right of the people to be secure in their persons, houses, papers, and effects, against unreasonable searches and seizures, shall not be violated, and no warrants shall issue, but upon probable cause." While many Americans tend to view the Fourth Amendment as merely an obstacle to effective law enforcement, it represents an important facet of an open society: the right of all persons to be free from arbitrary or oppressive governmental prying, spying, or intimidation in the name of "security" or public order.

The origins of the Fourth Amendment are found in early American experiences with the colonial authority's power to conduct searches and make arrests using writs of assistance; that is, general warrants that did not specifically name the person or premises to be searched or the property to be seized. British officials used general warrants to conduct broad and sweeping searches for criminals, for untaxed goods held in ships, and even for political or religious dissenters. The distaste for general warrants grew to include any form of unreasonable intrusions and the rallying cry that "[a] man's house is his castle; and while he is quiet, he is well guarded as a prince in [his] castle." Ultimately, this principle was expressed in Virginia Declaration of Rights in 1776 and the Fourth Amendment.[13]

In the area of criminal investigation, the Fourth Amendment demands that all evidence be obtained in a reasonable manner and that warrants are not to be issued unless a neutral judge or magistrate is convinced that the police have established probable cause that the suspect is involved in criminal wrongdoing. But the Fourth Amendment raises many more questions than it answers. *What exactly constitutes an "unreasonable" search, or a "seizure"? Are all warrantless searches and seizures unreasonable, or does the warrant clause merely require that probable cause must exist if a warrant is to be issued?*

Furthermore, while the words of the Fourth Amendment are undeniably eloquent, they are but a statement of constitutional theory. Principles are not self-enforcing—they lack the means to guard against unreasonable searches and seizures. How, then, do we provide the government with the incentive to respect our Fourth Amendment rights?

## The Exclusionary Rule

One powerful though controversial incentive is the exclusionary rule; it provides that evidence that is otherwise admissible may not be used in a criminal trial if it is the product of illegal police conduct. Under common law, as far back as the Magna Carta, a judge was never obligated to exclude illegally seized evidence from trial. But the U.S. Supreme Court changed that time-honored practice in 1914 in *Weeks v. United States*, 232 U.S. 383, where it ruled that evidence seized in contradiction to the Fourth Amendment was "excluded," or inadmissible, in a federal trial. A unanimous Court hoped that the exclusionary rule would deter federal law enforcement officials from conducting unreasonable or illegal searches and seizures. However, since the Fourth Amendment had yet to be incorporated, the exclusionary rule applied only to the federal government.

The Fourth Amendment was finally incorporated through the due process clause of the Fourteenth Amendment in *Wolf v. Colorado*, 339 U.S. 25 (1949). The Court ruled that the security of one's person and privacy protected by the Fourth Amendment was "implicit in the concept of ordered liberty" and therefore enforceable to the states via the Fourteenth Amendment. But strangely, Justice Frankfurter went on to say that the "ways of enforcing such a basic right raise questions of a different order," and were therefore left up to the states. A state court was free to continue to admit illegally seized evidence so long as it could show that it had devised some other way of protecting the defendant's Fourth Amendment rights. Thus, the Fourth Amendment was central to due process and applicable to the states, but the exclusionary rule applied only to federal court proceedings and was not constitutionally mandated in state criminal proceedings.

An early attempt by the Court to define the scope of state discretion came in *Rochin v. California*, 342 U.S. 165 (1952). Having been given "some information" that Antonio Rochin was selling narcotics, three deputy sheriffs entered his residence by forcing open the door. They found him half-dressed and sitting at the edge of his bed. On the nightstand were several capsules later identified to contain morphine. When the police asked, "Whose stuff is this?" referring to the capsules, Rochin lunged for the pills and swallowed them. After several unsuccessful efforts to physically force Rochin to vomit the drugs, the deputies handcuffed Rochin and dragged him to a hospital where his stomach was pumped. At the direction of the officers, a hospital physician forced an emetic solution through a tube into Rochin's stomach against his will. After the capsules of morphine were recovered, the defendant was convicted and sentenced to sixty days in prison. His conviction was affirmed by two higher state courts on the grounds that although the search would have been unconstitutional under *Wolf* had it been conducted by the federal government, the California Constitution did not prohibit the admission of such evidence in state trials. Rochin could sue the police for civil damages, but the fruit of the search would still be admissible at his criminal trial.

On appeal, the U.S. Supreme Court reversed the California court's ruling. Writing for the majority, Justice Frankfurter attacked the state's countenance of such draconian methods of law enforcement. The deputies illegally broke into the privacy of Rochin's home, stuck their fingers down his throat, and dragged him to a hospital where they forcibly extracted the contents of his stomach. Their actions were clearly in violation of the fundamental principles of fairness contained in the due process clause of the Fourteenth Amendment. Frankfurter wrote: "[W]e are compelled to conclude that the proceedings by which this conviction was obtained do more than offend some fastidious squeamishness or private sentimentalism about combating crime too energetically. This is conduct that shocks the conscience. . . . They are methods too close to the rack and the screw."

But Frankfurter was trapped by his own judicial philosophy. As a staunch advocate of judicial restraint, he was not inclined to broadly apply the due process clause as "a destructive dogma [to be used] against the states in the administration of their systems of criminal justice." He was not about to overturn *Wolf*, but there was only so much that he could stomach. In going far beyond the bounds of investigatory necessity, the officers forced the Court to take a long look at its own constitutional responsibilities. Citing Cardozo's words in *Palko*, Frankfurter recognized that the due process clause of the Fourteenth Amendment demands that state governments do not cross the threshold of "decency and fairness" and fundamental justice guaranteed to all Americans.

Yet, although the police had clearly violated Rochin's Fourth Amendment right against unreasonable search and seizure, as well as his Fifth Amendment right against self-incrimination (as Justice Black maintained in his concurring opinion), the majority adamantly refused to apply the Fourth and Fifth Amendments through the due process clause of the Fourteenth. Frankfurter would have no part of either a broad natural law concept of due process or some method of selective or total incorporation of the Bill of Rights. In a classic statement of judicial restraint, he reasoned:

> We [judges] may not draw on our merely personal and private notions and disregard the limits that bind judges in their judicial function. Even though the concept of due process of law is not final and fixed, these limits are derived from considerations that are fused in the whole nature of our judicial process. The due process clause places upon this Court the duty of exercising a judgment, within the narrow confines of judicial power in reviewing state convictions.

Cognizant of pressure on the Court to nationalize the Bill of Rights, Frankfurter called for a cautious case-by-case application of the High Court's power of judicial review in due process cases. In a testament to his own judicial restraint, Frankfurter wrote that while the definition of the due process clause may be indefinite and vague, the Court should not take a natural law approach to the Fourteenth Amendment. Instead, he advocated a case-by-case scientific "disinterested inquiry" mindful of reconciling the needs of tradition with society's desire for a more progressive approach to criminal justice.

In his concurring opinion, Justice Black argued that the case was rightly decided but for the wrong reasons. He was satisfied that the Court had overturned Rochin's conviction, but not that the majority reasoning was cautious and narrow. Black believed that the officers violated Rochin's Fourth and Fifth Amendment rights, and that those protections were at all times applicable to the states via the Fourteenth Amendment. Not only had the police conducted an illegal search of Rochin's home, but in forcing out the contents of his stomach compelled Rochin to bear witness against himself, implicating the right against self-incrimination as well. This privilege is violated not only when a person is compelled to confess or testify against himself or herself but by having incriminating evidence taken from within the body by "a contrivance of modern science." Black also attacked the "nebulous" standards of due process employed by the majority and argued instead for total incorporation of the Fourth and Fifth Amendments into the due process clause of the Fourteenth. Of paramount concern to civil libertarian Black was the Court's case-by-case application of a kind of minimalist notion of due process. As long as the states did not cross the threshold of fundamental fairness, the Court was willing to defer to them, thereby nullifying the protections of the Bill of Rights. Black believed the Court should take the position "that faithful adherence to the specific guarantees in the Bill of Rights ensures a more permanent protection of individual liberty than that which can be afforded by the nebulous standards stated by the majority." In 1949, about a third of the states used the exclusionary rule. By 1960, despite *Wolf*, more than half of the states had adopted some form of exclusionary rule through legislative or judicial action.

Twelve years after *Wolf*, in *Mapp v. Ohio*, 367 U.S. 643 (1961), the Court reversed its position in an attempt to end the lack of uniformity and confusion in Fourth Amendment law. The famous case originated in May 1957, when several police officers appeared at Dollree Mapp's doorstep looking for a fugitive whom they believed to be hiding in her apartment. After Mapp refused twice to admit them without a search warrant, the officers used force to gain entry. When Mapp grabbed a piece of paper that the officers had told her was a warrant, the officers physically assaulted and handcuffed her. Having subdued Mapp, the police then searched her entire house until they uncovered obscene books, pictures, and photographs. Her conviction under Ohio law for possession of obscene materials was upheld by the Ohio Supreme Court. On appeal to the U.S. Supreme Court, Mapp challenged her conviction on the ground that the evidence used to convict her was unlawfully seized. Citing *Wolf*, Ohio countered that even if the search were made without the authority of a warrant, the state was not proscribed from using the evidence at Mapp's trial.

The High Court reversed both the lower court's ruling and its own earlier ruling in *Wolf*. Writing for the 6–3 majority, Justice Clark stated that all evidence obtained by searches and seizures in violation of the Constitution is inadmissible in state court. Since the Fourth Amendment's right of privacy was made applicable to the states in *Wolf*, it was only logical that the *Weeks* "sanction of exclusion" used against the federal government was also applicable to state law enforcement officials. Were it otherwise, reasoned Clark, the Fourth Amendment's guarantee of the right of privacy would be empty. The most important constitutional privilege guaranteed by the Fourth Amendment is the exclusion of evidence that has been forced or coerced from the accused. To rule that we are protected by the Fourth Amendment only to with-hold the benefits of the exclusionary rule is, in Clark's words, "to grant the right but in reality to withhold its privilege and enjoyment."

Thus, the purpose of the exclusionary rule is to compel respect for the Fourth Amendment by removing the incentive to disregard it; without this judicially created mechanism, we have no guarantee that the police will respect the Fourth. The rule and the Fourth Amendment are inextricably linked. To do away with the rule is to undermine the prohibition on unreasonable searches and seizures.

By admitting evidence unlawfully seized into state trials, disobedience to the federal constitution is in essence encouraged, and two systems of due process are created. Clark pointed out that in nonexclusionary rule states, federal officers would merely go to the state attorney with their unconstitutionally seized evidence. In doing so, prosecution on the basis of that evidence was "then had in a state court in utter disregard of the enforceable Fourth Amendment."

Clark then raised an issue that has been debated since the inception of the exclusionary rule. *Is the rule a mere "technicality" as its detractors contend? Will this rule benefit the criminal alone?* Is it true that, as Justice (then Judge) Cardozo said, "the criminal will go free because the constable blundered"? Clark reasoned that if a handful of criminals do go free in order to protect honest citizens by the promotion of professional and honest law enforcement, then so be it. He concluded: "Our decision, founded on reason and truth, gives to the individual no more than that which the Constitution guarantees him, to the police officer no less than that to which honest law enforcement is entitled, and to the courts, that judicial integrity so necessary in the true administration of justice."

Thus, in *Mapp* the Court adopted the view that because the Fourth Amendment does not expressly contain any provision or mechanism precluding the use of evidence seized in an unreasonable manner, the protections it guarantees require the enforcement of a judicially created exclusionary rule.

Critics of *Mapp* immediately blasted the Court for "handcuffing" law enforcement officials by making it easier for the defendant to get off on a technicality. Richard Nixon's 1968 presidential campaign focused more on the rulings of the Warren Court than on his Democratic opponent's policy proposals. As the "law and order" president, Nixon promised to nominate to the Supreme Court and federal judiciary only jurists who shared his conservative philosophy toward the rights of the accused. Four of Nixon's nominees—Warren Burger as chief justice, Harry Blackmun, Lewis Powell, and William Rehnquist—were confirmed, but while the Burger Court modified many of the Warren Court's rulings on obtaining evidence and procedural safeguards, the landmark rulings were largely left intact. The counterrevolution that was expected never materialized under the leadership of Chief Justice Burger.[14]

Although the Burger Court left *Mapp* standing, it legitimized a number of exceptions to the exclusionary rule. The most important of these came in *United States v. Leon*, 468 U.S. 897 (1984). Proceeding on an anonymous tip of "unproved reliability," police officers in Burbank, California, began an investigation into Alberto Leon's alleged drug trafficking. A search warrant was issued after several deputy district attorneys reviewed an affidavit summarizing the officers' surveillance of Leon's activities. The searches turned up large quantities of narcotics and drug paraphernalia. After Leon and codefendants were indicted on federal drug charges, a federal judge granted a motion to suppress evidence on the grounds that the affidavit was insufficient to establish probable cause. The government countered that the exclusionary rule should not be applied where evidence is seized by the police in good-faith reliance on what they believe to be a valid warrant. Because the police were proceeding on the assumption that the warrant was valid, the evidence seized should not be excluded from the trial even though the warrant was not valid. The exclusionary rule is designed to deter police from flouting the Fourth Amendment, not to punish the incompetence of the magistrate who issued the warrant. Why punish the police? *Should there be a good-faith exception to the exclusionary rule in such circumstances?* What about the related issue of whether the magistrate was neutral? Suppose the magistrate acts merely as a rubber stamp for the police?

The U.S. court of appeals affirmed the district court's ruling to suppress the evidence on the grounds that the magistrate erred in issuing the warrant and the affidavit was not sufficient to support the officers' application for a warrant. However, the Supreme Court disagreed and reversed the court of appeals. Writing for the majority, Justice White ruled that the exclusionary rule should be modified to allow the use of evidence obtained by police officers acting in good faith on a search warrant issued by a neutral magistrate even though the warrant is ultimately found to be unsupported by probable cause. White reasoned that since the Fourth Amendment contains no specific provision precluding the use of evidence at a defendant's trial, the exclusionary rule is not set in stone but is purely a creation of the Court. As established in earlier cases, this judicially created remedy is not itself a constitutional right but merely a means to safeguard Fourth Amendment rights through its deterrent effect on police.[15] The Court has never recognized an unbending application of the exclusionary sanction; to do so, ruled the Court, would constitute excessive interference with the criminal justice system and truth-finding functions of the judge and jury.[16] Thus, *Leon* established a good-faith exception to the exclusionary rule. But as Justice White pointed out, there are limits to the good-faith exception.

> We do not suggest, however, that exclusion is always inappropriate in cases where an officer has obtained a warrant and abided by it terms. . . . [T]he officer's reliance on the magistrate's probable cause determination and on the technical sufficiency of the warrant he issues must be objectively reasonable, . . . and it is clear that in some circumstances the officer will have no reasonable grounds for believing the warrant was properly issued.

Furthermore, if the magistrate who issued the warrant was intentionally misled by the officer, then the fruits of the search may be suppressed. And the good-faith exception does not apply in cases where the magistrate acts as a rubber stamp or where the warrant is not based on probable cause or fails to specify the place to be searched and items to be seized.

In his dissenting opinion, Justice Brennan, joined by Justice Marshall, attacked the majority's position on several fronts. He took issue with the contention that since the exclusionary rule is not expressly found in the Fourth Amendment and is merely a judicially created remedy, it can be limited, weakened, or abolished in the name of efficient law enforcement. According to the logic of the majority opinion, wrote Brennan, the protections of the Fourth Amendment apply only when the police unlawfully invade an individual's privacy. After that point, when the government seeks to use evidence obtained by that search, the Fourth Amendment may not necessarily apply. Such logic returned us to the time before *Weeks* established the exclusionary rule. For Brennan, the right to be free from the initial invasion of privacy and the right to exclude evidence resulting from that invasion were "coordinate components of the central embracing right to be free from unreasonable searches and seizures."

By making exceptions to the exclusionary rule, the power of the judiciary to protect the Fourth Amendment rights of individuals is weakened and, concomitantly, the hand of law enforcement is strengthened. If courts are not constitutionally bound to exclude illegally seized evidence because the Fourth Amendment is silent with respect to admissibility of evidence, then the judiciary's power to protect against unreasonable searches and seizures is significantly undermined. Brennan reasoned:

> Because the only constitutionally cognizable injury has already been "fully accomplished" by the police by the time the case comes before the courts, the Constitution is not itself violated if the judge decides to admit the tainted evidence. Indeed, the most the judge *can* do is wring his hands and hope that perhaps by excluding such evidence he can deter future transgressions by the police.

In the companion case to *Leon, Massachusetts v. Shepard*, 468 U.S. 981 (1984), the Court extended the good-faith exception to a defective warrant. In this case, a police officer used an incorrect warrant application form and altered the form so that the judge would authorize the search. The judge authorized the search, indicating to the officer that he would make the necessary clerical corrections. The officer then conducted the search and seized the evidence believing that he was acting on a valid warrant. However, because the judge never made the necessary corrections, the seized evidence was excluded from trial. The Supreme Court reversed and ruled that the good-faith exception applied to the officer's conduct and not to the judge's error. Since the mistake was the judge's and not the officer's, the evidence was admissible.

The Court has also ruled that the exclusionary rule does not apply when the police, through an honest mistake, find drugs while searching the wrong apartment;[17] or where a computer error showing an outstanding warrant on the wrong person leads to a vehicle search that happens to turn up a bag of marijuana that results in the arrest and conviction of that person.[18]

## Exceptions to the Warrant Requirement

***Does the Fourth Amendment demand the issuance of a warrant before every search or does meeting the standard of reasonableness alone suffice?*** We know that the framers of the Bill of Rights drafted the Fourth Amendment in response to the unreasonable law enforcement practices they had experienced while being subjects of the British Crown. They believed that the decision to invade the privacy of a person's home and personal effects should be made by a neutral magistrate rather than by an agent of the executive branch. The warrant requirement was also a way of immunizing officials from lawsuits for trespass and injury. If a jury found that the agent acted reasonably in conducting a search, a colonial peace officer proceeding without a warrant could not be sued by the defendant for damages. Some scholars and jurists argue that the framers were not so much concerned about warrantless searches as they were about the kinds and number of warrants that could be issued. According to this view, of more immediate concern to the framers was the "general" or overreaching warrant; that is, a search or arrest order that does not specify or particularize the person to be arrested or the property to be seized.[19]

The vague wording of the Fourth Amendment has come to mean that the issuance of a warrant from a neutral magistrate is one way of keeping a search or seizure reasonable. A police officer seeking a warrant from a neutral magistrate must demonstrate probable cause[20] that an individual has committed a crime, that a specific weapon or stolen goods are located in a particular place, and when the officer intends to make the search.[21] Justice Jackson succinctly summarized the purpose of the warrant requirement:

> The point of the Fourth Amendment, which often is not grasped by zealous officers, is not that it denies law enforcement the support of usual inferences which reasonable men draw from evidence. Its protection consists in requiring that those inferences be drawn by a neutral magistrate instead of being judged by the officer engaged in the often competitive enterprise of ferreting out crime. [Any assumption that evidence alone justifies a warrantless search] would reduce the Amendment to a nullity and leave the people's homes secure only in the discretion of police officers.[22]

But the Fourth Amendment does not demand a warrant; it merely prohibits searches and seizures that are unreasonable. Consequently, throughout most of the twentieth century, and particularly since the creation of the exclusionary rule in *Weeks* in 1914 and application of the warrant requirement to the states in *Wolf* in 1949, the Supreme Court has vacillated between a categorical warrant requirement and a reasonableness test. The Court proceeds from the assumption that searches conducted without a warrant are unreasonable under the Fourth Amendment, but it has made several specific exceptions to the warrant rule. In *Chimel v. California*, 395 U.S. 752 (1969), for example, the Court allowed a warrantless search "incident to arrest" but stipulated that the officer must confine the search only to what is in "plain view" and in "the immediate area" surrounding the suspect. Delivering the opinion of the Court, Justice Stewart argued:

> There is ample justification . . . for a [warrantless] search of the arrestee's person and the area "within his immediate control"—construing that phrase to mean the area from within which he might gain possession of a weapon or destructible evidence. . . . There is no comparable justification, however, for routinely searching any room

other than that in which an arrest occurs. . . . Such searches, in the absence of well-recognized exceptions, may be made only under the authority of a search warrant.

## The Confusing World of Automobile Searches

Most Americans come in contact with the police only after minor violations of traffic codes or, to a lesser extent, because they have been driving while intoxicated. We are, therefore, concerned less about the fateful knock on the door of our home than we are about being pulled over on the road after our late night revelries. The scenario may be familiar to some: An officer shines a light into your car and asks that you open the glove box or the trunk: "Step out of your car please." *Does the warrant requirement extend to automobiles? Does an officer have unlimited discretion when conducting an auto search?*

For most of us, a motor vehicle is merely a means of transportation and not a place of residence. The state's legitimate interest in public safety determines what we may or may not do with (or in) our cars when we are motoring. Furthermore, unlike houses, apartments, and other stationary structures, automobiles may whisk away evidence before a warrant can be obtained. Given these considerations, should the police have a greater degree of flexibility in deciding to search a vehicle prior to the issuance of a warrant?

In 1925 in *Carroll v. United States*, 267 U.S. 132, the Supreme Court easily distinguished automobiles from "houses, papers, and effects" in order to establish the auto exception to the warrant requirement. The Court ruled that the police were permitted to conduct a warrantless search of an automobile if they had probable cause to believe that the vehicle contained evidence of a crime and that it was likely the vehicle would be driven away before a warrant was issued. Chief Justice Howard Taft reasoned:

> The guaranty of freedom from unreasonable searches and seizures by the Fourth Amendment has been construed, practically since the beginning of government, as recognizing a necessary difference between a search of a store, dwelling house, or other structure in respect of which a proper official warrant readily may be obtained and a search of a ship, motor boat, wagon, or automobile for contraband goods, where it is not practicable to secure a warrant, because the vehicle can be moved out of the locality or jurisdiction in which the warrant must be sought.

However, while the police do have greater discretion in conducting searches of automobiles, Taft observed that citizens still retain "a right to free passage without interruption or search." Unless officers can show probable cause that a vehicle is carrying contraband, all persons "lawfully using the highways" shall not be subjected to a search.

Thus, *Carroll* established that acting on probable cause an officer may search a car without first obtaining a warrant. *What about closed containers within the car?* Suppose the officer searches your car (which we can assume includes the trunk) and finds a locked or sealed container. Does the auto exception apply to the container as well? In *United States v. Chadwick*, 433 U.S. 1 (1977), the Burger

Court established the rule that prohibits the police from conducting warrantless searches of closed containers found in automobiles unless the police have either probable cause or a warrant to search the entire automobile. The Court rejected the government's view that the Fourth Amendment warrant clause "protects only interests traditionally identified with the home." It further ruled that the privacy interest in luggage is "substantially greater than in an automobile," since luggage is intended to safeguard the privacy of personal effects, while the purpose of an automobile is primarily transportation.

In *Arkansas v. Sanders*, 442 U.S. 753 (1979), the Court found that the police had acted unconstitutionally when, without a warrant, they seized and opened a suitcase that had been placed in the trunk of a taxi. While the police had probable cause to seize the suitcase, they failed to demonstrate the necessity of conducting a warrantless search of luggage taken from an automobile. Since there was no danger that the suitcase would be removed or lost once it was in their possession, there was no reason the police couldn't wait for a warrant before forcing it open and examining its contents. The auto exception does not apply to luggage merely because the luggage was placed in an automobile.

Within a two-year period, the Court had postulated two rules. In *Chadwick*, it ruled that the police could not conduct a warrantless search of a closed container found in automobiles unless they had either probable cause or a warrant to search the entire automobile. In *Sanders*, the Court established that the auto exception does not apply to luggage simply because it was placed in an automobile. Were the two rules contradictory? Those responsible for implementing the Court's theories—namely the police and other local officials—believed that they were.

In *United States v. Ross*, 456 U.S. 798 (1982), the Burger Court attempted to distinguish among *Chadwick*, *Sanders*, and its earlier ruling in *Carroll*. It ruled that the *Carroll* doctrine applied to searches of automobiles when the police had probable cause to search the entire vehicle and that the *Chadwick-Sanders* rule applied to searches of luggage when the police had probable cause to search only a container within the vehicle. *Ross* established that if the police conducted a search of an automobile under the auto exception rule, closed containers found by the police during the warrantless search could also be searched without a warrant merely because of their presence within the vehicle. *Ross* rejected *Chadwick*'s distinction between containers and automobiles by reasoning that the expectation of privacy that one has in one's car is equal to the expectation of privacy that one has in a piece of luggage or a container of some kind. The Court also recognized that "the privacy interests in a car's trunk or glove compartment may be no less than those in a movable container."

*Ross* was clear enough, but because the Court did not explicitly overturn *Chadwick-Sanders*, no clear and unequivocal guideline emerged. What resulted over time was a dizzying array of rules governing automobile searches. The ambiguity of the closed container rule in particular became the source of trouble for courts and law enforcement officers alike. Suppose that you are a police officer with probable cause to believe that a package contains cocaine and you observe a suspect place that package in the trunk of a car. *Are you prohibited from opening the trunk and searching the package in the car because you lack probable cause to search the car itself? Doesn't the act of placing the package of cocaine in the trunk give you the requisite probable cause? Are you prohibited from searching until you obtain a warrant to unlock the car?*

In the 1991 case *California v. Acevedo*, 500 U.S. 565, the Rehnquist Court decided that the time had come to reexamine the logic of earlier cases and determine whether there were discrepancies among *Chadwick-Sanders, Carroll*, and *Ross*. In 1987, Officer Coleman of the Santa Ana, California, police department received a telephone call from a Drug Enforcement Agency (DEA) agent in Hawaii informing him that the DEA had intercepted a Federal Express package of marijuana that was intended for J. R. Daza of Santa Ana. A plan was devised whereby the DEA agent would send the package to Coleman, who would in turn take it to the Federal Express office and arrest the person who claimed it. As planned, Daza claimed the package and officers followed him to his apartment. After Daza was observed discarding the paper and box that had contained the marijuana, Officer Coleman quickly departed the scene to obtain a search warrant. However, before Coleman returned, Charles Acevedo unexpectedly left Daza's apartment carrying a brown paper bag the size of one of the marijuana packages mailed from Hawaii. He then locked the bag in the trunk of his car and started to drive away. Warrantless, but fearing the loss of evidence, police officers stopped him, opened the trunk and the brown paper bag, and found the marijuana.

Based on this evidence, Acevedo was convicted in a trial court, but the California Court of Appeals moved to suppress the marijuana found in the car. The state court ruled that under *Chadwick* the officers had probable cause to believe that the paper bag contained drugs, but they lacked probable cause to suspect that Acevedo's car itself contained marijuana. Since the probable cause was directed at the bag and not the car, the court ruled the case should be decided under *Chadwick* and not *Ross*.

The U.S. Supreme Court disagreed with the California court and ruled 6–3 that the police may conduct a warrantless search of a container within an automobile, even though they lack probable cause to search the entire vehicle, if they have probable cause to believe that the container holds contraband. They are not justified, however, in searching the entire vehicle merely on the grounds that they have probable cause to search the container.

Writing for the majority, Justice Blackmun recognized that the *Chadwick-Sanders* rule not only failed to provide adequate safeguards on privacy but also "confused courts and police officers and impeded effective law enforcement." For example, officer X has probable cause to believe that vehicle A contains cocaine. The officer begins to search the vehicle and discovers a closed box. Which rule applies, *Chadwick-Sanders, Carroll*, or *Ross?* Justice Blackmun believed that the best way to resolve this problem was to overturn the warrant requirement for closed containers set forth in *Sanders*.

As a result, *Ross* now applies to all searches of containers discovered in automobiles. The police may search a container without a warrant if their search is supported by probable cause. However, they may not search the entire car if they believe that a container in the trunk contains contraband; they must focus their search on the container. So while the police were justified in searching the bag in the trunk of Acevedo's car, they could not have extended their search to the entire vehicle because they did not have probable cause to believe that marijuana could be found in any other part of the car. Blackmun concluded: "Until today, this Court has drawn a curious line between the search of an automobile that coincidentally turns up a container and the search of a container that coincidentally turns up in an automobile. The protections of the Fourth Amendment must not turn on such coincidences."

Thus, all automobile searches are now to be governed by one interpretation of *Carroll*: "The police may search an automobile and the containers within it where they have probable cause to believe contraband or evidence is contained."

The dissenters—Stevens, White, and Marshall—attacked the majority for over-turning well-established precedent and for paying lip service to the Fourth Amendment. How could the majority recognize the "cardinal principle" that searches conducted without prior approval by judges are in most instances unrea-sonable while greatly enlarging the auto exception to this principle? In doing so, the majority had created this paradox: A briefcase is not subject to a warrantless search when a person is carrying it down the street, but it may be subject to a warrantless search once it is locked in a car. One would expect that the privacy interest in the contents of one's briefcase should increase rather than diminish when one takes the extra precaution of locking it in one's car.

Did *Chadwick-Sanders* impede effective law enforcement? To some extent, it probably did impose some inconvenience. But even if it did, Stevens reasoned, the inconvenience is merely the price we must pay in order to preserve our precious free-doms:

> It is too early to know how much freedom America has lost today. The magnitude of the loss is, however, not nearly as significant as the Court's willingness to inflict it without even a colorable basis for its rejection of prior law.
>
> Under the Court's holding today, the privacy interest that protects the contents of a suitcase or briefcase from a warrantless search when it is in public view simply vanishes when its owner climbs into a taxicab. Unquestionably the rejection of the *Sanders* line of cases by today's decision will result in a significant loss of individual privacy.

In a case involving the search of an automobile, *Florida v. Jimeno*, 500 U.S. 248 (1991), the Rehnquist Court ruled 7–2 that if a driver of an automobile is stopped by the police and gives permission to search the car, the police do not need a search warrant to open any containers found inside the car. The Fourth Amendment demands reasonableness and proscribes only intrusions that are unrea-sonable, the majority asserted. It is reasonable for an officer to consider a suspect's consent to search his car to include consent to examine a paper bag lying on the floor of the car.

*If you are a passenger in a car that is pulled over by the police for a routine traffic stop, may the police order you out of the car as well as the driver?* The Court answered in the affirmative in *Maryland v. Wilson*, 519 U.S. 408 (1997). Jerry Wilson was a passenger in a car travelling at a high rate of speed. The police pulled the car over and ordered a very nervous-looking Wilson out of the car. As Wilson exited a quantity of cocaine fell to the ground. He was then arrested and charged with possession of cocaine. The Baltimore County Circuit Court agreed with Wilson's lawyers that the cocaine was inadmissible because although police may order a driver out of a lawfully stopped car,[23] they may not order the passenger to do so. However, the Supreme Court disagreed and ruled (7–2) that in the interest of the officer's safety either the driver or the passenger may be ordered to step out of the car. Writing for the majority, Chief Justice Rehnquist cited that in 1994 alone there were 5,762 officer assaults and eleven officers killed during traffic pursuits and stops. Although there is not the same constitutional basis for ordering the passengers out of the car as there is for the driver, the additional intrusion on the passengers rights are minimal.

## Searches of Mass Transportation

Consider the following scenario: Upon arrival at your local airport after a long flight, you are startled from your sleep by the fact that the police have just boarded the cramped airplane. They randomly scan the aisles and finally decide to ask you if you would be terribly upset if they searched your carry-on luggage, advising you of your right to refuse. With everyone's eyes upon you and the police hovering over you, endless questions run through your mind. *May the police board a plane and ask at random for consent to search passengers' luggage even in the absence of an emergency and even though their search is not supported by reasonable suspicion? Does the passenger have the right to refuse to consent to the search? Does the officer's request constitute a search and seizure? If contraband is found as a result of this kind of search, could the exclusionary rule be used to suppress the evidence?* Given the heightened interest in airline safety following the September 11, 2001 terrorist attacks these issues have never been more germane.

The Supreme Court addressed these issues in *Florida v. Bostick*, 501 U.S. 429 (1991), where it ruled that suspicionless dragnet- style sweeps of buses in intra- and interstate travel are constitutional. On a routine bus sweep, without probable cause or individualized suspicion, two officers from the Broward County Sheriff's Department boarded a bus at a scheduled stop in Ft. Lauderdale, Florida, and asked Terrance Bostick for permission to see his identification, inspect his ticket, and search his luggage. The officers, wearing their bright green "raid" jackets, stood blocking the aisle, and one officer held a gun in a weapons pouch. Though he was not "arrested," Bostick consented to a search, which ultimately led to the discovery of cocaine.

At his trial he was unsuccessful in his attempt to suppress the cocaine as illegally seized evidence. However, on appeal, the Florida Supreme Court moved to suppress the cocaine on the grounds that the Broward County Sheriff's practice was unconstitutional. Prosecutors argued that the exclusionary rule did not apply because Bostick had not been seized prior to his relinquishment of the cocaine. But the Florida high court reasoned that a seizure had occurred because Bostick, like any reasonable passenger in such a situation, did not feel free to refuse the officers and leave the bus. Since he was in custody from the moment the officers asked to search his luggage, his Fourth Amendment rights were in play. The Florida court recognized that while the police may approach persons at random in most public places and ask consent for a search, they may not use the same tactics on a cramped bus because a suspect, who may be far from home, does not feel free to refuse, get up, and leave.

The U.S. Supreme Court has ruled on several occasions that a seizure does not occur simply because a police officer approaches a person and asks a few questions.[24] However, as the Florida court pointed out, on a cramped bus, with police towering above, would any reasonable person simply stand up and walk away? Because a seizure occurred the moment that Bostick felt he was not free to leave the bus, the Fourth Amendment was in play while the police searched his luggage. Since they searched without any probable cause, the fruits of their search should be suppressed.

The Supreme Court rejected this line of reasoning and ruled 6–3 to reverse the Florida high court. Writing for the majority, Justice O'Connor reasoned that the case did not turn on whether Bostick was free to leave, but rather on whether he was free to decline the officer's request and terminate the encounter.[25] A seizure does not occur simply because an officer approaches an individual and asks a few questions, nor do the police need to have a reasonable suspicion of criminal activity to approach a person and ask questions. Bostick, as a reasonable person, was free to disregard the police and walk away. Thus, since Bostick was not seized, the Fourth Amendment did not apply. Furthermore, because his decision to cooperate with the officers was voluntary, the officers were authorized to conduct a search without first obtaining a warrant. If the decision to give consent to the search had been a product of police intimidation or harassment, then the search would have been unconstitutional. O'Connor pointed out that the officers did not point their guns at Bostick.

O'Connor's reasoning begs the question of what would have happened to Bostick if he had gotten off the bus after declining the officer's request to search his luggage. One could reasonably assume that the officers would have seized him at that point. While that assumption is probably valid, O'Connor contended that a refusal to cooperate with the police does not furnish "the minimal level of objective justification needed for a detention or seizure." Bostick could have walked away and the police would have had to obtain a warrant to search his suitcase, unless they had reasonable suspicion that his suitcase was a bomb or some device that posed a threat to public safety.

Does this decision apply to buses in particular or to all forms of transportation? O'Connor contended that the ruling in this case applied equally to police encounters on trains, planes, or city streets. She also challenged the dissenter's view that the Court's decision was a departure from past precedent. She believed that four cases— *Terry, Royer, Rodriguez,* and *Delgado*—supported the logic of *Bostick*.[26]

Justice O'Connor also fended off charges that the majority was willing to suspend constitutional guarantees so that the government had a blank check to wage a draconian war on drugs. She countered:

> If that war is to be fought, those who fight it must respect the rights of individuals, whether or not those individuals are suspected of having committed a crime. By the same token, *this Court is not empowered to forbid law enforcement practices simply because it considers them distasteful* [emphasis added].

The dissenters were amazed and incensed at the majority's willingness to justify suspicionless police sweeps of buses simply because such a practice is an effective law enforcement technique. Justice Marshall, joined by Justices Blackmun and Stevens, attacked the practice as violating the Fourth Amendment. Marshall argued that the issue was not whether Bostick was free to refuse permission to search his luggage, like the majority argued, but whether he felt free to terminate his encounter with the police. If Bostick remained seated while obstinately refusing to answer the officers, then he knew that the officers would only grow suspicious and intensify their search. Indeed, according to police testimony, this is likely to be the effect of a passenger's recalcitrance. If Bostick attempted to terminate the encounter with the police, he would have had to "squeeze past the gun-wielding inquisitor who was blocking the aisle of the bus." Since the bus was preparing to leave, Bostick would have had to purchase another ticket to his destination in Atlanta. Marshall pointed out that it would be permissible for the police to approach Bostick on the street or after reaching his destination at a bus terminal, but not while traveling on a bus midway to his destination. A coercive element is added to the encounter when the person is in unfamiliar territory far from home. In theory, Bostick could have exercised his Fourth Amendment rights by walking away from the police, forcing them to show probable cause or to obtain a warrant. However, he was afraid to squeeze past the officers and leave the bus so far from home. Recall that the police were not proceeding under any probable cause or individualized suspicion, but were conducting a dragnet search hoping to turn up something. Marshall was not suggesting that the police must obtain a warrant every time they wish to question someone, but that they must have a "reasonable, articulate basis to suspect criminal wrongdoing" before they approach passengers.

## The "Seizure" Question Revisited

The precise scope of our Fourth Amendment right against unreasonable seizures by the government depends largely on how the Court defines a seizure and at what point a seizure occurs. ***Does a seizure occur when a police officer detains a person for a moment to ask a question or only when physical contact of some kind occurs?*** The answer is central to the Fourth Amendment's guarantee against unreasonable seizures and the application of the exclusionary rule to deter the police from unreasonable law enforcement tactics. In *Katz v. United States*, 389 U.S. 347 (1967), discussed later in this chapter, the Court held that electronic eavesdropping conducted without any physical conduct and without the seizure of any material object fell within the protection of the Fourth Amendment. Contrary to the older common law definition of seizure, where physical touching occurs, in *Katz* the Court extended the concept of seizure to the electronic recording of sounds. In *Terry v. Ohio*, 392 U.S. 1 (1968), the Court expanded this definition of seizure to include official restraints on individual freedom short of actual common law arrest. By increasing the variety of police-citizen interactions that are covered by the Fourth Amendment, the Court has forced the police to show reasonable suspicion—if not probable cause—before detaining a suspect or seizing a piece of evidence. Unreasonable seizures—those not preceded by a showing of reasonable suspicion—could lead to the exclusion of evidence at trial.

But the police don't live in a theoretical world. The guidelines set forth in cases like *Terry* become difficult to follow in tense situations where the police, without a reasonable suspicion that a person is involved in wrongdoing, see a person suddenly run wildly down the street at their approach. Since the police have absolutely no idea what this person has done, should they turn away in fear that their pursuit and possible discovery of evidence could constitute an unreasonable seizure? Does the fact that this person has bolted for no apparent reason other than the sight of their patrol car justify their pursuit? Most would say that it does. Suppose further that as this person sprints away objects of all kinds are strewn from his backpack and are collected as evidence by the companions of the pursuing officer. The objects are small chunks of plastic explosive and the now-subdued runner confesses to be a terrorist. Since the officers proceeded without the reasonable suspicion that this person is a terrorist, can the plastic explosives be used as evidence at trial? A defense attorney could argue that under existing Fourth Amendment jurisprudence the evidence should be suppressed.

Is there a "street pursuit" exception to the reasonable suspicion rule? The Court revisited these questions in *California v. Hodari D.*, 499 U.S. 621 (1991). The case originated when a group of youths, including Hodari D., were hanging out around a car in a high-crime area of Oakland, California. Upon seeing an unmarked police car, Hodari and his friends started running away. Judging that the teenagers must be up to something, the police chased them. As the officers drew near, Hodari jettisoned his cargo—a small rock of crack cocaine. After he was subdued, the officer also discovered $300 in cash and a pocket pager, commonly used by drug dealers. At the juvenile proceeding, the judge rejected Hodari's argument that the crack should be excluded as evidence because it was seized in violation of the Fourth Amendment's requirement that the police must have at least a "reasonable suspicion" before they stop and interrogate suspects. A California state appeals court reversed, ruling that the police had begun the chase prior to establishing that Hodari had committed a crime, and that the cocaine should be suppressed as evidence.

The U.S. Supreme Court reversed the state appeals court, ruling 7–2 that the police need not show reasonable suspicion to justify the pursuit of a fleeing individual, for a pursuit is not the same as a seizure. A pursuit becomes a seizure when the police make physical contact with a defendant or when they show that the defendant yielded to any "show of authority" by the police during the chase. Since Hodari did not comply with the officers' show of authority, he was not seized until after the cocaine was dropped and the officers tackled him. Thus, the cocaine was not the fruit of an unconstitutional search: Hodari voluntarily "gave" the cocaine to the police.

Even if the police do not have a reasonable suspicion—much less probable cause—to detain or question a suspect, abandoned evidence seized by the police incident to a chase or questioning may be used against the defendant without violating the Fourth Amendment. Employing a pre-*Terry* analysis, Justice Scalia reasoned that under the Fourth Amendment, a seizure occurs when an officer uses either physical force or a show of authority to obtain compliance to his or her will. Finding abandoned or discarded evidence pursuant to a chase is not a seizure. Street pursuits are not seizures under the Fourth Amendment and, therefore, are exempt from the reasonable suspicion rule that governs situations where persons are just standing around in a park or other public place. Since it is not the purpose of the Fourth Amendment to deter the police from questioning or pursuing suspects who have fled down a street or a sidewalk, recovered evidence from a street pursuit cannot be excluded under the exclusionary rule. The purpose of the exclusionary rule is to deter the misconduct of the police, and Scalia asked how this purpose would be furthered by extending the rule to evidence seized as a result of a street pursuit. What would be gained by deterring the police from pursuing or questioning a group of teenagers who scatter when a patrol car comes into view? Scalia wrote: "We do not think it desirable, even as a policy matter, to stretch the Fourth Amendment beyond its words and beyond the meaning of arrest as respondent urges. Street pursuits always place the public at some risk, and compliance with police orders to stop should therefore be encouraged."

In their dissent, Stevens and Marshall blasted the majority's narrow definition of a seizure as "seriously flawed," "profoundly unwise," and "unfaithful to a long line of Fourth Amendment cases." Was the majority's ruling a departure from precedent or an unreasonable reading of the Fourth Amendment? Citing *Terry* and *Katz*, Stevens argued that a seizure occurs "whenever an objective evaluation of a police officer's show of force conveys the message that a citizen is not entirely free to leave." This broad definition of seizure might include a situation where a police officer taps you on the shoulder with a nightstick and says, "Step over here, now!" *Katz* and *Terry* expanded Fourth Amendment protection by extending the definition of seizure from the common law requirement of "grasping," or physical conduct, to a show of authority or force by the police resulting in the submission of a citizen to that show of force. In order to constitute a seizure under Scalia's interpretation, the police officer would have to handcuff the citizen or fire a shot overhead. All interaction up to that point would not implicate the Fourth Amendment. Stevens added that the consequences of the majority's logic will "encourage unlawful displays of force that will frighten countless citizens into surrendering whatever privacy rights they still may have." Law enforcement officials could now walk into a shopping mall with their guns drawn and wait for a reaction to justify their investigation.

## Clarifying *Terry*

*Do activities such as running, loitering, or even waiting for a bus in a high-crime area create a reasonable suspicion of wrongdoing that allows the police to stop and question someone?* In *Illinois v. Wardlow*,[27] in 2000, the Court addressed this question and revisited the stop-and-frisk doctrine established in *Terry*. Recall that under *Terry*, the police must have a reasonable suspicion of criminal behavior to stop and detain a person for investigative purpose. To conduct a frisk, the police must have reasonable suspicion that the suspect is armed and dangerous.

Around noon on September 9, 1995, Sam Wardlow was standing next to a building in an area of Chicago known for heavy narcotics trafficking. He was holding an "opaque" plastic bag. At the same time, a four-car caravan of Chicago's finest was patrolling the area on the lookout for people who might be engaged in drug trafficking. When Wardlow saw a patrol car, he bolted down the street. Two officers caught up with him, stopped him, and conducted a pat-down search for weapons. The search revealed a .38–caliber handgun that the suspect was carrying in his plastic bag. The officers arrested Wardlow.

An Illinois trial court convicted Wardlow of unlawful use of a weapon by a felon, but the Illinois Appellate Court reversed his conviction on the grounds that under *Terry* the officers did not have reasonable suspicion sufficient to justify an investigative stop. The Illinois Supreme Court affirmed, ruling that sudden flight in a high-crime area does not create a reasonable suspicion justifying a stop because running away may simply be an exercise of the right to "go on one's way." The state of Illinois then appealed to the U.S. Supreme Court.

The Supreme Court ruled 5–4 to reverse the Illinois high court's ruling and held that the officers' did not violate the Fourth Amendment. Writing for the majority, Chief Justice Rehnquist reasoned that an officer does not need probable cause to stop a suspect, but rather a "reasonable articulable suspicion" that a criminal activity is occurring. Although reasonable suspicion is not as demanding a standard as probable cause, an officer needs to show "at least a minimal level of objective justification" for the stop.

*By what means, then, should an officer determine reasonable suspicion?* Through common sense, says the Court. Wardlow's flight gave the officers a "particularized suspicion of criminal activity." Nervous, evasive behavior is another relevant factor in determining reasonable suspicion. *May location have any impact on an officer's determination?* Yes. The Court states that while police cannot stop someone simply for being present in a high-crime area, a location's characteristics are relevant in determining whether the circumstances are suspicious enough to warrant further investigation. Thus, no one rule determines reasonable suspicion—it is the totality of the circumstances that must be considered by officers. This totality of circumstance test is supported by all nine justices.

*What about the argument that the Fourth Amendment demands that the police use a more rigorous and less subjective standard in establishing reasonable suspicion?* Rehnquist does not believe that such a standard exists and refused to burden the police and the courts with the requirement that suspicious behavior be established scientifically. Absent some mathematical equation or formula, the police are permitted to use common sense judgments and inference about human behavior.

*Does this approach make it more likely that the police will stop innocent people?* Yes, but this kind of stop—a so-called *Terry* stop—is a minimal intrusion that allows the officer to conduct a brief investigation. If the officer does not learn facts rising to the level of probable cause, the individual must be allowed to go on his or her way.

*What about simply running away at the sight of a police officer? Does this action by itself warrant police action?* No, said the Court, rejecting Illinois's request that the Court create a rule that authorized the temporary detention of anyone who flees at the mere sight of a police without respect to the totality of circumstances.

In his dissenting opinion, Justice Stevens[28] praised the Court for adhering to the "totality of circumstances" rule and rejecting the proposition that "flight" is an indication of criminal activity. However, he was not persuaded by the facts of this case that the officer had reasonable suspicion to stop Wardlow. A reasonable person who resides in a high-crime area may run at the sudden appearance of the police for a variety of reasons, including a fear of getting caught in the crossfire of an arrest or merely because he fears the police. Stevens wrote:

> Among some citizens, particularly minorities and those residing in high crime areas, there is also the possibility that the fleeing person is entirely innocent, but, with or without justification, believes that contact with the police can be dangerous, apart from any criminal activity associated with the officer's sudden presence. For such a person, unprovoked flight is neither "aberrant" nor "abnormal."

## Media Ride-Alongs

The media have often accompanied the police on "busts" in order to provide dramatic images for the evening news. "Real-life" law enforcement programs that combine news and entertainment have also gained in popularity. It is now commonplace to see shaky zoomed-in camera shots of police breaking down doors and rousing suspects out of their beds in early-morning raids. The First Amendment protects the media's right to document the actions of law enforcement, and the Fourth Amendment allows the police to enter and search out home unless they do so in an unreasonable way. *But may the police bring along reporters and photographers when making busts? Are media ride-alongs constitutional? Can it be argued that the media's presence during a search violates the Fourth Amendment even though it is the police and not the media that are executing a warrant?* This question was addressed for the first time by the U.S. Supreme Court in *Wilson v. Layne* in 1999.[29]

The case originated with "Operation Gunsmoke," a national fugitive apprehension program that combined the efforts of U.S. federal marshals, state and local law enforcement, and the media. The program was very effective, resulting in more than 3,000 arrests in forty metropolitan areas. One of the dangerous fugitives targeted was Dominic Wilson. Computer records accurately showed that he was likely to be armed, to resist arrest, and assault police. However, the computer incorrectly listed Wilson as living at an address that was actually his parent's address. So, in the early-morning hours, the Gunsmoke team of marshals, local police officers (dressed in street clothes), and a reporter and photographer from the *Washington Post* entered the home of Wilson's parents and subdued an angry Charles Wilson (Dominic's father), believing him to be the suspect. The officers soon learned that they had the wrong man, apologized and departed. The *Washington Post* photographer took pictures but the paper never published them.

Wilson's parents then sued the law enforcement officials for monetary damages on the grounds that the officers' actions in bringing members of the media to observe and record the attempted arrest violated their Fourth Amendment rights. Attorneys for the police argued that the officers were protected by the doctrine of "qualified immunity" because they had not knowingly violated any constitutional rights by allowing the media to ride along. The district court rejected the immunity defense, but the court of appeals reversed, granting the police immunity but refusing to address the Fourth Amendment question because at the time of the Wilson search there was no guiding precedent on media ride-alongs.

On appeal, the U.S. Supreme Court held 8–1 that a media ride-along *does* violate the Fourth Amendment, but because the law on this matter was not settled at the time of the arrest, the officers are immune from lawsuits. On the one hand, the law allows citizens to sue federal officials for violating the citizens' Fourth Amendment rights, but law enforcement officials, like all government officials performing their official duties, are generally granted a qualified immunity that shields them from liability for civil damages resulting from mistakes—unless it can be shown that they knowingly violated clearly established rights.[30] The police were immune from lawsuits in this case because the courts had never ruled on whether media ride-alongs were constitutional.

Writing for the majority Chief Justice Rehnquist held that the officers had a valid warrant to enter the Wilsons' home in order to arrest Dominic Wilson, but they were not entitled to bring the media with them. Rehnquist agreed with the officers' argument that the police have some degree of discretion when they are executing a warrant. They may sometimes go beyond the precise wording of the warrant in order to advance legitimate law enforcement objectives. The Court has held in the past that while not every police action inside the home must be explicitly authorized by the text of the warrant,[31] the Fourth Amendment does require that police actions in execution of a warrant be related to the objectives of the authorized intrusion.[32] But the reporters inside the home were not related to any of the objectives of the intrusion and "ignore[d] the importance of the right of residential privacy at the core of the Fourth Amendment." Rehnquist wrote:

> It may well be that media ride-alongs further the law enforcement objectives of the police in a general sense, but it is not the same as furthering the purposes of the search. Were such generalized "law enforcement objectives" themselves sufficient to trump the Fourth Amendment, the protections guaranteed by that Amendment's text would be significantly watered down.

The interest in promoting the public's awareness of crime fighting and good public relations for the police is not sufficient to justify the ride-along intrusion into a private home. The police, themselves, may videotape searches, arrests, or even routine traffic stops in the name of improving law enforcement techniques or preserving evidence. Even the presence of third parties during the execution of a warrant may be constitutionally permissible in some circumstances; but media ride-along intrusions into private homes so that reporters can work on stories for their own purposes are not constitutional.

Notwithstanding all of the exceptions to the warrant requirement embraced by the Court in recent years, the chief justice concluded by reiterating the "centuries-old principle of respect for the privacy of the home." Given the "overriding respect for the sanctity of the home that has been embedded in our traditions since the origins of the Republic," absent a warrant or "exigent circumstances" the police may not enter a home to make an arrest.

## ELECTRONIC EAVESDROPPING

The framers of the Fourth and Fifth Amendments (ratified in 1791) could never have imagined technology that allows the government to electronically obtain incriminating statements from a suspect in his home, much less conduct a computer search of a person's "papers and effects" from a distant location. But advances in science eventually made it possible for the government to, in Justice Louis Brandeis's words, "obtain disclosure in court what is whispered in the closet." In his famous *Harvard Law Review* article in 1890, Brandeis presaged the time when searches of private papers and thoughts would be conducted by means far more sophisticated than even wiretapping. Long before the computer age, Brandeis predicted:

> Ways may some day be developed by which the government, without removing papers from secret drawers, can reproduce them in court, and by which it will be enabled to expose to a jury the most intimate occurrences of the home. . . . *Can it be that the Constitution affords no protection against such invasions of individual security* [emphasis added]?[33]

Twenty years after Brandeis' prediction, new technology made it possible to electronically tap into telephone conversations. At the height of Prohibition in the 1920s, the government used this technology for the first time to pursue bootleggers. Roy Olmstead and several accomplices were prosecuted and convicted under the National Prohibition Act after they were apprehended by federal agents for importing and selling liquor. The agents acted on incriminating evidence obtained by the wiretapping of telephone lines. Over counsel's objections that the evidence was inadmissible under the Fourth and Fifth Amendments, Olmstead and codefendants were convicted in federal district court. A U.S. court of appeals affirmed the convictions. ***Does the Fourth Amendment's prohibition of unreasonable searches and seizures extend to the electronic wiretapping of telephone conversations and to other forms of electronic surveillance?*** In *Olmstead v. United States*, 277 U.S. 438 (1928), the Supreme Court reversed the court of appeals decision and ruled that the Fourth and Fifth Amendments do not apply to electronic eavesdropping of telephone conversations. Writing for the 5–4 majority, Chief Justice Taft reasoned that by no stretch of the imagination could the Fourth Amendment's protection against unreasonable searches and seizures be made to apply to telephone conversations. The purpose of the Fourth Amendment, wrote Taft, is to prevent the use of unreasonable governmental force to search material things, such as a person, a house, or one's papers and effects. Telephone conversations are none of these things, and the evidence at issue was secured through the sense of hearing and not by force. If Congress wished to protect telephone conversations by making them inadmissible it could do so, but the courts could not adopt such a policy by twisting the meaning of the Fourth Amendment.

Taft also refused to accept Olmstead's Fifth Amendment self-incrimination challenge because there was no evidence that Olmstead and the others were compelled to divulge information concerning their bootlegging activities over the telephone. The chief justice was adamant in his refusal to extend or expand the language of the Fourth or the Fifth Amendment to include telephone conversations. He reasoned:

> The reasonable view is that one who installs in his house a telephone instrument with connecting wires intends to project his voice to those quite outside, and that the wires beyond his house, and messages passing over them, are not within the protection of the Fourth Amendment. Here those who intercepted the projected voices were not in the house of either party to the conversation.

The behavior of the federal agents may have been unethical but it was not unconstitutional. The courts could not exclude evidence because it was obtained solely through unethical means.

In his dissent, Justice Brandeis attacked Taft's unduly literal construction of the Fourth and Fifth Amendments. Reminiscent of his famous *Harvard Law Review* article[34] thirty-eight years earlier, Brandeis argued that the framer's intent in adopting the Fourth Amendment was to provide a comprehensive "right to be let alone" and not merely to protect against physical entry into the homes of citizens. The Court had already set the stage for this idea in *Boyd v. United States*, 116 U.S. 616 (1886), where it held that individuals have an "indefeasible" common law and Fourth Amendment right of private property that protects not only one's home and effects, but the "privacies of one's life." While *Boyd* expanded privacy protection beyond houses, papers, and effects—thus setting the tone for broader Fourth Amendment protection—the Court had refused to recognize an invasion as a search or a seizure unless an actual physical trespass or taking occurred.

In order to protect that broadened privacy interest, reasoned Brandeis in *Olmstead*, "every unjustifiable" invasion of privacy by the government must be considered a violation of the Fourth Amendment and, concomitantly, that any evidence obtained by such an intrusion and used against the individual must be deemed a violation of the Fifth Amendment.

Justice Brandeis's position was not to be adopted by the Court until *Katz v. United States*, 389 U.S. 347 (1967). Charles Katz, a bookie, was convicted in a federal district court for telephoning bets and wagers from a glass-enclosed public telephone booth in Los Angeles to his accomplices in Boston and Miami. FBI agents used an electronic listening device attached to the outside of the booth to make recordings of the telephone conversations. Rejecting Katz's contention that the recorded conversations were obtained in violation of his Fourth Amendment rights, the U.S. court of appeals affirmed the lower court's ruling. Katz appealed to the Supreme Court. Citing *Olmstead*, the government argued that because the telephone booth from which Katz made his calls was constructed of glass—rendering him visible to the FBI agents—he had no Fourth Amendment rights while in the booth. Although they did not believe that they needed a warrant, the agents took care that they did not begin their surveillance until they had probable cause to believe that Katz was conveying gambling information to persons in other states in violation of federal law. Furthermore, the surveillance was limited in purpose to his gambling activities. Thus, the tapping of his telephone call from the booth did not constitute an illegal search under the Fourth Amendment.

Katz responded that because the public telephone booth is "a constitutionally protected area," the evidence obtained without a warrant was obtained in violation of the Fourth Amendment. Contrary to the trespass doctrine espoused by Chief Justice Taft in *Olmstead*, nonphysical penetration of a constitutionally protected area violates the Fourth Amendment.

Writing for the majority, Justice Stewart rejected the government's position and Katz's formulation of the issue as well. Stewart reasoned that the Fourth Amendment protects persons and not places. It does not create a "constitutionally protected area" around the booth, but protects a person's "reasonable expectation of privacy." By entering the telephone booth and closing the door, Katz made an effort to keep what he said private. Thus, even though the area of surveillance was neither a private residence nor a hotel room but a glass booth, Katz had a reasonable expectation of privacy in his conversation.

Stewart dismissed the government's claim that because the booth was made of glass Katz abandoned any expectation of privacy. What Katz sought to exclude when he entered the booth, however, was not the "intruding eye" but the "uninvited ear." Contrary to the trespass rule set forth in *Olmstead*, electronic eavesdropping and recording constitute a search under the Fourth Amendment, and it is not necessary to penetrate the wall of the booth in order for a search to occur. Having established this rule, Stewart then turned to whether the search conducted was constitutional. Even though the agents relied on *Olmstead*, acted with restraint, and narrowly tailored their "search," they nevertheless conducted the search without presenting their probable cause to a neutral magistrate who would decide whether to issue a warrant.

The constitutional standard established in *Katz* held that the limits on Fourth Amendment protection are not determined objectively by where the subject is, but rather subjectively by the expectation of privacy that the subject has in a particular situation. Furthermore, since electronic eavesdropping constitutes a search, it is therefore bound by the probable cause and warrant requirements of the Fourth Amendment.

***Must the police always secure a warrant before they "bug" a residence or a telephone booth?*** Wouldn't a rigid warrant requirement tend to tip off the suspect and perhaps lead to the destruction of critical evidence? In *Dalia v. United States*, 441 U.S. 238 (1979), the Burger Court ruled 5–4 that the police need not announce their purpose before installing a legal listening device. The Court relied on Title III of the Omnibus Crime Control and Safe Streets Act of 1968, which provides a "constitutionally adequate substitute" for advance notice by requiring the police to notify the authorizing judge once the eavesdropping is complete. The judge, in turn, must then notify those persons subjected to the surveillance. The Court reasoned that a Title III electronic surveillance order allows the police discretion in determining how the search will take place.

***Does a person using a telephone enjoy a reasonable expectation in every instance?*** The police often use a pen register; that is, a device that records the telephone numbers of outgoing calls. Does the use of this device amount to a search under the Fourth Amendment? In *Smith v. Maryland*, 442 U.S. 735 (1979), the Court ruled 6–3 that the use of a pen register by police does not constitute a search under the Fourth Amendment. A person using a telephone does not enjoy a reasonable expectation of privacy in this instance because telephone companies regularly use such devices to obtain billing information. While the telephone user enjoys an expectation of privacy in the content of his or her conversations, there is no such protection for the numbers that are called. By calling your bookie on the telephone, you have voluntarily given this information to the telephone company and assume the risk that this information may be given to the police.

***What about cordless telephones and cell phones?*** The proliferation of cordless telephones and cell phones raises interesting Fourth Amendment questions. When you use a conventional telephone at home or in an office you have a reasonable expectation that your conversation is private and that the Fourth Amendment applies to any attempt to eavesdrop. In order to hear your conversation, the police must attach a listening device to the telephone or phone line. But suppose you make your call poolside from a cordless phone and the police accidentally overhear your conversation over their radio as they pass your house. The mobile handset of a cordless phone uses an FM signal just like a walkie-talkie and may be overheard on any ordinary FM radio. The police drive past again and record your conversation with an officer's microcassette recorder. They then use the tape recording to obtain a warrant to search your house. Does *Katz* apply? Does the exclusionary rule apply because the police recorded your conversation and plan to use it to bring charges against you? Or did you give up your reasonable expectation of privacy by using a cordless phone?

Although the U.S. Supreme Court has not yet ruled directly on such a case, the Kansas Supreme Court addressed similar questions in *State v. Howard* in 1984.[35] While tuning his FM radio, Howard's neighbor overheard conversations between Howard and others that transpired over a cordless phone. The neighbor recorded one conversation and gave the recording to the police, who in turn provided the neighbor with a more sophisticated recording device and asked if he would record additional conversations. The police then obtained a warrant to install a pen register to record the telephone numbers Howard called, even though they never had a warrant to record the conversations. After a warrant to search Howard's house was issued on the basis of the recordings, the police discovered a cache of narcotics in Howard's possession.

The prosecution suffered a setback when the trial court suppressed the recorded conversations. But on appeal, the Kansas Supreme Court reversed, holding that because a conversation over a cordless phone constitutes an oral communication rather than a wire communication under federal law, the exclusionary rule does not apply. The defendant had no reasonable expectation of privacy under *Katz* because he was using a cordless phone—if he read the phone's operating manual, he knew the risk of being overheard. The person to whom Howard was speaking, however, did have a reasonable expectation of privacy because he was using a conventional phone and did not know that Howard was using a cordless phone.

In 1993, the U.S. Supreme Court denied certiorari and thus left standing the ruling of a federal court of appeals in a case dealing with the expectation of privacy in cordless phone conversations. In *United States v. Smith*,[36] a federal appeals court ruled that no reasonable expectation of privacy exists in cordless phone transmissions "due to the ease with which they can be monitored." Defendants "knowingly expose" their conversations to the public by using a means of communication that can be easily intercepted.

## AERIAL SURVEILLANCE

*Would a random aerial flyover of a backyard or field by police officers in a small plane or helicopter constitute a search under the Fourth Amendment?* The question that emerges in this category of cases is: *At what point does a person's reasonable expectation of privacy diminish because of the actions or carelessness of that person?* Suppose that Grandma Daniels decides to build a still and produce moonshine whiskey in her backyard. She surrounds her yard with a tall fence, and around the fence plants dense evergreen bushes. The only way the still can be spotted is from above. Does her expectation of privacy extend to areas not hidden from view? The U.S. Supreme Court wrestled with these issues in 1986 in *California v. Ciraolo*, 476 U.S. 207.

The Court granted certiorari to review the California Court of Appeals ruling that a warrantless aerial observation of a person's yard that leads to the issuance of a warrant violates the Fourth Amendment. The following events led to the ruling. On September 2, 1982, Santa Clara police received an anonymous tip that Ciraolo was growing marijuana in his backyard, but a six-foot outer fence and ten-foot inner fence prohibited them from observing the contents of the property. The police then secured a small plane and flew over Ciraolo's yard at an altitude of 1,000 feet, from which they photographed marijuana plants eight to ten feet in height growing in the suspect's yard. Based on an affidavit and the supporting photographs, the officers obtained a warrant to search Ciraolo's property. The search netted seventy-three marijuana plants, which were used to convict the defendant on a charge of cultivation of marijuana. The trial court judge refused to suppress the evidence as fruits of an illegal search. However, the California Court of Appeals reversed on the grounds that under *Oliver v. United States*, 466 U.S. 170 (1984), Ciraolo's backyard was within the curtilage of his home. In sum, he had a reasonable expectation of privacy in his yard.

The U.S. Supreme Court reversed the California court's ruling. Writing for the 5–4 majority, Chief Justice Burger applied the two-part *Katz* test. First, did Ciraolo have a subjective expectation of privacy in his yard? Second, was that expectation "reasonable"? The defendant had no difficulty in satisfying the first part of the test. However, Burger concluded that Ciraolo's expectation that his marijuana garden was protected from aerial police surveillance was unreasonable and was "not an expectation that society is prepared to honor." While he could reasonably expect that a ten-foot fence would keep people at street level from peering into his backyard, it does not follow that the fence would necessarily shield his gardening hobby from the eyes of a citizen or police officer climbing a tree or standing on top of a truck. It is not enough to assert that one's expectation of privacy is reasonable under *Katz*; one must also question whether the government's intrusion infringes upon the personal and societal values protected by the Fourth." Such values include the fundamental privacy interests essential to the physical and psychological well-being of the person and the family. Clearly, cultivation of marijuana falls outside of those interests. While Ciraolo's yard was within the curtilage of his home, that area did not bar all police observation. The police are not expected to avert their eyes when they walk or ride on a public street past one's home. The officers flew over Ciraolo's house in public airspace in a nonintrusive manner and were able to view the plants with the naked eye. Indeed, anybody flying over would have seen Ciraolo's garden.

Justice Powell, joined by Justices Brennan, Marshall, and Blackmun, attacked Burger's reasoning as a major departure from the *Katz* standard. Powell pointed out that had the officer climbed over the fence or used a ladder to look over the fence without a warrant, the majority certainly would have agreed that the search would have been unreasonable. Why then is the use of an airplane to conduct a search reasonable? Powell was curious as to why the majority would concede that Ciraolo had a reasonable expectation of privacy from a camera mounted on a long pole, for instance, but not from aerial observation. Deciding the case by relying on the manner of surveillance rather than a subjective expectation of privacy was directly contrary to *Katz*.

For Powell it appeared that the majority's holding rested solely on the fact that Ciraolo's expectation of privacy was unreasonable because "members of the public fly in planes and may look down at homes as they fly over them." In other words, by not building a dome over his backyard, Ciraolo ran the risk every day of someone in an airplane looking down and seeing his marijuana plants. Powell dryly commented:

> This line of reasoning is flawed. First, the actual risk to privacy from commercial or pleasure aircraft is virtually nonexistent . . . The risk that a passenger on such a plane might observe private activities, and might connect those activities with particular people, is simply too trivial to protect against . . . Therefore, contrary to the Court's suggestion, people do not "knowingly expos[e]" their residential yards "to the public" merely by failing to build barriers that prevent aerial surveillance.

## THE "NO-KNOCK" WARRANT

*Does the Fourth Amendment require police officers to knock and announce their presence before executing a warrant and entering a residence? Is there an "announcement" requirement in the Fourth Amendment? What if the police destroy property during an no-knock execution of a warrant?* The U.S. Supreme Court addressed these questions in *United States v. Ramirez*, 523 U.S. 65 (1998).

The case originated when a reliable informant notified Alcohol Tobacco and Firearms (ATF) agents that Alan Shelby, an extremely dangerous escaped prisoner, was hiding at Hernan Ramirez's home. The informant's observation was corroborated by a federal agent who saw Shelby outside of the residence.

Based on this information a deputy U.S. marshal obtained a "no-knock" warrant granting permission to enter and search the Ramirez home. The police will often ask a judge for a no-knock warrant to enter and search a home when they believe that announcing their presence would be dangerous or inhibit the investigation of a crime. A no-knock entry usually means that officers must break a window or break down a door.[37]

The informant had also told the agents that Ramirez might have guns and drugs hidden in his garage. Early in the morning while the Ramirez family slept, forty-five officers arrived to execute the warrant. They first announced over a portable loud speaker that they had a search warrant before breaking a single window in the garage so that they could point a gun through the opening. Assuming that his house was being burglarized, Ramirez grabbed a pistol and fired into the ceiling of his garage. The officers fired back and shouted, "Police." When Ramirez realized that it was the police entering his home, he dropped his pistol and threw himself on the floor. He waived his *Miranda* rights, confessing that he had fired the weapon, that he owned the gun, and that he was a convicted felon. The agents then obtained another warrant to search the house for additional weapons. The escaped convict, Alan Shelby, was not found.

Ramirez was indicted for being a felon in possession of a firearm, but the district court granted his motion to suppress evidence regarding his possession of weapons, ruling that the agents had violated the Fourth Amendment because there were "insufficient exigent circumstances" to justify the police officers' destruction of property (breaking the window) in the execution of the warrant. The court of appeals affirmed, concluding that while a "mild exigency" (some risk or possibility of mistake) is sufficient to justify a no-knock entry that can be accomplished without the destruction of property, a "more specific inference of exigency" is necessary when property is destroyed. In other words, the police must be held to a higher standard and show specific examples of the possibility of danger or error if they plan to destroy property during a no-knock entry. The ATF agents in this case had conducted an unreasonable search because they had failed to meet the higher standard.

The U.S. Supreme Court unanimously reversed the court of appeals ruling and attempted to clarify the standards to be used for no-knock entries. The Court had already ruled in earlier cases that in some circumstances an officer's unannounced entry into a home might be unreasonable but that there was no rigid rule requiring announcement in all instances.[38] In order to justify a no-knock entry the police must have a reasonable suspicion that knocking and announcing their presence, under the particular circumstances, would be "dangerous or futile," or that it would interfere with the investigation of the crime by allowing the destruction of evidence.[39] But the Court felt that neither of these cases directly addressed whether the reasonableness of a no-knock entry depends on property damage. So, in *Ramirez* the Court decided that the Fourth Amendment does not hold officers to a higher standard when a no-knock entry results in the destruction of property. An entry's lawfulness does not depend on whether property is damaged; a no-knock entry is justified if police have reasonable suspicion that knocking and announcing their presence would be dangerous, futile, or inhibit the effective investigation of the crime. Excessive or unnecessary property destruction during a search may violate the Fourth Amendment even though the entry itself is lawful and the evidence was obtained lawfully. If this standard is applied in Ramirez's case, then it is obvious that no Fourth Amendment violation occurred. The agents certainly had a reasonable suspicion that knocking and announcing their presence might be dangerous to themselves and others. Furthermore, the police broke only a single window in the garage to discourage Shelby or Ramirez from rushing to get the weapons that the informant had told them were in the garage.

## THE RIGHT TO COUNSEL

As early as 1701, many of the American colonies took steps to guarantee the privilege of counsel. Pennsylvania's Charter of Privilege (1701), for example, provided that "all criminals shall have the same Privilege, of Witnesses and Counsel as their Prosecutors." By 1720, Pennsylvania and Delaware required the appointment of counsel in capital and treason cases. Soon after, South Carolina extended this right to murder and felony cases. By 1750, Connecticut had adopted the custom of paying lawyers to defend indigent defendants charged with serious crimes.[40] The new federal government strengthened the right to counsel by passing the Judiciary Act of 1789, the same year that James Madison drafted the Sixth Amendment to the Bill of Rights. In 1790, one year before the Bill of Rights was ratified, Congress passed the Federal Crimes Act, requiring the federal courts to appoint counsel to defendants in capital cases. Although in the vast majority of cases the typical defendant argued his own case, it is clear that early Americans recognized the importance of the right to counsel.[41]

The Sixth Amendment provides that "In all criminal prosecutions, the accused shall enjoy the right . . . to have the assistance of counsel for his defense." Like many other provisions in the Bill of Rights, the phrase is deceptive in its simplicity. Did the framers actually intend for the right to counsel to apply in all criminal cases? Do the words "enjoy the right" imply an obligation on the part of the government to appoint a lawyer if the defendant is indigent, or do they mean only that a defendant cannot be forbidden from seeking the assistance of counsel? The Sixth Amendment, when ratified, was understood as providing only the right of retaining an attorney in a federal trial—a right that was not enforceable against the states.[42]

The U.S. Supreme Court did not have an opportunity to rule directly on the meaning of the Sixth Amendment right to counsel and its applicability to the states until the cases *Powell v. Alabama*, 287 U.S. 45 (1932), and *Johnson v. Zerbst*, 304 U.S. 458 (1938). In *Powell*, the Court ruled that the right to counsel is a fundamental right in state criminal proceedings, but refused to incorporate the right to counsel into the due process clause of the Fourteenth Amendment. The Court recognized the fundamental nature of the right to counsel, but maintained its adherence to its traditional nonincorporation case-by-case approach, occasionally ordering new trials with the assistance of counsel for poor defendants but usually abiding by the decisions of the state courts. Nonetheless, *Powell* was a great breakthrough. On the importance of counsel and the pitfalls of the common practice of defendants acting as their own counsel, Justice George Sutherland wrote:

> The right to be heard would be, in many cases, of little avail if it did not comprehend the right to be heard by counsel. Even the intelligent and educated layman has small

and sometimes no skill in the science of law. . . . He lacks both the skill and knowledge adequately to prepare his defense, even though he has a perfect one. He requires the guiding step of counsel at every step in the proceedings against him. Without it, though he be not guilty, he faces the danger of conviction because he does not know how to establish his innocence.

In *Johnson v. Zerbst* six years later, the Court stated categorically that in both capital and noncapital federal cases the federal government must provide counsel for the indigent defendant. Citing *Powell*, the Court argued that the Sixth Amendment withholds from federal courts in all criminal proceedings the authority to deprive an accused of life or liberty unless the accused has counsel or has waived the right to counsel. While *Johnson* is a landmark decision because it broadened the right to counsel in federal cases, it did little to help the infinitely larger number of defendants standing trial across the street in the state courthouse. There was little doubt that a dual system of justice existed. Surely the concept of fundamental fairness demanded that the Court make the right of indigents to counsel enforceable against the states by incorporating the Sixth through the Fourteenth Amendments.

A decade later, in *Betts v. Brady*, 316 U.S. 455 (1942), the Court ruled that a refusal to appoint counsel for an indigent defendant charged with a felony did not necessarily violate the Fourteenth Amendment. Betts was indicted of robbery in a trial court in Maryland. During arraignment he asked the judge to appoint counsel for him, but he was told that it was not the policy in that county to appoint counsel except in murder and rape cases. As was the custom of that time, Betts was expected to conduct his own defense. He was found guilty and sentenced to prison for eight years. On appeal to the U.S. Supreme Court, Betts argued that he had been denied the right to assistance of counsel in violation of the due process clause of the Fourteenth Amendment. However, adhering to its narrow case-by-case approach, the Court rejected his appeal:

> Asserted denial [of due process] is to be tested by an appraisal of the totality of facts in a given case. That which may, in one setting, constitute a denial of fundamental fairness, shocking to the universal sense of justice, may, in other circumstances, and in light of other considerations, fall short of such denial.

Examining the constitutional, legislative, and judicial histories of the states from the ratification of the Bill of Rights to that time, the Court extrapolated that "appointment of counsel is not a fundamental right, essential to a fair trial." Therefore, the Sixth Amendment's guarantee of counsel is not "made obligatory" on the states via the Fourteenth Amendment.[43] This position would stand for another twenty-one years before it was attacked and finally discarded by the Warren Court in the celebrated case *Gideon v. Wainwright*, 372 U.S. 335 (1963).[44]

Clarence Earl Gideon was tried and convicted in a Florida court for having broken into a poolroom with the intent to commit a misdemeanor—a felony offense under Florida law. He appeared before the bench without counsel and asked the court to appoint counsel for his defense. His request was denied on the grounds that under *Betts*, the state was not required to appoint counsel for indigent defendants unless they were charged with a capital offense. Gideon then proceeded to conduct his own defense "about as well as could be expected from a layman." He made an opening statement to the jury, cross-examined the state's witnesses, presented witnesses in his own defense, and closed with an assertion of his innocence. However, Gideon was convicted by the jury and sent to jail. With the aid of the prison's law library and in his own handwriting, he unsuccessfully petitioned the state supreme court for a writ of habeas corpus on the grounds that "I, Clarence Earl Gideon, was denied the rights of the 4th, 5th and 14th amendments of the Bill of Rights."

On his second appeal, the U.S. Supreme Court granted certiorari to review the pervasive problem of a defendant's federal constitutional right to counsel in a state court, a problem, wrote Justice Black, that "has been a continuing source of controversy and litigation in both state and federal courts." The Court appointed Abe Fortas as Gideon's counsel. (Two years after *Gideon*, in 1965, Fortas was appointed to the U.S. Supreme Court and served until his resignation in 1969.)

Writing for a unanimous court, Justice Black began his landmark opinion with a simple query: Should this Court's holding in *Betts v. Brady* be reconsidered? Black believed that it should. He reasoned that the Court in *Betts* had erred in concluding that counsel was not one of the rights fundamental to a fair trial. In *Powell v. Alabama* and in *Grosjean v. America Press Co.*, 287 U.S. 45 (1932), the Court had already established that the assistance of counsel was among the fundamental rights safeguarded against state action by the due process clause of the Fourteenth Amendment. Therefore, the Court's decision in *Betts* was actually a deviation from older precedents. Black espoused the following axiom:

> Not only these precedents but also reason and reflection require us to recognize that in our adversary system of criminal justice, any person hauled into court, who is too poor to hire a lawyer, cannot be assured a fair trial unless counsel is provided for him. This seems to be an obvious truth.

For Black, lawyers were not luxuries but necessities. The state spends a great deal of money to hire lawyers to prosecute those accused of crime. Similarly, defendants who are charged with a crime attempt to hire the very best lawyers they can afford. But the constitutional ideal of a fair trial cannot be realized if only the state and the well-off have access to lawyers. As twenty-two states argued in their *amicus curiae* briefs, *Betts* was "an anachronism when handed down" and should be overruled. Can you imagine yourself, with a few months of preparation, having to select jurors, cross-examine witnesses, and wrestle with the Byzantine world of criminal procedure and rules of evidence? Would you know how to impeach the credibility of a state's witness or when to object to the introduction of evidence?

*But how meaningful is the right to counsel if long before trial a defendant makes incriminating statements to the police during secretive custodial interrogations at the police station prior to obtaining counsel?* One function of the right to counsel is to discourage the police from coercing or manipulating the suspect into making incriminating statements contrary to the "right to remain silent." While most of us want effective policing in our community, few of us would like to see the police given the authority to establish guilt through coerced confessions before a case goes to trial. Thus, what is at stake is more than the right to have the assistance of counsel, but the Fifth Amendment's privilege against self-incrimination.

## POLICE INTERROGATIONS AND THE FIFTH AMENDMENT

The Fifth Amendment provision that "[n]o person . . . shall be compelled in any criminal case to be a witness against himself" reflects a time-honored common law principle that no person is bound to betray himself or herself or can be forced to give incriminating evidence. After all, under the physical or emotional abuse of the whip, the hot iron, or simply the crafty prosecutor, even the strongest person can be made to admit anything. The precise scope of protection afforded by the privilege against self-incrimination is not carved in stone, but at its core lies a respect for human dignity joined with the ideal that a person is innocent until proven guilty. By remaining silent, the defendant forces the prosecution to produce evidence and testimony proving guilt beyond a reasonable doubt.

The U.S. Supreme Court has generally interpreted the self-incrimination clause of the Fifth Amendment broadly enough to protect against a host of questionable police practices.[45] It has also applied the clause to grand jury proceedings[46] and congressional hearings.[47] However, the Court did not incorporate the Fifth Amendment into the due process clause of the Fourteenth Amendment until *Malloy v. Hogan*, 378 U.S. 1 (1964). The case had its origins in the conviction of a gambler named Malloy who was imprisoned when he refused to testify in a state investigation of gambling activities in and around Hartford, Connecticut. He unsuccessfully petitioned for habeas corpus relief on the grounds that his privilege against self-incrimination was violated when he was thrown in jail for refusing to cooperate with the government's investigation. The Warren Court reversed (5–4) the lower court's ruling, holding that the Fifth Amendment's exception from compulsory self-incrimination is also protected by the Fourteenth Amendment's due process clause. In doing so the Court overturned the 1908 case *Twining v. New Jersey*, 211 U.S. 78.

Writing for the majority, Justice Brennan reasoned that contrary to the state's claim, it was irrelevant that Malloy was a witness in a legislative inquiry and not a defendant in a criminal trial. While providing testimony on gambling activities around the state, there was a possibility that Malloy might disclose evidence linking himself to a more recent crime for which he might still be prosecuted. Thus, the Fifth Amendment applied to testimony during legislative proceedings. The only other way around this problem is through a grant of immunity.[48]

The privilege against self-incrimination evokes a dramatic image of the defendant "taking the Fifth" while on the witness stand. But the overwhelming amount of incriminating evidence is obtained not in a courtroom setting but in the station house or patrol car. Many overzealous or overworked law enforcement officials, acting in good faith, may seek to facilitate their investigation by encouraging the suspect to either confess or implicate others. Police do not have to employ "third degree" or "rubber hose" tactics in order to elicit conflicting stories or statements of guilt; for some persons, a visit to the police station alone may result in a confession of guilt. This is why the right to remain silent and the right to an attorney are central to the Fifth Amendment's protection against self-incrimination. Having an attorney present during questioning makes it less likely that the police will attempt to coerce a suspect into making incriminating statements. The police most certainly have the right to question the suspect, but it often happens that during interrogation defendants may be coerced into signing confessions or making incriminating statements admitting guilt. Proceedings such as these work on the ignorance or fear of suspects. The information gained is then used to build a case before the suspect even speaks with an attorney. The police know that any competent lawyer will tell a client to make no statement during the period between arrest and indictment. If the right to counsel is provided prior to indictment, the ability of the police to obtain confessions will be weakened. But if the police are empowered to establish guilt during a pretrial interrogation, the trial itself would be a sham—no more than an appeal from an interrogation.

The Warren Court addressed this problem in *Escobedo v. Illinois*, 378 U.S. 478 (1964), where it was asked this question: *Does refusal by police to honor a suspect's request to consult with a lawyer during questioning constitute a denial of the right to counsel and violate the privilege against self-incrimination?* Escobedo was arrested for the suspected murder of his brother-in-law. Shortly after he reached the police station, Escobedo's lawyer arrived, but during the interrogation the police denied requests from both suspect and lawyer to confer with each other. While the police had only a vague idea that Escobedo was connected with the murder, they told him that they had "convincing evidence" that he had fired the fatal shots. He was free to go home if he "pinned" it on another suspect being held by the police. Without being informed of an Illinois law that made mere complicity in a murder plot as damaging as firing the fatal shot or of his Fifth Amendment to remain silent, Escobedo was coerced into making a number of incriminating statements implicating himself in the murder plot and ultimately leading to his conviction for the murder of his brother-in-law. His motion to suppress the incriminating statements at his trial was denied.

The U.S. Supreme Court reversed Escobedo's conviction and ruled that assistance of counsel was as fundamental during interrogation as it was during trial. That so many confessions of guilt are obtained during interrogation attests to the need for counsel during questioning, for whatever happens at this stage affects the outcome of the whole criminal proceeding. Indeed, the right of counsel would be an empty right if it applied only after the defendant was formally indicted. Justice Arthur Goldberg reasoned that the "guiding hand of counsel" was essential to advise Escobedo of his rights during the interrogation by the police. Writing for the 5–4 majority, Goldberg concluded:

> In *Gideon v. Wainwright* . . . we held that every person accused of a crime, whether state or federal, is entitled to a lawyer at trial. The rule sought by the state here, however, would make the trial no more than an appeal from an interrogation; and the "right to use counsel at the formal trial [would be] a very hollow thing [if], for all practical purposes, the conviction is already assured by pretrial examination."

The rule established in *Escobedo* is as follows: The Fifth and Sixth Amendments are implicated when the investigation is no longer a general inquiry into an unsolved crime but an interrogation of a particular suspect in police custody and where the suspect has requested but has been denied counsel and has not been advised of the right to remain silent.

Two years later, in the famous case *Miranda v. Arizona*, 384 U.S. 436 (1966), the Court extended the *Escobedo* rule by requiring police to read an elaborate set of warnings before conducting custodial interrogations. The *Miranda* warning has become an integral part of police practice as well as popular lore. *But what constitutional purpose is served by reading an arrestee his or her rights?*

On March 3, 1963, an eighteen-year-old woman was kidnapped and raped near Phoenix, Arizona. Ernesto Miranda was arrested ten days later and taken to the police station. Miranda was young and poor and had reached only the ninth grade in school. He was emotionally ill though legally sane, and, as far as we know, was ignorant of his Fifth and Sixth Amendment rights. At the station house, after Miranda was picked out of a police lineup by the victim, two officers took him into a separate room and interrogated him. He was not informed of his right of counsel or privilege against self-incrimination. At first Miranda denied his guilt, but within a short time gave a specific and detailed oral and written confession. The question taken up in *Miranda* is whether this privilege against self-incrimination is as fully applicable during a period of custodial interrogation as it is during a trial.

As illustrated by the majority opinion, the Court was sensitive to a long legacy of psychological abuses by police during custodial interrogation of suspects. Such tactics include everything from giving false legal advice to the "third degree" in order to extract a confession. Since all of these tactics transpire in private, there is little incentive for the police to respect the suspect's right against self-incrimination and right to counsel. How, then, do you provide such incentives to the police? The answer is by threatening to suppress confessions as evidence unless officers can show that they followed certain procedural safeguards.

In *Miranda*, the Court held that the right against self-incrimination does indeed apply to custodial police interrogation. Writing for the 5–4 majority, Chief Justice Warren reversed Miranda's conviction and pointed out that the Fifth Amendment right is applicable outside of criminal court proceedings and protects all persons in custody from being compelled to incriminate themselves. To make this right enforceable, all persons in custody must be informed of their right to remain silent. The police are not to assume that the accused knows about this right or has waived this right. Warren wrote: "[W]ithout proper safeguards the process of in-custody interrogation of persons suspected or accused of crime contains inherently compelling pressures which work to undermine the individual's will to resist and to compel him to speak where he would not otherwise do so freely."

In order to mitigate these pressures and protect the privilege against self-incrimination, the accused must be read his or her rights. Prior to any questioning after a person has been taken into custody, the person must be warned that "he has the right to remain silent, that any statement he does make may be used as evidence against him, and that he has a right to the presence of an attorney, either retained or appointed." The suspect may waive any of these rights, provided that the waiver is

made "voluntarily and intelligently." However, at any time the defendant may rein-
voke these rights and refuse to answer additional questions. It follows that the prosecution may not use any of the defendant's statements unless it demonstrates the
application of the *Miranda* rules during the custodial interrogation. If the state fails
to follow these rules, the evidence gained through the interrogation may be ruled
inadmissible at trial.

Chief Justice Warren anticipated the negative reaction that the ruling produced.
Do the procedural safeguards on custodial interrogation tie the hands of law enforcement officials, as many were prepared to argue? Warren contended that it was not his
intention to "hamper the traditional function of police officers in investigating
crime." *Miranda* did not affect the process of obtaining evidence in the field by questioning witnesses at the scene of the crime. It applied only to in-custody interrogations where a coercive atmosphere exists and where the power of the state may be
wielded in an arbitrary or heavy-handed manner. Warren continued:

> [O]ur decision does not in any way preclude police from carrying out their traditional
> investigatory functions. Although confessions may play an important role in some
> convictions, the cases before us present graphic examples of the overstated "need" for
> confessions. In each case, authorities conducted interrogations ranging up to five days
> in duration despite the presence, through standard investigating practices, of consid-
> erable evidence against each defendant.

In what might be called a hostile dissent, Justice Harlan (joined by Justices
Stewart and White) attacked the majority's ruling as "poor constitutional law" and
harmful use of judicial power to make public policy. Harlan clearly believed that the
decision would seriously impair the ability of law enforcement to solicit confessions
through legitimate means. For him the majority's "experimentation" was at minimum a handicap on policing and at worst a "hazard" to society's welfare. Harlan
believed that the Court should defer to the law enforcement establishment in the
name of public safety. He wrote:

> Society has always paid a stiff price for law and order, and peaceful interrogation is
> not one of the dark moments of the law. . . .
> 　　Nothing in the letter or the spirit of the Constitution or in the precedents squares
> with the heavy-handed and one-sided action that is so precipitously taken by the
> Court in the name of fulfilling its constitutional responsibilities.

The sharply divided Court in *Miranda* was in many ways a reflection of the
division in society regarding the Warren Court's expansion of the rights of the
accused. As a former governor of California, Earl Warren knew that many state law
enforcement officials took great pride in second-guessing, circumventing, or flouting Supreme Court rulings. The *Miranda* warning would make it more difficult for
the police to evade the procedural safeguards governing interrogations that were set
forth in earlier cases. He predicted that with time the *Miranda* ruling would become
an accepted part of police procedures.[49]

In the 1968 presidential campaign, Republican Richard Nixon promised that if
elected he would appoint to the Supreme Court justices who would overturn Warren

Court rulings that "coddled" criminals. After Warren retired in 1969 and President Nixon appointed Warren E. Burger to be chief justice, the Burger Court began to limit the scope and applicability of earlier rulings on coerced confessions. For example, the Court upheld the use of the testimony of a witness who was found by the prosecution as a result of an interrogation of a defendant who had not been read the *Miranda* warning.[50] Also upheld was the use of incriminating statements made to officers in a police car after the defendant requested an attorney but was told that none could be telephoned until the defendant and police had reached the station house.[51] The Burger Court continued this process by ruling that it was not necessary for a suspect to expressly waive his rights during an in-custody interrogation, and that it was not necessary for the police to use the exact language of the *Miranda* warning when reading suspects their rights.[52]

When conservative Republican Ronald Reagan was elected to the presidency in 1980, he continued Nixon's policy of appointing justices likely to overturn the rulings of the Warren Court. Reagan elevated Associate Justice Rehnquist to the Chief Justiceship in 1986, and also appointed Sandra Day O'Connor (1981), Antonin Scalia (1986), and Anthony Kennedy (1988) to the Court during his two terms in office. George H. W. Bush, Reagan's vice president and eventual successor, also hoped to narrow *Miranda* and other Warren Court rulings by appointing two conservative judges: David Souter in 1990 and Clarence Thomas in 1991.

Further modifications of *Miranda* were made by the Rehnquist Court when it ruled 5–4 that the police, after reading a defendant his or her rights, may tape any telephone call made by a defendant and use that recording as evidence at trial.[53] The Court also ruled 8–1 that a jailed, though not yet arraigned, defendant had no right to be read the *Miranda* warning by an undercover agent who was posing as a fellow inmate and attempting to encourage the defendant to make incriminating statements.[54]

In 1990, the Rehnquist Court was asked to overturn *Miranda* in *Minnick v. Mississippi*, 498 U.S. 146. Robert Minnick, who was suspected of burglary and murder, was ordered to answer the sheriff's questions after his attorney left the police station. In the absence of his attorney, Minnick made several incriminating statements that were used to convict him in Mississippi courts. The state supreme court argued that *Miranda* and *Edwards v. Arizona* (451 U.S. 477 (1981))[55] require only that police allow a suspect to confer with a lawyer at least once. After that one conference, the police may begin a new interrogation of the suspect—even in the absence of the suspect's attorney. This second round of interrogation is undertaken with the hope that after the attorney leaves, the suspect may be convinced to change his or her mind and confess to the crime. *Does this approach amount to a mere exception to* Miranda *or does it render it meaningless?*

Over the objections of Rehnquist and Scalia, the majority overturned the state court's ruling, holding that once a person in custody requests an attorney, police may not initiate further questioning until the attorney is present. Under *Edwards*, incriminating statements obtained during a police interrogation in the absence of a lawyer may not be used at trial. Writing for the majority, Justice Kennedy reasoned that the purpose of *Edwards* was to prevent police from badgering a defendant into waiving previously asserted *Miranda* rights. The rule seeks to ensure that statements made in subsequent questioning are not the result of coercion or duress. Kennedy wrote:

A single consultation with an attorney does not remove the suspect from persistent attempts by officials to persuade him to waive his rights, or from the coercive pressures that accompany custody and that may increase as custody is prolonged. . . . We decline to remove protection from police-initiated questioning based on isolated consultations with counsel who is absent when the interrogation resumes.

However, in *Arizona v. Fulminante*, 499 U.S. 279 (1991), the Rehnquist Court ruled 5–4 that coerced confessions may sometimes be used as evidence in criminal trials without necessarily invalidating a conviction. The admission at trial of coerced confessions may be excused as harmless error if it can be shown that other evidence—obtained independently of the confession—is adequate to support a guilty verdict.

Suppose that a suspect is in jail and has been charged with two crimes: counterfeiting and drug trafficking. He has spoken to his attorney regarding the counterfeiting charge, but not the drug charge. May the police question him on the second charge without his attorney being present? By doing so, do they implicate his Fifth Amendment privilege against self-incrimination? In *McNeil v. Wisconsin*, 501 U.S. 171 (1991), the 6–3 majority held that under the Sixth Amendment police may question a suspect who is in jail on another charge in the absence of his attorney. The suspect's Fifth Amendment *Miranda* right is not violated if the police question him about a crime when his court-appointed lawyer in another case is not present. Barring such police questioning, Scalia wrote, would seriously impede effective law enforcement. Scalia also made a highly significant break from established jurisprudence when he asserted that if the Sixth Amendment right to counsel carries with it a Fifth Amendment right, then that right is extremely narrow.

By affording the accused the right to remain silent, the Fifth Amendment places the burden of proving guilt on the state. It forces the government to produce evidence against the accused through honest effort rather than through the expedient method of compelling an admission of guilt by means of a rubber hose or psychological pressure. But more than that, this privilege protects a general right to privacy that limits the state's ability to force from us embarrassing or incriminating facts about our personal lives.

## *Miranda* Revisited

During its 1999–2000 term, the Rehnquist Court was again urged to overturn *Miranda* in *Dickerson v. United States*.[56] The conflict involved the Omnibus Crime Control Act enacted by Congress in 1968, just two years after *Miranda* was decided. One provision of the law, section 3501, stated that all voluntary confessions made by suspects during custodial interrogation could be admitted as evidence, regardless of whether the suspect was given an explicit warning about the right to remain silent. While coerced confessions could still be excluded as evidence, under section 3501, the trial judge, in the presence of the jury, was instructed to look at the totality of the circumstances to determine whether a confession was given voluntarily or whether it was coerced. Congress's intent in 1968 was to narrow *Miranda*, but the law was never enforced by the executive branch.

The case began when Thomas Dickerson was indicted for a 1997 bank robbery. Before his trial in 1999 Dickerson asked a U.S. district court to suppress a statement that he had voluntarily made to FBI agents on the grounds that he had not received *Miranda* warning before making his statement. The district court granted his motion to suppress under *Miranda*, but the court of appeals reversed, ruling that under section 3501 Dickerson's statements could be admitted as evidence. The Court of Appeals for the Fourth Circuit then concluded that *Miranda v. Arizona* was no longer the law of the land because it was Congress's intent in section 3501 to supercede *Miranda*.

The U.S. Supreme Court granted certiorari to address two very important questions. *First, who has the final say on the matter of admissibility of evidence: Congress or the Supreme Court? Second, what then is the status of* Miranda? *Is it good law? Should it be modified or, perhaps, overturned?* No one was surprised when the Court granted certiorari—after all, the court of appeals had just overturned a landmark precedent—but there was much speculation about whether *Miranda* had seen its final hours.

The Supreme Court voted 7–2 to uphold *Miranda* as the law of the land. Writing for the majority, Chief Justice Rehnquist, who has in the past been critical of *Miranda*, argued that while Congress has the ultimate authority through constitutional amendment to modify or overturn any judicially created rules of evidence and procedure that are not required by the Constitution, Congress may not *legislatively* supercede the Court's decisions interpreting the Constitution. In other words, since *Miranda* is based on the Court's enforcement of the Fifth Amendment privilege against self-incrimination, Congress cannot modify or overturn it unless two thirds of both houses propose and the three fourths of the states ratify a constitutional amendment. In addition, Rehnquist continued, the Court's discretion to mandate *Miranda*'s constitutional protections is based on its authority to prescribe rules of evidence and procedure for the federal courts.

*Why did the court of appeals take the unusual action of overturning a Supreme Court decision?* Because the court of appeals fully expected the Supreme Court to agree. The judges on the Fourth Circuit Court of Appeals in Richmond, Virginia, are considered to be among the most conservative activist judges in the country. These judges were keenly aware that over years the Supreme Court has gone out of its way to bash and weaken *Miranda* by (1) creating exceptions (as in *Arizona v. Fulminante*), (2) citing examples of criminals going free, and (3) diminishing its importance by referring to the *Miranda* warnings as "not themselves rights protected by the Constitution.[57] So it seemed that the stage was set for its reversal. Chief Justice Rehnquist himself has often led the fight to do so. But strangely in *Dickerson*, Rehnquist voted to uphold *Miranda*. The chief justice wrote: "We disagree with the Court of Appeals' conclusion, although we concede that there is language in some of our opinions that supports the view taken by that court. But first and foremost of the factors on the other side—that *Miranda* is a constitutional decision. . . . "

Over the years, Rehnquist has been eager to point out the shortcomings of *Miranda*, and many interpreted these criticisms as a willingness to overturn it. Conservative groups thought that this was their chance to change the law. But at the last minute, Rehnquist balked, conceding that the principle of *stare decisis* "weigh[s] heavily against overruling it now." In other words, since *Miranda* has been around since 1966 and most (if not all) law enforcement officers were trained under it, there is no point in overturning well-established precedent. Six of his colleagues agreed.

A furious Justice Scalia, dissenting (joined by Justice Thomas), rejected the majority's position outright, arguing that the majority had just established a new rule: The laws of Congress can be disregarded not only when they conflict with the Constitution but when they conflict with a decision of the Court that creates a constitutional rule. Relying on a more limited view of judicial power, Scalia pointed out that the Court exhibits the "frightening and antidemocratic" power to not merely apply the Constitution but to expand it through judge-created rules and doctrines (but not rights) like those in created by *Miranda*.

In his own unmistakably sardonic but entertaining style, Scalia scolds the majority for its "judicial arrogance."

> Today's judgment converts *Miranda* from a milestone of judicial overreaching into the very Cheops' Pyramid (or perhaps the Sphinx would be a better analogue) of judicial arrogance. In imposing its Court-made code upon the States, the original opinion [*Miranda*] at least asserted that it was demanded by the Constitution. Today's decision does not pretend that it is—and yet still asserts the right to impose it against the will of the people's representatives in Congress.

The irony of *Dickerson* is that not only did the narrowly decided *Miranda* ruling survive another challenge, seven justices, led by one of its harshest critics, bolstered *Miranda* against future challenges. *Miranda*, with all of its flaws, is now even more firmly established in American law.

Note that the Court refers to the guarantee against self-incrimination as a privilege rather than a right. While the Court has never offered a lengthy explanation of this choice, it may be suggesting that unlike a right, which inheres in the person and limits the power of government, a privilege can be granted or suspended by the government through its power to interpret the vague words of the Constitution.

## CRUEL AND UNUSUAL PUNISHMENT

The Eighth Amendment's prohibition of the infliction of cruel and unusual punishment is based on a common law concern for the dignity of persons—even that of the most vilified of criminals. Prior to the ratification of the Eighth Amendment, the Virginia Bill of Rights (1776) as well as the earlier English Bill of Rights (1689) had already sought to guarantee against barbaric or excessive punishments, such as burning at the stake, crucifixion, breaking on the wheel, and grossly disproportionate prison sentences. The phrase "cruel and unusual punishment" was also intended to limit the kinds of conduct that can be considered a criminal offense and to ensure the fair and equal imposition of justice.[58]

***What constitutes cruel and unusual punishment?***    Unfortunately (or perhaps fortunately), this phrase is not easily defined. When the Eighth Amendment was ratified in 1791, citizens routinely witnessed public executions for more than a dozen different offenses. Public hangings and debtors' prisons were widely accepted forms of punishment. During the Revolutionary period in South Carolina, for instance, criminals could be hanged for 113 separate offenses. However, in the northern states, murder and rape generally were the only crimes for which an offender could be hanged, and by the early nineteenth century there was a growing movement to abolish capital punishment.[59] It is clear that the framers envisioned each new generation of Americans grappling with this phrase in the context of the social mores and unique problems of the day.

Throughout much of our history, the judgment of whether a sentence or punishment was cruel and unusual was left to the discretion of the states, with the U.S. Supreme Court entering the fray only on rare occasions. In 1878, in *Wilkerson v. Utah*, 99 U.S. 130, the Court upheld public execution by firing squad, and in *In re Kemmler*, 136 U.S. 436 (1890), the Court held that electrocution was not cruel when compared to hanging and other contemporary measures. (On August 6, 1890, Kemmler was given the dubious honor of being the first criminal executed by electrocution.)[60]

In *Weems v. United States*, 217 U.S. 349 (1910), the Court ruled that the Constitution does prohibit Congress and the federal judiciary from imposing cruel and unusual punishments and that the definition of the clause "is not fastened to the obsolete, but may acquire meaning as public opinion becomes enlightened by humane justice." But until recently the Court has been reluctant to challenge Congress and hesitant to address whether the Eighth Amendment should be applied to the states via the Fourteenth Amendment. Since most states took it for granted that the death penalty was an acceptable and constitutional form of punishment, most appeals challenging capital punishment as cruel and unusual took the form of procedural rather than substantive due process claims—challenging the method or procedure by which a person was sentenced to death or put to death and not the death penalty per se. For example, in the late 1940s, a young African American man in Louisiana was sentenced to death in the electric chair after being convicted of murder. While there was nothing unusual about his sentence, the fact that he was ordered to face death a second time after the electric chair malfunctioned on the first attempt prompted some to believe that his punishment might possibly be cruel and unusual under the Eighth Amendment. But the U.S. Supreme Court allowed the execution to take place, as it ruled that the young man was not made to suffer a cruel and unusual form of punishment when he was made to face death twice.[61]

In 1962, the Supreme Court handed down a landmark Eighth Amendment decision that has had a significant impact on the states' discretion to determine what kinds of offenses may be punished by criminal sanctions. *Robinson v. California*, 370 U.S. 660 (1962), came to the Court not on appeal from a death sentence but on appeal from a ninety-day prison term. Lawrence Robinson was convicted in Los Angeles Municipal Court for violating a state law that made it a misdemeanor to be addicted to narcotics. (The main purpose of the statute was to cure "volitional" users by giving them time to dry out or go "cold turkey" while incarcerated.) Robinson was not arrested and convicted for possession or trafficking, but for having needle marks and scars on his arms. Under the California statute, a person could be continuously guilty of this offense regardless of whether or not that person had ever used any narcotics within the state. In *Robinson*, the Court ruled that the statute violated the Eighth and Fourteenth Amendments because it made a status or condition—rather than conduct—a criminal offense. The state sought to punish Robinson for being an addict even though it had no evidence that he had ever touched a drug while residing in California. While the punishment of ninety days in jail was neither cruel nor unusual, being sentenced for merely having a condition of some kind violates the Constitution. Writing for the majority, Justice Stewart quipped, "It is unlikely that any state at this moment in history would attempt to make it a criminal offense for a person to be mentally ill, or a leper, or to be afflicted with a venereal disease." A state may legitimately require medical or psychological treatment or some form of quarantine, but it may not make having an illness a criminal offense.

*Robinson* is important for two main reasons. First, it set a standard whereby states were prohibited from enacting criminal punishments on the basis of the status of the alleged offender rather than for his or her conduct. Second, it applied the constitutional protection against cruel and unusual punishment to the states via the Fourteenth Amendment.

However, in *Powell v. Texas*, 392 U.S. 514 (1968), the Supreme Court refused to extend *Robinson* to overturn the conviction of a man who argued that his drunken behavior was "not of his volition" but rather the result of the "disease of chronic alcoholism." A Texas court had found Leroy Powell guilty of public intoxication, noting that he was a chronic alcoholic who had been convicted of public intoxication more than 100 times. The Court narrowly rejected (5–4) Powell's argument, since he was convicted not for being a chronic alcoholic but for being intoxicated in public. Powell's argument went beyond seeking exculpation from drunkenness on the basis of his disease: He contended that his behavior in public was a result of factors that he could not control.

The majority was concerned that had the Court not rejected this claim of "not of his own volition" it would have created a kind of Eighth Amendment insanity plea that could have been used to alter the standards of criminal responsibility throughout the nation. For example, it would be possible to challenge the constitutionality of a law requiring mandatory prison sentences for child molesters on the grounds that their behavior was the product of a disease of some kind. Writing for the majority, Justice Marshall reasoned:

> I cannot say that the chronic alcoholic who proves his disease and a compulsion to drink is shielded from conviction when he has knowingly failed to take feasible precautions against committing a criminal act, here the act of going to or remaining in a public place. On such facts the alcoholic is like a person with smallpox, who could be convicted for being on the street but not for being ill, or, like the epileptic, who would be punished for driving a car but not for his disease.

## The Death Penalty

It is always difficult to pinpoint the precise day or year that a social or political movement is born. But in the early 1960s many prominent individuals and groups launched a strategy aimed at overturning the death penalty. The Legal Defense Fund of the NAACP and the ACLU attempted to convince the Court that the death penalty was unconstitutional under the Eighth and Fourteenth Amendments. They argued that not only was capital punishment "cruel and unusual" under the Eighth Amendment, but also that contrary to the equal protection clause of the Fourteenth Amendment, disproportionately more blacks convicted of murder or rape received the death penalty than whites convicted of the same offenses. This was especially true when the victim was white. *Is the death penalty cruel and unusual in itself, or does the manner of application determine its constitutionality?*

In the 1972 case *Furman v. Georgia*, 408 U.S. 238, the Court granted certiorari to review three state court decisions imposing the death penalty. In a Georgia court, William Furman was convicted for murder and sentenced to death. Lucius Jackson was convicted for rape and also sentenced to death. A third defendant, Elmer Branch, was convicted in a Texas court for rape and sentenced to death. They appealed to the U.S. Supreme Court after unsuccessful appeals to the high courts of Georgia and Texas. The question raised was whether the imposition and implementation of the death penalty in the three cases constituted cruel and unusual punishment in violation of the Eighth and Fourteenth Amendments. Hanging in the balance were the laws of thirty-nine states, several federal death penalty provisions, and the lives of more than 600 prisoners on death row.

In *Furman*, a 5–4 majority ruled that "the imposition and carrying out" of the death penalty under the present system constituted cruel and unusual punishment. Since each of the five justices in the majority wrote separate concurring opinions, *Furman* contained five different reasons for the Court's invalidation of the death penalty. Justice Douglas began by arguing that the death penalty was cruel and unusual when applied selectively to minorities, the poor, and social outcasts for whom society has no pity. Since empirical evidence showed that judges and juries imposed the penalty in a selective and arbitrary manner, the death penalty as administered violated the Eighth Amendment and the principle of equal protection in the Fourteenth Amendment. According to Douglas, the Eighth Amendment requires legislatures to write penal laws that are "evenhanded, nonselective, and nonarbitrary, and to require judges to see to it that general laws are not applied sparsely, selectively, and spottily to unpopular groups." Douglas likened capital punishment in the American system to that existing under ancient Hindu law where a Brahman was exempt from capital punishment. In a caste system, the severity of punishment increases as social status diminishes. However, Douglas stopped short of addressing whether the death penalty per se is unconstitutional.

Justice Brennan took a different approach to defining "cruel and unusual." He elucidated several principles that a court might use to determine whether a challenged punishment violates the Constitution. First, the clause prohibits the infliction of uncivilized and inhuman punishments. In doing so it compels the state, even as it punishes, to treat the convicted "with respect for their intrinsic worth as human beings." Thus, a punishment was cruel and unusual, according to Brennan, when it did not "comport with human dignity." While the punishment could involve physical and psychological pain, it should not be degrading to the dignity of human beings. Second, the clause demands that, in the name of human dignity, the state refrain from inflicting punishment arbitrarily or unevenly; namely, imposing the death penalty on some but not on others who are guilty of the same crime. Brennan wrote: "Indeed, the very words 'cruel and unusual punishments' imply condemnation of the arbitrary infliction of severe punishments. And, as we now know, the English history of the Clause reveals a particular concern with the establishment of a safeguard against arbitrary punishments." Third, Brennan argued that the clause requires that a punishment must not be "unacceptable to contemporary society." Does this mean that the form of punishment in question is not found anywhere else in civilized societies or that it is not a method approved by the majority of citizens? Brennan said that one indication would be that it is not found in any jurisdictions other than those before the Court. Another indication would be that it offends "contemporary human knowledge," such as the law at issue in *Robinson* that made it a criminal offense to be a drug addict.

The fourth and final principle inherent in the cruel and unusual clause is that a punishment must not be excessive. A punishment is excessive if it is an "unnecessary" or "pointless infliction of suffering." If there is a less-severe form of punishment that will adequately accomplish society's penal goals, then the present form of punishment is probably excessive.

Summing up his opinion, Brennan concluded that the death penalty is inconsistent with these four principles:

> Death is an unusually severe and degrading punishment: there is a strong probability that it is inflicted arbitrarily; its rejection by contemporary society is virtually total; and there is no reason to believe that it serves any penal purpose more effectively than the less severe punishment of imprisonment. The function of these principles is to enable a court to determine whether a punishment comports with human dignity. Death, quite simply, does not.

Justice Stewart, concurring, did not agree with Brennan's conclusion that the death penalty was cruel and unusual, but he did believe that the Eighth and Fourteenth Amendments "cannot tolerate the infliction of a sentence of death under legal systems that permit this unique penalty to be so wantonly and freakishly imposed."

Justice Marshall was the only member of the Court other than Brennan who argued that the death penalty per se was unconstitutional. He concluded that even if capital punishment was not excessive, it was cruel and unusual "because it is morally unacceptable" by contemporary societal standards. Marshall attacked the conventional wisdom that since public opinion polls indicated that a majority of Americans supported the death penalty in some instances, capital punishment was not incompatible with contemporary societal norms. He believed this logic to be misleading. While many citizens supported the death penalty in the abstract, they were painfully uninformed about its effectiveness as a deterrent, its arbitrary implementation, and the fact that the cost of executing a capital offender exceeded that of life in jail. The citizenry's support for capital punishment was based solely on its desire for retribution, even though the legislature did not ground its support for it solely on retributive theory. Marshall wrote:

> While a public opinion poll obviously is of some assistance in indicating public acceptance or rejection of a specific penalty, its utility cannot be very great. This is because whether or not a punishment is cruel and unusual depends, not on whether its pure mention "shocks the conscience and sense of justice of the people," but on whether people who were fully informed as to the purposes of the penalty and its liabilities would find the penalty shocking, unjust, and unacceptable.

Marshall argued that if the average citizen had adequate knowledge of all the facts regarding capital punishment, he or she would find it unfairly administered, ineffective, and unjust.

The dissenting justices (Burger, Blackmun, Powell, and Rehnquist) did not believe that the death penalty as administered was unconstitutional, and that the Court should defer in the matter of capital punishment to the state legislatures. But brushing past his objection to the majority's activism, Chief Justice Burger appeared to praise the fact that legislatures would now have to provide better standards for judges and juries to follow when the death sentence was meted out. He wrote:

> While I cannot endorse the process of decision-making that has yielded today's result and the restraints that that result imposes on legislative action, I am not altogether displeased that legislative bodies have been given the opportunity, and indeed unavoidable responsibility, to make a thorough reevaluation of the entire subject of capital punishment.

Justice Blackmun's dissenting opinion was a classic illustration of the tension between a judge's perception of his or her proper role and the personal beliefs of a devoutly moral person who opposes the death penalty. The role of the Court, wrote Blackmun, is to pass upon the constitutionality of legislation and not upon the particulars of policy-making. It was clear to him that the cruel and unusual clause of the Eighth Amendment did not prohibit legislatures from imposing the death penalty if they so chose, and the Court could rule only if the method of execution or punishment was being challenged, not capital punishment per se. It should not rule on when it can be imposed or on the basis of whether or not it is an effective form of punishment. However, Blackmun did not come to this conclusion easily:

> Cases such as these provide for me an excruciating agony of the spirit. I yield to no one in the depth of my distaste, antipathy, and, indeed, abhorrence, for the death penalty, with all its aspects of physical distress and fear and of moral judgment exercised by finite minds. . . . For me, it violates childhood's training and life's experiences, and is not compatible with the philosophical convictions I have been able to develop. . . . Were I a legislator, I would vote against the death penalty.

*Furman* was a watershed case in the capital punishment debate. On the one hand, the Court admitted that it was willing to strike down a state's capital punishment sentencing procedure if a state imposed the death penalty in an arbitrary or capricious manner. On the other hand, it directly ruled for the first time that the death penalty per se is not cruel and unusual punishment in violation of the Constitution.

Yet, the Court did not resolve the argument. Four justices argued that capital punishment was not unconstitutional per se, and only two—Brennan and Marshall—held that the death penalty was inherently unconstitutional. Three justices agreed that the challenged statutes were unconstitutional as applied, but said nothing directly on the question of whether the death penalty could ever be imposed.

In the years immediately following *Furman*, legislatures in thirty-five states enacted new statutes that brought their sentencing procedures in line with the Court's ruling. None of these statutes banned capital punishment itself. In fact, in 1972, after a popular referendum, California passed a constitutional amendment authorizing capital punishment. In 1974, Congress added aircraft piracy to the list of federal crimes punishable by death. This legislative response to *Furman* gave rise to several new disputes that were ultimately addressed by the Supreme Court in six cases in 1976. While these disputes involved various challenges to the states' post-*Furman* reforms to sentencing procedures, two overarching constitutional questions surfaced: *Is the death penalty for the crime of murder cruel and unusual under all circumstances? Is a mandatory death sentence for a broad category of offenses unconstitutional?*

The first question was answered in the negative by the Court's 7–2 decision in *Gregg v. Georgia*, 428 U.S. 53 (1976),[62] where it upheld a complex Georgia bifurcated, or two-stage, sentencing procedure under which the jury's attention is focused on the "particularized nature of the crime and the particularized nature of the individual defendant." The trial was divided into the verdict stage and the sentencing stage, both taking place before the same jury. At the sentencing stage, the jury is allowed to consider any aggravating or mitigating circumstances, but must find the defendant guilty of at least one of ten statutory aggravating circumstances beyond a reasonable doubt before it may impose the death penalty. Furthermore, under the Georgia statute, the state supreme court was required to review every death sentence to determine whether it was imposed under the influence of "passion or prejudice" and whether it was excessive or disproportionate to the penalty imposed in similar cases. Writing for the majority in *Gregg*, Justice Stewart first reiterated that capital punishment was not per se unconstitutional. He then went on to say that the Georgia statute satisfied the concerns of the Court in *Furman* because there was sufficient proof that the death penalty was no longer being imposed in an arbitrary or capricious manner.

Stewart was also convinced that society as a whole had endorsed the death penalty for murder and, in doing so, had demonstrated that capital punishment does not violate the principles of decency demanded by the cruel and unusual clause of the Eighth Amendment. He pointed out: "The most marked indication of society's endorsement of the death penalty for murder is the legislative response to *Furman*. The legislatures of at least 35 states have enacted new statutes that provide for the death penalty for at least some crimes that result in the death of another person."

The second question raised by the 1976 capital punishment cases was whether a mandatory death sentence constitutes cruel and unusual punishment. A North Carolina statute made death the mandatory sentence for all first-degree murder convictions. In *Woodson v. North Carolina*, 428 U.S. 280 (1976), the Supreme Court ruled 5–4 that a mandatory death sentence for certain crimes is unconstitutional because it allows no standards to guide the jury in its determination of which first degree murderers will be sentenced to death or life in prison. North Carolina's mandatory death penalty statute suffered from the same problems identified in *Furman*: It did not provide a check on the arbitrary and capricious exercise of the jury's discretion, there were no objective standards to guide and rationalize the process of imposing a death sentence, and there was no provision under the North Carolina law for the judiciary to review the sentence imposed by the jury.

In the decade following the landmark cases *Furman* and *Gregg*, the Court ruled that capital punishment was an excessive punishment for the crime of rape;[63] that states may not limit the mitigating factors that juries may consider when the death penalty applies;[64] that the Eighth Amendment prohibits the imposition of capital punishment on a person who aided and abetted, but did not commit, a felony in which a person was murdered;[65] and that the execution of a prisoner who has gone insane on death row violates the cruel and unusual punishment clause.[66]

Groups such as the NAACP, Amnesty International, and the ACLU continued to argue after *Furman* and *Gregg* that juries are more likely to impose the death penalty on minority defendants who murder white victims than on white defendants convicted of murdering white or minority victims. An empirical study of more than 2,000 murder cases in Georgia in the 1970s was undertaken by Professors David C. Baldus, George Woodworth, and Charles Pulaski. The Baldus study found that African American defendants charged with killing white victims were 4.3 times more likely to receive the death sentence than those charged with killing blacks. In other words, six out of every eleven defendants convicted of killing a white person would not have received the death penalty if their victims had been African American.[67]

*If the death penalty is not cruel and unusual per se, but is administered in a discriminatory manner—disproportionately on certain groups—would it be possible to mount a Fourteenth Amendment equal protection challenge in addition to an Eighth Amendment attack on a state's sentencing process?*

Warren McClesky, an African American, was convicted and sentenced to death for murdering a white police officer during a robbery. He was sentenced to death in a Georgia trial court but sought federal habeas corpus relief on the grounds that Georgia's capital sentencing process was administered in a racially discriminatory manner in violation of the Eighth Amendment and the equal protection clause of the Fourteenth Amendment. To support his challenge, McClesky's counsel cited the Baldus study, but the federal district court refused to grant relief on the basis of a single piece of research.

The U.S. court of appeals affirmed, ruling that even assuming the validity of the Baldus study, the statistics were insufficient to demonstrate discriminatory intent (Fourteenth Amendment analysis) or irrationality or arbitrariness in sentencing under the *Furman* standard.

On appeal in *McClesky v. Kemp*, 481 U.S. 279 (1987), the Supreme Court dismissed McClesky's argument outright. Writing for the 5–4 majority, and citing *Furman* and *Gregg*, Justice Powell argued four major points. First, McClesky could not show that for his crime the death penalty was disproportionate to other death sentences imposed in Georgia. In other words, other persons convicted for committing the same crimes had received the death penalty. Second, he could not show that the state's sentencing process operated in an arbitrary or capricious manner. McClesky could not prove that the Georgia legislature enacted the death penalty statute because of an anticipated intentional discriminatory effect. There was no evidence suggesting that the state tried to put more blacks than whites to death. Third, Justice Powell pondered the negative policy impact of a ruling in favor of McClesky's claim. If McClesky's claim were taken to its logical conclusion, argued Powell, our nation's entire criminal justice system would be in jeopardy: "The Eighth Amendment is not limited in application to capital punishment, but applies to all penalties. Thus, if we accepted McClesky's claim that racial bias has impermissibly tainted the capital sentencing decision, we would soon be faced with similar claims as to other types of penalty."

Claims could then be made on the basis of other racial or ethnic characteristics, or on the basis of sex, handicap, physical attractiveness, or type of accent. If the legislatures wish to make policy on the basis of statistical evidence showing that racism influences the sentencing process they are free to do so, argued Powell, but the Court can rule only on whether the law was properly applied.

Fourth, Justice Powell rejected the contention that the Baldus study proved that racial considerations influence capital sentencing decisions in Georgia. If there is a risk of racism influencing a jury's decision, at what point does that risk become constitutionally unacceptable? While the Court recognized that there is some risk of racial prejudice influencing the outcome of any jury's deliberations, it would not accept the Baldus study as "the constitutional measure of an unacceptable risk of racial prejudice influencing capital sentencing decisions." In other words, the Court would not strike down an entire system of sentencing just because one study suggests that racial prejudice may influence a jury's decision. In order to get a favorable ruling, McClesky would have had to prove that the law of Georgia was applied in his case on the basis of race or that the jurors, attorneys, or judges were motivated by racism.

In his dissenting opinion, Justice Brennan (joined by Justices Marshall, Blackmun, and Stevens) recognized the importance of Powell's four points but did not see them as compelling enough to completely obviate the fact that "race casts a large shadow on the capital sentencing process." Brennan believed that all actors in the sentencing process were aware that race "would play a prominent role in determining if [McClesky] lived or died"; it did not matter that this risk could not be proven. Since *Furman*, the Court had been concerned with the risk of the imposition of an arbitrary sentence, rather than the proven fact of arbitrariness. Therefore, if *Furman* was the guiding standard, the fact that McClesky could not prove the influence of race is irrelevant in evaluating his argument.

Brennan was not so willing to reject the findings of the Baldus study. When the statistical evidence was combined with the reality of Georgia's notorious "legacy of a race-conscious criminal justice system," the study provided enough proof that "McClesky's claim is not a fanciful product of mere statistical artifice":

> History and its continuing legacy . . . buttress the probative force of McClesky's statistics. Formal dual criminal laws may no longer be in effect, and intentional discrimination may no longer be prominent. Nonetheless, as we acknowledged in *Turner*

*v. Murray*, 476 U.S. 28 (1986), . . . "subtle, less consciously held racial attitudes" continue to be of concern, and the Georgia system gives such attitudes considerable room to operate.

Brennan dismissed the majority's fear that accepting McClesky's claim would invite countless challenges to sentencing procedures on the basis of personal characteristics or sex. There is no history of discriminatory sentencing based on hair color or even gender, while there is ample evidence of racially motivated accusations and convictions.

During the 1990s, the Court handed down at least one (and often more) capital punishment case per term. Although none of these cases are as fundamentally important as *Furman, Gregg,* or *McClesky*, the Court regularly addressed a number of key issues. For example, in 1995 a divided Rehnquist Court (5–4) ruled that inmates on death row may challenge their convictions on the grounds that exculpatory evidence (favorable to their defense) was wrongly suppressed by prosecutors *if* there is a "reasonable probability" that the disclosure of the evidence would have produced a different verdict in the trial.[68] A year later, the Court unanimously upheld provisions of the Antiterrorism and Effective Death Penalty Act of 1996 that limit state prisoners to one habeas corpus petition (appealing death sentence) if no new claim, or argument for appeal can be made.[69] The Court also made it more difficult (5–4) for federal courts to reverse state death row inmates' convictions on federal constitutional grounds.[70]

## THE CONSERVATIVE AGENDA AND THE EIGHTH AMENDMENT

### Penalties for Drug Offenses

The war on drugs has also profoundly affected Eighth Amendment jurisprudence. During this twenty-year campaign Congress has dramatically increased the penalties for drug possession and expanded the authority of law enforcement officials. Mandatory minimums and "three-strike" laws have been imposed, curtailing the sentencing discretion of judges and turning many federal district courts into drug courts. Although the population of violent and nonviolent drug offenders in federal prisons has soared, few believe that these aggressive policies have diminished the supply or the demand for drugs. The "zero-tolerance" school of thought has also raised the possibility of imposing the death penalty on drug dealers.[71]

*Just how far can Congress go? Are there constitutional limits on the government's power to fix punishments for drug offenses?* In the 1991 case *Harmelin v. Michigan*, 501 U.S. 957 (1991), the Rehnquist Court rejected an Eighth Amendment challenge to a mandatory lifetime sentence without parole for the possession of 650 grams of cocaine (approximately 40,000 individual doses). Writing for the 5–4 majority, Justice Scalia reasoned that the sentence was not "significantly disproportionate," nor was it unconstitutional merely because it was mandatory and did not give the trial court an opportunity to consider mitigating circumstances. In other words, severe sentences may seem cruel but are not necessarily unusual in the constitutional sense. Scalia argued that while the Eighth Amendment does encompass noncapital disproportionate sentences—such as a thirty-year prison term for possession of one marijuana cigarette—it does not require strict proportionality between the crime and the sentence. The Eighth Amendment merely forbids extreme sentences that are grossly disproportionate to the crime.

## Limiting Prisoner Lawsuits

During the past decade the prison population in the United States has grown dramatically to nearly two million inmates in federal and state correctional institutions.[72] The number of prisoner lawsuits has also increased. In the past twenty years the number of lawsuits filed each year by inmates has tripled.[73] These suits run the gamut from serious complaints about lack of access to the courts and unhealthy prison conditions to frivolous complaints about salad bars, peanut butter, and designer athletic shoes.[74]

Prior to the 1960s, prisoners had few rights and the federal courts rarely intervened in matters of prison administration.[75] In the late 1960s and 1970s, however, the Court rejected this "hands-off" policy and recognized that "there is no iron curtain drawn between the Constitution and the prisons of this country."[76] The Court also spoke of no longer turning a blind eye to inhuman conditions[77] and came close to classifying prisoners as a protected minority.[78] Federal judges took control of prisons until conditions improved.

By the 1980s, however, as the crime rate rose and thousands of frivolous lawsuits filed by prisoners overwhelmed the dockets of federal courts, the U.S. Supreme Court began to uphold restrictions on prison's rights. Restrictions were upheld on prisoners' free exercise of religion[79] and general First Amendment claims[80] and the authority of prison officials to segregate (separate)[81] or "double-cell" inmates.[82] In 1991, in *Wilson v. Seiter*, 501 U.S. 294, the Court ruled (5–4) that prisoners filing complaints over prison conditions on Eighth Amendment grounds must show "a culpable state of mind on the part of prison officials." Writing for the majority, Scalia reasoned that implicit in the Eighth Amendment's protection against cruel and unusual punishment is the concept of intent. Prisoners must show that the conditions of confinement are the result of deliberate indifference on the part of prison officials and not merely the effect of a stingy legislature or lack of tax revenue.

Justices White, Marshall, Blackmun, and Stevens concurred in the judgment but dissented to the standard. They argued that the majority's use of the deliberate indifference standard was both unwise and inconsistent with previous rulings. Under this standard it would be virtually impossible to successfully challenge prison conditions. The majority's ruling was a departure from precedent, which demanded that prisons comport with the contemporary standard-of-decency rule.

In 1996, in *Lewis v. Casey*, 518 U.S. 343, the Court rejected a class action claim brought by Arizona inmates who claimed that their constitutional right of access to the courts was limited by inadequate prison libraries. Prisoners do have the right to file lawsuits to gain access to the legal system, but this right does not guarantee a library, the justices concluded.

Even in light of the Court's efforts to limit prisoners' claims, the number of lawsuits filed in federal courts continued to rise dramatically to 68,235 by 1996.[83]

Although 95 percent of these suits were frivolous and not successful, they placed an extraordinary burden on the criminal justice system. As a result, Congress passed the Prison Litigation Reform Act[84] (PLRA) of 1995, placing major restrictions on inmate access to the federal courts. PLRA limits the number of suits that can be filed and requires that prisoners "exhaust available administrative remedies prior to bringing suit."[85]

***What about prisoner appeals from death row?*** For more than twenty years as associate justice and chief justice, Rehnquist has ardently and publicly argued for a limit on the number of appeals sought by death row inmates. His efforts finally bore fruit in 1991 in *McClesky v. Zant*, 481 U.S. 279. According to the 6–3 majority, in all but exceptional cases, the prisoner's second or subsequent habeas corpus petition can be dismissed. By limiting the number of successive petitions, states are able to carry out death sentences more quickly and more cost effectively. *McClesky v. Zant* redefined the "abuse of the writ" rule so that second and subsequent petitions raising new constitutional claims could be dismissed as abusive unless the inmate shows that there was sufficient cause for not raising the claim earlier or that the inmate suffered actual prejudice.

## Victims' Rights

One dimension of the very successful movement to protect the rights of the victims of crime is the use of victim impact statements during the sentencing phase of a criminal trial. Many states allow juries and judges to hear testimony from the victim of a crime (or the victim's survivors) before final sentencing. In this way, the person who is raped or murdered is not seen merely as an objectified or faceless victim, but rather as a distinct individual whose loss uniquely affects family, friends, and society. Rape victims, for instance, have given dramatic testimony on the persistent emotional scars that haunt them long after the convicted rapist is released from prison.[86]

But many critics argue that victim impact statements serve only a political purpose: satisfying voters and thus reelecting local district attorneys. After all, the objective of a trial is to prove the guilt of the defendant, not the moral character or "worth" of the victim. The defendant is either guilty or innocent, and is not more guilty because the victim was an upstanding citizen or good parent. Furthermore, in capital trials victim impact statements may violate the Eighth Amendment because, contrary to *Furman* and *Gregg*, such testimony may lead to an arbitrary imposition of the death penalty, particularly where the victim is an affluent, middle-class, productive, or esteemed member of society. *If victim impact statements allow the socioeconomic or racial status of the victim to have a bearing on whether the jury imposes the death penalty, then isn't the death penalty being administered in an arbitrary and capricious manner contrary to the Eighth Amendment?*

In the past, the Supreme Court prohibited the use of victim impact statements during the penalty phase of a capital trial. In *Booth v. Maryland*, 482 U.S. 496 (1987), and *South Carolina v. Gathers*, 490 U.S. 805 (1989)—both very close decisions—the Court established that the evidence relating to a particular victim or to the harm that a capital defendant causes a victim's family has no relevance to the question of guilt or to the capital sentencing decision. In addition, the admissibility of victim impact evidence was not to be determined on a case-by-case basis: Such evidence per se was impermissible. The only exception that the Court allowed was where such evidence related directly to the circumstances of the crime. However, in *Payne v. Tennessee*, 501 U.S. 808 (1991), the Rehnquist Court reversed the previous position, ruling 6–3 that there is nothing in the Eighth Amendment prohibiting the state from admitting victim impact evidence if it so chooses. Chief Justice Rehnquist wrote:

> A state may legitimately conclude that evidence about the victim and about the impact of the murder on the victim's family is relevant to the jury's decision as to whether or not the death penalty should be imposed. There is no reason to treat such evidence differently than other relevant evidence is treated.

The Court had changed its mind and was now of the opinion that a state may allow the jury to use all evidence of the harm caused by the defendant in its determination of the defendant's "moral culpability and blameworthiness." It is only logical and fair that if the defense has the right to humanize the defendant by telling of an unfortunate past and emotional hardships, then so too has the state the right to remind the jury that the victim was a human being "whose death represents a unique loss to society and in particular to his family." Such evidence may be used unless it can be shown that it is so "unduly prejudicial that it renders the trial fundamentally unfair" under the due process clause of the Fourteenth Amendment.

Dissenting in *Payne*, Justices Marshall, Blackmun, and Stevens blasted the majority's ruling as a flagrant departure from the doctrine of *stare decisis* and from established capital sentencing jurisprudence. By overturning two recent rulings on the grounds that they were narrowly decided, the Court had abnegated the proper function of the judiciary. Marshall pointed out that contrary to what the majority suggested, *stare decisis* was important to stability in the law and to the legitimacy of the Supreme Court. If the Court keeps changing its mind, its decisions will go unheeded. Marshall wrote:

> This truncation of the Court's duty to stand by its own precedents is astonishing. By limiting full protection of the doctrine of *stare decisis* to "cases involving property and contract rights," . . . the majority sends a clear signal that essentially *all* decisions implementing the personal liberties protected by the Bill of Rights and the Fourteenth Amendment are open to reexamination.

If the chief justice was actually advocating that a precedent may be overruled if it was decided by only a 5–4 margin "over a spirited dissent," then, Marshall pointed out, "the continued vitality of literally scores of decisions must be understood to depend on nothing more than the proclivities of the individuals who *now* comprise a majority of this Court." Rehnquist's reasoning would invite all state and federal officials to reinstate policies that were previously deemed unconstitutional in the hope that the Court would reverse its decisions on controversial questions ranging from capital sentencing to abortion.

Justice Stevens, also dissenting, argued that even if *Booth* and *Gathers* had never been decided, *Payne* would still represent a dramatic departure from precedent. Victim impact evidence in the capital sentencing process serves no purpose other than to encourage jurors to vote in favor of the death penalty solely on the basis of their emotions. Throughout history, the character of the victim has been irrelevant to the defendants' guilt. Furthermore, "open-ended reliance" by a capital sentence jury on victim impact statements promotes arbitrary and capricious sentencing contrary to *Gregg v. Georgia.*

Stevens's concluding comments in *Payne* are evocative of a pervasive issue in American government. Should the judiciary be accountable to public opinion? Should it follow the election returns? Stevens had little doubt that given the present popularity of capital punishment, the majority's ruling would enjoy widespread political support. But it "is a sad day for a great institution" when the Court throws precedent and common sense to the wind because of what Justice Holmes called the "hydraulic pressure" of public opinion.

Since *Payne*, judges have often expressed concern that victim impact testimony turns the courtroom into a media circus and makes it difficult for jurors to deliberate in an objective and fair manner. During the trial of Timothy McVeigh for the 1995 Oklahoma City bombing, the judge banned from the courtroom victims and victim's family members who wished to give victim impact testimony during the sentencing phase of the trial. In essence, they could either attend the trial or testify during the sentencing phase, but not both. Judges often bar witnesses from a trial until they are called upon to testify in order to prevent them from being unduly influenced by the proceedings. In McVeigh's trial, the judge felt that by the end of the trial the victim impact testimony would be influenced and prejudiced by the gripping testimony of eye witnesses and experts. A court of appeals upheld the judge's decision over the vociferous protests of victims rights groups.[87] However, the drama did not end there. In the court of public opinion the judge was bound to lose. In 1997, victims rights advocates persuaded Congress to enact the Victim Rights Clarification Act, which prohibits district courts from excluding any victim of an offense from a trial because the victim plans to offer victim impact testimony during the sentencing hearing.[88]

## CONCLUDING COMMENTS

Some have argued that only the guilty have reason to fear the police and that the inconvenience resulting from some of the aforementioned law enforcement practices is a small price to pay for victory against criminals. Even if you have nothing to lose and everything to gain from these practices, do you really want the police to detain you after a long trip and inspect your luggage without probable cause or individualized suspicion? What if you were carrying erotic photos of a friend or, worse, a pill case containing a variety of prescription and over-the-counter drugs? Unless you could immediately produce the prescription, the police would probably detain you until a physician or pharmacist corroborated your story. In either of these situations, you would suffer humiliation or fear before you were offered a terse apology and released. Furthermore, are you willing to endure helicopters hovering over your house, random sobriety checkpoints, mandatory drug testing, and warrantless searches of your luggage and communications in order to fight the war on drugs? What about coerced confessions or random house searches in your neighborhood?

This "small price to pay" argument misses the point of our due process rights. The prohibition on unreasonable searches and seizures or coerced confessions was not intended to shield criminals from prosecution or harassment, but to prevent the emergence of an oppressive environment much like that in Algeria, for instance, where every ten or twenty kilometers you must show your papers and hope that you appear innocent under the piercing gaze of the police.

# Finding the Full Text of the U.S. Supreme Court Opinions Cited in Chapter 5

The full opinion of the U.S. Supreme Court's rulings discussed in this chapter can be found at the Findlaw URL address following each case listed below, or, by using the case name (e.g., *Schenck*) or citation (e.g., 249 U.S. 47). Other web sites where opinions can be found are listed at the end of chapter 1.

## Due Process and Incorporation

*Hurtado v. California* (1884), http://laws.findlaw.com/us/110/516.html

*Twining v. New Jersey* (1908), http://laws.findlaw.com/us/211/78.html

*Palko v. Connecticut* (1937), http://laws.findlaw.com/us/2320/319.html

## Searches and Seizures

### The Exclusionary Rule

*Weeks v. United States* (1914), http://laws.findlaw.com/us/232/383.html

*Wolf v. Colorado* (1949), http://laws.findlaw.com/us/339/25.html

*Rochin v. California* (1952), http://laws.findlaw.com/us/342/165.html

*Mapp v. Ohio* (1961), http://laws.findlaw.com/us/367/643.html

*United States v. Leon* (1984), http://laws.findlaw.com/us/468/897.html

*Massachusetts v. Shepard* (1984), http://laws.findlaw.com/us/468/981.html

### Exceptions to the Warrant Requirement

*Chimel v. California* (1969), http://laws.findlaw.com/us/395/752.html

### The Confusing World of Automobile Searches

*Carroll v. United States* (1925), http://laws.findlaw.com/us/267/132.html

*Continued*

# Finding the Full Text of the U.S. Supreme Court Opinions Cited in Chapter 5 *Continued*

*United States v. Chadwick* (1977), http://laws.findlaw.com/us/433/1.html
*Arkansas v. Sanders* (1979), http://laws.findlaw.com/us/442/753.html
*United States v. Ross* (1982), http://laws.findlaw.com/us/456/798.html
*California v. Acevedo* (1991), http://laws.findlaw.com/us/565/111.html
*Florida v. Jimeno* (1991), http://laws.findlaw.com/us/500/248.html
*Maryland v. Wilson* (1997), http://laws.findlaw.com/us/519/408.html

### *Searches of Mass Transportation*

*Florida v. Bostick* (1991), http://laws.findlaw.com/us/501/429.html

### *The "Seizure" Question Revisited*

*Katz v. United States* (1967), http://laws.findlaw.com/us/389/347.html
*Terry v. Ohio* (1968), http://laws.findlaw.com/us/392/1.html
*California v. Hodari D.* (1991), http://laws.findlaw.com/us/499/621.html

### *Clarifying* **Terry**

*Illinois v. Wardlow* (2000), http://laws.findlaw.com/us/000/98-1036.html

### *Media Ride-Alongs*

*Wilson v. Layne* (1999), http://laws.findlaw.com/us/000/98-83.html

## Electronic Eavesdropping

*Olmstead v. United States* (1928), http://laws.findlaw.com/us/277/438.html
*Boyd v. United States* (1886), http://laws.findlaw.com/us/116/616.html
*Katz v. United States* (1967), http://laws.findlaw.com/us/389/347.html
*Dalia v. United States* (1979), http://laws.findlaw.com/us/441/238.html
*Smith v. Maryland* (1979), http://laws.findlaw.com/us/.442/735html

## Aerial Surveillance

*California v. Ciraolo* (1986), http://laws.findlaw.com/us/476/207.html
*Oliver v. United States* (1984), http://laws.findlaw.com/us/466/170.html

## The "No-Knock" Warrant

*United States v. Ramirez* (1998), http://laws.findlaw.com/us/523/65.html

## The Right to Counsel

*Powell v. Alabama* (1932), http://laws.findlaw.com/us/287/45.html

*Johnson v. Zerbst* (1938), http://laws.findlaw.com/us/304/458.html

*Betts v. Brady* (1942), http://laws.findlaw.com/us/316/455.html

*Gideon v. Wainwright* (1963), http://laws.findlaw.com/us/372/335.html

*Grosjean v. America Press Co.* (1932), http://laws.findlaw.com/us/287/45.html

## Police Interrogations and the Fifth Amendment

*Malloy v. Hogan* (1964), http://laws.findlaw.com/us/378/1.html

*Twining v. New Jersey* (1908), http://laws.findlaw.com/us/211/78.html

*Miranda v. Arizona* (1966), http://laws.findlaw.com/us/384/436.html

*Minnick v. Mississippi* (1990), http://laws.findlaw.com/us/498/146.html

*Arizona v. Fulminante* (1991), http://laws.findlaw.com/us/499/279.html

*McNeil v. Wisconsin* (1991), http://laws.findlaw.com/us/501/171.html

### Miranda *Revisited*

*Dickerson v. United States* (2000), http://laws.findlaw.com/us/000/99-5525.html

## Cruel and Unusual Punishment

*Weems v. United States* (1910), http://laws.findlaw.com/us/217/349.html

*Robinson v. California* (1962), http://laws.findlaw.com/us/370/660.html

*Powell v. Texas* (1968), http://laws.findalw.com/us/392/514.html

### The Death Penalty

*Furman v. Georgia* (1972), http://laws.findlaw.com/us/2108/238.html

*Gregg v. Georgia* (1976), http://laws.findlaw.com/us/428/53.html

*Woodson v. North Carolina* (1976), http://laws.findlaw.com/us/428/280.html

*McClesky v. Kemp* (1987), http://laws.findlaw.com/us/481/279.html

## The Conservative Agenda and the Eighth Amendment

### Penalties for Drug Offenses

*Harmelin v. Michigan* (1991), http://laws.findlaw.com/us/501/957.html

### Limiting Prisoner Lawsuits

*Wilson v. Seiter* (1991), http://laws.findlaw.com/us/501/294.html

*Lewis v. Casey* (1996), http://laws.findlaw.com/us/518/343.html

*McClesky v. Zant* (1991), http://laws.findlaw.com/us/499/467.html

### Victims' Rights

*Booth v. Maryland* (1987), http://laws.findlaw.com/us/482/496.html

*Payne v. Tennessee* (1991), http://laws.findlaw.com/us/501/808.html

## NOTES

1. For more detailed discussion of the Fourteenth Amendment and nationalization of the Bill of Rights, see Richard C. Cortner, *The Supreme Court and the Second Bill of Rights: The Fourteenth Amendment and the Nationalization of Civil Liberties* (Madison: University of Wisconsin Press, 1981).
2. 32 U.S. (7 Pet.) 243 (1833).
3. Among Chief Justice John Marshall's celebrated opinions expanding the power of the federal government are *Marbury v. Madison*, 1 Cranch 137 (1803); *Gibbons v. Ogden*, 6 Wheat. 1 (1824); and *McCulloch v. Maryland*, 4 Wheat. 316 (1819).
4. In *Dred Scott v. Sanford*, 19 How. 393 (1857), the Taney Court declared that the framers did not intend blacks to be part of the sovereign people of the United States. Therefore, black people could never claim the right of citizenship or any of the rights, privileges, and immunities protected by the Constitution.
5. For further discussion, see the classic work by Jacobus tenBroek, *The Antislavery Origins of the Fourteenth Amendment* (Berkeley: University of California Press, 1951).
6. 83 U.S. (16 Wall.) 36 (1873).
7. *Fisk v. Kansas*, 274 U.S. 380 (1927).
8. *Near v. Minnesota*, 283 U.S. 697 (1931).
9. *Hamilton v. Regents of the University of California*, 293 U.S. 245 (1934).
10. *Powell v. Alabama*, 287 U.S. 45 (1932).
11. *Everson v. Board of Education*, 330 U.S. 1 (1947).
12. *In re Oliver*, 333 U.S. 45 (1932).
13. See the classic work by Nelson B. Lasson, *The History and Development of the Fourth Amendment to the United States Constitution* (Baltimore: Johns Hopkins University Press, 1966).
14. See Vincent Blasi, *The Counterrevolution That Wasn't* (New Haven, CT: Yale University Press, 1983).
15. *United States v. Calandra*, 414 U.S. 338 (1974); and *Stone v. Powell*, 428 U.S. 465 (1976).
16. *United States v. Payner*, 447 U.S. 727 (1980).
17. *Maryland v. Garrison*, 480 U.S. 79 (1987).
18. *Arizona v. Evans*, 514 U.S. 1 (1995).
19. See Taylor, "Two Studies of Constitutional Interpretation," cited by Justice Stevens in *Marshall v. Barlow's*, 436 U.S. 307 (1978).
20. The Court outline the basis for establishing probable cause in *Spinelli v. United States*, 393 U.S. 410 (1969).
21. *Wong Sun v. United States*, 371 U.S. 471 (1963).
22. *Johnson v. United States*, 333 U.S. 10 (1948).
23. *Pennsylvania v. Mimms*, 434 U.S. 106 (1977).
24. See *Terry v. Ohio*, 392 U.S. 1 (1968); *Florida v. Royer*, 460 U.S. 491 (1983); and *California v. Hodari D.*, 111 S. Ct. 1547 (1991).
25. O'Connor relied on *INS v. Delgado*, 466 U.S. 210 (1984).
26. *Terry v. Ohio*, 392 U.S. 1 (1968); *Florida v. Royer*, 460 U.S. 491 (1983); *Florida v. Rodriquez*, 469 U.S. 1 (1984), and *INS v. Delgado*, 466 U.S. 210 (1984).
27. http://www.laws.findlaw.com/us/000/98-1036.html.
28. Joined by Justices Souter, Ginsburg, and Breyer.
29. 119 S. Ct. 1692.
30. See *Harlow v. Fitzgerald*, 457 U.S. 800 (1982).
31. *Michigan v. Summers*, 452 U.S. 692 (1981).
32. *Arizona v. Hicks*, 480 U.S. 321 (1987); and *Maryland v. Garrison*, 480 U.S. 79 (1987).

33. Samuel Warren and Louis Brandeis, "The Right to Privacy," 4 *Harvard Law Review* 193 (1890).
34. Warren and Brandeis, "The Right to Privacy"; see also chapter 6.
35. 679 P.2d 197.
36. 978 F.2d. 171 (5<sup>th</sup> Cir. 1992).
37. Such entries are permitted under federal law governing felons who are in possession of firearms, 18 U.S.C. § 3109.
38. *Wilson v. Arkansas*, 514 U.S. 927 (1995).
39. *Richards v. Wisconsin*, 520 U.S. (1997).
40. For further discussion, see W. M. Beany, *The Right to Counsel in American Courts* (Westport, CT: Greenwood Press, 1972).
41. For further analysis, see F. Heller, *The Sixth Amendment to the Constitution of the United States* (Lawrence: University of Kansas Press, 1951).
42. Heller, *The Sixth Amendment*.
43. Though the Court refused to extend the Sixth Amendment to all criminal cases, it did rule that in capital cases and in "special circumstances," the government must appoint counsel for indigent defendants. Such special circumstances included cases where the defendant was young, ignorant, or incompetent (*DeMeerleer v. Michigan*, 329 U.S. 633 [1947]); in legally complex cases (*Cash v. Culver*, 358 U.S. 633 [1959]); and where the trial judge's conduct was called into question (*Townsend v. Burke*, 334 U.S. 736 [1948]).
44. See Anthony Lewis's classic account of this case in *Gideon's Trumpet* (New York: Vintage Books, 1966).
45. See *Counselman v. Hitchcock*, 142 U.S. 547 (1892).
46. Scc *Leftkowitz v. Cunningham*, 429 U.S. 893 (1970).
47. See *Watkins v. United States*, 354 U.S. 178 (1957).
48. Grant of immunity have been sanctioned by the Court since *Brown v. United States*, 161 U.S. 591 (1896). See also *Ulman v. United States*, 350 U.S. 422 (1956); and *Kastigar v. United States*, 406 U.S. 92 (1972).
49. See Earl Warren, *The Memoirs of Chief Justice Earl Warren* (New York: Doubleday, 1977), 315–318; and Bernard Schwartz, *Super Chief: Earl Warren and His Supreme Court—A Judicial Biography* (New York: New York University Press, 1983), 588–595.
50. *Michigan v. Tucker*, 417 U.S. 433 (1974).
51. *Oregon v. Haas*, 420 U.S. 714 (1975).
52. *North Carolina v. Butler*, 441 U.S. 369 (1979).
53. *Arizona v. Mauro*, 481 U.S. 520 (1987).
54. *Illinois v. Perkins*, 110 S. Ct. 2394 (1990).
55. In *Edwards v. Arizona*, 451 U.S. 477 (1981), the Burger Court ruled that under *Miranda* a suspect cannot be questioned further "until counsel has been made available to him."\
56. http://laws.findlaw.com/us/000/99-5525.html.
57. *Michigan v. Tucker*, 417 U.S. 433 (1974).
58. See Hugo Bedau, ed., *The Death Penalty in America*, 3<sup>rd</sup> ed. (New York: Oxford University Press, 1982); and John Laurence, *A History of Capital Punishment* (New York: The Citadel Press, 1960).
59. See Lawrence M. Friedman, *American Law* (New York: W.W. Norton, 1984), 213–217; and Ernest van de Haag's classic, *Punishing Criminals* (New York: Basic Books, 1975).
60. See Laurence, *A History of Capital Punishment*, 64.
61. *Louisiana ex rel. Francis v. Resweber*, 329 U.S. 459 (1947).
62. Two other cases decided shortly after *Gregg* that upheld the capital sentencing laws in Florida and Texas are *Proffitt v. Florida*, 428 U.S. 242 (1976); and *Jurek v. Texas*, 428 U.S. 262 (1976).

63. *Coker v. Georgia*, 433 U.S. 584 (1977).

64. *Lockett v. Ohio*, 438 U.S. 586 (1978).

65. *Enmund v. Florida*, 458 U.S. 782 (1982).

66. *Ford v. Wainwright*, 477 U.S. 399 (1986).

67. This study is cited in *McClesky v. Kemp*, 481 U.S. 279 (1987); see also R. Kennedy, "*McClesky v. Kemp*: Race Capital Punishment and the Supreme Court," 1010 *Harvard Law Review* 1388 (1988).

68. *Kyles v. Whitley*, 514 U.S. 419 (1995).

69. *Felker v. Turpin*, 518 U.S. 651 (1996).

70. *Calderon v. Coleman,* 525 U.S. 141 (1998).

71. For background reading on the war on drugs, see Stephen P. Thompson, ed., *The War on Drugs: Opposing Viewpoints* (San Diego, CA: Greenhaven Press, 1998); and James A. Inciardi, *The War on Drugs III* (Boston: Allyn and Bacon, 2002).

72. Allen J. Beck, U.S. Department of Justice, *Prisoners in 1999*, http://www.ojp.usdoj.gov/bjs/pubala2.htm#prisoners (August 2000).

73. John Scalia, U.S. Department of Justice, *Prisoner Petitions in the Federal Courts, 1980–96*, http://www.ojp.usdoj.gov/bjs/pub/ascii/ppfc96.txt (October 1997).

74. See http://www.ojp.usdoj.gov/bjs/pub/ascii/ppfc96.txt.

75. See John A. Fliter, *Prisoner's Rights: The Supreme Court and Evolving Standards of Decency* (Westport, CT: Greenwood Press, 2001).

76. *Wolff v. McDonnell*, 418 U.S. 539 (1974).

77. *Hutto v. Finley*, 437 U.S. 678 (1978).

78. See *United States v. Carolene Products*, 304 U.S. 144 (1938).

79. *O'Lone v. Estate of Shabazz*, 482 U.S. 342 (1987).

80. *Turner v. Safley*, 482 U.S. 78 (1987).

81. *Hewitt v. Helms*, 459 U.S. 460 (1983).

82. *Rhodes v. Chapman*, 452 U.S. 337 (1981).

83. See Scalia, *Prisoner Petitions in the Federal Courts*.

84. 18 U.S.C. 3626.

85. See Joseph T. Lukens, "The Prison Litigation Reform Act: Three Strikes and You're Out of Court—It May Be Effective But Is It Constitutional?" 70 *Temple Law Review* 471 (1997). The Court is presently reviewing a challenge to one provision of the act in *Booth v. Churner*, 206 F.3d 289 (3d Cir.), *cert. granted*, 121 S. Ct. 377 (2000).

86. For a detailed examination of this subject, see George P. Fletcher, *With Justice for Some: Protecting Victims Rights in Criminal Trials* (New York: Addison-Wesley Publishers, 1996); and Sara Faherty, *Victims and Victims Rights* (New York: Chelsea House, 1999).

87. *United States v. McVeigh*, 106 F.3d 325 (10 Cir. 1997).

88. 18 U.S.C. 3510 (1997).

# CHAPTER SIX

# Privacy: "The Right to Be Let Alone" or "The Right to Choose"?

*We deal with a right of privacy older than the Bill of Rights—older than our political parties, older than our school system. . . . Would we allow the police to search the sacred precincts of the marital bedroom for telltale signs of the use of contraceptives? The very idea is repulsive to the notions of privacy surrounding the marriage relationship.*

Justice William O. Douglas in *Griswold v. Connecticut*, 381 U.S. 479 (1965)

*I believe the framers would be appalled by the vision of mass governmental intrusions upon the integrity of the human body that the [Rehnquist] majority allows to become reality.*

Justice Thurgood Marshall, dissenting in *Skinner v. Railroad Executives Association*, 489 U.S. 602 (1989)

The definition of the right of privacy, as well as its scope of protection, is one of the most debated concepts in American law. Many prominent legal scholars and practitioners argue that the right of privacy extends only to our right to be "let alone" from the prying eyes of the state or other private citizens. Others argue for a much broader right of privacy, which can be understood as the right to choose whether to perform a specific act (such as an abortion) or to refuse to undergo a particular experience (such as unwanted medical treatment). Though the U.S. Supreme Court has adopted both interpretations of privacy, concerns about the specific kinds of activities and lifestyles protected by the constitutional right to privacy are still vigorously debated.[1]

## TORT LAW AND FOURTH AMENDMENT ORIGINS OF THE PRIVACY RIGHT

As early as sixty years before the Supreme Court elevated the right of privacy to constitutional status in 1965, guarantees of limited privacy interests were found in a body of case law surrounding the common law tort doctrines of trespass, defama-

229

tion, and nuisance. As might be expected, however, this early expression of a legal claim to privacy was very narrow or limited, and it was used only to protect against the disclosure of personal information or the unauthorized use of one's name or photograph for the purpose of selling a product or a service, such as life insurance. The full legal expression of the right of privacy in its modern form developed slowly, incrementally building upon this existing body of tort law.[2]

The first argument for a broader common law protection of the right of privacy was set forth by Samuel Warren and Louis Brandeis in a famous essay published in the *Harvard Law Review* in 1890.[3] Warren and Brandeis argued that the existing body of case law already contained the necessary elements for what they believed to be a broader, more comprehensive right of privacy—a "right to be let alone." The essay was written out of concern about an irritating trend of overzealous press accounts of the private activities of prominent families, Warren's family being among those subjected to this profitable "yellow journalism." The authors wrote of the importance of privacy in civilized societies, arguing that the invasion of privacy constituted an independent tort, or injury, because it violated the individual's dignity, intruded upon a person's independence, and sullied the uniqueness of the individual's personality.[4]

It is difficult to assess Warren and Brandeis's impact on the eventual legal recognition of the right of privacy. However, as early as 1890 their essay was cited in an opinion by the New York Superior Court. The court ruled against the publication of an unauthorized photograph of an actress who appeared on stage in tights. The court argued that the publication of the photograph constituted a violation of the woman's right of privacy because the newspaper exploited the actress's fame or notoriety without her permission.[5] But in 1899, the Michigan high court refused to recognize an asserted right of privacy at all when the family of a deceased public official named Atkinson sued to enjoin a cigar company from selling a brand of cigar bearing his name and boasting of his endorsement.[6]

An important case that stands out in the early debate over the existence of the right of privacy was *Roberson v. Rochester Folding Box Co.*, 64 N.E. 442 (1902). The litigation involved the unauthorized use of a young woman's photograph to sell flour. The advertisement on which the picture appeared contained an awful pun about "the flour of youth." In denying recovery to the family of the unfortunate young woman, the New York Court of Appeals went to great length to reject Warren and Brandeis's argument that an independent and very broad right of privacy existed. The court ruled on the grounds of lack of precedent, the purely mental nature of the alleged privacy violation, the danger to freedom of press, the problem of discerning the line between private and public persons, and the problem of the immense volume of litigation that would ensue if such a right were recognized.

During the decades following these early cases, American society experienced rapid industrialization, massive waves of immigration, and urban crowding and conflict. Within this context of social and technological change, judges continued to argue over the legal recognition of the right of privacy. Ever so cautiously, state courts began to recognize the principle that Warren and Brandeis had written about.[7]

The adage, "A man's house is his castle," symbolizes our society's traditional concern for constitutionally protected places, such as our homes or personal space.

Indeed, the Fourth Amendment was intended to protect all citizens from arbitrary and unreasonable invasions by the government. The framers of the Fourth Amendment, however, could not imagine a time when technology would make it possible for a search to go beyond a mere physical intrusion into a home and a seizure to go beyond the taking of a tangible object of evidence. Current technology now makes it possible to violate privacy with an electronic listening device, a hidden camera, or a computer-assisted device that "reads" the vibrations that the human voice produces on a window pane. As early as 1886, the U.S. Supreme Court recognized that the Fourth Amendment protects limited privacy interests. In *Boyd v. United States*, 116 U.S. 616, the Court ruled that both the Fourth and Fifth Amendments extend to

> all invasions on the part of the [federal] government and its employees of the sanctity of a man's home and the privacies of life. It is not the breaking of his doors, the rummaging of his drawers, that constitutes the essence of the offense, but it is the invasion of his indefeasible right of personal security, personal liberty, and private property.

When Warren and Brandeis published their essay, they prophesied that "mechanical devices" would ultimately be used to intrude upon our private lives. Twenty-five years after this prophesy, Brandeis was appointed to the U.S. Supreme Court by President Woodrow Wilson. It was during Brandeis's tenure that the Supreme Court would face an electronic eavesdropping case for the first time.

In *Olmstead v. United States*, 277 U.S. 438 (1928), the Court was asked to consider whether wiretapping constituted a search or seizure within the meaning of the Fourth Amendment. Over Justice Brandeis's strong dissent, the majority of the Court answered that it did not, arguing that if a person installs a telephone for the purpose of projecting his or her voice outside of the home, then the person gives up an expectation of privacy in the conversation. The Fourth Amendment applied to unreasonable physical intrusions, the majority argued, and not to electronic eavesdropping on telephone conversations. Therefore, the exclusionary rule, which holds that evidence illegally obtained may not be used in a criminal prosecution, did not apply in this instance.

Brandeis insisted that new discoveries and inventions made it necessary to move beyond the Court's traditional interpretation of Fourth Amendment protection: "Discovery and invention have made it possible for the government, by means far more effective than stretching upon the rack, to obtain disclosure in court of what is whispered in the closet."

The Fourth Amendment, said Brandeis, was broad enough to encompass a right to privacy and thus to protect the "most intimate occurrences of the home." Brandeis was again way ahead of his time, for his views would not be vindicated until *Katz v. United States*, 389 U.S. 347 (1967), discussed in chapter 5.

Recall that the government argued that because the telephone booth from which Katz placed his bets was constructed of glass, therefore rendering him visible from the street, Katz had no Fourth Amendment rights while in the booth. But the Court found that Katz, by going into the telephone booth and closing the door, had made an effort to keep what he said private. Thus, he had a reasonable expectation of privacy in his conversation. *Katz* was significant because the area under surveillance was not a private residence or a hotel room, but rather a public telephone booth.

Reasonable expectation, as one of the dominant legal theories in privacy cases, has come to be defined as a commonsense understanding of the precautions needed to keep one's actions and affairs private. For example, one should stay in one's house, apartment, or dormitory room; go into a telephone booth; or talk in the presence of only trustworthy individuals if one expects to have privacy. What is sought to be kept private, even outside the home, is protected by the Fourth Amendment's prohibition of unreasonable searches.

*Is this expectation of privacy absolute?* At what point do we forfeit this right? Suppose that Katz, Jr. uses his cellular phone in his convertible sports car to make a drug deal. He does so while parked at a doughnut shop frequently patronized by police officers. Does he abandon his expectation of privacy because of his reckless behavior? The Court uses the concept of assumption of risk to deal with this kind of situation. For example, the Court held in *United States v. White*, 401 U.S. 745 (1981), that a person contemplating illegal activities undertakes the risk that his or her conversations might be reported to the authorities. A failure to realize the risk is a failure of judgment, from which one does not deserve protection. The Court ruled that James White's public conversations, overheard by a "wired" government agent, could be used as evidence at White's criminal trial. White's assumption of risk resulted in forfeiture of his reasonable expectation of privacy. In sum, the reasonable expectation of privacy doctrine is significant because it supports the concept that the Fourth Amendment protects people and not just places. Thus, privacy protection extends beyond the walls of dwellings to wherever people have a reasonable expectation of privacy.

## DRUG TESTING

*Do compulsory breath, urine, and blood tests for the purpose of detecting drug use violate one's reasonable expectation of privacy?* Or are the inconveniences of drug testing offset by society's interest in clear-minded citizens and drug-free workplaces? While some may shrug off drug testing as a small price to pay in the war on drugs, others contend that compelling a person to give blood samples or subjecting a person to supervised urination is the worst intrusion on a person's dignity and privacy. Many civil libertarians who oppose drug testing argue that in addition to the initial intrusion, drug testing further implicates privacy rights by necessitating the creation of data files that persist long after the test itself.

The Supreme Court has recognized that a compelled physical intrusion, penetrating beneath the skin, for alcohol or drug testing constitutes a search under the Fourth Amendment (*Terry v. Ohio*, 392 U.S. 1 [1968]), and that the ensuing lab analysis to obtain physiological data is a further invasion of the individual's privacy interests (*Arizona v. Hicks*, 480 U.S. 321 [1987]). Breathalyzer tests and blood alcohol tests administered to motorists suspected of driving while intoxicated raise similar privacy interests and are considered to be searches under the Fourth Amendment (*California v. Trombetta*, 467 U.S. 479 [1984]). In addition, any restriction on an employee's freedom of movement that is necessary to obtain breath, urine, or blood samples is also a factor in the Court's assessment of the intrusiveness of the testing program (*United States v. Place*, 462 U.S. 696 [1983]). There is no question that drug testing raises a Fourth Amendment privacy issue. However, there is much dispute concerning precisely how that privacy interest will be balanced with the government's asserted interest in public safety or with its war on drugs. Is the privacy of a worker in a nuclear power plant, for instance, completely eclipsed by society's desire to take every precaution against negligent behavior or drug use? Is our interest in safety so compelling that the worker should stand ready to submit to all kinds of biological and psychological tests at a moment's notice and without probable cause? Furthermore, if the Fourth Amendment is implicated by drug testing, does its fundamental privacy protection apply to civil searches—the actions of private parties—or only to the searches by police who are pursuing a criminal investigation?

The Rehnquist Court addressed these questions in *Skinner v. Railway Labor Executives Association*, 489 U.S. 602 (1989), in which it ruled 6–3 in a complex opinion that mandatory drug testing of employees in "safety-sensitive" jobs is not in itself unconstitutional even if the employer fails to show probable cause.[8]

The case originated when members of the Railway Labor Executives Association and various other labor organizations brought suit against Secretary of Transportation Samuel Skinner challenging the constitutionality of Federal Railroad Administration (FRA) regulations governing drug and alcohol testing of employees. Congress had enacted the Federal Railroad Safety Act of 1970, authorizing the FRA to require blood and urine tests for employees who violate safety rules or who are involved in train accidents. In 1983, the FRA took this policy a step further by permitting railroads to require breath or urine tests of any employee under "reasonable suspicion" by a supervisor of being under the influence of alcohol. Under FRA regulations, these tests could be administered without a warrant, probable cause, or "individualized suspicion." Whenever the results of either of these tests are intended to be used in a disciplinary proceeding, the employee must be given an opportunity to submit to a blood test at an independent medical facility. If the employee declines to take the blood test, the railroad may then presume impairment and take the appropriate actions.[9]

The labor organizations challenging the FRA drug-testing policy argued that by authorizing compelled urine and blood tests without probable cause or individualized suspicion, the government violated the railroad employees' reasonable expectation of privacy and bodily integrity protected by the Fourth Amendment. The government responded to these charges by pointing out that the Fourth Amendment did not apply in this case because the drug testing was undertaken by a private party—the railroad company—and not by the government itself. Even if the employees did have a Fourth Amendment privacy right that protected them from their employer, that right was outweighed by the compelling public interest in promoting safety for railroad workers and passengers.

The Supreme Court ruled that while it is true that the right of privacy guaranteed by the Fourth Amendment does not apply to private parties acting on their own initiative, it does protect against such intrusions if the private party acted as an instrument of the government. In other words, even though the drug testing was undertaken by the railroad company, the Fourth Amendment privacy guarantee still applies. Writing for the majority, Justice Kennedy reasoned:

> The fact that the Government has not compelled a private party to perform a search does not, by itself, establish that the search is a private one. Here, specific features of the regulations combine to convince us that the Government did more than adopt a passive position toward the underlying private conduct.

The FRA's regulations made it clear that the government not only wanted to see private companies implement drug testing, but it also wanted to use the fruits of the search as evidence in a federal criminal action against the employee.

The decision, however, took an unfavorable turn for the railroad workers when Justice Kennedy reasoned that although drug tests do raise privacy concerns, the collection and testing of breath, urine, and blood samples from workers do not entail the degree of intrusion that would constitute an unreasonable violation of the right of privacy. The collection of a breath or urine sample is by no means as intrusive as a blood-testing procedure or some other test that involves a compelled intrusion into the body. The Court had already sustained the constitutionality of taking blood samples in *Schmerber v. California*, 384 U.S. 757 (1966). In *Schmerber*, the Court ruled that a state could order a blood sample taken from a motorist suspected of driving while intoxicated despite his refusal to consent to the procedure.[10] Nevertheless, intentional governmental intrusions upon the privacy of the workers must be deemed a search under the Fourth Amendment. However, since the Fourth Amendment proscribes only searches and seizures that are unreasonable, it must be established whether drug tests constitute reasonable or unreasonable searches. To do so, the individual's right of privacy is balanced with a compelling or legitimate governmental interest. In this case, it is the government's "special need" to regulate the conduct of railroad employees in safety-sensitive jobs that outweighs the employee's expectation of privacy.[11]

The courts have long recognized the government's need to restrict the privacy and freedom of movement of public school children, parolees and prisoners, and workers in hazardous industries. In these special situations, government has been exempted from the traditional probable cause and warrant requirements for search and seizure. Since we cannot rely on all employees to adhere to the rules, and since in the time it takes to establish probable cause or secure a warrant the substances would no longer appear in the bloodstream, mandatory drug tests following all accidents are the necessary means by which the FRA's goal of a safe workplace is implemented.

The question remains, however, whether the railroad company may impinge upon the employee's privacy without the use of a warrant or an individualized suspicion. It is not surprising that given the circumstances of the workplace the Court was willing to invoke the warrant exception as it had in *Schmerber*. But the Court went beyond merely applying the warrant exception. In light of the high-risk and safety-sensitive nature of the railway worker's responsibilities, the Court waived the probable cause and individualized suspicion requirements as well, thus enabling the railroad to require breath, urine, and blood testing solely on the basis of "reasonable suspicion." Kennedy argued: "In limited circumstances, where the privacy interests are implicated by the search are minimal, and where an important governmental interest furthered by the intrusion would be placed in jeopardy by a requirement of individualized suspicion, a search may be reasonable despite the absence of such suspicion."

Thus, in safety-sensitive positions, utility clearly outweighs privacy. Is this a reasonable position? Are there alternatives to this approach? The railroad unions advocated employing individuals trained to detect employees who are impaired by drugs or alcohol rather than resorting to such invasive tests. The government opposed that approach and argued that requiring railroad officials to show evidence of impairment before ordering a test would be tantamount to waiting until the engineer is observed pushing a few wrong buttons or making poor judgments before any action is taken. In most cases, impaired workers rarely show any outward signs of alcohol or drug use.

Regardless of how intrusive these tests may appear to the average person, railroad employees, like airline pilots and others in safety-sensitive jobs, understand that they have a diminished expectation of privacy by virtue of their employment in a high-risk occupation. Thus, it is constitutionally permissible for employers, acting under governmental regulations, to demand that their employees submit to drug testing even in the absence of probable cause or individualized suspicion. This policy is justified by the special need of the government to regulate the conduct of individuals in safety-sensitive occupations. The problem, then, is to determine whether the 'special needs' rule applies in a particular set of circumstances or how broadly the government is permitted to define "safety-sensitive." (We can assume that the rubric encompasses security-sensitive positions as well.) Are physicians and other health care providers included? What about an elementary school teacher or a Little League coach? How far can this line of reasoning be taken? Can a hospital administrator or a school principal order drug testing on demand? Under the Court's ruling, employers may use the special needs exception in conducting searches in a way that exceeds that which is needed for law enforcement. Is the government's interest in deterring drug use in the workplace as compelling as its interest in policing the streets for criminal activity?

The two lone dissenters, Justices Marshall and Brennan, attributed the majority's support of these draconian measures to a new hysteria over the threat of drugs. While they recognized the importance of a sound drug policy, they reminded us that many tragic events in American history, such as the relocation of Japanese-Americans or the McCarthy witch-hunts during the 1950s, resulted from similar overreactions to perceived threats. Marshall wrote:

> Precisely because the need for action against the drug scourge is manifest, the need for vigilance against unconstitutional excess is great. History teaches that grave threats to liberty often come in times of urgency, when constitutional rights seem too extravagant to endure. . . . In permitting the government to force entire railroad crews to submit to invasive blood and urine tests, even when it lacks any evidence

of drug or alcohol use or other wrongdoing, the majority today joins those short-sighted courts which have allowed basic constitutional rights to fall prey to momentary emergencies.

Marshall then attacked the Court's widening of the special needs exception—applied previously in the area of law enforcement—to justify the FRA's testing of all workers without any evidence of malfeasance and regardless of the fact that every worker appears to be sober and alert. While admitting that some exceptions to the probable cause rule could be justified by the particular needs of police when conducting criminal searches, Marshall and Brennan could not countenance the application of a special needs exception to civil searches "beyond the normal need for law enforcement." Recall that in this case the invasion of privacy was not a result of the actions necessitated by a police criminal investigation, but rather from the action of an employer investigating the cause of a workplace accident. Drug use by workers in safety-sensitive jobs is an undeniably important issue, but is the drug problem of such a magnitude that we should afford greater privacy protection to suspected drug dealers than to workers in high-risk occupations who are not even suspected of drug use? Quoting Justice Brandeis's dissent in *Olmstead v. United States*, Marshall lashed out: "Because abandoning the explicit protections of the Fourth Amendment seriously imperils 'the right to be let alone—the most comprehensive of rights and the right most valued by civilized men,' . . . I reject the majority's 'special needs' rationale as unprincipled and dangerous."

Marshall and Brennan believed that by empowering agents of the government to eclipse an individual's right of privacy by virtue of some special need, the majority's decision completely abandoned the established framework under which Fourth Amendment claims have traditionally been evaluated. In contrast to permissible warrantless searches in recent cases involving agents of the state acting in circumstances requiring special needs, *Skinner* did not demand individualized evidence "suggesting the culpability of the persons" whose privacy was invaded. Those in the majority believed that their decision was compatible with recent precedent.[12]

Are drug tests really that intrusive? Marshall argued that compelling a person to have his or her skin pierced by a hypodermic needle for the purpose of extracting blood or requiring a person to urinate while someone else looks on are not merely annoyances, as the majority contended, but are substantial intrusions on privacy and bodily integrity. To characterize these intrusions as minimal, argued Marshall, "is nothing short of startling." Drug testing may be necessary, but since these intrusions are full-scale searches under the Fourth Amendment they should be subject to the requirements of probable cause and individualized suspicion. In other words, a supervisor must suspect that employee X is under the influence of marijuana, and then have X tested only to prove that he was under the influence of that particular drug. The alternative is for all employees to go to work every day under the shadow of a possible breath, urine, or blood test.

Since *Skinner* was decided in 1989, drug testing for employees, athletes, and others has become commonplace and largely accepted without complaint. However, the Court decided the issue was worth revisiting in *Chandler v. Miller*[13] in 1997, where it struck down as unconstitutional a Georgia law that required candidates for public office to submit to a drug test. As part of its war on drugs, the state required all candidates (thirty days prior to qualifying for nomination or office) to submit to a urinalysis test. The law was enacted not because there was evidence that public officials were using drugs, but out of a need to make a symbolic statement against drug use.

Libertarian candidates for state office filed suit against the governor, arguing that the law violated the First, Fourth, and Fourteenth Amendments to the U.S. Constitution. However, both a federal district court and an appellate court affirmed the law, relying on the Supreme Court's earlier rulings in *Von Raub*,[14] which upheld random drug testing of customs officials; *Skinner*, which sustained a drug-testing program for railway employees; and *Veronia School District v. Acton*,[15] which supported drug tests for student athletes. The lower courts argued that the state's interest in the drug-testing program superceded the individual's privacy expectations and the Fourth Amendment's protection against suspicionless searches. But the Supreme Court strongly rejected this argument outright, ruling 8–1 that the lower courts had misapplied the earlier rulings. Even if the drug test was not excessively intrusive, Georgia failed to show a special need that was substantial or important enough to override privacy interests and sufficiently vital to suppress the Fourth Amendment requirement that individualized suspicion must be present before a search is undertaken. Indeed, during oral argument the counsel for the state of Georgia admitted that there was no evidence that Georgia officeholders have a problem with drug use.

The Court had upheld drug testing in earlier cases because it was shown that those tests were a necessary means to advance a clear objective, such as maintaining safe rail travel and drug-free customs officers. However, the Georgia legislature's need to "get tough" or display a commitment to the war on drugs does not justify a whole new range of suspicionless searches. The Fourth Amendment protects persons from state action that diminishes personal privacy for the sake of making a symbolic statement.

Writing for the majority, Justice Ginsberg concluded that Georgia's symbolic drug-testing statute "diminishes personal privacy for a symbol's sake. The Fourth Amendment shields society against that [kind of] state action." She also reiterated:

[W]here the risk to public safety is substantial and real, blanket suspicionless searches calibrated to the risk may rank as "reasonable"—for example, searches now routine at airports and at entrances to courts and other public buildings. But where, as in this case, public safety is not genuinely in jeopardy, the Fourth Amendment precludes the suspicionless search, no matter how conveniently arranged.

## PRIVACY AS AUTONOMY AND REPRODUCTIVE FREEDOM

Privacy as autonomy represents a more comprehensive and controversial definition of privacy. This concept of privacy is not merely the right to be let alone, to be free from governmental invasions, but also the personal right to determine for oneself whether to perform a specific act or undergo a particular experience. Thus, while the right to be let alone can be understood as a negative right—to be free from intrusion—privacy as autonomy empowers the person with a positive right to make autonomous choices. This expanded theory of privacy has its origins in the Court's application of substantive due process as a means of protecting fundamental, though unwritten, personal freedoms. Substantive due process allows the Court to "discover" implied rights within the text of the Constitution by reading into the due process clauses of the Fifth and Fourteenth Amendments fundamental values or natural law concepts.[16] The Court had initially used substantive due process to strike down early attempts to regulate economic relations on the grounds that such regulations violated the fundamental right to economic liberty, or liberty of contract. The substantive due process approach enabled the Court to take a broad view of "liberty" and "property," and thus find protected interests not specifically enumerated in the Constitution.

While this substantive due process concept of economic liberty was ultimately abandoned by the Court, the judicial reasoning employed set the stage for the Court's eventual elevation of the concept of privacy as autonomy to a constitutional right. Two early cases illustrate this point: *Meyer v. Nebraska*, 262 U.S. 390 (1925), and *Skinner v. Oklahoma*, 316 U.S. 535 (1942). In *Meyer*, the Court employed a broad view of liberty to overturn the conviction of a public school teacher who taught the German language contrary to a state law prohibiting the teaching of foreign languages to young students. Justice James McReynolds argued that the law interfered with the profession of language teachers, with the educational opportunities of students, and with the power of parents to control the education of their children. The state's interest in promoting a common language and "American ideals" was not a justified restraint on those interests. Thus, the Court defined liberty as not only freedom from physical restraint but also the freedom to acquire knowledge, to marry, to bring up children, to work, and to pursue happiness.

In *Skinner v. Oklahoma*, the Court combined this concept of liberty with an equal protection argument to produce a much broader basic right. The Court struck down an Oklahoma law requiring mandatory sterilization after a third conviction for a felony involving moral turpitude, such as chicken stealing, but not for felonies such as embezzlement from one's employer.[17] Under the law, if a jury found that the defendant was an "habitual criminal," the court could order the sterilization of the defendant by vasectomy for a male and by salpingectomy for a female. Although the distinction between the kinds of felons who could be sterilized appeared to be arbitrary, the Court might have sustained the law if it had not felt that the law violated one of the basic human rights—procreation. Writing for the majority, Douglas reasoned that the law violated the due process guarantee of liberty:

> [M]arriage and procreation are fundamental to the very existence and survival of the race. The power to sterilize, if exercised, may have subtle, far-reaching and devastating effects. In evil or reckless hands it can cause races or types which are inimical to the dominant group to wither and disappear. Any experiment which the state conducts is to his irreparable injury. *He is forever deprived of a basic liberty* [emphasis added].

The law violated the equal protection clause of the Fourteenth Amendment because it called for the sterilization of one kind of individual (the chicken thief) and not for the other (the embezzler), even though both individuals had committed the same quality of offense. This violated the constitutional guarantee of equal protection. Douglas wrote: "[S]trict scrutiny of the classification which a state makes in a sterilization law is essential, lest unwittingly or otherwise invidious discriminations are made against groups or types of individuals in violation of the constitutional guarantee of just and equal laws."

Douglas's discussion of fundamental or basic personal liberties was a portent of things to come during the Warren Court. Not since the *Lochner* era's substantive due process arguments to protect fundamental economic liberty had the Court applied strict scrutiny to a law in order to protect an unenumerated fundamental liberty.

## Elevation of Privacy to a Constitutional Right

The Court's recognition of the fundamental right to marry, procreate, and choose how to raise children presages the ultimate recognition of privacy as a constitutionally protected right in the landmark case *Griswold v. Connecticut*, 381 U.S. 479 (1965), in which the Supreme Court invalidated a Connecticut law prohibiting the use of contraceptives. The state law made it a criminal offense to use or counsel the use of any drug or instrument for the purpose of preventing conception. Mary Griswold, then executive director of the Planned Parenthood League, and Dr. C. Led Buxton, medical director of the League's New Haven Center, violated the law by giving birth control information and prescribing contraceptives to married people. On November 10, the New Haven police ordered the center closed. Griswold was found guilty and fined $100. The high court of Connecticut affirmed her conviction, whereupon she appealed to the U.S. Supreme Court.

The Supreme Court overturned the Connecticut law, arguing that the law directly and adversely affected the intimacy of the marital relationship and represented an unwarranted governmental intrusion into the sphere of private matters. But the Court was initially undecided on how to approach the Connecticut law. Griswold and Buxton had originally argued that the Connecticut statute violated their freedom of association, but this approach met with some opposition from the justices. Justice Black was quick to oppose this view on the grounds that "[t]he right of association is for me a right of assembly and the right of the husband and wife to assemble in bed is a new right of assembly for me."[18] Justice Douglas disagreed with Black, arguing that the First Amendment right of association did not merely protect the right of assembly, but extended to the marital relationship. Ultimately, Douglas adopted a privacy argument and convinced the majority that the law placed severe limitations on a woman's personal autonomy, or freedom to enter into the most fundamental sort of personal and intimate relations.[19] Moreover, the law placed constraints on a woman's ability to decide whether or not to have children. In a broader sense, such constraints restricted her right to freely choose her own life plans and moral convictions concerning the fundamental issues of sexual relations and the control of her private life. In sum, the law was an invasion of a woman's constitutional right to privacy. Justice Douglas stated:

> We deal with a right of privacy older than the Bill of Rights—older than our political parties, older than our school system. Would we allow the police to search the

sacred precincts of the marital bedrooms for telltale signs of the use of contraceptives? The very idea is repulsive to the notions of privacy surrounding the marriage relationship.[20]

A reading of the Constitution reveals that no such right of privacy is enumerated. According to Justice Douglas, although the right of privacy is not among the rights specifically enumerated in the Constitution, the right is implied by several constitutional amendments and by the concept of liberty most assuredly found in the due process clauses of the Fifth and Fourteenth Amendments. Even more controversial than the right of privacy itself was Douglas's methodology of "finding" this new right. He argued that this unenumerated right was found in the following provisions of the Bill of Rights, and that it applied to the states through the Fourteenth Amendment:

1. The "penumbras" of liberty; in other words, the inherent guarantees of the specific protections of the Bill of Rights. The right of association found in the First Amendment is one example.
2. The Third Amendment, in its prohibition against the quartering of soldiers in any house in time of peace without the consent of the owner, is another facet of the right of privacy.
3. The Fourth Amendment—which affirms the right of the people to be secure in their persons, houses, papers, and effects against unreasonable searches and seizures—implies the right of privacy.
4. The Fifth Amendment, in its prohibition of self-incrimination, enables the person to create a zone of privacy.
5. The Ninth Amendment provides that the enumeration in the Constitution of certain rights shall not be construed to deny or disparage others retained by the people. In other words, just because the Constitution does not mention a right, it does not imply that the right does not exist.

Despite the confusion created by the legal reasoning in *Griswold* and by the four majority and two dissenting opinions, there is no question that the case established a new right of privacy. This new right, which came to be known as "privacy as autonomy" or "privacy inhering in a relationship," is much different from the reasonable expectation of privacy theory found in Fourth Amendment search and seizure cases. Unlike the older formulation of privacy, the new right does not seem to have any clear definition of what kinds of activities it protects, nor does it have any bounds on the scope of its protection.

The new broadened right of privacy set forth in *Griswold* was immediately subject to debate. *If privacy is fundamental to the marital relationship, then what about unmarried couples or homosexual couples? Could it be used to negate state laws proscribing particular sexual acts? If the new right is fundamental to personal choice in the intimate matter of contraception, what about a woman's right to terminate a pregnancy?*

In *Eisenstadt v. Baird*, 405 U.S. 438 (1972), the Supreme Court addressed whether the right of privacy extended to unmarried couples in matters of conception and procreation. A Massachusetts law made it a felony to give anyone other than a married couple or a married person contraceptive medicines or devices. William Baird was arrested and convicted of illegally distributing contraceptives to a group of students at Boston University. Writing for the majority of the Court, Justice Brennan argued that the intent of the Massachusetts law was not altogether clear. Was it the purpose of the law to regulate contraceptive devices as such or was it to regulate premarital sex? The Court believed it was the latter and struck down the law as unconstitutional.

In its decision, the Court relied on the *Griswold* precedent—the right of privacy protected the marital relationship. In *Eisenstadt*, however, the Court destroyed the distinction between married and unmarried couples, arguing that a married couple is not a single and independent entity but an association of two autonomous persons. If the right to privacy means anything, wrote Brennan, it is the right of the individual, married or single, to be free from unwarranted intrusion of the state into personal areas of conduct.

## Abortion

In 1973, in one of the most controversial decisions in American history, the Supreme Court extended the right of privacy to a woman's decision to terminate a pregnancy. In *Roe v. Wade*, 410 U.S. 113, the Court applied the right of privacy and the due process clause of the Fourteenth Amendment to strike down a Texas law making it a felony to abort a fetus except "upon medical advice for the purpose of saving the life of the mother." The Texas law was typical of abortion statutes then in effect in most states, though, beginning in the 1960s, many states had begun to reform (decriminalize) their abortion laws.[21]

Jane Roe (a pseudonym) and three other persons brought suit challenging the constitutionality of the Texas law on the grounds that it denied equal protection and due process under the Fourteenth Amendment and violated a woman's right of privacy. Justice Blackmun, writing for the majority, began by examining some of the reasons criminal abortion laws had been enacted over the past hundred years.[22] He found a variety of justifications. Some anti-abortion laws were enacted not out of a desire to protect the fetus or the health of the mother but because of the Victorian desire to discourage sexual promiscuity in women. He dismissed this rationale outright. Other laws were aimed at protecting pregnant women from primitive and dangerous abortion techniques. In the early 1900s, before the development of modern antibiotics, the mortality rate from abortion was high. Even as late as 1940, women developed serious health problems or died as a result of botched abortions. However, changes in medical technology negated this justification for criminal abortion laws. Although the risk to the woman increases as the pregnancy continues, the mortality rates for women undergoing abortions early in pregnancy are no higher than the mortality rates associated with normal childbirth.

The third and most controversial rationale for criminal abortion laws reflected the state's interest in protecting prenatal life. Many such laws were based on the belief that life begins at conception and that the fetus is a person in possession of constitutional rights. While no one refutes the view that human life begins at conception, the Court has never ruled that a fetus is a legal person protected by the Constitution. The Court has ruled that while a state may determine the point at which a fetus becomes a person, it may not do so prior to the point at which the fetus is medically viable. A fetus is considered viable when it has the capability of living independently of the mother's womb, or after twenty-three and a half or twenty-four weeks of gestation. Today, dramatic changes in medical technology, such as the development of an artificial womb, could change how the courts view this matter. But the law has never recognized a fetus to be a legal person in the sense that it recognizes a newborn baby or an adult to be a legal person.[23]

The Court argued that although the state does have an interest in protecting prenatal life, its interest must be balanced with a woman's right to privacy. Prior to the end of the first trimester, the abortion decision must be left up to the woman and her attending physician. During the second trimester, the state may regulate the abortion procedure in ways that are "reasonably related to maternal health." At the stage subsequent to viability, however, the state may regulate or prohibit abortion on the grounds of its interest in the "potentiality of human life." Thus, it is only at the point of viability—when the fetus has the capability of "meaningful life" outside of the mother's womb—that the state's interest is compelling enough to ban all abortions if it so chooses.[24]

The Court overturned the Texas law on the grounds that the right of privacy was found to be "broad enough to protect a woman's decision to terminate her pregnancy." Citing Brandeis's dissenting opinion in *Olmstead* and the majority's opinions in *Katz* and *Griswold*, the Court articulated a right of privacy that protects a woman's exclusive claim on her body. The Court argued that by denying a pregnant woman a choice in this matter, the state may force upon a woman

> a distressful life and future. Psychological harm may be imminent. Mental and physical health would be taxed by child care. There is also the distress, for all concerned, associated with the unwanted child, and there is the problem of bringing a child into a family already unstable, psychologically and otherwise, to care for it.[25]

Justice Douglas, offering an even broader definition of privacy in a concurring opinion, wrote that the right may also be understood as a right of autonomous control over the development and expression of one's intellect, interests, tastes, and personality. It is the right to care for one's own health and to be free from bodily restraint or compulsion in the basic decisions of procreation and contraception. It is the "freedom to walk, stroll, or loaf."

Thus, in addition to legalizing abortions, *Roe v. Wade* dramatically expanded the right of privacy. Yet, contrary to the views of many people on both sides of the abortion debate, no absolute right to an abortion anytime during pregnancy was established by *Roe v. Wade*. Only during the first three months of pregnancy is a woman's right to an abortion beyond the reach of the state. As the fetus develops, the state's interest in protecting prenatal life becomes more compelling and the woman's privacy interest diminishes.[26] Thus, the trimester framework established in *Roe* is central to the protection of a woman's right of privacy. Any tampering with that framework by the Court could ultimately lead to weakening *Roe*'s protection.

Justice Blackmun's argument in *Roe* was intended to strike a balance between individual freedom and the state's concern for prenatal life. It was also an attempt to secure a moral compromise and, in doing so, resolve the abortion debate once and for all. However, quite the opposite occurred. By the late 1970s and early 1980s, a vocal and politically influential anti-abortion rights movement had formed, pressuring Congress and many state legislatures to enact a variety of new restrictions on abortion rights. After *Roe*, Congress enacted the Hyde Amendment, which forbids the funding of nontherapeutic abortions under the Medicaid program; the Adolescent Family Life Act, which prohibits federal funding of organizations that advocate abortions; and an amendment to Title VII of the 1964 Civil Rights Act so that employers are not required to fund health insurance benefits for abortion except to save the mother's life.

Among the restrictions that states have enacted on abortion rights are bans on the use of public funds or facilities, laws requiring parental or spousal notification and consent, bans on the advertising of abortion, fetal protection laws, and mandatory hospitalization rules. These restrictions were intended to place major obstacles in the way of women seeking to exercise their constitutional rights without explicitly challenging the fundamental right established in *Roe*.

This strategy has drawn a mixed response from the Court. In *Beal v. Doe*, 432 U.S. 438 (1977), the Supreme Court upheld a Pennsylvania law stating that the Social Security Act does not require the state to use Medicaid funds to pay for elective abortions for the poor. The Court also upheld Connecticut's refusal to reimburse Medicaid recipients for elective abortion expenses[27] and the city of St. Louis's denial of access to public hospitals to indigent women seeking nontherapeutic abortions.[28]

Some states enacted various forms of spousal or parental notification and consent statutes. However, in *Planned Parenthood of Central Missouri v. Danforth*, 428 U.S. 552 (1976), the Court ruled 5–4 to invalidate provisions of a statute requiring a husband's consent to an abortion and the parent's consent when the woman is an unmarried minor. On whether the state could give the spouse a veto over the woman's decision, Justice Blackmun wrote:

> [T]he state cannot delegate to a spouse a veto power which the state itself is absolutely and totally prohibited from exercising during the first trimester of pregnancy. . . .
> Since it is the woman who physically bears the child and who is more directly and immediately affected by the pregnancy . . . the balance weighs in her favor.

Nor could the state give a parent or a guardian absolute and possibly arbitrary veto over the decision of a patient and her physician to terminate a pregnancy. This does not mean that the state is prohibited from placing any restrictions on minors, but only restrictions that are absolute or arbitrary. If the state requires a pregnant minor to obtain parental consent, it must also provide an alternative procedure for procuring authorization for the abortion. This may include a confidential judicial proceeding in which the minor can show that, in consultation with her physician, an abortion is in her best interests.[29] Two years after *Danforth*, the Court upheld (6–3) a Utah law that required physicians to notify parents if possible before performing an abortion on a minor when she is living with and dependent on her parents and is

unemancipated by marriage. Chief Justice Burger reasoned: "[As] applied to immature and dependent minors the statute plainly serves a significant state interest by
providing an opportunity for parents to supply essential medical and other information to a physician. . . . [T]he Constitution does not compel a state to fine-tune its
statutes so as to encourage or facilitate abortions."[30]

In the 1980s, the Court was perceived as becoming more conservative after
President Reagan appointed three new justices: Sandra Day O'Connor (1981),
Antonin Scalia (1986), and Anthony Kennedy (1988). Reagan also elevated
Justice William Rehnquist to the chief justiceship in 1986. Many Court-watchers
believed that these appointments would dramatically alter the Court's collective
stand on privacy rights. A more conservative court could turn back the clock on
the kinds of relationships and conduct protected by the Constitution and possibly
overturn *Roe v. Wade*.

However, in *Akron v. Akron Center for Reproductive Health*, 462 U.S. 416
(1983), and *Thornburgh v. American College of Obstetricians and Gynecologists*,
476 U.S. 747 (1986), the Court reaffirmed the general principles laid down in *Roe v.
Wade*. In *Akron*, the Court held (6–3) that women have a constitutional right to terminate a pregnancy and that this right may be restricted only by the most compelling
state interest in health and medical standards. In doing so, the Court overturned a city
ordinance that made a woman's right to an abortion contingent on five provisions:
(1) All abortions after the first trimester must be performed in a hospital, (2) parental
notification must be secured before an abortion is performed on an unmarried minor,
(3) the physician can perform the abortion only after a mandated and specified discussion occurred between patient and physician, (4) there is a twenty-four-hour waiting period between the patient's signing of the informed consent form and the
physician's performance of the abortion, and (5) fetal remains must be disposed of
in a "humane and sanitary manner."

In *Thornburgh*, the Court struck down (5–4) as unconstitutional provisions of a
Pennsylvania law that required a woman seeking an abortion to be informed of the
name of the physician performing the procedure, of the medical risks of the abortion
procedure to be used, and of the possible psychological and physical effects of an
abortion. In addition, the law required the physician to report information about the
woman and the procedure to the state. Justice Blackmun, writing for the majority,
argued again that the states are not free, under the guise of protecting the health of
the mother or potential life, to "intimidate women into continuing pregnancies." The
provisions of the law, wrote Blackmun, were placed above privacy interests and were
intended solely to "deter a woman from making a decision that, with her physician,
is hers to make." A slim majority of the Court once again recognized that persons
have a constitutionally protected "private sphere of individual liberty."

The pivotal case in the post-*Roe* debate is *Webster v. Reproductive Health
Services*, 492 U.S. 490 (1989). With the retirement of Justice Powell in 1987 and the
confirmation of Justice Anthony Kennedy in 1988, the fifth vote in the slim majority, which had thwarted numerous attempts to overturn *Roe*, was no longer assured,
and the stage was set for significant restrictions on abortion rights or for an overturning of *Roe*. Shortly after Justice Kennedy's confirmation, the Reagan administration encouraged Missouri's attorney general, William Webster, to appeal a court

of appeals ruling that struck down a restrictive Missouri anti-abortion statute. The U.S. Supreme Court granted certiorari in order to review the constitutionality of four provisions of the Missouri law. First, the preamble of the law promulgated "findings" by the state that "[t]he life of each human being begins at conception," and that "unborn children have [constitutionally] protectable rights in life, health, and well-being." Anti-abortion forces hoped that if the preamble passed constitutional muster, the trimester framework of *Roe* would be weakened by allowing the state to assert an interest in protecting the fetus during the first trimester.

Second, the statute required that prior to performing an abortion on any woman twenty or more weeks pregnant, the physician must perform a viability test to ascertain the gestational age, weight, and lung maturity of the fetus. Third, the statute made it unlawful to use public funds, facilities, or employees to perform abortions not necessary to save a woman's life. Fourth, the statute prohibited the use of public funds, facilities, or employees for the purpose of "encouraging or counseling" a woman to have an abortion except when the woman's life was threatened.

So it has been with many recent abortion cases argued before the Rehnquist Court. *Webster* was expected to be the case to overturn *Roe* outright, so oral argument took place amidst a great deal of media coverage. Demonstrators lined the sidewalks around the Supreme Court building. In addition, a record seventy-eight *amicus* briefs were filed by individuals and groups representing both sides of the debate. In a 5–4 decision, a very fragmented Court upheld the Missouri statute. Delivering the opinion of the Court, Chief Justice Rehnquist left the preamble untouched on the grounds that by itself the preamble did not regulate abortion or proscribe behavior in any way. He refused to adopt the court of appeals' view that the purpose of the preamble was to justify abortion regulation in the name of potential life, interpreting it as merely a statement of the legislature's philosophy or view of when life began.

The Court also upheld the prohibitions on the use of public funds, facilities, or employees to perform abortions not necessary to save the life of the mother. Relying on earlier decisions, Rehnquist adhered to his long-standing opinion that there is no such thing as a constitutional right to public dollars even if governmental aid is necessary to the exercise of a constitutional right.[31] He reasoned:

> Just as Congress's refusal to fund abortions in *McRae* left "an indigent woman with at least the same range of choice in deciding whether to obtain a medically necessary abortion as she would have had if Congress had chosen to subsidize no health care costs at all," Missouri's refusal to allow public employees to perform abortions in public hospitals leaves a pregnant woman with the same choices as if the State had chosen not to operate any public hospitals at all.

Even though a prohibition on the use of all public funds, facilities, and employees would work to deny most indigent women access to an abortion, the denial of such aid would not technically violate their constitutional right to an abortion. In sum, there is no constitutional right of access to public dollars or facilities for the purpose of securing an abortion. Rehnquist admitted that a different line of reasoning might be followed if the state had a program of socialized medicine where all hospitals and physicians were government funded and all abortions were subsidized.

The Court also accepted Missouri's terse explanation of why the gag rule of the third provision was constitutional. Missouri maintained that the prohibition on encouraging or counseling was not unconstitutionally overbroad because it was not aimed at the speech or conduct of any physician or health care provider, but directed only at those who were responsible for administering government-funded health care.

Finally, the Court upheld the provision of the act that required all physicians to conduct viability tests on the fetus if in the physician's judgment the patient is twenty or more weeks pregnant. In other words, the physician had to determine that the fetus was not viable before performing an abortion. The law's challengers argued that by requiring physicians to administer these expensive and often unreliable tests, the state had intruded upon the physician's discretion and had placed an additional obstacle in the path of all women seeking abortions. But Rehnquist believed that the state's test for viability was a legitimate means of furthering its interest in protecting potential human life—an interest, he argued, that exists throughout a woman's pregnancy and not just from the point of viability on. Unlike the second trimester mandatory hospitalization rule struck down in *Akron* as a "heavy, and unnecessary burden," viability testing did not, in O'Connor's words, "impose an undue burden on a woman's abortion decision."

Rehnquist then proceeded to attack the very core of the *Roe* decision—the trimester framework. Since 1973, when *Roe* was handed down, the trimester framework had served as a barrier against state restrictions on abortion during the first three months of pregnancy and had limited the state's ability to assert its interest in protecting potential life until after the fetus was considered viable at twenty-three and one half to twenty-four weeks. But contrary to *Roe*, a plurality of justices concluded that Missouri's interest in protecting the fetus was compelling even before twenty weeks or viability. In doing so, *Webster* discards what Blackmun had called *Roe*'s "analytic core" without explicitly overturning *Roe*. Attacking what he believed to be a straitjacket on the legislatures and the courts, Rehnquist wrote:

> In the first place, the rigid *Roe* framework is hardly consistent with the notion of a Constitution cast in general terms, as ours is. . . . The key element of the *Roe* framework—trimesters and viability—are not found in the text of the Constitution or in any place else one would expect to find a constitutional principle.

Is there a fundamental right to abortion after *Webster?* More specifically, was *Roe v. Wade* still "good law"? The chief justice refused to even mention either the right of privacy or the fundamental right to an abortion, and clearly called for the abandonment of the *Roe* trimester framework because it had led to "a web of legal rules . . . resembling a code of regulations rather than a body of constitutional doctrine." Rehnquist recognized the state's interest in protecting potential human life throughout pregnancy, but refused to overrule *Roe* outright, as Missouri and the Reagan administration had urged, because the issue at stake in *Webster* was different from the issue in *Roe*. In *Webster*, the issue was whether the state could ban abortions at the point of viability, whereas in *Roe*, the issue was whether Texas could criminalize the performance of all abortions.

Justice Scalia went on record as the only justice calling for an outright overruling of *Roe*, largely on the grounds that abortion is a political issue to be resolved by the legislatures and not by the courts. Why not go beyond the specific issues in *Webster* and overturn *Roe?* Scalia argued:

> Alone sufficient to justify a broad holding is the fact that our retaining control, through *Roe*, of what I believe to be, and many of our citizens recognize to be, a political issue, continually distorts the public perception of the role of this Court. We can now look forward to at least another Term with carts full of mail from the public, and streets full of demonstrators, urging us—their unelected and life-tenured judges . . . to follow the popular will.

But Scalia did not make clear why he thought abortion was purely a political issue. Was it because Scalia is an advocate of judicial restraint and was deferring to the legislative process? Perhaps he was frustrated by the huge amount of mail concerning abortion that bombards the Court. Was it because abortion is not an enumerated right, or because the Court has been burdened with interpreting concepts such as "viability" and "undue burden"? Scalia did not address these issues in his concurring opinion in *Webster*.

Justice Blackmun, the author of the *Roe* opinion, wrote a scathing dissent against what he believed to be a deceptive interpretation of the Missouri statute and an underhanded approach to the entire constitutional issue of abortion. He dismissed Rehnquist's assertion that the preamble of the law was "abortion-neutral": It demanded that the rights of the unborn be protected by the U.S. Constitution to the fullest extent possible. He noted that the law did more than remove the state from the business of providing abortions; by broadly defining "public facility," it took steps to assure that abortions were not performed by many private physicians. Under this provision, the state could prohibit the performance of abortions even in private facilities located on property leased from the state.

In *Webster*, a majority refused to recognize the existence of the right of privacy, completely glossing over whether the Constitution protects a woman's decision to have an abortion. Blackmun understood this strategy as one intended to cast doubt on the Court's commitment to a constitutional right of privacy, thus sending a message to the states that they were free to experiment with new restrictions on abortion rights. Rather than addressing the issue head on, Rehnquist attacked it by challenging the trimester framework—a judicially created method of protecting a woman's privacy interest against state action. Blackmun recognized that if the trimester framework is weakened, the interests protected by the right of privacy begin to crumble. He wrote:

> The plurality repudiates every principle for which *Roe* stands; in good conscience, it cannot possibly believe that *Roe* lies "undisturbed" merely because this case does not call upon the Court to reconsider the Texas statute, or one like it. . . . It is impossible to read the plurality opinion and especially its final paragraph, without recognizing its implicit invitation to every State to enact more restrictive abortion laws, and to assert their interest in potential life as of the moment of conception.

In an unusual and thought-provoking dissent, Justice Stevens offered two reasons the statute's preamble should be declared unconstitutional. First, since the law implied that the state has the power to protect life from the point of conception, defining conception as the "fertilization of the ovum of a female by the sperm of a male," the law threatened to place serious restrictions not only on a woman's right to terminate her pregnancy but also on her right to use contraceptives to prevent conception. Contrary to the Court's rulings in *Griswold* and *Eisenstadt*, the preamble could be used to ban the use of common forms of contraception, such as the morning-after pill and the IUD, and it would certainly proscribe the introduction of the controversial French abortion pill (RU–486). If RU–486 is widely used in the United States, the legal distinction between contraception and abortion may become even more blurred: Legislatures and courts would then have to ascertain when conception takes place and when pregnancy begins. Some forms of contraception prevent the sperm from fertilizing the egg, while others stop the fertilized egg from implanting in the uterus.[32] *Do we accept a medical definition of pregnancy or a religious-moral one? At what point does the act of contraception (protected by* Griswold *) become an act of abortion? Could the weakening of* Roe *affect the right to privacy as set forth in* Griswold?

Stevens also believed that the preamble of the Missouri law violated the establishment clause of the First Amendment. Because the state legislature's assertion that life begins at conception threatened a woman's choice of contraceptives, and since it had absolutely no purpose except to advance a religious opinion, the preamble violated the establishment clause by threatening to encroach upon reproductive freedom for solely religious considerations. The preamble was "an unequivocal endorsement of a religious tenet of some but by no means all Christian faiths, [and] serves no identifiable secular purpose." Stevens pointed out that several *amicus* briefs for the state had even argued for the statute on religious grounds. While there was a clear secular interest in protecting the life of a nine-month, fully sentient fetus, the state had no legitimate secular or medical interest in protecting a newly fertilized egg.

Justice Stevens was alone in his adoption of an establishment clause approach to the problem, and very few legal scholars and practitioners have seriously entertained mounting a challenge to restrictive abortion statutes on the grounds that such laws are religiously motivated. Nevertheless, abortion rights advocates welcomed Stevens's articulation of an "entanglement" rationale to their fight against restrictive abortion laws.

While most legislative attempts to place restrictions on contraception and abortion are justified in terms of the state's interest in protecting potential human life, individuals and groups that sponsor such legislation generally proceed from a religious perspective. Why then isn't there more serious consideration of the establishment approach? One reason may be that it can be argued that restrictions on abortion are based not on religious opinions alone, but also on the moral preferences of a majority of citizens who rightfully are interested in punishing murder, child abuse, and adultery. Such laws may reflect the religious views of some, but they are also justified by a general moral abhorrence to such behavior that transcends the religious teachings of any particular faith. So, while many groups oppose abortion for religious reasons, many others do so on strictly moral or philosophical grounds. In any event, the majority of justices skirted the issue by concluding that the preamble was nothing more than a philosophical statement having no real effect on human conduct.

The irony of *Webster* is that while the Court continued to recognize a woman's right to have an abortion, it left the door open for almost any kind of restriction short of an outright ban. It seems as if the Court was saying that a woman has the right to an abortion, but that the state may effectively offset that right with some sort of reasonable interest. The only remaining threshold recognized by the majority to prohibit the complete negation of a woman's right to an abortion was Justice O'Connor's rather conservative undue burden standard. While it prevents a complete ban on abortions, it is flexible with regard to the variety of state interests that are constitutionally permissible. It is conservative also because it does not presuppose a particularly strong liberty interest in the face of attempts to restrict what a woman may or may not do with her own body.

While Justice O'Connor found none of the provisions of the Missouri law unduly burdensome, she attacked one restriction on this ground in *Hodgson v. Minnesota*, 1497 U.S. 417 (1990). *Hodgson* raised several questions regarding the right of women under age eighteen to undergo an abortion. *Can a state require a young women under age eighteen to secure parental approval before undergoing an abortion?* Is the minor's privacy interest always outweighed by her parents' wishes? Stated somewhat differently, to what degree may the state interfere in the decisions of the family? May it require the parents to follow some mandated process of decision-making concerning their child's health (i.e., the consent of both parents rather than just one)?

In *Hodgson*, the Court addressed a Minnesota abortion law that required unemancipated minors to notify both parents within a forty-eight-hour waiting period before undergoing an abortion. The state did not require the parents' consent, but merely their notification.[33] Challengers of the law argued that even notification requirements place an undue burden on the woman because she may have to face hostile or abusive parents. However, under a subdivision of the law, the minor was guaranteed access to a "judicial bypass" of the two-parent rule if the young woman had been subject to parental abuse or neglect or her health was at risk. A federal district court struck down the statute in its entirety, but the U.S. court of appeals reversed on the grounds that the bypass provision saved the law from placing an undue burden on the young woman's right to due process.

In *Hodgson*, one of its most divided and confusing opinions, the Supreme Court ruled that (1) the law's forty-eight-hour waiting period was *not* unconstitutionally burdensome because it did not cause an unreasonable delay; (2) the requirement that both parents be notified of the young woman's decision to undergo an abortion, whether or not both parents were responsible for the young woman, was unconstitutional because it did not advance any legitimate state interest; and (3) both the two-parent notification and the forty-eight-hour waiting period were constitutional when a judicial bypass was provided.

A majority—consisting of Justices Stevens, Brennan, Marshall, Blackmun, and O'Connor—argued that without the bypass the two-parent requirement did not further the state's interests in protecting the pregnant minor or in maintaining family integrity. This was particularly true when the parents were divorced or separated, and especially so when family violence was present. A minor had a right to terminate her pregnancy, but the state had a strong interest in making sure that "immaturity, inexperience and lack of judgment" did not impair her "ability to exercise [her] rights wisely." Responsible parents also had enough of a liberty interest in their child's upbringing and welfare that they could supersede their child's decision to undergo or forgo a particular medical procedure.

Since the state did not have any reason to doubt the first parent's judgment concerning the health and welfare of the child, it was enough to have one parent notified. The judgment of one parent combined with the privacy of the minor outweighed both the state's interest in family unity and the second parent's objection to the abortion. Thus, it was constitutional for the state to require the minor to notify one parent prior to undergoing an abortion, but unconstitutional for the state to require the minor to secure the approval of both. Citing her dissent in *Akron*, O'Connor wrote:

> It has been my understanding in this area that "[i]f the particular regulation does not 'unduly burde[n]' the fundamental right, . . . then our evaluation of that regulation is limited to our determination that the regulation rationally relates to a legitimate state purpose. . . . Minnesota has offered no sufficient justification for its interference with the family's decision-making processes.

The opinion became even more confusing when O'Connor joined a second majority—including Kennedy, Rehnquist, White, and Scalia—to uphold the two-parent notification on the grounds that its intrusiveness was obviated by the judicial bypass rule. Under the Minnesota statute's bypass provision, a court could authorize an abortion without parental notice if it found that the minor was mature and capable of giving informed consent or if an abortion was in the best interest of the minor.

Furthermore, the forty-eight-hour rule was deemed constitutional because it reasonably furthered the legitimate state interests in ensuring that the minor's decision was sound by giving time for family discussion or consultation with the family physician.

Only four justices—Kennedy, Rehnquist, White, and Scalia—believed that the two-parent notification rule without judicial bypass was constitutional.

Justices Marshall, Brennan, and Blackmun dissented from the judgment of the Court that the judicial bypass makes the restrictions constitutional. The requirements of the law were unconstitutional because without any compelling interest the state was usurping a young woman's control over her body by allowing either parent or a court the power to veto her decision to undergo an abortion. The notification requirement could create "severe physical and psychological effects" because it could lead to parental anger and rejection. The law compelled many young women to become teen mothers, to travel to a state without such requirements, or to attempt self-abortion or seek an illegal abortion in order to avoid telling a parent. Justice Marshall reasoned that even with the bypass rule, the two-parent notification requirement

> forces a young woman in an already dire situation to choose between two fundamentally unacceptable alternatives: notifying a possible dictatorial or even abusive parent

and justifying her profoundly personal decision in an intimidating judicial proceeding to a blackrobed stranger. For such a woman, this dilemma is more likely to result in trauma and pain than in an informed and voluntary decision.

Thus, under *Hodgson*, parental notification requirements are constitutionally permissible if the law provides the minor with the opportunity to substitute the consent of a judge when it is impossible or harmful, due to domestic violence, to obtain consent from her parents. Also upheld (by six justices) was the requirement that a minor wait forty-eight hours after notifying one of her parents before having the abortion.

One dimension of a woman's right to terminate her pregnancy is the opportunity to discuss the abortion procedure with her physician. Restrictions on the patient-physician relationship run the risk of implicating not only the patient's right of privacy but also the free exchange of ideas protected by the First Amendment. Imagine having to seek medical help at a federally subsidized cancer clinic. Imagine further that the attending physician is prohibited by law from performing or even discussing an experimental cancer treatment because it utilizes fetal tissue. The government has ordered these prohibitions at publicly funded facilities ostensibly to prevent a mass exodus of cancer patients to Mexico, where the risky treatment is performed, and because of moral opposition to the use of fetal tissue for scientific experiments. Are the government's actions constitutional? Is this a First Amendment issue or a question of privacy? Does the fact that the law applies only to physicians who receive governmental support obviate all constitutional objections? Suppose the same physician is also prohibited by Congress from even mentioning abortion to a patient who has come for family planning advice. The Court has upheld bans on governmental funding for abortions; would the same logic apply to counseling or referral as well?

In 1988, Secretary of Health and Human Services (HHS) Louis Sullivan issued regulations based on a new interpretation of Title X of the Public Health Service Act of 1970. Enacted three years before *Roe*, the act was intended by Congress to assist in the establishment and operation of family planning projects. The act mandated that no funds could be used in programs where abortion was a method of family planning. The new regulations were specifically intended to bar physicians and other employees of federally financed family planning clinics from all discussion of abortion with their patients. If a woman asked about terminating a pregnancy, the regulations required the clinic to inform her that "the project does not consider abortion an appropriate method of family planning" even if the physician believed that it was in her best interest to seek counseling on abortion.

Dr. Irving Rust, medical director of a Planned Parenthood clinic in New York, challenged the HHS regulation on the grounds that it violated (1) the privacy of the patient-physician relationship, (2) the medical ethics that require doctors to provide patients with complete information about their health care choices, (3) the First Amendment free speech rights of Title X fund-recipients and their medical staffs by imposing ideological conditions on the receipt of public funds, and (4) a woman's right to choose whether to terminate a pregnancy. How closely does this case parallel our hypothetical cancer case? Do any earlier Court cases shed light on these issues?

In *Rust v. Sullivan*, 500 U.S. 173 (1991), the Court voted 5–4 to uphold the HHS regulations, with Justice Souter (serving his first term) casting the deciding vote. It was no surprise that the Court agreed with the proposition that the government had no constitutional duty to subsidize abortion even though a woman's decision to terminate her pregnancy is a constitutionally protected activity, for it had come to this conclusion in *Webster* and earlier cases. Writing for the majority, Chief Justice Rehnquist reiterated his view that the government's decision to fund activities related to childbirth but not abortion does not place any unconstitutional burden on a woman who wishes to terminate her pregnancy. He reasoned:

> Congress' refusal to fund abortion counseling and advocacy leaves a pregnant woman with the same choices as if the government had chosen not to fund family-planning services at all. The difficulty that a woman encounters when a Title X project does not provide abortion counseling or referral leaves her in no different position than she would have been if the government had not enacted Title X.

***Can the government subsidize one kind of medical advice (favoring childbirth) while refusing to subsidize another (discussion of abortion)?***    Can it constitutionally discriminate on the basis of viewpoint by threatening to withhold funds every time abortion is mentioned to a patient? The Court said yes: The government was not violating freedom of expression, but was merely legislating on the basis of a value judgment that childbirth is preferable to abortion. The regulations simply ensured that funds were not used for counseling abortion as an alternative in family planning. Women seeking advice on abortion would just have to go elsewhere, and physicians and other health care personnel who found the program ethically abhorrent could simply quit and work in a facility not funded by the federal government.

According to Rehnquist, Congress had simply chosen to fund one kind of activity over another. He used the National Endowment for Democracy as a parallel: When Congress established that program to encourage other nations to adopt principles of democratic government, it was not required by the First Amendment to fund a program to encourage competing philosophies, such as communism and fascism. The regulations did not require physicians to give up "abortion-related speech," but simply required that such activities be kept separate from Title X activities. Thus, technically, the regulations did not prohibit abortion counseling or abortions, they simply forbade the government from subsidizing either activity.

Did the Chief Justice go too far with his "no right to public funds" argument, or was he consistent with established thinking? The dissenters—including Justices Blackmun, Marshall (serving his last term), Stevens, and O'Connor—attacked the majority's ruling as a "viewpoint-based suppression of speech" allowing the regulation of speech between a pregnant patient and her doctor solely for the purpose of manipulating her decision to continue her pregnancy. Title X regulations forbid the encouragement, promotion, or advocacy of abortion, but they do not prohibit the advocacy of anti-abortion views. Because they permit anti-abortion views but proscribe pro-abortion rights, the regulations are content-based and seek to restrict one form of speech but not another. Blackmun argued:

[T]he provisions intrude upon a wide range of communicative conduct, including the very words spoken to a women by her physician. By manipulating the content of the doctor/patient dialogue, the regulations upheld today force each of the petitioners "to be an instrument for fostering public adherence to an ideological point of view [he or she] finds unacceptable."[34]

Under the majority's line of reasoning, the government could restrict communication in one of the most private relationships—between doctor and patient—so long as that restriction is limited to the funded workplace. But by knowingly omitting certain options in health care, wouldn't a physician be guilty of violating the Hippocratic Oath or perhaps acting in a manner that constitutes malpractice? Theoretically, the physician and the patient could meet later at a private facility to discuss abortion, but the woman would have to pay for such consultation out of her own pocket.

The dissenters maintained that the regulations also affected the woman's right of privacy as autonomy, or what Blackmun referred to as "bodily self-determination," by limiting the information necessary to make an intelligent choice. If she had no such information, she might be reluctant to exercise her rights. Indeed, that was the purpose and effect of the regulations. Prior to *Rust*, the Court had upheld numerous restrictions on abortion, but this was the first time since *Roe* that the Court had upheld a regulation aimed at influencing a woman's decision to continue her pregnancy. Similar coercive measures had been struck down in *Akron* and *Maher*.

Thus, *Rust v. Sullivan* joined a growing number of cases in which the Court acknowledged that a woman's right to undergo an abortion is constitutionally protected, but it then upheld restrictions that render the right virtually useless to a significant number of women. Such limitations include funding restrictions; consent and parental notification provisions; stringent regulations of the actual medical procedures, including informed consent requirements demanding that women be subjected to lengthy interviews and lectures on fetal development; restrictions on abortion counseling; and perhaps most significantly, an attempt to abandon the trimester framework, allowing the state to protect a fetus at any stage of gestation.

The retirements of Justice Brennan in 1990 and of Justice Marshall in 1991 provided the George H.W. Bush administration with the opportunity to make two appointments to the Court, perhaps presaging the outright reversal of *Roe v. Wade*. Seizing the moment, a number of states enacted a variety of restrictions on a woman's right to terminate her pregnancy. Although it did not ban abortions outright, the Pennsylvania Abortion Control Act required women before having an abortion to wait twenty-four hours after listening to a presentation intended to dissuade them from having an abortion, required teenagers to obtain consent from one parent or a judge, mandated physicians to make reports to the state, and included a provision ordering a woman to inform her husband before undergoing an abortion. It was expected that with the help of the two newest appointees—Justices Souter and Clarence Thomas—the Court would vote to overturn *Roe*.

However, in *Planned Parenthood v. Casey*, 505 U.S. 833 (1992), the Court upheld *Roe* by 5–4. Handed down during a presidential campaign, the ruling produced more high drama than new constitutional law. Of great significance was

Justice Kennedy's shift to the O'Connor bloc, which also included Souter, Blackmun, and Stevens. In sustaining all but the spousal notification provision of the Pennsylvania law, the majority adopted O'Connor's undue burden standard, defining an undue burden as a "substantial obstacle in the path of a woman seeking an abortion before the fetus attains viability."

In her opinion, Justice O'Connor reaffirmed what she believed to be the essence of *Roe*: A woman has the right to choose before viability without undue interference from the state. Before viability, a state's interests are not strong enough to support a prohibition of abortion or to impose a substantial obstacle to the right to elect the procedure. The state may not unduly assert its interest in fetal health before the fetus becomes viable.

The majority also demonstrated a willingness to rely on pragmatic and perhaps sociological reasons for reaffirming precedent. Overturning *Roe* would constitute a dramatic departure from *stare decisis*, thereby undermining the legitimacy of the Court. Furthermore, an entire generation had come of age under *Roe* expecting to have the right to make autonomous reproductive decisions. A change in course could bring about social chaos, something that the moderate justices were not willing to risk. Thus, in many ways the majority's position was a conservative one—judicial restraint in the context of well-established precedent.

The dissenters—Rehnquist, Scalia, White, and Thomas—argued that the Court should have overturned *Roe*. They were more willing to take an activist conservative position, to break with established law, and to allow group rights to prevail. Rehnquist argued that since *Roe* was wrongly decided in the first place, *stare decisis* did not apply. Furthermore, since the Court had already abandoned the *Roe* framework of analysis in *Webster*, *Roe* was merely a facade for an entirely new way of adjudicating abortion rights cases.

The question that remains is not whether the Court is likely to overturn *Roe*, but whether it will render *Roe* virtually useless to many women by continuing to allow new and creative restrictions on abortion rights. As Justice Blackmun concluded in *Rust*: "This [trend] is a course nearly as noxious as overruling *Roe* directly, for if a right is found to be unenforceable, even against flagrant attempts by government to circumvent it, then it ceases to be a right at all."

## "Partial Birth" Abortion

The standard that emerged from the *Casey* ruling can be understood as follows: A law is unconstitutional if, before fetal viability, it imposes an undue burden on the woman's decision to terminate her pregnancy. An "undue burden" is defined as a restriction or regulation imposed by the state that has the purpose of placing an "substantial obstacle in the woman's path." However, after the fetus becomes viable, the state may enact laws that protect human life and may, therefore, regulate or even prohibit abortion unless the woman's health or life is threatened.

*Casey* and earlier rulings give us an idea of the restrictions that states may or may not enact that place restrictions on a woman's right to an abortion. The Court revisited two such restrictions in the 1997 cases *Lambert v. Wicklund*[35] and *Mazurek v. Armstrong*.[36] In *Lambert*, the Court ruled 6–3 to uphold Montana's Parental Notice of Abortion Act because it contained a judicial bypass provision that the minor could use if it was not in her best interest to notify her parent or guardian. In *Mazurek*, the Court ruled 6–3 to uphold a Montana law prohibiting anyone but physicians from performing abortions.

In its 1999–2000 term, the Court heard *Stenberg v. Carhart*,[37] a case involving dilation and extraction (D&X), or as some call it, "partial birth" abortion. This form of abortion is particularly controversial because it is done very late in a woman's pregnancy and involves a procedure that is more disturbing than other forms of abortion. Public opinion runs the gamut, from an absolute ban on the procedure to support for a ban on the procedure as long as an exception to the ban is made to protect the health and life of the mother.

By the late 1990s, the most commonly used abortion procedure had become "vacuum aspiration," which is used during the first trimester of pregnancy (before twelve weeks of gestational age). About 90 percent of all abortions performed in the United States take place during the first trimester. During the second trimester (twelve to twenty-four weeks), the technique used is dilation and evacuation (D&E). D&E presents a greater health risk to the mother, especially if the abortion is performed later in the second trimester. To minimize the risk, some physicians use the D&X procedure. A rare procedure, D&X involves removing the fetus feet first from the uterus through the cervix all the way up to its head. The brain of the fetus is then "evacuated" so that a dead fetus is vaginally delivered. Thus, the term "partial birth." The procedure was invented as a way of minimizing the risk to the woman when it was necessary to abort a "nonviable" or abnormal fetus that had no chance of living outside of the womb.[38]

The state of Nebraska made it a felony to perform a D&X, "unless such procedure is necessary to save the life of the mother whose life is endangered by a physical disorder, physical illness, or physical injury." The law provided for the immediate revocation of a convicted physician's license to practice medicine. Dr. Leroy Carhart, a Nebraska physician, successfully challenged the constitutionality of the law in a federal district court. The U.S. Court of Appeals for the Eighth Circuit affirmed, and Nebraska' attorney general appealed to the U.S. Supreme Court.

On appeal, the Supreme Court ruled 5–4 that the Nebraska law violated a woman's constitutional right to have an abortion as established by *Roe* and *Casey* because the law (1) lacked the required exception for the "preservation of the health of the mother," (2) imposed an undue burden on the woman's ability to choose the safest form of abortion available, and (3) applied to both pre- and postviability stages of pregnancy. Writing for the slim majority, Justice Breyer argued that although the state has an interest in protecting fetal life after the first trimester, a regulation on abortion may promote but not endanger a woman's health or life. Citing numerous medical studies, Breyer was convinced that D&X is the safest way for a physician to terminate a late-term pregnancy.

It is important to note the difference between Nebraska's "life of the mother" exception and the "health of the mother" exception established by precedent. Nebraska argued that the procedure should be banned outright without the health exception because there was no evidence that the relatively rare D&X procedure significantly reduces a woman's risk of developing several complications associated with abortion. Under the Nebraska law, the D&X abortion could be lawful only if the woman's *life* was threatened, not just her health.

Furthermore, even if the law's basic aim was to ban D&X, its language could be construed to cover a much broader category of abortion procedures. For example, the law makes no exception for the performance of D&E and other commonly used procedures that might, in some circumstances, use techniques that are similar to D&X. The question then is not whether the Nebraska legislature intended to ban D&X but whether the law was intended to apply only to D&X. Justice Breyer concluded:

> In sum, using this law some present prosecutors and future Attorneys General may choose to pursue physicians who use D&E procedures, the most commonly used method for performing previability second trimester abortions. All those who perform abortion procedures using that method must fear prosecution, conviction, and imprisonment. The result is an undue burden upon a woman's right to make an abortion decision.

Breyer's opinion is in many places almost apologetic to both sides of the debate. He hoped that his graphic overview of modern abortion techniques did not seem "cold," "callous," or "horrifying" to readers, and he recognized the "virtually irreconcilable points of view" in the abortion debate.

The four dissenting justices—Rehnquist, Kennedy, Scalia, and Thomas—expressed their views in four separate dissenting opinions. The gist of their arguments can be understood as follows. Justice Kennedy and Chief Justice Rehnquist argued that the majority did not apply *Casey* properly in its decision to strike down the Nebraska law. Recall that under *Roe v. Wade*, the state's interest in protecting the fetus existed but was weak compared to the woman's right to elect an abortion. But under *Casey*, the Court balanced more evenly the state's interest in the life of the fetus and the woman's right to an abortion. The Nebraska law was compatible with *Casey* because it advanced a legitimate state interest in banning a controversial late-term abortion procedure while placing no undue burden on a woman's rights. Kennedy wrote:

> *Casey* is premised on the States having an important constitutional role in defining their interest in the abortion debate. It is only with this principle in mind that Nebraska's interests can be given proper weight. The State's brief describes its interest as including concern for the life of the unborn and "for the partially-born," in preserving the integrity of the medical profession, and in "erecting a barrier to infanticide." A review of *Casey* demonstrates the legitimacy of these policies.

There is no absolute right to an abortion. The Court has long recognized that states have an interest in enacting rules and regulations to encourage women to think about the alternatives to abortion and in forbidding medical procedures that might cause the medical profession or society as a whole to become "insensitive, even disdainful, to life, including life in the human fetus."

As they had done in the past cases, Chief Justice Rehnquist and Justices Scalia and Thomas rejected *Roe* and *Casey* outright. Nevertheless, they believed that under

*Casey* the Nebraska law easily passed constitutional muster. They could find no good reason to prevent the states from banning one rarely used form of abortion that is generally held to border on infanticide. In a rhetorical flourish, Justice Scalia damned the Court's ruling as one that would go down in history beside two of the Court's biggest mistakes—*Korematsu* (the interment of Japanese Americans) and *Dred Scott* (recognizing black persons as property). As he has maintained over the years, the Court's rulings have served only to exacerbate the national division over abortion. *Roe* has inflamed our national politics, has muddied the selection of Supreme Court justices, and has kept the Court in "the abortion-umpiring business."[39]

## PRIVACY AND HOMOSEXUALITY

Many civil libertarians have argued that, based on the substantive due process privacy argument set forth in cases such as *Griswold, Eisenstadt*, and *Roe*, the Court should extend the right of privacy to adult homosexual conduct. ***Does the right of privacy extend beyond the sphere of reproductive freedom into the area of sexual privacy or life style choices?*** Are laws proscribing or criminalizing homosexual conduct constitutional? *If privacy is fundamental to the marital relationship, to unmarried persons seeking contraceptives, and to a woman who wishes to terminate her pregnancy, what about the right of two consenting adults of the same sex to engage in sexual activity, marry, and adopt children?*

The argument that the right of privacy protects homosexual conduct had its first major setback in *Commonwealth's Attorney for the City of Richmond v. Doe*, 425 U.S. 901 (1976), when the Burger Court denied an appeal of a man who was convicted under a Virginia sodomy law for having homosexual relations in a public restroom. Ten years later, the attempt to extend the right of privacy was again defeated in *Bowers v. Hardwick*, 478 U.S. 186 (1986), in which the Court was asked to invalidate a Georgia sodomy law on the basis that it violated the "most intimate personal association with another consenting adult." The Burger Court refused on the grounds that the kinds of privacy interests relating to marriage, contraception, and abortion set forth in *Griswold, Eisenstadt*, and *Roe* bore no resemblance to the claimed constitutional right of persons to engage in homosexual conduct. While these earlier cases conferred a broad and fundamental individual right to decide whether or not to conceive or to have a child, the Court was in no way inclined to adopt an even broader definition of privacy in order to overturn state sodomy laws. In addition, Justice White wrote:

> Nor are we inclined to take a more expansive view of our authority to discover new rights imbedded in the Due Process Clause. The Court is most vulnerable and comes closest to illegitimacy when it deals with judge-made constitutional law having little or no cognizable roots in the language or design of the Constitution.

In fact, the majority refused even to mention the right of privacy as such. If there was, as the Court put it, a liberty interest found in the Fourteenth Amendment that protects intimate relationships, the majority of justices were in no mood to rule that this liberty interest was fundamental enough to prohibit states from criminalizing homosexual conduct. Chief Justice Burger wrote:

> [I]n constitutional terms there is no such thing as a fundamental right to commit homosexual sodomy. [To] hold that the act of homosexual sodomy is somehow protected as a fundamental right would be to cast aside millennia of moral teaching.
>
> This [ruling is essentially not a question of personal "preferences" but rather of the legislative authority of the State.

The dissenting justices—Blackmun, Brennan, Marshall, and Stevens—cast the issue in a somewhat different light. They argued that, contrary to the beliefs of the majority, this case was not about the right to engage in homosexual sodomy, but about the right to be let alone from the prying eyes of the state. The fact that time-honored moral judgments are often cast into legislative decree does not mean that the state should be permitted to deny individuals the right to decide for themselves whether to engage in private consensual sexual conduct. Homosexual conduct was really not the issue, since the statute, as written, applied to heterosexual activity as well—it was just that Georgia was not willing to apply the statute against heterosexuals. Blackmun also attacked the majority's selective application of *Griswold* and *Roe* only to matters affecting reproduction and heterosexual relationships and argued that the right of privacy extends to a "fundamental interest all individuals have in controlling the nature of their intimate associations with others."

*Bowers v. Hardwick* virtually ended attempts by gay rights activists to challenge state sodomy laws before the Supreme Court under the right of privacy or any other provision of the Constitution. As a result, challenges to such laws have been directed at state courts and legislatures. Interestingly, since *Bowers*, the Georgia Supreme Court—as well as three other state high courts[40]—struck down the state's 165-year-old sodomy statute at issue in *Bowers* as a violation of the state constitution. The court reasoned that "unforced sexual behavior conducted in private between adults" (homosexual or heterosexual) is protected by Georgia's constitutional right to privacy, which is wider in scope than that protected by the U.S. Constitution.[41]

While sodomy is still a criminal offense in nineteen states,[42] many state courts have adopted broad definitions of privacy to grant the same protections to adult homosexual conduct as are extended to adult heterosexual conduct. Since many states use sodomy laws to prevent gays from gaining custody of their own children, adopting children, or entering certain professions, the privacy argument may ultimately be replaced by an equal protection approach to the issue.[43]

## THE RIGHT TO DIE

In *Roe v. Wade*, the Court argued that the right of privacy guarantees the freedom to care for one's own health and body and protects the right to be free from bodily restraint or compulsion. Based on this reasoning, can one plausibly argue that the right of privacy protects the decision to discontinue life-sustaining treatment? *Is there a constitutional right to die?* There is no doubt that competent patients have the right to refuse any form of unwanted medical treatment, but what about patients who are comatose, brain dead, or severely retarded? Many states have asserted the right to keep incompetent patients alive even if there is no hope of recovery and it is against the wishes of the patient's family or loved ones. *What gives state authorities the right to act in such a manner? On what grounds and by what means can an incompetent person assert his or her right to refuse unwanted medical treatment?*

The Supreme Court did not address these questions until 1990. However, building upon the concept of privacy as autonomy set forth in *Griswold* and *Roe*, the New Jersey Supreme Court, in the famous 1976 *Quinlan* case,[44] broadened the right of privacy to "encompass a patient's decision to decline medical treatment." In doing so, the court opened the door for a new genre of cases that have come to be known as right to die cases.

In *Quinlan*, the father of a young woman who was in a permanent coma sought judicial action to have his daughter removed from a respirator so that she could die a natural death. Karen Quinlan's attending physicians agreed that she would never resume a cognitive life and that she needed round-the-clock life support. Even though such treatment served only to prolong her deterioration, Quinlan's physicians argued that she should remain on the respirator and that decisions to terminate life-sustaining treatment are best made by doctors. By tradition, the medical profession believed that when a terminally ill patient is comatose or incompetent, the physician must make the critical decisions rather than the patient or the patient's family. The state enters the controversy because it is the state's duty to support the physician's judgment, just as the state is justified in using force to preserve and protect life.

The New Jersey Superior Court agreed with the physicians' reasoning and ruled against the Quinlans, but upon appeal, the New Jersey Supreme Court reversed the lower court's decision, ruling that Quinlan had to be treated as a person in possession of the right of privacy. This right, as explained by the court, protects a person's decision to refuse unwanted medical treatment.

Life-sustaining treatment may be legitimately ordered by the state in cases where the patient's chances of recovery are good and contingent upon a minor procedure, such as a blood transfusion. But how does a comatose or mentally incompetent person exercise the right of privacy? According to the New Jersey high court, the right may be exercised even when the express wishes of the patient are not known. Quinlan's right of privacy could be asserted on her behalf by a legal guardian who knew her preferences, values, and morals: "We have concluded that Karen's right of privacy may be asserted on her behalf by her guardian under the peculiar circumstances present . . . it [privacy] should not be discarded solely on the basis that her condition prevents her conscious exercise of choice."

Building upon the precedents of *Griswold* and *Roe*, the New Jersey court ruled in *Quinlan* that the right of privacy as autonomy is broad enough to protect an incompetent person's decision to decline medical treatment in the face of the state's compelling interests in preserving life and maintaining medical standards.

Fourteen years later, the U.S. Supreme Court wrestled with the right to die controversy for the first time in *Cruzan v. Director, Missouri Department of Health*, 497 U.S. 261 (1990). In *Cruzan*, the parents of twenty-five-year-old Nancy Cruzan, who was in a persistent vegetative state as a result of an automobile accident, sought to discontinue life-sustaining treatment. Cruzan was able to breath on her own, but she received all of her nutrition and fluids directly through a tube surgically implanted in her stomach. When her parents realized that Nancy had no chance of recovery and might continue in this state for possibly thirty years, they petitioned the hospital and the state of Missouri to terminate tubal feeding and hydration. The Cruzans argued that even though Nancy had neither executed a living will nor appointed anyone to make health care decisions for her in the event she became incompetent, she had stated before the accident that she did not want to live as a "vegetable."

The hospital officials refused the request, forcing the Cruzans to file suit in a Missouri trial court. The trial court ordered the feeding and hydration tube removed, arguing that Cruzan had a fundamental right to refuse unwanted medical treatment and that no state interest outweighed her right to liberty. However, the Missouri Supreme Court disagreed and reversed the trial court's decision, finding Cruzan's remarks about not wanting to live as a vegetable to be too general and casual. In order to establish Cruzan's intention, clear, convincing, and reliable evidence of her wishes must be known.

In a 5–4 decision, the U.S. Supreme Court affirmed the Missouri high court's decision, leaving Cruzan's situation unchanged. However, in doing so the Court recognized a constitutionally protected significant liberty interest in refusing unwanted medical treatment. Justice Rehnquist wrote:

> The Fourteenth Amendment provides that no State shall "deprive any person of life, liberty, or property, without due process of law." The principle that a competent person has a constitutionally protected liberty interest in refusing medical treatment may be inferred from our prior decisions.
>
> But determining that a person has a liberty interest under the Due Process Clause does not end the inquiry; whether respondent's constitutional rights have been violated must be determined by balancing his liberty interests against the relevant state interests.

The decision seems to raise more questions than it answers. *First, if there is a right to die, why did the Court refuse to order the withdrawal of life support? Second, does this significant liberty interest extend to incompetent persons, like Cruzan, or only to competent persons who wish to decline medical care?* The Court recognized that under certain circumstances a surrogate may act to exercise the incompetent person's right to refuse medical treatment, as long as the action of the surrogate conforms to the wishes expressed by the patient while competent. According to the Court, Missouri acted properly in requiring that evidence of the incompetent's wishes concerning the withdrawal of the medical treatment be proved by convincing evidence.

*Third, in light of this constitutionally protected right to refuse life-sustaining medical care, what interest does a state have in keeping a person in Cruzan's condition alive?* The Court gave several answers. Great caution is required because an erroneous decision to terminate such treatment cannot be corrected—Cruzan would die. Another reason is based on the state's interest to guard against a hasty decision on the part of the patient's surrogate or guardian. After all, advances in medical science may occur and enable physicians to return the patient to a cognitive state, or perhaps new evidence regarding the patient's intent may surface. It is even possible that an unscrupulous spouse or family member might act solely on the basis of financial gain. For these reasons, most states simply forbid oral testimony entirely as the sole means of determining the wishes of an incompetent or deceased person.

Can the "substituted judgment" doctrine that enabled Quinlan to terminate her medical treatment by proxy be used in cases like *Cruzan?* The Court said no. The substituted judgment doctrine may be used in cases involving mentally retarded persons or minors but does not apply in Cruzan's situation because there was no automatic assurance that the views of family members would necessarily be the same as the patient's if she were competent. In fact, the majority's decision allowed a state to refuse to consider the decision of another person acting on behalf of the terminally ill patient. The dissenters, on the other hand, argued that the decision of a proxy or surrogate should be considered when determining whether to terminate medical treatment.

*The fourth question that* Cruzan *compels us to ask is: Why did the Court refuse to analyze the case in terms of the right of privacy?* Why did it embrace the liberty interest argument instead? Is *Cruzan* a privacy issue? Nowhere in the Court's opinion is the word "privacy" mentioned. It is only in a footnote that the Court mentions this point when it states that although many state courts have held that a right to refuse treatment is encompassed by a constitutional right of privacy, "we have never so held. We believe this issue is more properly analyzed in terms of a Fourteenth Amendment liberty interest."

What was Cruzan's fate? Shortly after the Court rendered its judgment, her friends and colleagues provided the Missouri trial court with clear and convincing evidence that she had not wanted to be kept alive by extraordinary means. The Missouri court then allowed Cruzan's guardians to terminate her nutrition and hydration, and she died on December 26, 1990. The impact of this drama has yet to be determined. In terms of the right of privacy, *Cruzan* represents a further attempt by the Court to define the boundaries of privacy protection. While the Court recognized a limited right to die for incompetent patients in *Cruzan*, the majority's opinion left the states with much discretion to determine the precise scope of this liberty interest.[45] Consequently, the rights of incompetent terminally ill patients vary from state to state.

## PHYSICIAN-ASSISTED SUICIDE

*Quinlan* and *Cruzan* involved persons who never had the prospect of regaining the ability to make decisions regarding their medical care. *But what about persons who are mentally competent and refuse all treatment?* The law has traditionally recognized that no competent adult can be forced to receive unwanted medical care even if the patient's family or physician insists upon further treatment. Terminally ill patients will often gladly embrace death rather than face the prolonged pain, anguish, and expense of long-term medical care.

Taken to the next level, some individuals decide not only to discontinue treatment but also to seek out active assistance in ending their life. In essence, they ask their physicians to assist them in committing suicide. Unlike instances where death results from a physician's failure to resuscitate or continue treatment—considered to be passive euthanasia—physician-assisted suicide, or active euthanasia, can be prosecuted as murder. Fearing a growing movement in the states to legalize the practice, Congress passed in 1997 the Federal Assisted Suicide Funding Restriction Act, which prohibits the use of Medicare or Medicaid funds in support of physician-assisted suicide.[46]

The issue of assisted suicide has been around since Hippocrates but was most recently put on the public agenda by Dr. Jack Kevorkian. Praised as an angel of death by some but derided as "Dr. Death" by others, Kevorkian helped more than one hundred patients to commit suicide in 1990 using his "mercy machine." Kevorkian was prosecuted in a number of states for active euthanasia, was acquitted several times, but eventually was convicted and sent to prison. But the issue did not end there. Many state legislatures have attempted to pass laws or constitutional amendments allowing for physician-assisted suicide, but as of 2002 only Oregon allows the practice. Oregon's Death With Dignity Act, approved by 60 percent of the voters in a ballot initiative, allows a terminally ill patient to obtain a prescription from a physician for a fatal drug overdose as long as it is the patient who initiates the discussion of suicide, and the patient waits at least fifteen days and is examined by a second physician before receiving the prescription for the drugs.

*If privacy as autonomy, or one's "liberty interest," allows a terminally ill person to "die with dignity" by instructing an administering physician to discontinue life-prolonging medical treatment, does it not also grant the right to ask a physician to take positive steps to end one's life?* The U.S. Supreme Court addressed this question in the 1997 companion cases *Washington v. Glucksberg* and *Vacco v. Quill.*[47] The Court heard oral argument for the two cases at the same time. *Washington v. Glucksberg* originated when the Court of Appeals for the Ninth Circuit struck down the state of Washington's law forbidding physician-assisted suicide on the grounds that it violated the right of privacy and substantive liberty protected by the due process clause of the Fourteenth Amendment. The Supreme Court granted cert. to hear *Vacco v. Quill* after the Court of Appeals for the Second Circuit struck down New York's ban on physician-assisted suicide, not on the basis of the right of privacy, but rather on the grounds that the law violated the equal protection clause of the Fourteenth Amendment. The appeals court's reasoning was that the New York law made an arbitrary and thus unconstitutional distinction between the terminally ill patient's right to terminate unwanted medical treatment and his or her claimed right to physician-assisted suicide.

The U.S. Supreme Court unanimously reversed both appellate court decisions. First, in *Washington v. Glucksberg*, Chief Justice Rehnquist began his opinion by stating that laws prohibiting suicide or assisted-suicide are long-standing expressions of the states' commitment to the protection and preservation of all human life. Despite changes in attitudes towards suicide itself and the enactment of laws emphasizing end-of-life decision-making, the Court is not prepared to overturn the traditional prohibition on assisting suicide. To do so, wrote Rehnquist, would be to establish a new constitutional right, something that the Court was not prepared to do.

The Court reaffirmed the principle that the due process clause of the Fourteenth Amendment provides "heightened protection against government interference with certain fundamental rights and liberty interests," but it also reaffirmed its cautious and restrained approach to constitutional interpretation. In a classic statement of judicial restraint, Rehnquist wrote:

> By extending constitutional protection to an asserted right or liberty interest, we, to a great extent, place the matter outside the arena of public debate and legislative action. We must therefore exercise the utmost care whenever we are asked to break new ground in this field . . . lest the liberty protected by the Due Process Clause be subtly transformed into the policy preferences of the members of this Court.

In *Vacco*, the court of appeal's equal protection argument was rejected as well. The equal protection clause of the Fourteenth Amendment commands that no state shall deny to any person equal protection of the laws. In enacting a law, a legislature creates legal categories or distinctions among people; for example, who is to be taxed, who must sign up for selective service, or who may or may not purchase alcoholic beverages. The question is whether these classifications are reasonable or whether they are based on prejudicial attitudes towards race, sex, ethnicity, or age. Classifications (or legal distinctions) on the basis of race "invidiously discriminate" and are therefore in violation of the Fourteenth Amendment. The equal protection clause can also be invoked if a legal classification places a burden on the exercise of a fundamental right. However, it does not *create* any substantive rights.

*Did the New York law treat terminally ill people differently? Wasn't it true that those who were on life support systems were allowed to hasten death by ending treatment but those who were not on life support were not allowed to hasten death through physician-assisted suicide? Isn't the refusal of continued life a type of assisted suicide? After all, the physician "pulls the plug," if you will.* The Supreme Court rejected this argument outright as an illogical distinction. Rehnquist argued that when a patient refuses life-sustaining treatment, he or she dies from the underlying illness. But if a patient ingests lethal medication prescribed by the physician, he or she is killed by the medication.

In sum, laws that outlaw assisting suicide are based on a rational interest in protecting life and do not infringe upon any fundamental right or treat people differently. The Court refused to extend its reasoning in *Cruzan* to physician-assisted suicide; nor was it prepared to acknowledge a new right found either in the concept of liberty or in the Fourteenth Amendment.

The standard that emerges from *Glucksberg* and *Vacco* can be understood as follows: A law may not prohibit a physician from: (1) honoring the patient's wishes not to begin life-sustaining medical treatment or to withdraw such treatment; (2) refraining from doing "useless and futile or degrading things to the patient when the patient no longer stands to benefit from them"; and (3) administering "aggressive palliative care," such as high doses of pain-killing drugs in order to hasten the patient's death as long as the physician's intent is to ease the patient's pain.

However, a state may punish a physician for administering "aggressive palliative care," such as high doses of pain-killing drugs, if the primary intent of the patient and physician is to kill the patient.

***Does the Court's ruling in* Glucksberg *and* Vacco *mean that states may not legalize physician-assisted suicide?*** No, it means that laws prohibiting the practice are constitutional; there is nothing in the Constitution that prohibits states from banning the practice. In 2000, the state of Oregon's Death With Dignity Act survived a court challenge and an attempt by Republican members of Congress to pressure President Clinton's Attorney General Janet Reno to stop physicians from prescribing drugs to assist in suicides by revoking their federal registration. The same year, the House Judiciary Committee proposed legislation that would make assisted suicide a federal crime, but as of 2002 no floor debate or further action had been taken on the measure. Although the issue fades in and out of the news, advocates and opponents of assisted suicide are closely watching Oregon's bold experiment. Proponents argue that as support grows for a right to die with dignity and autonomy, it will be only a matter of time before other states follow Oregon's lead. On the other hand, opponents, who tend to be religious conservatives, are fiercely lobbying legislators at the state and federal levels to pull the plug on the assisted-suicide movement.

## CONCLUDING COMMENTS

More than a century has passed since Warren and Brandeis published their famous essay on privacy in the *Harvard Law Review*, and nearly forty years have elapsed since Justice Douglas penned his complex and controversial opinion in *Griswold*, "finding" an unenumerated right of privacy in the penumbras of liberty. Yet the passage of time has not altered the fact that the right of privacy has never rested on solid ground; it has always balanced somewhat precariously on its constitutional foundation. To borrow Justice O'Connor's observation about *Roe v. Wade*, the right of privacy has always been on a collision course with itself. Jurists have argued in numerous court opinions and scholarly articles that because its definition is too vague and elusive, the right of privacy would ultimately have to be redefined or abandoned by the Court.

Ever since a slim majority on the Warren Court first elevated privacy to a constitutional right, members of the Burger and Rehnquist Courts have openly expressed their frustration and annoyance at the largely undefined parameters of this right and, as a result, have striven to limit the variety of interests that fall under its protection. More recently, a majority of the Rehnquist Court refused to even recognize the right of privacy in its earlier *Griswold* and *Roe* form. Chief Justice Rehnquist avoids the "P" word altogether, refusing to even mention privacy when an abortion case is argued before the Court.

The Court now evaluates claims that raise privacy issues from the standpoint of a number of subsidiary liberty interests protected by the due process clauses of the Fifth and Fourteenth Amendments, rather than through a broader privacy as autonomy approach. Unlike the expansive though admittedly more nebulous definition of privacy, the liberty interest approach permits the Court to remain flexible and non-committal, examining privacy claims on a case-by-case basis. Since each asserted liberty interest offers a different degree of constitutional protection, the Court finds it easier to reconcile legitimate state interests—such as morality, safety, and order—with the right to be let alone or the right to choose. Thus, a kind of sliding scale of liberty interests has emerged, protecting differing degrees of privacy or autonomy. These interests range from hair length[48] to the more fundamental interest in terminating unwanted medical treatment or a pregnancy. The liberty interest asserted by a person who refuses to cut his or her hair is clearly less fundamental than the liberty interest asserted by a woman who challenges a policy affecting her choices in reproduction and contraception.

At what point would an asserted interest be important or fundamental enough to receive protection on this sliding scale? The Court refused to extend constitutional protection to the privacy interests that a person has in a good reputation.[49] Chief Justice Rehnquist argued that the due process clause of the Fifth Amendment does not protect a person's liberty interest in his or her personal reputation against defamatory actions. Reputational privacy has been recognized by many state courts in tort cases where plaintiffs claim that their reputation was sullied by individuals who portrayed them inaccurately or in a false light. However, the Supreme Court has never extended constitutional protection to reputation, and there is little hope that this could be a successful claim.

Exactly what interests and activities does the right of privacy protect? There is no question that drug testing, for instance, raises privacy interests, but there is some disagreement on the Court concerning how that privacy interest should be balanced with various governmental needs. The Court's cautious decision in *Cruzan* clearly demonstrated this point. While half-heartedly recognizing a constitutional right to refuse unwanted medical treatment, the Court nevertheless argued strongly for the state's interest in protecting life and in maintaining the standards of the medical profession. The personal right that the Court balances with the state's interest is based on a very narrow or near-literal interpretation of the Fourteenth Amendment, rather than on the constitutional right of privacy as such. For many years, jurists and Court-watchers alike took for granted that it was just a matter of time before the Supreme Court applied the kind of reasoning found in *Griswold, Roe*, and *Quinlan* to issues such as the right to die and ultimately to homosexual conduct and other lifestyle issues. However, it is clear that the Rehnquist Court has no interest in either broadening the right of privacy or extending its protection to other forms of human activity. Terms such as "autonomous choice" and "private sphere" are likely to remain absent from the Court's language for some time to come.

*Who then will resolve the issues of physician-assisted suicide, homosexual privacy, informational privacy in the Internet age, or unforeseen bio-ethical privacy issues of the twenty-first century?* If the Court intends to develop a more narrow and restrictive definition of the right of privacy or to avoid the issue entirely by leaving it to the states, then so be it. But history teaches us that the contrary to professions of judicial restraint, the Court is ultimately called on to resolve society's most fundamental and profound constitutional questions.

# Finding the Full Text of the U.S. Supreme Court Opinions Cited in Chapter 6

The full opinion of the U.S. Supreme Court's rulings discussed in this chapter can be found at the Find law URL address following each case listed below, or by using the case name (e.g., *Schenck* ) or citation (e.g., 249 U.S. 47). Other web sites where opinions can be found are listed at the end of chapter 1.

## Tort Law and Fourth Amendment Origins of the Privacy Right

*Boyd v. United States* (1886), http://laws.findlaw.com/us/116/616.html

*Olmstead v. United States* (1928), http://laws.findlaw.com/us/277/438.html

*Katz v. United States* (1967), http://laws.findlaw.com/us/389/347.html

*United States v. White* (1981), http://laws.findlaw.com/us/401/745.html

## Drug Testing

*Terry v. Ohio* (1968), http://laws.findlaw.com/us/392/1.html

*Arizona v. Hicks* (1987), http://laws.findlaw.com/us/480/321.html

*California v. Trobetta* (1984), http://laws.findlaw.com/us/467/479.html

*United States v. Place* (1983), http://laws.findlaw.com/us/462/696.html

*Skinner v. Railway Labor Executives Association* (1989),
     http://laws.findlaw.com/us/489/602.html

*Schmerber v. California* (1966), http://laws.findlaw.com/us/384/757.html

*Chandler v. Miller* (1997), http://laws.findlaw.com/us/000/96-126.html

## Privacy as Autonomy and Reproductive Freedom

*Meyer v. Nebraska* (1925), http://laws.findlaw.com/us/262/390.html

*Skinner v. Oklahoma* (1942), http://laws.findlaw.com/us/316/535.html

### Elevation of Privacy to a Constitutional Right

*Griswold v. Connecticut* (1965), http://laws.findlaw.com/us/381/479.html

*Eisenstadt v. Baird* (1972), http://laws.findlaw.com/us/405/438.html

### Abortion

*Roe v. Wade* (1973), http://laws.findlaw.com/us/410/113.html

*Beal v. Doe* (1977), http://laws.findlaw.com/us/432/438.html

*Planned Parenthood of Central Missouri v. Danforth* (1976),
     http://laws.findlaw.com/us/428/552.html

*Akron v. Akron Center for Reproductive Health* (1983), http://laws.findlaw.com/
us/462/416.html

*Thornburgh v. American College of Obstetricians and Gynecologists* (1986),
http://laws.findlaw.com/us/476/747.html

*Webster v. Reproductive Health Services (1989)*, http://laws.findlaw.com/
us/492/490.html

*Hodgson v. Minnesota* (1990), http://laws.findlaw.com/us/497/417.html

*Rust v. Sullivan* (1991), http://laws.findlaw.com/us/500/173.html

*Planned Parenthood v. Casey* (1992), http://laws.findlaw.com/us/505/833.html

### *"Partial Birth" Abortion*

*Stenberg v. Carhart* (2000), http://laws.findlaw.com/us/000/99-830.html

### Privacy and Homosexuality

*Commonwealth's Attorney for the City of Richmond v. Doe* (1976),
http://laws.findlaw.com/us/425/901.html

*Bowers v. Hardwick* (1986), http://laws.findlaw.com/us/478/186.html

### The Right to Die

*Cruzan v. Director, Missouri Department of Health* (1990),
http://laws.findlaw.com/us/497/261.html

### Physician-Assisted Suicide

*Washington v. Glucksberg* (1997), http://laws.findlaw.com/us/000/95-1858.html

*Vacco v. Quill* (1997), http://laws.findlaw.com/us/000/95-1858.html

## Notes

1. See Alan Westin's classic work, *Privacy and Freedom* (New York: Athenaeum Press, 1970).
2. Westin, *Privacy and Freedom*, and see William Prosser, "Privacy," 48 *California Law Review* 338 (1960).
3. Samuel Warren and Louis Brandeis, "The Right to Privacy," 4 *Harvard Law Review* 193 (1890).
4. Warren and Brandeis, "The Right to Privacy."
5. Prosser, "Privacy," 338.
6. Prosser, "Privacy," 338.
7. Westin, *Privacy and Freedom*.
8. See also *National Treasury Employees Union v. Von Raab*, 489 U.S. 602 (1989), in which the Court ruled 5–4 to uphold the U.S. Customs Service's drug-testing policy for employees.

9. It was reported in *Skinner* that a study of alcohol abuse by employees of seven major railroads found that during the course of a year, about one of every eight workers drank a least once while on duty, 5 percent reported to work "very drunk," 13 percent reported to work at least a "little drunk" one or more times, and 23 percent of the operating personnel were "problem drinkers." The FRA also reported that from 1972 to 1983, 25 fatalities, 61 nonfatal injuries, and about $20 million in property damage resulted from 21 train accident attributed to alcohol or drug use by railroad employees.

10. The test had to be performed in a "reasonable manner." See also *Camara v. Municipal Court*, 387 U.S. 523 (1967).

11. The Court applied the special needs rule to a civil (as opposed to a criminal) search in two earlier cases: *New Jersey v. TLO*, 469 U.S. 325 (1985), and *Donovan v. Dewey*, 552 U.S. 594 (1981).

12. Brandeis, dissenting in *Olmstead v. United States*, 277 U.S. 438 (1928).

13. http://laws.findlaw.com/us/000/96-126.html: 117 S. Ct. 1295 (1997).

14. *Treasury Employees v. Von Raub*, 489 U.S. 656 (1989).

15. *Veronia School District v. Acton*, 515 U.S. (1995).

16. There are two kinds of due process of law—procedural and substantive. Procedural due process refers to the manner in which a law is applied regardless of the content of the law. Substantive due process refers to the subject matter or content of the law. If a court applies substantive dues process to a law, it is reviewing the content of that law independently of the procedures by which its was applied. The Supreme Court originally used substantive due process during the "*Lochner* era" (based on *Lochner v. New York*, 198 U.S. 45 [1905]) to strike down economic regulations on the ground that they violated liberty of contract. In modern times, the Court has abandoned its use of substantive due process to review economic regulations but has applied it to strike down governmental restrictions on individual rights and liberties. In doing so, the Court has broadly interpreted the due process clauses of the Fifth and Fourteenth Amendments, as well as the Bill of Rights as a whole, to "find" rights not enumerated or to expand rights in ways that are reflective more of fundamental values than of constitutional text or the original intent of the framers. There is a voluminous body of literature on this subject; for a good overview, see Gerald Gunther, *Constitutional Law* (New York: Foundation Press, 1985), 448–585; see also Robert McCloskey, "Economic Due Process and the Supreme Court," in the *Supreme Court Review: 1962*, Phillip Kurland, ed. (Chicago: University of Chicago Press, 1962), 34–62; and Bernard Seigan, *Economic Liberties and the Constitution* (Chicago: University of Chicago Press, 1980).

17. Compare this case with *Buck v. Bell*, 274 U.S. 200 (1927), which sustained a state law permitting the sterilization of institutionalized mental patients.

18. See Bernard Schwartz, *Super Chief: Earl Warren and His Supreme Court—A Judicial Biography* (New York: New York University Press. 1983), p. 577.

19. Justice Brennan advanced a similar approach in the earlier case *Lamont v. Postmaster General*, 381 U.S. 301 (1965).

20. *Griswold v. Connecticut*, 381 U.S. 479 (1965).

21. For a comprehensive study of the abortion debate in the early years, see Raymond Tatalovich and Byron Daynes, *The Politics of Abortion: A Study of Community Conflict in Public Policymaking* (New York: Praeger Publishers, 1981).

22. Earlier in his career, Justice Blackmun had served as legal counsel for the Mayo Clinic.

23. For a short but excellent discussion of this issue, see Barry Furrow, et al., *Health Law* (St. Paul, MN: West Publishing, 1991), 884–911.

24. *Roe v. Wade*, 410 U.S. 113 (1973).

25. *Roe v. Wade,* 410 U.S. 113.

26. Decided along with *Roe* was its companion case, *Doe v. Bolton*, 410 U.S. 179 (1973). In *Doe*, the Court ruled 7–2 that the state may not require abortions to be performed in hospitals or be subject to approval by hospital committees. Nor could the state require that two physicians agree with the abortion decision.
27. *Maher v. Roe*, 432 U.S. 464 (1977).
28. *Poelker v. Doe*, 432 U.S. 59 (1979).
29. In *Bellotti v. Baird*, 428 U.S. 132 (1976), the Court struck down (9–0) a statute requiring a minor to secure the consent of both parents before undergoing an abortion.
30. *H. L. v. Matheson*, 450 U.S. 398 (1981).
31. *DeShaney v. Winnebago County Department of Social Services*, 489 U.S. 656 (1989); *Poelker v. Doe*, 432 U.S. 59.
32. See Furrow, *Health Law*, 935–936.
33. The Court previously upheld similar parental notification requirements in *H. L. v. Matheson*, 450 U.S. 398 (1981), and *Akron v. Akron Center for Reproductive Health*, 462 U.S. 416 (1983).
34. Blackmun cited *Wooley v. Maynard*, 430 U.S. at 715.
35. 177 S. Ct. 1169 (1997).
36. 117 S. Ct. 1865 (1997).
37. http://laws.findlaw.com/us/000/99-830.html
38. See *Harris v. McRae*, 448 U.S. 297 (1980). The majority opinion contains a detailed overview of abortion procedures for those who are not too squeamish. See also H. Grimes, "The Continuing Need for Late Abortions," 280 *JAMA* 747 (August 26, 1998).
39. *Korematsu v. United States*, 323 U.S. 214 (1944); *Dred Scott v. Sandford*, 19 H.W. (60 U.S.) 393 (1857).
40. See *Commonwealth v. Wasson*, 842 S.W.2d 487 (Ky. 1992); *Gryczan v. State*, 942 P.2d 112 (Mont. 1997); and *Campbell v. Sundquist*, 926 S.W.2d 250 (Tenn. App. 1996).
41. *Powell v. State*, 510 S.E.2d 18 (Ga. 1998); see also Wendy Stein, "*Powell v. State*: An Auspicious Decision in a Culture of Affectional/Sexual Orientation Discrimination," 27 *Florida State University Law Review* 897 (2000).
42. For a concise table of states that have criminalized and decriminalized sexual acts between consenting adults of the same sex, see Craig R. Ducat, *Constitutional Interpretation*, 7th ed. (Belmont, CA: Wadsworth/Thompson, 2000), 807.
43. See Stein, "*Powell v. State*: An Auspicious Decision in a Culture of Affectional/Sexual Orientation Discrimination."
44. 355 A.2d 647 (1976) (N.J.).
45. For a collection of articles written shortly after *Cruzan*, see 20 *Hastings Center Report* 5 (September/October 1990).
46. For an excellent discussion of this complex issue, see Melvin I. Urofsky, "Justifying Assisted Suicide: Comments on the Ongoing Debate," 14 *Notre Dame Journal of Ethics & Public Policy* 893 (2000).
47. http://laws.findlaw.com/us/000/95-1858.html.
48. In *Kelly v. Johnson*, 425 U.S. 238 (1976), the Court upheld a police department's regulation concerning the hair length of its officers.
49. *Siegert v. Gilley*, 111 S. Ct. 1789 (1991).

# CHAPTER SEVEN

# Equal Protection of the Laws

*We conclude that in the field of public education the doctrine of "separate but equal" has no place. Separate educational facilities are inherently unequal. Therefore, we hold that the plaintiffs and others similarly situated for whom the actions have been brought are, by reason of the segregation complained of, deprived of the equal protection of the laws guaranteed by the Fourteenth Amendment.*

Chief Justice Earl Warren in *Brown v. Board of Education,*
347 U.S. 483 (1954)

## RACIAL DISCRIMINATION

### Separate But Equal

On May 18, 1896, the U.S. Supreme Court ruled 8–1 in *Plessy v. Ferguson*, 163 U.S. 537, that state laws requiring segregation on the basis of race are constitutional under the Fourteenth Amendment. In upholding the "separate but equal" doctrine, a predominantly northern Court cast a pall over the struggle for civil rights. Not since the infamous *Dred Scott*[1] ruling of the Taney Court in 1857—which held that blacks were not entitled to the rights and privileges of citizenship—had any opinion of the Supreme Court come to represent racial intolerance more than *Plessy v. Ferguson.*

*Plessy* originated in 1890, when the Louisiana legislature enacted a law requiring railroad companies to provide separate but equal accommodations for white and "colored" passengers. Homer Plessy, who was "seven-eighths Caucasian and one-eight African blood," was arrested for refusing to leave a seat in a whites-only railroad coach. He challenged the law on the grounds that it violated the Thirteenth Amendment, which abolished slavery, and the Fourteenth Amendment, which guaranteed equal protection of the laws. But the Court rejected Plessy's Thirteenth Amendment argument outright on the grounds that slavery implied involuntary servitude or a state of bondage, and thus the Thirteenth Amendment did not apply to laws that merely separated the races. A statute that made a legal distinction between the races on the basis of color did not destroy the legal equality of the races or create a condition of slavery; it merely reflected the social distinctions based on color

270

that existed in society. Furthermore, while the objective of the Fourteenth Amendment was to enforce the absolute legal and political equality of the two races, it was not intended to abolish distinctions based on color or to enforce social equality and the "commingling of the two races upon terms unsatisfactory to either."

Contrary to Plessy's assertion that the Louisiana statute fostered or implied inferiority of blacks, the Court argued that the law merely reflected already existing social mores and traditions. Writing for the majority, Justice Henry Brown argued that the legislature was well within its right to enforce those social attitudes through legal distinctions between blacks and whites. Nothing in the Constitution prohibited the states from making such distinctions as long as equal facilities or accommodations were provided for each race. Indeed, as Justice Brown pointed out, such distinctions existed in the practices of even the most progressive states. He wrote:

> The most common instance of [separation] is connected with the establishment of separate schools for white and colored children, which have been [upheld] even by courts of states where the political rights of the colored race have been longest and most earnestly enforced. [Laws] forbidding the intermarriage of the two races may be said in a technical sense to interfere with the freedom of contract, and yet have been universally recognized as within the police power of the state.

Brown concluded that social prejudices could not be overcome by mere legislation or a single order to integrate railroad cars. Equality would come about only when time and custom eradicated prejudices and not before.

In his famous lone dissent, Justice John Marshall Harlan,[2] a former slaveowner, wrote that the Constitution was "colorblind, and neither knows nor tolerates classes among citizens." He objected to the law on the grounds that it interfered with the personal freedom of citizens and created superior and inferior classes of persons under the Constitution: a caste system, if you will. He compared the Court's decision to *Dred Scott*, arguing that it would prolong racial tension in the nation by "permit[ting] the seeds of race hate to be planted under the sanction of law." Harlan also recognized the hypocrisy of celebrating our freedom while relegating an entire class of persons to inferiority. In a stirring passage, he wrote:

> [We] boast of the freedom enjoyed by our people above all other peoples. But it is difficult to reconcile that boast with a state of the law which, practically, puts the brand of servitude and degradation upon a large class of our fellow citizens,—our equals before the law. The thin disguise of "equal accommodations" [will] not mislead any one, nor atone for the wrong this day [has] done.

By elevating the separate but equal doctrine to constitutional status, *Plessy* provided the legal and moral justification for policies of segregation and second-class citizenship for millions throughout the United States. Indeed, in 1927 the Court unanimously extended *Plessy* to uphold a Mississippi law that required Chinese children to attend black schools.[3]

By the 1930s, judicial rulings were beginning to chip away at the separate but equal doctrine. For instance, the Court ruled in 1938 that a Missouri policy paying blacks to attend law school out of state rather than admitting them to an in-state law school denied them the "equal opportunity for legal training."[4] In the 1940s, the Court ruled that a black with a first-class train ticket could not be constitutionally ordered to sit in the second-class section,[5] and that a black must be admitted to an all-white law school if there is no other law school in the state.[6]

The 1950 case *Sweatt v. Painter*, 339 U.S. 637, offered another ray of hope. In *Sweatt*, the Court applied the Fourteenth Amendment to the whites-only admission policy of the University of Texas College of Law; in doing so, it substantially weakened the separate but equal doctrine. By ruling that the word "equal" applied not only to tangible factors (such as university buildings, books, and faculty) but also to intangible qualities (such as institutional reputation and opportunity to interact with a cross-section of the legal profession), the Court made it more difficult for states to maintain and justify separate but equal, or "dual," school systems.[7]

## Brown v. Board of Education

The ongoing struggle for racial equality began long before the Warren Court's celebrated decision in *Brown v. Board of Education*, 347 U.S. 483 (1954). Yet, more than any other case, *Brown* has come to symbolize a great victory for the American civil rights movement; perhaps because the ruling was so long overdue or because it served as a catalyst for congressional and presidential action. The Court's unanimous and resounding attack on racial segregation demonstrated to those without hope that after hundreds of years of segregation, change was possible. Whatever the reason, and in light of criticism from both liberals and conservatives, there is no underestimating the legal and symbolic importance of *Brown*.

Like many landmark rulings, *Brown* originated in the hopes and desires of human beings who had long endured unequal treatment under the law. Oliver Brown brought suit against the board of education in Topeka, Kansas, for refusing to admit his eight-year-old daughter Linda to an all-white school located only five blocks from her house. Because of the board's policy of segregating elementary schools, Linda was forced to travel twenty-one blocks to the nearest all-black school. Brown's suit was one of four lawsuits brought by blacks seeking admission on a nondiscriminatory basis to the public schools of their community in Kansas, South Carolina, Virginia, and Delaware. In each instance, black children were denied admission to all-white schools under laws permitting or requiring segregation on the basis of race. With the exception of Kansas, the states involved in the suit required mandatory segregation of all public schools. The board of education in Topeka, Kansas, elected to establish segregated elementary schools, but operated other schools in the city on a nonsegregated basis.

*Does the equal protection clause of the Fourteenth Amendment provide a remedy to state-sponsored segregation in the public schools? Can segregated public schools be made equal under the Fourteenth Amendment when the races are provided with substantially equal facilities? Or does the segregation of children in public schools solely on the basis of race deprive the children of the minority group of equal education opportunities?* Although the *Brown* ruling was handed down on May 17, 1954, under the leadership of newly appointed Chief Justice Earl Warren, the case was originally argued in December 1952 shortly before the death of Chief Justice Frederick M. Vinson. Just prior to reargument, Warren was appointed to the chief justiceship by President Eisenhower. Before his death, Vinson had openly proclaimed that he was not ready to overturn the pernicious separate but equal doctrine of *Plessy v. Ferguson*, and had even hinted that he would vote to affirm several lower court rulings that upheld segregation. However, at least five of his colleagues were ready to abandon the separate but equal doctrine.[8]

Working their way up from the lower federal courts, the plaintiffs argued that segregation deprived them of equal protection of the laws under the Fourteenth Amendment. Even if Linda Brown and the other children were provided with substantially equal facilities, books, and teachers, segregated public schools could never be equal under the Fourteenth Amendment. A three-judge federal court in each of the states except Delaware denied relief to Brown and the others on the grounds that statutes mandating or permitting segregated schools were constitutional under the separate but equal doctrine. The Delaware Supreme Court also adhered to the separate but equal doctrine, but nevertheless it ordered the admission of the black students on the grounds that the state's black schools were substantially inferior to the white schools.

When oral argument was heard the second time, the Court focused its inquiry largely on the meaning of the equal protection clause of the Fourteenth Amendment and the circumstances surrounding its adoption. The Fourteenth Amendment provides: "No State shall . . . deny to any person within its jurisdiction the equal protection of the laws." The Delaware attorney general confidently argued that a decision against segregation in the public schools would contradict the intent of the framers of the Fourteenth Amendment. For Warren, however, the legislative history of the amendment was "inconclusive"; thus, the problem with relying on its history to discern its meaning was that it was unclear what the proponents and opponents of the amendment intended and, at the time of its ratification in 1868, no system of tax-supported public schools had taken root in the South. In fact, education of white children was left to parents, churches, and private organizations; and in many places in the South, education of blacks was prohibited by law. Yet Warren was unwavering in his drive to overturn separate but equal; it was just a matter of finding support for his position.

Warren then looked at the *Slaughterhouse* Cases[9] of 1873. There, the Court had interpreted the Fourteenth Amendment as prohibiting all "state-imposed discriminations against the Negro race." It was questionable, however, whether equal protection extended beyond political and legal equality to the issues concerning personal liberty and the social relations between blacks and whites.

Although *Sweatt* made it much more difficult for the states to justify segregated facilities, when *Brown* came to the Court, *Plessy* was still good law. Thus, a novel approach to the problem had to be employed if separate but equal was to be overturned. As Chief Justice Warren observed:

[W]e cannot turn the clock back to 1868 when the Amendment was adopted, or even to 1896 when *Plessy v. Ferguson* was written. We must consider public education in the light of its full development and its present place in American life throughout the Nation. Only in this way can it be determined if segregation in the public schools deprives these plaintiffs of the equal protection of the laws.

The testimony indicated that in some communities black and white schools were being equalized with respect to tangible factors, such as buildings, curricula, and teacher qualifications. Many communities were working to this end so that they could maintain segregated schools. But the Court refused to base its ruling merely on a comparison of tangible factors. Instead, it focused on the actual effect of segregation on educational opportunities for the children. Writing for the unanimous Court, Warren argued that separating black children from other children of similar age and ability solely because they were black generated feelings of inferiority among black children, causing psychological scars and adversely affecting the quality of public education in America. This sense of inferiority affected not only children's emotional health, but also their motivation to learn and succeed in society. Since public education was compulsory—a social good mandated by law—legally sanctioned segregation in education deprived a class of people of equal protection of the laws. In a now-famous passage, Warren wrote:

> We conclude that in the field of public education the doctrine of "separate but equal" has no place. Separate educational facilities are inherently unequal. Therefore, we hold that the plaintiffs and others similarly situated for whom the actions have been brought are, by reason of the segregation complained of, deprived of the equal protection of the laws guaranteed by the Fourteenth Amendment.

At the heart of the Court's decision rested the belief that segregated schools engendered feelings of inferiority in millions of American citizens. However, many of the justices cringed at the thought of handing down a landmark decision based largely on social science rather than on constitutional doctrine. In fact, the opinion's celebrated footnote eleven cited seven studies conducted by social scientists. Several justices, including Justice Jackson, believed that the entire issue of segregation was beyond the legitimate concern of the judiciary, as it was a political, not a constitutional, issue.[10] But the chief justice would not let such judicial rigidity stand in his way. He was sufficiently convinced by the NAACP's attorney Thurgood Marshall and the research of eminent psychologists and sociologists, such as Kenneth B. Clark and Gunnar Myrdal, that millions of black children would continue to suffer emotional harm at the hands of the state as long as segregated public education was permitted.

But before the Court could convince American communities to desegregate their public schools, Warren had to convince his colleagues that a ruling of such magnitude would have to be the handiwork of a unanimous Court. When he joined the Court, Warren knew that four justices—Black, Douglas, Burton, and Minton—would vote to strike down segregation. His task was to convince Justices Reed, Clark, Jackson, and Frankfurter to join the majority. After Frankfurter was convinced, he assiduously worked with Warren to convince the remaining justices to join also.[11]

*Brown* is unquestionably one of the most important statements of constitutional law in American history. But the phrase "[s]eparate educational facilities are inherently unequal" is merely a statement of principles—it offers no precise remedy to the problem of segregation. School systems are not agents of the federal government, but rather localized and autonomous institutions influenced by the traditions and prejudices of the surrounding community. It was unlikely that compliance would be a serious problem in Kansas, but the Court expected militant noncompliance in the Deep South. Justice Black, a native Alabaman, believed that it would be best to leave enforcement to the federal district courts in the states.[12] A direct order from the Supreme Court compelling southern states to admit black students immediately into all-white schools would hurt rather than help desegregation. Now that African Americans had standing to sue segregated school systems, the best approach to implementation was a strategy of lawsuits in the lower courts. Thus, although the Court voted unanimously to overturn segregation in the public schools, it was quite divided over the proper means of implementation. This is illustrated by the vagueness of the opinions in both *Brown* and "*Brown II*." In a classic understatement, Warren wrote: "Because these are class actions, because of the wide applicability of this decision, and because of the great variety of local conditions, the formulation of decrees in these cases presents problems of considerable complexity."

In other words, under the decision Linda Brown and others similarly situated in this class action now had standing to sue school boards for relief. But there was little hope that they would prevail, for if anything, local and state officials were even more adamant in their efforts to maintain segregation. Therefore, to address the issue of compliance, the Court requested further argument in *Brown II*, 349 U.S. 294 (1955), where it invited the U.S. attorney general and the attorneys general of all states requiring or permitting racial discrimination in public education to present their ideas to the justices.

Warren recognized the formidable social and political obstacles to be overcome by local officials in implementing *Brown*, but nevertheless ordered the states to "make a prompt and reasonable start toward full compliance with our . . . decision" and "to admit to public schools on a racially nondiscriminatory basis with all deliberate speed the parties to these cases."

The issue of public schools in the District of Columbia was addressed in *Bolling v. Sharpe*, 347 U.S. 497 (1954), where the plaintiffs challenged the segregated school system there. Because the equal protection clause of the Fourteenth Amendment applies to the states and not to the federal government, the Court adopted the due process clause of the Fifth Amendment as a remedy to discrimination. Chief Justice Warren reasoned:

[T]he concepts of equal protection and due process, both stemming from our American ideal of fairness, are not mutually exclusive. The "equal protection of the laws" is a more explicit safeguard of prohibited unfairness than "due process of the law," and, therefore, we do not imply that the two are always interchangeable phrases. But, as this Court has recognized, discrimination may be so unjustifiable as to be violative of due process.

Warren used *Bolling* as an opportunity to articulate his views on equal protection theory. Many laws "classify" or discriminate among people. For example, a law may provide entitlements to the aged but not to the young. A selective service law requires men to register but places no such obligation on women. In these cases, the Court asks only that the classification be reasonable and that it further some legitimate governmental interest. However, classifications on the basis of race are considered constitutionally suspect or unreasonable because they bear no rational relationship to any proper governmental objective. Such classifications must be given strict judicial scrutiny. Thus, segregation in public education is not reasonably related to the legitimate governmental interest in universal public education, and it serves no purpose other than accommodating racism. Furthermore, racial discrimination is a deprivation of liberty under the due process clause of the Fifth Amendment as well as the equal protection clause of the Fourteenth. Warren continued: "In view of our decision that the Constitution prohibits the states from maintaining segregated public schools, it would be unthinkable that the Constitution would impose a lesser duty on the federal government." Although the explicit purpose of *Bolling* was to prohibit the federal government from discriminating in the public schools, Warren's reasoning implied that strict judicial scrutiny must be applied to government-sponsored discrimination in all public institutions.

The initial response to *Brown* and *Bolling* from the southern states reflected a wait-and-see attitude. The chief justice received only 700 of the kinds of hate letters that usually bombard the Court after any controversial ruling.[13] The response to *Brown II*, however, was not quite as subdued. Almost immediately, resolutions of "interposition" were passed by several southern legislatures, declaring null and void the two desegregation rulings. Congress did nothing, as the issue was too hot to handle. Although President Eisenhower refused to say or do anything to support the desegregation rulings, he later sent federal troops into Little Rock, Arkansas, to protect black children from angry white mobs.

Southern state legislators and citizens adamantly resisted any attempt on the part of the federal government to "violate their rights." By 1956, the Citizens' Council, a group aimed at placing economic sanctions on all who supported desegregation, had 250,000 members throughout the South. African American and white civil rights activists were threatened, beaten, bombed, and murdered by various groups, including the Ku Klux Klan. In 1956, angry mobs prevented black students from enrolling in the University of Alabama and in the public schools of Mansfield, Texas, and Clinton, Tennessee. When Birmingham, Alabama, attempted to implement the Court's ruling, a black man was castrated by a group of whites as a warning to those who would desegregate their schools. Going beyond nullification laws, several states demonstrated their artful resolve by providing subsidies to communities that closed public schools and opened all-white private academies.[14]

Throughout the late 1950s, civil rights activists brought numerous lawsuits before federal district courts with the help of the NAACP's Legal Defense Fund. In these cases, the Constitution's granting of life tenure to federal judges cut both ways. In many southern districts, federal judges rose above personal prejudice to follow *Brown*, but the majority of southern judges, secure in their lifetime position, either flatly challenged the Supreme Court's decree or merely repeated *Brown*'s vague "with all deliberate speed" admonition with a wink and a nod and did nothing to encourage remedial action.[15]

In reaction to a 1957 federal district court's order to desegregate Central High School in Little Rock, Arkansas, Governor Orval Faubus ordered the National Guard to thwart any attempt by African American students to get inside the school. The federal district court issued an injunction against the governor's action, and nine students, including John Aaron, were allowed to enter the school. However, they were later evacuated when a mob of angry whites threatened to remove the students by force. In response to continuing violence, President Eisenhower sent units of the U.S. Army's 101st Airborne Division to Little Rock to protect the children and to enforce the district court's order. Federal troops remained with the black students for the entire 1957–1958 school year.

In 1958, William Cooper and other members of the Little Rock school board convinced the district court that a two-and-one-half year delay in the desegregation order was needed to diffuse the tense situation. However, after the U.S. court of appeals reversed the district court's order, Cooper was forced to take his case to the U.S. Supreme Court in *Cooper v. Aaron*, 358 U.S. 1 (1958), the "Little Rock case." Infuriated by noncompliance to the principles set forth in *Brown*, the Supreme Court ruled that school board members and all other public officials in the state, including the governor, could be held directly liable for hardships and injuries suffered by the black students. No longer was the abstract "state" the guilty party; all conditions in the public schools—segregation, discrimination, harassment, and substandard education—were ruled to be directly traceable to the actions of legislators and executive officials of Arkansas. Through their own noncompliance to *Brown*, these Arkansas officials were responsible for bringing about violent resistance to the Constitution. The members of the school board had boldly argued that they were not bound by *Brown* and openly sought to oppose and vilify federal law and federal courts. Thus, what was at stake in *Cooper* was more than desegregation; it was the supremacy of the Constitution, the maintenance of federalism, and the power of judicial review. Citing the 1880 case *Ex parte Virginia*,[16] Warren commanded that any person who acts in the name and for the state, "and is clothed with the state's power," is prohibited by the Constitution from denying equal protection of the laws. "This must be so, or the constitutional prohibition has no meaning," he stated. Thus, the Fourteenth Amendment extends not merely to nebulous concepts such as "state" or "school board" but also to governors and individual members of the school board. Discrimination may be traced directly to them. In sum, *Brown* could not be openly and directly nullified by state officials nor indirectly "through evasive schemes for segregation."

The chief justice then concluded his opinion with a lesson in constitutional law, attacking those who would attempt to nullify the decisions of the Supreme Court and, in John Marshall's words, "wage war against the Constitution." He argued: "It follows [the reasoning of *Marbury v. Madison*] that the interpretation of the Fourteenth Amendment enunciated by this Court in the *Brown* case is the supreme law of the land, and Art. VI of the Constitution makes it of binding effect on the states."

As Chief Justice Marshall reasoned: "If the legislatures of the several states may, at will, annul the judgments of the courts of the United States, and destroy the rights acquired under those judgments, the constitution itself becomes a solemn mockery."[17]

## Implementing *Brown*

Throughout the 1960s, while the Court was working to dismantle the last vestiges of de jure, or legal segregation, school systems in the North and South were still perfecting the art of foot-dragging. Federal courts had already heard dozens of cases dealing with issues ranging from outright noncompliance to technical disputes over the best way of dismantling segregation based on population patterns. Resistance to *Brown* was not always calculated. Honest efforts to desegregate schools were thwarted by national demographic trends—the exodus of middle-class whites to the suburbs in the 1960s and the concomitant decay of the inner cities. The issue of desegregation was moot in many communities, since blacks and whites traditionally lived miles apart in distinct parts of town and in different school zones. In other communities, new schools were built only in areas of white suburban expansion, leaving the old schools predominantly black. Gerrymandering, or redrawing attendance zones to exclude African Americans, was another common method of circumventing *Brown*. To address these problems, federal courts ordered fixed racial ratios for both student bodies and faculties, redrawn attendance zones, and—the most controversial—compulsory busing. Next to the Court's initial order to desegregate, no policy has been met with more acrimony and fierce resistance than forced busing. The political fortunes of many candidates in the North as well as in the South were often dependent on this single issue.

The election of President Nixon in 1968 had an impact on desegregation efforts. When Earl Warren retired in 1969, President Nixon replaced him with conservative Warren Burger, who was expected to lead a counterrevolution in constitutional law. Nixon also appointed Associate Justices Blackmun, Powell, and Rehnquist. As with due process, conservatives hoped that the new appointees would overturn many of the Warren Court's liberal civil rights decisions. The Nixon administration was quick to act on public sentiment toward busing. As antibusing protesters rallied in the North and South, the Nixon administration's Justice Department brought numerous suits in federal courts throughout the country with the intent of delaying the implementation of *Brown*.

In 1969, approximately 29 percent of the students in the Charlotte, North Carolina, school systems' were black. Two thirds of these students attended schools that were 99 percent African American even though the city was operating under a four-year-old desegregation order. The school board did employ some token desegregation, but little had changed since *Brown* was handed down in 1954. Acting on the Warren Court's decree in the 1968 case *Green v. County School Board*[18] to "take whatever steps necessary" to end desegregation, a federal district judge proposed a radical plan to desegregate Charlotte's schools. Judge McMillan ordered 13,000 of the school district's 84,000 students to be bused and attendance lines redrawn so that a meaningful ratio (71 percent to 29 percent) of white to black students would eventually be achieved in each of the city's schools.

Judge McMillan's radical plan was challenged by the Charlotte school board in
*Swann v. Charlotte-Mecklenburg Board of Education*, 402 U.S. 1 (1971), on the
grounds that the remedies were unworkable and that the federal district court exceeded
its power under the Constitution and the Civil Rights Act of 1964. The fate of one-race
schools that existed purely because of population patterns within the city was also at
stake in the case. In an unexpected unanimous opinion, the Burger Court upheld Judge
McMillan's order and ruled that because local authorities had failed "to meet their
constitutional obligations," the Court was now compelled to set forth specific guidelines to desegregate the city's schools once and for all. Chief Justice Burger asserted
that, contrary to the position of the school board, the Civil Rights Act of 1964 was
enacted not to limit the federal courts' power of equitable relief, but to define the federal government's role in providing remedies under *Brown*. Disposing of that issue,
Burger then asked: "[What are] the responsibilities of school authorities in desegregating a state-enforced dual system in light of the equal protection clause?" The following standard was promulgated: A constitutional violation has occurred where each
school does not have a ratio of black to white students reflecting the proportion of the
district as a whole; and, independent of student assignment, it is possible to identify a
white school or a black school simply by reference to the racial composition of the faculty and staff, the quality of school buildings and equipment, or the organization of
sports activities. The permissible remedies available to the federal district courts
include: (1) racial balances or quotas for the numbers of students and teachers, (2)
redrawing attendance zones, and (3) compulsory busing. The district court's use of the
71 percent to 29 percent ratio, reflecting the racial proportion in the community, was
constitutional though not, according to Burger, fixed in stone. The pairing and group-
ing of noncontiguous school zones for the purpose of achieving racial balance was permissible as well. Most controversially, busing could be required when it served as a
meaningful tool of school desegregation and did not create an excessive burden on the
school system or the children. The Court believed that busing was necessary because
the African American population was concentrated in the northwestern part of the city.

    Was it permissible for a school system to have a small number of one-race
schools? Burger said yes. Until new schools were built or until neighborhood patterns changed, one-race schools were permissible only if those schools resulted from
demographics and not intentional discrimination. Burger expressed some level of
sympathy for the position that the courts had imposed unreasonable burdens on the
day-to-day operations of public schools. Nonetheless, he wrote:

> All things being equal, with no history of discrimination, it might well be desirable
> to assign pupils to schools nearest their homes. But all things are not equal in a sys-
> tem that has been deliberately constructed and maintained to enforce racial segrega-
> tion. The remedy for such segregation may be administratively awkward,
> inconvenient, and even bizarre in some situations and may impose burdens on some;
> but all awkwardness and inconvenience cannot be avoided in the interim period when
> remedial adjustments are being made to eliminate the dual school systems.

    After *Swann*, there was one last desperate and open challenge to the Court's
authority in the form of a North Carolina law prohibiting compulsory busing and

"racial balancing" in schools. However, relying on its reasoning in *Swann*, a unanimous Court struck down the state law.

Contrary to the expectations of many conservatives, the Burger Court remained faithful to the Warren Court's commitment to desegregation. In many of the Burger Court's school desegregation rulings involving cities in the North and West, the issue of unintentional segregation resulting from white flight to the suburbs was addressed. In *Milliken v. Bradley*, 418 U.S. 717 (1974), involving the Detroit public school system, the Court ruled (5–4) that compulsory busing was impermissible where segregation resulted from population patterns and not from de jure discrimination. But in two Ohio cases, the Court upheld a federal district court's order for extensive busing plans because it was found that 70 percent of all students attended schools that were either 80 percent black or white.[19] School districts were not required to rearrange attendance zones every year so that a determined racial balance could be maintained.[20] Yet, in another case the Court held that the allocation of teachers within a school system may be found to have a discriminatory impact on minority children.[21]

Suppose a segregated school system fails to raise the revenue necessary to comply with a desegregation order. May a federal district court order an increase in the school district's tax rate in order to fund busing, for example? How far does the remedial power of the federal courts go? Almost a decade after *Swann*, the Rehnquist Court ruled 5–4 in *Missouri v. Jenkins*, 495 U.S. 33 (1990), that although the district court abused its discretion by imposing the tax itself, the court does have the power to order the appropriate officials to levy taxes in order to desegregate schools. The dissenters—Kennedy, Rehnquist, O'Connor, and Scalia—argued that a finding of discrimination cannot be used as the basis for "a wholesale shift of authority" over the operation of a school system from parents, teachers, and elected officials to unelected, life-tenured federal judges.

In some communities, legal desegregation was ended by decree years ago and compliance secured through one of many remedies. But as the years passed and new, mostly white suburbs developed, schools became resegregated as a result of population patterns, not governmental action. Indeed, this trend has extended into the twenty-first century. Many contend that modern resegregation is not purely a result of persons deciding to move to the suburbs; the paucity of economic opportunities for African Americans and discriminatory real estate practices have contributed to these new patterns of segregation. The latter issues notwithstanding, when can a decree to desegregate be lifted? Does a court order exist in perpetuity even though a school system has abided by the original order?

In 1972, a federal district court ordered the school board of Oklahoma City to adopt a master plan for desegregation. After the city had complied with the desegregation order for five years, the district court ordered the case closed. By the mid-1980s, however, the exodus of whites to the suburbs created a new de facto segregated system. In order to remain faithful to the original order, the city would have had to embark upon a more extensive system of busing African American students a great distance from their inner-city homes to white suburban schools. The school board decided instead to adopt a new plan that allowed students in kindergarten through fourth grade to attend neighborhood schools. It further permitted any student who was in the majority in one school to voluntarily transfer to a school where he or she would be in the minority. The city continued some busing of students in grades five through twelve and remained committed to the racial diversity of faculty and staff in the schools. But Robert Dowell and other African American students and their parents were unhappy with the new plan and reopened the original desegregation case. They argued that under the new plan, 17 percent of the sixty-four elementary schools in the city would be 90 percent black. In response to the plan, the federal district court ruled that since a "unitary" (desegregated) system had been achieved under the original plan, the original decree had expired and the issue was now back in the hands of the local school board. The old system, which had operated under de jure discrimination, no longer existed. Any new segregation was not a result of a history of discrimination but of certain demographic changes and economics.

After a court of appeals reversed the district court, the school board appealed to the U.S. Supreme Court in *Board of Education of Oklahoma City Public Schools v. Dowell*, 498 U.S. 237 (1991). The Rehnquist Court agreed with the district court that the desegregation degree was not intended to operate in perpetuity. The school board had complied with the original order for a reasonable period of time (thirteen years). Writing for the 5–3 majority,[22] Chief Justice Rehnquist stressed that once an old system of de jure segregation is eliminated, the courts should return control of the operation of the city's schools to local authorities. As important as it is to have a school system free from discrimination, it is equally important to respect the democratic process at the local level. The importance of localism/federalism is a common theme that runs though most of Chief Justice Rehnquist's opinions.

Dissenting, Justice Marshall—joined by Justices Blackmun and Stevens—argued that a desegregation decree cannot be lifted so long as "conditions likely to inflict the stigmatic injury condemned in *Brown* persist" and there are feasible ways of ameliorating such conditions. Attacking de jure segregation alone is not enough to eliminate stigmatization and discrimination. Complete relief depends on going after any negative effects of segregation that are traceable to the old system of de jure segregation. Marshall wrote: "In sum, our school segregation jurisprudence establishes that the *effects* of past discrimination remain chargeable to the school district regardless of its lack of continued enforcement of segregation, and the remedial decree is required until those effects have been finally eliminated."

He concluded by attacking the majority's trivialization of segregation resulting from "private decision-making." The "private decision" to send a child to an all-white school or to move to the suburbs may be beyond the decision-making process of the government, but the ability of people to make such choices is part of a calculated attempt by school authorities to allow for segregated schools. According to Marshall, by lifting the decree, the majority allowed the process to start all over again.

## Desegregating Other Public Facilities

*What about public facilities other than schools? Do the principles set forth in* Brown *apply to facilities having little or nothing to do with education, such as public swimming pools and golf courses?* If segregation in the public schools *creates a feeling of inferiority in African Americans, the same must be true for public facilities such as recreational facilities*[23] and bus systems.[24] Thus, the next crucial step in the process of desegregation was extending the concept of public facilities to many restaurants and hotels. Seven years after *Brown*, in *Burton v. Wilmington Parking Authority*, 365 U.S. 715 (1961), the Court ruled that a privately owned restaurant operated in a city parking garage could not turn away African American patrons. The city argued that the restaurant was privately owned and therefore the "state action" required to bring an equal protection claim was absent. However, the restaurant had acted under a state law that allowed the owner to refuse to serve persons who would be offensive to the majority of customers. Furthermore, the garage in which the restaurant was located was constructed with tax dollars and operated with a tax exemption. More than enough state action was present to classify the restaurant's policy as violative of the equal protection clause.

When President Kennedy took the oath of office in 1961, civil rights leaders anticipated great changes. But early in his term, Kennedy and his brother Robert, the attorney general, were nearly as cautious as President Eisenhower. Although Kennedy made a number or pro-civil rights appointments to the judiciary[25] and the executive branch, he was reluctant to ask Congress for a comprehensive civil rights act or to challenge recalcitrant southern officials head on.

However, President Kennedy could no longer remain passive in the face of outright noncompliance to federal court orders. In 1962, he changed his approach somewhat by calling out U.S. marshals to protect James Meredith from an armed mob intent on preventing him from being the first African American to enroll at the University of Mississippi. Setting the stage for presidential action and the eventual passage of the Civil Rights Act of 1964 was the Birmingham campaign of Martin Luther King, Jr., during the winter of 1962–1963. King's successful strategy of sit-ins at lunch counters and boycotts of white-owned businesses initially met with fierce violence. Peaceful demonstrations were countered with police brutality. City jails were filled to capacity. Television and newspaper images of the brutal treatment of ordinary black men and women created a rising tide of public sentiment in favor of federal action. Ultimately, King succeeded in desegregating the South's most segregated city. Spurred on by these successes, but at the same time frustrated by the rate of change, militant black leaders such as Malcolm X began to urge violent resistance to racism. The Kennedys preferred to work with southern leaders behind the scenes, but as the situation grew more tense, the president worked openly for the passage of a new civil rights act. After Kennedy was assassinated in November 1963, the act was quickly passed in 1964 under the leadership of President Johnson. Building on the Civil Rights Acts of 1957 and 1960, the 1964 law was designed to eradicate most forms of segregation and discrimination. It banned discrimination in voter registration and in public accommodations, and it authorized the federal government to bring lawsuits to desegregate schools and public facilities and to withhold federal funds from programs that were unfairly administered. The act further established sweeping protection against employment discrimination and set up a community relations service to mediate civil rights disputes. In 1965, Johnson deftly garnered support in Congress for a comprehensive voting rights act that empowered the federal government to attack the literacy tests and other obstacles to African

American registration and voting. By 1965, it appeared that the concept of equal protection set forth by the Warren Court in *Brown* was to be implemented in a uniform and enforceable manner.[26]

## Private Facilities

*Does the equal protection clause of the Fourteenth Amendment extend to privately owned motels, restaurants, and stores?*    There is little dispute that the freedom of association, right to privacy, and right to property empower me to turn you away from my house. Suppose that my restaurant and motel are adjacent or attached to my home. Don't I reserve the right to refuse you refreshment and lodging? Arguments of this kind were used to deny accommodations and service to African Americans traveling on business or vacation. Because of the uncertainty of finding lodgings in all parts of the country—not just the South—African Americans were often forced to sleep in their cars, stay with friends, or not travel at all. Can you imagine forgoing a potentially lucrative sales convention for fear of being denied lodging on account of race? Or saying to your family, "The only colored hotel in Ft. Lauderdale is booked up, so we have to go somewhere else on vacation this year." What legal mechanisms guard against this form of discrimination?

The Court addressed this complex issue in *Heart of Atlanta Motel v. United States*, 379 U.S. 241 (1964). The owner of an Atlanta motel in a busy section of town refused to rent rooms to blacks, contrary to Title II, section 201, of the Civil Rights Act of 1964. Based on Congress's power to regulate interstate commerce, including local activities having a bearing on commerce, Title II was enacted to remedy "the deprivation of personal dignity that surely accompanies denials of equal access to public establishments." Section 201 declared that the racially discriminatory operation of a motel of more than five rooms for rent or hire adversely affected interstate commerce. The owner of the motel challenged an injunction as well as the constitutionality of Title II on the grounds that the operation of the motel was of purely local concern, having nothing to do with Congress's interstate commerce power. The act, he contended, deprived him of liberty and property under the Fifth Amendment. The Court disagreed. Congress's power to promote interstate commerce found in Article I of the Constitution includes the power to regulate local activities related to that commerce in the states of origin and destination. In addition, Congress has a rational basis for finding that racial discrimination by motels affects commerce as well as for devising the means to eliminate such discrimination. The motel owner's right or personal liberty to select his guests as he sees fit was outweighed by the interests asserted in Title II. Second, since it was doubtful that the motel would suffer an economic loss as a result of the act, there were no grounds to claim that the act deprived the owner of liberty and property under the Fifth Amendment. Justice Clark concluded: "[T]he action of the Congress in the adoption of the Act as applied here to a motel which concededly serves interstate travelers is within the power granted it by the commerce clause of the Constitution, as interpreted by this Court for 140 years." Prior to passage of the Civil Rights Act, the Court had already ruled that the Interstate Commerce Act prohibited segregation in bus terminals and buses used in interstate transportation.[27]

In his concurring opinion, Justice Douglas was unhappy with the means by which the Court offered relief to the problem of private discrimination. He reasoned that the Court should have based its ruling not on the commerce clause (which was Congress's basis for the act) but on a broad reading of the Fourteenth Amendment. He wrote: "A decision based on the Fourteenth Amendment would have a more settling effect, making unnecessary litigation over whether a particular restaurant or inn is within the commerce definitions of the Act or whether a particular customer is an interstate traveler." Under Douglas's interpretation, the Civil Rights Act would apply to all customers in all public motels and restaurants, thereby "put[ting] an end to all obstructionist strategies and finally close one door on a bitter chapter in American history."

Some of the most poignant photographs from the early civil rights struggle were of young African Americans defying the "No Colored" signs at Woolworth's lunch counters. In *Katzenbach v. McClung*, 379 U.S. 294 (1964), argued at the same time as *Heart of Atlanta Motel*, the Court ruled that Ollie's Barbecue, a family-owned business in Birmingham, Alabama, fell within the aegis of the Civil Rights Act and therefore could not decline to serve black customers. Counsel for Alabama contended that the act could not be applied under the Fourteenth Amendment because the state was in no way involved in the restaurant's refusal to serve African Americans; it was a purely private decision. But the Court found a way to resolve the issue by focusing on how the refusal to serve a class or a race of people adversely affects the overall interstate sale of food and disrupts the interstate travel of blacks. Ollie's bought 46 percent of its food from out-of-state suppliers. By preventing blacks from buying prepared food from clean and easily accessible restaurants while on business or pleasure trips, the owners of Ollie's discouraged travel, obstructed interstate commerce, and prevented professional and skilled people from moving into a community.

One could argue that the total amount of business at Ollie's had little impact on interstate buying, selling, and transporting of food products, and it would be extremely difficult to show a correlation between Ollie's practices and the interstate flow of food. Nevertheless, the Court reasoned, if left unchecked, hundreds of such discriminatory establishments would certainly have a detrimental impact on interstate commerce and the national economy.

Why did the Court employ the interstate commerce argument rather than the equal protection clause to ban racial discrimination in hotels and restaurants? One reason was that in order to invoke the Fourteenth Amendment the plaintiff had to show state action. The Court could grant relief only if it could be shown that there had been some involvement of the government or agent of the government in the discriminatory action. This clearly placed private businesses beyond the scope of the Fourteenth Amendment. While the federal commerce power approach was perhaps tenuous and insensitive to human dignity, as Douglas felt, it did allow Congress and the courts to attack discrimination in all but the smallest, most isolated motels and eateries. In fact, at times the Court has had to stretch the concept of interstate commerce to ferret out discriminatory practices. Suppose that you use several hundred acres of your own property to build a segregated recreation area. Your park is in a remote area of the state, far from all major routes of travel and centers of economic activity. Would you be exempt from Title II of the Civil Rights Act? Probably not, since under *Daniel v. Paul*, 395 U.S. 298 (1969), Title II applies if any amount of food or goods sold at a private facility's snack bar came from out of state or if any of the park's visitors were from out of state. This line of reasoning makes it virtually impossible to circumvent the law.

But the Court did not feel constrained to rely on the state action doctrine or the interstate commerce argument to strike down private discrimination in the important case *Runyon v. McCrary*, 427 U.S. 160 (1976). Michael McCrary brought suit under the Civil Rights Act of 1866 (amended in 1970) against the Runyons, husband and wife proprietors of a private school that refused admission to African Americans. The Civil Rights Act provides that all persons within the jurisdiction of the United States shall have the same right in every state to make and enforce contracts as is enjoyed by white citizens. The Runyons argued that the act did not extend to the prerogative of private, commercially operated sectarian schools. But the Supreme Court ruled 7–2 that the act did prohibit racial discrimination in the making of private contracts. Since the Runyons' school was engaged in making and enforcing private contracts with the parents of students, their conduct of exclusion constituted a form of prohibited discrimination under the law. Justice Stewart based this conclusion on the fact that Congress had refused to reject an earlier Supreme Court ruling that the 1866 act afforded private-sector employees a right to sue employers for racial discrimination.[28] Congress was very clear in its desire to extend the act to private acts of racial discrimination.

Does this finding suggest that the need to guard against discrimination outweighs a person's rights of free association and privacy? Do parents have the right to send their children to schools of their choice even if those schools promote undesirable beliefs, such as the view that racial segregation is acceptable? According to Justice Stewart, the Runyons had the right to operate a private school that teaches racism, and parents had the right to send their children to such a school. But those rights in no way empowered the Runyons from excluding students on the basis of race. The case did not address whether a private organization could exclude on the basis of religion or sex. Stewart wrote: "[W]hile parents have a constitutional right to send their children to private schools that offer specialized instruction, they have no constitutional right to provide their children with private school education unfettered by reasonable government regulation."

Since private discrimination is far from being a settled area of law, the Court has come under intense political pressure to reexamine its ruling in *Runyon*. Although the Rehnquist Court narrowly reaffirmed *Runyon* in *Patterson v. McLean Credit Union*, 485 U.S. 617 (1988), it ruled 5–4 that under the Civil Rights Act of 1866, private employers could be held liable only for racial discrimination in hiring and firing and not for racial harassment in the workplace. Writing for the majority, Justice Kennedy refused to extend *Runyon*'s interpretation of the 1866 Civil Rights Act beyond making and enforcing the contract between employer and employee, thus forcing aggrieved employees to seek other legal remedies for racial discrimination on the job. Two of the dissenting justices in *Patterson*—Brennan and Marshall—have since retired and have been replaced by Justices Souter and Thomas.

## AFFIRMATIVE ACTIONS AND QUOTAS

Remedies such as busing and fixed race ratios among students and teachers in public schools represent measures that go beyond the mere prohibition of discrimination. Such measures are intended to actively bring about a degree of integration that normally would not have occurred even if the doors were open to all. Cases such as *Green* and *Swann* reflect this principle. Having used various federal and state civil rights statutes to pry open the doors of academia, civil rights advocates were hopeful that minorities would receive the same higher educational and professional opportunities available to whites. As more minorities entered the professions and gained economic and political clout, the last vestiges of segregation and discrimination would certainly disappear. But simply opening the doors to prominent graduate schools was not enough. Something was needed to help minority students overcome the cultural, academic, and financial obstacles to attending the nation's best universities. Federal financial aid programs, enacted during the Great Society programs of the Johnson years, further opened the doors to a more diverse population in the various professions. But because progress was so slow, various state and federal laws were enacted requiring institutions to take affirmative action beyond simple equal opportunity in order to promote minority enrollment in undergraduate and professional degree programs. Working from a broad grant of administrative discretion, universities and colleges devised a host of affirmative action programs aimed at implementing the principle of equal opportunity. The initial assumption was that equal opportunity means more than the absence of discrimination—it means taking positive steps to redress past discrimination, thus giving certain classes of people an opportunity to make up for lost time. Other justifications for affirmative action reflect utilitarian concerns that a vast untapped pool of human resources is underutilized or that the professions need to more closely reflect the pluralistic population of our society. For example, in 1970, when blacks made up 11.1 percent of the total population, the number of black physicians constituted only 2.2 percent of the total number of physicians, a percentage that had not changed in twenty years.[29]

While the ideals underlying race-based remedies are not particularly controversial, the various measures adopted to implement these ideals have generated acrimonious debate. Institutions have adopted measures ranging from using race or gender as one factor in a variety of admission or hiring criteria to a fixed number of slots (a quota) to be filled with members of underrepresented classes by a certain target date. But since there is a finite number of admissions slots or positions in a firm or an organization, some members of classes who are not underrepresented—such as white males—will not receive equal consideration. Thus, in the name of redressing past discrimination (compensatory justice), nonminority males are forced to suffer a form of discrimination. This has led many to charge that such preferential treatment constitutes reverse discrimination in violation of the equal protection clause of the Fourteenth Amendment and Title VI of the Civil Rights Act of 1964. Opponents of preferential treatment of minorities and women argue that the very form of discrimination that the courts set out to eliminate is proactively fostered by affirmative action programs. Persons who have never discriminated against anyone are made to suffer deprivations in the name of diversity on campus, societal discrimination, or compensatory justice. Even some minority members, such as Thomas Sowell, argue that affirmative action does more harm than good insofar as it engenders new reasons for African Americans and whites to resent each other and because it stigmatizes bright young African Americans and women as "affirmative action types" even though they would have succeeded without any kind of preferential treatment.

Proponents of affirmative action programs respond that after hundreds of years of societal discrimination, the least white males can do is tolerate a few years of inconvenience until racial and gender parity is achieved in the professions. Very few people will ever suffer any substantive injury as a result of affirmative action programs, and opposition to such programs is more a result of the rhetoric of conservative politicians than denial of admission or loss of a job. Many conservatives have gone on record that they are not opposed to all forms of affirmative action per se, but only programs that employ some form of quotas or "set asides."

***Does affirmative action constitute reverse discrimination and therefore represent an unconstitutional use of state power?***    The first definitive ruling on affirmative action was *Regents of the University of California v. Bakke*, 438 U.S. 265 (1978). The medical school of the University of California at Davis adopted two admissions policies: one for minority applicants and one for nonminorities. Under both policies, admissions decisions were based on overall and science grade point averages (GPA), Medical College Admissions Test (MCAT) scores, letters of recommendation, extracurricular activities, and other biographical data. However, under a special admissions program, a committee made up predominantly of members of minority groups asked applicants if they wished to be classified as "economically or educationally disadvantaged." If applicants fell into this category, they were neither required to meet a 2.5 GPA cutoff nor to compete against other applicants in the regular admissions process.

Eighty-four of the 100 slots allotted were filled through regular admissions criteria, but sixteen were set aside for members of disadvantaged groups. This policy resulted in the admission of some minority applicants who were of lower academic standing than many "regular" applicants who were denied admission. Over a period of four years, sixty-three minority students were admitted under the affirmative action program and forty-four under the regular admissions program. Although numerous disadvantaged whites applied, none were accepted. Alan Bakke, a white male, applied under the regular program in 1973 and again in 1974 but was denied admission. In both years minority applicants were admitted with substantially lower scores than Bakke's. After he was rejected for the second time, Bakke sued to compel the medical school to admit him, alleging that the special admissions policy excluded him solely on the basis of his race. He alleged that this treatment deprived him of his rights under the equal protection clause of the Fourteenth Amendment, the California Constitution, and Title VI of the Civil Rights Act of 1964, which maintains that no person shall, on the grounds of race or color, be excluded from any program receiving federal financial assistance.

The state trial court ruled that the special program violated Title VI as well as the federal and state constitutions. Because the minority applicants competed only against one another for a fixed number of slots that were allotted solely on the basis of race, the whole scheme was an unconstitutional racial quota system. But since there was no proof that Bakke would have been admitted even in the absence of the affirmative action program, the trial court did not order the university to take any action regarding Bakke's candidacy. The California Supreme Court agreed, adding that under the strict scrutiny standard, the special admissions program was not the least intrusive means of achieving the state's legitimate interest of integrating the medical profession and increasing the number of minority doctors willing to administer to minority patients. However, the state's high court ordered the medical school to admit Bakke.

In a highly complex and fragmented 5–4 decision, the U.S. Supreme Court upheld the state high court's order to admit Bakke as well as its invalidation of the medical school's affirmative action program, but it struck down the state court's ruling that race may not be taken into account as a factor in admissions decisions. Writing for a bloc of five justices who agreed only that the plan was unconstitutional, Justice Powell reasoned that under the equal protection clause, racial and ethnic classifications of any kind call for strict judicial scrutiny. He would not tolerate a double standard of equal protection.

Such classifications could exist only if they served some compelling state interest that could not be achieved by any other means. Although special admissions programs do classify on the basis of race, in some circumstances they are permissible if the goal of such programs is "sufficiently compelling." While the medical school's interest in racial diversity in the medical profession was compelling, its quota-based special admissions program was not the least intrusive means of achieving racial diversity. Justice Powell wrote:

> [A quota system] prefers the designate minority groups at the expense of other individuals who are totally foreclosed from competition for the 16 special admissions seats in every Medical School class. Because of that foreclosure, some individuals are excluded from enjoyment of a state-provided benefit—admission to the Medical School—they otherwise would receive.

Thus, because a racial classification was made, Bakke was deprived of an opportunity enjoyed by others solely on the basis of his race. He was subject to reverse discrimination. Minority status may be used as a consideration in the admissions decision, but it may not be the only consideration. If it is the sole consideration, then the medical school is sending the message that persons like Bakke need not even apply. Furthermore, the university's practice of admitting certain kinds of people solely to achieve a specified percentage was unconstitutional because it preferred members of one group for no reason other than race. This kind of policy constitutes an illegal quota. In the absence of an act of discrimination specifically proscribed by statute or the Constitution, a classification that punishes innocent individuals like Bakke in order to remedy something as amorphous as "societal discrimination" is unconstitutional. Unless a member of a minority group can demonstrate that he or she has been subject to an act of discrimination, a remedy as drastic as a quota cannot be used.

The medical school asserted that its goal of improving health care services to the community was sufficiently compelling to support the use of a racial classification, but the Court disagreed because the school could not prove that the special admissions policy was the only way of improving health care for minorities.

Isn't racial or ethnic diversity on campus a legitimate goal? If such a goal is legitimate, may race or sex be used as a factor in the admissions decision? The Court said yes, but not through a quota system. The appropriate way of achieving this goal is through an affirmative action program that uses race or sex as one factor among many in the admissions process. Powell applauded the system then used by Harvard University. Under the Harvard plan, when the admissions committee met to review a large "middle group" of applicants who were deemed admissible, race, sex, ethnicity, and geographical origin were some of the factors used to tip the scales in an applicant's favor. No quota existed for the number of African Americans or people from rural backgrounds that should be admitted, but being African American or a rural resident had a positive impact on the academically qualified candidates that the committee would favor. In such an affirmative action program, race, sex, or ethnicity may be deemed a plus, but the applicant was still judged in comparison to all other applicants of similar academic standing. This kind of plan treated the applicant as a person and not merely as an instrument through which a fixed percentage of minority students could be achieved. The prospective student who lost out on the last admissions slot to another candidate receiving a plus because of sex was not foreclosed from all consideration simply because he was male but rather because given all the factors—academic as well as nonacademic—his qualifications did not outweigh those of the female applicant. In contrast, under the Davis medical school plan, regardless of their qualifications, applicants not of the desired minority groups were completely foreclosed from consideration. A social benefit was withheld from them solely on the basis of race.

The University of California urged the Court to adopt a two-class theory of equal protection holding that the Fourteenth Amendment's equal protection guarantee protects only disadvantaged or underrepresented minorities. Thus, any reverse discrimination against the white majority was not suspect if it was benign in nature. Unlike invidious discrimination, benign discrimination advances a social good, such as the integration of the medical profession.

But the majority of the Court refused to embrace this formulation of the equal protection clause. Justice Powell reasoned that racial classifications of any sort are inherently suspect and call for strict scrutiny. Nothing in the Constitution supports the notion that persons may be asked to suffer "otherwise impermissible burdens" (i.e., discrimination) in the name of compensatory justice. Furthermore, the rights established by the Fourteenth Amendment are individual rights, not group rights. He wrote:

> The guarantees of the Fourteenth Amendment extend to all persons. Its language is explicit. . . . It is settled beyond question that the "rights created by the first section of the Fourteenth Amendment are, by its terms, guaranteed to the individual. The rights established are personal rights." *Shelly v. Kraemer*, 334 U.S. 1 [(1948)]. *The guarantee of equal protection cannot mean one thing when applied to one individual and something else when applied to a person of another color. If both are not accorded the same protection, then it is not equal* [emphasis added].

Why should Bakke have to bear the burden of redressing past wrongs not of his own making? If minority applicants could show that they suffered discrimination at the hands of the university or the state, then the Court might approve drastic measures to remedy an equal protection violation, as it had in *Swann*. But unlike cases such as *Brown* or *Swann*, neither the university nor Bakke was accused of discrimination. The university's special admissions program was not aimed at fighting acts of individual discrimination but at combating societal discrimination. Thus, race-based remedies are not permissible where such discrimination is alleged. Furthermore, Powell pointed out that as a matter of social policy, preferential programs may actually work against a disadvantaged group by reinforcing common stereotypes that certain groups cannot achieve success without special favors or protection.

Justices Burger, Rehnquist, Stewart, and Stevens—concurring in part and dissenting in part—joined in the judgment of the Court only insofar as it admitted Bakke to medical school and struck down the minority admissions policy. They refused to rule on whether race could ever be used as a factor in an admissions policy, but asserted that reverse discrimination is unconstitutional whether it is based on notions of compensatory justice or societal discrimination.

Another bloc of justices—Brennan, White, Marshall, and Blackmun—concurring in part and dissenting in part, concluded that the affirmative action plan at the Davis medical school was constitutional. They did not believe that the Civil Rights Act and the Fourteenth Amendment barred the preferential treatment of racial minorities as a means of remedying past societal discrimination. Brennan argued that without some preferential treatment the principles set forth in *Brown* could never be fully implemented. Therefore, the purpose of overcoming pervasive minority underrepresentation in the medical profession was sufficiently important to justify the university's use of quotas. In fact, Brennan did not see how the Davis plan differed significantly from the Harvard scheme touted by Powell. Brennan further argued that because there was a need for compensatory justice, a two-class equal protection analysis could be applied. Bakke, then, could not recover for reverse discrimination. Brennan reasoned that the inconvenience suffered by Bakke was in no way like that suffered by African Americans. Bakke was neither stamped as inferior nor segregated from the rest of society. If anything, he was advantaged by past societal discrimination. Unlike discrimination against racial minorities, the use of racial preferences for remedial purposes does not inflict a pervasive injury upon individual whites in such a way that wherever they go or whatever they do there is a significant likelihood that they will be treated as second-class citizens. Furthermore, Brennan added, it was not as if the program admitted applicants who were substantially less qualified than nonminority applicants. All were more or less qualified applicants to the program.

If we can glean anything from this fractious opinion it is that the issue was far from resolved. The Court did not promulgate any one model of affirmative action nor did it preclude the use of quotas in cases where past discrimination could be shown. *Bakke* allowed universities and organizations to use affirmative action but at the same time established standing for white males to bring reverse discrimination suits if affirmative action was taken too far. If anything, *Bakke* left university administrators, state agencies, and private businesses with a great deal of discretion. As a result, a wide variety of preferential hiring and admission programs have been adopted.

*How much discretion do schools, colleges, or governmental entities have in formulating preferential admissions or hiring policies? At what point do such policies run afoul of the Constitution? Are there any situations that justify quotas?* Suppose that a formerly segregated city has taken all measures available to combat race discrimination in its allocation of jobs, benefits, and services, Equal opportunity rules are enacted and violators vigorously prosecuted. Five out of seven seats on the city council are filled by African Americans. However, even in this ideal scenario, absent any intentional or de jure discrimination, the lingering effects of past discrimination are evidenced by the fact that very few blacks work for the city and no minority-owned businesses receive contracts from the city to pave roads, build airports, or do electrical work. If the city decides that this represents a problem worthy of its attention, what kinds of preferential schemes may the city adopt without running afoul of the law? The Rehnquist Court addressed this question in the *City of Richmond v. J. A. Croson*, 488 U.S. 469 (1989).

The case originated in April 1983 when Richmond, Virginia, adopted the Minority Business Utilization Plan requiring contractors to whom the city awarded construction contracts to subcontract at least 30 percent of the dollar amount of the contract to one or more minority-owned contractors, called minority business enterprises (MBEs). Typically, contractors utilize numerous subcontractors at various stages of a project. The 30 percent set-aside did not apply to city contracts awarded to minority-owned contractors. The city's remedial plan was in response to the small number of contracts (less than 1 percent) awarded from 1978 to 1983 to minority-owned businesses in a city that was 50 percent African American. It was also in response to the fact that there were virtually no minority businesses belonging to any of the city's various contractors' associations, which collectively wielded considerable political clout in city politics. Although there was no direct evidence of race discrimination on the part of the city in awarding contracts, the plan was enacted to remedy past discrimination as evidenced by the significantly lower number of contracts awarded to minorities.

In September 1983, the city awarded a contract to the J. A. Croson Company, a heating and plumbing contractor. The company then contacted five or six MBEs to work as subcontractors, but none expressed an interest in the project. Because Croson had not received any MBE bids, he filed a request for a waiver of the 30 percent set-aside. Twenty-one days after the deadline, an MBE finally submitted a bid, but the bid pushed the total cost of the project significantly higher than the overall bid that the city had accepted from Croson. In the end, the city decided to rebid the project and the Croson Company sued the city, challenging the constitutionality of the plan. Opponents of the plan argued that the disparity between the number of contracts awarded to MBEs and the total minority population of Richmond had little value in determining whether there was evidence of discrimination. Since there was no real evidence of direct race discrimination in awarding the contracts, the quota remedy was unconstitutional. A federal district court upheld the city's plan, but the court of appeals struck down the set-aside program as violative of the equal protection clause of the Fourteenth Amendment.

In *Croson*, the Supreme Court affirmed the decision of the court of appeals, ruling that the city of Richmond must limit any race-based remedies, such as the set-asides, to only those aimed at eradicating the effects of its own prior discrimination. Where no prior discrimination could be shown, race-based remedies were unconstitutional. Had the city shown that it was a participant in a system of racial exclusion practiced by the local construction industry, then it could have used set-aside plans to dismantle such a system. The Court would not accept the argument that because the effects of past discrimination could still be seen, the city was justified in depriving nonminorities of equal protection. Five of the nine seats on the city council were held by African Americans. O'Connor would not accept the two-class equal protection argument advocated by Justices Marshall and Brennan. She wrote:

> Classifications based on race carry a danger of stigmatic harm. Unless they are strictly reserved for remedial settings, they may in fact promote notions of racial inferiority and lead to a politics of racial hostility. We thus affirm the view expressed by the plurality in *Wygant* that *the standard of review under the Equal Protection Clause is not dependent on the race of those burdened or benefited by a particular classification* [emphasis added].

O'Connor reiterated what the Court expressed in *Bakke*: The guarantee of equal protection cannot mean one thing when applied to a member of a minority group and another thing when applied to a person of a nonminority group. The level of judicial scrutiny that the Court must apply should not vary according to the ability of different groups to "defend their interests in the representative process." In sum, since there was no evidence of discrimination in the construction industry, the city failed to demonstrate a compelling interest in awarding contracts on the basis of race.

**Are race-based remedies ever permissible?**  O'Connor pointed out that had the city demonstrated that nonminority contractors were systematically excluding minority businesses from subcontracting opportunities, then the city could have taken action. Or, if it could be shown that there was a statistically significant disparity between the number of qualified minority contractors willing and able to provide a particular service and the number of contractors actually engaged by the city or by the city's prime contractor, then an action for discrimination could be filed. Under these circumstances, the city could dismantle the closed system by taking action against those who discriminated. Only in the extreme case, wrote O'Connor, can some form of "narrowly tailored racial preference" be used to break down the pattern of deliberate discrimination.

Concurring, Scalia concluded that strict scrutiny must be applied to *all* racial classifications. Therefore, no racial quotas or preferences are allowed except to eliminate a system of intentional discrimination.

Dissenting, Justice Marshall, joined by Brennan and Blackmun, stated that *Croson* was a "deliberate and giant step" backward in the Court's affirmative action jurisprudence. They believed that race-conscious classifications designed to redress past discrimination are constitutional. The city of Richmond may not be intentionally discriminating against minorities, but its routine spending decisions and interactions with private companies might be "reinforcing and perpetuating" the exclusionary effects of past discrimination. Marshall attacked the majority for paying lip service to remedying the effects of past discrimination. He wrote:

> But our decisions have often emphasized the danger of the government tacitly adopting, encouraging, or furthering racial discrimination even by its own routine operations. . . . When government channels all of its contracting funds to a white-dominated community of established contractors whose racial homogeneity is the product of private discrimination, it does more than place its imprimatur on the practices which forged and which continue to define that community.

Unlike the majority, Marshall argued that the interest in preventing companies working under city contract from discriminating against minority contractors is as strong as the interest in eliminating private discrimination by restaurants and motels. Marshall reiterated his position that a two-class or two-tier theory of equal protection is constitutional. In sum, racial classifications drawn on the presumption that blacks are inferior to whites are unconstitutional; in contrast, racial classifications drawn for the purpose of remedying the effects of discrimination against blacks are constitutional because they serve a compelling governmental interest in compensating for past injustices.

In 1971, minorities owned only ten of the approximately 7,500 radio stations in the country and none of the more than 1,000 television stations. In 1977, in an attempt to increase the "diversity of broadcast viewpoint," the Federal Communications Commission (FCC) adopted a policy aimed at encouraging minority ownership in the broadcast industry. Although the FCC found no overt discrimination in the industry, very few minorities were willing or able to enter the broadcasting business. The FCC reasoned that unless minorities are encouraged to enter mainstream commercial broadcasting, a large part of the American public will remain underserved and the larger nonminority audience will be deprived of the minority viewpoint. One year after the plan had been implemented, minorities still owned less than 1 percent of the nation's radio and television stations even though they constituted one-fifth of the U.S. population. By 1986, minorities owned 2.1 percent of the 11,000 radio and television stations in the United States.

The FCC's affirmative action plan used minority status as one factor among several in deliberations to grant new licenses. Minority ownership and day-to-day operation were considered pluses to be weighed together with other relevant factors. Metro Broadcasting, Inc. challenged this plan on the grounds that contrary to the Court's past affirmative action rulings, the FCC used unconstitutional race-conscious measures not justified by a compelling governmental interest. But the Supreme Court disagreed and upheld the FCC plan in *Metro Broadcasting, Inc. v. FCC*, 497 U.S. 547 (1990). The Court narrowly sustained (5–4) the use of preferential treatment in awarding radio and television licenses. Writing for the bare majority, Justice Brennan reasoned that Congress has the power to employ race-based measures even if they are not remedies to past discrimination. Congress and the FCC did not justify the affirmative action policy strictly as a remedy for past discrimination but as a way of promoting programming diversity in two mediums having a limited number of frequencies and dominated by a majority viewpoint. Thus, the policy serves a legitimate governmental objective that is in many ways independent of the issue of discrimination. Even though the plan classified persons on the basis of race, Brennan refused to apply strict scrutiny. Recall that for Brennan, racial classifications were suspect only when minorities were adversely affected. His conservative colleagues, however, contended that all classifications were suspect.

Brennan further reasoned that just as a "diverse student body" contributing to a "robust exchange of ideas" is a constitutionally permissible goal on which race-based university admissions programs are based, the diversity of views and information on radio and television serves important First Amendment values. In order to achieve that diversity, minority ownership must be fostered. Brennan concluded that even if the FCC's affirmative action plan imposes a minor burden on nonminorities, it is a burden that innocent persons must sometimes bear in order to eradicate racial discrimination.

Dissenting, Justice O'Connor—joined by Rehnquist, Kennedy, and Scalia—argued that the FCC policy violated the equal protection clause by not treating applicants for licenses as individuals judged on their own merits, but merely as a means to bring about some vague notion of racial parity in broadcasting. In doing so, O'Connor charged, the majority departed from the established requirement that racial classifications are permissible only if they are "necessary and narrowly tailored to achieve a compelling state interest." What the FCC had done was provide benefits to some members of society and deny benefits to others solely on the basis of race or ethnicity.

The sole proponents of the two-tiered theory of equal protection—Brennan, Marshall, and Blackmun—never mustered enough votes to thwart the doctrine of reverse discrimination, which is now a well-established constitutional doctrine. Absent a second liberal revolution on the Supreme Court or lower federal courts, the two-tiered theory of equal protection will fade into history. The predominant judicial philosophy on the Court in 2002 makes it very difficult to justify preferential treatment in the absence of direct evidence of intentional discrimination. In a passage that set the tone for later rulings on affirmative action, Justice O'Connor wrote in *Metro Broadcasting:*

> Except in the narrowest of circumstances, the Constitution bars such racial classifications as a denial to particular individuals, of any race or ethnicity, of "the equal protection of the laws." The dangers of such classifications are clear. They endorse race-based reasoning and the conception of a Nation divided into racial blocs, thus contributing to an escalation of racial hostility and conflict. Such policies may embody stereotypes that treat individuals as the product of their race, evaluating their thoughts and efforts—their very worth as citizens—according to a criterion barred to the government by history and the Constitution.

By 1991 a conservative majority had solidified on the Court. That year also marked the retirement of Justice Brennan—once called the most powerful liberal in America—who retired from the Court after serving thirty-four years. President

George H. W. Bush filled the vacancy with David Souter, a moderately conservative justice from the New Hampshire Supreme Court. President Bush had an opportunity to make a second appointment when Justice Thurgood Marshall, the first African American justice, announced his retirement in 1991. Bush then appointed Clarence Thomas, also an African American, who served as a chair of the Equal Employment Opportunity Commission (EEOC) during the Reagan administration. Bush's appointments of Souter and Thomas promised two more voices of opposition to affirmative action.

In 1993, Justice Byron White, an opponent of most affirmative action programs, retired after serving thirty-one years on the Court. His successor, Ruth Bader Ginsburg, was named by President Clinton in 1993. Clinton also appointed Stephen Breyer in 1994, replacing retiring Justice Harry Blackmun. Both Ginsburg and Breyer were expected to be supporters of moderate affirmative action plans.

The newly configured Court had its first opportunity to address affirmative action in *Adarand Constructors, Inc. v. Pena*, 515 U.S. 200 (1995). The case originated in 1989, when Mountain Gravel and Construction Company was awarded a lucrative construction contract from the Central Federal Lands Highway Division (CFLHD), which is part of the U.S. Department of Transportation (DOT). The terms of the contract provided that Mountain Gravel would receive additional compensation in accordance with the Small Business Act if it hired subcontractors certified as small businesses owned by "socially and economically disadvantaged individuals." "Socially disadvantaged" is defined as having been subjected to racial or ethnic prejudice or cultural bias simply because of membership in a group without regard to individual qualities. "Economically disadvantaged" individuals are those who have been unable to compete in the free enterprise system due to "diminished capital and credit opportunities" that were a result of being socially disadvantaged. This latter classification had been adopted by the government with the hope of avoiding claims of reverse racial discrimination.

The contract that led to the dispute was the result of one provision of a federal highway project stipulating that not less than 10 percent of highway construction funds go to construction companies owned by minorities and women who have submitted a bid on the contact. Mountain Gravel then solicited bids from subcontractors for the guardrail portion of the project. Although Adarand, a Colorado-based highway construction company, submitted the lowest bid, Mountain Gravel awarded the subcontract to Gonzales Construction Company, a minority-owned business. Mountain Gravel would have accepted Adarand's low bid had it not been for the additional compensation it received from DOT for hiring Gonzales instead.

After losing the guardrail contract to Gonzales, Adarand filed suit in the U.S. district court, claiming that the program was unconstitutionally race-based and seeking to end all such programs that would affect the company in the future. Citing *Metro Broadcasting*, the district court rejected Adarand's argument and granted the government's motion to drop the case. The U.S. court of appeals affirmed, upholding the use of the subcontractor compensation clause as an appropriate means of advancing a legitimate governmental interest. The U.S. Supreme Court disagreed, reversing the lower courts' rulings.

The issues in *Adarand* were threefold. First, did Adarand have standing to sue to prevent the future application of the subcontractor compensation clause? The Court said yes. Since Adarand bids on every guardrail project in Colorado, sometime in the near future it would bid on another government contract that offers financial incentives for hiring disadvantaged contractors. Second, since Adarand sued the federal government, it based its action on the due process clause of the Fifth Amendment rather than on the equal protection clause of the Fourteenth Amendment. Does the Fifth Amendment contain an equal protection clause that protects against discriminatory legislation passed by Congress? The Court said yes, since it has been long-established that equal protection obligations imposed by the Fifth and Fourteenth Amendments are the same.

Third, and most importantly, is the program actually based on the status of being disadvantaged, as the government argued, or on race? If the program is not based on race, then it is subject to the lowest level of judicial scrutiny and is a constitutional means of advancing an important governmental interest. If it is race-based, the Court will apply a much stricter form of scrutiny, demanding that the program advances a compelling governmental interest.

As we have seen, certain narrowly tailored programs that are designed to remedy the effects of past discrimination are permitted. The issue here is whether the Fourteenth Amendment requires strict scrutiny of all raced-based actions by government. If it does, then few, if any, of these remedies can survive.

Writing for the 5–4 majority, Justice O'Connor argued that the lower courts inappropriately relied on *Metro Broadcasting* to decide the case. She argued that *Metro* incorrectly departed from *Croson* by abandoning strict scrutiny for intermediate scrutiny. In *Croson*, the Court ruled that any person of any race has the right to demand that any governmental racial classification that subjects a person to unequal treatment be subjected to strict scrutiny. So, in *Adarand*, the Court returned to *Croson* rather than breaking new ground. Throwing out *Metro*, the Court ruled that all affirmative action programs will henceforth be analyzed under strict scrutiny and be permitted only if they are narrowly tailored measures that further compelling governmental interests.

***How do we determine if affirmative action programs are constitutional? It is not enough to say that the project is benign—that it has good intentions and makes up for past wrongs?***    Government must clearly articulate the exact need for the program and then tailor the program to meet the need. In other words, the Court would be more likely support a narrow, or limited, affirmative action policy where there is a record of "pervasive, systematic, and obstinate" discriminatory conduct.[30]

Although Justice Scalia was in the majority, he wrote separately to categorically reject any instance where the government has a compelling interest in discriminating on the basis of race in order to "make up" for past discrimination. He argued that individuals who have been wronged by unlawful racial discrimination should be "made whole," but under our Constitution there can be no such thing as a "creditor or debtor race." He stated: "In the eyes of government, we are just one race here. It is American."

In a brief but vitriolic concurring opinion, Justice Thomas took the opposite view of his predecessor Thurgood Marshall. Thomas argued that not only do these remedial racial preferences violate the principle of equal protection, they also exacerbate racism in the form of liberal paternalism, teaching Americans that minorities are so chronically handicapped that they cannot compete "without their patronizing indulgence."

Thomas has come to be a spokesman, of sorts, for the evils of affirmative action. He believes that such programs engender attitudes of superiority among nonminorities who must "care" for disadvantaged groups and feelings of resentment by those who are injured by such programs; in addition, they stamp minorities with a badge of inferiority. In his opinions as well is in speeches, Thomas argues that rulings like that in *Adarand* only exacerbate rather than reduce racial prejudice and will delay the time when race becomes truly irrelevant or insignificant.

The dissenting justices attacked the majority justices' view that affirmative action is just another form of racism and their logic that equated the desire to foster equality in society by using race-based preferences with the same racist sentiments underlying segregation and Jim Crow. The minor measures at issue in *Adarand* are not racist; nor do they promote racism, as Justice Thomas believes. It is twisted logic to equate these benign forms of discrimination that enable a small number of newcomers to enter the marketplace with racism, reverse or otherwise.

The dissenters also believed that the Court should have upheld the programs because they were a good-faith effort by the government to create an affirmative action program based not on race or sex but on social or economic status. Indeed, a minority contractor is disqualified from consideration if he or she was not economically or socially disadvantaged. Unlike earlier set-asides, the preference program in *Adarand* was designed to overcome social and economic disadvantages that are usually associated with race. And, unlike earlier programs, the new program did not contain a quota or numerical goal. The dissenters also dismissed as naïve Justice Scalia's assertion that we are just one race—Americans—in the face of the reality that minorities still encounter discriminatory treatment by employers, realtors, and banks, as well as contract-granting cities or agencies.

## *Hopwood* and Race-Based College Admission Decisions

***What about race-based admission decisions by colleges and universities intended to promote a more diverse student body?*** The U.S. Supreme Court has not addressed that issue directly since *Bakke*. However, the issue has surfaced in lower federal courts around the country. In *Hopwood v. State of Texas* (78 F.3d 932 (1996)),[31] the U.S. Court of Appeals for the Fifth Circuit relied on *Adarand* in its ruling that race-based programs can be only a narrowly constructed remedy to a specific instance of discrimination and not a means to promote diversity. In that controversial case, affirmative action in college admissions was handed a major setback when the Supreme Court refused to hear a challenge to the appeals court's ruling striking down a race-based admission policy at the University of Texas (UT) Law School.

To promote diversity, the law school adopted a segregated application evaluation process in order to admit more African Americans and Mexican Americans.

When the admissions office received an application it was color-coded according to race, and minority applicants were then reviewed for admission using lower scores than the scores used for white applicants.

Cheryl Hopwood and three other white residents of Texas applied for admission in 1992. Their applications were rejected while minorities with significantly lower scores were admitted to the program. Hopwood then challenged the constitutionality of the UT plan on the grounds that any consideration of race or ethnicity by the law school for the purpose of achieving a diverse study body is unconstitutional under the Fourteenth Amendment. Relying on the fractious *Bakke* ruling, a federal district court upheld the race-based admissions plan. However, the court of appeals struck it down, holding that the law school presented no compelling justification under the Constitution or Supreme Court precedent that allows it to elevate some races over others even for the purpose of correcting the racial imbalance in the student body. The appeals court argued that *Adarand* had superceded *Bakke* and that no case since *Bakke* has accepted "diversity" as a compelling enough state interest to justify racial classifications.

Circuit Court Judge Jerry Smith wrote that the classification of persons on the basis of race frustrates rather than promotes the goals of equal protection and that "we see the caselaw as sufficiently established that the use of ethnic diversity simply to achieve racial heterogeneity, even as part of the consideration of a number of factors, is unconstitutional."

Judge Smith was sensitive to the fact that a large number of colleges and universities in Texas are genuinely committed to the goal of a diverse student body. Therefore, he suggested that while the use of race per se is not permitted, state-supported schools may consider a range of factors ("some of which may have some correlation with race") in making admissions decisions. Among such factors are whether an applicant's parents attended college or the applicant's socioeconomic background.

In sum, the only way to use race as a consideration in the admissions process is if it is found that "past segregation has present effects." If this is true, then the legislature would have to determine the extent of those effects and then create a narrow and limited remedy that is directly related to past harms—"to limit carefully the 'plus' given to minority applicants to remedy that harm."

*So, are affirmative action programs of any kind constitutionally permissible after* **Croson, Adarand,** *and* **Hopwood?**    Yes, but only on a very limited basis. A governmental program that calls for some type of racial preference could be used if it is proved that a public or private agency or business intentionally discriminated against a minority group. Unfortunately, the Court does not provide examples of a specific instance where affirmative action can be used. It says only that such policies are permissible if they are aimed at eradicating the effects of prior intentional discrimination by an organization, company, or city and that the policies must be narrowly tailored. Justice O'Connor has recognized the unfortunate persistence of both the "practice and lingering effects of racial discrimination" and has noted that government "is not disqualified from acting in response to it." So, unless Congress or state legislatures abolish affirmative action outright, some limited forms of race- and gender-based programs will probably persist for some time. The question is what forms such policies will be allowed to take.

Had President Clinton made a third appointment to the Court or had Vice President Gore won in the 2000 election we might have witnessed a Court that was marginally more supportive of affirmative action. But since it is likely that the Court will grow even more conservative during the tenure of President George W. Bush—since he will have the opportunity to appoint two or three new justices—we should not expect *Adarand* or *Hopwood* to be overturned or dramatically modified. Yet, the issue will not go away. Affirmative action still draws strong support from the African American community, over 90 percent of which voted for Al Gore in the 2000 election. Secretary of State Colin Powell, an African American who is a Republican, has publicly endorsed limited forms of affirmative action. Many local and state agencies, universities and colleges, and corporations still tenaciously cling to affirmative action policies.

The debate reveals much not only about race relations in the United States but also about our apparent inability to reach a consensus on the legitimate scope of governmental intervention in economic and social relations. Nevertheless, as we enter a new phase of the civil rights epoch, we cannot simply rely on solutions that are nearly twenty-five years old. We must challenge ourselves to develop new and imaginative ways to guarantee and advance equal opportunity in an increasingly diverse and competitive society.

## SEX DISCRIMINATION

While organized political and legal efforts to eliminate sex discrimination began well before the end of the nineteenth century, in many respects the true revolution in women's rights occurred only within the last three decades. Indeed, many professional women in their twenties and early thirties have reaped the rewards of women's liberation and the feminist movement without much awareness of the battles that were fought while they were babies. Much like the civil rights movement, the evolution of women's rights in the 1960s and 1970s took place within a context of deeply rooted paternalism, stereotyping, and resentment. Regardless of one's interpretation of the feminist movement and the role of women in society, there is little doubt that there has been a long and tragic history of sex discrimination in the United States.[32]

Until quite recently, women who sought to enter the world of arts and letters, law, politics, and commerce were shut out by a variety of statutes and court decisions reflecting centuries of what has been called "romantic paternalism." With the exception of the right to vote, granted by the Nineteenth Amendment in 1920, women were barred from virtually all professional activities by numerous laws reinforcing stereotypical distinctions between men and women. Even the Supreme Court reflected the prejudices of the day and openly fostered not only notions of "the lesser man" but also binding legal distinctions based on "natural law." Justice Joseph Bradley wrote in 1873:

> Man is, or should be, woman's protector and defender. The natural and proper timidity and delicacy which belongs to the female sex evidently unfits it for many of the occupations of civil life. The constitution of the family organization, which is

founded in the divine ordinance, as well as in the nature of things, indicates the domestic sphere as that which properly belongs to the domain and functions of womanhood. The harmony . . . of interests and views which belong, or should belong, to the family institution is repugnant to the idea of a woman adopting a distinct and independent career from that of her husband. . . . The paramount destiny and mission of woman are to fulfill the noble and benign offices of wife and mother.[33]

Great strides were made in securing opportunities and rights for women after World War II, but overt government-sponsored discrimination in education, the workplace, and the political arena existed until the mid-1970s. Although sex-based classifications were by no means completely eliminated by early reforms, the Equal Pay Act of 1963 and Title VII of the Civil Rights Act of 1964 established the legal means for women to take action against any employer or labor union covered by the act that discriminated on the basis of sex. The ill-fated Equal Rights Amendment, passed by Congress in 1972, was intended to end sex discrimination once and for all. Supported by at least two thirds of the states, the ERA read: "Equality of rights under the law shall not be denied by the United States or any state on account of sex." However, influential conservative organizations—such as the National Council of Catholic Women, the Mormons, and Phyllis Schlafly's Eagle Forum—were able to mobilize enough support in state legislatures to prevent the ERA's ratification by three fourths of the states.[34] But the Supreme Court's ruling in *Reed v. Reed*, 404 U.S. 71 (1971), more than compensated for the defeat of the ERA.

*Reed* was the first in a long string of rulings attacking sex discrimination under the equal protection clause of the Fourteenth Amendment. The case originated on March 29, 1967, when Richard Reed, the adopted son of Sally and Cecil Reed, died in Ada County, Idaho, without leaving a will. Sally Reed filed a petition seeking to be appointed administrator of her son's estate, which amounted to less than $1,000. Her petition was denied under an Idaho law stipulating that when two individuals otherwise equally entitled to be administrator seek appointment, the male must be preferred to the female. The state did not deny this power to women altogether, but gave preference to men when both were equally entitled. For example, a wife of a husband who dies intestate (without will) has a preference over a son, brother, father, or any male relative, but in the case of a brother and sister, the brother would be preferred.

Sally Reed challenged the law on the grounds that it violated the equal protection clause of the Fourteenth Amendment by giving a mandatory preference to males over females without regard to their individual qualifications as potential estate administrators. A state district court ruled in her favor, but the Idaho Supreme Court reversed. On appeal, the U.S. Supreme Court overturned the law, concluding that Idaho's arbitrary preference of males established a classification subject to scrutiny under the equal protection clause. The Court did not employ strict scrutiny, as in race-based classifications, or reasonableness, the lowest level of scrutiny that is normally applied to non-race-based distinctions. Instead, it created a middle tier of scrutiny called "intermediate," or "close," scrutiny for sex-based classifications. Recall that under the logic of *Brown*, when a law creates a suspect classification (different treatment on account of race), the state must show a compelling reason for such a law and demonstrate that the classification is necessarily related to the state's objective in enacting the law. If less burdensome means to achieve that objective are available, the equal protection clause requires that they be used. Minimal scrutiny, or the reasonableness test, is applied where race or fundamental rights are not involved or where mutable characteristics, such as wealth or age, are the basis for the classification. Under minimal scrutiny, the state must show only that the classification is rational or that it serves a legitimate interest, such as prohibiting persons under age twenty-one from drinking alcohol.

Idaho based its statute not on any desire to exclude women from the administration of estates, but on what it thought to be a reasonable assumption that women had less experience than men with legal and business affairs. In a terse though unanimous opinion, the Court found the preference for men to be arbitrary and in violation of the equal protection clause of the Fourteenth Amendment. Although the amendment does not deny the states the power to treat different classes of persons in different ways, it does prohibit classification on an irrational basis—on "criteria wholly unrelated to the objective of that statute." The classification must bear a substantial relation to the objective of the legislation, so that all persons similarly situated are treated alike. What was the objective of the Idaho statute? Cecil Reed argued that the mandatory preference for male applicants was reasonable, since "men [are] as a rule more conversant with business affairs than . . . women." Perhaps at the time the law was passed that assumption was correct, but in modern times, presumably due to the greater longevity of women, surviving widows administer a large number of estates, both intestate and under wills of their departed spouses. Thus, if you give preference to a man without first demonstrating that a women is incompetent to serve as administrator of an estate, then you are providing "dissimilar treatment for men and women who are . . . similarly situated." Chief Justice Burger wrote:

> To give a mandatory preference to members of either sex over members of the other, merely to accomplish the elimination of hearings on the merits [of who is best suited to become administrator] is to make the very kind of arbitrary legislative choice forbidden by the Equal Protection Clause of the Fourteenth Amendment; and whatever may be said as to the positive values of avoiding intrafamily controversy, the choice in this context may not lawfully be mandated solely on the basis of sex.

Without fanfare or any explicit acknowledgment of this historic accomplishment, the Court moved sex-based classifications from minimum judicial scrutiny toward strict scrutiny. Two years later, in *Frontiero v. Richardson*, 411 U.S. 677 (1973), the Court would have to hammer out the details of its new equal protection theory and decide whether or not to elevate sex to the suspect category along with race.

Sharon Frontiero, an officer in the U.S. Air Force, challenged an act of Congress stipulating that wives of male armed forces personnel are automatically considered dependents for purposes of increased housing and medical benefits, but that the husbands of female personnel are not considered dependents unless they are dependent on their wives for more than 50 percent of their support. Frontiero had to prove to the Air Force that her husband was her dependent while the female spouses of her male colleagues automatically received benefits. Frontiero's husband did not qualify as her dependent because he was receiving veterans benefits while attending college. Thus, the regulation was based on the assumption that since the husband was the primary breadwinner of the family, the couple did not need the same benefits as a traditional married couple. Since benefit packages are considered part of one's overall compensation, women members of the armed forces whose husbands worked full-time received less overall compensation than their male counterparts. *Does this kind of unequal treatment constitute unconstitutional discrimination against servicewomen?* Since Frontiero was suing the secretary of defense, an agent of the federal government, the case was brought on due process grounds under the Fifth Amendment, as in *Bolling v. Sharpe*, rather than under the equal protection clause of the Fourteenth Amendment.

Striking down the benefits scheme, the Court held 8–1 that classifications based on sex are suspect and are to receive the same level of scrutiny as those based on race,[35] alienage,[36] and national origin.[37] Since sex, like race and national origin, is an immutable characteristic determined by nature or chance, the imposition of special burdens on a particular sex—solely because of sex—constitutes an arbitrary distinction in violation of the equal protection clause. Like race, sex is different from non-suspect statuses, such as intelligence, age, or physical limitations, because it "frequently bears no relation to ability to perform or contribute to society." Legal distinctions between the sexes will often have the effect of relegating an entire class of people to inferior status without regard to the abilities of its individual members.

The government's rationale for the dual set of qualifications was based on the breadwinner theory, which assumes that wives in our society are more often dependent on their husbands than husbands are on their wives. But to satisfy the standards of strict scrutiny, the government cannot merely cite tradition—it must show some rational purpose for the regulation. For example, it must be shown that it is administratively simpler and more cost efficient to have this dual standard than to apply the same dependency requirement to all spouses. In fact, many of the wives who automatically receive benefits would fail to qualify under the 50 percent rule. Justice Brennan concluded:

> [Our] prior decisions make clear that, although efficacious administration of governmental programs is not without some importance, "the Constitution recognizes higher values than speed and efficiency." . . . And when we enter the realm of "strict scrutiny," there can be no doubt that "administrative convenience" is not a shibboleth, the mere recitation of which dictates constitutionality.

Not all of the justices accepted the position that all sex-based classifications are unconstitutional. In his concurring opinion, Justice Powell agreed that the challenged statute was unconstitutional, but rejected Brennan's view that all classifications based on sex, like those classifications based on race, are inherently suspect and must be subject to strict scrutiny. For Powell, the Court's ruling in *Reed v. Reed* offered adequate relief to Frontiero without adding sex to the group of classifications that are inherently suspect. Justices Powell and Blackmun, as well as Chief Justice

Burger, were satisfied that the equal rights amendment, pending ratification by the states at that time, would resolve the problem without the Court's decree. However, the ERA was never ratified, and support for applying strict scrutiny for sex-based classifications has never garnered support of a majority of justices.

*May legislatures create legal distinctions between men and women if such distinctions are based not on some outdated stereotype but on a factual and measurable difference between men and women?* For example, may the state prohibit women from working in environments that could prove dangerous to them if they become pregnant? Wouldn't such a law be based solely on biology rather than on social prejudice? Statistics show that among drivers between the ages of sixteen and twenty-five, fewer women than men are involved in serious traffic accidents and women are less likely to drive while intoxicated. Based on these findings, wouldn't it be reasonable for a state to allow women to drive at age sixteen, but prohibit men from driving until they reach age eighteen? Would this differentiated driving age requirement pass muster under the equal protection clause?

Oklahoma sought to promote the important interest of highway safety by enacting a statute prohibiting the sale of 3.2 percent beer to males under age twenty-one and to females under age eighteen. The law was based on statistical evidence showing that eighteen-to-twenty-year-old male arrests for driving while intoxicated significantly exceeded female arrests for the same age group. Thus, the question in *Craig v. Boren*, 429 U.S. 190 (1976), was whether such a sex-based differentiation denies males from eighteen to twenty-one years of age equal protection under the Fourteenth Amendment.

According to the Court's rulings in *Reed* and subsequent cases, to withstand a constitutional challenge, sex-based classifications must serve important governmental objectives and must be substantially related to those objectives. Reducing the number of traffic fatalities is clearly an important objective; and a differentiated drinking age is rationally related to that objective. The Court recognized that although the law advanced the important state objective of saving lives on the state's highways, it ruled 7–2 that the classification was not substantially related to the achievement of that goal. In other words, there were less restrictive ways of promoting highway safety than creating a differentiated drinking age. Writing for the majority, Justice Brennan would not countenance the use of a sex-based classification as a means of regulating drinking and driving. Surely there had to be a better way. Furthermore, to limit the protection of the Fourteenth Amendment solely on the basis of a few (possibly flawed) statistical studies was simply unacceptable. Thus, applying the intermediate level of scrutiny to the Oklahoma beer statute, the Court held that the law "invidiously discriminates" against males eighteen to twenty-one years of age. Brennan wrote: "In sum, the principles embodied in the equal protection clause are not to be rendered inapplicable by statistically measured but loose-fitting generalities concerning the drinking tendencies of aggregate groups."

In his dissenting opinion, Justice Rehnquist objected to the majority's reasoning on two grounds. First, he thought it was unprecedented to apply heightened scrutiny to a law that disadvantaged males—a group that has never suffered from discrimination. Because the equal protection clause protects only disadvantaged groups, only minimal scrutiny should be applied to the law. Second, Rehnquist reasoned that the majority's rule that classifications by sex must serve important governmental objectives and must be substantially related to those objectives was overly general and irresponsible. He wondered how the Court would determine what objectives are important or whether a particular law is substantially related to an objective. Rehnquist wrote: "Both of the phrases used are so diaphanous and elastic as to invite subjective judicial preferences or prejudices relating to particular types of legislation, masquerading as judgments whether such legislation is directed at 'important' objectives or, whether the relationship to those objectives is 'substantial' enough."

*What about prohibitions on women serving in combat or not being subject to the draft or draft registration?*    Although thousands of women serve in the armed forces and many have fought in near-combat situations in Grenada and in the Persian Gulf War, Congress remains ambivalent about women in combat situations. Female military professionals have claimed that this distinction has served as a "glass ceiling," denying them the prestige, rank, and pay of their male counterparts. While this issue is likely to remain the province of Congress and the executive branch, the Court has ruled on the constitutionality of a male-only draft registration law in *Rostker v. Goldberg*, 453 U.S. 57 (1981).

At the end of the Vietnam War in 1975 draft registration was discontinued by presidential proclamation. But following the Soviet Union's invasion of Afghanistan in 1979, President Carter asked for a joint resolution of Congress to reactivate the registration process under the Military Selective Service Act (MSSA). Although he recommended that Congress amend the MSSA to permit the registration and possible conscription of women as well as men, Congress allocated only enough funds to register men and declined to amend the MSSA. Consequently, a lawsuit was brought by several men challenging that the act's sex-based classification amounted to discrimination in violation of the due process clause of the Fifth Amendment. They were joined by several women's groups, such as the National Organization of Women (NOW) and the Women's Equity Action League, which submitted *amicus* briefs urging the Court to overturn the MSSA. Just three days before registration was to commence, a federal district court permanently enjoined the government from requiring registration of men under the MSSA.

In a 6–3 ruling, the Supreme Court reversed and sustained the constitutionality of Congress's decision. Writing for the majority, Justice Rehnquist applied minimum scrutiny to the classification under the MSSA, reasoning that the Court should maintain its traditional respect and deference to congressional authority in military and national security matters. Rehnquist cited *Schlesinger v. Ballard*, 419 U.S. 498 (1975), where the Court upheld the U.S. Navy's policy of allowing women a longer period of time in which to attain the promotions necessary for continued service. The Navy's extension policy was based on the fact that in light of combat restrictions, women did not have the same opportunities for promotion. Thus, the Navy's distinction was not based on antiquated generalizations about sex roles but rather on "the demonstrable fact that male and female officers are *not* similarly situated with respect to opportunities for professional service."

Congress is not free to disregard the Constitution when it acts in the name of military affairs, but the level of judicial scrutiny of sex-based distinctions will differ because of the military context of the dispute. In other words, the Court will not automatically apply the *Reed* or *Frontiero* standard. Furthermore, Rehnquist believed that unlike earlier cases, Congress's decision not to call for the registration of women was not based on blind prejudice or stereotype, but rather on well-established military policy of restricting women from combat situations. Since women are excluded from combat, and registration serves as a prelude to the induction of combat troops in an emergency, Congress concluded that women draftees would not be needed in the event of an emergency. Thus, there was no need to appropriate money for registering women. The more controversial issue of women in combat was not addressed by any of the justices.

Nothing in the MSSA prevents women from volunteering for military service or denies them opportunities while serving. In sum, the Court found that administrative necessity justified the sex-based classification. Rehnquist concluded that the exemption from registration is sufficiently and closely related to Congress's purpose in authorizing registration:

> As was the case in *Schlesinger v. Ballard*, "the gender classification is not invidious, but rather realistically reflects the fact that the sexes are not similarly situated" in this case. The Constitution requires that Congress treat similarly situated persons similarly, not that it engage in *gestures of superficial equality* [emphasis added].

Based on its landmark rulings in *Reed, Frontiero*, and *Craig*, the Burger Court also invalidated an Alabama law making husbands but not wives liable for alimony payments;[38] a New York law empowering unmarried mothers, but not unmarried fathers, who had put their children up for adoption to withhold consent if they did not approve of the adoptive parents;[39] and a Missouri workman's compensation plan that provided full benefits to widows, but denied benefits to widowers unless it could be shown that the man was either mentally or physically handicapped.[40]

One of the more significant, and controversial, sex discrimination cases heard by the Rehnquist Court involved a "fetal protection" policy adopted by a company that manufactured automobile batteries. The policy excluded fertile women from certain jobs that exposed them to high levels of lead, since the development and health of a fetus are threatened by prolonged exposure to that substance. The direct effect of the policy was to deny employment to a number of women because they were fertile. If a woman wanted to keep her job, she would have to demonstrate that she could not get pregnant. If she failed to do so or did not submit to sterilization, she would be dismissed.

In *International Union, Automobile Workers, Aerospace, Agricultural Implement Workers of America, UAW v. Johnson Control, Inc.*, 499 U.S. 187 (1991), a unanimous Rehnquist Court struck down the policy on the grounds that it classified on the basis of gender and childbearing capacity, rather than on the basis of fertility alone. The fertility of men is also negatively affected by exposure to lead, but since the company was concerned exclusively with the health of the fetus, the policy did not apply to men who did the same kind of work as the woman. The Court relied heavily on the Pregnancy Discrimination Act of 1978, in which Congress expanded the definition of "sex discrimination" to include discrimination "because of or on the basis of pregnancy, childbirth, or related medical conditions." In essence, unless a woman could demonstrate that she was infertile or sterilized, the company would treat her as potentially pregnant and, therefore, disqualified from certain jobs.

Writing for a Court unified in its judgment but not in its reasoning, Justice Blackmun rejected the company's claim that the policy represented a bona fide occupational qualification (BFOQ) because there was no evidence that pregnant women could not participate in the manufacture of batteries as well as men. A BFOQ could be used to prohibit pregnant women from climbing twenty-foot ladders, for instance. But the company's policy was based solely on its moral and ethical concerns about fetal life (and its anti-abortion position) rather than on concerns about safety in the workplace. Blackmun concluded:

> Decisions about the welfare of future children must be left to the parents who conceive, bear, support, and raise them rather than to the employers who hire those parents. Congress has mandated this choice through Title VII, as amended by the Pregnancy Discrimination Act. It is no more appropriate for the courts than it is for individual employers to decide whether a woman's reproductive role is more important to herself and her family than her economic role. Congress has left this choice to the woman as hers to make.

## Single-Sex Colleges: The VMI Case

One of the most politically controversial sex discrimination rulings of the 1990s involved Virginia Military Institute (VMI), an historically all-male public university. Founded in 1839, VMI was the last remaining single-sex college or university in the state of Virginia. Its mission was to produce men who are "citizen-soldiers," prepared to be leaders in civilian life as well as in the military. To this end, VMI uses an "adversative method" of education that subjects its students to "[p]hysical rigor, mental stress, absence of privacy, minute regulation of behavior, and indoctrination in desirable values." Cadets live under constant surveillance in spartan barracks and are regularly tormented and punished by other cadets. Not exactly a party school.

Nevertheless, VMI's unique educational philosophy—which has produced military generals, members of Congress, and business leaders—has earned the loyalty and support of alumni and has attracted many talented prospective students, both male and female. VMI admitted only young men because it believed that the adversative method is inherently unsuitable to women, although its policies were attributable more to the traditional values of its wealthy alumni than to scientific evidence.

In 1990, a female high school student applied and was denied admission to VMI. The U.S. Department of Justice responded to her complaint and sued Virginia and VMI, alleging that VMI's exclusively male admission policy violated the equal protection clause of the Fourteenth Amendment. By being denied admission to VMI, women were being deprived of unique opportunities to develop skills and make the kinds of personal connections that are conducive to professional success.

VMI claimed that very few women were interested in attending, but the record showed that in the two years preceding the suit, VMI had received 347 inquiries from women (which were ignored) and that the women could potentially achieve at least 10 percent of the school's 1,300 enrollment. Experts also testified that based on studies of physical training in the armed forces, there are exceptional women who are capable of all of the activities required of VMI cadets, and that given the realities of a mixed-gender armed forces, the VMI ROTC program would be improved by the admission of women.

However, the U.S. district court ruled in favor of VMI. The court based it decision on the only U.S. Supreme Court precedent addressing the constitutionality of single-sex public universities: *Mississippi University for Women v. Hogan*, 458 U.S. 718 (1982). In that case, the Supreme Court struck down an all-women policy at a state-supported nursing school, establishing a rule that classifications based on sex are allowed only when they serve as an "exceedingly persuasive justification" for a compelling governmental interest.

The state of Virginia argued that it had an important interest in maintaining VMI's unique single-sex environment because it yielded substantial benefits— including "autonomy and diversity"—especially where all of its other state public universities and colleges are coeducational. If women were admitted, then many aspects of VMI's distinctive educational methods would be severely altered. VMI, as it had existed since 1839, would cease to exist.

The U.S. court of appeals, however, reversed the district court, ordering the state to pursue three options: (1) admit women to VMI, (2) establish a parallel institution or program, or (3) abandon state support, leaving VMI free to pursue its policies as a private institution. In response, Virginia proposed to create and support a parallel program for women: Virginia Women's Institute for Leadership (VWIL) located at Mary Baldwin College, a small private liberal arts college for women. VWIL students would participate in ROTC programs but would not employ VMI's adversative approach; rather VWIL would use "a cooperative method which reinforces self-esteem." Upon review, both the district court and court of appeals found the two programs "sufficiently comparable" and therefore constitutional.

However, the U.S. Supreme Court rejected the VWIL remedy and held that Virginia's exclusion of women from the educational programs that VMI provides denies equal protection to women. Writing for the 7–1 majority, Justice Ginsburg held in *United States v. Virginia*, 518 U.S. 515 (1996), that the constitutional violation in this case is the categorical exclusion of women, regardless of their individual merit, from an extraordinary educational opportunity afforded to men. Virginia had shown no "exceedingly persuasive justification" for excluding all women from the citizen-soldier training afforded by VMI. The Court did not buy the state's "VMI would cease to exist" argument nor its "promotion of diversity" justification. The state had argued that VMI would cease to exist because its program would have to be "softened" to account for "female sensitivities." Ginsberg admitted that it can be assumed that most women would not choose VMI's method of education; but it is also highly probable that most men would not want to be educated in such an environment. But that is not the issue. The issue is whether the state can constitutionally deny to women who have the will and capacity the kinds of opportunities made available at VMI. Ginsburg wrote:

> The notion that admission of women would downgrade VMI's stature, destroy the adversative system and, with it, even the school, is a judgment hardly proved, a prediction hardly different from other "self-fulfilling prophecies" once routinely used to deny rights or opportunities. When women first sought admission to the bar and had access to legal education, concerns of the same order were expressed.

What about the state's "diversity" argument? Virginia argued that since all of the state's other public institutions of higher education were coeducational, why not maintain one all-male school to recognize the needs of one element of the state's population: young men who wish to be educated in the tradition of the old military academies. But the Court felt that the state was using the diversity argument rather cynically. The state policy calling for diversity was not intended to keep an historically all-male institution segregated but rather to allow women to be admitted to many of the state's preeminent universities that had been closed to women as late as the 1970s. Today, it seems remarkable that the University of Virginia was not coeducational until 1972.

Ginsburg also attacked VWIL as a "pale shadow" of VMI in terms of the range of challenges, curricular choices, faculty reputation, funding, prestige, and alumni support and influence. It did not provide equal opportunity, but rather a separate but equal remedy Texas proposed in 1946 for Herman Sweatt.

Although he concurred with the majority's judgment, Chief Justice Rehnquist objected to the introduction of a new legal standard in gender classification cases. In the past, any classification based on gender had to "serve important governmental objectives and must be substantially related to the achievement of those objectives." Under the VMI ruling, the government must show an *"exceedingly persuasive justification"* to support a gender-based classification. Rehnquist found this new standard—which is an attempt to clarify the old standard—to be too vague and confusing. "Important governmental objectives" is vague enough; now we have "exceedingly persuasive." Nevertheless, Rehnquist believed that VMI's justification for the single-sex policy—maintenance of the adversative method—did not serve an important enough governmental interest to continue to deny admission to women.

Rehnquist also stated that he believed that a state may establish separate institutions for men and women as long as the two institutions "offered the same quality of education and were of the same caliber." However, in this case he agreed with the majority that VWIL was distinctly inferior to VMI.

## SEXUAL HARASSMENT

When Justice Marshall retired from the Court in 1991, President Bush announced that he would appoint another black jurist to the High Court. Although Clarence Thomas had somewhat limited experience as a judge, he had established a reputation for himself as chair of the EEOC during the Reagan administration. Since many feared that Thomas would move the conservative Court even further to the right, a tumultuous Senate confirmation process was expected, but no one dreamed of the controversy that unfolded. In the midst of the Senate Judiciary Committee's questioning of Thomas, a confidential FBI report was leaked to the media. The report contained allegations by a law professor named Anita Hill that Thomas had made numerous unwanted sexual advances toward her when she was a staff attorney in Thomas's EEOC office in the 1980s. Overnight, as Anita Hill and "sexual harassment" became household words, Thomas's confirmation hearings evolved into a national debate on sexual harassment while a disconcerted Senate Judiciary Committee looked on.

After Thomas was narrowly confirmed by the full Senate in early 1992, the media lost interest in sexual harassment and focused its attention elsewhere. Nevertheless, there is no gainsaying the impact of Hill's graphic testimony on our awareness of sexual harassment in the workplace and in schools and colleges. Indeed, it often requires one well-publicized event to rivet the eyes of Americans on a social problem. Americans began asking, "What is sexual harassment?" "How long has this been going on?" "Have I ever been guilty of this offense?"

What legal recourse is available to victims of harassment? As we have seen, over the past twenty-five years the Supreme Court and Congress have taken steps to eliminate sex discrimination. In enacting Title VII of the Civil Rights Act of 1964, Congress sought to make it unlawful for an employer to discriminate against any individual with respect to his or her salary or conditions of employment because of that individual's race, color, religion, sex, or national origin. Title IX of the Educational Amendments, enacted by Congress in 1972, is intended to eliminate sex discrimination in any educational program receiving federal funding. The Court's rulings in *Reed* and *Frontiero* also represent milestones in the quest for equality. But what about sexual harassment? *Does sexual harassment constitute sex-based discrimination under the Fourteenth Amendment, Title VII, or Title IX?*

Suppose that Jane, a recent college graduate, is seeking employment as an airline pilot. She encounters no state law prohibiting such employment and, in fact, is strongly encouraged to apply under the airline's affirmative action plan. In addition, she is given comparable salary, benefits, and advancement opportunities. But the airline's record is tarnished because almost every day for five years, her supervisor, who is male, has asked her for dates and has made unwanted sexual advances and jokes. Her job security and promotions are not at all affected, but she is miserable because of the hostile environment in which she must work. She files a grievance with the personnel office, but the treatment continues. Can she bring a discrimination suit against the airline, or is this merely a personal problem she must resolve with her supervisor? Does sexual harassment constitute sex discrimination as such, or merely the kind of unfortunate interpersonal conflict that many have experienced at their jobs?

Until the late 1970s, the vast majority of federal courts dismissed sexual harassment suits on the grounds that such conduct did not amount to discrimination under Title VII or any other legal provision or doctrine. Judges argued that sexual harassment claims were not like traditional Title VII cases because the conduct had no relationship to the nature of the employment. Since employers themselves were not creating a condition of employment based on gender, victims could not recover under Title VII. Furthermore, unlike harassment on the basis of race or national origin, harassment in the form of sexual advances fell outside the scope of traditional legal protections because both men and women could be harassed and because it was considered merely personal sexual conduct on the part of the supervisor and not conduct that the company was liable for. How could the sexual advances of one person be construed as employment discrimination? If the advances amounted to assault, criminal charges could be filed. Employers could take action if they wished, but they were not compelled to do so under law. Though unlikely, they could fire the supervisor who harassed the employee, but the company itself had no incentive to stop such behavior because it could not be held legally liable for its employee's actions.

It was possible for a woman to bring a personal injury or wrongful discharge action if she could demonstrate that a sexual act was a precondition for employment or continued employment,[41] but no court was ready to award civil damages under federal discrimination law for sexual advances. After all, the victim was not discriminated against because she was a women, as in a conventional sex-discrimination case, but rather because she refused to engage in sexual relations.[42] The acts of harassment were not sufficiently related to the conditions of the workplace or the policy of the employer; they were merely the result of the personal proclivities of individuals. It was assumed that if a male supervisor took retaliatory action against a woman because she spurned his attentions, he was not acting on the basis of gender but on the basis that she refused his advances. While harassment was recognized as a horrible abuse of authority and privilege, judges were very reluctant to extend Title VII protection to this form of conduct.

The first successful sexual harassment suit in a federal court was *Williams v. Saxbe*[43] in 1976, in which a federal district court ruled that retaliation for the refusal to grant sexual favors does constitute sex discrimination under Title VII. Explaining how harassment amounts to discrimination, the court reasoned that the conduct of the supervisor created an "artificial barrier to employment" placed before one gender and not the other, despite the fact that "both genders were similarly situated." Title VII prohibits all discrimination affecting employment based on gender and not merely discrimination based on stereotypical or outdated views of women.

A year after *Williams*, in *Barnes v. Costle*,[44] the District of Columbia Circuit Court ruled that abolishing, or threatening to abolish, a woman's job because she refuses her supervisor's sexual advances constitutes a discriminatory "job retention condition" in violation of Title VII. Women who are harassed are seen as sexual fair game to the men who are their supervisors; and once such harassment occurs, the women have the choice of giving in to the demands or suffering adversely as an employee. Thus, although the victim is not denied economic benefits because of her sex, she is discriminated against merely because as a woman she became the target of her supervisor's sexual desires. Unlike a man, who is expected merely to be a competent employee, a woman who is harassed is expected to be competent as well as an object of sexual gratification. In sum, contrary to the principle of equal protection, two different conditions of employment are imposed on two persons who are similarly situated.

*What about employer liability for sexual harassment?*  Unless an employer is held liable for the actions of its employees, the employer has little or no incentive to root out sexual harassment from the work environment. In *Tompkins v. Public Service Electric and Gas*,[45] a federal appeals court ruled that Title VII does not exempt employers from liability for the actions of their employees. Title VII is violated when the employer does not take prompt remedial action after being informed that a supervisory employee has made sexual advances or demands toward a subordinate employee.

In 1980, the EEOC established clear guidelines regarding sexual harassment. The EEOC determined that sexual harassment constitutes sex discrimination in violation of Title VII and that conduct amounting to sexual harassment includes unwelcome sexual advances, requests for sexual favors, and other verbal or physical conduct of a sexual nature.

The first sexual harassment case to come before the U.S. Supreme Court was *Meritor Savings Bank, FBD v. Vinson*, 477 U.S. 57 (1986). This celebrated case originated twelve years earlier when Mechelle Vinson was hired as a teller trainee by Sidney Taylor, vice president of the Meritor Savings Bank. Over a four-year period, she was promoted to teller, head teller, and assistant branch manager. It was undisputed that her advancement was based solely on merit. However, she was mysteriously fired in 1978 after notifying the bank that she was taking sick leave for an indefinite period. It was revealed that over a period of four years, Vinson was propositioned, fondled, assaulted, and raped by Taylor. She eventually had consensual intercourse with him after he threatened to fire her. She left because she could no longer stand the abuse. Vinson brought suit against Taylor and the bank charging that during her employment, she was subjected to constant sexual harassment by Taylor in violation of Title VII of the Civil Rights Act of 1964. As in many sexual harassment cases, Vinson failed to file a grievance with her direct supervisor, since it was her direct supervisor who was the source of harassment.

Vinson argued, and the court of appeals affirmed, that unwelcome sexual advances by Taylor created an offensive or hostile working environment amounting to a form of discrimination on the basis of sex. The bank apparently did not challenge this contention, but instead argued that Vinson could not recover for damages because in enacting Title VII Congress was concerned with tangible factors, such as unequal pay, and not purely psychological aspects of the workplace environment.

Writing for the unanimous Court, Justice Rehnquist rejected the bank's contention and asserted that Title VII is not limited to economic or tangible discrimination, but rather extends to the entire spectrum of discriminatory treatment of women in the workplace. Rehnquist reasoned that sexual harassment encompasses both quid pro quo conduct and the creation and maintenance of a "hostile environment." Quid pro quo harassment occurs when a supervisor or any person in authority requires sexual favors from an employee in return for some form of economic or professional advantage. Hostile environment or condition of work harassment occurs in an environment where the employee is regularly subjected to sexual comments, innuendo, or propositions, but is never promised or denied anything connected with employment.

The rule set forth in *Vinson* can be understood as follows. In order to bring an action against an employer, an employee must show that the harassment affected a "term, condition, or privilege" of employment, within the meaning of Title VII, and must be "sufficiently severe or pervasive" to alter the conditions of the victim's employment and create an abusive working environment. In addition, "voluntariness" or the fact that the victim was not forced against her will into a sexual situation or act is not a defense to a sexual harassment suit brought under Title VII. The victim need show only that the sexual advances were unwelcome and that the conduct met the requirements of Title VII in order to bring a claim. Rehnquist pointed out that the district court had erroneously focused on the voluntariness of Vinson's participation in the sexual encounters with her boss. The correct inquiry was whether her words or conduct indicated that her supervisor's sexual advances were unwelcome and not whether her participation in the sexual activity was consensual.

Could the bank be held vicariously liable for Taylor's actions? If the harasser alone is held liable, then institutions such as banks or law firms have little incentive to maintain workplaces free of sexual harassment. The district court held that since the bank was unaware of Taylor's conduct it was not liable. The court of appeals, however, embraced the opposite view; it held that an employer is always strictly liable for a hostile environment caused by the action of an employee even though the employer neither knew nor could have foreseen the misconduct. The Supreme Court refused to take a definitive stand on the issue of employer liability because it did not want to imply that employers are always automatically liable. The Court preferred to have all allegations of sexual harassment under Title VII examined on a case-by-case basis. Thus, although employers are not always automatically liable for the actions of supervisors, they cannot absolve themselves of liability simply by showing that a nondiscrimination policy was in place or because the victim failed to take advantage of the company's grievance procedure.

*Vinson* guaranteed without equivocation that victims of sexual harassment can find relief under Title VII of the Civil Rights Act not only for discriminatory hiring or promotion decisions, but also for unfair conditions that result from a hostile environment. The majority's ruling is far from perfect, however. Four justices—Marshall, Brennan, Stevens, and Blackmun—were not entirely happy with the majority's position that, in some cases, the employer could escape liability by showing that the victim failed to give notice of her supervisor's conduct.

The sexual harassment of students by teachers and professors in schools and colleges has existed as long, if not longer, than the harassment of employees by supervisors in the workplace. Under Title IX of the Education Amendments of 1972, schools and colleges receiving federal financial assistance (including student financial aid) may lose that assistance if they engage in sex discrimination. Congress defined sex discrimination as the denial of any benefits or the exclusion from any program on the basis of sex. Sexual harassment as such was not included in this formulation, nor was it stipulated whether a victim of discrimination could bring a private lawsuit against an institution or sue for monetary damages. However, the Supreme Court has ruled that remedies for sex discrimination under Title IX are not limited to injunctive relief and the termination of federal aid, but include the right to bring a private lawsuit against a university,[46] as well as the claim to monetary damages if attendance in a public institution or participation in a sport or activity is prohibited.[47]

*But does Title IX offer protection against the kind of sexual conduct toward students that falls outside the traditional definition of sex discrimination?* Suppose that Prudence is admitted to State University. She participates in all of the activities of her choice and is not denied any educational opportunities. However, during her junior year, while enrolled in a course required for her degree, she endures repeated sexual advances by one of her professors. In this hypothetical case, the harassment can take the form of a quid pro quo situation or a hostile environment. She has fended off numerous sexual advances, and feels that unlike her classmates she must not only be academically competent, but must also serve as an object of sexual attention or perhaps gratification. Let us further suppose that she must continue the relationship with her professor until she completes her degree program. This kind of problem would be exacerbated in a high school, for example, where the relationship between teachers (or administrators) and students is much more paternalistic. What recourse does Prudence or the high school student have?

In response to this problem, many universities and colleges have established internal grievance procedures through which students can seek administrative relief. However, by their very nature and composition, grievance committees are slow and unreliable means of dealing with sexual harassment; in many cases, the student graduates before the committee completes its investigation and makes its ruling. Committees have occasionally disciplined or dismissed professors or administrators, but such rulings have had a limited effect on sexual harassment campuswide. Many argued that until universities could be held liable for the actions of their faculty or staff, there would be little incentive to take affirmative steps to heighten awareness or to adopt real deterrents to such conduct. In addition, courts are very reluctant to hear these disputes until all administrative remedies are exhausted. For the most part, judges have been predisposed to defer to the outcome of administrative hearings.

Although a federal court has recognized the right to bring a sexual harassment action under Title IX in 1977, victims have had little incentive to sue because they could not recover monetary damages.[48] In 1991, however, the Supreme Court changed this equation in *Franklin v. Gwinnett County Public Schools*, 503 U.S. 60. In a unanimous opinion, joined by Justice Thomas, the Court ruled that students in schools and colleges may sue for monetary damages for sexual harassment under Title IX. The Gwinnett County (Georgia) school system was sued by Christine Franklin, a high school student, after she had been subjected to continual sexual harassment, including coercive intercourse, by Andrew Hill, a sports coach and teacher at North Gwinnett High. Teachers and administrators were aware of the problem but took no action. In fact, they encouraged Franklin not to press charges. Eventually, the school dropped its investigation after Hill resigned. Franklin had filed a complaint with the Office of Civil Rights (OCR) of the U.S. Department of Education, but the OCR ruled that although her rights had been violated under Title IX, the federal government could take no further action because Hill had resigned and the county had conducted an investigation. Franklin then unsuccessfully sought to convince the U.S. district court and the U.S. court of appeals that Title IX authorizes an award of monetary damages.

Arguing the position of Gwinnett County, the Bush administration reasoned that in enacting Title IX, Congress did not intend for the courts to award monetary damages to victims of sexual discrimination, but only to cut off any federal dollars going for special programs at the affected schools or colleges. Under that interpretation of the law, funds would be withheld until the school or college took action to stop the harassment by disciplining or terminating the teacher or professor. The problem with this construction of the law was that by the time that happened, the injured student would have graduated or withdrawn from school. By allowing victims to sue for damages, the Court provided schools and colleges with the incentive to eliminate hostile conditions at the school or to take action before (or soon after) a complaint was filed by the student. Prior to *Gwinnett*, civil rights legislation made it possible for victims of sex discrimination in the workplace to sue for damages, but the law did not apply to students.

Writing for the Court, Justice White attacked the position that because Congress did not specify appropriate relief for sex discrimination the courts were prohibited from taking action prescribing remedies. In the workplace, it may be appropriate to enjoin the supervisor from making sexual advances or to award back pay to the victim, but in an educational environment these remedies are inappropriate. The Court had already ruled in *Cannon v. University of Chicago* in 1979 that relief under Title IX was not limited to withdrawal of federal funds, but that private individuals could sue for damages for sex discrimination.[49] *Gwinnett* is important because it extended the Court's 1979 ruling to sexual harassment as a form of discrimination. Relying on the reasoning of *Meritor*, Justice White wrote:

> Unquestionably, Title IX placed on the Gwinnett County Schools the duty not to discriminate on the basis of sex, and "when a supervisor sexually harasses a subordinate because of the subordinate's sex, that supervisor 'discriminate[s]' on the basis of sex."
>
> . . . We believe the same rule should apply when a teacher sexually harasses and abuses a student.

White believed that the department of education's position that the appropriate remedies are back pay and injunctive relief was illogical and meaningless because Franklin was a student, not an employee, and that since she was no longer attending the school, injunctive relief did nothing for her. By paying a monetary award to Franklin, the school system would not only compensate her for her suffering, but would also send a message to the schools and colleges that tolerate or ignore sexual harassment on the part of their employees.

Another practical benefit of *Gwinnett* can be understood as follows. Since the Seventh Amendment grants a right to a jury trial in all suits involving monetary damages, and since jurors are generally more willing than judges to hand down favorable rulings in sex discrimination cases, *Gwinnett* may also make it easier for plaintiffs to win sexual harassment suits because such cases will now be tried before juries rather than before judges.

The Court returned to the issue of sexual harassment in 1998 in *Faragher v. City of Boca Raton*,[50] where it ruled not on the definition of sexual harassment but on the circumstances under which an employer may be held liable under Title VII.

Beth Ann Faragher was an ocean lifeguard for the city of Boca Raton, Florida, from 1985 to 1990. She brought a lawsuit in a federal district court against the city alleging that her two supervisors created a "sexually hostile atmosphere." The supervisors, Bill Terry and David Silverman, had subjected Faragher and other female lifeguards to "uninvited and offensive touching" and had made lewd and offensive remarks. The record showed that Terry, chief of the Marine Safety Division, had once said that he never would promote a woman to the rank of lieutenant and that Silverman had said to Faragher, "Date me or clean the toilets for a year." The city had a sexual harassment policy, but it completely failed to disseminate its policy among employees of the Marine Safety Division.

The district court ruled that the harassment was sufficiently serious to alter the conditions of Faragher's employment in violation of Title VII of the Civil Rights Act and that the city was liable for the actions of its employees. The district court ruling was reversed, however, by the U.S. Court of Appeals for the Eleventh Circuit on the grounds that under the rules of liability set forth in *Meritor* the city was not liable for the actions of the supervisors because the two men were not acting "within the scope of their employment" and with the city's knowledge or assistance.

Since there was obvious confusion among the two courts as to the precise rule to determine when an employer is to be held liable, the U.S. Supreme Court decided to grant appeal and address several related questions. *Is an employer vicariously liable for harassment of an employee caused by a supervisor no matter what the circumstances? What is the difference between vicarious and automatic liability? What defense may an employer use against a sexual harassment claim brought as a result of the actions of one of its employees?*

The Court held 7–2 that the city of Boca Raton was vicariously liable for the sexual harassment caused by Terry and Silverman. The rule that emerged from *Faragher* can be understood as follows: An employer is subject to vicarious liability for the harm to an employee resulting from a hostile environment created by a supervisor with immediate (or successively higher) authority over the employee. The supervisor's authority—which flows from the employer—makes it possible to alter the terms or conditions of employment of the employee.

But an employer is not automatically liable. There are defenses to counter automatic liability: The employer may have a valid defense against the claim when it can be shown that no tangible employment action is taken. The defense consists of two conditions: (1) that the employer exercised reasonable care to prevent or promptly correct the harassing behavior (e.g., disseminated a policy); (2) that the employee (victim) unreasonably failed to take advantage of any preventive or corrective opportunities provided by the employer to avoid harm. This does not mean that the dissemination of a policy or the victim's failure to complain will get the employer off the hook in all instances. Nor will this defense work when the supervisor's harassment culminates in a tangible employment action, such as firing, demotion, or undesirable reassignment.

In sum, the Court found that the conduct of Faragher's two supervisors did indeed create a hostile environment, that the supervisors were granted virtually unchecked authority over her and that she was completely isolated from the city's higher management, that the city failed to disseminate its sexual harassment policy among beach employees and failed to monitor the behavior of supervisors, and, therefore, the city was liable for the actions of its employees.

Although the main purpose of the ruling was to clarify the murky rules of liability, the Court did briefly revisit its definition of hostile environment sexual harassment that has been developed in *Harris, Meritor*, and *Oncale v. Sundowner Offshore Services* (1998). The Court concluded in *Faragher* that when sexual harassment is alleged, courts and agencies must to determine whether:

> A sexually objectionable environment is both objectively and subjectively offensive—one that a reasonable person would find hostile or abusive, and one that the victim in fact did perceive to be.
>
> An environment is sufficiently hostile or abusive by looking at all the circumstances, including: (a) the frequency of the discriminatory conduct; (b) its severity; (c) whether it is physically threatening or humiliating, or a mere offensive utterance; (d) it unreasonably interferes with an employee's work performance.

In *Oncale v. Sundowner Offshore Services*,[51] however, the Court clarified this standard by stipulating that Title VII does not prohibit "genuine but innocuous differences in the ways men and women routinely interact with members of the same and opposite sex" and that "simple teasing," "offhand comments," and "isolated incidents (unless extremely serious) do not amount to sexual harassment because they do not amount to discriminatory changes in the terms and conditions of employment under Title VII.

In his dissenting opinion in *Faragher,* Justice Thomas (joined by Scalia) argued that an employer can be held liable *only* when an employee suffers adverse employment consequences from the actions of a supervisor. Since Faragher suffered no adverse employment consequences, the city is not liable for the conduct of Terry and Silverman, the two lifeguard supervisors. He also disagreed with the majority's view that the city should be liable merely because it did not disseminate its sexual harassment policy. The city should have been given the opportunity to defend itself by showing (1) that there was a reasonable way for Faragher to complain to a city official who supervised Terry and Silverman, but that she did not attempt to do so, and (2) that it never would have learned of the harassment even if the policy had been distributed.

## DISCRIMINATION ON THE BASIS OF SEXUAL PREFERENCE: AN EQUAL PROTECTION QUESTION?

*Does the equal protection clause of the Fourteenth Amendment prohibit discrimination on the basis of sexual preference as it does race- and sex-based discrimination? Do gays and lesbians as a legal class of persons have the same constitutional right against discrimination as do racial minorities and women?* The answer is no, since the Supreme Court has never ruled on these questions; however, it will be only a matter of time before these issues are argued before the Court.

Today, gay and lesbian rights groups are growing in number and strength. They are well funded, well organized, and have won some pivotal legal battles. Sexual orientation discrimination complaints are now being litigated in state and federal courts. Many cities and counties have enacted laws and ordinances that prohibit discrimination against gays and lesbians.[52] On the cultural level, American society continues to grow more tolerant of openly gay men and women and less tolerant of discrimination. A national survey conducted in 2000 by *Newsweek* magazine found that 83 percent of the American public believes that homosexual and bisexuals should be protected from discrimination in employment.[53] Even candidates for national office are voicing their support for antidiscrimination measures. Vice President Al Gore, who won more of the national popular vote than the ultimate victor in the 2000 presidential race, George W. Bush, strongly supported the passage of federal legislation that would ban sexual-orientation discrimination. If enacted, the Employment Non-Discrimination Act (ENDA) would extend some of the federal protections to gays and lesbians enjoyed by other protected groups, such as African Americans and women, but would include various exemptions for private and religious organizations that exclude homosexuals.[54]

But the nation remains divided. On the other side of the debate, there are large numbers of well-organized social and religious conservatives who believe that homosexuality is immoral if not illegal. They oppose same-sex marriage, benefits for same-sex partners, and a range of other rights and protections for homosexuals. Conservatives have successfully enacted the military's "Don't Ask, Don't Tell" policy, which allows the discharge of openly homosexual service personnel, and the Defense of Marriage Act (DOMA), which legally defines marriage as a union of a man and a woman. DOMA also gives states the authority to refuse to recognize same-sex marriage licenses issued in other states.[55]

Since *Bowers v. Hardwick* in 1989, where the Court refused to apply the right of privacy to strike down state sodomy laws, the justices have given us only a glimpse of their thinking on the legal status of homosexuals. Thus, the only way to predict how the issue might be addressed in the future is to examine cases that have raised the issue of unequal treatment of gays and lesbians.

In 1996, the Supreme Court heard a case involving an equal protection challenge to a state constitutional amendment that was designed to invalidate local ordinances in Aspen, Boulder, and Denver, Colorado, that prohibited discrimination against homosexuals. In *Romer v. Evans*, 517 U.S. 620 (1996), the Court ruled 6–3 that the equal protection clause prohibits a state from passing a constitutional amendment that forbids local governments from enacting measures to protect homosexuals from discrimination. Supporters of Constitutional Amendment 2, passed by a ballot referendum, argued that the amendment was not antigay but intended only to deny these cities from creating "special rights" for homosexuals—to elevate homosexuals to a protected class of persons, like African Americans and women. But the Court struck down the amendment because it "impose[d] a special disability" on one group alone. Under the equal protection clause, a state cannot identify a class of persons (any persons) by a single trait and then deny them legal protection. Applying an equal protection standard to the language of the amendment, the Court concluded that the amendment bore no rational relation to a legitimate governmental purpose. Its only discernable purpose, according to the Court, was to harm an unpopular group.

Writing for the majority, Justice Kennedy pointed out that Amendment 2 not only barred homosexuals from seeking protection from existing public accommodations laws, it also nullified specific legal protections for this "targeted class" in all transactions in housing, sale of real estate, insurance, health and welfare services, private education, and employment. Kennedy wrote:

> It is not within our constitutional tradition to enact laws of this sort. Central both to the idea of the rule of law and to our own Constitution's guarantee of equal protection is the principle that government and each of its parts remain open on impartial terms to all who seek its assistance.
>
> A law declaring that in general it shall be more difficult for one group of citizens than for all others to seek aid from the government is itself a denial of equal protection of the laws in the most literal sense.

He concluded that Amendment 2 classified homosexuals not to further a proper legislative end but to make them unequal to everyone else. "A State cannot deem a class of persons a stranger to its laws," Kennedy concluded.

In his dissenting opinion Scalia—joined by Rehnquist and Thomas—argued that Amendment 2 was simply a modest attempt to protect traditional moral values from the efforts of a politically powerful minority to change those values. Scalia believed that by holding that homosexuality cannot be singled out for disfavorable treatment, the majority had overturned *Bowers* and advanced the rule that opposition to homosexuality is the same as racial or religious bias. Since Bowers was good law at the time of the amendment's passage, it was still permissible for a state to make homosexual conduct criminal. If so, then it surely was permissible for a state to pass laws disfavoring homosexual conduct, which is what Amendment 2 sought to accomplish.

Scalia believed that the majority of voters in Colorado approved Amendment 2 because they felt threatened by a political minority residing in the more urban areas in Colorado imposing pro-homosexual views upon the rest of Colorado's residents. A growing number of communities were passing pro-gay ordinances. The governor, then Roy Romer (a Democrat), had signed an executive order prohibiting discrimination based on sexual preference. According to Scalia, gays and lesbians are free "to use the legal system for reinforcement of their moral sentiments . . . but they are subject to being countered by lawful, democratic countermeasures as well." The Court, wrote Scalia, was caught in the middle of the a *kulturkampf* (culture war), a place were it did not belong.

*Is* Romer *an important ruling for homosexuals?* Notwithstanding Scalia's comments, the Court did not overturn *Bowers* or place homosexuals into the same constitutionally protected class with minorities and women. However, by ruling that a state cannot single out a specific group and make it more difficult for that group to pursue its policy goals, *Romer* makes it very difficult for states to thwart the efforts of communities that wish to enact antidiscrimination measures. The statewide population will have to accept that there will be some communities within their state that will be very supportive of a homosexual lifestyle and others that will not.

Another reason *Romer* is important is that although the majority gave no indication that sexual preference should be elevated to a suspect classification, the language used by the majority is nonjudgmental, tolerant, and sympathetic.

*There are many civic and religious organizations that oppose homosexuality. Can these organizations be forced to tolerate and include gays and lesbians as members or employees if a state law or city ordinance prohibits discrimination on the basis of sexual preference? Would the organization's freedom of association under the First Amendment supercede the antidiscrimination law?* The Court addressed this issue in *Boy Scouts of America v. Dale*[56] in 2000. In 1989, the Boy Scouts of America informed James Dale, a life-long scout, that he could not serve as a scout master. Dale had been involved in scouting since he was a cub scout at the age eight. Ten years later, he earned the Boy Scout's highest rank of Eagle Scout. A year later, he was granted adult membership in the Scouts and was given the position of assistant scoutmaster. Dale was considered an exemplary Boy Scout, who was committed to the organization.

However, when it was learned in 1989 from a newspaper article that he is an avowed homosexual and an activist in the gay rights movement, the Boy Scouts revoked Dale's membership. In response, Dale filed a suit under a New Jersey law that prohibits discrimination on the basis of sexual preference in all public accommodations. The state supreme court rejected the argument that the Boy Scouts is a private group exempt from the public accommodations law. Instead, it ruled that the Boy Scouts is a place of public accommodation that discriminates on the basis of sexual orientation.

On appeal to the U.S. Supreme Court, the Boy Scouts argued that its First Amendment freedom of "expressive association" outweighs New Jersey's discrimination statute. The Supreme Court agreed. Delivering the opinion of the 5–4 majority, Chief Justice Rehnquist wrote that although the freedom of expressive association is not absolute, the New Jersey law places an unconstitutional burden on the Boy Scouts' ability to carry out its mission of inculcating its members with a value system of its own choosing. In other words, by forcing the Scouts to accept Dale the government was telling the Boy Scouts that the organization could no longer advocate its traditional message embodied in the Boy Scouts' oath. The organization does not want to promote homosexual conduct by allowing an openly gay man and activist to remain a scout leader.

The Court has long recognized that implicit in the right to engage in First Amendment activities is a corresponding right to associate with others in pursuit of a wide variety of political, social, economic, educational, and cultural ends. This right of "expressive association" is necessary to prevent the majority from imposing its views on groups that would rather express other ideas. This right prevents the government from forcing a group to accept members it does not like. For example, how could the Jewish Anti-Defamation League continue to advocate toleration for Judaism if a law or governmental regulation forces it to extend membership to Nazis or other anti-Semites. Such a regulation would impair the group's ability to express only the views that it chooses.

However, the freedom of expressive association is not absolute. This freedom not to include unwanted members may be overridden by regulations that serve compelling state interests that are unrelated to the suppression of ideas. For example, the Court has ruled that the compelling interest in prohibiting sex discrimination prevents private organizations such as the Jaycees from excluding women.[57]

***What kinds of groups are protected by the First Amendment's expressive association right? Does it extend only to advocacy groups, such as the NAACP, or to other kinds of organizations as well?***    The Boy Scouts is not technically an advocacy group but it does have a clear mission: to instill good morals, reverence for God, and patriotism. Although sexual preference is not expressly mentioned in the Scout Oath and Law, young men are encouraged to be "morally straight" and "clean." On numerous occasions, Scout leaders have concluded that homosexual conduct is contrary to the mission of the organization. Since 1978, the official position of the Boy Scouts was that avowed homosexuals were not to be scout leaders. Allowing Dale to stay on as an adult member would place a burden on the organization's ability to express its ideals. The forced inclusion of Dale—a gay rights advocate—as a scoutmaster would significantly affect the Boy Scouts' ability to advocate its viewpoint.

On this point the Court referred to the earlier case *Hurley v. Irish-American Gay, Lesbian, and Bisexual Group of Boston*, 515 U.S. 557 (1995). *Hurley* established that notwithstanding a state public accommodations law, the organizers of a private St. Patrick's Day Parade in Boston could not be forced to include among the marchers an Irish-American gay, lesbian, and bisexual group (GLIB). The parade organizers did not wish to exclude the GLIB members because of their sexual orientation, but rather because they wanted to carry a GLIB banner in the parade, thus proclaiming a message that the parade organizers did not share. Rehnquist wrote:

> As the presence of GLIB in Boston's St. Patrick's Day parade would have interfered with the parade organizers' choice not to propound a particular point of view, the presence of Dale as an assistant scoutmaster would just as surely interfere with the Boy Scout's choice not to propound a point of view contrary to its beliefs.

One could argue that the Boy Scouts' ability to promote its message was not significantly affected by the forced inclusion of Dale because, after all, the purpose of the Boy Scouts is not to promote the debate of sexuality of any kind. Indeed, its leaders are discouraged from speaking out on issues other than those relating to the mission of the Scouts. Furthermore, as the New Jersey Supreme Court pointed out, the numerous sponsors and members of the Boy Scouts subscribe to different views of homosexuality.

But Rehnquist disagreed and posited two rules that are helpful in understanding the First Amendment rights of private organizations. First, associations do not have to associate for the purpose of disseminating a certain message in order to be entitled to First Amendment protections. For example, the purpose of the St. Patrick's

Day parade was not to espouse any views about sexual orientation but to celebrate the day. Therefore, the organizers had a right to exclude certain participants. Second, the First Amendment does not require that every member of a group agree on every issue in order for the group's policy to be "expressive association." For example, it is irrelevant that some heterosexual scout leaders disagree with the Scouts' policy. What is relevant is the presence of an avowed homosexual and gay right activist in a scoutmaster's uniform. Regardless of the divergent views of its members, it is sufficient for the organization to take an official position on an issue. An organization has a First Amendment right to choose to send one message but not another.

Rehnquist did not directly address the New Jersey law that prohibits discrimination on the basis of sexual preference in public accommodations. He did state that New Jersey's definition of "public accommodation" is "extremely broad," extending not only to traditional public places like restaurants and shopping malls but also to places that may not be open to the general public. States are free to enact laws that protect groups that are targets of discrimination unless such laws impose a serious burden on a private organization's rights of expressive association.

The reason the Court ruled that private organizations like the Jaycees or the Rotary Club may not exclude women from membership is that neither club adequately demonstrated that admitting women would affect the organizations' mission: providing a network to promote success in the business world.

So, for Rehnquist, this case had nothing to do with homosexuality—it had to do with denying First Amendment protection to individuals or private groups that refuse to accept the view that homosexuality is acceptable. Rehnquist wrote:

> We are not, as we must not be, guided by our views of whether the Boy Scouts' teachings with respect to homosexual conduct are right or wrong; public or judicial disapproval of a tenet of an organization's expression does not justify the State's effort to compel the organization to accept members where such acceptance would derogate from the organization's expressive message.

***Does this mean that groups can claim "expressive association" when they wish to avoid abiding by antidiscrimination laws? Could the Jaycees or the Rotary Club exclude homosexuals?*** The four dissenting justices—(Stevens, Souter, Ginsburg, and Breyer)—framed the dispute differently from the majority. They were interested primarily in how it is possible to enforce the New Jersey discrimination law without running afoul of the constitutional rights of the Boy Scouts. Writing for the dissenters, Justice Stevens argued that the right of expressive association is not absolute; that is, the right does not protect every club or organization in which members exercise discrimination in choosing associates. For example, the Court has rejected the claims of organizations with discriminatory membership policies, such as private schools, law firms, and labor organizations. But until now, wrote Stevens, the Court has never once found that a right to associate in the selection of members supercedes a state's antidiscrimination law. Indeed, the Court held that a Minnesota antidiscrimination law superceded the Jaycees right to restrict membership to males between the ages of eighteen and thirty-five.[58] Like the Boy Scouts, the Jaycees also had claimed that the antidiscrimination law placed a burden on its ability to communicate or foster a message of civic mindedness. The Court had not accepted the Jaycees's argument that, because the organization had taken public positions on a number of diverse issues (freedom of expressive association), it had the right to conclude that the admission of women would impede the organization's ability to engage in constitutionally protected activities.

Stevens believed that the Boy Scouts were unable to show that by admitting an avowed homosexual the group would be unable to carry out its various purposes. The relevant question is whether the inclusion of a kind of person would "impose any serious burden," "affect in any significant way," or be "a substantial restraint upon" the organization's "shared goals," "basic goals," or "collective efforts to foster beliefs." It would not because the Boy Scouts as a national organization have never had any stated policy or shared goal of opposing or disapproving of homosexuality; in fact, the organization was silent on the subject. So, the antidiscrimination law does nothing to impair the Boy Scouts' mission or purpose. It was not as if the law were being applied to a rabidly antihomosexual religious organization. Stevens wrote: "An organization can adopt the message of its choice, and it is not this Court's place to disagree with it. But we must inquire whether the group is, in fact, expressing a message (whatever it may be) and whether that message (if one is expressed) is significantly affected by a State's antidiscrimination law."

In sum, to be successful in defending a group from the charge of violating an antidiscrimination law, an organization must show that it has adopted and advocated an unequivocal position inconsistent with a position advocated or epitomized by the person whom the organization seeks to exclude. Members of the Boy Scouts engage in expressive activities outside of the troop but are asked by the organization not to bring religious or political views into the organization. Any disobedient member who ignores the policy may be dismissed. It follows that there is no basis for the Scouts to presume that a homosexual will be unable to comply with this rule. If he did talk about his sexuality, he could be dismissed. But the Boy Scouts argued that even if Dale said nothing, the mere presence of an avowed homosexual would send a distinct message that the Boy Scouts accepts homosexuality. Again Stevens disagreed. There was no evidence that Dale's open declaration of his homosexuality, reported in a local newspaper, would force the Boy Scouts to covey the message that the organization advocates or accepts homosexuality.

The dissenters concluded with a frank discussion of homosexuality in our society. Over the years, homosexuality has enjoyed greater acceptance and understanding from the scientific community, some religious communities, and society as a whole. Nevertheless, bigotry toward homosexuals has "ancient roots" like "equally atavistic opinions" about certain racial groups." Stevens concluded: "[S]uch prejudices are still prevalent and . . . they have caused serious and tangible harm to countless members of the class New Jersey seeks to protect. . . . That harm can only be aggravated by the creation of a constitutional shield for a policy that is itself the product of a habitual way of thinking about strangers."

Citing Justice Blackmun's classic dissenting opinion in *Bowers v. Hardwick*, Stevens recognized that unfavorable attitudes towards homosexuals are reinforced by the political authority of the state, including the actions of the Court that prevent New Jersey from protecting members of this "class" of people. The dissenters also took the important step of comparing discrimination on the basis of sexual orientation with that of race- or sex-based discrimination and applauded New Jersey's attempt to protect homosexuals as a legal class of persons—something that a majority of justices has never done.

## VOTING, ELECTIONS, AND THE EQUAL PROTECTION CLAUSE

### The Principle of "One Person, One Vote"

The right to vote in a free and open election is the essence of a democratic system. Yet, sadly, for much of our nation's history that right was denied to many citizens because of their race or sex. After the Civil War, the Fifteenth Amendment was ratified in 1869 to guarantee that "[t]he right of citizens of the United States to vote shall not be denied or abridged by the United States or by any State on account of race, color, or previous condition of servitude." Even after the ratification of the Fifteenth Amendment, many states continued to use both direct and indirect means—such as white primaries and literacy tests—to prevent African Americans from registering and voting.

The U.S. Supreme Court entered the fray in 1944 when it struck down white primaries in *Smith v. Allwright*[59] and "good character" tests in *Louisiana v. United States*.[60] The Twenty-Fourth Amendment and the Supreme Court ended the poll tax;[61] and Congress finally got serious about implementing the Fifteenth Amendment by enacting the Voting Rights Act in 1965,[62] intended to end all forms of discriminatory schemes designed to keep African Americans and others away from the ballot box.

But guaranteeing equal access to the polling place was not sufficient to end all racially discriminatory voting practices. The right to vote can be affected not only by an obstacle to ballot access but also by a dilution of voting power (e.g., when election schemes are adopted for the purpose of reducing or nullifying a minority group's ability to elect the candidate of its choice). A racial gerrymander occurs when the state deliberately distorts the boundaries of a legislative district to prevent African Americans from electing representatives to legislative bodies. For example, in the 1950s Alabama redefined the boundaries of the city of Tuskegee from a square to a weird twenty-eight-sided figure in order to exclude black voters from the city limits.[63]

Under the leadership of Chief Justice Earl Warren (1954–1969), the Supreme Court handed down some of the most important rulings in our nation's history. Best known for its ruling in *Brown v. Board of Education*, as well as other racial discrimination cases, the Warren Court also expanded freedom of expression, the right to privacy, voting rights, and rights of the accused. Yet, when Chief Justice Warren was once asked which ruling was the most important of his tenure, he replied that it was the Court's ruling on legislative malapportionment in *Baker v. Carr*, 369 U.S. 186 (1962).[64]

Legislative apportionment is the distribution of a state's legislative seats according to population. For example, if a state's population is evenly distributed across ten legislative districts (each district sending one representative to the state capitol), then we could conclude that legislative seats are apportioned equally and that all segments of the state's population are equally represented in the legislature. However, malapportionment might exist if a majority of a state's population migrated to an urban area in one district but the legislative district lines were never redrawn to reflect the population shift. The majority of voters in the urban area are underrepresented because even though the majority of the state's population resides in the urban area, it is represented by only one seat, whereas the rural (or nonmetropolitan) areas are represented by nine seats. Thus, the state legislature would be dominated by representatives from rural or nonmetropolitan areas who would have little incentive to address the problems of the urban area. The strength of the urban vote would be "diluted" by the way the district lines were drawn, thus creating a form of political discrimination against urban dwellers. Even though each citizen gets only one vote, the city dweller's vote would count less because he or she would have little impact on the policymaking of a legislature dominated by representatives from rural districts. These representatives would be less likely to address urban problems, such as poverty, racism, crime, and crumbling infrastructure.

Malapportionment, also called "gerrymandering," results when state legislatures either do not respond quickly enough to demographic changes in their states or from the intentional desire of politicians to dilute the strength and influence of the urban (typically minority) voter. Although this problem dated back to the late 1800s, the courts refused to address this concern because it was considered a "political question" (rather than a legal or constitutional one) that was left up to the state legislatures to resolve.

The political question doctrine was turned on its head in 1962 when the Supreme Court decided to hear *Baker v. Carr*, 369 U.S. 186. Baker and other citizens of the state of Tennessee brought a Fourteenth Amendment challenge to the state's legislative apportionment scheme. They argued in a federal district court that because their votes had been "debased," or diluted, Tennessee deprived them of the equal protection of the laws. The state was required under a 1901 law to redistribute its legislative districts every ten years, but even in light of a migration to urban areas for more that sixty years, the legislature refused to order reapportionment of its general assembly. The *Baker* lawsuit also asked the court to order the state either to hold an at-large election of legislators (without the use of district or counties) or redistrict the state in accordance with the 1950 federal census. The federal district agreed that although a civil rights violation existed, the courts did not have jurisdiction in what was considered a political matter.

The U.S. Supreme Court, however, rejected the notion that this was a political question beyond the scope of judicial review. Simply because the suit sought protection of a political right (voting) it did not mean that it presented a purely political question. Writing for the majority, Justice Brennan argued that this was a justiciable constitutional issue appropriately heard by a court because vote dilution as a result of malapportionment violates the equal protection clause of the Fourteenth Amendment. Baker and the other appellants were entitled to a trial in a federal district court. A citizen's right to vote free of "arbitrary impairment" by state action has been recognized as a constitutional right, particularly when such impairment resulted from dilution by a false tally of votes,[65] by the refusal to count votes from certain precincts,[66] or by stuffing the ballot box.[67]

Just as the Constitution prohibits a state from disqualifying a voter on the basis of race (Fifteenth Amendment) or sex (Nineteenth Amendment), it also prohibits the state from weighing one person's vote more heavily than it does another's. When the Supreme Court remanded *Baker* to the district court, the question for the lower court to determine was whether Tennessee violated the Fourteenth Amendment by discriminating against a class of voters. However, the Court focused all of its energy on the question of standing and jurisdiction and offered no test or standard by which it could be determined whether the election system or districting scheme in a state violated the Constitution. A year later, in *Gray v. Sanders*, 372 U.S. 368 (1963), the Court established this standard when it struck down a Georgia election plan that created districts that were not "substantially equal" in representing voters.

In 1962, the Court also struck down a racially motivated gerrymander in *Gomillion v. Lightfoot*, 364 U.S. 339. The Alabama legislature redrew the boundaries of the city of Tuskegee from an existing square to a twenty-eight sided shape with the obvious intent to exclude from the city limits most black voters. Unlike *Baker* and other malapportionment cases, *Gomillion* involved a very obvious attempt not to dilute but to eliminate the voting strength of black voters.

Immediately after *Baker v. Carr*, lawsuits were brought in more than 30 states challenging the constitutionality of legislative apportionment. States were put on notice that they had to show a compelling reason to justify apportionment schemes that were not based on population alone and deviated from the principle of one person, one vote. One such case, decided by the Warren Court, that has had a lasting impact on the reapportionment debate is *Reynolds v. Sims*, 377 U.S. 533 (1964). The case originated in Alabama where the state constitution required that the legislature must be reapportioned on the basis of population every ten years. However, even in light of major populations shifts from rural to urban centers, no reapportionment had taken place since 1901. As a result, representation was based more on geography than on population. Roughly 25 percent of the state's population (mostly rural and white) could elect a majority of state senators and a majority of state representatives—clearly diluting the voting strength of three fourths of the state's population (which included a large bloc of urban black voters). Under the existing scheme, the votes of certain citizens (rural) had five to ten times the weight of others voters (urban) in the state.

Feeling the heat, Alabama adopted a new apportionment plan, but a federal district court held it to be a violation of the principle of one person, one vote under the equal protection clause of the Fourteenth Amendment.

On appeal, the Supreme Court ruled that the plan was in violation of the Fourteenth Amendment, reasserting that diluting the weight of votes (as a result of place of residence) impairs basic constitutional rights just as much as direct discrimination based on race. It is not enough to allow every citizen a vote. Equal protection requires the state to make "an honest and good faith effort" to construct legislative districts "as nearly of equal population as is practical" so that the relative influence of all citizens' votes are roughly equal. Warren wrote: "Legislators represent people, not trees or acres. Legislators are elected by voters, not farms or cities or economic interests." Because the lines were drawn based on geography rather than on population, sparsely populated districts were apportioned the same number of seats in the legislature as were densely populated districts. Warren continued: "Logically, in a society ostensibly grounded on representative government, it would seem that a majority of the people of a State could elect a majority of that State's legislators."

It was no surprise that the state of Alabama basically told the Court to "butt out"—that the judiciary had no role to impose a different political philosophy or theory of representation on its citizens and that apportionment was a "political question" traditionally not addressed by the courts. This, along with the state's rights argument, was the standard southern response to any of the Court's attempts to bring about equal protection of minorities; but, as in *Baker v. Carr*, the Court quickly dismissed the state's reasoning, arguing that a denial of constitutional protection demands judicial protection.

Just as the Court was attempting to bring about a revolution in representative government through its malapportionment rulings of the 1960s, another type of revolution was under way: the massive baby boom exodus to the suburbs. As more suburbs sprang up overnight, the redistricting ordered by the courts under the principle of one person, one vote actually increased legislative representation for predominantly white suburban voters. A new constituency was born—concerned not with the decaying infrastructure of the big city, but with lower taxes, improved highways, and new schools.

Regardless of this demographic shift, the Court went on to apply strict scrutiny to legislative apportionment in cases involving local government,[68] community college districts,[69] and congressional districting.[70] The Court, growing more conservative by the mid-1970s, continued to hear malapportionment cases throughout the 1970s and 1980s but began to relax the level of scrutiny placed on state and local election schemes. For instance, the Burger Court relaxed the one person, one vote standard to allow a reapportionment plan that guaranteed each of the majority political parties a minimum number of "safe seats" in the legislature[71] and protected the seniority of incumbent representatives.[72]

As a result of litigation subsequent to the Supreme Court's racial gerrymandering rulings, many states were ordered by federal district courts to redraw legislative districts so that more minority candidates would get elected. For instance, at one point forty of North Carolina's 100 counties were under court order to comply with the Voting Rights Act of 1965.

Counties may not change voting practices or reapportion legislative seats without federal approval. As a result of the 1990 census, North Carolina gained a twelfth seat in the U.S. House of Representatives and state authorities enacted a plan that included one majority-black congressional district. In accordance with the Voting Rights Act of 1965 any state that wishes to make changes in a "standard, practice, or procedure with respect to voting" must secure authorization form the U.S. Attorney General (at that time, Janet Reno). The Attorney General objected to the plan submitted by North Carolina because it created only one majority-black legislative district: Reno believed that a second district would increase minority voting strength in the south-central to southeastern region of the state. At the time of the reapportionment, 20 percent of the state's population was black, 1 percent was Native American, and 1 percent was Asian. The black population was relatively dispersed, constituting a majority in only five of the state's 100 counties.

The state revised its plan, creating two majority-black districts. The first of the two odd-shaped districts as described by the Court was hooked-shaped and tapered to a narrow band with finger-like extensions reaching into the southern part of the state. The second majority-black district was created in the north-central region of the state, stretching snake-like 160 miles along Interstate 85. For much of its length, the odd-shaped district was only as wide as the I–85 corridor, which contained tobacco-producing areas, financial centers, and manufacturing areas. It was drawn so that it would meander like a river into all-black neighborhoods.

Reno liked the plan, but many North Carolinians did not. The North Carolina Republican Party and several white voters brought suit against state and federal officials, claiming that North Carolina had created two congressional districts made up of an arbitrary concentration of black voters. This action constituted an unconstitutional racial gerrymander in violation of the Fourteenth Amendment. They argued that the two legislative districts were created along racial lines simply to create congressional districts so that two black representatives would be elected to Congress.

By a 2–1 vote, the federal district court dismissed the complaint, arguing that the appellants were not discriminated against because the redistricting favoring minority voters did not lead to underrepresentation of white voters statewide.[73]

On appeal in *Shaw v. Reno*, 509 U.S. 630 (1993), the U.S. Supreme Court reversed the district court's ruling. Writing for the 5–4 majority, Justice O'Connor argued that the reapportionment plan was an effort to unjustifiably segregate voters into separate districts solely on the basis of race. She wrote: "Classifications of citizens based solely on race are by their nature odious to a free people whose institutions are founded upon the doctrine of equality, because they threaten to stigmatize persons by reason of their membership in a racial group and to incite racial hostility."

According to equal protection precedent, any law that makes distinctions on the basis of race must serve a "compelling governmental interest" or else it will struck down as unconstitutional. According to O'Connor, the "bizarre" North Carolina redistricting legislation is unexplainable on grounds other than race because it created oddly shaped districts that did not correspond to any established geographical boundaries or political subdivisions. Therefore, the law must be subjected to strict scrutiny under the Fourteenth Amendment. A racial gerrymander should receive the same level of scrutiny as other laws that classify citizens on the basis of race. While it may have the noble purpose of enhancing minority representation in Congress, the law is suspect because it is based on the stereotypical assumption that members of the same race have the same political opinions and prefer the same candidates. O'Connor continued: "It also sends to elected representatives the message that their primary obligation is to represent only that group's members, rather than their constituency as a whole."

*What if the racial gerrymander favors or helps the minority that has suffered electoral discrimination?*    The Court rejects any gerrymander because it regards the Fourteenth Amendment as "color blind"; that is, equal protection is not dependent on the race of those benefited or burdened by a particular classification. The Fourteenth Amendment applies to minorities and nonminorities alike. This is the same reason the Rehnquist Court has consistently struck down affirmative action plans as reverse discrimination.[74]

The states have a legitimate interest in creating majority-black districts in order to comply with the Voting Rights Act, but they may not use racial gerrymandering to do so. So, racial redistricting is permissible but racial gerrymandering is not. *What is the difference? What constitutes racial gerrymandering?* The Court defines it as drawing boundary lines of dramatically irregular shape, having no relationship to existing political subdivisions or geographical boundaries in order to send a member of one particular race to a legislative body. Not all reapportionment statutes that concentrate members of one race in one district are unconstitutional. Lines may be drawn for legitimate demographic reasons, placing members of a racial group that live in a community into one legislative district. How does the Court tell the difference? Sometimes just looking at how a district is drawn on a map will indicate that it may be unconstitutional. Some districts take the form of barbells, with a thin zone connecting two black communities twenty miles apart, others are octopus-shaped. Justice O'Connor wrote:

> [W]e believe that reapportionment is one area in which appearances do matter. A reapportionment plan that includes in one district individuals who belong to the same race, but who are otherwise widely separated by geographical and political boundaries, and who may have little in common with one another but the color of their skin, bears an uncomfortable resemblance to political apartheid.

The four dissenting justices[75] thought that it was absurd for the Court to argue that the political influence of members of the white majority in North Carolina had been unfairly diluted or cancelled. Since there is only one black representative to Congress from North Carolina, it strains credulity to suggest that North Carolina's purpose in creating a second majority-black district was to discriminate against white voters.

The bloc of four dissenters made several other points. First, they argued that the conscious use of race in redistricting does *not* violate the equal protection clause *unless* the effect of the plan is to deny a particular group equal access to the political process or to unduly minimize its voting strength. Second, the dissenters did not believe that the shape of the district should not be used as a standard or test to determine whether an election plan violated the equal protection clause. The Constitution does not impose a requirement of "contiguity or compactness" on how the states draw their electoral districts, nor does it prevent a state from drawing district lines for the purpose of helping one group of voters elect one of its own unless the sole purpose is to make it more difficult for members of a minority group to win an election. It is not a violation of the Constitution when the majority acts to facilitate the election of a member of a group that lacks power because it remains underrepresented in the state legislature.

After *Shaw* the racial gerrymandering battle continued. Responding to the results of the 1990 census, the Florida legislature adopted a new reapportionment plan. However, the Department of Justice refused to approve the plan under the Voting Rights Act because the plan did not create a minority-majority district in the Tampa metropolitan area. After the Florida legislature failed to reach an agreement on a new plan, the Florida Supreme Court carved an oddly shaped legislative district out of four counties with a population that was 45.8 percent black and 9.4 percent Hispanic. In 1994, nonminority residents challenged the proposed district under the Fourteenth Amendment as an unconstitutional racial gerrymander that diluted the voting strength of nonminority voters and violated the sovereignty of the state of Florida. The U.S. Supreme Court narrowly (5–4) rejected the challenge, but the plan was ultimately altered through a mediated settlement that reduced the black voting-age population of the district from 45.8 to 36.2 percent by incorporating only three counties instead of four.[76] In 1997, however, the Supreme Court agreed with a federal district court decision to strike down a Virginia plan that created an irregularly drawn majority-black (64 percent) district as an unconstitutional racial gerrymander.[77] The district would have been Virginia's only congressional district in which African Americans made up a majority of the voting-age population. Now that the results of the 2000 census have been analyzed, a new redistricting fight will likely commence.

## BUSH V. GORE: RECOUNTS, "ONE PERSON, ONE VOTE," AND THE 2000 PRESIDENTIAL ELECTION

It is safe to say that *Bush v. Gore* will likely be remembered as the most aptly named case ever to be decided by the U.S. Supreme Court. Not only did the case determine the outcome of one of the closest and most bitterly contested presidential elections in our nation's history, it also expressed, on a deeper level, the stark and bitter partisan divisions in American society. The case led to an incredible scenario never envisioned by constitutional scholars, politicians, and pundits: the U.S. Supreme Court resolving a stalemated presidential contest through the application of the equal protection clause of the Fourteenth Amendment. It sounds farfetched, but it happened; and the legitimacy of the outcome of that election as well as the wisdom of the Court's role in its outcome will undoubtedly be debated for many years. What follows is a discussion of the facts, outcome, and implications of this landmark decision.

### Stormy Forecast for the Sunshine State

As election day 2000 approached, political commentators predicted a close outcome but no one dreamed of the infamous photo finish in Florida, where the presidential race hinged entirely on Florida's twenty-five electoral votes. As the polls closed that evening the major networks prematurely called the race for Vice President Al Gore but then quickly retracted their projection when it was realized that only a fraction of the results were in. Early the next morning, the networks declared that Florida's electoral votes had pushed Texas Governor George W. Bush over the top to become the forty-third president. Gore then placed the traditional concession call to Bush.

A short time later, much to everyone's surprise, Gore called Bush to withdraw his concession after learning that the vote was so close that under Florida law an automatic machine recount was required (if the margin was under one half of 1 percent). On the day after the election, Bush led by 1,784 votes, but after the machine recount his lead dropped to 537 votes. Gore then exercised his right under Florida law to request manual recounts by the canvassing boards of any county. Due to voter error and technical glitches in old punch-card voting machines, thousands of votes were not counted. As the nation waited, election judges stared at partially punched "chads" hanging from punch cards in order to ascertain voter intent. Weeks passed and no resolution was in sight. Recounts were started, stopped, and started again amidst charges of fraud, deception, and a lack of uniform standards to guide the recount. To make matters worse, thousands of Gore supporters in Palm Beach County charged that poorly constructed ballots had tricked them into voting for Reform Party candidate Pat Buchanan.

When it became obvious that several counties would not complete their recounts by the November 14 deadline, they petitioned the Florida secretary of state for an extension. The extension was denied, and Gore filed suit in the state court arguing that the secretary of state had acted illegally. The Florida Supreme Court agreed, ordered the secretary of state not to certify the election, and ordered a full manual recount because of a discrepancy between a sample manual recount and machine returns. The Florida Supreme Court then set the recount deadline for November 26. Since this recount would exceed the time frame for submitting election returns under state law, the Bush team appealed the decision to the U.S. Supreme Court.

## Developing a Constitutional Argument

In *Bush v. Palm Beach County Canvassing Board*,[78] the Court agreed with the Bush attorneys that the Florida Supreme Court may have misinterpreted Florida election law and interfered with the right of the state legislature to regulate the electoral process under Article II, Section 1, clause 2, of the U.S. Constitution. Without offering a definitive ruling, the Supreme Court remanded the case to the Florida Supreme Court on December 4, asking the Florida high court to clarify its reasons for ordering a new recount. On December 11, the Florida Supreme Court issued a response to the remand and reinstated the recount. In a separate state court action, *Gore v. Harris*,[79] the Florida Supreme Court ordered a hand recount of 9,000 ballots in Miami-Dade County.

With each passing day new speculation emerged over how the contested election would be resolved and whether the resolution would be fair or totally partisan. The Florida Supreme Court, dominated by Democrats, supported an expanded recount of votes. The Florida secretary of state, a Republican who had campaigned for Bush, certified the election for Bush even while the recount continued. The Republican-dominated Florida legislature threatened to bypass the voters and select a new slate of twenty-five Bush electors. Some speculated that if Florida's electoral vote were still up for grabs in January 2001, the U.S. House of Representatives would decide the election when it convened for its new legislative session. If Florida wound up sending two slates of electors—one Bush and one Gore—both houses of Congress would have to agree on which slate to accept. The U.S. Supreme Court would have the final say if the Bush lawyers could make a convincing argument that the dispute constituted a "case or controversy" under the Constitution rather than (as the Gore team argued) a matter for the state courts to decide.

The case *Bush v. Gore*[80] began to make its way to the U.S. Supreme Court after the Florida Supreme Court ordered a full recount of 45,000 "undervotes"— a process that could give the advantage to Gore (at that point Bush held on to a slim lead of 537 votes statewide). But the Bush lawyers convinced the U.S. Supreme Court to order a stay of the recounts and hear the case a week later. The Bush team argued that the Florida Supreme Court violated the state legislature's right (under Article II, Section 1, clause 2 of the U.S. Constitution) to determine the manner in which presidential electors are appointed by : (1) broadly interpreting Florida election law to establish new standards and dates for resolving the presidential election; (2) failing to comply with federal election law; and (3) violating the equal protection clause through its sanction of a standardless manual recount.

In a per curiam opinion, the U.S. Supreme Court ruled that the Florida Supreme Court's order to continue the recount violated the equal protection clause of the Fourteenth Amendment. The Court began its opinion by pointing out that the individual citizen has no federal constitutional right to vote for electors for the president unless the state legislature chooses a statewide election as the means to implement its power to appoint electors under Article I, Section 1 of the Constitution. If the state legislature decides to vest the right to vote for president in its people, the right to vote is fundamental and it must make sure that "equal weight is accorded to each vote and equal dignity owed to each voter." The principle of equal protection applies not only to who gets to vote but also to the manner in which people vote. The state may not "by arbitrary and disparate treatment, value one person's vote over that of another." The Court went out of its way to point out that in the past it has ruled that once the state grants the right to vote, distinctions cannot be made that are inconsistent with the equal protection clause;[81] and that the right to vote can be denied by a "debasement" or "dilution" of the weight of a citizen's vote just as effectively as by wholly denying the right to vote itself.[82]

The recount procedures ordered by the Florida Supreme Court violated the Constitution because they treated voters in an arbitrary and disparate manner. The reason primarily has to do with the "chad"—a small rectangular piece of the ballot card that is designed to be pushed out completely by a stylus pen. In some instances, the chad was not pushed out with the necessary precision for a machine to count the remaining perforation or hole in the card. Therefore, some chads were hanging by a corner or two; some chads were not punched out at all but simply "dimpled" by the stylus. The problem that the U.S. Supreme Court had with the Florida Supreme Court's order was not that one is unable to ascertain the intent of the voter, but rather the lack of specific standards with which to determine the voter's intent. The recount mechanism ordered by the Florida, court did not satisfy the requirement for nonarbitrary treatment of voters.

Again the Court cited it past rulings to support its findings. In *Gray v. Sanders*, 372 U.S. 368 (1963), the Court ruled that a state violated the principle of one person, one vote when it treated voters in an arbitrary and disparate manner. In *Moore v. Ogilvie*, 394 U.S. 814 (1969), the Court invalidated a countywide procedure that diluted the influence of citizens in larger counties in the process by which presidential candidates were nominated. In *Moore*, the justices observed that the idea that the citizens of one county can be granted greater voting strength than voters in another county "is hostile to the one man, one vote basis of our representative government."

The Florida Supreme Court sanctioned this kind of uneven treatment when it ruled that the recount totals from two counties, Miami-Dade and Palm Beach, be included in the statewide certified total of votes. It even ruled that the recount totals from Broward County were to be considered part of the official vote totals even though the county certification had not been challenged by Gore. Each of these counties used varying standards to determine what was a legal vote. Broward County used a more lenient standard than Palm Beach County and, therefore, uncovered almost three times as many new votes even though the populations of the two counties are about even.

Another problem was that although undervotes (no vote for president) and overvotes (two votes for president) are not read by the machine, the hand recount was counting undervotes (when intent could be established) but not overvotes.

In addition to the problem with how the votes were counted, the Court also had a problem with the actual process by which the votes were to be counted under the Florida Supreme Court's ruling. The ruling did not specify who would recount the ballots. The canvassing boards were forced to quickly assemble ad hoc teams of people who had no training in handling and counting ballots.

The Court concluded that given all of these difficulties the recount could not be conducted in compliance with the requirements of equal protection and due process without "substantial additional work" and by December 12, the day that the state is required to certify its electors. New statewide standards for determining a legal vote would have to be adopted, a plan to implement the standards would have to be devised, and then judicial review of any disputed matters would undoubtedly be necessary. This could not be done by December 12 because the Court delivered its opinion in *Bush v. Gore* on December 12. The Court concluded:

> None are more conscious of the vital limits on judicial authority than are the members of this Court, and none stand more in admiration of the Constitution's design to leave the selection of the president to the people, through their legislatures, and to the political sphere. When contending parties invoke the process of the courts, however, it becomes our unsought responsibility to resolve the federal and constitutional issues the judicial system has been forced to confront.

In his concurring opinion, Chief Justice Rehnquist cited a number of additional precedents to strengthen the Court's argument. He began by pointing out that in ordinary cases the Court defers to the decisions of state courts on issues of state law but there are some instances where the Constitution imposes a duty or confers a power on a particular branch of state government. In this instance, Article II, Section 1, clause 2 requires that state legislatures participate in the presidential election by choosing the electors for president and vice president. Pursuant to that provision, Congress enacted a law (3 U.S.C. Section 5) that requires that the state's selection of electors "shall be conclusive, and shall govern in the counting of the electoral votes" if the electors are chosen under laws enacted prior to election day and if the selection of electors is completed six days prior to the meeting of the electoral college. Thus, election law cannot be changed after the fact by the state legislature, state courts, or Congress. In other words: "[I]f we are to respect the legislature's Article II powers, therefore, we must ensure that post-election state court actions do not frustrate the legislative desire to attain 'safe harbor' provided by §5." This is what the Florida Supreme Court did. It pushed the vote counting past the safe-harbor date of December 12, which is the last day under federal law to appoint electors and six days prior to the meeting of electors on December 18. Four days prior to this deadline the Florida Supreme Court ordered the standardless recount discussed above. There was simply not enough time to do this without moving passed the safe-harbor provision of the law. Rehnquist, and four of his associates, were not going to allow this to happen.

Seven justices of the Court agreed that there were constitutional problems with the recount ordered by the Florida Supreme Court that demanded a remedy. But without ordering a remedy, the Court reversed the Florida high court's ruling and remanded it for further proceedings. But there were no further proceedings. At that point, the clock had run out and Gore conceded the election to Bush.

## A Divided and Partisan Court

The election was finally over but the controversy did not end with Gore's concession speech. Although seven of the nine justices agreed that the recount was fraught with constitutional problems, only five of the nine—Rehnquist, Scalia, Thomas, Kennedy, and O'Connor—believed that the recount should not continue under a new plan that was compatible with the equal protection clause. Four justices—Stevens, Ginsburg, Breyer, and Souter—believed that the Court could and should offer a remedy and that it was possible to continue the recount. Thus, it was a comfortable 7–2 ruling on the constitutionality of the recount, but a slim 5–4 split on whether a recount should continue.

Dissenting, Justice Stevens—joined by Justices Ginsburg and Breyer—did not believe that the federal questions that emerged in this case were substantial enough for the Court to intervene in the election and that the Florida Supreme Court's exercise of judicial review over the election was consistent with the Florida and U.S. Constitutions. Florida law holds that all ballots that reveal the intent of the voter constitute valid votes. Therefore, it is the constitutional right of all Florida voters to have their vote counted. The appropriate course of action is to remand the case to Florida so that a recount consistent with the equal protection clause can continue.

The dissenting justices joined Stevens in his assessment that the majority was more interested in finality than fairness. The dissenters pointed out that while there were 170,000 uncounted votes statewide, the statewide total of undervotes was only about 60,000. So, there was no reason why in six days the Florida courts could not establish uniform standards to review the uncounted votes. Four of the justices were ready to remand the case to the Florida courts with instructions to create uniform standards for evaluating the several types of ballots that prompted differing and unfair treatment. They were not worried about the safe-harbor provision of Section 5 because they did not believe that Congress had intended for the deadline to be carved in stone or to prevent the state from counting legal votes until a "bona fide winner" is determined. Indeed, in 1960, Hawaii appointed two slates of electors and Congress chose to count the one state appointed on January 4, 1961, long after the safe-harbor deadline of Section 5.

Stevens concluded by attacking the majority for its lack of confidence in the impartiality of the Florida Supreme Court—a view that "can only lend credence to the most cynical appraisal of the work of judges throughout the land." Finally, making a subtle suggestion about the Supreme Court's own impartiality, Stevens stated:

> Time will one day heal the wound to that confidence that will be influenced by today's decision. One thing, however, is certain. Although we may never know with complete certainty the identity of the winner of this year's Presidential election, the identity of the loser is perfectly clear. It is the Nation's confidence in the judge as an impartial guardian of the rule of law.

## Ramifications

Five-to-four is a slim margin indeed for one of the Court's most controversial decisions. A narrow margin by itself is not enough to question the legitimacy of the Court's ruling. However, a 5–4 vote along what appears to be distinctly partisan lines to end all recounts and, thus declare Bush the winner, was certainly not an ideal way to resolve a political if not constitutional crisis. The justices who ruled to stop the recount—Rehnquist, O'Connor, Scalia, Thomas, and Kennedy—are conservative Republican appointments to the bench. President Bush is comfortable with most of their positions and has talked of elevating Justice Scalia to the chief justiceship when Rehnquist steps down. Both O'Connor and Rehnquist have made no secret of their eagerness to retire during a Republican administration. The justices who argued for a recount—Stevens, Souter, Ginsburg, and Breyer—are moderate-to-liberal jurists who would most likely be at odds with the Bush administration. Justice Stevens, who has served on the Court since 1975, is close to retirement and will most likely be succeeded by a Bush appointee.

The deep division begs the question of whether the ruling was based on partisan politics or rooted in some consistent and identifiable differences in constitutional interpretation. The suspicion of partisan motivations is strengthened by the fact that the five conservatives who have fiercely fought for state's rights voted for a federal judicial resolution to Florida's unsettled election, while the four liberal-to-moderate justices were uncharacteristically decrying the Court's intrusion into state prerogatives.

Another explanation of the majority's reluctance to abide by a recount might be that the majority was more interested in finality than fairness, as Justice Stevens charged. No doubt the justices feared that it would likely take weeks if not months of further litigation and review before an amenable recount plan was adopted. So, there was clearly an interest in finality.

What about fairness? Seven of the nine justices held that the recounting was unfair—that it violated the principle of one person, one vote required by the equal protection clause. But in order to apply the equal protection clause in this case the Court had to break new ground in its one person, one vote jurisprudence, since there was no definitive precedent that directly applied to the constitutionality of the manner in which a hand recount takes place. The Court adopted the Bush team's ingenious albeit improvised equal protection claim and then justified its ruling by cobbling together an opinion from a few old vote-dilution rulings of the 1960s. In doing so, the Rehnquist Court broke entirely new ground in the area of equal protection. In fact, the opinion was reminiscent of the Warren Court's willingness to extend the equal protection clause to a wide range of social and political problems. There is absolutely no evidence that any of the justices had any prior inclination to embark down this new path. Nor is there any evidence of this new theory of voting rights in lower court opinions or in academic writing. It appears to have originated in the Bush legal team's strategy to put an end to the recounts, which were slowly but surely eroding Bush's lead. On the other hand, Gore's strategy was to keep the count going before the clock ran out to find the uncounted votes. To stop this counting and recounting, the Bush team had to convince the Court that Gore was attempting to change the way votes are counted after the election was over and that the resulting lack of uniformity of vote counting was anathema to the principle of equal protection. The majority agreed, and the clock ran out.

**What is the nature and scope of this new one person, one vote standard and what are its possible ramifications?**    The new standard holds that the principle of one person, one vote is violated when, during a count or recount, there is an absence of a specific and uniform standard of establishing the intent of the voter. A vote recount must be carried out according to the principle of equal treatment and fundamental fairness so that one person's vote is not valued more than that of another. A system of counting or recounting votes cannot grant more voting strength to one person than to another; it cannot "debase" or "dilute" the weight of a citizens vote relative to other citizens. Under this new standard, many existing laws concerning the manner in which votes are recounted may be challenged. Theoretically, one could sue a state if it allows counties to use different kinds of voting or vote tabulation methods. For example, some wealthier counties use optical scanning while other counties still have the old punch-card systems. The ruling certainly opens the door for a greater role for the federal courts in overseeing state and local elections.

Bush v. Gore also opens the door to political attacks on the Supreme Court, since the decision regarding who would be president was based on a slim 5–4 vote. The ruling will be scrutinized and lambasted by the media, scholars, and members of the bench and bar, as well as by senators during the next set of confirmation hearings. While the justices are accustomed to political fallout from controversial rulings on school prayer or abortion, rarely does the public question the justices impartiality—the cornerstone of the Court's legitimacy. As Justice Stevens pointed out in his dissenting opinion, the majority's ruling shakes the public's confidence in the judge as an impartial guardian of the rule of law.

## CONCLUDING COMMENTS

### Equal Protection Counterrevolution or Expansion?

The 1992 confirmation of the controversial Thomas—an outspoken critic of affirmative action—led many scholars and Court-watchers to predict that the Rehnquist Court now had the votes to back away from the principle of equal protection. After all, the Rehnquist Court had already been all too willing to defer to conservative politicians and had shown an open hostility to race- and sex-based remedies to societal discrimination.

However, the Court's rulings during the 1990s do not square with this charge and, in fact, demonstrate that the Court is still seriously committed to the principle of equal protection. Shortly after Thomas's confirmation, the Rehnquist Court handed down a surprising 8–1 ruling (Scalia dissenting) in the pivotal case *United States v. Fordice*, 505 U.S. 717 (1992). In that case, the Court ruled that according to the principles laid down in *Brown* and *Green*, public universities and colleges in Mississippi must go much further than merely establishing racially neutral admissions policies.

When the *Fordice* opinion was reported by the media, many Americans were shocked to learn that nearly thirty years after *Brown*, Mississippi's major comprehensive and regional universities remained predominantly (80–90 percent) white, while its historically black universities were between 92 and 99 percent black. The state attributed this fact solely to student choice, since legal segregation had been dismantled long ago. But in *Fordice* the Court placed the blame squarely on the state's policy of relying on standardized test scores as the single factor in making admissions decisions. Even the companies that administered these tests cautioned against the use of test scores alone, since black students tend to score lower than white students on such exams. Experts suggest that admissions decisions should factor high school or college GPAs into the admissions equation. The black students who did not have the required scores could attend one of the historically black universities or a community college with the hope of transferring to a predominantly white institution. The Court also attributed the present system to the fact that the state still maintained duplicate academic programs in white and black universities, as it had in the days of legal segregation. Consequently, while the universities were technically open to all, subtle mechanisms were in place to encourage black students to take the path of least resistance. The Court ordered Mississippi to do more than show a good-faith effort to encourage diversity in its traditionally all-white institutions. If the state perpetuates a policy or practice traceable to its prior legal system that continues to have discriminatory effects, and that policy is without sound educational justification, then the state violates the equal protection clause. Thus, the Supreme Court adopted a standard of review more rigorous than that adopted by the lower federal court, the latter having ruled that a less strict standard of review was permissible for college segregation disputes because, unlike students attending elementary and secondary schools, college students are free to attend the school of their choice.

Despite the *Fordice* ruling, many civil rights advocates continued to criticize the Court, particularly for its refusal to adopt the two-class theory of equal protection advanced by justices Brennan and Marshall. Recall that the two-class theory applies a lesser degree of judicial scrutiny to discrimination against white males, thus making it more difficult to bring reverse discrimination challenges to preferential treatment policies. But others have praised the Court for embracing the "color-blind" theory of equal protection.

On the issue of affirmative action, however, the Rehnquist Court has braved a direct and solidly conservative path. Race-based remedies, such as set-asides, can be used only as legal remedies when it can be proved that intentional discrimination can be traced directly to the actions of decision-makers.

Aside from affirmative action, the counterrevolution never did materialize. There is no evidence that the Rehnquist Court has abdicated its duty to implement the principles of equal protection and the ideals established by the Warren Court in *Brown v. Board of Education*. It has broadened protections against sex discrimination in the VMI ruling, by introducing a new legal standard in gender classification cases. In the past, any classification based on gender had to "serve important governmental objectives and must be substantially related to the achievement of those objectives." Now, under the VMI ruling, the government must show an "exceedingly persuasive justification" to support a gender-based classification.

During the 1990s the Court also embraced and broadened the concept of sexual harassment and made it less difficult to hold an employer liable in sexual harassment cases. The Court has also made it more difficult for a state to thwart efforts by local governments to protect against discrimination on the basis of sexual preference, and it has broken totally new ground in its one person, one vote jurisprudence.

---

 # Finding the full text of the U.S. Supreme Court Opinions Cited in Chapter 7

The full opinion of the U.S. Supreme Court's rulings discussed in this chapter can be found at the Findlaw URL address following each case listed below, or by using the case name (e.g., *Schenck*) or citation (e.g., 249 U.S. 47). Other web sites where opinions can be found are listed at the end of chapter 1.

## Racial Discrimination

### Separate But Equal

*Plessy v. Ferguson* (1896), http://laws.findlaw.com/us/163/537.html

*Sweatt v. Painter* (1950), http://laws.findlaw.com/us/339/637.html

### Brown v. Board of Education

*Brown v. Board of Education* (1954), http://laws.findlaw.com/us/347/483.html

*Brown II* (1955), http://laws.findlaw.com/us/349/294.html

*Continued*

## Finding the full text of the U.S. Supreme Court Opinions Cited in Chapter 7    *Continued*

*Bolling v. Sharpe* (1954), http://laws.findlaw.com/us/347/497.html

*Cooper v. Aaron* (1958), http://laws.findlaw.com/us/358/1.html

### *Implementing* Brown

*Green v. County School Board* (1968), http://laws.findlaw.com/us/391/430.html

*Swann v. Charlotte-Mecklenburg Board of Education* (1971),
   http://laws.findlaw.com/us/402/1.html

*Milliken v. Bradley* (1974), http://laws.findlaw.com/us/418/717.html

*Missouri v. Jenkins* (1990), http://laws.findlaw.com/us/495/33.html

*Board of Education of Oklahoma City Public Schools v. Dowell* (1991),
   http://laws.findlaw.com/us/3498/237.html

### *Desegregating Other Public Facilities*

*Burton v. Wilmington Parking Authority* (1961), http://laws.findlaw.com/us/
   365/715.html

### *Private Facilities*

*Heart of Atlanta Hotel v. United States* (1964),
   http://laws.findlaw.com/us/379/241.html

*Katzenbach v. McClung* (1964), http://laws.findlaw.com/us/379/294.html

*Daniel v. Paul* (1969), http://laws.findlaw.com/us/395/298.html

*Runyon v. McCrary* (1976), http://laws.findlaw.com/us/427/160.html

*Patterson v. McLean Credit Union* (1988),
   http://laws.findlaw.com/us/485/617.html

## Affirmative Action and Quotas

*Regents of the University of California v. Bakke* (1978), http://laws.findlaw.com/
   us/438/265.html

*City of Richmond v. J. A. Croson* (1989), http://laws.findlaw.com/us/488/
   469.html

*Metro Broadcasting, Inc. v. FCC* (1990), http://laws.findlaw.com/us/497/547.html

*Adarand Constructors, Inc. v. Pena* (1995), http://laws.findlaw.com/us/515/200.html

### Hopwood *and Race-Based College Admissions Decisions*

*Hopwood v. State of Texas* (1996), http://laws.findlaw.com/us/000/u20033.html

## Sex Discrimination

*Reed v. Reed* (1971), http://laws.findlaw.com/us/404/71.html

*Frontiero v. Richardson* (1973), http://laws.findlaw.com/us/411/677.html

*Craig v. Boren* (1976), http://laws.findlaw.com/us/429/190.html

*Rostker v. Goldberg* (1981), http://laws.findlaw.com/us/453/57.html

*Schlesinger v. Ballard* (1975), http://laws.findlaw.com/us/419/498.html

*International Union, Automobile Workers, et al. v. Johnson Control, Inc.* (1991), http://laws.findlaw.com/us/499/187.html

### Single-Sex Colleges: The VMI Case

*Mississippi University for Women v. Hogan* (1982), http://laws.findlaw.com/us/3458/718.html

*United States v. Virginia* (1996), http://laws.findlaw.com/us/518/515.html

## Sexual Harassment

*Meritor Savings Bank v. Vinson* (1986), http://laws.findlaw.com/us/477/57.html

*Franklin v. Gwinnett County Public Schools* (1991), http://laws.findlaw.com/us/503/60.html

*Faragher v. City of Boca Raton* (1998), http://laws.findlaw.com/us/000/97-282.html

*Oncale v. Sundowner Offshore Services* (1998), http://law.findlaw.com/us/000/96 568.html

## Discrimination on the Basis of Sexual Preference: An Equal Protection Question?

*Romer v. Evans* (1996), http://laws.findlaw.com/us/517/620.html

*Boy Scouts of America v. Dale* (2000), http://laws.findlaw.com/us/000/99-699.html

*Hurley v. Irish-American Gay, Lesbian, and Bisexual Group of Boston* (1995), http://laws.findlaw.com/us/515/557.html

## Voting, Elections, and the Equal Protection Clause

### The Principle of "One Person, One Vote"

*Baker v. Carr* (1962), http://laws.findlaw.com/us/369/186.html

*Gray v. Sanders* (1964), http://laws.findlaw.com/us/372/368.html

*Westberry v. Sanders* (1964), http://laws.findlaw.com/us/376/1.html

*Gomillion v. Lightfoot* (1962), http://laws.findlaw.com/us/364/339.html

*Reynolds v. Sims* (1964), http://laws.findlaw.com/us/377/533.html

### Bush v. Gore: Recounts, "One Person, One Vote," and the 2000 Presidential Election

*Bush v. Gore* (2000), http://laws.findlaw.com/us/000/00-949.html

## Notes

1. *Dred Scott v. Sanford*, 19 Howard 393 (1896).
2. The first Justice John Marshall Harlan served from 1877 to 1911, while the second Justice John Marshall Harlan (grandson of the first) served from 1955 to 1971.
3. *Gong Lum v. Rice*, 275 U.S. 78 (1927).
4. *Missouri v. Ex rel. Gaines v. Canada*, 305 U.S. 337 (1938).
5. *Morgan v. Virginia*, 328 U.S. 373 (1946).
6. *Sipuel v. Board of Regents*, 332 U.S. 631 (1948).
7. *Mclaurin v. Oklahoma State University*, 339 U.S. 637 (1950).
8. J. Kluger, *Simple Justice: The History of* Brown v. Board of Education *and Black America's Struggle for Equality* (New York: Knopf, 1975), 614.
9. 83 U.S. (16 Wall.) 36 (1873), and see discussion in chapter 5.
10. For a fascinating account of the interpersonal dynamic of this case, see Bernard Schwartz, *Super Chief: Earl Warren and His Supreme Court—A Judicial Biography* (New York: New York University Press, 1983), chapter 3.
11. Schwartz, *Super Chief*, 90–91.
12. Schwartz, *Super Chief*, 90–91.
13. Schwartz, *Super Chief*, 110.
14. See Donald G. Nieman, *Promises to Keep: African-Americans and the Constitutional Order, 1776 to the Present* (New York: Oxford University Press, 1991).
15. Nieman, *Promises to Keep*, chapter 6.
16. 100 U.S. 339 (1880).
17. *United States v. Peters*, 5 Cranch 115 (1809).
18. 391 U.S. 430 (1968).
19. *Columbus Board of Education v. Penick*, 433 U.S. 449 (1979), and *Dayton Board of Education v. Brinkman*, 433 U.S. 526 (1979).
20. *Pasadena City Board of Education v. Spangler*, 427 U.S. 424 (1976).
21. *Board of Education of City School v. Harris*, 444 U.S. 130 (1979).
22. Justice Souter did not participate in this case.
23. *Mayor of Baltimore v. Dawson*, 350 U.S. 877 (1955).
24. *Gayle v. Browder*, 352 U.S. 903 (1956).
25. Thurgood Marshall was appointed to the U.S. court of appeals in 1961. He would later be the first African American to serve on the Supreme Court after he was appointed by President Johnson in 1967.
26. Nieman, *Promises to Keep*, 170.
27. *Boynton v. Virginia*, 364 U.S. 454 (1960).
28. See *Jones v. Alfred H. Mayer Co.*, 392 U.S. 409 (1969). In passing the Equal Employment Opportunity Act of 1972, Congress specifically rejected a proposed amendment that would have repealed *Jones*.
29. For a solid discussion of the issue as it first unfolded, see Nathan Glazer, *Affirmative Action* (New York: Basic Books, 1976).
30. See *United States v. Paradise*, 480 U.S. 149 (1987).
31. The U.S. Supreme Court denied cert., 518 U.S. 1033 (1996).
32. See Jo Freeman, *The Politics of Women's Liberation* (New York: David McKay, 1975); Joyce Gelb, *Feminism and Politics* (Berkeley: University of California Press, 1989); and Judith Baer, *Equality Under the Constitution* (New York: Cornell University Press, 1983).
33. Justice Bradley, concurring in *Bradwell v. State*, 16 Wall. 130, 141 (1873).
34. See Mary Francis Berry, *Why ERA Failed* (Bloomington: Indiana University Press, 1986).
35. *Loving v. Virginia*, 388 U.S. 1 (1964).

36. *Graham v. Richardson*, 403 U.S. 365 (1971).

37. *Oyama v. California*, 332 U.S. 633 (1948).

38. *Orr v. Orr*, 440 U.S. 268 (1979).

39. *Caban v. Mohammed*, 441 U.S. 380 (1979).

40. *Wengler v. Druggists Mutual Insurance Co.*, 446 U.S. 142 (1980).

41. *Tompkins v. Public Service Electric Co.*, 422 F. Supp. 553 (D.N.J. 1976).

42. See *Corne and DeVane v. Bausch & Lomb*, 390 F. Supp. 161 (D. Ariz. 1975); and *Miller v. Bank of America*, 418 F. Supp. 233 (N.D. Cal. 1976).

43. 422 F. Supp. 654 (D. D.C. 1976).

44. 561 F.2d 983 (D.C. Cir. 1977).

45. *Tompkins v. Public Service Electric and Gas Co.*, 568 F.2d 1044 (3$^{rd}$ Cir. 1977).

46. *Cannon v. University of Chicago*, 441 U.S. 677 (1979).

47. *Pennhurst State Schools and Hospitals v. Halderman*, 451 U.S. 1 (1981).

48. See *Moire v. Temple University School of Medicine*, 800 F.2d 1136 (1986).

49. *Cannon v. University of Chicago*, 441 U.S. 677 (1979).

50. 118 S. Ct. 2275 (1998); http://laws.findlaw.com/us/000/97-282.html.

51. 118 S. Ct. 998 (1998).

52. See Lambda Legal Defense and Education Fund for the breakdown of states, cities, and counties that prohibit sexual orientation discrimination at http://www.lambdalegal.org.

53. *Newsweek*, March 20, 2000, at 46–48.

54. For an excellent overview of the subject of sexual orientation discrimination, see J. Banning Jasiunas, "Note: Is ENDA the Answer? Can a 'Separate But Equal' Federal Standard Adequately Protect Gays and Lesbians From Employment Discrimination?" 61 *Ohio State Law Journal* 1329 (2000).

55. Jasiunas, "Note: Is ENDA the Answer?"

56. 120 S. Ct. 2446 (2000).

57. *Roberts v. United States Jaycees*, 468 U.S. 609, 622 (1984).

58. Justice Stevens relied on the principles set forth in *Board of Directors of Rotary International v. Rotary Club of Duarte*, 482 U.S. 537 (1987); and *Roberts v. United States Jaycees*, 468 U.S. 609 (1984).

59. *Smith v. Allwright*, 321 U.S. 649 (1944).

60. *Louisiana v. United States*, 380 U.S. 145 (1965).

61. The Twenty-fourth Amendment was ratified in 1964. In 1966, the Supreme Court ruled in *Harper v. Board of Elections*, 383 U.S. 663 (1966), that the equal protection clause of the Fourteenth Amendment prohibits a state from imposing a poll tax as a requirement to vote in *any* state election.

62. The Voting Rights Act was expanded and strengthened in 1970, 1975, and 1982.

63. The Court struck down this scheme in *Gomillion v. Lightfoot*, 364 U.S. 339 (1960).

64. See Schwartz, *Super Chief*, p. 410.

65. *United States v. Classic*, 313 U.S. 299 (1941).

66. *United States v. Mosley*, 238 U.S. 383 (1915).

67. *Ex parte Siebold*, 100 U.S. 371 (1880).

68. *Avery v. Midland County*, 390 U.S. 474 (1968).

69. *Hadley v. Junior College District*, 397 U.S. 50 (1970).

70. *Kirkpatrick v. Preisler*, 394 U.S. 526 (1969).

71. *Gaffney v. Cummings*, 412 U.S. 783 (1973).

72. *Karcher v. Daggett*, 462 U.S. 725 (1983).

73. The U.S. district court relied on *Jewish Organization of Williamsburgh, Inc. v. Carey*, 430 U.S. 144 (1977).

74. See *Richmond v. J. A. Croson Co.*, 488 U.S. 469.

75. Justices White, Blackmun, Stevens, and Souter.
76. *Lawyer v. Department of Justice*, 117 S. Ct. 2186 (1997).
77. *Meadows v. Moon*, 117 S. Ct. 2501 (1997).
78. http://laws.findlaw.com/us/000/00-836.html.
79. Facts and finding as stated in http://laws.findlaw.com/us/000/97-282.html.
80. http://laws.findlaw.com/us/000/97-282.html.
81. *Harper v. Virginia Board of Elections*, 383 U.S. 663 (1966).
82. *Reynolds v. Sims*, 377 U.S. 533 (1964).

# CHAPTER EIGHT

# The Rehnquist Court: Counterrevolution or Respect for Precedent?

## THE CHANGING COMPOSITION OF THE COURT

The Warren Court brought about a revolution in civil rights and liberties through a philosophy of liberal judicial activism—using the power of judicial review to act as an agent of social and political change. It saw itself as the guardian of civil rights and liberties, a champion of the forgotten man and the unpopular minority. The Warren Court refused to be bound by a literal construction of the Constitution, seeing the document as a living incarnation of the ideals of liberty and equality. Thus, it was just a matter of moving the nation closer toward those ideals.

When Chief Justice Earl Warren ended his sixteen-year tenure on the U.S. Supreme Court and was succeeded by Nixon appointee Warren Burger in 1969, hopeful conservatives and anxious liberals predicted the end of the liberal judicial activism of the Warren era. Under Warren's leadership, the Supreme Court had brought about an unprecedented revolution in civil rights and liberties. Upon his retirement, however, conservatives hoped to return the Court to an idealized time when judicial restraint prevailed and the decisions of state legislatures were respected. Nixon's appointment of three other justices—Harry Blackmun, Lewis Powell, and William Rehnquist—seemed to presage an imminent counterrevolution in constitutional law. President Nixon boasted that his appointees, all adherents to the ideas of original intent and strict interpretation of the Constitution, would lead the Court down a new path toward judicial restraint and deference to the majoritarian process. But as history has shown, presidents have been less than successful at predicting how their nominees will behave once they are secure on the bench. President Eisenhower, a conservative Republican, appointed Earl Warren and William Brennan, justices who ultimately became the most influential liberal activists to serve on the Supreme Court. Eisenhower once quipped that his appointment of Warren was the biggest mistake he had ever made. And so it was that Nixon's prediction of an impending counterrevolution in civil rights and liberties was premature. As we have seen, the Nixon appointees brought about a few modest limitations on the scope of due process rights, but, in balance, the Burger Court left intact the constitutional handiwork of the Warren Court and actually expanded many of the Warren Court's rulings on reproductive freedom, church-state relations, freedom of expression, and discrimination. Those expecting a counterrevolution were gravely disappointed.

Although he did not "lead" the Court as Warren had, Chief Justice Burger proved to be a pragmatic jurist who balanced his deep respect for the Constitution with the demands of a nascent "new federalism" that reached its zenith during the Reagan years. Burger was neither a civil libertarian nor a conservative radical bent on overturning precedent. Nor was Blackmun destined to move the Court to the right. During his first two terms on the Court, Blackmun criticized the Warren Court's liberal judicial activism in the area of criminal due process, voting consistently with Chief Justice Burger and the other conservatives. However, after several terms, Blackmun began to move away from Burger toward the liberal Justices Brennan and Marshall. Though still somewhat conservative on criminal due process issues, Blackmun established a reputation as a moderate-to-liberal jurist following his controversial opinion in *Roe v. Wade*.

Justice Powell earned the reputation of an independent conservative while serving on the Court from 1971 to 1987. Powell voted more consistently with Burger and Rehnquist than any other justice on the Burger Court. Although a staunch advocate of judicial restraint, Powell was not afraid to break from his conservative colleagues in defense of *Roe v. Wade* or to support the Warren Court's stand on school prayer and governmental aid to parochial schools.

Of the four Nixon appointments, only William Rehnquist has lived up to the expectations of the counterrevolutionaries. Rehnquist brought to the Court a solidly conservative philosophy developed during his tenure as assistant attorney general in charge of the Office of Legal Counsel during the Nixon administration, and has remained true to that cause for more than twenty years as associate and chief justice. A well-known critic of the Warren Court, Rehnquist immediately developed a reputation as the "Lone Ranger," penning iconoclastic dissenting opinions reflecting a judicial philosophy comprised of original intent, states' rights, and a narrow interpretation of the Bill of Rights and the Fourteenth Amendment. In his dissents, Rehnquist left very few of the Warren Court's decisions unchallenged, but since he was virtually alone in his thinking, his arguments served only as a harbinger of things to come. Rehnquist could influence the Court only by assembling a bloc of like-minded justices.

The judicial appointments of President Reagan pushed the Court in Rehnquist's direction. When Justice Stewart stepped down in 1981, Reagan kept his promise to nominate the first woman to the high bench by appointing Sandra Day O'Connor, a former Arizona legislator and state court of appeals judge. In her first term, she fell in line with Rehnquist, her Stanford Law School classmate, and Chief Justice Burger. Her early opinions demonstrated an eagerness to defer to the legislative process and to narrowly interpret the Bill of Rights and the Fourteenth Amendment. When Chief Justice Burger retired in 1986, Reagan nominated William Rehnquist to the chief justiceship with the hope of implementing a clear-cut conservative agenda. Rehnquist was narrowly confirmed by the Senate despite fierce and acrimonious debate. Reagan also appointed Antonin Scalia, a former law professor and D.C. Circuit appeals court judge. It was hoped that through his intellectual power Scalia would lead the Court down the path of conservatism.

Between 1988 and 1992, President Reagan and his successor, President George H. W. Bush, made a number of appointments that solidified a conservative majority. In 1988, after Reagan's nomination of Robert Bork was rejected by the Senate, conservative court of appeals judge Anthony Kennedy was confirmed, replacing retiring Justice Powell. Court-watchers predicted that Kennedy, purported to be even more conservative than Bork, would fall in line with Scalia's strict interpretation of the Constitution.

In 1991, Justice Brennan, once called the most powerful liberal in America, retired from the Court after serving thirty-four years. President Bush filled the vacancy with Judge David Souter, a moderately conservative justice from the New Hampshire Supreme Court. President Bush had an opportunity to make a second appointment when Justice Thurgood Marshall, the first African American to serve on the Supreme Court, announced his retirement in 1991. Marshall had long postponed his retirement with the hope that a Democratic president would appoint his successor. Bush replaced Marshall with Clarence Thomas, also an African American, who had served as chair of the Equal Employment Opportunity Commission (EEOC) during the Reagan administration and as a court of appeals judge for one year prior to his appointment to the Court. The similarities between Thomas and Marshall go no further than race and humble origin, for most of Thomas's views are often nearly diametrically opposed to Marshall's not only on policy issues but also on the proper application of judicial power. It seemed that the stage was finally set for the counterrevolution.

However, the fortunes of the Republican Party changed in 1992 when Bill Clinton defeated President George H. W. Bush. Had Thurgood Marshall held out for just another year President Clinton would have chosen his successor and the Court's composition would have been dramatically different. After Republican presidents had made ten consecutive appointments, President Clinton was in a position to shape the Supreme Court and federal judiciary. When Byron White stepped down in 1993, Clinton filled the vacancy with Ruth Bader Ginsburg, a moderate-to-liberal U.S. court of appeals judge who easily sailed through the Senate confirmation process. In 1994, Justice Blackmun announced his retirement, and Clinton appointed Steven Breyer, a moderate U.S. court of appeals judge who was easily confirmed by the Senate. Clinton won a second term in 1996 but did not have an opportunity to make a third appointment. As we have seen in the preceding chapters, the Court took a dramatic conservative turn under the leadership of Chief Justice Rehnquist and the Reagan and Bush appointees. However, the question was whether the two Clinton appointees could forge a moderate bloc of justices and prevent the Court from drifting further to the right or, perhaps, bring the Court back to the center.

*Did the Rehnquist Court lead a counterrevolution by bringing about a dramatic shift in civil rights and liberties? Were the celebrated rulings of the Warren and Burger eras abandoned? Or, notwithstanding the tenure of the conservatives, such as Rehnquist, Scalia, and Thomas, did the principle of* stare decisis, *or respect for precedent, forestall or prevent dramatic change in the voting patterns of the Court? What impact did the Clinton appointees have on the Court?* A review of selected cases from earlier chapters will help to answer these questions.

## FREEDOM OF EXPRESSION: NEW STANDARDS OF REVIEW

Amidst the patriotism of the 1980s, the flag-burning cases provided the Court's new conservative coalition with an excellent opportunity to reexamine past rulings on symbolic conduct. It was clear that the new conservative bloc, led by Chief Justice Rehnquist, would work to limit the scope of First Amendment protection of symbolic and expressive conduct. The conservatives had long advocated applying a lesser degree of scrutiny to laws that restrict symbolic conduct, a kind of expression thought to exist only on the periphery of First Amendment protection. However, with the help of Reagan appointee Anthony Kennedy, the Court narrowly overturned the Texas flag desecration statute, thus establishing the rule that the state may not ban flag burning merely because it is offensive to a majority of its citizens.

Chief Justice Rehnquist—joined by O'Connor, White, and Stevens—based his dissenting argument on a narrow reading of "expression" and on the state's prerogative to remove the flag from the list of symbols and objects that can be used or abused for the purpose of symbolic expression. The bloc of four dissenters embraced the position that Johnson's actions were of such minimal value that they were far outweighed by state interests in preventing breach of peace. Surprisingly, and no doubt greatly disappointing to the counterrevolutionaries, was the moderate position taken by Justice Kennedy. Kennedy refused to join with the Rehnquist–O'Connor bloc, joining instead the three liberals—Brennan, Marshall, and Blackmun. Kennedy argued in support of extending First Amendment protection to flag burning, admitting that sometimes "we make decisions we do not like" and that many Americans will be "dismayed" by the decision.

The flag-burning issue is far from settled. The new patriotic fervor that has swept the nation following the terrorist attacks of September 11, 2001, is likely to reinvigorate interest in laws that protect the American flag from desecration. Given this new national mood and the fact that the flag-burning cases were so narrowly decided (5–4), it is likely that the Court will revisit this issue in the near future.

The Court's willingness to limit the protection afforded to symbolic conduct by reexamining established standards of review is evident in its rulings on nude dancing. Although exotic dancing enjoys some protection, when speech and nonspeech elements combine in an activity such as dancing, "a sufficiently important governmental interest" in restricting the nonspeech element—public nudity—can justify limitations on the expression. The majority's position was clearly a break from the standard that the state must demonstrate a "compelling interest" if it wishes to restrict expression. Like many of the Rehnquist Court's rulings, the nude dancing decision brought mixed reviews. Civil libertarians were pleased with the Court's acknowledgment that exotic dancing is a protected activity, but were distressed by the break from the compelling interest standard and by the fact that the Court has recently made it easier for communities to combat the negative secondary effects of nude dancing. Thus, one trademark of the Rehnquist Court's jurisprudence is the subtle doctrinal shift rather than the radical departure from precedent.

Nevertheless, the Court's 7–2 ruling in *Reno v. ACLU* that online speech and publications receive the same constitutional protections as do newspapers and books was a clear indication that the Court has grasped the importance of the Internet as a new marketplace of ideas.

## CHURCH-STATE ISSUES

### Free Exercise of Religion

Chief Justice Rehnquist has never concealed his criticism of the Court's interpretation of the religion clauses of the First Amendment. Both he and Justices Scalia and Thomas have taken a literalist-majoritarian position that where the interests of a religious minority clash with the needs of the majority, the free exercise clause protects only against direct restrictions on religious liberty and not against indirect burdens placed on religious conduct by laws that advance a legitimate state interest. The Rehnquist-Scalia position hearkens back to a pre-*Sherbert* view that in order to live in society one must often subordinate the need to engage in religiously motivated conduct to the needs of the majority, especially when that conduct is not particularly appreciated by the majority.

Rehnquist's perseverance once again paid off, for in the *Goldman* yarmulke case, the majority uncritically accepted the contention of the U.S. Air Force that Captain Goldman's religiously motivated conduct posed a threat to discipline and esprit de corps. In the *Smith* peyote case, it was Justice Scalia who carried the mantle for Rehnquist, reasoning that although a state is prohibited from banning conduct solely because it is religiously motivated, the state may forbid religious conduct if the law does not directly target the practice and is evenly applied to those who commit the same activity for nonreligious reasons. Scalia ignored two well-established cases, *Sherbert* and *Thomas*, relying instead on Felix Frankfurter's reasoning in the 1940 *Minersville v. Gobitis* case to support his argument. Justice Brennan called this approach a "subrational-basis standard" of judicial review: an absolute uncritical deference to the military's discretion. Interestingly, in both *Goldman* and *Smith*, Reagan appointee O'Connor, once a close ally of Rehnquist, vigorously attacked the Rehnquist-Scalia approach as a dramatic break from established precedent and an abdication of the judicial role. She emerged from these two cases as a voice of moderation, distancing herself from the conservative bloc. In both cases, the majority abandoned the compelling interest test, which requires the government to justify any substantial restriction on religiously motivated conduct by showing that it has a clear and compelling interest and that this interest is achieved by means that are narrowly drawn. O'Connor was incensed by what she saw as a complete deference to military doctrine in the case of Captain Goldman and to law enforcement in the case of the two Native Americans. Justice Blackmun went one step further, calling Scalia's interpretation of the free exercise clause "distorted" and bordering on an abdication of judicial authority. However, in the unanimous *Lukumi Babalu* case, the Rehnquist Court ruled that when a religious practice (animal sacrifice) is burdened by a law that is not neutral or not of general application, the law must undergo the most rigorous of scrutiny. To satisfy the commands of the First Amendment, a law must advance "interests of the highest order" and must be narrowly tailored.

## Establishment of Religion

Despite predictions of a counterrevolution in establishment clause doctrine, the Burger Court found few faults with the Warren Court's key rulings and reaffirmed the principle that government ought to remain neutral with regard to religious instruction. However, the Burger Court began backing away from the wall of separation metaphor, hinting that it would be more willing to accommodate various incursions of religion into state-sponsored activities.

By the mid-1980s, the Court's criticism of the murky nature of the three-pronged *Lemon* test resulted in a long line of inconsistent church-state rulings. Several justices hinted that the *Lemon* test had outlived its usefulness. Indeed, Justice O'Connor's initial exploration of this possibility in *Wallace v. Jaffree* in 1985 led many to believe that it was only a matter of time before the Court adopted a less exacting standard in church-state disputes, ultimately reinstating school prayer. The Reagan and George H. W. Bush administrations were hopeful that O'Connor would join with Justices Rehnquist and Scalia to call for a complete abandonment of *Lemon* and a reassessment of the establishment clause doctrine. This never materialized, and Rehnquist and Scalia remained in isolation, as evidenced by their dissenting opinion in the 1987 Louisiana creationism case.

The appointments of Justices Kennedy, Souter, and Thomas had pundits predicting an imminent move to reestablish school prayer, but again this was not to be. Justice Kennedy disappointed many in the 1992 case *Lee v. Weisman*, voting to affirm the Court's long-standing ban on prayer in public school by striking down prayers at graduation ceremonies. Resisting pressures exerted by the federal government to overrule the twenty-year-old *Lemon* test, Kennedy joined O'Connor in the moderate center of the Court. Just three years earlier, Kennedy had joined Rehnquist, Scalia, and White in calling for a reexamination of *Lemon*, but in *Lee* Kennedy changed his mind and broke from the Rehnquist-Scalia-Thomas conservative bloc. Furthermore, Kennedy was joined by Souter in refusing to reexamine establishment clause precedent. Souter, voting in his first establishment clause case, surprised conservatives by embracing a firm stand against any violation of the separation of church and state—a position compatible with that of retired Justice Brennan. "The state may not favor or endorse either religion generally over nonreligion or one religion over others," Souter wrote, concluding that "[o]ur aspiration to religious liberty, embodied in the First Amendment, permits no other standard." Souter, who has served on the Court since 1990, staked out a moderate position quite early and has excoriated the most conservative members of the Court—Rehnquist, Scalia, and Thomas—for their radical positions. Justices White, Rehnquist, and Thomas joined with Scalia to signal their readiness to adopt a more accommodating position toward traditional religious practices, a position that Rehnquist has been arguing since his arrival in 1971. *Lee v. Weisman* demonstrated how near the Court came to uprooting twenty years of church-state precedent in favor of a more accommodationist position that would allow local communities to placate religious interests. However, with Clinton's appointments of Ginsburg and Breyer, the continued moderation of Souter, and the stamina of Stevens (serving since 1975), such an upheaval in church-state doctrine did not materialize. Indeed, as we saw in the

Court's 2000 ruling on prayer at football games, six justices strongly reaffirmed *Lee v. Weisman* to rule that students' free exercise of religion does not supercede the limitations imposed on the government by the establishment clause.

## DUE PROCESS

No area of constitutional law has changed more over the past fifty years than the due process rights of persons suspected or accused of criminal conduct. Through an unprecedented use of judicial power, the Warren Court reined in the archaic, overzealous, and heavy-handed law enforcement techniques of the day by expanding the protection against unreasonable searches and seizures, providing new mechanisms to strengthen the right against self-incrimination, and extending the right to counsel to noncapital crimes. In doing so, Warren also led the greatest revolution in constitutional law—the nationalization of the Bill of Rights through selective incorporation. This dramatically altered not only the relationship between the individual and the state but also the nature of federalism. The Rehnquist Court has not directly commented on the wisdom of selective incorporation, largely because the doctrine is too firmly entrenched in constitutional law.

The Burger Court modified many Warren Court rulings, but the landmark rulings were left intact and the predicted counterrevolution never occurred. However, as a conservative majority solidified on the Rehnquist Court, substantial doctrinal changes as well as outright reversals of precedent occurred. By the late 1980s, Chief Justice Rehnquist, no longer the lone dissenter, was successful in building coalitions of justices willing to reexamine the underlying doctrines and principles of well-established due process protection. Changes in due process jurisprudence has taken the form of both subtle doctrinal shifts and departure from numerous precedents.

Several significant changes have come about in search and seizure law. For instance, in the area of drug testing of individuals in safety-sensitive jobs, the Court has waived all probable cause and individualized suspicion requirements, thus allowing invasions of privacy solely on the basis of reasonable suspicion and the special needs of a situation. As a result, the government is no longer expected to show a compelling interest in waiving these requirements, nor does it need to use the least-intrusive or least-restrictive means available when the right to privacy is at stake.

The Rehnquist Court has also departed from the long-standing *Carroll* doctrine by ruling that the police may conduct a warrantless search of the containers found within an automobile if there is probable cause to believe contraband or evidence is contained therein. The new logic creates a paradox: A briefcase is not subject to a warrantless search when a person is carrying it down the street, but may be subject to a warrantless search once it is locked in the person's car. Going one step further, the Court expanded this exception by ruling that once a driver of a vehicle gives police permission to search the car, the police do not need a warrant to open any containers found inside the automobile.

The Rehnquist Court also demonstrated an eagerness to break from precedent in order to help the states fight the war on drugs by authorizing warrantless, suspicion-less, dragnet-style searches of mass transportation in intrastate and interstate travel and by its ruling that the Fourth Amendment does not apply to situations where police are pursuing a fleeing individual. In the dragnet search case, Justice O'Connor loosely interpreted established precedent to justify what three members of the Court believed to be an outcome based not on reason but on deference to the exigencies of the war on drugs. In the street pursuit case, Justice Scalia relied on a pre-Warren-era definition of seizure in order to justify an exception to the reasonable suspicion rule that police must follow before chasing someone down the street.

While the Rehnquist Court has refused to overturn *Miranda* outright, it has ruled that a coerced confession may be used as evidence in a criminal trial if it can be shown that the confession was the result of a "harmless error" on the part of the police. In doing so, the Court undermined its earlier rulings that coerced confessions could never really be harmless. The Court has also loosened the restrictions on the admissibility of coerced confessions by ruling that recorded conversations containing incriminating statements made after a defendant has been read his or her rights may be admitted as evidence at trial. These are but two of many cases that illustrate a tendency of the Rehnquist Court to adopt the narrowest possible interpretation of a settled precedent such as *Miranda* without actually overturning it. Over the years, the Court has gone out of its way to weaken *Miranda* by creating exceptions and by diminishing its importance through references to the *Miranda* warnings as "not themselves rights protected by the Constitution." It came as a surprise, therefore, when Chief Justice Rehnquist joined the majority in *Dickerson* to uphold *Miranda* because of the principle of *stare decisis*, or established precedent.

The Court's eagerness to support the war on drugs and the zero tolerance approach to drug enforcement policy is illustrated by its recent affirmation of a mandatory life sentence without parole handed down against a man convicted of possessing 650 grams of cocaine. In a ruling that significantly alters Eighth Amendment law, Justice Scalia reasoned that the sentence is not significantly disproportionate to the crime, and therefore cruel, merely because it is mandatory or because the jury is denied the opportunity to consider mitigating circumstances.

In the midst of the national debate over prison overcrowding and an outcry over early releases of inmates, the Rehnquist Court broke with the long-standing "contemporary standard of decency" rule by holding that prisoners filing complaints about prison conditions must show a deliberate indifference or culpable state of mind on the part of prison officials before corrective action must be taken by the state. Prison officials of many states who have been operating under federal court orders for years welcomed the ruling, since under this standard it will be virtually impossible for inmates to successfully challenge prison overcrowding.

Sympathetic to many Americans' frustration with the seemingly endless number of appeals available to inmates on death row, Chief Justice Rehnquist has on occasion broken from the Court's taboo on airing personal viewpoints in public to speak out on his desire to limit the number of death row appeals. As an associate justice and as chief justice, Rehnquist has fought for a change in direction in the Court's habeas corpus policy. His efforts finally bore fruit in a number of cases in which a majority voted to limit the number of petitions for habeas corpus relief. In all but exceptional cases, a prisoner's second or subsequent habeas corpus petition can now be easily dismissed by federal judges, thus allowing states to carry out executions more quickly and cost effectively.

In a significant break from established capital sentencing doctrine, and a boon for the victim's rights movements, the Court ruled that the Eighth Amendment does not prohibit the use of victim impact statements during the sentencing phase of a capital trial. The Supreme Court's change of heart concerning such statements came after nearly two decades of intense political pressure to offset some of the rights enjoyed by defendants with rights that protect crime victims. The dissenters attacked the Court's foolhardy deference to widespread popular support for victim's rights, a position they saw as an abdication of the traditional judicial role. By overturning two rulings, the Court was in many ways encouraging further challenges to narrowly decided rulings by sending the message that it was willing to reexamine established doctrine.

The Court also made it easier for the police to stop and question someone by modifying the stop-and-frisk standard established in the 1960s. For years, law enforcement officials complained that the Court hamstringed their power to stop and question a suspicious person either loitering in a high-crime area or running away at the sight of police. Rehnquist reasoned that an officer does not need probable cause to stop a suspect, merely a "reasonable articulable suspicion" that criminal activity is occurring. The ruling does make it more likely that the police will stop innocent people, Rehnquist admitted, but it is a minimal intrusion justified by Americans' desire for safer streets.

## PRIVACY: TRANSFORMATION FROM A CONSTITUTIONAL RIGHT TO A LIBERTY INTEREST

The right of privacy established in *Griswold v. Connecticut* and expanded by *Roe v. Wade* has been virtually abandoned by the Court. Despite the fact that the Court has not openly overturned *Griswold*, no other constitutional right has been subjected to the kind of narrowing than the right of privacy. Ever since Justice Douglas led a majority to elevate privacy to constitutional status, it has been under attack by conservative forces. From the very beginning, Rehnquist attacked the right as purely an act of judicial invention and sought to narrow its largely undefined parameters. If the right of privacy does exist in Rehnquist's jurisprudence, it is only in the narrowest possible terms. The Burger Court began its drive to narrow the right when, in *Bowers v. Hardwick*, Justice White refused to extend the right of privacy to homosexual conduct. In cases affecting personal privacy, the majority refused even to mention the right of privacy as such, instead applying a Fourteenth Amendment "liberty interest" analysis to governmental intrusions, as in the instance of drug testing. Chief Justice Rehnquist adopted this approach in the controversial *Cruzan* right to die case. He recognized a constitutionally protected significant liberty interest to refuse unwanted medical treatment, but refrained from analyzing the issue in terms of the right of privacy as state courts had done since the famous *Quinlan* decision in 1973. Rehnquist also adopted this approach in the matter of assisted suicide, arguing that laws outlawing assisted suicide are based on a rational interest in protecting life and do not infringe upon any fundamental right. By employing the sliding scale of liberty interest in questions involving drug testing, sexual relations, the termination of unwanted medical treatment, and abortion, the Court has given the states more discretion to judge how privacy is to be balanced with legitimate governmental interests in safety and morality. The Court now analyzes privacy claims from the standpoint of a number of subsidiary liberty interests that are protected by the due process clauses of the Fifth and Fourteenth Amendments rather than through a fundamental privacy right approach. This approach permits the Court to remain flexible and noncommittal. Thus, while the Court has not openly rejected the existence of a constitutional right of privacy, it has gradually chipped away at its fundamental status, leaving the right as a ghost of its former self.

## ABORTION RIGHTS

The weakened right of privacy has also made it easier for the Court to allow greater restrictions on abortions. It was in *Webster* that newly appointed Justice Kennedy cast the fifth vote to uphold a highly restrictive anti-abortion statute, thus undermining the foundations of *Roe v. Wade*. Because the trimester framework was regarded as a straitjacket on state autonomy, the Court adopted Justice O'Connor's undue burden standard allowing the states to assert an interest in potential life before twenty weeks or viability. According to this standard, states may restrict abortions unless the restrictions impose an undue burden on a woman's abortion decision. Satisfied by the O'Connor standard, the Court refused to overturn *Roe* outright. Only Justice Scalia, who would have little to do with implied rights and balancing tests, called for an outright overruling of *Roe* largely on the grounds that abortion is a political issue to be resolved by the legislatures.

The retirement of Justice Brennan in 1990 and Justice Marshall in 1991 set the stage for a possible outright reversal of *Roe*. Encouraged by the confirmation of Justices Souter and Thomas, and egged on by the federal government, a number of states boldly enacted a host of new restrictions on abortion. One such law was the Pennsylvania Abortion Control Act. While not banning abortions outright, the law required women to wait for twenty-four hours after listening to a presentation intended to dissuade them from having an abortion before undergoing an abortion. The law also required teenagers to obtain consent from one parent or a judge, physicians to make reports to the state, and a married woman to notify her husband before undergoing an abortion. The prediction was that a majority of justices—Rehnquist, Scalia, White, Kennedy, and Thomas—would vote to overturn *Roe*, while O'Connor, Blackmun, Stevens, and perhaps Souter would vote to reaffirm the 1973 ruling. However, in a surprising move, Justice Kennedy reversed his earlier position and shifted to the O'Connor bloc, upholding *Roe* by the slimmest of margins. In sustaining all but the spousal notification provision of the Pennsylvania law, the majority in *Casey* adopted a version of O'Connor's undue burden standard, defining an undue burden as a "substantial obstacle in the path of a woman seeking an abortion before the fetus attains viability." Four of the nine justices—Rehnquist, Scalia, White, and Thomas—argued that the Court should have overturned *Roe*. Strangely, both proponents and opponents of abortion rights hailed the ruling as a victory, albeit a dubious one. Proponents were obviously relieved that *Roe* was not overturned, but they were dismayed by the Court's willingness to allow additional restrictions on abortion. Opponents of abortion rights were relieved that the Court had no intention of returning to its earlier doctrinal approach to abortion rights—the *Roe* trimester framework.

Justice O'Connor's position in the Pennsylvania case was a departure from her more conservative position in *Webster* that the state had a compelling interest in fetal life at any stage of gestation. Indeed, when O'Connor was first appointed to the Court in 1981, she indicated a willingness to abandon *Roe*. But in *Casey* she reaffirmed what she believed to be the essence of *Roe*: A woman has the right to choose before viability without undue interference from the state.

In many ways the majority's position was a cautious one—judicial restraint in the face of well-established precedent. The dissenters—led by Chief Justice Rehnquist—were more willing to take a conservative activist position to break with established law. Rehnquist argued that since *Roe* was wrongly decided in the first place, the doctrine of *stare decisis* did not apply. Furthermore, since the *Roe* framework of analysis was already abandoned in previous cases, *Roe v. Wade* was merely a facade for an entirely new way of adjudicating abortion rights cases.

Over the years, Scalia, embracing the role of legal purist, remained true to his position that since the decision to terminate a pregnancy is not explicitly protected by the U.S. Constitution and abortion has traditionally been prohibited by the states, the Court should wash its hand of the entire issue and return it to the states where the people can make the political compromises necessary to resolve the issue. While Scalia's arguments are well reasoned, containing the forceful logic of a constitutional scholar, he has been unable to muster the consistent support of a bloc of justices who wish to follow his intellectual lead. As made evident by a number of his lone dissenting opinions, Scalia appears to be more interested in logic than compromise or coalition-building. One could also argue that his logic and constitutional purity are merely a veneer for his own brand of conservative activism—a bending of the Constitution in favor of the majoritarian process and socially conservative morality.

At the time of *Casey* in 1992, many believed that only one justice stood in the way of completing the counterrevolution in the area of women's reproductive rights that began with *Beal v. Doe* in 1977. At the center of this highly divided Court was eighty-three-year-old Harry Blackmun, author of the *Roe* opinion. It was believed that if Blackmun, or Justice Stevens for that matter, were to be succeeded by a justice willing to vote with the conservative bloc, a constitutional right would surely cease to exist. Yet, the appointments of Ginsburg and Breyer by Clinton, the moderation of Souter, the commitment of O'Connor to *Roe* as settled precedent, and the reluctance of Stevens to retire seem to have solidified support for the right to abortion for some years to come. However, Justice Kennedy did break from the O'Connor bloc to vote with Rehnquist, Scalia, and Thomas in the "partial birth" abortion decision in 2000. Kennedy maintained his support for *Casey* in principle, but yielded to Nebraska's asserted interests in "erecting a barrier to infanticide" and in the integrity of the medical profession. As they have done in the past, Chief Justice Rehnquist and Justices Scalia and Thomas rejected *Roe* and *Casey* outright.

## EQUAL PROTECTION: RESPECT FOR PRECEDENT

*Has the Court remained committed to the principle of equal protection of Brown?* Justice Clarence Thomas's controversial confirmation in 1992 led many to predict that the Rehnquist Court now had the votes to back away from the principle of equal protection. After all, the Rehnquist Court had already been willing to narrow the Warren and Burger Courts' positions on race- and sex-based discrimination.

However, the Court's rulings during the 1990s do not square with this charge and, in fact, demonstrate that the Court is still seriously committed to the principle of equal protection. Shortly after Thomas's confirmation, the Rehnquist Court handed down a surprising 8–1 ruling (Scalia dissenting) in the pivotal *Fordice* case, where the Court ruled that according to the principles laid down in *Brown* and *Green*, public universities and colleges in Mississippi must go much further than merely establishing racially neutral admissions policies to achieve equal protection?

Despite the *Fordice* ruling, many civil rights advocates continued to criticize the Court, particularly for its refusal to adopt the two-class theory of equal protection advanced by retired justices Brennan and Marshall. Recall that the two-class theory applies a lesser degree of judicial scrutiny to discrimination against white males, thus making it more difficult to bring reverse discrimination challenges to preferential treatment policies. But others have praised the Court for embracing the "color-blind" theory of equal protection.

On the issue of affirmative action, however, the Rehnquist Court has braved an unwavering and solidly conservative path. Race-based remedies, such as set-asides, can be used only as legal remedies when it can be proved that intentional discrimination can be traced directly to the actions of decision-makers.

Aside from affirmative action, the counterrevolution in equal protection jurisprudence never did materialize. There is no evidence that the Rehnquist Court has abdicated its duty to implement the principles of equal protection and the ideals established by the Warren Court in *Brown*. It has broadened protections against sex discrimination in the Virginia Military Institute (VMI) ruling, by introducing a new legal standard in gender classification cases. In the past, any classification based on gender had to "serve important governmental objectives and must be substantially related to the achievement of those objectives." Now, under the VMI ruling, the government must show an "exceedingly persuasive justification" to support a gender-based classification.

During the 1990s, the Court also embraced and broadened the concept of sexual harassment and made it easier to hold an employer liable in sexual harassment cases. Applying the equal protection clause, the Court has also made it more difficult for a state to thwart efforts by local governments to protect against discrimination on the basis of sexual preference. Finally, in *Bush v. Gore* in 2000 the Court expanded its one person, one vote jurisprudence established by the Warren Court in *Baker v. Carr.*

## COMPETING JUDICIAL PHILOSOPHIES AND THE DIRECTION OF THE COURT

As stated at the outset of this book, judicial philosophy refers to an amalgam of a justice's substantive policy choices, beliefs about the proper application of judicial review, and approach to constitutional interpretation. The competing judicial philosophies on the Warren, Burger, and Rehnquist Courts have been critical to the development and evolution of our civil rights and liberties. Although judicial philosophies on the Burger Court often pulled in opposite directions, the Burger era was one of moderate judicial restraint, generally characterized by a somewhat narrow reading of the Constitution; an effort to defer to the legislative process (mostly in the area of criminal due process); and where no precedent interceded, a respect for the moral traditions in the states. The fact that the Burger years left the Warren Court's major rulings intact (and in some instances expanded upon them) can be attributed more to Burger's integrity and respect for the principle of *stare decisis* than to any discernable philosophy. Burger was a conservative in the traditional sense of the word: He sought to conserve, or maintain, legal, constitutional, and political traditions. He was a passionate defender of Constitution as well as of the integrity and independence of the judiciary.

No single collective judicial philosophy has emerged on the Rehnquist Court. However, it is possible to identify several characteristics or tendencies shared by distinct blocs of justices. The arch-conservative bloc consists of Rehnquist, Scalia, and Thomas. While they are by no means identical in their views, they share a willingness to apply judicial review to promote the interests of the majority over the rights of the individual. In this sense, they can be regarded as conservative activists. As with adherents to judicial restraint, their interpretation of the Bill of Rights and Fourteenth Amendment tends to be quite narrow, but they cannot easily be classified as judicial restraintists because they do not necessarily feel constrained to follow precedent. Conservative activists are as unabashed in their agendas as are liberal activists, but where liberals champion civil liberties and rights and are suspicious of majorities, conservatives tend to promote state sovereignty and defer to the political branches of government when there is no clear constitutional proscription against doing so.

The term "Rehnquist Court" itself may be misleading, since Chief Justice Rehnquist has neither successfully "led" the Court (in the style of Earl Warren) toward a discernible goal or philosophy, nor enjoyed the consistent support of a coalition of justices across a range of issues. This is particularly true since the shift of Justices O'Connor and Kennedy away from the arch-conservative bloc and more toward the conservative-moderate center. Rehnquist's impact on the Court has been largely confined to the area of due process, where many of his positions, once dismissed as unorthodox or radical, are now enjoying majority support. It is in this area of law that Rehnquist has been successful in convincing a majority of justices that *stare decisis* should not stand in the way of conservative activism and that the Court should not be afraid to overturn precedents decided by 5–4 margins.

The principle of *stare decisis* is strongest for the chief justice in cases involving property and contract rights for, as he reasons, people would be fearful to enter into commercial transactions if the law were to constantly change. On the other hand, *stare decisis* has less force in cases involving implied procedural rights and in narrowly decided cases where a great deal of disagreement exists among the justices. However, Rehnquist's decision to uphold *Miranda* in *Dickerson* contradicts such a characterization. While this approach to constitutional adjudication may seem somewhat unorthodox, we should not underestimate its impact on civil rights and liberties, since the chief justice can use his agenda-setting and opinion-assignment role to encourage a plurality of his conservative associates to approach narrowly decided precedents in the same manner. Rehnquist has also worked tirelessly to bring about subtle doctrinal shifts resulting in the application of lesser degrees of judicial scrutiny, the retreat from the compelling interest test, and the adoption of the sliding scale of liberty interests approach to privacy questions. If the policies of the Reagan-Bush (1981–1992) era can be understood as a reaction to liberal politics rather than as a revolution of new ideas, Rehnquist has had a tendency to use the Court to clear the path of obstacles blocking the political branches from implementing conservative reforms.

Justice Scalia's opinions are nearly as cryptic as they are erudite. On the surface, his arguments demonstrate a predisposition toward legal purism and judicial restraint, but upon further study, they illustrate his conservative moralism and willingness to uphold laws reflecting the moral interests of the community. His emphasis on the importance of majoritarian rights can be seen in his criticism of the Court's ban on prayer at public school graduation ceremonies and football games as contrary to "long-standing American tradition." Thus, Scalia's judicial philosophy is an amalgam of judicial restraint, scepticism of earlier rulings, and conservative moralism. As we saw in his dissent in the Louisiana creation science case, Scalia argued that the Court should not let the establishment clause interfere with legislators expressing their religious convictions through law. Regardless of the value or veracity of those convictions, or whether they promulgate religious doctrine, legislators have the right to advance the moral teaching of their choosing. This conservative moralism, also evident in his opinions on abortion and obscenity, is more likely to be employed in cases involving rights or issues that either are not explicitly defined in the Bill of Rights or are resolved by earlier rulings. This is not to imply, however, that Scalia is loathe to break from well-established constitutional doctrine.

It is not likely that Scalia's forceful intellect will lead the Court to a conservative promised land unless President George W. Bush fulfills his promise to elevate Scalia to the chief justiceship and appoint a few more like-minded justices. We might then see a revolution not only in civil rights and liberties but also in nearly every area of constitutional law. For now, Scalia often seems somewhat philosophically isolated from many of his associates. Justice Clarence Thomas, who demonstrates a similar kind of conservative moralism and votes with Scalia 80 percent of the time, is much more pragmatic on a range of issues, particularly equal protection. Nevertheless, we can predict from Justice Thomas's record that he will likely remain in the arch-conservative bloc rather than gravitating toward the moderate center.

The second bloc of justices consists of Stevens, Souter, Ginsburg, and Breyer—the most liberal members of the court, who all vote with each other more than 75 percent of the time. This bloc of justices is more likely to uphold and expand upon the Warren and Burger Court's rulings on freedom of expression, privacy, due process, and equal protection. Justice Stevens, appointed by President Ford in 1975, is considered the leader of the liberal bloc of the Court. As we have seen, Stevens has written some of the most scathing dissents when the conservatives are in the majority. By the same token, he can be a nonideological jurist who attempts to build a consensus among justices.

Justice Souter, appointed by President George H. W. Bush in 1990 began his tenure as a moderate conservative but has leaned more toward the liberal-to-moderate justices with each new ruling. A libertarian (rather than a social) conservative in the New England tradition, Souter is willing to respect traditional community values, but is highly suspicious of governmental intrusion on personal rights. During his first term in 1990, he voted with the chief justice nearly 90 percent of the time, but very quickly severed this connection in order to join with the more moderate Justices O'Connor and Kennedy. Justice Souter demonstrates a reverence for precedent that has placed him at the Court's moderate center, voting with Stevens approximately 70 percent of the time and with Breyer and Ginsburg about 80 percent of the time. However, many of these alliances are issue-specific.

The third bloc of justices consists of Justices O'Connor and Kennedy (both moderate conservatives) who vote with the arch-conservatives about 70 percent of the time. However, on numerous occasions O'Connor and Kennedy have provided the liberal bloc with the crucial fifth or sixth vote to uphold well-established precedent. O'Connor typically joins with the liberal bloc in abortion cases, such as the controversial "partial birth" abortion ruling in 2000. Much like former Chief Justice Burger, O'Connor and Kennedy are more respectful of precedent and seek a pragmatic balance between individual and group rights. They also tend to read the Constitution narrowly, but unlike their arch-conservative associates they are more respectful of the Court's historic role of guardian of the Bill of Rights. Since they have no obvious political or ideological agenda, it is unlikely that the O'Connor-Kennedy bloc will attempt to lead the Court in any particular direction. The two justices believe that the Court should remain a largely reactive (rather than proactive) body unless the political process fails to resolve a difficult social or political problem, such as abortion or sexual harassment. Furthermore, unless a fundamental right is directly abridged, O'Connor and Kennedy are more likely to approach a challenged statute neither from a presumption of constitutionality nor unconstitutionality. Instead, they focus on the nature of the burden placed on the freedom relative to the importance of the governmental interest advanced. While they are not likely to place particularly onerous burdens on lawmakers seeking to advance legitimate state interests, neither will they allow political forces to seriously debilitate fundamental rights.

With the help of Justices O'Connor and Kennedy, the liberal bloc presently seems to have the arch-conservatives at bay, keeping the Court from moving further to the right. This configuration of justices helps account for a spate of moderate rulings after a series of departures from precedent and politically conservative rulings. Without speculating on future appointments, but based rather on the evidence at hand, it is likely that the Court will remain on this path of moderation. Perhaps, with time, even Justice Thomas will move to the center and join his moderate associates.

On the Supreme Court, moderation rather than radicalism is the norm. Although there are many reasons that may account for this tradition, one explanation rests in the concept of role perception. A justice's perception of the proper role of the Supreme Court weighs heavily on the development of his or her judicial philosophy and may account for a justice's "moderation" while on the Court. A liberal or conservative policy agenda or political ideology may be tempered somewhat by the realization that *stare decisis* is a core value of our system of law. So too is the fact that a justice is under pressure to justify each decision through logic and a host of well-respected constitutional norms. Personal preferences may pale in light of the awesome role of guardian of the Constitution thrust upon each of the justices. Even the most ardent ideologue would hesitate to abdicate the power of judicial review, something that O'Connor often accuses Rehnquist of doing.

As we have seen, the Rehnquist Court has left undisturbed many of the Warren and Burger Courts' equal protection cases and has not overturned the controversial rulings on abortion and symbolic conduct. However, it has assiduously worked to eviscerate much of the doctrinal underpinnings of these earlier opinions. Very few opinions have remained untouched by this reexamination. The celebrated precedents still exist, but in many instances only as shells of their former being, as in the case of the right of privacy and search and seizure law. The Rehnquist Court has asserted the existence of a right, but then proceeds to allow almost every conceivable governmental restriction or limitation on it. Perhaps it is in this light that we can fully understand the counterrevolution. By rethinking established modes of constitutional adjudication, the Rehnquist Court has tipped the scales more in the direction of states' rights, community interests, law and order, and majority rule, bringing us, in some instances, nearly full circle to many of the judicial doctrines of the pre-Warren era. In cases where the most conservative justices are able to muster a majority, the Court resembles a reverse mirror-image of the Warren Court—that is, a conservative activist body, not reluctant to revisit established precedent, break new ground, and boldly assert itself into the political process.[1]

The changing fortunes of the two political parties, the long-term evolution of a particular justice's philosophy, and the unforeseen kinds of issues that will be heard in the next ten or twenty years make it nearly impossible to predict the Court's direction in the twenty-first century. In fact, history teaches us that the Court tends to defy the predictions of presidents, pundits, and legal scholars. It is safe to predict, however, that the Court 's influence will not be diminished during its third century and will likely continue to grow as it has since Chief Justice John Marshall penned *Marbury v. Madison* in 1803.

## NOTES

1.  It is noteworthy that outside the area of civil rights and liberties—and thus beyond the scope of this book—lies another dimension of constitutional law: state-federal relations. It is in this area that the Rehnquist Court is taking an even more conservative—perhaps radical—path. A dominant conservative bloc of justices is in the process of developing a new theory of federalism. In a number of recent cases dealing with congressional power to regulate matters such as radioactive waste, political term limits, Indian gaming,

employment law, and gun control, the Court has adopted some very provocative ideas in order to place limits on the regulatory power of the federal government.

However, the Court's 5–4 split, its deep philosophical divisions, and external practical politics all have an effect on how far the conservative majority can go in its redefinition of state sovereignty. The world of federalism as we know it may be turned upside down. A highly ideological Court armed with a broad concept of state sovereignty would make it very difficult for Congress or the president to develop and implement a range of solutions to pressing problems—even if such federal solutions enjoy widespread popularity with the people and are supported by the states themselves.

# Selected Further Readings

Abernathy, Glen. *The Right of Assembly and Association*. New York: Columbia University Press, 1981.

Abraham, Henry J. *Freedom and the Court: Civil Rights and Liberties in the United States*. 6th ed. New York: Oxford University Press, 1988.

_____. *The Judicial Process*. 7th ed. New York: Oxford University Press, 1998.

_____. *Justices and Presidents*. 2nd ed. New York: Oxford University Press, 1985.

Alley, Robert S. *The Supreme Court on Church and State*. New York: Oxford University Press, 1988.

Arthur, John. *The Unfinished Constitution*. Belmont, CA: Wadsworth Publishing, 1989.

Baer, Judith. *Equality Under the Constitution*. New York: Cornell University Press, 1983.

Barnes, Catherine. *Journey From Jim Crow: The Desegregation of Southern Transit*. New York: Columbia University Press, 1983.

Berger, Raoul. *Death Penalties: The Supreme Court's Obstacle Course*. Cambridge, MA: Harvard University Press, 1982.

_____. *Government by Judiciary: The Transformation of the Fourteenth Amendment*. Cambridge, MA: Harvard University Press, 1977.

Black, Hugo. *A Constitutional Faith*. New York: Alfred Knopf, 1969.

Blasi, Vincent (ed.). *The Burger Court: The Counterrevolution That Wasn't*. New Haven, CT: Yale University Press, 1983.

Bodenhamer, David J. *Fair Trial: Rights of the Accused in American History*. New York: Oxford University Press, 1992.

Bork, Robert. *The Tempting of America: The Political Seduction of the Law*. New York: Free Press, 1990.

Cannon, Mark, and David O'Brien (eds.). *Views From the Bench: The Judiciary and Constitutional Politics*. Chatham, NJ: Chatham House, 1985.

Cooper, Phillip J. *Battles on the Bench*. Lawrence: University of Kansas Press, 1995.

Cox, Archibald. *The Court and the Constitution*. Boston: Houghton Mifflin Co., 1987.

Davis, Derek. *Original Intent: Chief Justice Rehnquist and the Course of American Church/State Relations*. Buffalo, NY: Prometheus Books, 1991.

Dionne, E. J., and Kristol, William (eds.). *Bush v. Gore: The Court Cases and Commentary.* Washington, D.C.: Brookings Institution Press, 2001

Downs, D. A. *Nazis in Skokie: Freedom, Communication and the First Amendment.* South Bend, IN: Notre Dame University Press, 1985.

Ducat, Craig. *Modes of Constitutional Interpretation.* St. Paul, MN: West Publishing, 1978.

Dworkin, Ronald. *Taking Rights Seriously.* Cambridge, MA: Harvard University Press, 1982.

Epstein, Lee, and Knight, Jack. *The Choices Justices Make.* Washington, D.C.: Congressional Quarterly Press, 1998.

Fellman, David. *The Constitutional Right of Association.* Columbia: University of South Carolina Press, 1963.

Forer, Louis. *A Chilling Effect: The Mounting Threat of Libel and Invasion of Privacy Actions to the First Amendment.* New York: Norton, 1987.

Glazer, Nathan. *Affirmative Action.* New York: Basic Books, 1976.

LaFave, Wayne. *Search and Seizure: A Treatise on the Fourth Amendment.* Mineola, NY: Foundation Press, 1978.

Levy, Leonard. *The Establishment Clause: Religion and the First Amendment.* New York: Macmillan, 1986.

Lewis, Anthony. *Gideon's Trumpet.* New York: Random House, 1964.

Lofgren, Charles. *The* Plessy *Case.* New York: Oxford University Press, 1987.

Maltz, Earl M. *The Chief Justiceship of Warren Burger.* Columbia: University of South Carolina Press, 2000.

McCann, Michael W., and Gerald Houseman. *Judging the Constitution.* Glenview, IL: Scott, Foresman and Co., 1989.

McCloskey, Robert G. *The American Supreme Court.* Chicago: University of Chicago Press, 1960.

MacKinnon, Catherine. *Sexual Harassment of Working Women.* New Haven, CT: Yale University Press, 1979.

Meiklejohn, Alexander. "The First Amendment *IS* an Absolute," in *The Supreme Court Review.* Chicago: University of Chicago Press, 1961.

Mezey, Susan Gluck. *In Pursuit of Equality: Women, Public Policy, and the Federal Courts.* New York: St. Martin's Press, 1992.

Momeyer, Richard W. *Confronting Death.* Bloomington: Indiana University Press, 1988.

Nelson, Harold (ed.). *Freedom of the Press From Hamilton to the Warren Court.* New York: Bobbs-Merrill, 1967.

Nieman, Donald G. *Promises to Keep: African-Americans and the Constitutional Order, 1776 to the Present.* New York: Oxford University Press, 1991.

O'Brien, David M. *Storm Center: The Supreme Court in American Politics,* 5th edition. New York: Norton, 2000.

Perry, H. W., Jr. *Deciding to Decide: Agenda Setting in the United States Supreme Court.* Cambridge: Harvard University Press, 1991.

Pritchett, C. Herman. *Constitutional Civil Liberties.* Englewood Cliffs, NJ: Prentice-Hall, 1984.

Rehnquist, William H. *The Supreme Court*. New York: Morrow, 1987.

Schwartz, Bernard. *Super Chief: Earl Warren and His Supreme Court—A Judicial Biography*. New York: New York University Press, 1983.

Sowell, Thomas. *Affirmative Action Reconsidered: Was It Necessary in Academia?* Washington, D.C.: American Enterprise Institute, 1975.

Strum, Phillipa. *When the Nazis Came to Skokie*. Lawrence: University of Kansas Press, 1999.

Tribe, Lawrence. *Abortion: A Clash of Absolutes*. New York: Norton, 1990.

_____. *American Constitutional Law*. New York: The Foundation Press, 1988.

_____. *God Save This Honorable Court*. New York: Random House, 1985.

Warren, Samuel, and Louis Brandeis. "The Right to Privacy," in *Harvard Law Review* 4:193 (1890).

Watson, George L., and Stookey, John A. *Shaping America: The Politics of Supreme Court Appointments*. New York: HarperCollins, 1995.

Weinstein, James. *Hate Speech, Pornography, and the Radical Attack on Free Speech Doctrine*. Boulder, CO: Westview Press, 1999.

Westin, Alan. *Privacy and Freedom*. New York: Atheneum Press, 1970.

White, G. Edward. *The Marshall Court and Cultural Change, 1815–1835*. New York: Macmillan, 1988.

# The Constitution of the United States

We the people of the United States, in Order to form a more perfect Union, establish Justice, insure domestic Tranquility, provide for the common defence, promote the general Welfare, and secure the Blessings of Liberty to ourselves and our Posterity, do ordain and establish this CONSTITUTION for the United States of America.

## ARTICLE I

**Section 1.**   All legislative Powers herein granted shall be vested in a Congress of the United States, which shall consist of a Senate and House of Representatives.

**Section 2.**   The House of Representatives shall be composed of Members chosen every second Year by the People of the several States, and the Electors in each State shall have the Qualifications requisite for Electors of the most numerous Branch of the State Legislature.

No person shall be a Representative who shall not have attained to the Age of twenty-five Years, and been seven Years a Citizen of the United States, and who shall not, when elected, be an Inhabitant of that State in which he shall be chosen.

Representatives and direct Taxes shall be apportioned among the several States which may be included within this Union, according to their respective Numbers, which shall be determined by adding to the whole Number of free Persons, including those bound to Service for a Term of Years, and excluding Indians not taxed, three fifths of all other Persons. The actual Enumeration shall be made within three Years after the first Meeting of the Congress of the United States, and within every subsequent Term of ten Years, in such Manner as they shall by Law direct. The Number of Representatives shall not exceed one for every thirty Thousand, but each State shall have at Least one Representative; and until such enumeration shall be made, the State of New Hampshire shall be entitled to chuse three, Massachusetts eight, Rhode-Island and Providence Plantations one, Connecticut five, New-York six, New Jersey four, Pennsylvania eight, Delaware one, Maryland six, Virginia ten, North Carolina five, South Carolina five, and Georgia three.

When vacancies happen in the Representation from any State, the Executive Authority thereof shall issue Writs of Election to fill such Vacancies.

The House of Representatives shall chuse their Speaker and other Officers; and shall have the sole Power of Impeachment.

**Section 3.**    The Senate of the United States shall be composed of two Senators from each State, chosen by the Legislature thereof, for six Years; and each Senator shall have one Vote.

Immediately after they shall be assembled in Consequence of the first Election, they shall be divided as equally as may be into three Classes. The Seats of the Senators of the first Class shall be vacated at the Expiration of the second Year, of the second Class at the Expiration of the fourth Year, and of the third Class at the Expiration of the sixth Year, so that one-third may be chosen every second Year; and if Vacancies happen by Resignation, or otherwise, during the Recess of the Legislature of any State, the Executive thereof may make temporary Appointments until the next Meeting of the Legislature, which shall then fill such Vacancies.

No Person shall be a Senator who shall not have attained to the Age of thirty Years, and been nine Years a Citizen of the United States, and who shall not, when elected, be an Inhabitant of that State in which he shall be chosen.

The Vice President of the United States shall be President of the Senate, but shall have no vote, unless they be equally divided.

The Senate shall chuse their other Officers, and also a President pro tempore, in the absence of the Vice President, or when he shall exercise the Office of the President of the United States.

The Senate shall have the sole Power to try all Impeachments. When sitting for that purpose, they shall be on Oath or Affirmation. When the President of the United States is tried, the Chief Justice shall preside: And no person shall be convicted without the Concurrence of two thirds of the Members present.

Judgment in Cases of Impeachment shall not extend further than to removal from Office, and disqualification to hold and enjoy any Office of honor, Trust, or Profit under the United States: but the Party convicted shall nevertheless be liable and subject to Indictment, Trial, Judgment, and Punishment, according to Law.

**Section 4.**    The Times, Places and Manner of holding Elections for Senators and Representatives, shall be prescribed in each state by the Legislature thereof; but the Congress may at any time by Law make or alter such Regulations, except as to the Places of Chusing Senators.

The Congress shall assemble at least once in every Year, and such Meeting shall be on the first Monday in December, unless they shall by Law appoint a different Day.

**Section 5.**    Each House shall be the Judge of the Elections, Returns and Qualifications of its own Members, and a Majority of each shall constitute a Quorum to do Business; but a smaller number may adjourn from day to day, and may be authorized to compel the Attendance of absent Members, in such Manner, and under such Penalties, as each House may provide.

Each House may determine the Rules of its Proceedings, punish its Members for disorderly Behavior, and, with the Concurrence of two thirds, expel a Member.

Each House shall keep a Journal of its Proceedings, and from time to time publish the same, excepting such Parts as may in their Judgment require Secrecy; and the Yeas and Nays of the Members of either House on any question shall, at the Desire of one fifth of those Present, be entered on the Journal.

Neither House, during the Session of Congress, shall, without the Consent of the other, adjourn for more than three days, nor to any other Place than that in which the two Houses shall be sitting.

*Section 6.*    The Senators and Representatives shall receive a Compensation for their Services, to be ascertained by Law, and paid out of the Treasury of the United States. They shall in all Cases, except Treason, Felony, and Breach of the Peace, be privileged from arrest during their Attendance at the Session of their respective Houses, and in going to and returning from the same; and for any Speech or Debate in either House, they shall not be questioned in any other Place.

No Senator or Representative shall, during the Time for which he was elected, be appointed to any civil Office under the Authority of the United States, which shall have been created, or the Emoluments whereof shall have been increased, during such time; and no Person holding any Office under the United States shall be a Member of either House during his continuance in Office.

*Section 7.*    All Bills for raising Revenue shall originate in the House of Representatives; but the Senate may propose or concur with Amendments as on other bills.

Every Bill which shall have passed the House of Representatives and the Senate, shall, before it become a Law, be presented to the President of the United States; If he approve he shall sign it, but if not he shall return it, with his Objections, to that House in which it shall have originated, who shall enter the Objections at large on their Journal, and proceed to reconsider it. If after such Reconsideration two thirds of that House shall agree to pass the bill, it shall be sent, together with the objections, to the other House, by which it shall likewise be reconsidered, and if approved by two thirds of that House, it shall become a Law. But in all such Cases the Votes of both Houses shall be determined by Yeas and Nays, and the Names of the Persons voting for and against the Bill shall be entered on the Journal of each House respectively. If any Bill shall not be returned by the President within ten Days (Sundays excepted) after it shall have been presented to him, the Same shall be a Law, in like Manner as if he had signed it, unless the Congress by their Adjournment prevent its Return, in which Case it shall not be a Law.

Every Order, Resolution, or Vote to which the Concurrence of the Senate and House of Representatives may be necessary (except on a question of Adjournment) shall be presented to the President of the United States; and before the Same shall take Effect, shall be approved by him, or being disapproved by him, shall be repassed by two thirds of the Senate and House of Representatives, according to the Rules and Limitations prescribed in the Case of a Bill.

***Section 8.*** The Congress shall have Power To lay and collect Taxes, Duties, Imposts and Excises, to pay the Debts and provide for the common Defence and general Welfare of the United States; but all Duties, Imposts and Excises shall be uniform throughout the United States;

To borrow money on the credit of the United States;

To regulate Commerce with foreign Nations, and among the several States, and with the Indian Tribes;

To establish a uniform Rule of Naturalization, and uniform Laws on the subject of Bankruptcies throughout the United States;

To coin Money, regulate the Value thereof, and of foreign Coin, and fix the Standard of Weights and Measures;

To provide for the Punishment of counterfeiting the Securities and current Coin of the United States;

To establish Post offices and post Roads;

To promote the Progress of Science and useful Arts, by securing for limited Times to Authors and Inventors the exclusive Right to their respective Writings and Discoveries;

To constitute Tribunals inferior to the Supreme Court;

To define and punish Piracies and Felonies committed on the high Seas, and Offences against the Law of Nations;

To declare War, grant Letters of Marque and Reprisal, and make Rules concerning Captures on Land and Water;

To raise and support Armies, but no Appropriation of Money to that Use shall be for a longer Term than two Years;

To provide and maintain a Navy;

To make Rules for the Government and Regulation of the land and naval forces;

To provide for calling forth the Militia to execute the Laws of the Union, suppress Insurrections and repel Invasions;

To provide for organizing, arming, and disciplining the Militia, and for governing such Part of them as may be employed in the Service of the United States, reserving to the States respectively, the Appointment of the Officers, and the Authority of training the Militia according to the discipline prescribed by Congress;

To exercise exclusive Legislation in all Cases whatsoever, over such District (not exceeding ten Miles square) as may, by Cession of particular States, and the acceptance of Congress, become the Seat of Government of the United States, and to exercise like Authority over all Places purchased by the Consent of the Legislature of the State in which the Same shall be, for the Erection of Forts, Magazines, Arsenals, dock-Yards, and other needful Buildings;—And

To make all Laws which shall be necessary and proper for carrying into Execution the foregoing Powers, and all other Powers vested by this Constitution in the government of the United States, or in any Department or Officer thereof.

***Section 9.*** The Migration or Importation of such Persons as any of the States now existing shall think proper to admit, shall not be prohibited by the Congress prior to the Year one thousand eight hundred and eight, but a tax or duty may be imposed on such Importation, not exceeding ten dollars for each Person.

The privilege of the Writ of Habeas Corpus shall not be suspended, unless when in Cases of Rebellion or Invasion the public Safety may require it.

No Bill of Attainder or ex post facto Law shall be passed.

No capitation, or other direct, Tax shall be laid unless in Proportion to the Census or Enumeration herein before directed to be taken.

No Tax or Duty shall be laid on Articles exported from any State.

No Preference shall be given by any Regulation of Revenue to the Ports of one State over those of another: nor shall Vessels bound to, or from, one state, be obliged to enter, clear, or pay Duties in another.

No Money shall be drawn from the Treasury, but in Consequence of Appropriations made by Law; and a regular Statement and Account of the Receipts and Expenditures of all public Money shall be published from time to time.

No Title of Nobility shall be granted by the United States: And no Person holding any Office of Profit or Trust under them, shall, without the Consent of the Congress, accept of any present, Emolument, Office, or Title, of any kind whatever, from any King, Prince, or Foreign State.

*Section 10.*    No state shall enter into any Treaty, Alliance, or Confederation; grant Letters of Marque and Reprisal; coin Money; emit Bills of Credit; make any Thing but gold and silver Coin a Tender in Payment of Debts; pass any Bill of Attainder, ex post facto Law, or Law impairing the Obligation of Contracts, or grant any Title of Nobility.

No State shall, without the Consent of the Congress, lay any Imposts or Duties on Imports or Exports, except what may be absolutely necessary for executing its inspection Laws: and the net Produce of all Duties and Imposts, laid by any State on Imports or Exports, shall be for the Use of the Treasury of the United States; and all such Laws shall be subject to the Revision and Control of the Congress.

No State shall, without the Consent of Congress, lay any duty of Tonnage, keep Troops, or Ships of War in time of Peace, enter into any Agreement or Compact with another State, or with a foreign Power, or engage in War, unless actually invaded, or in such imminent Danger as will not admit of delay.

# ARTICLE II

*Section 1.*    The executive Power shall be vested in a President of the United States of America. He shall hold his Office during the Term of four years, and, together with the Vice President, chosen for the same Term, be elected, as follows:

Each State shall appoint, in such Manner as the Legislature thereof may direct, a Number of Electors, equal to the whole Number of Senators and Representatives to which the State may be entitled in the Congress; but no Senator or Representative, or Person holding an Office of Trust or Profit under the United States, shall be appointed an Elector.

The Electors shall meet in their respective States, and vote by Ballot for two persons, of whom one at least shall not be an Inhabitant of the same State with themselves. And they shall make a List of all the Persons voted for, and of the Number of

Votes for each; which List they shall sign and certify, and transmit sealed to the Seat of the Government of the United States, directed to the President of the Senate. The President of the Senate shall, in the Presence of the Senate and House of Representatives, open all the Certificates, and the Votes shall then be counted. The Person having the greatest Number of Votes shall be the President, if such Number be a Majority of the whole Number of Electors appointed; and if there be more than one who have such Majority, and have an equal Number of Votes, then the House of Representatives shall immediately chuse by Ballot one of them for President; and if no Person have a Majority, then from the five highest on the List the said House shall in like Manner chuse the President. But in chusing the President, the votes shall be taken by States, the Representation from each State having one Vote; a quorum for this Purpose shall consist of a Member or Members from two-thirds of the States, and a Majority of all the States shall be necessary to a Choice. In every Case, after the Choice of the President, the Person having the greatest Number of Votes of the Electors shall be the Vice President. But if there should remain two or more who have equal votes, the Senate shall chuse from them by Ballot the Vice President.

The Congress may determine the time of chusing the Electors, and the Day on which they shall give their Votes; which Day shall be the same throughout the United States.

No person except a natural-born Citizen, or a Citizen of the United States, at the time of the Adoption of this Constitution, shall be eligible to the Office of President; neither shall any Person be eligible to that Office who shall not have attained to the Age of thirty-five years, and been fourteen Years a Resident within the United States.

In Case of the Removal of the President from Office, or of his Death, Resignation, or Inability to discharge the Powers and Duties of the said Office, the same shall devolve on the Vice President, and the Congress may by Law provide for the Case of Removal, Death, Resignation, or Inability, both of the President and Vice President, declaring what Officer shall then act as President, and such Officer shall act accordingly, until the disability be removed, or a President shall be elected.

The President shall, at stated Times, receive for his Services a Compensation, which shall neither be increased nor diminished during the Period for which he shall have been elected, and he shall not receive within that Period any other Emolument from the United States, or any of them.

Before he enter on the execution of his Office, he shall take the following Oath or Affirmation:—"I do solemnly swear (or affirm) that I will faithfully execute the Office of President of the United States, and will, to the best of my Ability, preserve, protect, and defend the Constitution of the United States."

**Section 2.**    The President shall be Commander in Chief of the Army and Navy of the United States, and of the Militia of the several States, when called into the actual Service of the United States; he may require the Opinion, in writing, of the principal Officer in each of the executive Departments, upon any subject relating to the Duties of their respective Offices, and he shall have Power to Grant Reprieves and Pardons for Offences against the United States, except in Cases of Impeachment.

He shall have Power, by and with the Advice and Consent of the Senate, to make Treaties, provided two thirds of the Senators present concur; and he shall nominate, and by and with the Advice and Consent of the Senate, shall appoint Ambassadors, other public Ministers and Consuls, Judges of the supreme Court, and all other Officers of the United States, whose Appointments are not herein otherwise provided for, and which shall be established by Law: but the Congress may by Law vest the Appointment of such inferior Officers, as they think proper, in the President alone, in the Courts of Law, or in the Heads of Departments.

The President shall have Power to fill up all Vacancies that may happen during the Recess of the Senate, by granting Commissions which shall expire at the End of their next Session.

**Section 3.**   He shall from time to time give to the Congress Information of the State of the Union, and recommend to their Consideration such Measures as he shall judge necessary and expedient; he may, on extraordinary occasions, convene both Houses, or either of them, and in Case of Disagreement between them, with respect to the Time of Adjournment, he may adjourn them to such Time as he shall think proper; he shall receive Ambassadors and other public Ministers; he shall take Care that the Laws be faithfully executed, and shall Commission all the Officers of the United States.

**Section 4.**   The President, Vice President and all civil Officers of the United States, shall be removed from Office on Impeachment for, and Conviction of, Treason, Bribery, or other high Crimes and Misdemeanors.

## ARTICLE III

**Section 1.**   The judicial Power of the United States, shall be vested in one supreme Court, and in such inferior Courts as the Congress may from time to time ordain and establish. The Judges, both of the supreme and inferior Courts, shall hold their Offices during good Behaviour, and shall, at stated Times, receive for their Services, a Compensation, which shall not be diminished during their Continuance in Office.

**Section 2.**   The judicial Power shall extend to all Cases, in Law and Equity, arising under this Constitution, the Laws of the United States, and treaties made, or which shall be made, under their Authority;—to all Cases affecting ambassadors, other public ministers and consuls;—to all cases of admiralty and maritime Jurisdiction;—to Controversies to which the United States shall be a Party;—to Controversies between two or more States;—between a State and Citizens of another State;—between Citizens of different States,—between Citizens of the same State claiming Lands under Grants of different States, and between a State, or the Citizens thereof, and foreign States, Citizens or Subjects.

In all Cases affecting Ambassadors, other public Ministers and Consuls, and those in which a State shall be Party, the supreme Court shall have original Jurisdiction. In all the other Cases before mentioned, the supreme Court shall have appellate Jurisdiction, both as to Law and Fact, with such Exceptions, and under such Regulations as the Congress shall make.

The trial of all Crimes, except in Cases of Impeachment, shall be by Jury; and such Trial shall be held in the State where the said Crimes shall have been committed; but when not committed within any State, the Trial shall be at such Place or Places as the Congress may by Law have directed.

**Section 3.** Treason against the United States, shall consist only in levying War against them, or in adhering to their Enemies, giving them Aid and Comfort. No Person shall be convicted of Treason unless on the testimony of two Witnesses to the same overt Act, or on Confession in open Court.

The Congress shall have power to declare the Punishment of Treason, but no Attainder of Treason shall work Corruption of Blood, or Forfeiture except during the Life of the Person attained.

## ARTICLE IV

**Section 1.** Full Faith and Credit shall be given in each State to the public Acts, Records, and judicial Proceedings of every other State. And the Congress may by general Laws prescribe the Manner in which such Acts, Records and Proceedings shall be proved, and the Effect thereof.

**Section 2.** The Citizens of each State shall be entitled to all Privileges and Immunities of Citizens in the several States.

A Person charged in any State with Treason, Felony, or other Crime, who shall flee from Justice, and be found in another State, shall on demand of the executive Authority of the State from which he fled, be delivered up, to be removed to the State having Jurisdiction of the crime.

No Person held to Service or Labour in one State, under the Laws thereof escaping into another, shall, in Consequence of any Law or Regulation therein, be discharged from such Service or Labour, but shall be delivered up on Claim of the Party to whom such Service or Labour may be due.

**Section 3.** New States may be admitted by the Congress into this Union; but no new State shall be formed or erected within the Jurisdiction of any other State; nor any State be formed by the Junction of two or more States, or parts of States, without the Consent of the Legislatures of the States concerned as well as of the Congress.

The Congress shall have Power to dispose of and make all needful Rules and Regulations respecting the Territory or other Property belonging to the United States; and nothing in this Constitution shall be so construed as to Prejudice any Claims of the United States, or of any particular State.

**Section 4.** The United States shall guarantee to every State in this Union a Republican Form of Government, and shall protect each of them against Invasion; and on Application of the Legislature, or the Executive (when the Legislature cannot be convened) against domestic Violence.

## ARTICLE V

The Congress, whenever two-thirds of both Houses shall deem it necessary, shall propose Amendments to this Constitution, or, on the Application of the Legislatures of two-thirds of the several States, shall call a Convention for proposing Amendments, which, in either Case, shall be valid to all Intents and Purposes, as part of this Constitution, when ratified by the Legislatures of three-fourths of the several States, or by Conventions in three-fourths thereof, as the one or the other Mode of Ratification may be proposed by the Congress; Provided that no Amendment which may be made prior to the Year One thousand eight hundred and eight shall in any Manner affect the first and fourth Clauses in the Ninth Section of the first Article; and that no State, without its Consent, shall be deprived of its equal Suffrage in the Senate.

## ARTICLE VI

All Debts contracted and Engagements entered into, before the Adoption of this Constitution, shall be as valid against the United States under this Constitution, as under the Confederation.

This Constitution, and the Laws of the United States which shall be made in Pursuance thereof; and all Treaties made, or which shall be made, under the Authority of the United States, shall be the supreme Law of the Land; and the Judges in every State shall be bound thereby, any Thing in the Constitution or Laws of any State to the Contrary notwithstanding.

The Senators and Representatives before mentioned, and the Members of the several State Legislatures and all executive and judicial Officers, both of the United States and of the several States, shall be bound by Oath or Affirmation to support this Constitution; but no religious Test shall ever be required as a qualification to any Office or public Trust under the United States.

## ARTICLE VII

The Ratification of the Conventions of nine States shall be sufficient for the Establishment of this Constitution between the States so ratifying the same.

Done in Convention by the Unanimous Consent of the States present the Seventeenth Day of September in the Year of our Lord one thousand seven hundred and Eighty seven, and of the Independence of the United States of America the Twelfth. In Witness whereof We have hereunto subscribed our Names.

Go. Washington, *President and deputy from Virginia*; *Attest* William Jackson, *Secretary*; *Delaware*: Geo. Read* Gunning Bedford, Jr., John Dickinson, Richard Basset, Jaco. Broom; *Maryland*: James McHenry, Daniel of St. Thomas' Jenifer, Danl. Carroll; *Virginia*: John Blair, James Madison, Jr.; *North Carolina*: Wm. Blount, Richd. Dobbs Spaight, Hu Williamson; *South Carolina*: J. Rutledge, Charles Cotesworth Pinckney, Charles Pinckney, Pierce Butler; *Georgia*: William Few, Abr. Baldwin; *New Hampshire*: John Langdon, Nicholas Gilman; *Massachusetts*:

Nathaniel Gorham, Rufus King; *Connecticut*: Wm. Saml. Johnson, Roger Sherman*
*New York*: Alexander Hamilton; *New Jersey*: Wil. Livingston, David Brearley, Wm.
Paterson, Jona. Dayton; *Pennsylvania*: B. Franklin* Thomas Mifflin, Robt. Morris*
Geo. Clymer* Thos. FitzSimons, Jared Ingersoll, James Wilson, Gouv. Morris.

   *Articles in Addition to, and Amendment of, the Constitution of the United States
of America, Proposed by Congress, and Ratified by the Legislatures of the Several
States, Pursuant to the Fifth Article of the Original Constitution.*

## AMENDMENT I [1791]

Congress shall make no law respecting an establishment of religion, or prohibiting
the free exercise thereof; or abridging the freedom of speech, or of the press; or the
right of the people peaceably to assemble, and to petition the Government for a
redress of grievances.

## AMENDMENT II [1791]

A well regulated Militia, being necessary to the security of a free State, the right of
the people to keep and bear Arms shall not be infringed.

## AMENDMENT III [1791]

No Soldier shall, in time of peace, be quartered in any house, without the consent of
the Owner, nor in time of war, but in a manner to be prescribed by law.

## AMENDMENT IV [1791]

The right of the people to be secure in their persons, houses, papers, and effects,
against unreasonable searches and seizures, shall not be violated, and no Warrants
shall issue, but upon probable cause, supported by Oath or affirmation, and particularly describing the place to be searched, and the persons or things to be seized.

## AMENDMENT V [1791]

No person shall be held to answer for a capital or otherwise infamous crime, unless
on a presentment or indictment of a Grand Jury, except in cases arising in the land
or naval forces, or in the Militia, when in actual service in time of War or public danger; now shall any person be subject for the same offence to be twice put in jeopardy
of life or limb; nor shall be compelled in any criminal case to be a witness against
himself, nor be deprived of life, liberty, or property, without due process of law; nor
shall private property be taken for public use, without just compensation.

---

*Also signed the Declaration of Independence.

## AMENDMENT VI [1791]

In all criminal prosecutions, the accused shall enjoy the right to a speedy and public trial, by an impartial jury of the State and district wherein the crime shall have been committed, which district shall have been previously ascertained by law, and to be informed of the nature and cause of the accusation; to be confronted with the witnesses against him; to have compulsory process for obtaining witnesses in his favor, and to have the Assistance of Counsel for his defence.

## AMENDMENT VII [1791]

In suits at common law, where the value in controversy shall exceed twenty dollars, the right of trial by jury shall be preserved, and no fact tried by a jury, shall be otherwise reexamined in any Court of the United States, than according to the rules of the common law.

## AMENDMENT VIII [1791]

Excessive bail shall not be required, nor excessive fines imposed, nor cruel and unusual punishments inflicted.

## AMENDMENT IX [1791]

The enumeration in the Constitution, of certain rights, shall not be construed to deny or disparage others retained by the people.

## AMENDMENT X [1791]

The powers not delegated to the United States by the Constitution, nor prohibited by it to the States, are reserved to the States respectively, or to the people.

## AMENDMENT XI [1798]

The Judicial power of the United States shall not be construed to extend to any suit in law or equity, commenced or prosecuted against one of the United States by Citizens of another State, or by Citizens or Subjects of any Foreign State.

## AMENDMENT XII [1804]

The Electors shall meet in their respective States and vote by ballot for President and Vice-President, one of whom, at least, shall not be an inhabitant of the same State with themselves; they shall name in their ballots the person voted for as President, and in distinct ballots the person voted for as Vice-President, and they shall make distinct lists of all persons voted for as President, and of all persons voted for as Vice-President, and of the number of votes for each, which lists they shall sign and certify, and transmit sealed to the seat of the government of the United States, directed to the President of the Senate;—The President of the Senate shall, in the presence of the Senate and House of Representatives, open all the certificates and the votes shall then be counted;—The person having the greatest number of votes for President, shall be the President, if such number be a majority of the whole number of Electors appointed; and if no person have such majority, then from the persons having the highest numbers not exceeding three on the list of those voted for as President, the House of Representatives shall choose immediately, by ballot, the President. But in choosing the President, the votes shall be taken by states, the representation from each state having one vote; a quorum for this purpose shall consist of a member or members from two-thirds of the states, and a majority of all the states shall be necessary to a choice. And if the House of Representatives shall not choose a President whenever the right of choice shall devolve upon them, before the fourth day of March next following, then the Vice-President shall act as President, as in the case of the death or other constitutional disability of the President.—The person having the greatest number of votes as Vice-President, shall be the Vice-President, if such number be a majority of the whole number of Electors appointed, and if no person have a majority, then from the two highest numbers on the list, the Senate shall choose the Vice-President; a quorum for the purpose shall consist of two-thirds of the whole number of Senators, and a majority of the whole number shall be necessary to a choice. But no person constitutionally ineligible to the office of President shall be eligible to that of Vice-President of the United States.

## AMENDMENT XIII [1865]

*Section 1.*    Neither slavery nor involuntary servitude, except as a punishment for crime whereof the party shall have been duly convicted, shall exist within the United States, or any place subject to their jurisdiction.

*Section 2.*    Congress shall have power to enforce this article by appropriate legislation.

## AMENDMENT XIV [1868]

*Section 1.*    All persons born or naturalized in the United States, and subject to the jurisdiction thereof, are citizens of the United States and of the State wherein they reside. No State shall make or enforce any law which shall abridge the privileges or immunities of citizens of the United States; nor shall any State deprive any person of life, liberty, or property, without due process of law; nor deny to any person within its jurisdiction the equal protection of the laws.

*Section 2.*    Representatives shall be apportioned among the several States according to their respective numbers, counting the whole number of persons in each State, excluding Indians not taxed. But when the right to vote at any election for the choice of electors for President and Vice-President of the United States, Representatives in Congress, the Executive and Judicial officers of a State, or the members of the Legislature thereof, is denied to any of the male inhabitants of such State, being twenty-one years of age, and citizens of the United States or in any way abridged, except for participation in rebellion, or other crime, the basis of representation therein shall be reduced in the proportion which the number of such male citizens shall bear to the whole number of male citizens twenty-one years of age in such State.

*Section 3.*　No person shall be a Senator or Representative in Congress, or elector of President and Vice-President, or hold any office, civil or military, under the United States, or under any State, who, having previously taken an oath, as a member of Congress, or as an officer of the United States, or as a member of any State legislature, or as an executive or judicial officer of any State, to support the Constitution of the United States, shall have engaged in insurrection or rebellion against the same, or given aid or comfort to the enemies thereof. But Congress may by a vote of two-thirds of each House, remove such disability.

*Section 4.*　The validity of the public debt of the United States, authorized by law, including debts incurred for payment of pensions and bounties for services in suppressing insurrection or rebellion, shall not be questioned. But neither the United States nor any State shall assume or pay any debt or obligation incurred in aid of insurrection or rebellion against the United States, or any claim for the loss or emancipation of any slave; but all such debts, obligations, and claims shall be held illegal and void.

*Section 5.*　The Congress shall have the power to enforce, by appropriate legislation, the provisions of this article.

# AMENDMENT XV [1870]

*Section 1.*　The right of citizens of the United States to vote shall not be denied or abridged by the United States or by any State on account of race, color, or previous condition of servitude—

*Section 2.*　The Congress shall have power to enforce this article by appropriate legislation.

# AMENDMENT XVI [1913]

The Congress shall have power to lay and collect taxes on incomes, from whatever source derived, without apportionment among the several States, and without regard to any census or enumeration.

## AMENDMENT XVII [1913]

The Senate of the United States shall be composed of two Senators from each State, elected by the people thereof, for six years; and each Senator shall have one vote. The electors in each State shall have the qualifications requisite for electors of the most numerous branch of the State legislatures.

When vacancies happen in the representation of any State in the Senate, the executive authority of such State shall issue writs of election to fill such vacancies: *Provided*, That the legislature of any State may empower the executive thereof to make temporary appointments until the people fill the vacancies by election as the legislature may direct.

This amendment shall not be so construed as to affect the election or term of any Senator chosen before it becomes valid as part of the Constitution.

## AMENDMENT XVIII [1919]

*Section 1.*   After one year from the ratification of this article the manufacture, sale, or transportation of intoxicating liquors within, the importation thereof into, or the exportation thereof from the United States and all territory subject to the jurisdiction thereof for beverage purposes is hereby prohibited.

*Section 2.*   The Congress and the several States shall have concurrent power to enforce this article by appropriate legislation.

*Section 3.*   This article shall be inoperative unless it shall have been ratified as an amendment to the Constitution by the legislatures of the several States, as provided in the Constitution, within seven years from the date of the submission hereof to the States by the Congress.

## AMENDMENT XIX [1920]

The right of citizens of the United States to vote shall not be denied or abridged by the United States or by any State on account of sex.

Congress shall have power to enforce this article by appropriate legislation.

## AMENDMENT XX [1933]

*Section 1.*   The terms of the President and Vice-President shall end at noon on the 20th day of January, and the terms of Senators and Representatives at noon on the 3d day of January, of the years in which such terms would have ended if this article had not been ratified; and the terms of their successors shall then begin.

*Section 2.*   The Congress shall assemble at least once in every year, and such meeting shall begin at noon on the 3d day of January, unless they shall by law appoint a different day.

*Section 3.*   If, at the time fixed for the beginning of the term of the President, the President elect shall have died, the Vice-President elect shall become President. If a President shall not have been chosen before the time fixed for the beginning of his term, or if the President elect shall have failed to qualify, then the Vice-President elect shall act as President until a President shall have qualified; and the Congress may by law provide for the case wherein neither a President elect nor a Vice-President elect shall have qualified, declaring who shall then act as President, or the manner in which one who is to act shall be selected, and such person shall act accordingly until a President or Vice-President shall have qualified.

*Section 4.*   The Congress may by law provide for the case of the death of any of the persons from whom the House of Representatives may choose a President whenever the right of choice shall have devolved upon them, and for the case of the death of any of the persons from whom the Senate may choose a Vice-President whenever the right of choice shall have devolved upon them.

*Section 5.*   Sections 1 and 2 shall take effect on the 15th day of October following the ratification of this article.

*Section 6.*   This article shall be inoperative unless it shall have been ratified as an amendment to the Constitution by the legislatures of three-fourths of the several States within seven years from the date of its submission.

# AMENDMENT XXI [1933]

*Section 1.*   The eighteenth article of amendment to the Constitution of the United States is hereby repealed.

*Section 2.*   The transportation or importation into any State, Territory, or possession of the United States for delivery or use therein of intoxicating liquors, in violation of the laws thereof, is hereby prohibited.

*Section 3.*   This article shall be inoperative unless it shall have been ratified as an amendment to the Constitution by conventions in the several States, as provided in the Constitution, within seven years from the date of the submission hereof to the States by the Congress.

# AMENDMENT XXII [1951]

No person shall be elected to the office of the President more than twice, and no person who has held the office of President, or acted as President, for more than two years of a term to which some other person was elected President shall be elected to the office of the President more than once.

But this Article shall not apply to any person holding the office of President when this Article was proposed by the Congress, and shall not prevent any person who may be holding the office of President or acting as President, during the term within which this Article becomes operative from holding the office of President or acting as President during the remainder of such term.

# AMENDMENT XXIII [1961]

*Section 1.* The District constituting the seat of Government of the United States shall appoint in such manner as the Congress may direct:

A number of electors of President and Vice President equal to the whole number of Senators and Representatives in Congress to which the District would be entitled if it were a State, but in no event more than the least populous State; they shall be in addition to those appointed by the States, but they shall be considered, for the purposes of the election of President and Vice President, to be electors appointed by a State; and they shall meet in the District and perform such duties as provided by the twelfth article of amendment.

*Section 2.* The Congress shall have power to enforce this article by appropriate legislation.

# AMENDMENT XXIV [1964]

*Section 1.* The right of citizens of the United States to vote in any primary or other election for President or Vice President, for electors for President or Vice President, or for Senator or Representative in Congress, shall not be denied or abridged by the United States or any State by reason of failure to pay any poll tax or other tax.

*Section 2.* The Congress shall have the power to enforce this article by appropriate legislation.

# AMENDMENT XXV [1967]

*Section 1.* In case of the removal of the President from office or his death or resignation, the Vice President shall become President.

*Section 2.* Whenever there is a vacancy in the office of the Vice President, the President shall nominate a Vice President who shall take the office upon confirmation by a majority vote of both houses of Congress.

*Section 3.* Whenever the President transmits to the President pro tempore of the Senate and the Speaker of the House of Representatives his written declaration that he is unable to discharge the powers and duties of his office, and until he transmits to them a written declaration to the contrary, such powers and duties shall be discharged by the Vice President as Acting President.

*Section 4.*    Whenever the Vice President and a majority of either the principal officers of the executive departments, or of such other body as Congress may by law provide, transmit to the President pro tempore of the Senate and the Speaker of the House of Representatives their written declaration that the President is unable to discharge the powers and duties of his office, the Vice President shall immediately assume the powers and duties of the office asActing President.

Thereafter, when the President transmits to the President pro tempore of the Senate and the Speaker of the House of Representatives his written declaration that no inability exists, he shall resume the powers and duties of his office unless the Vice President and a majority of either the principal officers of the executive departments, or of such other body as Congress may by law provide, transmit within four days to the President pro tempore of the Senate and the Speaker of the House of Representatives their written declaration that the President is unable to discharge the powers and duties of his office. Thereupon Congress shall decide the issue, assembling within 48 hours for that purpose if not in session. If the Congress, within 21 days after receipt of the latter written declaration, or, if Congress is not in session, within 21 days after Congress is required to assemble, determines by two-thirds vote of both houses that the President is unable to discharge the powers and duties of his office, the Vice President shall continue to discharge the same as Acting President; otherwise, the President shall resume the powers and duties of his office.

## AMENDMENT **XXVI** [1971]

*Section 1.*    The right of citizens of the United States, who are 18 years of age or older, to vote shall not be denied or abridged by the United States or any state on account of age.

*Section 2.*    The Congress shall have the power to enforce this article by appropriate legislation.

## AMENDMENT **XXVII** [1992]

No law varying the compensation for the services of the Senators and Representatives shall take effect, until an election of Representatives shall have intervened.

# Index of Cases

# Index